Prometheme H...

THE
INTELLIGENT MAN'S REVIEW OF EUROPE TO-DAY

G. D. H. COLE

Reader in Economics in the University of Oxford
Member of the Economic Advisory Council

and

MARGARET COLE

———————○———————

THE
INTELLIGENT MAN'S
REVIEW OF
EUROPE TO-DAY

———————○———————

LONDON

VICTOR GOLLANCZ LTD

14 Henrietta Street Covent Garden

1933

Printed in Great Britain by
The Camelot Press Ltd., London and Southampton

PREFACE

To survey the affairs of contemporary Europe is bound to be a troublesome matter ; for in the world to-day the pace of change is disconcertingly rapid for the author, who must suffer an interval between the writing of his book, or even the passing of the final proofs, and the circulation of it to the public. He cannot avoid the danger that some of his facts may be facts no longer by the time his book appears, and, worse still, that some of his ventures into prophecy— for he cannot wholly avoid prophesying—may have been falsified already by the course of events. There are some who feel, on these grounds, that contemporary " history " should not be written, or should be left to the newspapers. But we believe that intelligent people do want a convenient summary of contemporary happenings and forces ; and that, risky as the attempt to sum them up may be, the risk is well worth taking in the interest of a wider diffusion of international understanding.

In one sense, our task of revision has been simpler than it might have been, though, in this matter, we are sorry for it ; for our good fortune is not the world's. This book had to be written in the months immediately before the meeting of the World Economic Conference. Until the Conference met, some people hoped that it would lay the foundations for a new period of world prosperity and a new system of international collaboration in the economic field. If this had in fact happened, we might have had to face the need for a hurried last-minute revision of the economic section of this book. But as things have turned out, the proceedings of the Conference have hardly caused us to alter a single phrase, and have certainly called for no revision of our general conclusions about the world economic situation. For the Conference has served, not to persuade the nations to act together, but rather to illustrate the futility of such great gatherings except when they come together for a clearly defined purpose, and on a basis of skilled and careful preparation. It has, moreover, brought plainly to the surface the depth and difficulty of the economic, as well as the political, antagonisms which hold the great countries apart. Economic Nationalism remains as strong as ever, or stronger, for it has been reinforced by recent developments in the United States, where President Roosevelt has been driven by the refusal of other countries to co-operate with him in an international policy of reflation to base his hopes of recovery purely on the domestic market. Moreover, current events in Europe make remoter than ever the prospect of overcoming it by an appeal to the spirit of international common sense.

Especially, the World Economic Conference has shown that fear, rather than hope, is still the dominant feeling among politicians in economic as well as in political affairs. The fear of inflation among the countries still on the gold standard, the fear of expenditure, even on the most useful productive objects, among the devotees of balanced budgets, the fear of imports among every sect of Protectionists and Economic Nationalists, the fear of higher costs among employers, the fear of too much production among the advocates of restrictive schemes—these and other fears have been the burden of one Conference oration after another. The consequence is that nothing can be done—at the Conference ; and the statesmen go home to do, in their own countries, yet more of the things they were called together to prevent.

In one country only—the United States—are active measures being taken in the hope of ending the depression ; and the affairs of that country fall, except incidentally, outside the scope of this book. What has become clear is that President Roosevelt, whether his experiment in controlled Capitalism be destined to succeed or fail, is likely to be left to try it out alone, with no help from Europe. The gold-standard countries obstruct him, though they will be ready enough to take the profit of his success, if he does succeed ; and Great Britain, poised between Europe and America, will sit on the fence till it breaks under her weight, on the one hand declaring her desire to raise world prices, and on the other proclaiming a policy of " national economy " which thrusts off upon others the entire burden of any action likely to bring the desired result about. As we write, there is, largely owing to events in America, some real improvement in commodity prices and even in employment ; but this is precarious and speculative, for it is based rather on the anticipation of what America is going to do than on any real change in economic conditions apart from the American reflation. But there is at any rate this of hope about the American situation. Mr. Roosevelt is seriously trying to raise wages, and does seem to realise that, without this, mere reflation of credit is certain to lead on, by way of speculation, to a fresh collapse.

Indeed, if Europe be considered apart, the outlook has grown much more threatening since we began to write this book ; for the Nazi *coup* came while we were in the middle of it, bringing a renewed threat of European war, intense though not perhaps immediate, and throwing into sharper relief the manifest failure of the Disarmament Conference. As we write this preface, the much amended Four-Power Pact—to be known henceforward as the Pact of Rome— has just been signed after negotiations which have profoundly altered its significance since the original draft was put forward by Signor Mussolini ; for it is no longer primarily an instrument for the revision of the Treaties of Peace, but rather, for the moment at least, of Franco-Italian *rapprochement*. The new Pact may even be held to lessen the war-danger, less because it indicates any change in the temper of Nazi Germany than because there does seem to be a slackening of the tension between Italy and France. Moreover, the Pacts of Non-Aggression recently made between the U.S.S.R. and most of her neighbours considerably diminish the danger of war in Eastern Europe. But the Nazi struggle for Austria goes on ; and the fears of Poland and the Little Entente have by no means been stilled by the reassurances that the Pact excludes Treaty revision save on a basis of agreement, and under the conditions laid down in the League Covenant.

For Nazism, denying every standard of civilised conduct and government, is still running its revolutionary course in Germany, persecuting Communists, Socialists, Jews, and even Catholics, and breathing the sound and fury of impending war. Nazism may indeed settle down as a force in the affairs of Europe, as Italian Fascism seems to have done ; but it will be far harder to quieten a Germany smarting under defeat and full of irredentist aspirations than an Italy merely disappointed of overweening Imperialist ambitions. Moreover, while Nazism has smashed German Social Democracy past repair, and dealt a heavy blow at European Socialism as a whole, who knows what forces of revenge and revolution are preparing within the new Germany of to-day ?

Before this book appears, much more may have happened. The Nazi Revolution, President Roosevelt's controlled Capitalism—these will both have moved on to new stages. Dr. Dollfuss may be still in power in Austria—who shall say ? Japan may have coveted a fresh slice of Chinese or Russian territory ; and we may be able to see better how the great Russian experiment is faring in its present difficult phase. These things we must leave, only hoping that we have given our readers, within the scope of our book, reasonable means of estimating the significance of new developments as they arise, and that in doing this, if we have not concealed, we have not unduly obtruded our own opinions, or allowed them to distort our picture of the facts.

For the use of most of the maps in this book—some of them amended to suit our purpose—we have to thank Mr. J. F. Horrabin ; for, with his maps to be had, who would wish to use others ? Certain of his maps have appeared in Mr. H. G. Wells's *Outline of History* ; and we have to thank Messrs. Cassell for the use of the plates. Others are from Mr. Horrabin's excellent *Plebs Outlines*, or from his *Plebs Atlas*, and here again our thanks are due to the publishers. Finally, in a book of this sort, errors are inevitable. We hope they are not too many ; but we apologise for them, and shall be glad to be told where they occur.

G. D. H. C.
M. I. C.

HAMPSTEAD,
July 1933.

CONTENTS

LIST OF TABLES, CHARTS, AND DIAGRAMS

LIST OF MAPS

FOREWORD

THIS BOOK is being written at a time when the economic life of every country in the world has been dislocated by a trade slump of unprecedented severity, and everywhere men in their deep distress are questioning the very foundations of the economic and political systems under which they live. By common consent, while other continents are suffering as greatly as Europe from the world-wide depression, it is in Europe that the troubles go deepest, and the accustomed course of everyday life is being most profoundly disturbed. Europe was the storm-centre of the Great War : Europe has been the scene of the most shattering and challenging Revolutions of the twentieth century ; Europe is still the continent in which the threat of renewed wars is chiefly centred, as well as the place where new experiments in government and industry are being carried out. Moreover, Europe, despite the continued dominance and even the marked recrudescence of nationalist ideas, is also the area where slowly the new ideas of peaceful and constructive internationalism are taking root.

Internationalism, however, as the tragic history of the League of Nations has already shown, cannot strike roots save in a soil prepared for it by the growth of international knowledge and understanding. The past few years have given a sufficient demonstration of the helplessness of mere utopian internationalism in face of the slump. For nation after nation, as the crisis has swept over its borders, has sought to protect itself by purely national measures of security, regardless of the fact that these measures for the most part only make worse the world situation as a whole, and react disastrously upon those who adopt them. Mounting tariffs, drastic restrictions on foreign trade and on the making of payments across national frontiers, can at the best only snatch for one country a partial and relative advantage at the expense of the rest, and at the cost of inflicting still worse poverty on the world as a whole. Nor are the political repercussions less disastrous ; for nations which live in perpetual economic fear one of another are incapable of political collaboration, or of a belief in one another's good faith. Rising armaments and repressive dictatorships follow mounting tariffs ; and to the many futilities of the League is added the crowning futility of the Disarmament Conference.

Meanwhile, unemployment stalks across the world unchecked. The agriculturist, unable to sell his product, eats it, and relapses to the primitive for lack of the power to buy industrial goods. The industrial nations, unable to sell their wares, pass from economic into financial crisis, and resort to desperate measures of " economy " in order to make their budgets balance. Prices fall, and the burden of international and internal debts, public and private, becomes unbearable in consequence of the changed value of money. There is perpetual wrangling over these debts, from reparations and war debts to ordinary commercial obligations and farm mortgages ; and this wrangling further embitters international relations. In the scramble to sell, standards of living are forced down ; and a world infinitely better equipped than ever before to supply the means of living to all its inhabitants acquiesces helplessly in a continuance of grinding poverty and unnecessary distress.

Under these economic strains and stresses, systems of political government give way. The established methods of parliamentary government are more and more discredited and undermined. Men fly from the older political parties— from orthodox Socialism as well as from Liberalism and traditional Conservatism—to one extreme or the other. On the one side Communism, master of the vast Russian experiment, stretches out its hands to Asia and to Western Europe ; and on the other, Fascism, taking in each country a distinctive shape of its own, seeks to rally the nationalist instincts of the peoples behind a programme which discards all true internationalism as fruitless.

Such is the Europe which this book sets out to study, in the hope that better knowledge of the facts and tendencies of to-day—of the much that is evil and of the something here or there that gives solid ground for hope in the future—may help to create in men's minds that international understanding without which there is plainly no issue out of our present troubles and perplexities. For this at least can be said with confidence where so much is doubtful—that the disease from which the world is suffering is a disease not of each separate country but of the whole world, and demands a cure that can be applied only by courageous action on a world-wide scale. To so much of bias in their presentation the authors of this book readily plead guilty ; but they have tried to present the facts and tendencies as objectively as they have been able, not disguising their own views, but seeking to give full weight to what makes against them, as well as to what tells in their favour. They do not hope to please everybody ; but at least they hope that the honesty of their purpose and presentation will be unassailed.

Part I: HISTORICAL OUTLINE

§ 1. WHAT IS EUROPE?

WHAT IS Europe? The *Encyclopædia Britannica* says that it is " the smallest of those principal divisions of the land-surface of the globe which are usually distinguished by the conventional name of continents " ; and that definition may serve as a start. But it is important to realise that " Europe," in the sense of a civilisation-group, has not always borne quite the same meaning at different periods. In some ages the northern parts of what we now call Europe were practically not part of it ; at other times portions of Northern Africa and of Northern or Southern Asia (or both) were included in the ambit of European civilisation. Even now, when Europe is commonly accepted as being bounded by the Urals, the Caucasus, the Black Sea, and the Mediterranean, we find that political reasons make it necessary for parts of Northern Asia to be brought within the scope of this book.

Europe, also, has had a long history. In point of civilisation, it is not the oldest of the continents ; there were civilised states in Asia when the inhabitants of Europe were still primitive. But, though European civilisation has not had the longest, it has had the most variegated history. The history of European civilisation is one of continual change and development—sometimes in a progressive, sometimes in a retrogressive sense—and the political map of Europe to-day is the product of a great number of historical factors. Europe has grown rather than been planned ; and when, at one time and another, efforts have been made to re-plan Europe by important treaties, such as the Treaty of Paris in 1816 or the Treaty of Versailles in 1919, the results have often been more unfortunate and less stable than those of natural growth.

If, then, we take Europe as defined in our first paragraph, and look at it as a whole, what do we find ? Physically, Europe is divided into two main contrasting portions—the great plain to the north, and the mountain masses to the south. Reading the map from west to east, we find the great plain beginning as a narrowish strip in Northern France, continuing, still narrow, through Holland and North Belgium into Northern Germany, where it begins gradually to widen out. East of the Bavarian and Austrian highlands this widening becomes much greater, taking in the whole of Poland and spreading northwards up the Gulf of Riga, until we reach the great plain of European Russia which stretches from the Arctic Ocean to the shores of the Black Sea and merges almost imperceptibly, save for the slow slopes of the southern Urals, into the huge spaces of central Asia. The traveller who is ignorant of language and indifferent to the works of man will, as he looks out of his carriage-window, find nothing in the shape of the land, and little in the vegetation, to tell him when he has passed from Germany into Poland, and from Poland into Russia.

South of this great plain region is the mountain mass of which the Alps are the central core. Westward this mountain mass spreads *via* Haute-Savoie and the Dauphiné into southern and central France, and *via* the Pyrenees to the high-ridged plateaux of Spain ; northward it flings out the Black Forest, the mountains of South Germany, Austria, and Czechoslovakia, and the great curving ridge of the Carpathians ; southward project the Apennines and the other mountains of Italy, as well as submerged ridges which occasionally rise above sea-level, as in Corsica and other Mediterranean islands ; while eastward an irregular mountain block covers practically the whole of the Balkan countries, extends, growing even more irregular, south to Greece and the Ægean islands, and reappears, after a very brief interruption, across the Straits in the highlands of Asia Minor. This mountain region, naturally, is not homogeneous like the plain. Within it, separate mountain chains, upland regions, and even separate peaks can be distinguished. Moreover, there are a number of subsidiary plains, large and small, enclosed or half-enclosed within the ranges, of which the plain of Hungary, encircled by the arm of the Carpathians, is the most obvious example ; and there are also many instances in which rivers, cutting through the mountain masses, have in the course of ages turned their beds into wide valleys or plains of their own. The Po, whose valley is the plain of Lombardy, and the Rhone in Provence, are cases in point ; and it often happens that such minor plains or valleys, sheltered by the mountains, are more fertile and more productive than the unprotected northern flats. North again, of the great plain lie more mountains, the highlands of Wales and Scotland—Eastern England is really a part of the plain—and the great mountain chains of Norway and Sweden, which extend *via* Finland into the northernmost parts of Russia.

We have said that the great plain stretches from the coast of Normandy to central Asia without a break. It should be observed, however, that the only swamp area of any size in Europe, the Pripet marshes which lie between Poland and Russia, though they do not make a break, do in effect constitute a considerable natural barrier ; while there is a somewhat similar barrier in Finland, where a very hard undersoil has caused to exist a large number of lakes. (Most of the inland water of Europe is in fact to be found in Finland.) Furthermore, though there is no visible natural barrier to the south between Russia in Europe and Russia in Asia, there is in fact a perceptible, though not strictly defined, climatic differentiation. In the summer, the warm damp winds from the seas and mountains penetrate far into central Russia and produce a rainfall that is more like that of Central Europe than that of Asia, so that a broad wedge of Russian territory whose apex is somewhere about Kazan may be said to be European in summer and more or less Asiatic in winter.

Along with the climatic differences go differences in crops. In the south, round the Mediterranean regions, is the traditional home of the vine and the olive, the former, which stands fairly cold winters but requires sun to ripen it, extending further north than the latter. North of the olive region comes the region of forest trees, mainly beech at first, then beech and oak, then oak alone, with ash and birch extending further north, and north of all pine. North of the pine area comes the area of frozen sub-soil, where even the pine will not grow, and the vegetation descends to Arctic scrub. The forest region extends over the bulk of Europe except the steppes of South Russia, where trees only grow along the banks of rivers. The famous " black earth belt " of mid-Russia is all oak country. But, of course, not all the forest region is now covered with forest, though there is much forest remaining. Two-fifths of the entire area of Russia and Germany, for example, is still forest.

Where the forest has been cleared, there follow the cereal crops—wheat, for the most part, in the warmer and more sheltered parts, rye north and east of the Rhine, the Austrian Alps and the Carpathians, with barley and oats as subsidiary crops. There is not, of course, a definite boundary between wheat-growing and rye-growing areas ; but the distinction between the countries which eat wheaten and those which eat rye bread is fairly marked. Two foodstuffs of considerable importance have been introduced from America, maize in the south and potatoes in the north of

Europe ; and there has also in recent times been a considerable development of root crops such as turnips, swedes, etc. (mainly for feeding cattle), and sugar-beet. Tobacco is grown in the south and cotton only in the Turkestan and Transcaucasian provinces of Russia.

Transport and Occupations. Europe's means of communication and transport are on the whole excellent. The natural means are plentiful : there is the sea, which by many bays and indentations, and such great arms as the Gulfs of Bothnia and Riga, brings widely separated districts within easy " sea-reach " of one another ; and there are plenty of navigable rivers, of which some, such as the Dnieper, the Danube, the Rhine and the Rhone, have been highways of traffic ever since there was any traffic to use them. The hand of man has added to these natural advantages—there are large and important canal systems in many areas, of which the French canals are the best ; and there is also, at least in the western and central parts, a network of railways which, though suffering in general efficiency from having been planned overmuch on pre-war national lines, still far surpasses the railway-systems of any other continent but North America. Roads vary much more, from the magnificent French pattern of *routes nationales* radiating out from Paris (and planned and built, in the main, to serve the military needs of France) to the appalling series of pot-holes that go by the name of roads in central Russia and some of the Balkan States. The arrival of the internal combustion engine seems to be forcing some road improvement in Central and Eastern Europe as the arrival of the stage-coach forced it on eighteenth-century England ; but road-building is so expensive, and the countries which need it so poor, that any improvement can only be very slow. Of aerial transport it is too soon to speak with confidence. At the moment, its part is negligible ; air lines do not pay ; where they exist, they are subsidised by governments, mainly from military motives. At first sight, the greatest future for the development of aerial transport would seem to be in Russia, where railway competition is slight and where the great plain removes the problem of landing. But, of course, further inventions may mitigate or wipe out the difficulties of landing in mountainous country. In the meantime, one can only observe that the development of air navigation tends to concentrate traffic more on the capitals of the several countries, and to remove, to that extent, the obsolete horrors of the " frontier station."

To the English reader, who is too often educated to regard Europe as an over-large, polyglot, ill-tempered country lying to the east and south of England, it comes natural to think of Europe as primarily industrial. This is not so. According to the latest available figures (1933) less than a hundred millions out of its 250 millions of occupied inhabitants get their living by ways other than agriculture, hunting or fishing. Even if Soviet Russia be excluded, less than 50 per cent are so occupied ; and in only five out of the 28 important States (Great Britain, Belgium, Germany, Holland and Switzerland), do the industrial workers exceed the land workers in number. The great majority of the industrial workers in Europe are concentrated in and about the coalfields, of which there are four main conglomerations —the English coal-measures, the coalfields of Belgium, Northern France and the Ruhr, the Silesian field, and the inadequately-developed Donetz basin in South Russia. Of these fields, two, Silesia and the Ruhr, have been the subject of bitter political contention. Coal being so bulky and expensive to transport, the tendency, noted by all economic historians, to concentrate productive industry, and hence population, in and about the great coalfields, has generally prevailed. There are, however, smaller coal areas which have attracted manufactures to them ; there are also industries, such as the silk industry of the Rhone valley, which have grown up independently of coal ; and there is, further, the comparatively recent development of hydro-electric power in industry, which is most marked in countries such as Italy, Switzerland, and Scandinavia, which have little coal but abundance of water-power. This development, however, is as yet in its infancy, and its future is a matter of guesswork.

Broadly speaking, industrial production is still the preserve of Western Europe. The only non-agricultural product in which Eastern Europe has at present the advantage is petroleum, which is hardly found in the west. It should be remembered, however, that this statement refers only to present-day statistics. The unused mineral resources of Russia are enormous ; they are only beginning to be tapped to-day ; and it may well be that another generation or two will see a very great transformation in the balance of European modes of life.

To-day, however, we must still regard Europe as mainly agricultural ; and Eastern Europe as almost wholly so. Agricultural, in the sense of living off land crops—wheat, rye, potatoes, butter, cheese, etc., according to climate and fertility—and exporting, in the case of the east, a perceptible, though not a very large surplus, to feed the mine and factory workers of the west. Certain highly developed areas have specialised in certain products—the dairy produce of the Danes, and the vineyards of Southern France, are examples which will occur to everyone. But, in general, the type of " mixed farming " which aims at supplying as a first charge the necessities of the producer and only thereafter exchanging for industrial goods prevails. (The English reader, however, must beware of assuming that this implies a universal system of scattered farms such as he sees in his own country. The village community—a phenomenon lost in England since the industrial revolution—clustering round its own centre, with frequently miles of unoccupied territory separating it from the next community, is a far more common mode of organisation in the peasant countries.)

Much of Europe, then, is peasant. Much of Europe, then, by English or American standards, is poor. How poor, relative to the standard of an " advanced industrial country," the economic chapters of this book will show. It is important to realise, at the outset, that the standard of life of a Hungarian, Polish or Yugoslavian peasant, even before the world slump, was one at which the industrial worker of the west would have scorned to live, would, in fact, have died—probably of scurvy. The rulers of Soviet Russia, whose people consist largely of peasants bred to the lowest of European standards, and whose quotient of political realism is perhaps the highest in present-day Europe, have recognised this fact by putting the foreign (i.e. imported Western) industrial worker in a preferential position as regards essential food supplies, because the Western worker, called upon to live at the Russian peasant standard, dies out of hand. Nevertheless, the European worker, industrialist or peasant, lives better than the worker of other continents, save Australia and North America. This book is not dealing with the lot of the Chinese coolie, the Indian ryot, or the native of Kenya Colony ; but the existence, in Asia and Africa, of millions far outnumbering the entire population of Europe in an economic condition below that of the poorest European is a fact which must not be forgotten.

For the last point which must be emphasised in this opening survey is that Europe does not live of itself alone. In spite of this preponderance of agricultural over industrial workers, Europe does not feed or clothe itself. About 10 per cent of the food of Europe, and a smaller percentage of the clothing of its population, are annually imported, to say nothing of the raw materials which the industrial areas draw from tropical or semi-tropical regions. Ever since the seventeenth century, the import of primary products from other continents, and the export to them of manufactured goods, has been an integral part of European economy. Nor can we quite ignore the steady export of human beings to the west which, until a very few years ago, formed an important factor in keeping up the European standard of life. The practical closing of the United States to Europe's unwanted mouths has undoubtedly had some effect on the post-war standard of life in countries, such as

Italy or Roumania, which before the war annually exported a considerable human surplus across the Atlantic.

More important, however, for European history and present-day politics is the business of material import and export, including the export of capital, by which European groups which have a surplus to invest lend it overseas for the purpose of development and manufacture in " undeveloped " or " uncivilised " countries, and receive therefor an annual tribute of interest whose preservation leads to complicated political relationships with extra-European lands. The Near East, the Far East, the South American States, and the tropical African territories, have all played an increasing part in the life of Europe. As it were a great shadow, the shadow of imperialism, has loomed for at least the last two hundred years over all European events. In studying either the history or the present condition of modern Europe, the reader will find, again and again, that some quite minor incident or dispute appears to have attached to itself national passions out of all proportion to the issues immediately involved ; and a further examination will often show that the clue lies, not in Europe, but far outside, on the route to India or the upper reaches of the Nile. Neither European history nor European politics can be understood if the rest of the world is forgotten.

§ 2. EUROPE IN THE TIME OF CHARLEMAGNE

As WELL as being a physical and economic entity, Europe is a congeries of national States, having among them many varieties of race, religion, occupation and political institutions. To describe these States, their likenesses and differences, will be the concern of Part Two of this book. Here we have now to consider how Europe " came about " —how the political map which we shall draw grew to its present appearance.

In one sense, all history is continuous ; and it would be reasonable to begin a survey of European history in the Stone Age. But it would not be very useful for our purpose ; it would take up a great deal of space, and the bearing of much of it upon the life of modern Europe would be very slight. It will therefore be more sensible to begin at the earliest point at which we can think of Europe as a whole without having to concern ourselves also with Northern Africa and the Levant, at a point, that is to say, when the earlier civilisation-grouping which centred around both shores of the Mediterranean—which in its last phase we call the Roman Empire—had definitely ceased to exist. Such an historical point seems to lie somewhere between A.D. 732, when the Frank leader Charles Martel stopped, finally, the rapid conquests of the Mohammedan armies at the battle of Tours in Southern France, and 800, when the Pope crowned his grandson Charlemagne as Emperor of Catholic Christendom. Let us therefore begin by looking at Europe in the latter half of the eighth century.

The first essential is that we should not look at it too much from the standpoint of the modern Westerner. The rapid economic advance of Western Europe since the discovery of America, coal, and steam power, tends to make modern readers think only in terms of the West, and ask of any age first, what was happening in Britain, France, Germany, as though these were the areas of outstanding importance. But in the eighth century this was not in the least true. A dispassionate observer from another continent (or another planet), looking at eighth-century Europe, would have certainly selected the Eastern Roman or Byzantine Empire, centred upon the splendid city of Constantinople, as the most important political unit. This Byzantine Empire, it is true, had been very much reduced in territory during the preceding hundred years by the conquests of the Arabs under Mohammed and his successors. It had lost Egypt, Northern Africa, Syria, and Mesopotamia, and its hold upon Asia Minor was precarious. Nevertheless, in Asia Minor, Greece, the Ægean islands, and much of what now forms the Balkan States its territory was extensive, and it was, moreover, still vital and able to expand and deliver the culture it had learned from Greece and the form of Christianity known as Orthodox among the half-civilised tribes to the north and east of its own dominions. Bulgaria, for example, and the communities which sprang up along the Dnieper River and whose centre was Kiev, were Christianised from Constantinople, and the extent of its medieval influence can partly be calculated by seeing in what modern countries the majority of the population belong to the Greek Orthodox Church.

Further, the civilisation of the Byzantine Empire was a great civilisation. It had a long tradition of culture, going back more than a thousand years to the early Greek cities ; it had a highly developed city life, with magnificent buildings, spectacles, art, decoration, etc., etc. Constantinople is estimated to have contained, at its height, two million people—as many as modern Paris, more than Imperial Rome and far more than any medieval European city. Its reputation spread far beyond the confines of the Empire ; by the firesides of Norway and Sweden tales were told of Micklegarth—the word means Great City, and the city is Constantinople. Nor was the civilisation, though stiff and to our modern eyes overridden with formalism, in any sense effete. The finance of Constantinople was sound ; its gold besant circulated unquestioned in all markets of Europe and the Near East—no small achievement in an age where debased and unacceptable currencies were the rule ; and in a military sense the Empire had proved itself again and again able to withstand the attacks of the full Moslem force and to hold the Straits against Moslem invasion.

The Byzantine Empire, then, was solid, rich and splendid. Western and Central Europe, however, had fallen into a chaos which the efforts of Charlemagne did little but throw into relief. As the Roman Empire in the West declined, so did the system of government which it had taught to its barbarian subjects decline also. It became more and more difficult to find persons who would undertake the task of civil administration and perform it with reasonable justice and honesty ; more and more the Government, instead of itself governing or defending its territories, tended to " farm out " this function, to give to a great chief or lord the task of himself policing or defending his estates, thereby relinquishing in effect any right of control over his actions ; towns began to decay and roads to be unsafe ; and the class of small freemen who had come into the Empire with the barbarian tribes, like the remaining middle-class of the old régime, began to be driven by insecurity more and more to come, willingly or by force, under the protection, and even under the absolute power, of some great man. Serfdom was beginning.

These tendencies were rapidly strengthened when the Arab conquests (which included all Northern Africa, Spain, South Italy and Sicily and the Mediterranean islands) practically cut off Roman Christendom from the rich lands of the Near East. As the war was a religious war, the Christians in effect ceased to trade with the Moslems ; and of all that we now call Europe only Spain, Constantinople, some of the islands, and Venice (which was exceptional in many ways) continued to participate in that Mediterranean trade which had been the life-blood of the Roman Empire. The result of this was quickly seen in the rapid impoverishment of " Christendom." Gold coins disappeared ; silver coinage, and that of every sort and standard of refinement, alone was to be found ; but there was everywhere a return to primitive standards of living eked out by barter. The Roman cities dwindled, and many of them, like Verulamium and Silchester in England, simply disappeared. Even so important a city as the great port of Marseilles dwindled to a fraction of its former self. City life had nearly come to an end, and the rising of the " burgs " of the Dark Ages, which many have regarded as a revival of city life, is so in very small degree. For the majority of the burgs were not cities in any real sense, but small clusters of cottages around castles built by barons or princes of the Church, housing the craftsmen—smiths, armourers, carpenters, masons, and the like—who were necessary to the upkeep of the castle.

With the decay of the towns and the impoverishment of country life went a decline in the arts of civilisation. It is hardly necessary to remind readers that in this beginning of the Middle Ages practically all that was preserved of science, art, and literature was preserved by the monasteries ; it should be noticed, however, that preservation is all that we owe them. The new contributions made to these subjects during the period are of interest only to antiquarians.

Before Charlemagne it is somewhat misleading to speak of the political government of this part of Europe ; for there was hardly any. There was a rough language-grouping, derived from the tribes who had originally invaded the Roman Empire ; and there were " kings " or " dukes," or " princes," who were more or less sovereign over territories of varying extent. But such political power as there was rested mainly in the hands of local lords, who had carved out for themselves small or large territorial spheres, in which they were practically supreme, paying some sort of service and tax to their nominal overlord, ruling over a congeries of lesser lords and peasant farmers who might be slaves, serfs, or free tenants, and living, in their turn, by services and tribute taken from these classes. Medieval histories, for want of a better word, speak of the " kingdoms " of Neustria, Lombardy, and the like ; but it is important to realise that such kingdoms bore practically no resemblance to the kingdoms of the modern world, or even of the seventeenth century.

Such, in the eighth century, was the condition of a large part of Europe, covering roughly the area occupied by modern France, England, Germany, the Low Countries, Austria, Switzerland, and Northern Italy. Charlemagne, the grandson of Charles Martel, made a great effort to introduce unity and at any rate the rudiments of ordered government. Beginning with a counter-attack upon the Moslems in the Spanish Peninsula (later known as Moors), which resulted in the formation of a couple of Christian principalities just south of the Pyrenees, he went on to unite under himself the two main divisions of the former Frankish kingdom, which were roughly separated by the Rhine, and continued by conquering Northern Italy and parts of Germany which had never been included in the Roman Empire at all, and were now, by the efforts of Charlemagne and his monks, brought within the pale of " Christendom." His coronation, in the year 800, by the Pope as " Holy Roman Emperor "—of the results of which more later— proclaimed him ruler, in idea though not in fact, of all the lands which had formed part of the Roman Empire of the West, and filled his contemporaries with the idea that a golden age for Christendom was about to dawn.

They had some justification for this. Charlemagne tried hard to introduce some sort of order into his wide dominions ; he sent round royal emissaries to check and control in some degree the behaviour of the local lords ; he extended the scope of royal justice ; he regularised, as far as possible, taxation ; and he laid the foundations of the feudal system under which much of Europe lived and worked for many generations. Further, he was a friend to culture and learning, and encouraged education. After his death, men looked back with longing to his times. So in England they did to the times of Alfred the Great, who, a hundred years after Charlemagne, performed, on a smaller scale, much the same service for his own poorer and smaller country. But Charlemagne's efforts failed politically, partly because his empire, like the Roman Empire in its later days, was too poor to stand the expense of a strong system of political government on a large scale. At his death, his Empire split into three sections, France, Germany, and the intervening strip which was called Lotharingia—the name is preserved in modern Lorraine ; and within these three sections weakness and confusion were widespread. For a century and a half after Charlemagne's death, the northern parts of what had been his empire were helpless to protect themselves from Scandinavian raiders from the north (the

Vikings), who pillaged and settled practically as they pleased. Some of Charlemagne's social work remained ; the schools he founded continued, and the feudal system grew and developed. But the political legacy of his reign to later Europe was of very doubtful value ; it consisted in two things, the Holy Roman Empire, and what we have learned to call the problem of Alsace-Lorraine.

South of " Christendom " lay the Spanish Peninsula, held by the Moorish Caliphate. Spain and Portugal at this time, therefore, were outside " Europe " and linked with the Near East. This meant that Spain and Portugal were not cut off from either the trade or the civilisation on which the Roman Empire had flourished ; and we find that the Dark Age of which we were writing in previous paragraphs was not shared by these countries. The fact that so much of our medieval history is derived from writers of the Christian Church who were bitterly hostile to Islam has hidden from the ordinary reader the fact that Moslem rule was neither oppressive nor unenlightened. The Moslem conqueror propagated his religion by the sword ; but once he had conquered a territory he did not use persecution or torture to make the inhabitants individually Moslems. It is true that the unbeliever was in an inferior position and was taxed more highly than the believer ; but beyond that he was free to pursue his normal activities and to retain his political institutions. For the Moslems did not possess a developed political system of their own, which they enforced upon conquered peoples. It would be almost true to say that they had no political system at all ; in any event, anything that could be called an Arab Empire collapsed almost as soon as it was made. Practically, the Spanish Caliphate was independent of any outside control. Further, the Moslems were friends to learning—it was not Moslems, but monks, who burnt the great Greek library at Alexandria—and during the period of their rule the Spaniards were in touch with all the culture of Moslem countries as far east as Persia and India. The universities of Spain, particularly Cordova, were famous for their scholars, and when learning began to revive in Christian Europe, two centuries and more before what we call the Renaissance, it was Arab and Spanish scholars who played the leading rôle.

North of Christendom lay the Scandinavian countries, with the brilliant warrior, seafaring civilisation which we call Norse, and know from the Tales of Edda and the Northern Sagas. Norway, Sweden, and Denmark were the homes of the Norsemen, who in the ninth and tenth centuries were pushing outwards in all directions They colonised Iceland and Greenland, and visited the shores of Labrador and possibly places further south ; eastward they colonised the Baltic, entered Russia, spread to Nijni Novgorod, Kiev, and many other places, and enlisted themselves in the Emperor's bodyguard at Constantinople ; they overran England, Northern France and the shores of the North Sea ; and they sailed right round the west coast of Europe, founded states in Sicily and Southern Italy, and challenged the Moslem power in the Mediterranean. At one time a Norse prince, Cnut or Canute by name, was ruler of a great sea-kingdom reaching from England to the Baltic ; and when the wave of invasion had ceased and the Norsemen had settled down in new quarters, such as Northern England, Normandy, and Sicily, the amount of re-vivifying energy which they had brought with them began to be immediately apparent in the life of Europe.

East were groupings of half-civilised peoples with which we need not detain ourselves for the moment, except to observe that the great plain was then, as it had been for centuries, the home of a great variety of wandering tribes whom natural cataclysms, such as failure of crop or water supply, every now and then drove to raid the territories of their neighbours and to force these, in turn, into the more settled western lands. Much of the history of Eastern Europe in its early days is concerned with the struggles of civilisation with these invaders, as Charlemagne struggled with the Avars, and with their subsequent Christianisation.

There remain two phenomena—the city of Venice, and the Church of Rome. Venice, founded in A.D. 552 by citizens of Roman Italy who fled from the invading Lombards into the lagoons on which they built their city, is unique in that it of all the cities of the west remained in touch with the eastern trade without being severed from Christendom, and that it was a free city, in the sense of having no master (unless we count a shadowy and fluctuating allegiance to the Emperor of Constantinople) at a time when such a thing was almost unknown in the West. Venice, however, was a pioneer among cities, a forerunner of the true Middle Ages, and only as a pioneer does it concern us at this moment.

Last is the Church of Rome, which is not, and was not, of its nature a political institution, but which, through a series of circumstances, became one of the most important, if not the most important, political institution of medieval Europe. This importance is due in the first place to the fact that the Church survived when the Empire fell. It was thus the only institution which kept in men's eyes continuity with a greater and more prosperous past ; and to the prestige which this gave it was added the fact, already mentioned, that in the Church, and particularly in the monasteries, was preserved what little of culture was preserved during the Dark Ages.

Further, the Church was never exclusively a spiritual body. Not only did the Pope hold lands of his own in Central Italy, which in course of time were increased until the " States of the Church " formed a respectable-sized principality ; bishops also became lords and held estates in their own right, as did monastic foundations.

At first the Church was not so much a single institution as a federal body composed of a number of autonomous churches. Gradually, however, reforming Popes reduced this autonomy and established the fact that the Pope was the supreme head of Christendom, and that every local or territorial bishop, no matter how large his lands or how wide his spiritual jurisdiction, was the subordinate of the Pope. This, as will be easily seen, at once sowed the seeds of infinite political dispute. For, if the bishop is a feudal lord, holding lands of a feudal superior such as a king, and at the same time the subordinate of the Pope and responsible to him, which party—king or Pope—is actually to select a new bishop, and which is he to obey when they are in dispute ? It is no real answer to say that the Pope is the authority in spiritual, and the king in temporal matters ; for in the first place temporal and spiritual questions cannot in practice be separated, and in the second place, the Church had always a tendency, whenever it felt strong enough, to claim authority over all departments of life. The weapon of excommunication, for example, was used on many occasions, both by Popes and bishops, to punish what nobody could have regarded as wholly spiritual offences.

This question of final authority was raised quite clearly when the Pope crowned Charlemagne as Emperor. It is said that Charlemagne received this honour unwillingly ; and well he might. For by assuming the right to crown the Emperor, the Pope openly declared that the imperial power—the inheritance of Cæsar and Augustus—was his to confer, and inferentially his to take away ; and this led in the end to a long and bitter conflict which was never settled, except by temporary practical compromises, as long as the Holy Roman Empire had any effective existence. Nor was the dispute confined to Pope and Emperor ; wherever a king or prince and a bishop existed, the same trouble might arise. The existence, therefore, of the Roman Church as an independent political institution is of great importance in European history up to the Reformation and even beyond.

It should be observed that this is not true of the Greek Church. The Greek Church was a State Church, in which the Emperor appointed the Patriarch or Bishop of Constantinople ; and where other countries were converted to Orthodox Christianity the same procedure was adopted, and the Metropolitan—the Greek equivalent of an archbishop—appointed by the king. The problem of " Church and State " has not existed in Orthodox countries.

§ 3. MEDIEVAL EUROPE

THE DETAILED history of Europe from the death of Charlemagne to the beginning of the Crusades (end of the eleventh century) is of interest to nobody but specialists. There is an endless and confusing struggle between princelings whose very names are hard and unnecessary to remember ; there is poverty, famine, and a continual exposure to invasion. Nevertheless, by the end of the period we can see an improvement, a steadying and shaping which is bringing to birth what we call the medieval world.

First and foremost, the raids of the Norsemen have ceased. The countrymen of Canute have settled down in their new homes and brought their vigour, their enterprise and their organising ability to the service of the civilisation they have entered. They have become Christianised, which in the Middle Ages indicates not so much a change in religious belief, as we should understand it, as a social change, an admission into the community which was called Christendom. They have challenged the power of the Moslems in the Mediterranean, so that the life-blood of trade begins to flow back to Europe, and communities of trading merchants, humble at first, but soon to grow in importance, begin to spring up on suitable sites—seaports, river crossings, road junctions, and so forth. A variety of luxury goods (most of which we should nowadays term necessities) becomes available, and among the upper classes the standard of life begins to rise.

Meanwhile the worst of the social anarchy is being tempered. The Church, now much stronger and better organised, is using its prestige to endeavour to discourage unlimited private warfare, and with the removal of some of the causes of this warfare life has become definitely more safe. Government is becoming both more efficient and more responsible ; it is recognised that princes and lords in general hold their estates and their offices in virtue of some function which they fulfil, and that if they do not fulfil this function their power should be forfeit. The medieval *system*, to which we shall return in a moment, is being slowly worked out.

This growing safety increases the population, sets men free for missionary and pioneering work. Everyone has heard of the Crusades, and knows, more or less, that the immediate cause of the Crusades was the interference of the Seljuk Turks, who had wrested Asia Minor from the Byzantine Empire, both with the newly restored Levantine trade and with the pilgrims making for the holy places in Palestine ; but everybody does not realise how far those who went crusading, gentle and simple, were a surplus population produced by the increased security of life and the decline in private war. The Crusades, therefore, were in one sense a remedy for potential unemployment which incidentally enlarged the knowledge, the initiative, and finally, in spite of their high cost, the wealth of Europe. Nor was the crusading spirit entirely confined to those who set out for Palestine. To this time belongs the formation by the Church of the fighting monastic orders—the Knights Templar, the Knights Hospitaller, the Teutonic Order, and the like—which, designed primarily to defend Christianity and to spread it by force of arms in pagan lands, also played a considerable part in developing and civilising those lands. Non-military bodies also, such as the monasteries proper, helped in the work. Monastic communities sent out offshoots to poor and unreclaimed territories, such as Eastern Germany, and by draining the marshes and cutting down the forests, brought a large area of practically useless territory under cultivation, and so within civilisation. One may say, in fact, that the age of the Crusades saw a large tract of land which had been hitherto only on the fringes of Europe brought well into the European group. Germany beyond the Elbe, Poland, Courland, Lithuania, are cases in North-Eastern Europe, while further south the conversion of the Hungarians, the Bulgars, etc., made a Christian *bloc* which extended *via* Kiev well into Russia. It should be remembered, however, that the Great Plain has no certain boundary upon the east. The eastern side was, and continued insecure.

What was this Europe which was shaping itself eight or nine hundred years ago ? Medieval Europe is at the root of the history of all European countries ; but it is in many ways so different from the Europe of our own times that it is often extremely difficult to understand, particularly, as will be shown later, for an English reader.

It is impossible to understand medieval Europe unless one grasps, first of all, that it was at once more of a unity and far more subdivided than modern Europe, and further, that the subdivisions were not mutually exclusive. In modern Europe things are comparatively simple. A man is a citizen of one country ; he cannot be a citizen of two ; and if, by some chance, he is a citizen of a country of which he does not wish to be a citizen—as certain Germans on the morrow of the Peace Treaties found themselves turned willy-nilly into Poles—this may be annoying and unpleasant for him, but he will not be able to help it. He cannot cease to be a Pole unless by a complicated procedure he re-nationalises himself as a German. Poland and Germany are mutually exclusive political institutions ; and this principle is accepted throughout Europe. Of course, there do exist institutions, or societies, which cut across political boundaries, whether national or local, from the Beekeepers' Association of Northern Ireland to the International Match Combine. But these are in no sense part of the political machine ; and it is assumed, by most people at all events, that the political, mutually exclusive grouping is the one that matters, and that any other grouping or any other loyalty is, as it were, a side-line which should be dropped in cases of political necessity.[1]

There is no logical need that this should be so ; it is only the exaggerated nationalism of the nineteenth century which has caused it to be accepted without question, and one of the best ways of understanding that it is not necessary is to look at a Europe which got along without it.

[1] For the special case of the League of Nations, see Part V.

The unifying force in medieval Europe was mainly, as has been already said, the Church of Rome. When a community accepted Christianity it entered an organisation which was European. Not only did it receive a church of the same pattern as other European churches, with a European ritual delivered in the European language of Latin ; it also received church officers who were at any rate in part under the control of a European head, paid taxes (as time went on, heavier and heavier taxes) for the upkeep of a European court, and might even find within itself groups of persons, such as the various orders of friars, who worked directly under the instructions of the Pope. It is thus clear that, whatever the territorial loyalty of the medieval man, whether to prince, gild, or city, it might at any moment conflict with his European loyalty to the Church ; and in fact, it often did. But the point is that this was not considered as unnatural or extraordinary, but merely as inconvenient. (In the Orthodox areas, for the reasons given above, this conflict of loyalty was less politically apparent ; and we notice that the Orthodox countries tended to be considered a doubtful part of Christendom.)

So much for the unity of medieval Europe. Now consider its particularism. Much of Western Europe, in the Middle Ages, was organised *feudally*, on a system whose standardised development can be most clearly seen in France, though it spread, as Europe spread, eastward. The essence of feudalism, for our purpose, is the idea that every piece of territory is in the possession of some person, to whom it has been granted upon certain conditions by a superior. The small landowner " holds the land of " the large landowner, who in turn holds his of the duke (or whatever title he may bear), who holds his of the prince or king. In theory, to make the social pyramid perfect, the prince should also hold his lands of the Emperor ; but when, in 962, the Empire (henceforward called the Holy Roman Empire) was revived again under a prince of German race, Otto I, the jurisdiction, even the nominal jurisdiction, of the Emperor had become much smaller than that of

Charlemagne had been. Large parts of Western Christendom, such as France and Great Britain, never acknowledged the Imperial authority throughout the Middle Ages.

About feudalism there are three main points to be noticed. First, it made for, and clearly envisaged, divided allegiance. A feudal lord might be granted land, in respect of service, by more than one overlord ; and as the early forms of feudal tenure generally included the promise of military support to the overlord, it is easy to see that a quarrel between two of his overlords might immediately involve a vassal in a difficult moral and political problem. Secondly, the lord or overlord, in any particular case, might be a spiritual person or body—a bishop, an abbey, or the chapter of a cathedral—in which case difficulties were bound to arise between the duties owed to the Church and the duties owed to the temporal power—difficulties which sometimes make a spectacular appearance in history on occasions such as that on which Pope Innocent III put a ban upon John of England and absolved all his subjects from allegiance to him, but which in much smaller guise run through much of medieval life. Nor, curious though it may sound to those brought up upon a unitary system, did this conflict of loyalties often result in a deadlock.

Thirdly, the medieval man did not, like the nineteenth century man, conceive of property right as absolute. In theory, no land belonged to anybody as of right, but only in virtue of his fulfilment of certain obligations, which if he failed to fulfil, the land could be taken away from him. This again is hard for moderns to grasp. We have slowly accustomed ourselves to the idea that a man may be restricted in the *use* of his property by social considerations, and that he may be forced to contribute some part of it to the upkeep of society ; but we nevertheless think of it as *his* property, owned absolutely by him and controlled, as it were, only at the edges. It is salutary to realise that over a long period of European history the opposite view was held, and was working.

This feudal " pyramid " was sustained and fed by the

labour of the peasants, the great mass belonging to the
" simple " (i.e. non-gentle) class, who cultivated the land.
These might be free cottagers, or tenants on a number of
different systems of tenure, or slaves, or even day-labourers.
But for the most part, in Western Europe, they were in
that half-free condition which we know as serfdom, in
which, broadly speaking, they lived on scraps of land which
they could not leave and from which they could not be
driven, whose produce was their own after certain proportions and dues (often very heavy indeed) had been paid to
their immediate overlord and to the Church. Most of these
dues were paid in kind, that is to say, either in produce or
in labour ; the medieval agricultural system made little
use of money.

Such was feudalism—an agricultural economy affecting
by far the majority of Europeans, since Europe then, as at
any time prior to the coming of the machine age, was almost
wholly occupied in agriculture. But feudalism has gone,
and though it left important legacies in the realm of law
and the idea of kingship, we do not *see* much relic of it, at
any rate, in England of to-day. What we can still see, and
what most people mean when they talk of " the legacy of
the Middle Ages," comes, in the main, from the medieval
towns.

Towns and Gilds. Medieval towns, like modern
towns, were of very different sizes, from an English townlet
that was no more than a glorified village to great cities like
Paris or Florence. Some, like the cities of Northern Italy,
and, to a less extent, those of Flanders and the Baltic
coast, actually owned or controlled a large slice of surrounding territory ; were, in fact, city-states rather than
cities. But most of them had at least two factors in common ;
they grew mainly by trade, and they were governed, as
trade and manufacture throughout medieval Europe were
governed, by groups of people.

We have noticed how trade, after the darkness of the age
of Charlemagne, began to creep back into Western Europe.

Companies of merchants, such as in the East would be called " caravans," began to move to and fro, bringing necessities, such as salt, and luxuries, such as silk and spices from the Levant, to the agricultural communities. Gradually, sometimes upon the site of Roman cities such as Lyons, sometimes at such convenient " natural stops " as a ford, the mouth of a river, the meeting-place of two highways of traffic, etc., these *merchant gilds*, as they were called, established permanent settlements which grew up into towns ; and, where towns grew up, there also grew up industry and manufacture of all the goods, from cathedrals to cloth, which we associate with medieval times.

Because we have mentioned merchant gilds, however, it should not be assumed that all medieval towns were founded or governed by merchant gilds, or that the merchant gild was the only type of gild known. The medieval gild, in essence, is a co-operative association, largely religious in origin and character, for mutual help and defence. The merchant gild is, possibly, the most noticeable form of early gild organisation, as the craft gild is of its later development ; but the gild type of organisation suited the medieval mind, and we find gild associations springing up for workers in every sort and kind of craft, and even for occupations which we should not nowadays term crafts. The great medieval universities, for example, such as the University of Paris, began life as gilds. It was an army largely made up of the gilds of Flanders which in 1214 at the battle of Bouvines put the feudal cavalry to flight. Some medieval towns were governed by gilds or groups of gilds ; the charters of others provided them with a special municipal corporation. But in all cases the ideas behind the gild organisation were so strong and so pervasive that they tended to colour the spirit of all town government, whatever might be its actual form. A medieval corporation, when it was not itself a gild, looked and behaved very much more like a gild than like a modern City Council.

Two things should be noticed about this gild society : first, that one of its fundamental ideas was that of equality between brothers—not, it should be made clear, between all members of the gild, but between all members of the same status. The whole basis of much of the gild statutes and regulations was that when once a man had secured admission to his society (not by any means too easy a thing to achieve) his rights were the same as those of any other member of his class in the society. He must not have his trade interfered with by competitors willing to sell below rate, work overtime, use shoddy materials, or corner supplies ; in fact, most of what the nineteenth century called " beneficent competition " was forbidden, in both theory and practice, to a medieval craftsman or merchant. Secondly, the motive of his society, the motive which was assumed to underlie all the regulations by which he was bound, was not purely " economic " in the modern sense. Medieval political and economic thought is rather difficult for moderns to grasp, partly because so much of it is stated in religious terms, with arguments, drawn from the Scriptures and the writings of the Church Fathers, whose validity we should not now accept. But its main point is easy enough to seize, viz. that " economic actions "—production, buying, and selling, etc.—cannot be decided by purely " economic " arguments, but depend upon general views, which are at least as much moral and political as they are economic, about what sort of society is desirable. This attitude of mind colours the whole of medieval life ; it went into eclipse for a while when industrial capitalism was at its height, but in this generation it seems to be returning —with the difference that we tend to judge economic actions not by the standard of Christianity, but by the standard, according to our particular views and upbringing, of Nationalism or Socialism.

The main bulk of the regulations and rights produced by this point of view applied to all gild members ; the difference between different classes in the same gild lay rather in the government of the gild and in the apportionment of privileges. To these class-distinctions, which become more important as the gilds grow richer, as well as to the class-distinctions between gild and gild, we shall return in a later section. Here it is important to notice that this town-and-gild system spread rapidly all over Western Europe, and to a certain extent eastward, through the Middle Ages ; and that it formed a part of the system of territorial grouping which we have mentioned before. A town or gild might be a vassal, or an overlord, or both at once, or it might be a free city owing feudal allegiance to nobody—towns often bought their freedom. It might hold its land of several lords at once, or of a lord and his overlord, who might be at loggerheads (which was often advantageous to the town). The point to grasp, however, is that it was the town which counted in a man's life. We remember the great medieval names as citizens of Bruges, Rouen, or Nuremburg, rather than as subjects of the Count of Flanders or of some German prince.

The Rise of Nations. All this network of associations, small and large, political, economic, and religious, make the history of the Middle Ages difficult to follow and, in detail, unprofitable except for specialists in history. Nevertheless, from that life so unlike our own, the modern world was shaping, and if we look at the broad lines and ignore the details, we can see the process.

Slowly, the territorial divisions which we now call countries were beginning to appear. This is first seen in England, both because England has well-defined natural boundaries, and because it was conquered as a whole by the Duke of Normandy in 1066 and ruled by him as his own estate without higher authority—although he held his Norman lands as vassal of the King of France. For some generations the poor and bleak land of England, to which Wales was added by Edward I, counted less with its rulers than their possessions in France ; but this situation gradually altered until by the end of the Hundred Years' War (1453) the amount of French territory held by England was negligible. By this time, also, the feudal system was disappearing from English society. Largely because of the political sagacity of William I in granting out his conquered lands only in small and separate parcels, the feudal lords in England had never had the wealth or power which they attained on the Continent ; nor were the towns, which generally speaking sided with the king against the barons, of sufficient size or strength to become his rivals. Only during a period of royal weakness, as in the reigns of Stephen and John and part of that of Henry III, did the barons really attain power, and they had not unity enough to hold it. Edward I, by appearing as the defender of the towns and the lesser gentry (i.e. the beginnings of a middle class) against the depredations of a quarrelsome nobility, was able to lay the foundations of a strong English monarchy based on middle-class support, and his calling together of a Parliament composed of these elements as well as of the barons and bishops, on the understanding that he would be granted supplies in exchange for redress of grievances, was the real beginning of English " constitutional monarchy." His building, however, nearly collapsed owing to Henry V's foreign adventures and the Wars of the Roses in the fifteenth century, and it was left to Henry VII and Henry VIII to build it up again. (Scotland, a monarchy from early times, resisted efforts to incorporate it with the English system ; and remained for generations semi-tribal in character).

France was much slower in breaking down the medieval system. The House of Capet, who called themselves Kings of France from the end of the tenth century, were much weaker and controlled far less territory than many of their large vassals. Not only were there the great provinces held by English kings ; there were also feudal lords such as the Counts of Flanders, Brittany, and Toulouse, and the Duke of Burgundy, who were practically princes in their own right. The French towns, also, were much richer and more important than those of England, and could not by any means always be relied upon to support the kings. Slowly, however—assisted in part by the advantages of an un-broken succession—the French kings ate into the territories of the feudal lords. The Hundred Years' War disorganised the country terribly and delayed the process, but after the defeat and rout of the English at the instigation of Joan of Arc, it proceeded rapidly, until by the death of Louis XI (1483) the territories of the French Crown included all modern France but Brittany, Burgundy, and Calais and Dunkirk (all of which were added shortly afterwards). At this time France was the richest country in Europe, and the French king the richest monarch. This was largely owing to the introduction, in 1439, of the *taille*, a special tax levied in the first instance to provide a standing army to fight the English. The *taille*, however, rapidly became permanent, and being entirely at the disposal of the king, put him in a position of financial independence which greatly affected the history of France for the next three hundred years. There was, indeed, in France a body, called the States-General, composed of the same elements as the early English Parliaments ; but as the Crown was not dependent upon it for supplies it never attained the same importance.

South of the Pyrenees little kingdoms grew up, which gradually became greater kingdoms under the spur of resistance to the Moors. The Spanish Peninsula being the one part of Western Europe which during the Middle Ages was still partly peopled by men of alien faith, the crusading spirit remained alive there long after it had died out in Europe as a whole. Consequently the discipline and control of the Church was far stronger in Spain than in any other country. The Spanish kings were, and increasingly became, above all other things faithful servants of the Church ; the Catholic institution which Protestants most execrate, the Holy Inquisition, was born in Spain, as was the Jesuit Order which succeeded it as defender of the Church. Meantime, the kingdoms grew and encroached upon the Moors. The kingdom of Portugal was set up in 1140 ; east of it, the kingdoms of Aragon, Leon, and Castile became of importance. Finally, in 1492, the marriage of Ferdinand and Isabella united the last three kingdoms into one, which by the conquest of Granada, the last Moorish stronghold, brought the whole peninsula under Christian rule, though a number of persons of Moorish race continued to live and trade there until their final expulsion in 1609. The daughter of Ferdinand and Isabella married the son of the Hapsburg Maximilian, and their son, who became the Emperor Charles V, thus brought Spain, the Netherlands, and Austria, as well as other territories, under a single Hapsburg domination.

The greatest subdivision, in the Middle Ages, was to be found in the territories which we now call Italy and Germany—Germany, in this case, covering a varying area, but including at times Austria, Hungary and Bohemia (the western part of modern Czechoslovakia). The central part of Italy was occupied by the temporal domains of the Pope, which increased considerably in the unrest which followed the death of Charlemagne. South were the kingdoms of Naples, Apulia, and Sicily, which, wrested from the Saracens in the eleventh century by the Norsemen, remained Norman kingdoms or dukedoms for some time, though towards the end of the period they were fought over by the kings of France and Spain, and finally came into the possession of the House of Bourbon, kings of Navarre in Northern Spain who succeeded to the crown of France. But the glory of medieval Italy lay in the cities of the north and northern central parts. There were the great medieval city-states—greater by far than any English town, greater than the growing cities of Flanders and the Baltic coast, and growing gradually greater than Constantinople in its decline. Venice, the pioneer, has already been mentioned ; but Milan, Pisa, Genoa, Florence, Padua, Bologna, to take only half-a-dozen names, were only less well known. These cities were states rather than cities ; they had large territories from which they drew their sustenance ; they stood midway between the reviving Eastern trade and the hungry northern districts ; their feudal nobles early took to merchanting and left their castles to build themselves fortified palaces in the towns, which the tourist in Florence or Venice can see to this day ; they took to banking and manufacture for export in advance of other states and peoples ; and, as everyone knows, their leading men were the great patrons of art and the new learning which we call the Renaissance. As shipping contractors for the Crusaders, the maritime cities made a handsome profit, and the discovery of America at the end of the period, though financed by other Powers, was made by Italian sailors.

These were free city-states, sometimes governed by a monarchical duke or prince, sometimes by an oligarchy of the richest or most important men, sometimes possessing a semi-democratic constitution. They had not, however, attained their freedom without a struggle with the Emperor, who claimed to be their overlord. The battle of Legnano (1176), in which the Lombard League of cities, led by Milan, decisively defeated the Emperor Frederick Barbarossa, was one of the earliest blows struck by the rising merchant class against feudal power. But, having achieved freedom by uniting, they, like the Greek cities many centuries before, did not retain unity. Trade and territorial rivalries divided them ; the Genoese sailors hated those of Venice, it was said, more than they did the Saracen corsairs. The strife between city and city was bitter, and it was intensified by their entanglement in the quarrels between Empire and Papacy (see next section) and by social disputes, as increasing wealth created wide class differences within the gild system. In Florence, for example, the " lesser gilds " were practically shut out from any share in the government. A great part of Dante's *Inferno* is concerned with civil strife in Florence, and the picture which he gives of the social and political hatreds there is certainly vivid enough.

Germany alone presents in the Middle Ages the picture of a country which is disintegrating rather than integrating ; and this is due as much to the existence of the Holy Roman Empire as to any other single cause. A period of confusion, during which the feudal system became fairly firmly established east of the Rhine, followed the break-up of Charlemagne's empire, and ended in the election of

Otto the Great of Saxony, one of the half-dozen large German duchies, as king of Germany. He then crossed the Alps and in 962 was crowned by the Pope as Emperor. Henceforward, until its demise at the hands of Napoleon in 1806, the Imperial crown was always held by a prince of German or Austrian birth ; but after Charlemagne France was never again included in the imperial territories. The German king thus became overlord both of the North Italian cities and the South Italian kingdoms ; but in addition to the awkward size and shape of his dominions he had to contend with two great disadvantages—his crown was elective and not hereditary, and he had to receive the imperial title at the hands of the Pope. Subsequent emperors spent much of their time and treasure in (a) securing their own crowns, (b) suppressing revolts in either Italy or Germany or both, and (c) struggling for supremacy with the Popes.

Church and State. The last-named struggle is only one aspect of the dispute between Church and State which has been mentioned earlier ; but it is a struggle which continued throughout medieval history, and was probably responsible for more waste of life and substance than anything else. At first the Papacy, the older and better-organised institution, had the better of it. Gregory VII, the great reforming Pope of the eleventh century, who claimed overlordship of all Christendom, including the right to depose " wicked " rulers, but in fact asserted this prerogative mainly in Germany, forced the Emperor Henry IV to do penance in the snow of Canossa and to receive his crown back as a penitent at the Pope's hands. But gradually the growth of nationalism and the decline in the prestige of the Church, as the Reformation drew nearer, caused the feeling of Europe to turn against the more extravagant claims of papal supremacy ; when Frederick II in 1239 defied excommunication and declared that " his cause was the cause of every king in Europe," the kings of France and England both rallied to him ; and at the beginning of the next century an obstinate Pope was carried off captive by French troops. With his death in 1303 the medieval Papacy, with its claim to universal overlordship, practically came to an end ; and when, after a long sojourn at Avignon in France, and a furious internal dispute, during which two rival Popes and at one time three were engaged in excommunicating one another, a united Papacy was again seen in Italy, the Pope had been practically reduced to the status of an Italian prince—with, however, the right to levy tribute upon the kingdoms of Christendom.

Before Frederick II, however, the Popes had interfered heavily in the elections of German kings, supporting, naturally, the candidate who was likely to accord most weight to their claims ; and at times, particularly during the twelfth century, half Europe was involved in the struggle between Guelfs (anti-papal) and Ghibellines (supporters of the Pope). That any kingship remained in Germany at all, under the circumstances, is due partly to the fact that the old feudal duchies were rapidly crumbling to pieces. Germany, during the Middle Ages, was splitting into smaller and smaller units—a tendency which the emperors, on the whole, encouraged as much as they discouraged the growth of towns.

Nevertheless, towns did arise, particularly along the Rhine and on the northern coasts, and even formed themselves into federations, of which the great Hanseatic League of the trading towns of the Baltic and the North Sea is the best known. Meantime, and almost unnoticed by the emperors, German Christendom was extending itself east of the Elbe, through the efforts of monks, Orders like the Teutonic Knights, and of unnamed agricultural colonisers. German barons " Christianised " and took over lands in Courland and Livonia, and many of the governing positions in Lithuania, Poland, and Hungary began to be held by persons of German birth. While Western Germany was collapsing into fragments, new and more stable States were appearing in the east, of which Brandenburg under the Hohenzollerns and Austria under the Hapsburgs were the

chief. In 1273, after a period of unusual disorder, a Hapsburg was elected Emperor, and a hundred and fifty years
later the imperial title became in effect hereditary in that
family. A less desirable result of the eastward expansion was
the introduction of feudalism and serfdom in an unpleasant
and decaying form to Eastern Europe, and eventually,
through Poland, to Russia.

In the fourteenth century, the first republic of modern
Europe modestly established itself. Two small territories
in the Alps, called the cantons of Uri and Schwyz, were purchased by Frederick II in order to keep open the Alpine roads
between the two halves of his empire. For defence against
aggression—particularly aggression by the Hapsburgs—
these two, with other cantons, formed themselves into a
confederation, more than once decisively defeated the feudal
armies sent against them, and finally, though not until 1501,
established the practical independence of the Swiss Confederation of any other power in Europe. The Swiss were for the
most part burghers and small cultivators ; the first republic
of modern Europe thus started as a republic of the middle
classes, and quickly began to make a living by hiring out its
citizens as mercenary soldiers to belligerent states. (The
production of waiters and hotel-keepers is a later development.)

The cities of Flanders (i.e. modern Holland and Belgium,
with a part of Northern France) were of importance second
only to the cities of Italy. It was the Flemish cloth-weavers
who taught the English to weave their home-grown wool,
made possible the big English sheep farms of the fifteenth
and sixteenth centuries, laid the basis of the fortunes of
great cloth merchants like Dick Whittington, and founded
the trade on which English prosperity rested until the
industrial revolution. Like the Italian cities they were rich
and prosperous and patrons of art and literature ; and like
the Italian cities they developed bitter class-struggles. The
attempts of the van Arteveldes in the fourteenth century to
democratise the government of Ghent form one of the
bloodiest passages of medieval history. But, unlike the

Italian cities, they did not gain their freedom. Subjects, first of the Counts of Flanders, and then of the Dukes of Burgundy, they passed, upon the death of the last Duke, into the possession of the Hapsburg Emperor Maximilian ; and their real struggle for freedom belongs outside the medieval period.

We have dealt with that part of medieval Europe which has received the most attention from medieval historians ; we must now briefly consider its " outlying " areas. The Scandinavian countries—Denmark, Norway, and Sweden— continued as semi-feudal kingdoms differing little, except in being more pacific, from their Viking days. Sometimes they were separate, sometimes two or all united under a single king ; their importance in European history lies mainly in their quarrels with each other and with the Hansa towns over the Baltic and North Sea trade.

The history of Eastern and South-Eastern Europe is difficult to grasp ; but the two words, Turk and Tartar, are the key. Kingdoms, half feudal and half barbaric, are to be found in Lithuania, Poland, Hungary, Serbia, and elsewhere ; but their relations are confusing ; intermarriage often unites one to another ; and the interest lies really in the pressure from the East.

The early advance of the Seljuk Turks, which all but destroyed the Byzantine Empire at the battle of Manzikert (1076) has already been mentioned. The Christian counter-offensive, the first Crusades, drove the Turks back, and founded a small and shortlived European settlement in Palestine and Syria. Thereafter a series of to-and-fro fluctuations achieved a kind of equilibrium ; and though the Turkish Sultan was regarded as outside the European pale, he became less and less of a dangerous foe. But in the middle of the thirteenth century a great movement in the inner plains of Asia sent an invading Mongol people, the Tartars under Jenghiz Khan, pouring into Europe. They overran Russia, destroyed the kingdoms of Poland and Hungary, and seemed at one time likely to reach the Rhine.

But with the death of Jenghiz Khan his enormous Tartar Empire began to collapse, and in Europe the Tartars retreated to Russia, which they held until, late in the fifteenth century, a non-Tartar line of princes, of whom Ivan III was the most important, began to build up a new Russian kingdom centred upon Moscow. The Tartars were not savages like the Huns of Attila ; the court of Jenghiz Khan was intelligent and interested in the things of the mind more than many of the courts of Christendom ; and they introduced novelties into Europe, of which gunpowder, mainly owing to its uses in destroying the castles of medieval barons, is perhaps the best known. As their stay in Europe was so short, however, their influence is rather that of a fertiliser than of a permanent element. A second invasion, made a hundred years later under Tamurlane, became involved with the Ottoman Turks.

It was these Ottoman Turks who finally destroyed the Byzantine Empire, and brought Turkey really into Europe. In 1329 an Ottoman Empire was founded at Brusa in Asia Minor, just across the Straits from Constantinople, and the older Turkish power collapsed before it. Shortly afterwards the Turks entered Europe and set about encircling Constantinople. They conquered Roumania and Serbia, and began the practice of training captured Christian children as Moslem cavalry—these were called the Janissaries. For a time they were checked by the Tartars under Tamurlane ; but after his death in 1405 they resumed the attack, took Salonica, and hemmed in the Byzantine Empire. It appealed for help to the West ; but in the fifteenth century there was no crusading spirit left anywhere but in Spain, and the Spaniards were busy with their own Moslems. Constantinople fell in 1453 ; and shortly afterwards Greece, Bosnia, and Albania were added to the Turkish Empire. From this time we have to add a new State, Turkey, to the States of Europe, though its dominions were of course never confined to Europe, and though, owing to the religious difference, it was for a long time scarcely accepted as a member of the European system. Practically, however, we

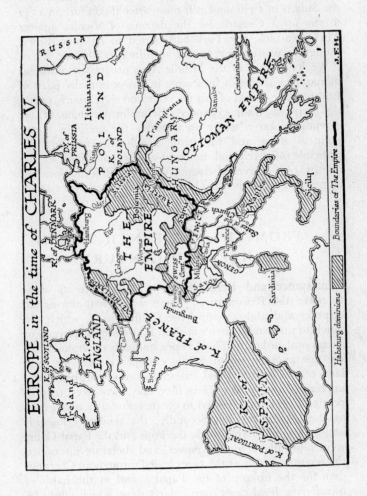

EUROPE in the time of CHARLES V.

RUSSIA

Dnieper

Lithuania

POLAND

Dr of PRUSSIA

Vistula

K. of POLAND

Dniester

Transylvania

Danube

Constantinople

OTTOMAN EMPIRE

K. of DENMARK

Oder

Elbe

Silesia

Bohemia

Moravia

Austria

HUNGARY

THE EMPIRE

Hamburg

Cologne

Worms

Swiss Confedn

French Comté

Savoy

Milan

Mantua

Venice

States of the Church

Florence

GENOA

Sicily

NETHERLANDS

Burgundy

Sardinia

K. of SCOTLAND

Ireland

K. of ENGLAND

Calais

Paris

Brittany

K. of FRANCE

K. of SPAIN

K. of PORTUGAL

J.F.H.

Habsburg dominions

Boundaries of The Empire

may say that after the treaty of Francis I of France with the Sultan in 1536, and still more after the failure in 1532 to stir up a Crusade for the defence of Vienna against Turkish attack, the Turk had ceased to be an outsider, though he was never regarded as quite a gentleman.

We have seen, as the Middle Ages progressed, national monarchies arising or increasing in power in many parts of Europe. The causes of this phenomenon were many, partly the desire, as trade expanded, for uniform systems of law extending over a wider area, partly the need for larger political units and for stronger government. But the principle of territorial monarchy was not lifted to the dignity of a universal dogma until the Reformation had come to signalise the final break-up of the medieval system.

§ 4. FROM THE FIFTEENTH TO THE EIGHTEENTH CENTURY

Renaissance and Reformation. Many currents went to make the Reformation. There were, first, the actual disputes and abuses within the Church itself, which did much to undermine men's faith in it as either a spiritual or a temporal authority. Three Popes, mutually excommunicating one another, could hardly enhance respect for their holy office ; and well-fed friars, poisoning cardinals, and unchaste nuns, however few they may have been in proportion to the total, served to create scandal as much then as they would to-day. Secondly, the tendency towards nationalism inevitably made the Pope and the Papal Court seem more like a foreign power, and therefore intensified the resentment felt at the taxes levied throughout Christendom for the upkeep of the Papacy, and at the habit of transferring legal cases (particularly those which might be remunerative) for trial to the Papal courts at Rome. Thirdly, the Humanists, the students of the Renaissance, were enraged at the hostility of the Church to the new learning, at its disposition to brand them as heretics, and to punish, even with death, attempts to study subjects or to think in terms which were not inside its traditional teaching ; and lastly, the economic structure was moving away from the medieval rules which the Church had drawn up and sanctioned. The equalitarian and communal system of the gilds was declining ; the capitalist *entrepreneur*, the big banker and trader, or partnership of bankers and traders, was coming to the fore ; and these were unwilling to be bound by rules forbidding high interest, forestalling, or trading in any way they chose. Thus economic, political, and cultural forces at the beginning of the sixteenth century were moved by a common discontent—a discontent which the Church did nothing to meet until it was too late.

When Martin Luther was excommunicated in 1521, few realised that a revolution had broken out ; it was not until the new nationalism really entered into the struggle—as evinced by the conversion of certain princes to Protestantism—that this became clear. For a brief while, also, it seemed to some that religious reform meant freedom of thought on religious matters ; but this was by no means the case, as the German peasants who in 1522 embraced a form of Protestantism rapidly discovered. They, however, were unwise enough to include in their religious programme certain proposals for social change which roused the wrath of their masters and gave rise to the bloody Peasants' War in Germany. It was the social aspect of the peasants' claims that finally decided Luther against them, and caused him to take the attitude that there was no right of private judgment against princes—an attitude later summed up in the famous phrase *Cujus regio ejus religio*. But, though the Peasants' War (in which, naturally enough, the peasants were completely and savagely crushed) was in a sense the first of the wars of religion, its causes were so much more social—resistance to feudal oppression, etc.—that it is not usually so considered. For some time after Luther's excommunication, religious disputes continued without reaching the stage of national or civil war.

But gradually it became clear that the passions kindled by religious differences could not be resolved without fighting. About the middle of the sixteenth century what are called " the wars of religion " broke out, and raged for a hundred years. They were ended finally, partly through exhaustion of the combatants and partly through the blunting of the sharp edge of religious feeling, by the Treaty of Westphalia in 1648, which closed the Thirty Years' War in Germany ; and it is worth noticing that, unlike some treaties, this treaty did really put a stop to religious warfare—though not to religious persecution. The religious map of Europe, which was drawn in 1648, lasted unchanged for nearly a hundred and fifty years ; and though since then important countries such as France, Russia, and Spain have changed their official religion, this has happened in each case in connection with a social revolution, the Church being disestablished or destroyed because of its connection with a discredited governing class. Nor has the religious change, of itself, led to war.

The Reformation took different courses in the different countries. In England it was, comparatively speaking, bloodless and not much concerned with religion. Henry VIII desired, not to change his religion, but to be free of papal domination, and, in effect, bought the support of his leading subjects in his struggle against the Pope by granting them the monastery lands. After a short Catholic reaction under Mary, during which, it is significant to note, the sequestered property was not restored, the curious compromise known as the Church of England was reached ; this gave England a State Church headed by the king and having its own ritual, which was a Protestant ritual though with leanings towards the older forms. This compromise has lasted almost unchanged to our own day. In the second quarter of the seventeenth century a belief that the Stuart dynasty was attempting to bring the country back to Rome was one of the causes of the Civil War, in which Scottish Calvinists joined with the lawyers and middle-class men who disliked the arbitrary government of Charles I and his advisers. But though the Court was beaten and Charles I executed, domination by a Puritan government did not prove any more popular ; and the Church of England was brought back at the Restoration and confirmed by the Revolution of 1688. Scotland, in the sixteenth century Catholic and under a Catholic queen, who had for a time been married to the king of France, was converted, mainly through the efforts of John Knox, to an extreme form of Protestantism. After the Union of England and Scotland in 1603, Scottish influence added strength to the reaction against Charles I ; but the English Protestants, though pushed by the Scots, declined to be guided by them. Nor was Scotland itself homogeneous ; the Highlands, in the main, remained Catholic and loyal to the Stuarts.

In France the struggle was long and bitter. The Court was Catholic ; but the nation was fairly evenly divided between Catholics and Protestants (called Huguenots), and civil war raged at intervals from 1562 onwards. Eventually, and partly owing to the extreme incapacity of the Court, the Huguenots won the victory, and their leader, Henry Bourbon of Navarre, became king of France as Henry IV (1589), but only, Catholicism being still so strong, at the price of becoming a Catholic. France thus remained Catholic ; but, as a make-weight, the Edict of Nantes (1598) granted the Huguenots not merely freedom of worship, but so much civil and political self-government as to make their communities semi-independent. After Henry's death, the French Government became more Catholic and more resentful of the privileged position of the Huguenots ; and in 1685 Louis XIV revoked the Edict of Nantes, with the result of expelling large numbers of the Huguenots, and making France uniformly Catholic once more. Nevertheless, it should be remembered that it was in France, during the civil wars, that the suggestion was made that differences in religion should be tolerated, in order that the State might not be torn to pieces in the struggle.

In Spain, Portugal, and Italy there was no Reformation. The Pope retained at any rate his power in his home country ; and Spain was the great stronghold of Catholicism, the source from which came the main forces defending the Church—the Inquisition and the Jesuit Order founded in 1534 by Ignatius Loyola. The Scandinavian countries went over to Protestantism with little difficulty. But in the Netherlands and Germany there were savage conflicts. The Netherlands, at the outbreak of the Reformation, were part of the dominions of the Hapsburg family, whose head was the Emperor Charles V. The northern provinces, in particular Holland and Zealand, became converted to Protestantism ; while the southern ones (modern Belgium) tended to remain Catholic. On the death of Charles V, his son Philip (husband of Mary of England), did not succeed to the Imperial Crown but did succeed to the throne of Spain and the Hapsburg Netherlands. Philip II was Spanish by upbringing, and as fanatical a devotee of the Catholic Church as any of his subjects. He therefore set about stamping out heresy in the Netherlands, reorganised the Church there and introduced the Inquisition, thereby causing to revolt against him even his Catholic subjects, who were not minded to be disciplined by Spanish clerics. The story of the fierce resistance of the Netherlanders to Philip's policy, which his general Alva was sent to enforce with fire and sword, has often been told ; the core of that resistance was the maritime provinces, which faced the drowning of their land by the cutting of the dykes sooner than give in, and maintained themselves by trade—partly also by piracy in the Spanish possessions, in which they were secretly aided by England ; its head, acting under very difficult circumstances, was William the Silent, Prince of Orange. He was assassinated in 1584 ; but the war continued. Eventually the Catholic south divided from the Protestant north and remained under the Hapsburgs. The seven United Provinces of the north maintained their resistance, and were formally freed from Spain by the Treaty of Bergen in 1609. Holland thus became a nation.

The application of the principle *Cujus regio ejus religio* to
the German-speaking lands resulted, since they were
divided among so many petty rulers, in a host of Catholic
and Protestant principalities, animated by mutual hatred ;
and the final battles of the religious wars were fought on
German soil. The original cause of the Thirty Years' War,
as this final phase is called, was a dispute over the succession
to the Bohemian throne, i.e., whether Bohemia was to be
Catholic or Protestant ; it rapidly developed into a struggle
between leagues of Catholic and Protestant States, and was
prolonged by the intervention of Gustavus Adolphus of
Sweden, leading what practically amounted to a Protestant
Crusade. Eventually it terminated in a kind of exhaustion.
The Treaty of Westphalia, as we have seen, settled the
religious map of Europe on a territorial basis, and settled it
for a very long time. But the devastation caused by the
Thirty Years' War had meanwhile put back the social
and economic development of large parts of Germany for
generations.

Cujus regio ejus religio did not mean religious toleration.
It did mean, however, that some possibility of religious
difference was recognised, since it was at any rate theoretically possible for a man to change his religion by changing his
country ; and gradually, in the Lutheran countries and in
England, the positive use of persecution began to decline.
Men suffered punishment and disability more because
their nonconformity with the State religion, whatever it
was, appeared to endanger the State, and less because it was
absolutely wicked and must be stamped out at all costs.
But one of the Reformed Churches held the contrary view
as strongly as any Inquisitor. The city of Geneva in 1541
committed itself to the administration of John Calvin, the
greatest and most ruthless of all the leading Reformers.
Calvin initiated the " Rule of the Saints," or the elect,
which demanded and fiercely enforced a strict conformity
in matters social and ethical as well as religious. Calvinism
wherever it went—and the power and logic of Calvin's
mind spread it far beyond the borders of Switzerland—was

always a persecuting creed, with the actual amount of persecution only limited by the strength of the particular Calvinistic Church. The civil government, in the view of the Calvinists, should be ruled by the elect, and should enforce the ideas and decrees of the Church.

Even to the Calvinists, however, religious toleration came in time and by force of events. Towards the end of the sixteenth century such people as the *Politiques* in France, Robert Browne in England, and Arminius in Holland were beginning to say that religious beliefs, if their holders were law-abiding, ought not to be the concern of the civil government ; the advent of the Quakers, who resisted persecution quietly but would not persecute, added to the general tendency, which was further reinforced as it became slowly clear that no persecution could really stamp out, for example, Catholicism in the Protestant States. Toleration, therefore, began to grow, more quickly in the Protestant than in the Catholic countries ; but in all its growth was slow, and the admission of tolerated persons to citizenship was slower still. In England, richest and safest of all the chief Powers, full Catholic emancipation was not secured until 1829, and events to-day remind us how far parts of " civilised " Europe are from even tolerating the Jews.

The New World.   Simultaneously with the Reformation and the wars of religion was taking place the political change from the medieval system to the system of national monarchies, to which we have already alluded, and the economic change to what is usually called Capitalism. Before we consider either of these changes, however, we must briefly explain the great change in the size of the known world which took place at the end of the fifteenth and the beginning of the sixteenth centuries.

One of the chief causes, no doubt, which led to the discovery of America was the closing, by the fall of Constantinople and the growth of the Ottoman Empire, of the trade routes to Asia. This gave a renewed impulse to adventurous sailors to test practically both the old legends—probably coming in their origin from Phœnician traders—of a lost continent lying far to the west of Europe, and the redis-covered knowledge that the world was round ; and the improvement of shipbuilding, such inventions as the mariner's compass, and the increased prosperity of Europe during the fifteenth century, made it possible to finance and provision such expeditions with reasonable hope of success. But the actual motive for the earliest " voyages of discovery " was religious. Dom Henriques of Portugal, often called Prince Henry the Navigator, sent his first expeditions out to West Africa as a semi-crusade, to convert the Moors and the native Africans to Christianity. Little of conversion was achieved ; but the expeditions and the settlements proved profitable, both in African products such as gold and ivory, and in African natives brought over to increase the labour force of Portugal. The African slave-trade, which was to prove so tremendous a social factor in the New World, began with the Portuguese expeditions in the latter half of the fifteenth century.

The Portuguese sailors continued their explorations southward from the mouth of the Senegal ; they rounded the Cape of Good Hope, and in 1598 Vasco da Gama landed in Calicut and thus established the " Cape route " to India and China. Meanwhile the Spanish State, under Ferdinand and Isabella, had taken the same course as regards the West. Columbus reached Hispaniola (Cuba) in 1492 ; the continent of America was discovered in 1498 ; Spanish expeditions conquered Mexico in 1517, and Peru in 1531 ; in 1519 to 1522 Magellan's voyage completed the circuit of the globe. The immediate result of the voyage of Columbus was the famous Papal Bull of 1493 dividing the New World between Spain and Portugal—a bull which the Reformation soon made inoperative.

The Italian cities, hitherto the leaders of sea-trading expeditions, played no part as such in the Discoveries, though Columbus and other navigators were of Italian birth. They were not so happily placed, geographically, as the countries with an Atlantic seaboard ; and they were further occupied in disputes with one another, with France and the Empire, and in defending themselves against Turkish aggression. But where Spain and Portugal had led, other countries, particularly England and Holland, followed. The Cabots discovered Newfoundland for England in 1497 ; the Dutch sailed to Trinidad and Guiana, planted colonists at the Cape of Good Hope, and attacked the Portuguese in the East Indies ; and during the sixteenth century many attempts were made to turn the flank of the Portuguese in the East Indies by discovering a North-West or a North-East Passage to India. The first of these goals proved hopeless and was finally abandoned after much loss ; the second led to the partial opening up of Russia to western trade *via* Archangel. But owing to the mineral wealth of South and Central America and to the Reformation, the main interest of the Protestant countries, in those years, lay, not in Canada or Moscow, but in plundering the Spanish and Portuguese monopolies. The defeat of the Armada in 1588 was only the largest single event in a campaign of anti-Spanish aggression.

The most noticeable *immediate* effects of the Discoveries were the great improvement in seamanship and ship-building which the long voyages necessitated, and the great influx of precious metals from the New World, which raised prices, and made possible a rapid expansion of trade and manufacture. But of course the long-term effects were very much greater. In the first place, the effect on men's minds of the sudden doubling of the size of the known world can hardly be exaggerated. Two new continents, to say nothing of India and the Spice Islands, now lay open to exploitation, and though their possibilities for the reception of settlers, as markets, and as sources for raw materials, were only slowly realised or exploited, they were at once sufficiently seen to fire the imaginations and to alter the assumptions of men, particularly those who lived on the western sea-board. The great change in the tone and spirit of English literature in Elizabethan days is sufficient proof of this.

Men did not know exactly what was happening or what was going to happen. But they knew that something was, and that it was enormous and fundamental.

The Rise of Capitalism.

Secondly, the New World gave additional impetus to the demand for new forms of economic organisation. This brings us to the subject of economic change to which we referred above. It is not possible to give any date for the introduction of " Capitalism " into Europe. All the features which we know as characteristic of Capitalism (except, of course, power-driven machinery) can be found in Europe before the Reformation, and changes from medieval economy were taking place before Columbus had been heard of. Nevertheless, the sixteenth century did see a rapid acceleration towards new forms. The gild system was breaking down, both from internal decay and from unsuitability to changing conditions. Internally, particularly in districts such as Northern Italy and Flanders, where the gilds had been wealthiest and strongest, bitter class-divisions had developed. The gilds had become, in effect, small oligarchies of rich men, keeping under their control both the lesser members of the gilds—and, in some cases, whole gilds which were, or were thought to be, of lesser importance—and also a quantity of hired labour which had no chance of rising to an independent position. This had already begun to give rise to class-struggles in gild cities, particularly in the districts mentioned above. Nevertheless, the growing narrowness of the gild oligarchy did not make it more flexible for undertaking the large-scale and long-distance operations which the new conditions required. For, though oligarchic, it was still in many respects bound by unsuitable traditions ; it had rules as to equality of opportunity among its members which prevented a would-be captain of industry from getting full play ; its control of the economy of the older towns largely hindered the development of new industries therein ; and it was still, in part at any rate, bound by Church theories about profit, price, and the payment of interest which seriously interfered with a rapid expansion of its operations elsewhere.

To sum up briefly a complicated subject, what the rising *entrepreneur* of the sixteenth century wanted was (*a*) command of ready money for investment without restriction in any enterprise in any place, and (*b*) a mobile labour force which could similarly be employed at any time and place without gild or feudal restrictions. The first he secured partly through the great expansion of the currency which was mentioned above, and partly by means of the regulated company, joint-stock company or partnership which operated, like the English East India Company, under charter but without gild restrictions. The second came to him through the break-up of feudalism in Western Europe, through the desire of the landowner to have money rather than hinds, to run his estate at a profit rather than to live off it in the old traditional way while supporting a large army of labour which might defend or aid him in private war. This tendency was most marked in England, where a large part of the land was deliberately turned over to the profitable business of sheep-farming, thus setting " free " a large mass of labour for employment either in new manufacturing enterprise or in the navy and merchant service of Elizabeth.

Neither gilds nor feudalism, naturally, died at once. Feudalism had received a blow from the ravages of the Black Death in 1348–51. It had practically disappeared in England and Holland ; but it survived, though with decreasing energy, in France, and was actually being introduced, in the form of degraded serfdom, into Eastern Europe (Poland in 1496, Russia in 1597, Austria in 1627). It may be noted, however, that even Western Capitalism had no objection to serfdom as such, as can be seen from its deliberate introduction into Scotland in the sixteenth century to provide labour for the Scottish mines.

The gild system in England, where it had never been very strong, and where the power of the new capitalists was greatest as compared with that of the Crown, was moribund by the end of the sixteenth century. On the Continent it remained, varying in strength and importance in different places, until after the French Revolution and Napoleon's conquests. But the future was not with it.

The new Capitalism, in objecting to gild regulation, tended also to object to the old system of town government and customary law, which was so bound up with it. This did not mean, however, that it desired no law at all, but that it desired law more simple, more uniform, more suited to its requirements, and operating over a wider area. Greater uniformity might be secured by the reversion to legal systems derived in part from the old Roman law—which did, in fact, take place to a considerable extent ; but the widening of the area of operation involves the creation of an effective authority which can enforce the law. This fact placed the new Capitalism in general upon the side of the national State as against the small, traditional, and cumbersome medieval unit. Put concretely, the capitalist wanted the king's writ and the king's arms to protect his operations, and he did not, fundamentally, care whether the king was acting in accord with Christian principles or not, so long as he gave security.

The Growth of States.   We have already given an account of the rise of the national monarchies in most European countries, and there is little to add to it for the century of the religious wars. Three things are of sufficient importance to merit separate mention : first, the disappearance, as free States, of all but a few of the cities of the Hansa League in the Baltic and the North Sea, partly because of economic decline after the Discoveries and the fall of Constantinople had lessened the importance of trade between the Baltic and the Levant, and partly through conflict with the national monarchies of Sweden and Denmark ; secondly, the rise of Prussia, united with Brandenburg in 1618, to a position among the German States only second to that of Austria ; and thirdly, the expansion of Russia to the East. Russia, not being a member of the

Roman communion, was unaffected by the Reformation ; but during that period she became appreciably more like the Russia we know to-day. The Tsars of Moscow, particularly Ivan IV, drove the Tartars steadily back, and incorporated the Tartar principalities of South Russia, as well as the older city-states, such as Pskov and Nijni-Novgorod and the district of Livonia, in their empire. Later in the century a great colonisation of Siberia took place, and showed, as has been shown both before and since, that the Urals do not in effect form any barrier between Europe and Asia. The successors of Ivan had to face a certain amount of semi-feudal revolt, which is generally connected with the name of Boris Godunov ; but early in the next century the empire was secure, and the first Romanov succeeded in 1613.

More important than these, however, was the appearance and working out of a theoretical basis and justification of the modern State (which has profoundly influenced thought and action ever since), and the defence of civil government upon lines which omitted the religious argument altogether. Curiously enough, this justification first appeared in a country which did not achieve a national State for hundreds of years. Machiavelli the Florentine in 1513 completed *The Prince*, which is a defence of the civil State—and of the employment by it, in order to secure social order, of methods which would be condemned by ordinary standards of personal morality—by arguments which are wholly secular. The State must exist, and must govern, by any and every means, for the sake of law and security ; and that is all that matters. This is the essence of Machiavellianism, and its simplicity has largely obscured both its fundamental nature and the completeness of its break with the past. Except for a brief period during which a childish doctrine called " the divine right of kings " attempted vainly to find a new religious sanction for national monarchies, no defender of absolutism from Hobbes to Mussolini has ever gone back to the arguments of religion. Though they may have added mystical and philosophic frills of varying value, they are all in essentials Machiavellians.

Some historians date the birth of modern Europe from the Treaty of Westphalia, some postpone it to the outbreak of the French Revolution or the battle of Waterloo. In 1648 there is, at any rate, much of modern Europe to be seen. The States which made the Treaty were all, except the Emperor, independent self-governing States in the modern sense—and the Emperor, though he survived, survived with sovereignty much curtailed. Their representatives met, for the first time, in a representative congress upon political questions. Its acts were drawn up in Latin as being the international language—this was subsequently replaced by French—and such diplomatic questions as the order of precedence among States were settled for the first time. Modern diplomacy, in fact, was really born at the signing of that treaty, a fact which may have some bearing on the extreme obsolescence of modern diplomacy.

The main difference between 1648 and 1815, considered as birth-dates for the modern world, lies in the idea of democratic nationalism, the creature of the French Revolution. National States, as we have seen, appeared in full strength during the Reformation period ; but they were, with but few exceptions, dynastic, autocratic States, among which territories, with their accompanying populations, were distributed according to strength, the limits to the acquisitions of any particular potentate being set by his own weakness or the willingness of his neighbours to combine against him. The principle of Luther with regard to religion was transferred to politics as religion waned, and it was not conceived that the common people had any right to choose in what national State they were incorporated, though it was observed, of course, that in certain cases the rule of an alien State might as a fact be so unpopular as to lead to rebellion—as, under any form or theory of government, a particular ruler may prove himself so obnoxious that he gets deposed or assassinated. No political system of any kind can deny the possibility, though it may deny the right, of insurrection. The revolt of the United Provinces, described in a previous section, is a clear case in point. Philip of Spain was an alien to the Dutch ; but it was not as an alien primarily, but as an oppressive and unpopular alien, that he succeeded in uniting against him all classes of his Dutch subjects in a resistance which had in the end to be recognised as a fact. There was also a recognition of nationalist feeling in certain of the territories of Eastern Europe which had been conquered by the Ottoman Empire (notably Serbia) ; but this was a recognition of religious rather than national oppression. It was as Christians held down by infidels rather than as Serbs held down by Turks that their inhabitants claimed sympathy. Nationalism, in the modern sense, together with political democracy, was taught to Europe by the French Revolution ; and, except within the Soviet Union, the years since Napoleon seem only to have increased its strength.

The outstanding features of the hundred and fifty years which followed the Treaty of Westphalia are, first, the development and crystallisation of the English social system to something very nearly resembling its present form ; second, the great changes in the overseas affiliations of the different countries ; third, the quarrels of the autocratic States in Europe, and the various attempts at hegemony, of which the French is the most important ; fourth, the beginnings of those ideals of democracy and equality which shaped, though they did not make, the French Revolution ; and fifth, the economic changes which were taking place above all in England, and which, speeded up to a sudden and epoch-making extent, turned rapidly into the machine age.

England was by far the most important exception to the statement that the national States of the seventeenth century were autocratic. Not that the Tudors and Stuarts would not gladly have been autocrats, but they could not for lack of cash. Henry VIII having in effect created a rich *bourgeoisie* as a price for assistance in breaking free from the

Pope and becoming a power in Europe, in which he received the hearty co-operation of Wolsey with results unfortunate both for Wolsey and the Crown, his successors had to put up with the situation, and either rule in accord with the views of a Parliament of squires and merchants or lose their own crowns or heads. Charles I, appealing to traditional loyalties, kept up a fight for some time ; but he was beaten as much by the power of the City of London as by anything else ; and in 1688 it was actually the City which called William III to the throne. Thus was the constitutional monarchy in England firmly established, safeguarded by the king's coronation oath, the financial control of Parliament, and the refusal to sanction a standing army ; and the merchants and landowners who had made the Revolution agreed not so much to share the spoils of government as jointly to receive and distribute them. The new system was fastened firmly on the country by the institution in 1694 of the Bank of England and the National Debt, which gave to the leading Whigs a direct interest in the financial and political stability of the country. It is significant that, after the death of Queen Anne, few of the English Jacobites raised a finger or put their hands in their purses to help either of the Pretenders ; and after 1745 the Government, by encouraging road-building and by a savage clearance of the economically backward Highlands, insured against a second repetition of the invasions.

More interesting, perhaps, is the stereotyping of the English class system somewhere about the reign of Anne. A modern reader, studying either Locke, the father of modern English political thought, or Defoe, the first modern novelist, must surely feel that here is the modern Englishman at last, a very different fellow from passionate controversialists like Milton or Bunyan, or the florid, word-loving *romancier* of the seventeenth century. Mind and temper and language, all seem to be changed. How has this happened ?

The clue to the English class system is that, owing to the comparative weakness and the early break-up of feudalism,

the various sections of the *bourgeoisie*—landowners, merchants, and the higher ranks of the army and the professions—were all fused together, often, indeed, all represented
in the same family ; that the landowners, as a class, many
of them being merchants by origin, treated their land as a
property to be improved and made to pay, not purely as an
endowment to be lived off, while the merchants (who frequently married into the families of the landowners),
tended to put their money into the land, either by contribution or by purchase. Sheep, further, provided a direct
economic link between the merchant and the landowners ;
the landowner bred the sheep, whose wool was the merchant's stock-in-trade. England, therefore, never developed
a functionless aristocracy, as did eighteenth-century France
or nineteenth-century Russia, and there was no real antagonism between the landowning and merchant classes.
A merchant risen from humble origins was readily accepted
into the governing class, and there was no general bar to
the acceptance of a manufacturer, though in the days of
the industrial revolution the manufacture of manufacturers
took place with such rapidity that they could not be absorbed with ease, and a situation of momentary difficulty
was created.

In Defoe's time, however, there was this wealthy and
homogeneous governing class, sharing the government out
among its members, with the Crown as a useful asset, differing at times over the spoils of government and details of
administration, but not at all in fundamentals. Below them
was a steady middle class, consisting on the one hand of
small yeomen and tenant farmers, and on the other of
small tradesmen and manufacturers, of whom Defoe was
one, disposed, like the English middle class at all times, to
grumble against its rulers, but on the whole quite contented. Below, again, was a populace of cottagers, hired
labourers, mine-workers, cloth-weavers, artisans and unskilled labourers in the towns, of whom no one cared, save
for the fear of strikes or bread riots, whether they were contented or not. In fact, their standard of living was, during

the major part of the eighteenth century at all events, rising sufficiently to keep them in acquiescent subjection.

This society was governed locally by Justices of the Peace, and in some of the old towns, also by closed and generally unrepresentative corporations deriving from ancient charters ; and nationally by a Parliament whose unrepresentative character had been obvious even by Cromwell's day. A surprising fact, to foreign observers, is that this Parliament was suffered to continue to exist in that form right until 1832. The explanation is quite simply that as a governing body it worked, and worked reasonably to satisfaction, until nearly the end of the century. After the accession of George III, it became for a time clear that a Parliament of unrepresentative, corruptible objects might be an inconvenience if the king decided to use it against the general will of the governing class, and proposals for reform therefore assumed some importance. But the outbreak of the French Revolution frightened the reformers into realising that an unrepresentative Parliament was far preferable to no Parliament at all, in the sense in which they had known it ; and reform was therefore postponed until fear of revolution had died away, and the inconvenience of a Parliament in which the manufacturing areas were almost entirely unrepresented, and too high a proportion of the voting machines were, or could be, at the command of too few persons, drove the manufacturing classes to join with the radicals and their own employees in a demand for reform. Which reform, though drastic enough to scandalise its opponents nearly out of their wits, proved, when applied to the British class-system, to involve quite small immediate alterations, and has been able to survive, with alterations in electorate and minor adjustments of procedure, right to the present time. Students, and admirers, of British " Parliamentary democracy " too often forget that the phrase should be pronounced with the stress on the word Parliamentary, not on the word democracy.

Colonies and Empire.   This book is not intended to trace
the history of Europe overseas, nor should we have space to
treat it adequately. But the *possession*, by European Powers,
of various territories and interests outside Europe so much
affects their policy and therefore the course of modern
European history, that the facts of the case must be briefly
taken into account. The main feature of our present period
is the rapid decline of Spain, the pioneer in New World expansion, and, to a less degree, of Portugal (from 1580 to
1640 Portugal was under the Spanish Crown) ; and the rise
of England, Holland and France as colonial Powers, the
first of these becoming, after vicissitudes, by far the most
important.

The question of Spain can be very shortly dealt with. As a
State, Spain declined and declined from Philip II's time
onwards. The defeat of the Armada was not an accident,
though luck played a part in it, as the winning of the toss
may assist a cricket team, but essentially the defeat of an inefficient by an efficient Power. This was due in part to
foolish economic policy, which rendered the bullion of the
New World a loss instead of a gain to the country which
brought it in, prevented the growth of manufacture, and
impoverished the agriculture of Spain ; and partly to the
bigotry of the Church in Spain and its close control over
government policy. These two factors combined disastrously
at times, as when in 1609 seventy thousand persons of
Moorish descent, including many of the most productive
elements of the Spanish population, were driven out of
Spain by order of the Church and salved by the Turks. But
the signs of this decline were far more visible in European
politics than in America, partly because the very economic
stagnation and poverty drove masses of Spaniards (50,000,
it was said, in one year) to emigrate, and so to assist in developing and retaining the New World possessions. Spanish
America was still open to plunder, but Spain retained all
her colonies until the nineteenth century, and even her exclusive right to trade with them until the Treaty of Utrecht
in 1713, when it was invaded by England. Portugal in the

seventeenth century lost the bulk of her East Indian possessions to the Dutch, but retained those on the African coast, and (except for a brief interval from 1624 to 1642) the vast territory of Brazil.

As is well-known, the colonial possessions of England, until after the Seven Years' War (1756–1763) consisted mainly of the North American colonies, founded at various dates from 1621 onwards, Newfoundland, the sugar islands of the West Indies, of which Jamaica was the most important, and certain trading stations in other parts of the world, notably on the Indian and African coasts. The French possessions were somewhat similarly distributed; French Canada and Louisiana in North America, sugar islands such as Guadeloupe and Martinique, and African and Indian trading stations. The Dutch, on the other hand, were all over the place—in New Amsterdam on the North American continent, in Brazil in South America, at the Cape of Good Hope, in Van Diemen's Land at the Antipodes, and in various places in the East Indies, from which, in the middle of the seventeenth century, they were gradually ousting the Portuguese. None of these possessions, however, was nearly as important as the Dutch carrying trade, which, in the early stages, was far greater than that of the English. The Dutch were the international carriers ; they were all but born on the water, and their ships, particularly after they were finally freed from Spain, went everywhere. Only gradually did England catch up to a point at which she could become a rival. In the early days of the English Protectorate, it is interesting to note, Cromwell made a proposal to the Dutch for the federation of the two Protestant, maritime, and now republican Powers—a proposal which was favourably received at first, but broke down, not altogether surprisingly, upon the question of the headship of the new federation. The English reprisal was the Navigation Act of 1651, which forbade English or colonial merchandise to be carried in any but English bottoms. This indicates at any rate some strength in English shipping ; yet sixteen years later the Dutch fleet was in the

Medway, coolly burning English ships at their moorings. By the end of the century, however, England, in spite of having accepted a Dutch king, had definitely gained the upper hand ; but this was due less to any inherent or acquired superiority than to increasing material wealth, and still more to her island position freeing her from constant fear of invasion and from the necessity of Continental entanglements. England could afford to keep out of Continental wars until it suited her interest to take part ; Holland could not, and the economic strain eventually wore her out.

In the eighteenth century, then, the colonial struggle transfers itself to England *versus* France. In that struggle France might be held to have many advantages ; she was still the richest country ; her colonies enjoyed (though intermittently, it is true) more support from the home Government than did the English possessions in America and India ; and her colonists seemed in many cases better able to secure native goodwill. The English American States, for example, whose record in treatment of Indians (with exceptions such as that of the Quakers who ruled Pennsylvania) is somewhat unsavoury, found that the French were far better trusted, and lived for long in terror of a French encirclement from the St. Lawrence to the Missouri letting loose raging tribes of Indians on their rear.

Nevertheless, the French Government, slipping down into the financial morass which preceded the Revolution, was unable both to hold an Empire and to carry out its European designs. Dupleix in India, and Montcalm in Canada, were both left without adequate support. In the one *annus mirabilis* of 1759 both India and Canada were lost, and the French colonial empire reduced to very small dimensions. (The present empire is nearly all post-Napoleonic.) England became pre-eminently *the* colonial Power ; the end of the eighteenth century saw Australia and the early nineteenth New Zealand painlessly becoming possessions of the British Crown ; and from 1815 onwards Great Britain takes part in European peace conferences with her eye on territorial acquisitions not in Europe but at the ends of the earth.

The political history of the Continent after 1648, for at any rate half our period, centres round the name of Louis XIV. The government of Henry IV and his minister Sully had successfully united France and repaired the economic losses of the wars of religion. Following upon them a succession of able Ministers reduced the nobles and the towns to complete dependence upon the king—the States-General, the only body in France resembling the English Parliament, met in 1614 for the last time before the Revolution ; and Louis XIV, at his accession in 1643, found himself the absolute ruler of the most populous kingdom in Europe, with the highest and most stable tax revenue, the largest army, the most experienced generals and diplomatists, and the highest reputation for art and culture. Armed with all these assets, the *Roi Soleil* set out, not long after the conclusion of the Treaty of Westphalia, to dominate Europe. The principal plank in his programme was to be the uniting of France with Spain, which was already in a state of decline, and whose king was a sickly imbecile unlikely to have children. This main object, however, though his generals made minor conquests upon his eastern borders, Louis was unable to achieve, mainly through the resistance of Holland. The Dutch intervened first in 1668, when he was invading the Spanish Netherlands, and the ensuing forty years were occupied in a series of coalitions organised against him by the Dutch, much as Pitt and his successors subsequently organised coalitions against Napoleon. The accession of William III, by bringing England into the war, finally settled it ; the victories of Marlborough at Blenheim and elsewhere (whose importance Southey's poem seems rather to under-estimate) depleted Louis' resources and forced him in the Treaty of Utrecht to give up both his conquests and his pretensions to Spain. Two years later he died, not without having drained the French exchequer to exhaustion. Meanwhile Austria, which had

acquired Bohemia in 1526, after a war with the Turks
conquered from them in 1699 the great area of Hungary,
and thus was formed the Austro-Hungarian Empire which
lasted until 1918, and gained, in 1713, Belgium, part of
North Italy, and Naples. Of the German Powers only the
united State of Brandenburg-Prussia (which owed a good
deal to the wise economic policy of its rulers) was at all
comparable to it ; and Prussia was still much poorer and
weaker than its neighbour.

Late in the century, an attempt somewhat similar to the
French attempt was made in Eastern Europe by the free-
booter Charles XII of Sweden, who endeavoured to make
the Baltic into a Swedish lake, to overrun Poland, and
even invaded Russia. Here, however, he met with the
obstacle of Peter the Great, who in 1685 had begun his
colossal task of westernising Russia. In that encounter
Charles was completely worsted, and by his death Sweden
had lost nearly all her possessions on the Baltic except
parts of Finland. Following up his advantage, Peter the
Great made an agreement with the king of Poland which
gave him some control over that country. In his reign, and
still more in that of Catherine II (1762–1796), another
westerniser, Russia definitely becomes part of what is subsequently called the Concert of Europe. One may also
note that a small kingdom, the kingdom of Sardinia, considerably increased in importance through the Treaty of
Utrecht. This is of significance for later European and
Italian history.

The Treaty of Utrecht left France beaten, but with
French territory unimpaired ; and the remainder of the
eighteenth century, until the Revolution, is occupied with
dreary diplomatic marchings and counter-marchings which
sometimes issue in war. Three things only are of importance
during the whole period—the survival of the kingdom of
Prussia under Frederick the Great from attack by Austria,
Russia, and France, and its acquisition of Silesia (a territory
nearly as much disputed as Alsace-Lorraine) from Austria ;
the alliance between France and Austria which may be

remembered by the marriage of Marie Antoinette to Louis XVI ; and the first partition of Poland between Prussia, Russia, and Austria, made in 1772.

§ 5. THE FRENCH REVOLUTION AND AFTER

THE FRENCH Revolution did not fall out of the air, either as regards its circumstances or the theories which guided it. As regards the circumstances, the most important are the financial bankruptcy caused by the long wars (and, to a much less extent, the extravagance of the Court and the governmental machine), the effects of an absolutist policy as regards trade and industry, and the persistence of an outworn feudalism and a functionless aristocracy. The natural resources of France were such that there was no real reason why industry and trade should not have developed there fast during the seventeenth and eighteenth centuries, and so created a solid basis on which the Continental wars could have been fought, as England fought the wars with Napoleon. And so, from time to time, they were developed. But trade and industry in France, as everywhere except in England and Holland, were under despotic control, and were therefore liable to sudden changes of policy either from political reasons or from pure caprice. The classic example is the revocation of the Edict of Nantes in 1685, which upset the entire silk industry by banishing thousands of Protestant textile workers from France. As a result, French industry, like French colonial expansion, was subjected to alternative over-stimulation and neglect, and magnificent opportunities were lost. Further, the remains of the medieval system were admirably calculated to hamper, discourage, and infuriate that class of would-be merchants and manufacturers whose support was of such importance to the government of eighteenth-century England ; while at the same time the continuance of feudal dues and exactions for the support of the Church and a landed aristocracy which, whether it resided at the Court or on its estates, did on the whole nothing to earn its keep, was felt to be more and more oppressive. The business of government, as in the Roman Empire, became more expensive as the taxes grew harder to collect ; by the reign of Louis XVI the State finances were in hopeless confusion, and as the privileged classes refused to be taxed to meet the deficit, the only remaining expedient was to call together the States-General. When the Third Estate of this body (the Commons) refused to cast their votes as a separate estate and so be outvoted by the remaining two estates of nobles and clergy, the Revolution had begun.

To a considerable extent, at any rate, these small *bourgeois* (many of them lawyers and lesser clergy) who made up the Third Estate knew what they intended to do as well as what they were doing. The Revolution did not happen without a great deal of discussion and propaganda, some of it native, some of it derived from English and American sources. The idea of the Rights of Man was not new in the eighteenth century ; in some sort, the idea of a limit beyond which no Government has a right to interfere with its subjects goes back beyond the Absolute State to medieval times, and it turns up with great vigour in the English Civil War. But after 1688, when the government in England ceased to be generally obnoxious, this idea became more and more negative, a mere statement that there were certain points beyond which government became tyranny. Discussion did not altogether cease ; but it became quiet and inconspicuous until the revolt of the American colonies gave a new and positive content to the idea of natural rights.

The North American States, separated from Great Britain by three thousand miles of sea and united to it only by a vague loyalty to the King and a Crown governor whose hopes of a quiet life and a prosperous return depended largely upon his conciliating the residents during his term of office, had been practically free to evolve their own forms of political machinery, and many of them were composed, like the Puritan settlements, of individuals who had fled from England actually to escape from interference with what they conceived to be their natural rights. Feudalism, chartered towns, and other varieties of privilege had never been found in America ; on the contrary, political democracy and complete religious toleration appeared there long before they were seen in Europe.

Under these circumstances, as soon as the conquest of Canada had removed the need for British protection against French aggression, the control of the British Parliament began to be felt by the colonists as an interference with their natural rights. The British Government would not make concessions, and a dispute which began over an unimportant tax resulted, in a few years, in open and successful war, and the resounding phrases of the Declaration of Independence. " We hold these truths to be self-evident ; that all men are created equal ; that they are endowed by their Creator with certain inalienable rights ; that among these are life, liberty, and the pursuit of happiness. That, to secure these rights, governments are instituted among men, deriving their just powers from the consent of the governed ; and that, whenever any form of government becomes destructive of these ends, it is the right of the people to alter or abolish it, and to institute new government, laying its foundation on such principles, and organising its powers in such form, as to them shall seem most likely to effect their safety and happiness."

In England, these words struck chords in the minds of Whigs like Burke and Fox and Radicals like Paine and Priestley, and revived on all sides a demand for the reform of Parliament so as to make it more in accordance with natural rights ; but in France the effect was far greater. In France, the government had long been obnoxious to " enlightened persons " as well as to those who were directly oppressed and inconvenienced ; and the discussion of natural rights and the prevention of arbitrary oppression had consequently never died down. Many of the ideas of Jefferson and others of the American revolutionists were actually derived from discussions in French circles. Now, in 1776, the doctrine of the Rights of Man was actually proclaimed by a nation under arms as its primary objective. The French Government, in revenge for its defeat in the Seven Years' War, sent help to the rebels ; many future revolutionaries, such as Lafayette, went out with the French reinforcements, and saw with their own eyes this nation not merely victorious but preparing to translate the Rights of Man into constitutional terms. (Incidentally, they mostly returned to France before some of the difficulties of this translation were realised.) American independence was not the only factor in the situation. In 1764 Rousseau, the most inspiring and influential of French thinkers, had published his *Social Contract*, and all over Europe a new consciousness of the existence of the masses was arising. John Wesley discovered that even colliers had souls to be saved ; movements towards educating the ragged poor, towards improving the lot of felons and suspected persons, even towards recognising the humanity of slaves, were being born ; even such autocrats as Joseph of Austria and Catherine of Russia were fain to call themselves " enlightened despots," and, while abating no whit of their despotism, did at any rate do something to mitigate brutalities in its employment. At the same time, Jeremy Bentham, hardly out of Oxford, found in a book of philosophy the phrase " the greatest happiness of the greatest number," and set about applying that devastating criterion to the existing institutions of the world. Bentham, it is true, cared nothing for the Rights of Man ; he thought natural rights " nonsense," and natural and imprescriptible rights " nonsense upon stilts " ; but his insistence on the value of the individual and his happiness gave additional arguments for the destruction of systems which cared for neither. In 1789 it was possible, as it would not have been possible a century earlier, to conceive of the Rights of Man as something at once universal and positive, to imagine a state of society in which the whole people should really partake in the government—and to set about bringing it into being.

Not that the delegates to the assembly of the Third Estate intended all this when they met. They aimed first at the redress of their most glaring grievances, and secondly at the abolition of privilege and the establishment, probably, of something like English constitutional government. Even at this early stage, though, the people of Paris, by destroying the Bastille and forming a National Guard, had proved themselves a somewhat alarming ally ; and shortly afterwards the peasants throughout the country set about liquidating privilege in their own way, by burning the *châteaux* and expelling their owners. The new constitution and the disestablishment of the Church (the greatest owner of privilege) were pushed rapidly on ; and when the Court, in fear, appealed to other dynastic Courts to help it in restraining the excesses of its subjects, and the Courts of Austria and Prussia, albeit slowly, responded, the Revolution was in full swing. Republican armies appeared in answer to the foreign invasion, and as the usual economic and financial difficulties of revolution showed themselves, and the inevitable counter-revolution began in such places as Lyons and the Vendée, so the right wing and moderate revolutionaries found themselves pushed out by the Jacobin left, who were determined at all costs to save the Revolution by strong measures, while pushing it as far as it would go. It would not, however, go beyond political equality ; its heads were men of the middle class, who wanted the abolition of privilege and the introduction of equal political rights. So, though the constitution of the First Republic gave political equality to more persons than did the English Reform Act of 1832, any attempt to follow this with economic equality was promptly crushed, as in the case of Babeuf's *Conspiration des Egaux* (1795).

The French revolutionary wars began in 1792. At first beaten, the armies of the Revolution then had a brief period of success ; but, as the wars, particularly after the execution of the king and queen, were more fiercely prosecuted, and as other Powers, such as England, took a hand, the revolutionary forces began to crumble. Military considerations came to override others, and the Jacobin Government was superseded, first by the Directory, then by Napoleon as First Consul, and finally by Napoleon as Emperor. Even after his first rise, Napoleon had to spend some time in pulling his forces together and reorganising them, in fighting rearguard actions and indecisive actions ; it was not until after the battles of Marengo and Hohenlinden (1800) that the French Revolutionary army was really recognised as a new and formidable force. The immediate result of these battles was the conclusion of peaces, or rather truces, between Napoleon and his chief opponents.

Napoleon. From this point dates the real drive of the French Revolution into Europe, which, however, soon becomes indistinguishable from the military and dynastic ambitions of Napoleon himself. As has so often been the case in the course of history, Napoleon's foreign policy was disastrously out of date, and in his later years at all events was simply an insane revival of the projects of Louis XIV. The idea of proselytising the Revolution by arms, however, did not begin with Napoleon ; it began early, as a counter to the invasions, and in 1793 the French drove the Austrians out of Brussels, never effectively to return. Nor should it be forgotten that where the French armies went, the principles of the Revolution did in fact go with them. Feudalism, in the conquered countries, particularly in Western Germany, was brought to an end ; republics were set up in such places as Holland and the Lombard plain ; the *Code Napoléon* was introduced. The legal uniformity which is to be found to-day over large parts of the Continent is due to the French invasions.

At first, except for the defeat at Trafalgar, which conclusively showed that French command of the sea was not to be achieved, Napoleon carried all before him, defeating Prussia and Austria, seizing the latter's Italian possessions, setting up vassal kingdoms in Holland, Naples, and all over Western Germany, destroying the Holy Roman Empire,

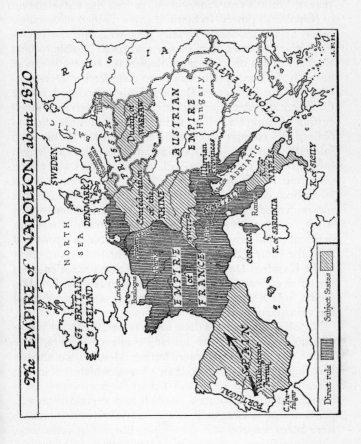

capturing the Pope, and overrunning Spain. But 1809, the year of Murat's entry into Spain, proved the highest point of Napoleon's power. In Spain the new French nationalism raised up a nationalism equally persistent, and the Peninsular War drained him of money and men. Unable to beat England at sea or to do more than make empty threats of invasion, he was equally unable to conquer her economically, for the boycott of English goods introduced by his Continental System was countered by the Orders in Council cutting off supplies, which so injured his allies that he was obliged to connive at extensive smuggling in his own interests. Further, his Continental conquests at length brought him into conflict with the Tsar, and led to the disastrous march on Moscow (1812). From Moscow check after check caused him to fall back until his abdication and the return of Louis XVIII, under the protection of the Allies, in 1814. Even then, after all the strain of war, his personal popularity was such that he was able to return and fight the campaign of Waterloo ; but the immediate effect of the Hundred Days, for France, was a severe stiffening of the terms of peace, and the fastening upon her of a Bourbon régime which was responsible for much of the troubles of the next thirty years.

Napoleon's wars have done much to obscure in the minds of historians and students his civil changes ; yet these were in fact no less great and more lasting. Mention has already been made of the Civil Code of 1802–3, which was in fact a reaffirmation in clear and definite terms of the social changes of the Revolution, though to a certain extent its political institutions, such as a greatly restricted franchise, were borrowed from the old régime. But, at the same time, Napoleon found opportunity enormously to improve the road and canal system of France, to institute an effective system of taxation, and to encourage industry as it had not been encouraged for a long time past. The prosperity and brilliance of France, particularly of Paris, just after the 1802 Peace of Amiens, were sights which the world came to see. All this, however, was achieved before the great invasions began ; if Napoleon had not been " the slave of history," Germany would have remained longer in the bonds of feudalism ; but France would have been enormously the gainer.

England and the Industrial Revolution.

Three causes of Napoleon's failure have already been mentioned—the failure to control the sea, the provocation of Spanish nationalism, and the attempt to make a French hegemony in Europe. To these a fourth should be added—the economic and financial strength of Great Britain, which enabled her, not only to maintain her sea power intact both in open conflict, as at Trafalgar, and by such measures as the repeated destruction of the Danish fleet, but also to keep the war going on a number of fronts (sometimes with singular ill-success) and to finance, with money and supplies, a perpetual opposition among other Powers. The European coalition which finally forced Napoleon's abdication is called by historians the Seventh Coalition ; had it not been for England's persistent pressing and England's financial power, the Seventh Coalition, and indeed several preceding coalitions, might easily never have been formed.

This economic power of England was chiefly the result of the economic development of the preceding century. The extraordinary growth of the last quarter of that century, which historians call the beginning of the industrial revolution, has obscured the progress made during the earlier years, but Defoe, writing of England about 1725, has no doubt about it. Again and again, in his *Tour* through England, he refers to the amazing growth of such towns as Liverpool in the previous twenty or thirty years.

Commerce, of course, rather than industry, showed the greatest increase during the earlier part of the period. Everyone has heard of the mass of trade done with distant parts by the great companies such as the Hudson Bay Company, the Turkey Company, the British West African Company, and above all, the East India Company.

(In the latter part of the eighteenth century the fortunes made by servants of the last-named—the " nabobs "— actually played no small part in the social and political history of their native land.) Old ports, such as Bristol, and newer ports such as Liverpool and Glasgow enormously increased in size and importance ; and there was an appreciable change in the diet of the people owing to greater and more varied imports of foreign food, such as tea, oranges, coffee, and cheap sugar. The English pudding— now, as some think, unfortunately common—was born under Queen Anne.

But manufacture was also proceeding rapidly, helped by greater financial stability and by the improvement of roads and the building of canals. Coal, mined in increasing quantities since Elizabeth's day, was becoming an important industry, and was steadily replacing the depleted timber of Sussex and Kent in the manufacture of iron ; metal goods of all sorts were being made in such centres as Sheffield and Birmingham : and there was a whole host of minor industries, in addition to the great woollen trade which, right up to the outbreak of war, was still the backbone of England's foreign trade. Shipbuilding was improving fast. Meanwhile, scientific experimentation (the Royal Society received its charter from Charles II) was helping to prepare the way for more rapid changes.

After the first quarter of the century, the agricultural experiments began that were so shortly to change the face of agricultural England. " Turnip " Townshend, Bakewell, and later Coke of Norfolk and other large landowners introduced methods of crop rotation and systematic stock-breeding which enormously increased agricultural productivity. (The value of Norfolk land was said to have increased tenfold between 1730 and 1760 alone.) At once landowning and large-scale farming became profitable propositions.

This had two results. In the case of stock-breeding there was much enclosure, resembling somewhat the enclosures of the sixteenth century, of commons for pasture. But in

arable the change was more far-reaching. The " engros-
sing " of arable land into large farms under a single direction involved the abandonment of the old strip system of
cultivation, where it still existed, of the common meadow
and pasture of the village, and in fact, of the communal
village life as it had existed since the Norman Conquest
and before ; and the provisions of the various Enclosure
Acts usually resulted in the small man getting no part in the
enclosed land. This enclosure movement was in full swing
when the war broke out ; it secured, generally speaking, a
considerably increased level of production ; and the high
war prices, coming on top of the increased production,
sent up enormously the monetary yield of agricultural
land. For a while, farming and land-owning became highly
profitable pursuits ; and as for the dispossessed cottagers
and small yeomen, few cared what happened to them as
long as parish doles were available out of the farmer's
surplus profits to prevent them actually reaching the point
of riot. If their services were not required as agricultural
labourers or for stone-breaking on the roads, perhaps they
could go into the army, or into the new factories.

For by the outbreak of war the manufacturing age was
beginning to transform Northern England, and beginning
to replace the old predominance of the woollen industry by
a predominance of cotton and iron. Factories employing
hired labour had long been known, particularly in the
cloth-weaving of Western England ; machines worked by
water-power had also been known to some extent. (Lombe's
silk-throwing factory employed 300 workers in 1718.) But
now a great crop of mechanical inventions enormously
increased the output of factory production, and prepared
the way for the age of steam.

Kay's flying shuttle, first used in 1727, is generally taken
as the starting-point of these new inventions, though it was
not itself used for machine production, but to increase the
output of the domestic weaver ; but in point of fact cotton
and iron progressed side by side. An invention which speeded up weaving needed to be followed by an invention to

speed up spinning ; coal, wanted for the ironworks, could not be mined in sufficient quantities unless some engine could be contrived to pump the water out of the deeper levels ; Watt's steam-engine, patented in 1763, could not be exploited unless it were possible to cast iron tubes hard and true ; and so on.

The cotton trade, even before the war, grew with enormous rapidity. In 1781 only $5\frac{1}{4}$ million pounds of raw cotton were imported ; by 1789 the amount had grown to $32\frac{1}{2}$ million. And this was before the application of steam to cotton manufacture ; for, though the steam-engine had been used there by 1789, it was not in full use until the nineteenth century, while the woollen trade was much slower to adopt it. Simultaneously there grew up an entirely new industry, that of engineering ; and the ironworks, violently stimulated, of course, by the demand for war material, increased their production many times over. Experiments with iron ships and the like prepared the way for the steam-engine, in the nineteenth century, to be adapted to the haulage of goods by land and sea.

These developments, with the bubble of war prices added to them, produced enormous fortunes for men from the northern counties, such as Richard Arkwright. Of the humblest origins, these found it difficult, owing both to class and place of birth, to get into the close corporation of the governing group. When, as not infrequently happened, they found themselves at odds with the policy of this governing group, they began to reflect on how its power was exercised and obtained, and to demand representation of the new industrial centres in Parliament. They listened to Benthamite Radicals who asked what was the *utility* of this ancient and venerable institution, this ancient and corrupt Church, these ancient and privileged municipal corporations, and came to the conclusion that they had no utility. The fact that many of them were Dissenters, and so suffering under civil disabilities and social contempt, pointed the argument. Further, the policy of the war blockade, with the resulting interference with trade, and above all, the

American War of 1812, angered them and turned them into opponents of the Government ; though too many of them held large blocks of the immense war debt, or profited by large war contracts, for them to risk upsetting the constitution before the war was over.

The reform movement, large before the end of the war, became larger still when it was over. The new factories in the north were collecting to work in them large supplies of labour, composed partly of women and children, partly of paupers, partly of low-grade Irish workers, and for the rest, of unskilled labour of various sorts, including some country-men evicted from the enclosed villages. Herded together in towns hastily run up without plan, air, or sanitation, and brutally disciplined within the factory, these workers formed the first aggregations of industrial proletariat in England (except for the northern miners and the west-country weavers) ; and, as prices rose and fluctuated, they were a source of perpetual anxiety to the Government. The small radical movements of the intelligent artisans who sympathised with the American and French revolution-aries and were working for the reform of Parliament and of the system of society which William Cobbett called the *Thing*, were unimportant and easily crushed by means of repressive laws such as those which suppressed the Corres-ponding Societies and the Trade Unions ; it was when the Radicals (above all, Cobbett) began to go round the new manufacturing districts, preaching to the new proletariat that the existing system was responsible for their dear food, their ragged clothes, and their wretched conditions, that a great and explosive Radical movement began to grow up. The Government first countered by the institution of the yeomanry, mounted regiments to keep the crowds in check ; then, as after the war the movement did not die down but rather increased with post-war unemployment, it took to more violent methods of oppression. It is then that we find the host of Acts of Parliament (some still unrepealed) against conspiracy and unlawful assembly, the repeated prosecutions of editors and pamphleteers, the extensive government system of spies and *agents-provocateurs*, and massacres like that of Peterloo. It was some years before it was realised that the only answer to Reformers was Reform.

Europe after Waterloo. However undemocratic the personal government of Napoleon, and however dangerous and obsolete his European ambitions, Waterloo meant the triumph of pure reaction in Europe. The House of Bourbon returned to Paris, it is truly said, " having learned nothing and forgotten nothing " ; but it is not always emphasised that they returned under express instructions to do neither. The end of the war gave the control of Europe to three absolute princes, the rulers of Russia, Prussia and Austria. Great Britain, whose main interest in the peace settlement lay in being able to retain her non-Continental conquests important for a naval power, such as Malta, Ceylon, Mauritius, and the South African possessions taken from the Dutch, was content to act in the very congenial rôle of policeman, Wellington being put in command of the Allied military occupation of Paris.

Meanwhile, the victorious despots proceeded to divide up the European spoil among themselves and such of their allies as seemed worthy of reward. The Tsar Alexander desired to give a mystical colouring to his political affiliations ; and consequently there arose the Holy Alliance of the three sovereigns (to which Louis XVIII was soon admitted), by which they undertook to regard themselves as appointed by Providence to preserve the post-war political system in Europe. This curious revival of the theory of Divine Right struck men's imaginations at the time ; but it was a spiritual and not a practical alliance. The practical architect of the peace settlement and political controller of Europe was not the Tsar but the Austrian foreign minister, Metternich.

By the terms of the Treaty of Paris, Poland, which Napoleon had partly restored in the Grand Duchy of Warsaw, was again divided between the three despotic Powers. The last remaining piece, the district around

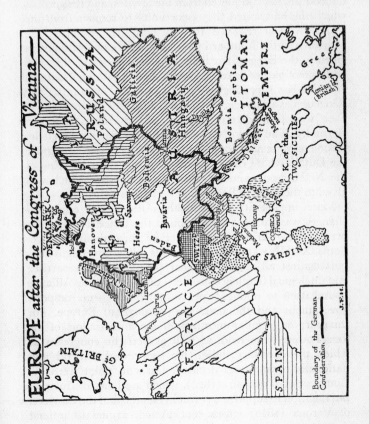

EUROPE after the Congress of Vienna

Gt BRITAIN
DENMARK
Holstein
Hanover
Saxony
Hesse
Bavaria
Baden
Luxem
Paris
FRANCE
SPAIN
CORSICA (French)
SWITZ.
Piedmont
Nice
Genoa
K. of SARDINIA
Modena
Lucca
Tuscany
Parma
K. of the
TWO SICILIES
Dalmatia
OTTOMAN EMPIRE
Bosnia
Serbia
Danube
Hungary
Bohemia
AUSTRIA
Galicia
Poland
RUSSIA
Gree
Ionian Is. (British)

Boundary of the German Confederation.
J.F.H.

Cracow, was finally absorbed by Austria in 1846. Russia retained Finland, conquered from the Swedes, and Bessarabia, which she had seized the opportunity to remove from the Turks. Austria received the northern part of Italy, i.e. Venetia and the Lombard plain, but not Genoa, which was given to the King of Sardinia. Prussia was enlarged by the addition of part of Saxony, Westphalia, the Rhine Province, and the last surviving piece of Swedish Pomerania ; the King of Bavaria received the Rhenish Palatinate ; and a Diet was formed representing all sovereign States in Germany. The minor German principalities destroyed by Napoleon were not restored. Finally, Belgium was put under the Dutch, whose ruler was raised to the status of King of the Netherlands, and the Danes lost Norway, which was given to the King of Sweden.

More important, perhaps, than the actual territorial changes was the creation, through the Peace Treaty, of a permanent instrument of reaction throughout Europe. Louis XVIII was promised by his fellow sovereigns support against all revolt, whether popular or Bonapartist ; and in logical sequence to this, the Quadruple Alliance bound itself to uphold " peace and quiet "—i.e. despotic government and the *status quo*—throughout Europe. For this purpose, regular meetings of the ambassadors of the four Powers were held, as well as periodic congresses at which the necessary action for suppressing Liberal and nationalist revolts was decided. Cases in point were the Congress of Troppau (1820) which authorised Austrian intervention to suppress a revolt in Naples, and the Congress of Verona (1822) which sent French armies to uphold despotic monarchy in Spain. The foreign invasions of Russia in the years immediately following the establishment of Communist rule were only a revival of the " interventionist " principles of 1816.

Two qualifications to this system should be noticed—the non-adhesion of Great Britain and the doubtful position of Turkey. Great Britain, having, as she believed, solved her own nationalist problems by the clearance of the Highlands and the purchase, in 1801, of the weak-kneed Irish Parliament, was a constitutional monarchy and proud of it, and very disinclined to force absolutist régimes on any European peoples. From the Treaty she wanted nothing but her naval conquests and the elimination of Napoleon and the danger of French attack. Both of these were early secured ; and, having got what she wanted, Great Britain, in effect, withdrew from the Continental *bloc*, and became, indeed, a potential source of support for Liberal and nationalist revolutions. The Sultan of Turkey, partly owing to remaining religious prejudices and partly owing to particular disputes at the time of the signing of the Treaty of Paris, was not a party to the Quadruple Alliance ; it was not until 1856 that Turkey formally became part of the Concert of Europe.

We thus have Europe nailed into an absolutist system in which territories were distributed with a fantastic disregard for the nationalist sentiments to which the French Revolution had given so large an impetus. The Treaty of Paris created seething storm-centres of national feeling, of which the most important were to be found in Belgium, Poland, Northern Italy, parts of the Austrian Empire such as Hungary and Bohemia, and certain of the Balkan provinces of the Turkish Empire. Side by side with these, however, there existed the strong Liberal movements in countries such as Spain, Portugal, France, and Western Germany, where there was no foreign oppression, but where the inhabitants had seen and even tasted the pleasures of constitutional government ; and—small now, but soon to grow —the protests of the new industrial proletariats against absolutism in the economic sphere. For the next thirty years the revolutionary movement in Europe was made up of nationalists, Liberals, and Socialists united in a harmonious hatred of all forms of oppression ; it was not until much later that the differences between these forces appeared, and it became clear that nationalism triumphant could be as illiberal as any autocracy, and that neither nationalism nor liberalism was necessarily in the least

favourable either to Socialism or to the working class. Until
1848, and indeed for some time afterwards, Marx and
Mazzini and a solid English Liberal Trade Unionist of the
type of William Allen could often work together.

It will be our task to trace the breaking up of the system
of 1815 until by 1870 it had disappeared for all practical
purposes ; but first we must turn aside to deal briefly with
the unique internal history of Great Britain.

When the immediate war reaction was over, and some
years before the Reform Act set the seal on change, the
British system had moved steadily in the direction of
liberalism. The worst of the repression was lightened after
1820 ; Trade Unions, suppressed in 1800, were restored,
almost casually, in 1824–25 ; the Catholics were emancipated, and the political (though not the economic or nationalist) grievances of the Irish thus redressed, in 1829 ; and
throughout the decade before the Reform Act Huskisson
and his colleagues, at the bidding of the northern manufacturers, were gradually removing governmental control
over trading operations. This last, of course, was an imperialist as much as a Liberal move; it was a recognition,
signalled by the removal of the embargo upon the export of
machinery and of skilled artisans, that it would for some
generations pay Great Britain to stimulate the economic
development of other nations as far as possible in order that
they might be in a position to buy her increasing surplus of
industrial goods. To this end the promotion of international
trade, the removal of tariff barriers, and the elimination of
war clearly contributed ; and until the 'eighties, at any rate,
it was perfectly possible for Liberals of the Cobden type to
regard the British system as the height of progressive
liberalism, and the British navy as only a police force necessary to ensure that this liberalism was not interfered with by
persons or groups of illiberal or unprogressive tendencies.

The 1832 Reform Act was carried by the manufacturing
classes with the aid of a discontented and hungry proletariat—of which the rural wing, attempting a protest by
itself in 1830, had been savagely crushed, thereby clearly

indicating that it was absolutism and foreign domination, not home repression, to which British Liberals objected. William Cobbett, who himself was accused of complicity in the 1830 risings, was one of the few Radicals to see in this the indication of the probable attitude of the middle-class reformers to their working-class allies when they should have gained their ends. The Reform Act, as a belated change, was drastic enough to surprise many. That is to say, it decisively removed the property rights of great land-owners in Parliamentary seats ; it brought the new indus-trial cities into the Parliamentary machine ; and it gave, impartially, votes to all the new *bourgeoisie* above a certain standard of living. The fact that it produced so little imme-diate change in either the method or the personnel of govern-ment, as, indeed, the fact that it succeeded in passing with the minimum of disorder, is a tribute to the adaptability of the British governing class. The political life of Wellington, that Iron Duke who in practice was such very malleable iron, is well worth studying from this point of view.

The Rise of the Working Class.

But the working classes, as a whole and immediately, got nothing out of the Reform Act. They did not get the vote ; in fact they actu-ally lost it in the few constituencies, such as Westminster, where they had possessed it before. In local affairs the Municipal Corporations Act of 1835 initiated a system of government in which they were no more represented than they were in Parliament. Wages and the cost of living were naturally unaffected by the political change ; and though the Reformed Parliament did make a small gesture in the direction of public education, and did, in the Factory Act of 1833, pass a useful measure which was more useful after its amendment in later years, the effects of these were small, and the Parliament was too much influenced by manufacturers and Liberals of the real *laissez-faire* school to interfere either with the horrible social conditions of such areas as Lancashire and South Wales or with the industrial despotism of the self-made factory owner. By far the most

obvious result of the Reform Act to the working classes was
the New Poor Law of 1834, which carried out an inevitable
economic change, the removal of surplus and stagnant
labour from the villages, by extremely harsh methods. The
triumph of liberalism, in England, came to mean to the
working classes the triumph of the workhouse—the English
Bastille.

Under these circumstances, the working-class organisations, Trade Unions, Co-operatives, and political societies,
which had been springing up rapidly for the previous ten
years, broke into open revolt, first in the great strikes of
1833–34, and then in the Chartist movement of 1836 onwards. Under the influence, largely, of Robert Owen, the
pioneer of factory legislation, the father of English Socialism
and Co-operation, as well as the initiator of many ideas upon
education, etc., whose fruit has yet to be fully gathered, most
of these movements had at any rate tendencies towards
Socialism in a pre-Marxian sense, i.e. towards equalitarian
communities of self-governing producers. Owen's direct
connection with the movement ceased with its industrial
defeat ; but many of the Chartist leaders were influenced by
him. Both protests failed, the industrial one immediately,
Chartism after a period of years. The constitution was never
really in the slightest danger from either. Apart from the
special economic circumstances (to which we shall return)
and the strength of the just-cemented alliance between
the old governing class and the new *bourgeoisie*, the movement failed from insufficient resources and divided counsels.
Particularly in the case of the Chartists, the division between
those who wished to educate by propaganda and those who
wished to prepare a revolution, was paralysing to both groups.
By the time of its final (and somewhat ludicrous) demonstration in 1848, Chartism was practically dead, though
Chartists, and members of the now reviving Trade
Unions, provided links with the revolutionists on the
Continent.

Apart from its inherent weaknesses, Chartism failed
partly because of changes in economic conditions, and

partly because some of its appeal was stolen by an organisation which was middle-class in aims and leadership. The Anti-Corn Law League, with its cry for cheap bread, seemed to promise what the working class had hoped to achieve from Reform, with more likelihood of success than through the Chartists ; and accordingly, membership fell away to take part in the great propaganda campaign of Bright and Cobden. Actually, the repeal of the Corn Laws, which was put through, under the immediate stimulus of the Irish famine, in 1846, did not bring cheap bread, for foreign wheat could not come in in sufficient quantities seriously to lower the home price until transport had been very much improved. All that free trade in corn did for some time after its introduction was to steady the level of prices so that a bad British harvest did not result in an immediate rise in the price of bread[1] ; and, in fact, as far as economic conditions were concerned, there was little reason why the Corn Laws should not have been repealed some years before. But the continuing support of a landowning class is not bought without a price.

Cheap food did not come in 1846. But better conditions were coming, partly owing to railway development. The middle of the 'forties was the great age of railway-building in Great Britain. In 1842 there were only 1,857 miles of railway ; by 1849 there were 6,031, and by 1854, 8,954 ; and the quantity of unskilled labour required for the building of all this mileage sensibly improved the state of employment. Further, the opening up of the New World, largely with the help of British capital, increased the opportunities for emigration. Money wages were not sensibly increased until after 1850, and then not very fast for some time ; but they were more regular, and they had fewer mouths to support. The British working class was moving towards the comparative prosperity of the mid-century ; and its ardour for revolt was waning. It did not receive the franchise until 1867, or, in the country districts, until 1884 ;

[1] With the exception of the year 1854–55 (the year of the Crimean War), in which there was a sharp rise.

Dr

but it was being well prepared to enter the *bourgeois* Parliamentary game of alternate Liberal and Conservative Governments which followed the Reform Act.

Nationalism in the Nineteenth Century.

The system of 1815 did not last long intact, though the two breaches first made in it might be strictly argued to be outside the system proper. In 1822–23 the Spanish and Portuguese colonies in South America declared their independence. The Powers, which had recently aided in stamping out a Liberal insurrection in Spain, desired to intervene ; but the United States unexpectedly took a hand, proclaiming in the Monroe Doctrine (1823) that intervention by European Powers on the American continent would no longer be tolerated ; and Canning, who desired to secure entry for British goods into the South American market, in the following year recognised the revolted States. The Spanish colonial empire was thus reduced to Cuba and the Philippines (which were lost in 1897 to the United States) and a few possessions on the coast of Africa.

In Europe, the Greeks in 1821 revolted against their Turkish masters. Little notice was taken at first until Mehemet Ali, pasha of Egypt and vassal of the Sultan, came to the rescue of his overlord and through his son Ibrahim began brutally putting down the revolt. Then a wave of anti-Mohammedan feeling appeared, and was reinforced, in England and France at any rate, by a sentimental republicanism which remembered the great days of classical Greece. (From 1802 to 1816, Lord Elgin had signalised English admiration for Greece by removing the best Parthenon sculptures from Athens to England.) Sympathy became widespread ; a Greek Loan, most of which never reached the Greeks at all, was raised ; the poet Byron went to their assistance and died at Missolonghi ; and finally England, France, and Russia joined in " mediating " with the Sultan to secure Greek independence. A small kingdom of Greece, presided over by a son of the King of Bavaria and guaranteed by all the Powers, was set up in 1832 ; but a concurrent revolt of Mehemet Ali against the Sultan had the un-expected result of rallying Russia to the protection of the latter and placing her, for the moment, in effective control of the Black Sea. One of the most difficult aspects of the " Near Eastern Question," the control of the Dardanelles, thus came to the front.

Turkey was not part of the Concert of Europe, and the Spanish colonies were far away. The events of 1830 to 1834, however, were more unmistakeable. In France the reac-tionary rule of Charles X, stupidest of all the Bourbons, had become intolerable to all but the extreme Right, and in July 1830 a brief revolution, accompanied by the mini-mum of street-fighting, turned him out and replaced him by Louis Philippe, son of a Revolutionist, who was intended to be a constitutional monarch of the English type. In the same year the Belgians revolted against Dutch domination. Great Britain and the new French monarchy supported them, and the Kingdom of the Belgians, with Leopold of Saxe-Coburg, uncle of Queen Victoria, at its head, was established in 1831. It was finally recognised by Holland in 1839 in the Treaty of London—the treaty by which all the leading Powers guaranteed to Belgium " perpetual neutral-ity." Further, in 1833–1834, there were liberal revolts in Spain and Portugal. These were successful, again with the support of England and France against the autocratic Powers, who backed the reactionaries—Carlists in Spain and Miguelists in Portugal. This, however, proved the end of liberal successes for the time being ; revolts in Italy and some of the small German States failed, and the Tsar seized the moment to take away most of the autonomy which had been granted to his Polish provinces. Nevertheless, the revolutionary movements, mostly under the inspiration of Mazzini, continued to develop underground.

It might have been expected that after 1830, and still more after 1832, England and France would stand in close alliance against a reactionary Europe. But Louis Philippe had too much of the French royal tradition in his blood to be an effective " head of a crowned republic." After a few years of indecision his government in effect became a veiled autocracy, which persistently embroiled itself with England over foreign policy, particularly in the Near East, where both countries had designs upon Egypt. A foolish attempt on his part to emulate the policy of Louis XIV by getting control of the Spanish throne completed the division. Nor did his government remain popular in France itself ; one party disliked his liberalism, another his autocracy, while the industrial proletariat, rapidly increasing in numbers, was furiously dissatisfied with the power given to the rich middle class and eagerly drinking in Socialist doctrines from the successors of Saint-Simon and Fourier, the French counterparts of Robert Owen. The people of Paris had made one revolution to free themselves from exploitation ; they were quite ready to make another.

The events of 1848 took all Europe by surprise. 1847 was a year of great distress and commercial panic ; it was also the year when the first international Socialist appeal, the *Communist Manifesto* of Marx and Engels, was drafted. (It was issued in 1848.) But in the main there was no particular cause for the " Year of Revolutions," except desperate discontent with the age of repression. It began with a rising in Sicily, which was quickly followed by insurrections in Paris, Vienna, Prague, Copenhagen, Berlin and many smaller German cities, a nationalist rising in Italy, led by the King of Sardinia, and another in Hungary, led by Louis Kossuth. In Belgium, Holland and Denmark, minor constitutional changes were demanded and received, in England, as related above, there was only a Chartist demonstration which was a failure, some Irish disturbances, which corresponded more to the continental upheavals, being suppressed easily and without publicity.

Taken by surprise and very much alarmed, the absolutist system at first yielded. The Hungarians gained their autonomy ; an Italian Republic was proclaimed in Rome and Tuscany ; several German princes hastened to grant constitutions ; and a republic, with avowed Socialists participating in the government, was set up in Paris. But reaction came swiftly and in arms. Everywhere, except in France, the risings were suppressed by the military, such concessions as a popular franchise, freedom of speech and freedom of assembly taken away, and monarchic and clerical despotism restored. In France, the liberal *bourgeoisie* resisted the attempt of the workmen and their leaders to give the revolution a Socialist aspect, and the workers under Louis Blanc and his colleagues were shot down by the Liberals under Cavaignac. The republic remained; but the reaction went so far as to enable Louis Napoleon, elected President in 1849, to make himself Emperor by the *coup d'état* of 1851. The German revolution collapsed; and the new Hungarian State was crushed in 1849 by Austrian arms. Nevertheless, though reaction triumphed it did not triumph completely. A few democratic gains remained; Napoleon III, elected by popular vote, could not occupy the position of a Continental despot, and England, though it had played so little part in the struggle, remained, under Palmerston, a tranquil home for exiled and active revolutionaries from all countries. (It may be noted that in 1847 the Protestant cantons of Switzerland, by defeating a Catholic League supported by the chief clerical powers and by France, had definitely put a stop to reaction in that country.)

Reaction emerged triumphant from the year of revolutions; but as has been said, it was not perfectly complete or very violent reaction. Only in Russia was the government entirely unaffected by liberalising ideas, and in Europe, partly owing to the economic conditions to be mentioned in the next section, there was, for a time, a definite tendency to pacific co-operation. The main interest of the next few years lies in the Near Eastern question, and the rise of Germany and Italy.

The story of Italian unity is quickly told. After the destruction of Garibaldi's Roman Republic in 1849, the Italian patriots had not in any way ceased their efforts, and within a few years, thanks largely to the diplomacy of Cavour, they had gained the partial support of Napoleon III, who until 1870 was prone to regard himself as commissioned to redraft the map of Europe on democratic lines. The struggle with Austria, which began in 1859, was short and decisive ; the Austrians were beaten, and a kingdom of Italy set up, after a plebiscite, with Victor Emmanuel of Sardinia as its king. Partly owing to the failure of Napoleon's support at the last moment, the unification of Italy was incomplete ; the Austrians were left in the possession of Venetia and the Pope of the Papal States, but during the distraction of the Franco-Prussian War the Italians redressed most, if not all, of these grievances. Italy thus became a national State on the parliamentary model ; but parliamentarism, as can be seen by events since the war, never obtained a strong hold on the minds of the Italians.

The history of German unity, until 1863 at all events, is the history of the growth of the German Zollverein or Customs Union, and its gradual control by Prussia. First formed in 1834, out of various smaller Customs Unions, the Zollverein gradually grew by the adhesion of more and more States, and developed a system of government and a policy of its own. At first hesitating, this policy was firmly taken in hand by Bismarck, who became Prussian Chancellor in 1862, and directed towards the establishment of Prussian supremacy and immediately at the definite removal of Austria from her path. In 1866, a dispute over Schleswig-Holstein (the German-speaking provinces of Denmark) was allowed to develop into a war in which Austria was immediately and decisively beaten, the neutrality of the Tsar having been secured three years before by giving him Prussian assistance to crush a Polish rising. Bismarck, however, did not wish for permanent enmity with Austria, and so demanded no territorial gains at the peace, contenting himself with uniting practically all the German States into the North German Confederation. The German Empire was now all but formed.

Its final consummation needed only a war, which Napoleon III kindly provided. Napoleon, in common with others, had been startled and alarmed by the revelation of the military strength of Prussia. When, in 1870, it was announced that a Hohenzollern was candidate for the throne of Spain, Napoleon visualised a new Holy Roman Empire under the Hohenzollerns instead of the Hapsburgs, and rushed to protest. Bismarck, who wanted war and had eyes, also, on the iron mines of Lorraine, situated so pleasingly near to the German coalfields, let him trip over his own feet. The Franco-Prussian War destroyed the belief in French military power which had existed since the seventeenth century, gave Alsace-Lorraine to Germany, and created the German Empire. Bismarck was then free, with the spectacular, if at times embarrassing assistance of William II, who became Kaiser in 1887, to develop a new orientation of European politics.

The Near Eastern question, from 1840 onwards, has always centred round the disposal of one or other part of the Ottoman Empire. In 1853 the Tsar Nicholas I, having failed to secure a general agreement to dismember Turkey, acted alone, seized the Roumanian provinces, and seemed about to get control of the Black Sea. This brought on the Crimean War, in which the Russians, in spite of the frightful inefficiency of the British war preparations, were finally defeated. The result was the neutralisation of the Black Sea and its closing to ships of war, the loss by Russia of a portion of Bessarabia including the mouth of the Danube, the admission of Turkey to the Concert of Europe (which meant, in effect, that the Great Powers announced that no one of them was to have a free hand in the Turkish dominions) and the erection of Roumania into a separate State (made independent in 1861). Meantime, the Sultan of Turkey promised better treatment for his Christian subjects, in which he disappointed them.

Russia was indignant at the Black Sea clauses of this treaty, which she denounced in 1870, when the attention of Europe was distracted by the Franco-Prussian War ; and she was also engaged in promoting Pan-Slavic movements in the Balkans, of which the centre was Serbia, and which were aimed, in the main, against Austria. In 1875 a Slav revolt in Herzegovina set the fire alight ; it was followed in the next year by a revolt in Bulgaria which the Turks endeavoured to stamp out by means of the " Bulgarian atrocities." Russia intervened, declared war on Turkey, and gained so thorough a victory that the Powers immediately took action to prevent her reaping the fruits. The Treaty of Berlin (1878), which Disraeli described as " Peace with Honour," settled the Near Eastern question in such a manner as to set the stage for the outbreak of 1914.

The main interest of the Treaty lay in its treatment of the Balkan States, which were left in great discontent. Roumania, though independent, was forced to cede the strip of Bessarabia gained in 1856 to Russia ; Bulgaria was practically cut in half, the northern part, Bulgaria proper, being made autonomous but tributary to Turkey, while Eastern Rumelia was left under direct Turkish government ; Serbia and Montenegro (now both parts of Yugoslavia) were made independent Turkish vassal States, but Serbia was in effect cut off from both Montenegro and the sea by an Austrian protectorate over Bosnia and Herzegovina and an Austrian garrison in the Sanjak of Novibazar. Great Britain, by a secret Treaty, laid hold of Cyprus, and with that and her shares in the newly made Suez Canal, was full set to dominate Egypt and control the new route to India.

Economic Changes. The first half of the nineteenth century was marked by the spreading of the industrial revolution from England to the Continent, the gradual removal of serfdom with its tying of men to the land, and the simplification and lightening of tariff barriers. In France, it is true, industrialisation had begun to a certain extent before the Revolution ; the Creusot ironworks, oldest of armament firms in Europe, was founded in 1780. But the Revolution had caused a great set-back, and all Napoleon I's passionate care for industry could not make France anything like the equal of England. Belgian industrial development also started early, especially (owing to her rich iron and coal resources) the iron industry. During the Napoleonic wars Belgium, then under French control, was largely used as an arsenal for the French armies. But Belgium was a small country ; during the early part of the nineteenth century Great Britain had no effective rival. After the war, however, and still more after 1830, French machine-production went ahead rapidly. Germany did not effectively " commence industrialist " till the 'fifties, and Russia not until the 'nineties.

To make any sort of factory production possible, however, it is necessary that there should be " free labour," not tied to the soil, but capable of being transferred to factory employment wherever the factory is set up. This meant that the remains of feudalism and serfdom had to be destroyed, and the peasant worker given complete freedom of movement. In those parts of Europe where Napoleon I had held effective control this had been done, and serfdom was not restored after his fall ; in other parts, however, emancipation was more slow. It gradually spread in Eastern Germany mainly through the efforts of Stein and Hardenburg in the first half of the century ; the Austrian serfs were freed in 1848, and the Russian in 1867. But this did not necessarily solve the peasant's problems, for the annual charge which his land (in countries other than France) had to bear in order to redeem the feudal dues—more simply, the tribute he had to pay to the landlords—was apt to be so heavy that, where there was no factory immediately ready for him to work in, he was often worse off immediately after emancipation than before. So, in all the great countries but Russia, considerable efforts were made to improve the land and to encourage the peasant to greater productivity. And there, at any rate, the labourer was, freed and ready to work ; and industrialisation began to advance.

Alongside of industrialisation went the reduction and simplification of tariffs. This can be regarded in three aspects, the first of which is the gradual abolition of the numerous and vexatious local tolls and tariffs which, like serfdom, were relics of medieval Europe, and no more than a tiresome hindrance to economic development. Second comes the abolition of tariffs between independent economic units, of which the German States are the great example. The German Customs Union played a larger part than any other single factor in bringing about German unity. Last was the lowering of tariffs between the great nations. Of this the Anglo-French commercial treaty of 1860 is the principal instance. Strong in the knowledge of the rapid progress of French industry, largely upon lines with which British products did not compete, and anxious to maintain the rôle of world architect of peace, Napoleon III carried through this treaty, largely against the opinion of his subjects, who regarded the economic ruin of France as the only possible result.

This result did not, as a matter of fact, occur. French prosperity continued to increase ; and for the next few years commercial treaties, with lowered tariffs, became the fashion among both politicians and economists. Of all economists, only the German, List, was opposed to free trade ; and List's influence at the time was slight. Bismarck, indeed, was not as whole-hearted as many, fearing the flooding in, over the eastern borders of Germany, of Russian grain exported at low prices to pay for the building of the railways which the Crimean War had shown to be so urgently needed. But in the late 'seventies there came a change which caused nearly all European countries rapidly to reverse their policy.

This change was immediately due to the improvement of railways and ocean transport, and at one remove to the inventions which made possible the production of steel on a large scale (such as the Bessemer process, patented in 1865, and the Gilchrist-Thomas process of 1876). The building of steel hulls, with far more effective engines, thus became practicable, and cargoes became bigger and voyages shorter and more profitable for perishable goods. Concurrently, the building of railways in the United States, largely with European capital, opened up the great corn-growing areas of the Middle West. The first American transcontinental line was opened in 1869, and steel rails, with a life many times that of iron rails, were effectively used in the 'seventies.

Immediately mass-produced corn, garnered at amazingly small cost, began to pour into Europe. In 1846 the cost of bringing corn from Odessa into London had been estimated as equal to a 10s. per quarter preference. Now this was swept away, and a study of the price of corn on the English market, year by year from 1875 to 1900, even when allowance is made for the fall in the general price-level, will give some indication of the meaning of American grain to Europe.

At once the countries with peasant populations dyked up against the flood, not merely for reasons of pure economics, but also because no country which intends, as both Germany and France after 1870 intended, to keep up a large land army with a great reserve of possible conscripts, can afford to let its peasantry be ruined. England alone, with no land frontiers to defend and a large city population delighting in cheap food, raised no tariffs. Besides, England had in effect no peasantry, and her landowners, being to start with comparatively well off and with access, in many cases, to alternative sources of income in commerce or manufacture, were in a better position to cope with rapidly falling prices. They were hard hit, it is true, both by the wheat imports, and in the next decade, after the invention of cold storage, by the competition of frozen meat from South America and the Antipodes; but they were not ruined. As to the agricultural labourer, his wages could not be lowered, for they were so low already; but he could be reduced in numbers. He could go into the cities, or he could emigrate; and he did. Only in one part of the British Isles—Ireland—was there a peasant population; and there the British Government had in the end to come to the rescue of the peasant by providing him with money both to buy his landlord out and to enable him to produce for himself.

The German tariff, the first example of this change of

policy, was passed in 1879, after an appallingly bad harvest. French opinion was moving in the same direction, and the French tariff of 1881 was also protective. Neither tariff was high ; but they increased gradually after 1900, when the age of really high tariffs begins. But these tariffs were not intended by any means solely for the protection of agriculture. Both France and Germany were developing iron and steel manufactures of their own (which, like the land armies, the Franco-Prussian War seemed to make more and more desirable), and were afraid of British competition. Other industries, such as French silk, threatened since the opening of the Suez Canal by competition from Japan, joined in the demand ; and the tariffs of these countries, reinforced by such additions as preferential railway rates, were in fact general tariffs. Thus, by the early 'nineties, in one of the quickest changes known to history, practically the whole of Europe, except Great Britain, had gone Protectionist. The United States, Protectionist from the start, after a brief experiment in the lowering of tariffs, returned to high protection after the Civil War of 1861.

§ 6. THE AGE OF IMPERIALISM

THE NEW tariff policy, however, was only one indication of the arrival of the age of economic nationalism and imperialism, whose beginning—in so far as the beginning of an epoch can be dated—is commonly set by historians at about 1880. Another sign is the great increase, in the older industrial countries, of the production of iron and steel and of what are called " constructional " goods. This is not to imply that consumption goods are not produced in ever increasing quantities ; but the prosperity of British industry as a whole, for example, comes to depend more upon the condition of the coal, iron and steel and engineering trades than, as fifty years back, upon that of cotton and woollen textiles. As the former both require more fixed capital, proportionately, and also have to face a more fluctuating demand, the result is a growing instability of industry, reflected, for a large part of the working class, in considerably increased ups-and-downs of employment. Furthermore, the rapid increase and improvement of European production as a whole demands wider markets outside Europe, secure access to sources of raw materials not found within the European continent, and governmental protection for the nationals of any country which engages in overseas trade, whether of their persons or their invested funds. For one of the largest items of European export, particularly in the case of Britain in the latter part of the century, was the export of capital, and its export not, as previously, to developing countries like the United States, but to countries practically undeveloped. This had unlooked-for results. Capital goods, and, to a less extent, goods of immediate consumption, cannot be sold outright to a totally undeveloped country, which will not be able to use, or, still more, to pay cash for them. Docks, harbours and railways are essential to a country which is to be brought within the ambit of commerce ; but docks, harbours, and railways are expensive. It is therefore necessary for the country which desires, say, to sell locomotives and railway equipment to the Argentine, first to lend the Argentine the money to pay for them—money which will only be repayable in instalments over a long period, as the railway begins to earn a profit. In point of fact, the industrial and transport development of Russia, the South American States, China, and many other areas was largely financed by European capitalists, who lent money in order to help provide a market for the goods which they or their fellows had to sell. This was more true of Great Britain than any other country, for the profits made by British industry in the mid-Victorian period were so great that there was more capital available than was required to finance home development, and as the surplus was not used to raise the standard of life of British workers, much of it had to seek investment overseas. It followed that those European countries whose nationals had lent money were continually interested in the financial and political stability of the countries to which it had been lent, in order that the capital might be safe and the interest punctually paid ; and a great deal of imperialist interference, both by diplomatic pressure and by direct threat of war, is attributable to the export of capital.

Along with political interference for the sake of preserving interest rights went political interference in order to safeguard supplies of essential raw materials, to secure exclusive rights of selling in a particular area, or simply to hold points that would be " strategic " in the event of war or any other interference with trading operations. We deal with this more fully in a later section ; here we need only observe that it is all part of a growing view, which is in direct contrast to the views of Cobden and the Free Traders, that it is the right and duty of Governments to act, both positively and negatively, so as to promote the economic interests of their subjects. The shift of opinion with regard to colonial possessions, which in the mid-century were regarded in the main as nuisances which would "drop away when ripe" without causing the mother country any inconvenience or diminution of trade, is a striking illustration. By the 'eighties, the desire to possess colonies was stronger among all Powers than it had been since the sixteenth century.

Lastly, we may note the tendency towards paternalism as well as to predatoriness on the part of Governments—an inclination to foster infant industries by means of subsidies, rebates, etc., as well as by tariffs, to regulate trades and associations within trades, and even, led by Bismarck, to secure the consent of the workers by such devices as social insurance. But present-day Communist and Fascist Governments have gone so much farther in the direction of universal State activity that this development may well be left to a later chapter.

Within the several countries, the growth of large-scale industrialism led immediately to combinations, both of capital and of labour ; but in Great Britain at any rate the working class fared rather differently from its continental neighbours. In Great Britain the workers had long been emancipated, and they participated to a certain extent in the general liberalising of institutions. Trade Unions were legal, and, though frowned upon when they sought to constrain men to act in concert in defiance of their employers, in so far as they could be looked upon as friendly societies—and in mid-Victorian days, after the collapse of Chartism, the friendly society aspect was very strong among them—they were encouraged as examples of the great Victorian virtue of mutual thrift. Money wages, and still more real wages, improved steadily after the middle of the century, and the Trade Unions became more and more " pillars of society." Even after the great depression of the late 'seventies, which opened their eyes again to the possibilities of unemployment and starvation, and even after the rise, from 1889 onwards, of " new " Unions of unskilled and semi-skilled workers led by men who were definitely hostile to Capitalism, the element of stolidity remained very large. Though they took part in Labour politics the Unions, as a whole, were not Socialist even at the outbreak of the European war. Nevertheless, partly as a result of the tendencies which were making for State paternalism on the Continent, and partly as a development of the theories of liberal thinkers such as John Stuart Mill, a peculiarly insular form of Socialism, mainly represented by the Fabian Society, did arise in England, and resulted, at the close of the century, in the formation of the Labour Party, Trade Union in its composition and support, Fabian in its main ideas.

The Continental workers—except, to a certain extent, the French—had never had this freedom ; in some countries they had been serfs, released from serfdom only to serve in the factories. In Germany and France, during the latter part of the nineteenth century, restrictions on combinations were to a certain extent removed ; but in the main it is still true that the continental worker was flung into an industry run on despotic lines. Of the continental, far more than of the British worker—and of the Russian worker most of all—Marx's words were true : " You have nothing to lose but your chains."

Under these circumstances, and particularly after 1850, Continental Trade Unionism and Socialism grew up in an atmosphere of bitter conflict, where working-class activity might at any moment end in imprisonment, death or exile. Its prophet and adviser was Karl Marx, who explained steadily the existence of the class-war, based on robbery by the owning class of the fruits of the labourer's efforts, and its inevitable termination in the conquest of power by the proletariat ; most of the Continental Socialist Parties are Marxian in their origin and terminology. In the realm of ideas, they had nothing in common with the British Labour movement ; they started with a different conception, and the attempt, in the 'eighties, to introduce Marxism into Great Britain barely gained a hearing. But the British worker knew a fellow-worker when he saw one, even though he did not understand what he said ; and, besides, he was by all training a liberal and an opponent of oppression, especially by foreigners. British Trade Unionists, then, willingly co-operated with Marx in the foundation of the First International in 1864, and indignantly sympathised with the victims of the 1871 Commune of Paris, the first attempt to set up a purely Socialist government—though they did not support the attempt itself. The attempt, made in the desperate circumstances of the end of the Franco-Prussian War, was hopeless from the start, and was speedily crushed ; but, such as it was, it has provided inspiration ever since for Communists all over the world.

The years between the Treaty of Berlin and the outbreak of the European War make more and more ironical reading. It is impossible not to contrast the armed camp of European diplomacy, with its growing fears and suspicions and its armaments increasing to the point at which alarmists even began to make feeble attempts to curtail war preparations and national sovereignty, and the steady parcelling out of the whole available world into colonial possessions, " spheres of influence," and areas of plain grabbing, with the enormous increase of productive power and material well-being producing on the one hand a much greater variety of life and freedom of choice and movement within a restricted area, and on the other a conviction born of prosperity that this freedom was bound to increase and that trifling difficulties such as imperialist rivalries would very soon be smoothed away. A small but very competent book published in 1912 ends with the words, " we can now look forward with something like confidence to the time when war between civilised nations will be considered as antiquated as the duel, and when the peace-makers shall be called the children of God." Within two years Europe was at war.

The salient features of these years are three : the pushing-on of imperialist expansion until there is no part of the world which is not the scene of imperialist rivalry in one form or other, the " armed peace " in Europe which drew by one " incident " after another closer to war, and, during the latter part, the increasing unrest, visible in all countries, of the working classes.

British imperialism, by an accident, began rather early, when in 1857 the Indian Mutiny forced the British Government to remove the East India Company, and to bring its Indian possessions directly under the British Crown. But it was not until after 1876, when Disraeli gave Queen Victoria the title of Empress of India, that the rapid expansion of British rule in that country really began. The French, in the next decade, followed suit by acquiring vast territories in Indo-China. But the great field of imperialism in the 'eighties was the African continent. The explorations of Stanley on the Congo, published in 1878, discovered enormous new possibilities of exploitation ; the International Congo Association, under Belgian influence, was formed in 1882, and within ten years the continent was practically divided up between the principal European Powers, the only serious set-back to imperialism being the defeat of Italy by the Abyssinians in 1896. For the most part, the partition of Africa, except north of the Sahara, was achieved without difficulty and without spectacular fighting ; but in 1899 Great Britain, becoming involved with the Cape Dutch in a quarrel which really derived from the discovery thirteen years earlier of the huge gold deposits on the Rand, entered upon the Boer War—the first important case in which imperialism had involved war between whites. Small in itself, the Boer War was important because of the interest it aroused and because of its plain disclosure of what imperialist policies were bound to lead to sooner or later. On the north coast, imperialism had begun with the French conquest of Algiers in 1830. Gradually, and not without many crises, the former possessions of Turkey along the coast were divided between Spain, France, Italy, and Great Britain. The share of the last-named was the protectorate over Egypt, which she established in 1882 jointly with France ; but France became in effect only a sleeping partner.

The new German Empire, coming late into the field and finding the best parts of Africa already in the hands of other Powers, but needing, none the less, raw materials, markets, and outlets for capital investment, turned its eyes eastward, through the Balkans to the Asiatic possessions of Turkey. The two most spectacular incidents were the speech of the Kaiser at Damascus in 1898, proclaiming himself " the friend of three hundred million Moslems," and the projection in 1902 of the Bagdad Railway, which was intended to provide a German-controlled route to Persia and the East. It was firmly believed, both before and during the European War, that Germany intended, through control of the Sultan, to put herself at the head of a world-wide Moslem movement.

In the case of the Far East, where effective imperialism began in the 'nineties, Germany was not left behind. India being closed, the most obvious field of exploitation was the helpless Chinese Empire, into which European Powers had been slowly pushing their way since the 'forties. But in the Far East there was Japan to be reckoned with. Japan, after the visit of Commodore Perry of the United States navy in 1854 had forced her to open herself to European traders, had rapidly transformed herself into a Power on the western model. It is true that Japan, in spite of her industrial growth, remained and still remains overwhelmingly agricultural as regards the occupations of her population ; it is true that her standard of living is far below that of the west, and that paternalism and the State control of economic life in Japan has been much greater even than in Germany. Nevertheless, as far as desire for markets, outlets for surplus population, opportunities for exploitation, and a strong naval and military force were concerned, Japan, by the 'nineties, closely resembled a Western Power, and the Sino-Japanese War of 1894-1895, with its result in the practical seizure of Korea by Japan, made this plain to the West. Great Britain, which had already recognised Japan, made an alliance with her in 1902.

The success of Japan in the war roused the European Powers to make an effort to check Japanese penetration into China, and a further scramble for concessions began. Russia, attempting to seize Manchuria in 1903, was badly beaten in the Russo-Japanese War, which startled the other Powers, including the United States, into full realisation of the economic and military strength of Japan. It proved, however, impossible to partition China as Africa had been partitioned, partly because of the jealousy of the Powers, and partly because the possible spheres of influence would not have been of anything like equal economic value. Nor could the immense population of China, poor and ill-governed as it was, be handed about like the almost uninhabited African territories. In 1912, therefore, mainly owing to the influence of the United States, a Six-Power Consortium was formed to exploit China under rules to be agreed. The opportunity for Japan did not recur until the European War had distracted the attention of most of her colleagues. Meantime, in Central Asia, apart from the German plans, Russia and Great Britain squabbled over Persia, Afghanistan and neighbouring areas.

Except in so far as the Balkan situation (which is attached to the Near Eastern problem) is concerned, political events in Europe were little more than a shadow of imperialist rivalries. In 1878 there were five Great Powers—Great Britain, France, Germany, Russia and Austria-Hungary; and the main question at issue was how, in the event of war, these Powers would be aligned. (Italy, poor, ill-equipped for industrialism, and suffering perpetual parliamentary crises, remained, as it were, only upon the fringe of the Concert of Europe.) The tradition of Great Britain since 1815, relying upon her sea-frontiers and her much greater wealth, had been to keep free of continental alliances except for purely *ad hoc* purposes, and to pursue her own policy ; but the coming of imperialism had altered all that. In Germany—and to a less extent in the United States—Great Britain saw a Power whose industrial development might make serious inroads on her foreign trade, particularly since the development of coal-mining in Germany had begun to threaten an export of which she had hitherto had a practical monopoly. Moreover, German naval development, as exemplified in the Von Tirpitz programme of 1900, was taken as a direct menace, aimed at cutting off British food supply in time of war. It was too late now to reverse the Free Trade policy so as to make Great Britain self-supporting ; Chamberlain's Tariff Reform scheme of 1903, which was rejected, only sought to secure to the British people at any rate the reversion of the food surpluses of the Dominions. But without command of the sea these would have been useless.

On the other hand, the traditional hostility between France and Britain was declining. French industry had developed on such different lines that it hardly competed at all with British ; the fear of French invasion or of French domination of Europe had finally vanished ; and except in the Nile valley, where the Fashoda " incident " of 1898 nearly led to war, the two States were not seriously at odds outside Europe. The inevitable *rapprochement* was delayed a little owing to the Germanic sympathies of Queen

Victoria ; but after her death events moved rapidly to the *Entente Cordiale* of 1904. The major points of disagreement were removed by the British Government's agreeing to support France in Morocco in exchange for a free hand in Egypt.

Germany and Austria were fairly firmly united, pursuing, on the whole, a joint policy as regards the Near East. There remained the question of Russia. The natural affinities of the Tsar were with the government of Bismarck and the Kaiser ; but there were personal difficulties on both sides, and there was also the strong desire on the part of France, fearing Germany and as yet unallied with Great Britain, to obtain an ally in Europe. (French capital, incidentally, played a great part in the industrialisation of Russia.) For nearly thirty years Russian policy wavered to and fro, making alliances and " understandings " (some secret and some open) now with this side and now with that. Eventually, in 1907, the *Triple Entente* was concluded between England, France and Russia, and Edward VII visited the Tsar at Reval. This *Entente* gave rise to great suspicion among English Liberals, and it did not remove the causes of friction between England and Russia in the Middle East ; nevertheless, the stage was now set for the war.

Lastly, we come to the Balkans. The provisions of the Treaty of Berlin were early infringed by the union of Bulgaria and Eastern Rumelia in 1885. In 1894 the Turkish massacres of Christians in Armenia caused British and French protests, of which, however, nothing came ; in 1897 the Greeks went to war with Turkey in order to incorporate Crete in the Greek kingdom. The Greeks were defeated, but through the intervention of the Powers Crete was put under a Greek High Commissioner. Disputes between the Balkan States about the territory of Macedonia were also becoming acute ; in 1903 the Macedonians revolted and for five years a portion of Macedonia was administered jointly by Russia and Austria.

The Young Turk revolution of 1908 brought matters to a crisis. In essence, the revolution made no change in the constitution or foreign policy of Turkey, but merely substituted a strong government for a weak one. There were even massacres of Christians in 1909. Under the circumstances, it became doubtful whether the system of semi-vassalage in the Balkans and other parts of the Turkish dominions could continue ; and interested parties took immediate action. Austria, supported by Germany, definitely incorporated Bosnia-Herzegovina in her Empire ; Bulgaria proclaimed its independence, and Crete its union with Greece. Three years later, when Germany had nearly precipitated war by sending a gunboat to Agadir to protest against the French protectorate of Morocco, Italy, in return, occupied Tripoli and declared war against the Sultan. The war, which might have dragged on for some time, was hastily settled by the yielding of Turkey, which was now faced with a greater danger. Italy retained Tripoli, Rhodes, and the Dodecanese.

For some time the Christian States of the Balkans had been discussing common action in view of their fear of renewed oppression by the Young Turk Government. Early in 1912 Greece, Serbia and Bulgaria, with the cognisance of the Tsar, signed mutual treaties for the partition of the Turkish possessions in Europe, and in October, after the outbreak of a rising in Albania, the various members of the Balkan League declared war. In the First Balkan War the Turks were completely defeated, and the subsequent treaty gave the allies all their demands except that, owing to the intervention of the Great Powers, in particular Austria, at the settlement, Albania was made into an independent guaranteed principality. But the allies fell out over the spoils ; the Second Balkan War (1913) found Bulgaria ranged against Greece, Serbia and Roumania. Bulgaria was defeated in her turn, and the Treaty of Bucharest took away her gains of 1912. Nevertheless, the other States were not satisfied, particularly Serbia, which while receiving large accessions of territory in Macedonia and Novibazar, had to allow Greece to take southern Macedonia and Salonica, thus losing access to the Ægean. The desire of the Serbs, stimulated by success in war and by the sympathy of Russia towards Pan-Slavic ambitions, was for the eastern Adriatic coast, which was in the hands of Austria-Hungary. The subsequent years were years of definite economic war between Austria-Hungary and Serbia, much to the disadvantage of both.

It is in some ways paradoxical that, in the period while nationalism and imperialism were growing so fast, there should yet have been a fairly steady trend towards greater personal freedom among the subjects of those nationalist and imperialist Powers. No liberal revolutions took place during the period except in Portugal, where, in 1910, King Carlos was assassinated and a republic established ; the revolutionary attempt in Russia which followed the Russo-Japanese War (1905) was crushed. Yet throughout Europe, even in Russia, there was a general movement towards democratisation of government, towards meeting the grievances of subject nationalities—and of women !—and towards greater recognition of Trade Unions and working-class activities. Labour and Social-Democratic Parties rose into prominence in many countries, and during the later years strikes, successful and unsuccessful, became frequent. Imperialist Capitalism, still rich in spite of the saturation of some markets and the beginning of Eastern competition, as industrialism grew in India, China and Japan, could yet spare enough to give the working class a share in prosperity, and neither war nor the threat of war was strongly enough felt to demand the curtailment of freedom where it had been won. There was superficial reason for believing that continental countries were in due course all destined to follow in the path of Great Britain.

The economic situation was not wholly satisfactory. Up to the end of the nineteenth century prices continued to fall, and real wages therefore to rise. In Great Britain the fall in prices was checked about 1896, and real wages fell slightly from 1900 to 1910. In practical effect, this fall was offset by the social gains of the first years of the Liberal

Government—old age pensions, an amended scheme of workmen's compensation, free meals for school-children, etc. But as the reforming energy of the Government died down and as its policy became in effect dictated by the Irish vote, the working classes began to lose patience, and their resentment at the failure of a radical victory to improve their standard of life found expression in the great series of strikes which began in 1911.

Nor was this strike wave without a guiding theory of its own. In part, it expressed simple mistrust of political action, and was under the influence of Syndicalist theories from France. The French Syndicalist movement was revolutionary, had no use for politics, and believed in overturning Capitalism by means of an infinite series of sudden strikes in different areas and industries. Alongside of Syndicalism went a set of theories formulated by American left-wing Trade Unionists, which also looked to strike action as a means of social change, but contemplated as a method the organisation of all workers into a single body—the One Big Union—which would then seize the power. Guild Socialism, a British Socialist doctrine influenced by Syndicalism, also appeared in 1912–13. Strikes were not confined to Great Britain, but took place in varying degrees all over Europe. In Sweden there was even a general strike. Where these strikes were serious they were generally defeated ; in the French railway strike of 1910 the one-time Socialist Minister Briand called the strikers to the colours ; but they indicated a general social ferment which made several of the Governments, in 1914, doubtful of the attitude of their working classes to the war.

It should be noted that in 1900, the various Social-Democratic Parties had formed a loose international federation, the International Socialist Bureau, which was officially opposed to war. Upon various occasions, notably at the Stuttgart Congress of 1907, this " Second International " made great efforts to frame a policy which in the event of war between nations could be adopted by the working classes of the world. The difficulties, however, were too great; the resolutions passed were not based on a sufficiently clear internationalist faith, and proved inoperative in the crisis of 1914.

As has been said, Portugal was the only country to go through a revolution during the early years of the twentieth century. Nationalist feeling, however, was growing in all States where nationalities were oppressed. But for the outbreak of war, a nationalist rising would very probably have taken place in Ireland.

§ 7. THE EUROPEAN WAR

THE EUROPEAN War broke out on July 28th, 1914. The immediate cause was the assassination of the Austrian Archduke Francis Ferdinand at Sarajevo, the capital of Bosnia, with weapons supplied from Serbian sources. The Austrian Government seized the opportunity to issue a violent ultimatum to Serbia, which the Serbian Government accepted in part, but not in whole. Germany and Russia both temporised, the former not desiring to interfere unduly with Austria, the latter wishing to uphold the Pan-Slav cause. The attitude of Great Britain was publicly uncertain, but privately she was committed to assist France, the ally of Russia, if war broke out, and if France were drawn in.

Events moved with great speed. On July 28th, Austria declared war on Serbia; on the 30th the Tsar ordered a general mobilisation, i.e. a mobilisation against the German as well as the Austrian frontier. This was interpreted in Germany as a definite act of aggression, and the German Socialists voted the war credits. On August 1st both Germany and France mobilised. The British Government hesitated, being uncertain of public opinion; but on August 3rd the German army, in order to attack the French before the Russians were ready, crossed the frontier of Belgium, thereby violating the 1839 Treaty of London and providing an excellent public war-cry. Great Britain declared war on

August 4th ; Japan, as Britain's ally, on August 23rd. During the progress of the war the combatants were reinforced on both sides ; the Central Powers by Turkey in November 1914, and by Bulgaria in September 1915 ; the Allies by Italy in April 1915 (though she did not declare war on Germany until the following year), Roumania in August 1916, Greece, after much vacillating, in 1917 and the United States in January 1917. Most of the South American States, as also China and Siam, took the same course, but without having any effect on the military operations.

Early in the war the Allied Powers held conferences in which they bound themselves not to make peace separately, and by the secret clauses of the Treaty of London (April 1915) and other agreements decided how, in the event of victory, the spoils should be divided. The Central Powers, on their side, were making equally fantastic plans. Japan, however, in the meantime seized the German port of Kiao-Chou, and presented various demands to China.

The military events of the war barely concern us here. The Allies held, almost from the start, a naval supremacy which the German use of submarines, though it caused anxiety about food supplies, did little to break. The navies of the Central Powers were useless except to keep the Allied fleet occupied, and it was thus fairly easy to blockade Germany and Austria from the sea. Similarly the German air-raids were a demonstration with no practical effect save to invite Allied reprisals. Essentially, the war was won through the exhaustion of the Central Powers by the length and cost of the struggle ; and the entry of the United States, with immense fresh resources of men and finance, at a moment when the Allies were near to financial collapse, made it impossible for the Central Powers to win. There were other actions fought, some to capture the German colonies in Africa, some in the attempt to cut off the Central Powers from communication with the east ; but the important field of war was always the Western Front.

Attempts at peace were made long before the Armistice,

and President Wilson was always ready to mediate. The first suggestion came from Germany in December 1916, and its rejection was followed by the unrestricted use of submarines against merchant and passenger vessels and the entry of the United States into the war. During the following spring the Austrian Government, which feared a Slav revolt, and believed that the Allied Powers desired to preserve the Austro-Hungarian Empire, made various peace overtures ; in July the German Reichstag passed a resolution in favour of peace by negotiation ; and in August the Pope endeavoured to mediate. All these efforts came to nothing. Meanwhile, in March 1917, the Tsarist régime in Russia had fallen ; a weak Provisional Government came into office ; and the attempt of the Allies to force Russia to continue the war resulted, immediately, in the complete failure of the June offensive, and, a few months later, in the Communist Revolution of October. Russia then concluded an armistice with Germany and her allies, and with Roumania, which had been defeated in the preceding year—an appeal for a general armistice having been rejected. After a certain amount of negotiation, during which it became clear that the Capitalist Powers would soon be ready to attack the Socialist State, the Russians were forced, in February 1918, to sign the treaty of Brest-Litovsk, by which Courland, Lithuania and Russian Poland were given up to the Central Empires, and independence promised to Finland, Estonia, Livonia, the Ukraine and parts of Caucasia. Russia was thus removed from the war, but the relief came too late for the Central Empires. The Slav propaganda, aided by Italy, was threatening to disrupt Austria ; the French, English and American governments recognised as a separate nation the Czechoslovak Council in Paris, presided over by President Masaryk ; the German offensive of March 1918, failed ; and Bulgaria, Turkey and Austria all announced their inability to face another winter of war. The Bulgarians were granted an armistice in September and the Turks in October. On November 11th, after General Ludendorff had tried in vain to organise a final resistance, and the Kaiser had fallen, the Provisional Government of Germany signed an armistice which was in effect a complete surrender.

§ 8. THE POST-WAR MAP OF EUROPE

NO EVENT, in all European history, has brought about such enormous changes in the political map of Europe, as regards both its boundaries and its methods of government, as the war of 1914–18, and the five Peace Treaties[1] which followed it. In the first place, by the end of the war there were only six neutral States in Europe—Spain, Switzerland, Holland, Norway, Sweden and Denmark. All the rest had joined in on one side or the other ; and as the Armistice constituted a virtual surrender by the Central Powers, in the hope (but under no guarantee) that the influence of the United States would mitigate the final terms, the Allies were practically in a position to dictate the peace. Only Turkey, of all the ex-German allies, resisted the terms imposed.

This meant that there were a very large number of claimants for the spoils, once a victory of spoliation had been assumed, for the number of Entente Powers was increased by the presence of certain " oppressed nationalities," notably the Poles and the Czechs, to whom freedom and territory had been promised. It is true that Russia, having not merely concluded a separate peace but gone over to Socialism, could now be reckoned as an enemy Power and available, therefore, for spoliation ; but even so there were difficulties, not lessened by the fact that certain secret treaties and agreements made to induce States to enter the Allied coalition contained terms that subsequent events had made it exceedingly difficult to fulfil. Notably was this the case with regard to Italy, where the fulfilment of the lavish

[1] Treaty of Versailles, with Germany; of St. Germain-en-Laye, with Austria; of Trianon, with Hungary; of Neuilly, with Bulgaria; of Sèvres, with Turkey. The last-named was never ratified, and has since been replaced by the Treaty of Lausanne (1923).

promises of the Treaty of London would have created great difficulties with both Serbia and Greece, to say nothing of France.

The story of the Versailles Conference, with its final imposing of the harshest possible terms upon the defeated countries, has been told more than adequately by Mr. Keynes in his *Economic Consequences of the Peace*. Here we are only concerned to note its effect upon the general appearance of Europe.

Five of the six neutral countries remained unchanged. So did Great Britain, which received its compensation for war services elsewhere, in the African possessions of Germany handed over under mandate, and in certain Pacific islands and New Guinea. Other Powers gained by Germany's colonial losses, but their share was insignificant compared with the British. The sixth neutral, Denmark, received the German-speaking part of Schleswig, which had been promised a plebiscite more than fifty years before. All the Allied States obtained accessions of territory. Belgium got some Flemish-speaking cantons which had been left in Prussian hands in 1815 ; France took back Alsace-Lorraine ; Italy, though disappointed of some of her claims, got *Italia irredenta* (the Trentino), the German-speaking South Tyrol, and part of Dalmatia. Still unsatisfied, the Italians in 1920 seized Fiume from the Serbs. In South-Eastern Europe considerable changes were made. Greece secured part of Macedonia, the Thracian coast practically up to Constantinople, and the coast of Asia Minor with Smyrna and its hinterland. But the Turkish revolution and revival of 1922 made it impossible for the Greeks to hold their new territories ; they were driven out of Asia Minor and in Thrace back as far as the Maritza River, leaving the Turks in possession of Adrianople. Roumania gained enormously in territory and considerably in resources by the addition of Bessarabia, seized from Russia, and the transference under the Treaties of Transylvania and the Banat from Austria-Hungary. On the west of the Balkan Peninsula, the small pre-war State of

Serbia, by uniting to itself the still smaller pre-war State of Montenegro, with Bosnia-Herzegovina, Croatia, part of Styria, the rest of Dalmatia, and other Austro-Hungarian territories, reappeared as the comparatively large State of Yugoslavia, and thus, much to the annoyance of Italy, realised the pre-war Serbian aspirations of free access to the Adriatic. Albania remained as an independent State, though " independence," in the case of a country situated in so strategic a position and having so poor and ignorant a population, may well be independence in little more than name.

All these territorial accessories, as well as the land occupied by the new States, came out of the territory of the defeated Powers. Of these Bulgaria suffered relatively least, losing some small areas to Yugoslavia on the west, and the eastern part of Thrace. (The latter loss, however, cut Bulgaria off from the Ægean.) Turkey, by the original settlement, was not merely to be confirmed in the loss of all her possessions in Europe except Constantinople itself, and to lose large parts of the Near East, but also to be deprived of the western part of Asia Minor. The Turkish revolutionaries under Mustapha Kemal, however, succeeded in reconquering Asia Minor and the part of Thrace round Adrianople. Germany, in addition to the territories transferred to Belgium, France and Denmark, lost West Prussia, Posen, the part of Upper Silesia which was given to Poland after a deferred plebiscite, the Polish Corridor to Danzig, and for a time, the Saar mining area. Danzig became a " Free City," as did for a time Memel, later acquired by Lithuania. Russia lost all her border States, including the Polish provinces, part of White Russia, and Bessarabia. At one time she had also lost the Ukraine ; but this, in spite of Polish attacks, was reconquered. As to Austria-Hungary, that Empire was completely dismembered. All the parts which did not speak German or Magyar were taken away, and the remaining partners, German Austria and Hungary, received separate treaties, which left one of them a small State with one huge city (Vienna) and practically no hinterland, and reduced the other to less than one half of its former size and population, many Magyar-speaking districts being transferred to alien rule.

Besides all these changes, we have to note the appearance of six new States. Four of these, Finland, Estonia, Latvia and Lithuania, were created directly out of the old Tsarist Empire. Poland, made out of the Polish provinces of Russia, Prussia and Austria, with additional increments sliced by the Russo-Polish war of 1920–21 off the western borders of Russia proper, was yet denied the " historic boundaries " which she demanded at the Peace Conference ; while the long and land-locked State of Czechoslovakia was formed almost entirely out of the former possessions of Austria-Hungary.

A comparison of the pre- and post-war maps of Europe will make all these changes clear, and may also suggest certain other reflections. Before the war there were five Great Powers, of approximately equal weight, in Europe— Great Britain, France, Russia, Germany and Austria-Hungary, with Italy as a doubtful sixth. Now Austria-Hungary has disappeared ; Russia has vanished from the Concert of Europe ; and Germany, though still a large State, has remained officially a beaten and partly tributary foe. There thus remain two Great Powers, with two of rather lesser importance. Against this, one must notice the increase among States of moderate size. Poland, Roumania, Czechoslovakia and Yugoslavia have all joined the category of Spain ; whereas against eleven small States there are now sixteen, including four carved off Russia, the autonomous Irish Free State, and two which were the brains of the great Austro-Hungarian Empire, and now find themselves reduced below Yugoslavia in importance. Iceland was made autonomous in 1918 under the Danish crown. This process has been sometimes described as the balkanisation of Europe ; it should not be forgotten that it is also the expansion of the Balkans. Roumania and Yugoslavia cannot any longer properly be described as Balkan States.

In addition to their retaliatory aspects, the Treaties, as is indicated by the creation of the new States, were intended to redraft the map of Europe more in accordance with ethnic and language boundaries. In some cases, this principle appears to have been deliberately flouted, as when the Germans of the South Tyrol were put under Italy, and large Magyar-speaking districts detached from Hungary ; but at any rate efforts were made to carry it out. The task, however, is obviously impossible, having regard to the way in which persons of different race and language live mixed up together in the States of Eastern and Central Europe. The reader who turns to the description of any one of these States in Part Two will find abundant examples. Nor would ethnic tidying always be in accordance with the wishes of the inhabitants ; in spite of the great strength of nationalist feeling men are still occasionally influenced by other than nationalist motives. There are Poles who would rather live in Germany than in Poland ; there are persons of Turkish race who do not want to live in Turkey. Something can be done to adjust a few of the difficulties by plebiscites in particular areas, or by exchange of the nationals of one State for the nationals of another, as in the case of Greece and Bulgaria. But, whatever is done, there must remain, in practically every State, a minority, sometimes several mutually hostile minorities, which are not homogeneous in language, race, religion, or all three, with the governing majority, and which, therefore, nationalism being what it is, will need special protection if the purpose of the Treaties is to be carried out. Only Soviet Russia, of all States in Europe, has had the courage to grant to her racial minorities full cultural autonomy, and to allow them freely to teach, write and print in their own languages. This is because the uniting power of a common Communist creed and Communist institutions is believed by the rulers of Russia to be strong enough to override the disruptive forces of nationality and of religious difference.

Accordingly, much of the activity of the League of

Nations has been directed to carrying out the provisions of the Treaties for the protection of minorities, to arranging conventions, and, equally if not more important, to seeing that these conventions are carried out. In the case of those victorious Powers which received little or no accession of territories, the services of the League of Nations have not been in request. Great Britain, after a short period of civil

Monarchies	Republics
Albania	Andorra
Belgium	Austria (Christian Social F. Dictatorship)
Bulgaria	Czechoslovakia
Denmark	Danzig (Nazi Government) F.
Hungary (Regency)	Estonia
Iceland	Finland
Italy (Fascist Dictatorship) F.	France
Liechtenstein	Germany (Nazi Dictatorship) F.
Luxembourg	Greece
Monaco	Latvia
Netherlands	Lithuania
Norway F.	Poland (semi-dictatorship) F.
Roumania (Monarchist Dictatorship)	Portugal
Sweden F.	San Marino
Yugoslavia (Monarchist Dictatorship)	Spain
United Kingdom	Switzerland
	Turkey (semi-dictatorship) F.
	U.S.S.R. (Communist)

war, yielded to the demands of her strong racial minority, and set up the Irish Free State, an autonomous Dominion within the Empire, which is at present demanding the right of secession. The problem of the Alsatians in France, of the Flemings in Belgium, and of the Catalans and other minorities in Spain is being handled by these States without outside interference. But in the new States of the east and south, there are all sorts of arrangements and suggestions for the protection of minorities, some of which appear to be working moderately well, some very badly indeed. Instances

Er

of peculiar difficulty are the welter of nationalities, claimed by Greece, Bulgaria and Yugoslavia, which is to be found in Macedonia, the condition of the Ukrainian and Russian minorities in Poland, and the almost insoluble problem of the Polish Corridor, which in order to give Poland an outlet to the sea divides the Germans in East Prussia from their neighbours on the west.

Not only has the political map changed ; the political complexion of the States has also altered enormously. Before the war there were only three republics in Europe (Switzerland, Portugal and France), and nineteen monarchies. Now, since the Spanish Revolution, there are fifteen republics and only twelve monarchies,[1] even if Hungary, which has a regent but no king, be included with the monarchical States. All the new States except Albania, which acquired a king in 1928, are republics ; and among the monarchies which have disappeared are the three ancient dynasties of the Romanovs, the Hohenzollerns, and the Hapsburgs, as well as the House of Castile.

But a mere division of the States of Europe into republics and monarchies does not adequately represent the situation. The position of the King of Italy, for example, is very different since Mussolini's seizure of power in 1922 ; and we must therefore add a new political category, that of dictatorship. Dictators are to be found in States nominally monarchical as well as in States nominally republican ; Mussolini in Italy, and, till recently, Primo de Rivera in Spain, found their respective monarchs no obstacle to their rule ; in certain of the Balkan countries, such as Roumania, the king himself has assumed dictatorial powers ; Horthy's régime in Hungary may be described as dictatorship or monarchy according to choice ; Pilsudski in Poland dictates through republican forms ; while recently Hitler in Germany must be added to the list of dictators in countries nominally republican. Greece has had a trial of several forms of government, monarchy, dictatorship, and

[1] Excluding the Irish Free State and States with under one million population.

constitutional republicanism. Of dictators, some, like Hitler and Mussolini, are heads of a definitely Fascist order of society ; others are despots unadorned. Mustapha Kemal in Turkey perhaps stands in a category all by himself ; he is dictator, but dictator of a country which has undergone violent social change. Turkish political institutions are not Communist ; but Kemal has more affinity with the Communist Party in Russia than with any of the above instances.

Nor are all of the republics by any means alike. An old-established republic, such as France or Switzerland, resembles more in character the republic of the United States, or, indeed, the British constitutional system if the King were removed. At the other extreme stands the Union of Socialist Soviet Republics, which is not merely a federal republic but a Socialist Federal Republic, under the dictatorship of the proletariat exercised through the Communist Party, with an economic system quite different from the rest of the world, and representative institutions (the Soviets) constituted on an entirely different basis. No other State in Europe has so far followed the Soviet example with success, though short-lived attempts, as in Hungary and Bavaria immediately after the Armistice, have been made. Midway come various Liberal-Democratic republics founded with the aid of the Social Democrats of the Right, of which Germany was, until recently, the chief example. These arose, mainly, out of conditions of defeat and economic collapse similar to, though less catastrophic than, those which produced the 1917 Provisional Government in Russia. That is to say, these Governments were brought to power by a working class in revolt against its old rulers, and had therefore to begin by aiming at an economic restoration of the working class. Thus, even when these republics were governed by coalitions between the right-wing Socialists and the *bourgeois* parties, something had to be done to satisfy, at least in part, the workers' demands. Hence the great increase of unemployment relief and social amenities, for example, in post-war Germany, the remarkable housing schemes of Socialist Vienna, and so on. But as the general economic situation proved an obstacle to a real increase in standards of life while nationalist and capitalist rivalries continued to exist, Governments of this type have found their task more and more impossible, and have either been driven out by violent reaction, as happened in Finland, or been forced to coalesce with other parties and become less and less socialistic. A clear example, in a non-republican country, was the 1931 defeat of British Labour. The Russian Revolution was made by the joint action of workers and peasants, but there has been no case of a purely peasant Government (though there have been peasant risings) since the failure of Stambuliski in Bulgaria in 1923.

Details about the constitutions of the various States, their parties, and their working, will be found in Part II. It may, however, be stated as a generalisation that, in the realm of politics, Europe has been and is being profoundly influenced by the two new ideas of Fascism and Communism. Of all the political *émeutes* which have disturbed Europe during the past fifteen years, with the exception of the revolution in Turkey, which is hardly now a European Power, and the long-delayed Spanish revolution, of which it is too soon to speak with confidence, there are only three that are of real interest, the Fascist revolution in Italy, the Nazist revolution in Germany, and the Communist revolution in Russia. Nationalism, during and since the war, has grown out of all recognition, and has even made its appearance outside the European system, to the embarrassment of certain Powers with colonial empires. (We may yet see the European system profoundly influenced by the growth of nationalist imperialism in the East.) But it is important to observe that it is a nationalism which has been fostered and increased during a time of great economic insecurity and economic decline, and that, therefore, the mass of the people have looked to nationalism to give them bread as well as freedom. The fear of starvation has reinforced the fear of oppression. This and the belief in the force of arms, which the war induced and the Peace Treaties approved, have produced an age of violence in Europe unprecedented since the Treaty of Westphalia. The settlement of 1816 resulted in a system of grim and secret oppression, that of 1918 in open and wholesale murder, both by individuals and by organised groups. Under the system of Metternich, persons obnoxious to the ruling powers disappeared into the dungeons of King Bomba or the distant parts of Siberia ; under that of Versailles they are shot by their political opponents, beaten up in droves by Fascist or Nazi thugs, or invaded, should the obnoxious group be in command of a State, by their neighbours. The system of setting bandits loose upon a State began in the middle of 1918, when such White generals as Denikin, Kolchak, Wrangel and Yudenich were encouraged to attack the Russian Communist Government ; but it has not stopped there, and against this tendency to violence, stimulated in part, as far as nationalist movements are concerned, by the international activities of armament firms, the pacifist elements, whether individual recusants, peace societies, or disarmament conferences, have so far struggled in vain. Even in countries which have not suffered revolution or invasion there is visible an intensification of nationalist feeling and a distinct tendency, in part a legacy of wartime regulations, to restrict the individual and group liberties associated with pre-war days, to control far more strictly the entry, movements and activities of foreigners, and to take or retain reserve powers, as exemplified in the British Emergency Powers Act used in the 1926 General Strike, for coping rapidly and without formalities with any social upheaval. This type of legislation by decree has gone much further on the continent than in Great Britain. Poincaré, in 1926, secured a considerable extension of the power to govern by emergency decree even in France. Brüning, under the stress of world depression and in face of a sharp conflict of opinion in the Reichstag, practically governed Germany by the extensive use of emergency powers of presidential decree between 1930 and 1932 ; and Pilsudski in Poland largely superseded the Seym by obtaining large and undefined powers of government by administrative edict. All over Europe, the effective authority of Parliaments has been weakened ; and Governments, under stress of the emergency, have claimed the power to act even without parliamentary sanction, in what they conceive to be the national interest.

Part II : THE COUNTRIES OF EUROPE

§ 1. POPULATIONS AND OCCUPATIONS

LET us begin with a few elementary facts.

The Continent of Europe, including its islands, covers an area of 4,400,000 square miles and had in 1930 about 506,000,000 inhabitants. Of this total area the European territory of the U.S.S.R. alone occupies more than one half, and the total territory of the U.S.S.R., including its territory in Asia, is nearly four times the size of the rest of the European countries put together. One quarter of all the inhabitants of Europe live in the U.S.S.R., and the total population of the U.S.S.R., including those who live in Asia, exceeds by about thirteen millions the combined populations of Germany, France and Italy. In terms of population the U.S.S.R. is the third largest country in the world, surpassed only by China and India. It has nearly forty million more people than the United States, and its territory is nearly three times as large. The U.S.S.R. covers not far short of one-sixth of the world's land surface and includes not far short of one-twelfth of the world's inhabitants.

Apart from the U.S.S.R., the territory of Europe is broken up among a very large number of separate and independent States of extraordinarily varying sizes. There are four " Great Powers," each with a population of more than forty millions. Of these, Germany, despite her territorial losses after the war, still comes easily first in number of inhabitants, with sixty-five million people ; but her area is now smaller than that of France, with her forty-two millions, or even Spain, with only twenty-four millions. Next to Germany in size of population comes Great Britain, with an area less than half that of either France or Spain, and not much more than half that of Germany. The United Kingdom, excluding the Irish Free State, has about forty-six million people. Then come France and, rapidly outdistancing France, Italy, with forty-two millions each.

These are the " Great Powers." Next them in number of inhabitants stands Poland with thirty-two million people, and then Spain with her twenty-four millions. The area of Poland, a State re-created after the war, is larger than that of Italy or the United Kingdom ; and Spain, as we have seen, is larger than any European country except the U.S.S.R. and France. Next in order of population follow Roumania with eighteen million people, Czechoslovakia with fifteen millions, and Yugoslavia with fourteen millions. No other European country has more than ten million inhabitants, unless account is taken of Turkey's fourteen millions, of whom only about one million live in Europe. Excluding Turkey, but including the U.S.S.R., we have

Populations of Europe in 1930
(in millions)

ICELAND

NORWAY 3

SWEDEN 6

FINLAND 3½

ESTONIA 1

LATVIA 2

LITHUANIA 2½

DENMARK 3½

U.S.S.R. 161 (Europe 127. Asia 34)

POLAND 32

DANZIG

GERMANY 65

HOLLAND 8

BELGIUM 8

SAAR

GREAT BRITAIN 46

IRISH F.S. 3

FRANCE 42

SWITZERLAND 4

CZECHO-SLOVAKIA 15

AUSTRIA 7

HUNGARY 9

ROUMANIA 18

BULGARIA 6

YUGOSLAVIA 14

ITALY 42

SPAIN 24

PORTUGAL 6

GREECE 6

ALBANIA 1

TURKEY 14 (Europe 1 Asia 13)

inhabitants, unless account is taken of Turkey's fourteen millions, of whom only about one million live in Europe.

Excluding Turkey, but including the U.S.S.R., we have so far five " Great Powers " in Europe, and five secondary Powers, each with more than ten million inhabitants. Next comes a substantial group of eight countries with populations exceeding five millions. These range from Hungary with its nine millions to Sweden and Bulgaria with a fraction over six millions each. Three more countries have between three and five million inhabitants ; four, including the Irish Free State, between two and three millions ; and two others about one million. Next follows a group of miscellaneous territories of varying degrees of independence, with populations ranging from 800,000 in the case of the Saar territory to 100,000 in that of Iceland ; and finally the rear is brought up by those territories with populations of less than 25,000, from Monaco with about 24,000 to Andorra with 5,000 inhabitants. This makes in all thirty-nine separate political units in Europe, including Turkey, or, if no account is taken of countries with under a million inhabitants, a total of twenty-eight, ranging in size and population from the U.S.S.R. with its 161 millions (127 millions in Europe) to Albania and Estonia with one million each.

Each of these twenty-eight self-governing territories (and some of the others) possesses its own customs administration and its carefully guarded frontier, and in each there is a separate Government claiming and, save in the case of the Irish Free State, actually exercising, complete and independent political sovereignty. Each of these twenty-eight countries has its own taxes, its own monetary system, its own railways, its own armed forces, and last but not least its own native supply of politicians and vested interests. Most of them have their own languages, often more than one, and their own separate and often aggressively nationalist systems of education. Many of them are troubled with " minority " problems, and a number of the newer States are devoting a large part of their energies to an attempt to

create a vigorous national consciousness out of the heterogeneous elements which the Peace Treaties have placed
under a common and exclusive political jurisdiction. Of
the twenty-eight leading European countries, some are
unitary States, governed with varying degrees of centralisation from a common centre, while others, such as Germany,
at any rate up to 1933, and the U.S.S.R., are federal, and
include within their territories smaller States possessing
varying degrees of autonomy and distinct Government
machines of their own. The only safe generalisation to make
about them all is that they are all intensely suspicious one
of another and suffering severely from the evil effects of the
world economic depression, and all busily engaged in
trying to thrust off as much as possible of the common
trouble upon their neighbours in the hope, doomed
inevitably to frustration, of bearing a lighter share of it
themselves.

These various countries are naturally very far from
homogeneous in their social and economic structure.
Indeed, within the borders of Europe are found countries
at almost every stage, from the intensified industrialisation
of Great Britain and Belgium to the overwhelmingly preponderant dependence on agriculture of certain of the
States of Eastern Europe. In more than half the European
countries for which figures are available—these include all
the most advanced—over 50 per cent of the occupied population is still engaged in agriculture and fishing. According to the latest available figures (which are in some cases
rather old) the proportion so engaged in two countries—
the U.S.S.R. and Bulgaria—is still over four-fifths of the
whole occupied population, and four other countries—
Roumania, Yugoslavia, Lithuania and Poland—have nearly
four-fifths of their occupied population engaged in agricultural pursuits. In Estonia, Latvia and Finland the proportion
is over two-thirds, and in Hungary, Portugal, Spain, Greece
and the Irish Free State over one half. Italy, also, despite
the development of industrialisation in recent years, has
still more than half its occupied population engaged in

agriculture. At the other extreme, in Great Britain the agricultural and fishing population is only about eight per cent of the total, whereas industry, commerce and transport together account for over two-thirds. Belgium again has two-thirds of her occupied population engaged in industry, commerce and transport, and Switzerland nearly two-thirds, while Holland, Germany and France all have over one half so engaged. In an intermediate group between the industrialised countries of Western Europe and the predominantly agricultural countries of Eastern Europe stand the Scandinavian States, Sweden, Norway and Denmark, and also Austria and Czechoslovakia, which have inherited the greater part of the industrial equipment of the pre-war Austro-Hungarian Empire. All these countries have between forty and fifty per cent of their occupied populations engaged in industry, commerce and transport as against between thirty and forty per cent in agriculture and fishing. They therefore approach nearly in terms of population to what is sometimes called a " balanced economy " ; but as the purchasing power of the urban classes considerably exceeds that of the rural population, all these countries have in fact a considerable surplus of industrial products to export, and need to import foodstuffs as well as raw materials for their industries. In fact the conception of a balanced economy is far more nearly realised in such a country as France, with fifty per cent of the occupied population in industry, commerce and transport as against thirty-eight per cent in agriculture. Germany, with fifty-eight per cent in the former and only thirty-one per cent in the latter group, comes into a different class and has been hitherto far more dependent than France on the export of manufactures in exchange for foodstuffs as well as raw materials, though of late high agricultural protection has brought her much nearer to autarchy.

The social structure of these various countries is further illustrated by the distribution of the remainder of their occupied populations. The percentage of the occupied population engaged in the armed forces ranges from a tiny fraction of one per cent in Austria and Switzerland to a maximum of two and a half per cent in Poland and Hungary ; and the great majority of countries have between one and two per cent of their occupied populations under arms. Much wider variations, illustrating the broad differences of social structure between the more and less developed countries, are to be found in the percentages of the occupied population engaged in the professions, in public administration and in domestic service. The proportion engaged in professions and public administration is highest in Austria, where the latest available figure gave it as eleven per cent ; for Austria inherited the large administrative equipment and professional personnel of the effective political and economic capital of the old Austro-Hungarian Empire. But the proportion is little lower in England and Wales, where it is ten per cent, though incidentally it is only six per cent for Scotland. At the other extreme Portugal, Roumania and the U.S.S.R. have only two per cent of their occupied populations in this group according to the latest available figures, and Lithuania only one and a half per cent. After Austria and Great Britain, the highest percentages, seven and a half and seven, are found in Holland and Belgium; while France, Germany and Denmark have all about six per cent.

The figures for domestic service tell much the same tale. In this case Denmark with thirteen per cent shows the highest figure, but this may be affected by the inclusion of farm servants. England and Wales comes next with twelve per cent,[1] and then again Austria with eleven per cent. On the other hand Poland, Greece, Finland and Estonia have only two per cent, and Bulgaria only one per cent. Norway, Holland and Sweden with nine, eight and seven per cent come next after England and Wales ; and again France and Germany with four and four and a half per cent respectively occupy an intermediate position. Apart from the special case of Austria, the proportion of the occupied population engaged in these latter groups serves as a fairly accurate

[1] Scotland nine per cent.

PERCENTAGES OF OCCUPIED
POPULATIONS ENGAGED IN

	Agriculture and Fishing	Industry, Trade, and Transport	Professions and Public Administration	Armed Forces	Domestic Service	Others
Austria (1920)	32	46	11	—(1)	11	—
Belgium (1920)	19	65	7	2	5	2
Bulgaria (1926)	81	13	3	1	1	—
Czechoslovakia (1920)	40	47	5	2	4	2
Denmark (1921)	35	44	6	1	13	1
England and Wales (1921)	7	68	10	1	12	2
Estonia (1922)	66	19	4	2	2	7
Finland (1930)	63	22	3	1	2	9
France (1926)	38	50	6	2	4	—
Germany (1925)	31	58	6	$\frac{1}{2}$	$4\frac{1}{2}$	—
Greece (1928)	54	26	4	1	2	8
Holland (1920)	24	59	$7\frac{1}{2}$	$\frac{1}{2}$	8	1
Hungary (1920)	58	28	$4\frac{1}{2}$	$2\frac{1}{2}$	4	3
Iceland (1920)	56	23	$4\frac{1}{2}$	—	15	$1\frac{1}{2}$
Irish Free State (1926)	52	26	6	1	10	5
Italy (1921)	56	35	$4\frac{1}{2}$	2	$2\frac{1}{4}$	—
Latvia (1925)	68	19	4	$1\frac{1}{2}$	$2\frac{1}{2}$	5
Lithuania (1923)	79	10	$1\frac{1}{2}$	$1\frac{1}{2}$	$5\frac{1}{2}$	$2\frac{1}{2}$
Norway (1930)	35	48	6	—(1)	10	$\frac{1}{2}$
Poland (1921)	76	15	$2\frac{1}{2}$	$2\frac{1}{2}$	2	2
Portugal (1911)	58	31	2	$1\frac{1}{2}$	$7\frac{1}{2}$	—
Roumania (1913)	80	13	2	2	3	—
Scotland (1921)	10	66	6	1	9	8
Spain (1920)	56	29	4	$2\frac{1}{2}$	$3\frac{1}{2}$	5
Sweden (1920)	41	45	5	$\frac{1}{2}$	7	$1\frac{1}{2}$
Switzerland (1920)	26	61	7	—(1)	6	—
U.S.S.R. (1926)	87	9	2	—(2)	—	2
U.S.A (1930)	22	51	8	$\frac{1}{2}$	10	8

(1) Included in previous column.
(2) Not included.
(3) Including clerks.

indicator of the size and wealth of the middle class in relation to the whole population of the country. The figures are of course subject to a certain margin of error, as they have not been compiled on a precisely uniform basis for all countries, nor do the latest figures relate always to the same year. But the discrepancies arising from these causes are not likely to be serious enough to invalidate the broad conclusions drawn in the preceding paragraphs.

§ 2. EASTERN EUROPE

IN 1930 Aristide Briand, then Foreign Minister of the French Republic, launched his project of the United States of Europe, in a memorandum which was sent simultaneously to all European Governments. What the French proposed, in terms kept carefully vague, was a federal organisation of all the States of Europe, designed both for the promotion of security and the prevention of war and for the furtherance of positive political and economic collaboration. The Briand project was conceived mainly in political terms ; for the French idea was that, if some sort of political federation could be established among the European States, economic co-operation between them would surely follow the achievement of political solidarity. Accordingly, the project in its first form contained no proposals for actual economic unification, but only for the building up, side by side with the League of Nations, of a far closer political body among the States of Europe alone. The relations of this new body to the League were not clearly defined, but it was to act somehow within the League framework ; and the Committee for European Union, which was formed as a result of Briand's initiative to study the project further, was brought into existence as a committee of the League of Nations.

When Briand launched his project, he was thinking primarily, not of the whole area of Europe in a geographical sense, but rather of all those countries of Continental Europe which lie between the Union of Socialist Soviet Republics on the east and the Atlantic Ocean on the west. It is true that Great Britain as a European member of the League of Nations was invited to take part in the discussions on European union and her entry into the proposed Union was contemplated as a possibility. But it had to be recognised at the outset that Great Britain, in face of her vast interests in other continents and of her imperial connections, stood to some extent apart from the nations of Continental Europe ; for these, even when they had empires of their own, stood to them in a relation substantially different from that of Great Britain to Canada or Australia or South Africa. Great Britain was but a doubtful and hesitant attendant at the discussions on European union. Perplexed between her lively interest in the development of political tranquillity and economic prosperity on the Continent and her fears of entering into any exclusive European arrangement that might prejudice her connections elsewhere, she could not be reckoned on as a whole-hearted member of any European family of States.

At the opposite end of the European continent stood the U.S.S.R., not a member of the League of Nations and in some sense the potential rallying point for a rival group of Continental forces. Briand was accused of endeavouring to make a *bloc* of Continental countries against Russia rather than a pacific federation of European countries for co-operative action in the political and economic field. Whether this was true or not, it is certain that Russian participation in the United States of Europe was neither expected nor desired. The federation was to have been one of countries living at one or another stage of economic development under the forms of government and economic organisation to which the Russian Communists had thrown out their fundamental challenge.

For certain purposes it is therefore best to think of Europe as a whole as divided into three sections—Great Britain, the U.S.S.R., and the rest ; for, despite their continual bickering

and the strong tendencies towards economic nationalism which they have manifested in recent years, the
countries of Continental Europe up to the new Russian
border do display to a considerable degree a real homogeneity of outlook. Between the democratic constitutions
of France and many of the new post-war States on the one
hand, and the Fascist or similar dictatorships of Italy,
Germany, Yugoslavia and to some extent Poland the cross
is far less wide in mental outlook than between any of these
systems and the quite different social arrangement which
has come into being in the U.S.S.R. From this standpoint
Great Britain forms of course a part of the European *bloc* ;
but even in this respect she stands to some extent outside
the concert of Continental anti-Bolshevism. British Socialism, for example, reformist as it is, has never shared
in the ferocious anti-Bolshevism of most of the Continental
Social Democratic Parties, and on the other hand, Communism in the Russian sense has found so far very little
foothold among the British workers. Let us therefore begin
our survey by leaving aside for the time being Great Britain
on the one hand and the U.S.S.R. on the other as far as
their internal conditions are concerned, and let us deal first
of all with the narrower Europe that lies between the
Russian frontier on the one hand, and the Atlantic Ocean
and the North Sea on the other.

Down the entire length of Continental Europe in the
east, from the Arctic regions to the Black Sea, stretches the
land frontier of the U.S.S.R. Along this eastern frontier of
Briand's Europe lie five States, four of them newly created
by the treaties of peace after the war, and the fifth so
enlarged in area and population as to be virtually a new
country. These five States are, from north to south, Finland,
Estonia, Latvia, Poland and Roumania. In addition, two
other States—Lithuania and Czechoslovakia—come within
a comparatively narrow distance of the Russian frontier ;
and Lithuania, at least, is only held apart from direct
contact with Russia by a territory placed on very questionable grounds of nationality under the Polish State. In the

Russia 1914
Germany   ”
Austria.
Hungary   ”

ESTHONIA
LATVIA
LITHUANIA
GERMAN
POLAND
GERMANY
RUSSIA
CZECHO-SLOVAKIA
AUSTRIA
HUNGARY
RUMANIA
ITALY
YUGO-SLAVIA
J.F.H.

THE NEW POST-WAR FRONTIER IN
CENTRAL AND EASTERN EUROPE

case of Czechoslovakia, the territory nearest Russia is occupied mainly by Ruthenians, closely akin in culture and nationality to the populations both of the neighbouring portions of the U.S.S.R. and to those of the Polish territory which lies between. Both Lithuania and Czechoslovakia, as well as the five border States, are therefore closely interested in the problems of the Russian frontier. Nor does this exhaust the geographical contacts of the U.S.S.R. with nations which have a foothold on the European Continent. To the south, Soviet territory marches with that of Turkey in the Transcaucasian region ; and the Turks, astride both sides of the exit from the Black Sea, command Russia's principal maritime outlet. Bulgaria, too, with her territory reaching the shore of the Black Sea, can fairly be regarded as another of Russia's geographical neighbours. Again in the north, where Russia's sea outlet is by way of the Baltic, Germany and the Scandinavian countries find themselves closely concerned in the problem of Russia's contacts with the West.

Let us, however, for the moment leave aside these wider contacts, and consider only the position of the countries lying along or near the western frontier of the U.S.S.R. It is important to realise at the outset that this enormously long land frontier is for the most part merely a line drawn on the map, and is not marked by any natural features which serve as clear physical boundaries between one geographical region and another. The border between Russia and Finland does indeed follow in the north for long distances the line of hills and mountain ranges, while in the south great lakes form to some extent a natural boundary. Estonia, too, is partly cut off from Russia by the long expanse of Lake Peipus, and in Central Poland the Pripet marshes serve for some distance, as was clearly shown in the late war, as a powerful geographical obstacle to military operations. Roumania, again, is parted from the territory at present under the jurisdiction of the U.S.S.R. by the River Dniester. But for long stretches of this eastern frontier of Briand's Europe there are no natural boundaries at all.

Nor are there clear cultural or ethnical frontiers. The line of post-war Russia has been pushed back a long way east of that of the pre-war Russian Empire ; and, while this has been done largely in accordance with the principle of national self-determination, the new frontiers include within the area of the Border States very many Russians and Ukrainians and other peoples far more closely akin in culture and outlook to the peasants of the U.S.S.R. than to the national majorities under whose political control they have been left by the Treaties of Peace and by the turmoils of the years immediately after the Great War. Finland, indeed, includes only a few Russians ; but in Estonia they form about eight per cent of the population, in Latvia fourteen per cent, in Poland probably twenty per cent, and in Roumania also a considerable though not easily ascertainable fraction. Czechoslovakia, as we have seen, also contains a substantial Ruthenian population closely akin to the Russians, and difficult to assimilate to the very different culture of the Czechs. Anyone who takes the trouble to look at one of the ethnographical maps of Europe and to compare it with the political maps of 1914 and of to-day will speedily realise that the application in the Peace Treaties of the principle of national self-determination—as far as it was applied—has by no means solved the problem of racial and national minorities in Eastern Europe. Indeed, this was so far recognised in the Treaties themselves that the new and enlarged States of post-war Europe have been compelled to include in their constitutions safeguards for the rights of minorities, and these rights are supposed to be upheld by international guarantees under the League of Nations. That they are by no means completely upheld the discontent in Poland, Roumania, Yugoslavia and several other States shows all too plainly.

We have, then, along the eastern borders of Briand's Europe a group of new countries whose frontiers are artificial both from the geographical and from the ethnical point of view. They were, moreover, when they were originally drawn, even more artificial from the economic standpoint. The border States which we are considering are all predominantly agricultural and inhabited mainly by peasants, though there were, at the time when the post-war settlements were made, large differences between area and area in the proportion of land cultivated in small holdings by peasant proprietors and that in the possession of large landed proprietors. But in the early years after the war the breaking up of large estates and the division of the land among the peasants, while it was carried out in different countries under widely varying conditions, tended everywhere to bring about a great increase in the proportion of small peasant holdings. This happened both in Russia and in the border States ; and until the Russians began their intensive drive for the socialisation of agriculture three years ago the peasants on both sides of the national frontiers continued to live under economic conditions which were very largely the same. The socialisation of agriculture in the U.S.S.R. may now be in process of creating a real economic frontier between it and the border States, but certainly no such economic frontier existed at the time when the new frontiers were made.

It follows from what has been said that the process of frontier-making in Eastern Europe was difficult in practice as well as in theory ; for the politicians at the Peace Conference, surrounded by rival nationalist experts in ethnography, could not in fact make frontiers simply in accordance with their interpretation of the principles of national self-determination as laid down by President Wilson. They had to consider what was actually happening in each of the territories which they were attempting to assign ; and more than once, after they had made their decision, it had to be altered in haste in face of a successful *coup d'état* by nationalists on the spot. The Poles got Vilna and the largely Lithuanian territory around it in the first place by forceful and unauthorised occupation. Lithuania got a bit of her own back by seizing Memel, and her *coup* duly received the recognition of the European Powers. The Pole

Korfanty seized a disputed area in Upper Silesia ; and successful Polish occupation undoubtedly affected the subsequent decision of the Powers. Moreover, before the new juridical frontiers were drawn at the Peace Conference, military occupation by nationalist forces had in many areas already determined the issue. For some time after the collapse of the Central Powers in the autumn of 1918 force and not diplomacy was successfully shaping the political structure of the countries of Eastern Europe.

Whenever an old empire or an old country is broken up as a political unit, and new States are created out of previously dependent areas, very difficult problems of economic as well as political reorganisation are bound to arise. Frontiers, on whatever principle or lack of principle they are drawn up, are almost bound to cut across economic areas which have hitherto possessed a high degree of interdependence. Railway systems, even if their construction has not been guided largely by considerations of military strategy, are almost always so devised as to bear a close relation to the political unity of the territories within which they are built. If national frontiers are altered railway systems cease to correspond to economic and social conditions ; and this is much more the case if the new States, animated by ideas of economic nationalism, proceed to build up high tariff walls around the territories placed under their control. The creation of a new country means the establishment of a new capital, not only as a seat of Government but also as the headquarters of a new Central Bank, and an elaborate set of financial institutions working in conjunction with it. The capital city almost inevitably becomes to some extent an economic and financial as well as a purely political capital. In the older countries railway systems and road systems converge upon the capital cities and upon the leading ports and other commercial centres falling within the national territory. But when new States are set up it is commonly found that their railway systems and their other means of communication are orientated not to their own capitals, or their own ports and commercial centres, but to the ports, capitals and commercial centres of the political units of which they previously formed a part. Thus the railway systems and the ports of Latvia and Estonia were essentially designed to serve the needs of Russian industry, commerce and administration. Riga and Reval were Russian ports engaged in the handling of imports and exports on behalf of the trading communities of pre-war Russia. In these countries the change of political sovereignty has involved and been accompanied by a tremendous change in the currents of trade ; and the equipment for transport lying within the territories of these new Republics does not correspond at all closely with their own conception of their new needs. Again, in Poland, built up as she has been out of territories previously divided between the three state systems of Russia, Germany and Austria-Hungary, the inherited system of transport is orientated not towards Warsaw as a national centre, but in separate sections towards Moscow, Kiev, Budapest, Vienna and Berlin, as well as towards Danzig and the Baltic ports of her northern neighbours. Enlarged Roumania finds her capital, away in the southern part of the country, quite inadequately linked up with her new territories on the other side of the Transylvanian Alps ; while Yugoslavia, the successor of pre-war Serbia and Montenegro, is in the worst position of all in her efforts to create a national economic unity based on a nationally unified system of transport.

Moreover, in face of the uncertainties of the political future, and of the clash of economic and political systems all along the frontier between Russia and the border States, it is impossible for economic development and reorganisation to proceed without a close regard for military considerations. Kiev is over 150 miles distant from the Polish frontier, but one reason why Ukrainian industry under the successive Five-Year Plans of the Soviet Union is being centred upon Kharkov rather than Kiev is that Kharkov is well out of reach of the threat of frontier wars. Russia is aiming at building up her new industrial system as far as she can out of the reach of her neighbours. Her leaders even speak of moving in process of time the economic capital of the U.S.S.R. from Moscow to the Urals, as they have moved it already from Leningrad to Moscow. All this frontier between the U.S.S.R. and Briand's Europe is still essentially an armed frontier, and on both sides of it the economic handling of the territories which lie along it continues to be governed, despite the conclusion of more and more pacts of non-aggression, by the sense of political instability and the threat of impending military conflict. This applies not only to the U.S.S.R. but with equal force to the new States on the opposite side of the frontier. They, too, want to put industrial development as far as possible out of the reach of warlike action by their neighbours. Accordingly, save under the most powerful and imperative inducements of economic opportunity, lands lying near the Russian frontier are likely for some time to remain industrially undeveloped, and to be given over to peasant agriculture, based on small peasant holdings on one side of the dividing line, and socialised farming on the other.

§ 3. FINLAND, ESTONIA, LATVIA, LITHUANIA

Finland.   The most northerly of Russia's neighbours is Finland, for more than a century a partly autonomous but discontented territory of the pre-war Russian Empire. When Finland was separated from Sweden and united to Russia in 1809 it was allowed to retain autonomy in the management of its internal affairs. But as the century advanced the Russian Empire became more and more aggressive in its attitude towards Finnish independence and in attempts to bring about the Russification of the country. This movement of Russian aggression went so far as to abrogate in 1899 the legislative power of the Finnish Diet, and Finland, by means of a " national strike," played an important part in the Russian revolutionary movement of

1905. Thereafter the powers of the Diet were restored and Finland was able to some extent to reassert its political liberty ; and the system of Parliamentary government with a single Chamber set up in 1906 prepared the way for the creation of an independent Finnish Republic when the Russian Empire collapsed in 1917. But in the years immediately before the war the Russian Government renewed its attempts at Russification, and the outbreak of war in 1914 found Finland in a condition of acute national discontent. It was impossible to compel the Finns to serve in the Russian army, and Finland remained in effect outside the sphere of military operations.

When the Russian army broke down in 1917, the Provisional Government set up after the first Revolution at once restored Finnish rights and representative government, and a temporary body based on equal representation of the Socialist and middle-class parties assumed power. Immediately after the Bolshevik Revolution this body proclaimed Finland's complete independence, which was at once recognised by the Bolshevik Government ; but thereafter a fierce struggle for power began. The Brest-Litovsk Treaty of March 1918 included a recognition of Finnish independence ; but whereas the majority of the Finnish Socialists sympathised with Communism, and desired to establish a Red Republic, the Finnish upper classes were on the side of Germany, and called in German help against the Communist Revolution. Through the spring of 1918 civil war raged in Finland. This ended with the victory of the White Army led by General Mannerhein and aided by the Germans ; and in the ensuing White Terror fifteen thousand Finnish Socialists and Communists were slaughtered, and no less than seventy-four thousand put in prison. The new Finnish Diet, which met in June 1918, altogether excluded the Socialists. It was strongly pro-German, and decided to offer the crown of Finland to a German prince, brother-in-law of the Kaiser. He accepted, but a few months later the collapse of the Central Powers altered the entire situation. The Germans were compelled to withdraw from Finland, and General Mannerhein became Regent and organised a coalition *bourgeois* Government, which was maintained in power by a civic guard a hundred thousand strong.

The elections of 1919, despite the disfranchisement of many Socialist voters, gave the Social Democrats eighty out of the two hundred seats in the new Chamber ; and in face of the changed political complexion of Europe Finland decided to become a republic and began gradually to settle down to constitutional government on much the same lines as the majority of the other new States of post-war Europe. The White anti-Socialist Government remained in power up to 1921, when it was displaced by an Agrarian-Progressive coalition which at length passed an amnesty on behalf of those convicted after the Civil War. Thereafter Finnish Communism revived, and secured a substantial representation in the Parliament of 1922 and the following years. The Social Democrats continued, however, as the strongest party, and were able to form a Socialist Government supported by the moderate *bourgeois* parties from 1925 to 1927. The fall of the Socialist Government in that year was followed by the return to power of the Agrarians, who have since governed the country. Communism has again been suppressed in Finland, but continues as a powerful force underground. Near neighbourhood to Russia, and the sharp division of political forces within the country, make the stability of Finnish politics continuously uncertain. Since 1920, when the Treaty of Dorpat was concluded, Finland has maintained diplomatic relations with the U.S.S.R., but her policy has been one of rejecting committal alliances with her neighbours. In 1922, Finnish rejection was responsible for bringing to nothing the proposed neutrality agreement with Estonia, Latvia and Poland, and the country has since tended to fall into line in its foreign affairs rather with the Scandinavian countries than with the border States. For some time close relations with Scandinavia were made impossible by the quarrel with Sweden over the Aaland Islands, and the position of the Swedish minority in Finland. But the Aaland Islands question was settled by the League of Nations, which recognised Finland's claim, but laid down conditions for the cultural autonomy of the Swedish population. The Swedes in Finland, who comprise about eleven per cent of the total population, still maintain a separate party of their own with over twenty members in the Finnish Chamber. But in recent years the animosity between the two nationalities has to a great extent died down. The Swedes, who belong mainly to the more well-to-do sections of the community and are concentrated in the south of the country, now work in alliance with the other *bourgeois* parties, and constitute a markedly conservative influence in Finnish politics.

Economically, Finland is a poor country greatly dependent on the prosperity of the timber trade. Of her land area, not including the great lakes which are dotted about the whole of her central region, over ninety per cent consists of woods and forests, and under seven per cent of arable land. She is therefore largely dependent on agricultural imports for the feeding of her population, though she exports butter and cheese as well as timber, wood-pulp and paper. Timber forms over one half of her total exports, and paper and wood-pulp together a further third. Despite her necessity to import foodstuffs, Finland now maintains, under the dominant influence of the Agrarians, a protective tariff in favour of agriculture as well as industry. A good deal of redistribution of land in favour of peasant holdings has taken place since the war, and there is a powerful movement of agricultural co-operation.

Whereas Great Britain has been in the past the chief buyer of Finnish exports, Finland has always drawn a large proportion of her imports from Germany. Thus in 1930 she sent nearly forty per cent of her exports to Great Britain, but drew therefrom only fourteen per cent of her imports, whereas thirty-seven per cent of her imports came from Germany, which took only twelve and a half per cent of her exports. These two countries preponderate overwhelmingly in Finland's external trade. Her only other important source of imports is the United States, and her trading relations both with Scandinavia and the border States and with Russia are comparatively small. Hence her policy of refraining from close political commitments to her immediate neighbours and her anxiety to maintain satisfactory relations with both Great Britain and Germany. Her relations with Russia are indeed greatly affected by the competition of the two countries in the timber market ; and it is from Finland, allied in this matter with Sweden, that the most lurid accounts of conditions in the Russian timber camps, and the bitterest complaints about Russian dumping, regularly emanate.

The Finnish regular army consists of only twenty-five thousand men ; but in addition the White Guard formed at the time of the Civil War maintains its existence as a Civic Guard a hundred thousand strong. Finland, in short, while she has settled down politically of late years, has still too lively a memory of the embittered civil conflict of 1918 and of the ensuing White Terror to be comfortable under her existing political system. She is, moreover, at present suffering acutely from the world depression, which reduced the gold value of her exports by more than one half between 1928 and 1932, while her imports over the same period have fallen by almost three-quarters, giving her what is known as a " favourable balance of trade " during the slump only at the cost of a great contraction of necessary imports, and a consequent fall in the standard of life of her people. Despite this improvement in the trade balance, Finland's dependence on exports to Great Britain forced her off the gold standard in 1931 in common with the rest of the Scandinavian countries, and thus decreased her power to purchase imports from Germany, which remained tied to gold. These conditions foreshadowed some readjustment in the direction of Finnish trade, but this is now liable to be influenced in an opposite direction by the Ottawa agreements concluded by Great Britain in 1932.

Estonia. On the opposite side of the Gulf of Finland, which commands the approach to Leningrad, lies the small Republic of Estonia, with a total population of little more than one million persons. The Estonians are a people of Finnish descent, and their language and culture are of Finnish type. Native Estonians form about eighty-eight per cent of the population of this new State, but within its boundaries are included minorities of Russians (8 per cent), and Germans (2 per cent). The country is predominantly agricultural, and about two-thirds of its occupied population live by agriculture, as against thirteen per cent engaged in industry. Estonia exports butter, bacon, potatoes, flax and linseed, but is an importer of cereals. Her chief customers are Great Britain and Germany, and she draws her imports chiefly from Germany and the United States.

Estonian nationalism is a product of modern times, and can hardly be said to have made its appearance before the Russian Revolution of 1905, when the demand for national autonomy was put forward by Estonian representatives in the Russian Duma. But this does not mean that Estonian political history has been uneventful ; on the contrary the territory has been handed to and fro for many centuries from one conqueror to another. In the thirteenth century it was shared between Denmark and the Knights of the Sword ; thereafter until the sixteenth century it was under German control ; it then passed to Sweden, and was finally ceded by Sweden to Russia in 1721. Thereafter it formed part of the Russian Empire, and its history in the nineteenth century was marked by a series of small peasant revolts and by a strong attempt at Russification by the Tsarist Government. The first Revolution of 1917 was immediately followed by the growth of a nationalist movement. In July of that year an Estonian Diet met, and prepared a scheme for an autonomous Estonia under Russian sovereignty, but immediately after the Bolshevik Revolution the Estonians proclaimed their independence and the Russian Government retaliated by dissolving the Estonian Diet. A large part of the country was at this time owned by

great German landowners—the so-called Baltic Barons—
and this section of the population, in face of the opposition
of the national Diet, called for German help. At this point
the Estonian nationalists were successful in driving the
Bolsheviks out of Reval, and a republic was definitely proclaimed. But this success was immediately followed by the
occupation of the country by the Germans in the interests
of the Baltic Barons. Russia was compelled to renounce her
rights in Estonia under the Brest-Litovsk Treaty , but after
the German collapse of the autumn of 1918 the German
forces had to withdraw, and the Russians promptly invaded
the country. The Finns thereupon came to the help of the
Estonians, and a British fleet arrived at Reval and took the
new Republic under its protection. With the aid of large
forces of Russian " Whites " the Bolsheviks were driven
out, and in 1919 Estonia was used as a base by the
' Whites " for an unsuccessful invasion of Russia. At the
same time an irregular German army from Latvia, under
the command of General von der Goltz, invaded Estonia,
but was successfully flung back with British help. An armistice with Russia was arranged at the end of 1919, and
peace definitely concluded at Dorpat in 1920. Full
Allied recognition of the Estonian Republic followed in
1921.

Before this, Estonia had begun to settle down to dealing
with her own internal problems. A law for the division of
the large estates hitherto held by the Baltic Barons was
passed in 1919, some measure of compensation for dispossessed owners being finally afforded in 1926. Under the
new conditions the peasants became definitely the dominant force in the country, but Communism retained considerable strength in the urban centres, and especially in
the large port of Reval (since rechristened Tallinn) which
served as an important outlet for Russian produce and as a
direct railway connection with Leningrad and Moscow.
At the end of 1924 there was at Reval a Communist
rising, and its defeat was followed by the suppression of the
Communist Party and the creation of a permanent Civic

Guard of thirty thousand men on the Finnish model.
Politically, Estonia maintains very close relations with her
neighbour Latvia, including, since the Treaty of 1923, a
defensive alliance and a unified tariff system. She is also
in treaty relations with the U.S.S.R. and closely dependent
politically on Great Britain. Estonia received a League of
Nations loan in 1926 for the purpose of stabilising her currency, and unlike her northern neighbour she maintained
the gold standard after the crisis of 1931. She has been
governed of late by a coalition between the Agrarians and
a *bourgeois* Centre Party, with a fairly strong Socialist contingent forming the opposition.

Latvia.   To the south of Estonia lies the Latvian Republic, including the great ice-free port of Riga, also known
to all newspaper readers as the chief centre from which
news about the impending collapse of the Soviet system
has been assiduously circulated in recent years. Latvia,
like Estonia, is a predominantly agricultural country, and
more than two-thirds of her total population depend
directly on agriculture for a living. Three-quarters of her
people are Letts by nationality, but she also includes a
strong Russian minority of about 14 per cent and substantial fractions of Jews and Germans. The majority of
the people are Protestants, but there is a Roman Catholic
minority of nearly 25 per cent, and the Orthodox Church
has also a considerable number of adherents. Latvia lost
nearly 40 per cent of her population during the war and
the period of acute disturbance which followed it ; for comparatively few of those who fled during this period ever
returned, and a great number of them actually perished.
Her population is now rather less than two millions in all.
Economically she has much in common with Estonia. Her
leading exports are timber, flax and butter, and she needs
to import cereals. Her chief source of imports is Germany,
and Germany also takes the leading place among her
markets, followed by Great Britain and Russia. Latvian
industries were severely damaged because all the available
plant, including most of the rolling stock of her railways,

was removed to Russian territory during the war or destroyed in the course of the civil troubles.

Latvia, like Estonia, was under German control during the greater part of the Middle Ages. In the sixteenth century her territory was parted between Poland and Denmark, and in the seventeenth century one of her provinces, Livonia, was annexed by Sweden. Livonia passed to Russia in 1710, and by the end of the century Latgalia and Courland had also been added to the Russian Empire. The usual discontents marked Latvia's connection with Russia during the nineteenth century. At the time of the Revolution of 1905, there was a vigorous national insurrectionary movement, which was savagely put down. In the Great War Lettish units served under a separate command in the Russian army, and after the Bolshevik Revolution of 1917 this Lettish army became a revolutionary force. The nationalist elements opposed to Bolshevism thereupon formed a *Landwehr* under British leadership to fight the " Reds," and this body gradually got control of the northern part of the country. Meanwhile the Latvian representatives at the Russian Constituent Assembly put forward a demand for independence ; but the Germans, under the Treaty of Brest-Litovsk, annexed and occupied Courland, the south-western province of Latvia, and proceeded to make an attempt at intensive German colonisation. The collapse of Germany was followed by a Bolshevik invasion of the country at the end of 1918, and thereafter by a devastating and tangled civil war between von der Goltz's German irregulars, the Russians, and the Lettish national forces. Courland, the great stronghold of the Baltic Barons, was von der Goltz's chief base of operations ; and not until his forces and the Bolsheviks had both been driven out with Allied help was Latvia in a position to settle down to dealing with her domestic problems.

The Republic had been definitely proclaimed at the end of 1918 ; but the first Latvian regular Parliament was not able to meet until 1922. In this Parliament and in its successors the characteristic feature of Latvian politics, aggravated by the system of proportional representation which all the new States of Europe have incorporated into their constitutions, has been the division of political forces into a large number of separate parties. In the first Latvian Parliament the Social Democrats formed the largest homogeneous group, with a membership of more than one-third of the Chamber. Since then Socialism has lost ground, and a system of consolidation among other parties has made more stable Governments possible. In the Chamber of 1933 the Agrarians are the leading party and exercise the chief control in the Government. But there are in addition to the Social Democrats a number of smaller conservative and *bourgeois* parties, and also a number of separate parties representing the various national minorities. Latvia, as we have seen, is in close treaty relations with Estonia, including the conclusion of a unified customs tariff. The large estates which covered a great part of the country before the war have been divided up among the peasants, and the domination of the Baltic Barons brought finally to an end. The social and economic structure of the country is thus closely akin to that of her immediate neighbours. Latvia, like Estonia, is a Republic of small peasant proprietors attempting to apply in her government the orthodox system of democratic Parliamentary institutions. These institutions, however, with no tradition behind them, and no strong hold upon the great mass of the people, possess little vitality ; and in Latvia as well as Estonia and Finland, the politics of government continue to be dominated by fear of Russia.

Lithuania. Lithuania, to the south of the Latvian Republic, is not strictly a border State of Russia, being cut off from direct contact with the Russians by the northern extremity of Poland. According to the original settlement of Lithuanian territory after the war, this separation between Lithuania and Russia was accomplished by assigning to Poland a long narrow stretch of territory running the entire length of the Lithuanian eastern border and obviously designed with the deliberate object of pushing a wedge between the small Lithuanian Republic and her great eastern neighbour. Since the forcible seizure of the city and province of Vilna by the Poles in 1920 the distance between Lithuania and Russia has become much greater, save at the extreme north. But the territorial settlement between the three countries has in it no element of finality, and Lithuanian politics and external relations continue to be dominated by the question of Vilna and of the border territories which shut the country off from direct contact with the U.S.S.R. On the west Lithuania adjoins East Prussia, and her chief trade both as importer and as exporter is with Germany. She is predominantly an agricultural country, and nearly 80 per cent of her population are directly dependent on agriculture for a living. Her chief exports are flax, linseed, timber, butter and pigs, and by far her largest imports are coal, other mineral products, and agricultural fertilisers and manures. Nearly half the whole area of the country consists of arable land and another quarter of grass land, the forest area being relatively small. By religion over four-fifths of the people are Roman Catholics, Protestants predominating only in the German city of Memel, which the Lithuanians seized in 1923 partly by way of retaliation for the act of the Conference of Ambassadors in recognising the Polish claim to Vilna.

Lithuania, unlike Latvia and Estonia, possesses a national history which lends strength to the nationalism of modern Lithuanian politics. She was a Grand Duchy in the thirteenth century, and from the fourteenth to the fifteenth century extended the great period of Lithuanian power, when her dominions spread from the Baltic to the Black Sea. In the sixteenth century Lithuania was united with Poland, and fell gradually under Polish domination, passing finally under Russian rule towards the end of the eighteenth century in connection with the partition of the old Polish kingdom.

The history of modern Lithuania, as of her neighbours,

begins with her part in the Russian Revolution of 1905. At that time the Lithuanians rose in revolt ; and they shared in the repression of the following years. During the war the Germans invaded Lithuania from East Prussia, and created a dependent Lithuanian State under promise of independence. In 1917 Russia was compelled to renounce all claim to Lithuania under the Treaty of Brest-Litovsk, and the Lithuanian State Council put forward a demand for independence, and actually proclaimed a republic in February 1918. The German withdrawal later in the year was followed by war with the Russians, who occupied Vilna and caused the removal of the Lithuanian national Government to Kovno. In the course of the subsequent war between Russia and Poland the Poles captured Vilna, only to be driven out again by the Russians, who in turn handed over the province to the Lithuanians in 1920 in order to save it from the Poles in the course of their retreat after their unsuccessful attack on Warsaw. But the Lithuanians were not long left in possession ; for despite the provisional assigning of the area to Lithuania, it was occupied later in the year by General Zeligowski's irregulars on behalf of Poland, and in 1923 this act of aggression was legalised by the Conference of Ambassadors, which gave recognition to the Polish occupation. The Lithuanian Government, however, refused to accept this decision ; and right up to 1927 Lithuania maintained a formal state of war with the Polish Government, only agreeing in that year to bring this condition to an end under strong pressure from the League of Nations.

In the meantime, as we have seen, the Lithuanians found partial compensation for their loss of Vilna by the forcible seizure of the town and territory of Memel, which had been constituted a free city at the end of the war ; and this act of aggression, which gave the Lithuanians an outlet to the Baltic, was also legally recognised in 1924 by the formal cession of Memel to the Lithuanian Republic. Hostility to Poland was largely responsible for the early conclusion of peace between Lithuania and Russia in July 1920, on terms which included Russian recognition of Lithuania's claim to Vilna. Largely on account of her attitude on this question Russia's relations with Lithuania have been throughout much better than with the other border States ; but Lithuania has also entered into close relations with her northern neighbours, and from 1924 has formed part of one customs system with Latvia and Estonia. Hostility to Poland and the desire to regain Vilna, which is regarded as the historical capital of the Lithuanian Republic, dominate Lithuanian politics. Before 1926 Lithuania was governed for a time by a coalition of parties of the Left, which in that year concluded a pact of non-aggression with Soviet Russia, but was immediately afterwards overthrown by a military *coup d'état*. This was followed by the formation of a strongly nationalist Government with a predominantly clerical complexion, under the leadership of Professor Valdemaras. But this Government was essentially dependent on military support, and the rule of Professor Valdemaras became in effect a dictatorship. Since his overthrow power has been held by a coalition of nationalist parties with a predominantly Agrarian composition, the Social Democrats and the various national minorities forming the principal elements in the opposition.

§ 4. POLAND

THE FRONTIER between Russia and Poland stretches in a long curving line from a point almost level with the northern part of Lithuania at one extreme to the confines of Bessarabia in the south. Save where the Pripet marshes form near the middle of this long line a great natural barrier, the frontier is from the geographical point of view almost everywhere purely artificial, neither rivers, nor mountains, nor even hills running along it for any considerable distances. In the south it cuts through the middle of the uplands of the Ukraine and Eastern Galicia ; and in the north it is an arbitrary line drawn across the plain which stretches right from the Urals to the North Sea. Nor does the Russo-Polish border correspond to any real division of races or peoples. In the north, White Russia extends racially right across Polish territory to the neighbourhood of Vilna, and further south, around the Pripet marshes, there is an inextricable mixture of races, in which, for a long way west of the existing frontier, Poles form only a tiny minority among White Russians and Ukrainians. Only in the extreme south do Poles live in large numbers near the frontier, and in this area they are mingled with a Ruthenian majority, though the predominant culture of Galicia, unlike its racial affiliations, can be regarded as mainly Polish. Even Lemberg, however, is but an island of Polish nationality set in the midst of a predominantly Ruthenian countryside, and the entire belt up to the frontier, in which Poles and Ruthenians live mingled together, cuts in between the Russians of the Ukraine and the closely kindred Ruthenians of the eastern part of Czechoslovakia. The new Polish State, even according to the Polish statistics, contains racial minorities amounting to over thirty per cent of the population. Fourteen per cent of the population are Ruthenians and Ukrainians, a further four per cent White Russians, four per cent in the western part of the country Germans, and eight per cent Jews.

This startling inclusion of seven million Russians and Ukrainians within the new Poland arises in part out of the action of the Allied Governments at the Peace Conference, but also out of the circumstances in which the Russo-Polish frontier was defined in 1920-21. The Treaty of Riga, entered into at the close of the war between Poland and the U.S.S.R., pushed the Polish frontier far to the east of the line originally contemplated by the Allies at Versailles. For Poland, after her success, with Allied help, in beating back the Russian advance upon Warsaw, was in no mood to forgo the opportunities for territorial aggrandisement which were presented to her by the military and economic embarrassments of the Soviet Union. She had claimed at Versailles her historical frontiers—a claim which would have involved the passing under her political control of vastly larger national minorities than are included in her present area. The Poles had been greatly dissatisfied with the reception accorded at Versailles to their claims, despite the backing which France gave to their pretensions in accordance with the desire of her statesmen to establish a powerful State in Eastern Europe, both as a counterpoise to Soviet Russia and as a permanent menace to Germany along her eastern frontiers. Disappointed at Versailles, the Poles, helped by France to roll back the Russians from Warsaw, seized their opportunity and thereby created for themselves an even more difficult and dangerous minorities problem than was bound to arise in any event out of the inextricable mingling of races in Eastern Europe. There has been constant trouble ever since 1918 over the treatment of racial minorities by the new Polish State ; for the Poles, strongly nationalist in outlook, want as far as possible to unify their country by imposing a Polish culture and outlook on all the minorities over which they rule. This has led to endless trouble and constant wrangling before the Minorities Commission of the League of Nations, which in this as in other cases has been able to do all too little to protect the minority groups, despite the safeguards included on their behalf in the Peace Treaties. It was a tragic irony that caused Poland to appear, in 1933, as the champion of the oppressed Jews against their still worse treatment in Nazi Germany. For Poland contains a very large Jewish population, estimated at 3,000,000 ; and there are close connections between Polish and German Jews all along the Polish-German frontiers and above all in Upper Silesia.

More than a hundred years had passed since the disappearance of Poland as a nation at the final partition of 1795 when the Poles found in the Great War an opportunity for the reassertion of their national claims. Napoleon had indeed revived for a short time the Grand Duchy of Warsaw ; but Napoleon's new Poland was swept away in the Peace Settlement of 1815, and thereafter Poland was a country divided under three distinct imperial sovereignties. Warsaw and the largest part of the country belonged to Russia, Austria-Hungary held Galicia, and Germany Posen. Of these three areas Galicia alone had obtained under Austrian rule some measure of autonomy ; and there the Polish elements in the population dominated the country with its partly Ruthenian peasant population. The outbreak of the Great War thus found the Poles enlisted in the armies of all the three Great Powers of Eastern Europe ; but the Russian part of the country was speedily overrun by the Austro-German armies, and from 1915 onwards practically all Poland fell under the occupation of the Central Powers. These Powers were well aware of the importance from their point of view of keeping the country quiet, and in 1916 Germany and Austria-Hungary united in promising some sort of Polish independence after the war as a reward for loyalty. In 1917 a Polish Regency Council was set up under the auspices of the Central Powers, and thereafter Polish nationalism found itself sharply divided between the elements in the country which were looking for the realisation of their independence to a German victory, and a Polish National Committee sitting at Paris which based its hopes rather on a French triumph. Marshal Pilsudski, who became after the war dictator of Poland, belonged to the former group. In 1914 he led the private Polish army which he had been organising for years before in Galicia into Russian territory, and in 1916 he continued to act on the side of the Central Powers. But in July of that year he fell foul of the German and Austrian authorities then in control of the territory of Poland, and proceeded to open up negotiations with the Allied Powers. He was nevertheless persuaded to become Minister of War in the Council of State formed by the Central Powers to administer Poland, and set to work to form his secret military organisation, which was able to take control of the country in 1918. Before long he again quarrelled with the Central Powers ; and he was arrested and imprisoned in Germany until his release by the German revolutionary authorities at the end of the war. He then returned to Poland and was at once elected Chief of State with dictatorial powers, his military record and his long period of revolutionary activity making him the natural leader of the new State.

There is no need to enter here into the extraordinarily tangled history of Polish affairs in the years immediately following the war. It is enough to say that when Marshal Pilsudski assumed power the future borders of the Polish State were still utterly unknown and indefinite. There was no agreed settlement of the frontier with Russia ; for the terms of the Brest-Litovsk Treaty had been wiped out by the defeat of the Central Powers. The relations of the Ukraine with Russia were still uncertain, and in Eastern Galicia an attempt was being made under the leadership of Petliura to establish an independent Ukrainian-Ruthenian State. There was incredibly confused and many-sided warfare throughout 1919 ; but the consolidation of the Russian power gradually reduced the combatants to two. Early in 1920 the Poles launched an offensive against Russia, advanced far into the Ukraine, and actually took Kiev. This onslaught was a material factor in unifying Russian sentiment, and it was followed by a Soviet counter-offensive which brought the Russian armies almost to Warsaw. This counter-invasion in turn roused the Poles to an intense national effort, and the French, who saw in the impending collapse of Poland the death-blow to the European system which they had endeavoured to establish at Versailles, rushed munitions and military advisers to the assistance of the Polish Government. The British Government, dominated by anti-Bolshevik sentiment, was also on the side of the Poles ; but the suggestion of British intervention on behalf of Poland was met by the threat of the Labour and Socialist bodies to declare a general strike, and Great Britain, unlike France, gave only passive support. The French aid, however, sufficed to enable the Poles to drive back the Russians in disorder ; and it was under these circumstances that the Soviet Union was compelled to agree to the preposterous frontier laid down in the Riga Treaty.

Thereafter the relations between the U.S.S.R. and Poland were those rather of an armed truce than of a definitive peace. Poland, intensely nationalistic, dominated in her politics by social classes which fear more than anything else the penetration of Communist influence among the Polish masses, and conscious of the weakness engendered by the presence of large dissatisfied national minorities in her midst, lives in permanent fear of Russia ; while France, her political projects reaffirmed by the defeat of the Russians, continued until lately to fortify her eastern dependent with both diplomatic and financial assistance—an association likely to be renewed in face of the recrudescence of German militarism. A Treaty between France and Poland was concluded in 1921 ; and in the dispute with Germany over the partition of Upper Silesia the Poles could always count on French sympathy. Not until 1924 were diplomatic relations established between Poland and the U.S.S.R., and even to-day, despite the conclusion of a mutual pact of non-aggression, Poland remains an armed camp watching jealously the movement of events in both Russia and Germany, and garrisoned against discontents within as well as against her larger neighbours. Since 1921 she has been allied with Roumania, which needs her help over the Bessarabian question. Indeed, these two countries have formed together the instruments of the French policy of the *cordon sanitaire*, designed to keep off the Russian menace from Western Europe.

The situation along the eastern frontier of Poland is thus unsettled enough to account for the persistence of a strongly militaristic attitude on the part of the governing classes in the new Polish State ; for, whatever treaties and non-aggression pacts may be concluded, nothing can remove the essential insecurity of a settlement so obviously devoid of principle as that which resulted from the Polish-Russian conflict of the years following the conclusion of the Great War. Poland's army of well over a quarter of a million men at peace strength and her heavy expenditure on armaments are in existing circumstances and in the existing temper of

European politics the inevitable outcome of her uncertain situation. Nor are her problems confined to the east. In the north, there is the vexed question of Danzig and the Polish " Corridor " ; and in the south, as we have seen, there is an inextricable mingling of races. There too the question of frontiers has been settled without any regard either to national conditions or to natural boundaries or even to the unity of economic areas. Poland sticks down like a wedge between the Ruthenians of eastern Czechoslovakia and the kindred peoples of the Ukraine. In the Teschen area an extraordinary frontier has been drawn, giving the Poles the town and the head waters of the Vistula, and the Czechs the valuable coal mines in the immediate vicinity. On the west the Polish frontier is even more arbitrary and extraordinary, and in the neighbourhood of the free city of Danzig and in Upper Silesia, emergency arrangements which have about them no guarantee of permanence or successful working have had to be concluded.

Upper Silesia presented, indeed, the most difficult of the problems of territorial adjustment at the end of the war, for in this region, with its valuable coal mines and iron and other mineral deposits developed by German enterprise before the war, Germans and Poles live mixed up together over a wide indeterminate area for which both countries put forward insistent claims. The Allied Governments attempted to deal with this vexatious problem by ordering a plebiscite to be taken in the disputed area ; but when this resulted in a majority of votes for union with Germany the question was referred to the Council of the League of Nations, which proceeded, instead of assigning the entire territory to either disputant, to draw a boundary clean through the middle of this industrial area, using as its chief canon of judgment the votes recorded in each distinct town or administrative district. While these readjustments were in progress the Poles attempted to deal with the situation in the same way as they had dealt with the Lithuanian claims to Vilna. Polish irregulars under Korfanty occupied Upper Silesia with the idea of presenting the Council of the

League with an accomplished fact. But in this case, in view of the result of the plebiscite, it was not possible for the Poles successfully to sustain their claim to the entire area. In the event they got most of the coal mines (53 out of 67, or, in terms of output 24 million tons out of 31 million), and Poland thus became one of the leading coal producing and coal exporting countries of Europe. Poland further got over two-thirds of the zinc and lead mines and a full half of the important iron and steel industry of Upper Silesia. But the settlement did not succeed in solving at all the problem of national minorities. Over half a million Poles were left on the German side of the frontier and over 350 thousand Germans on the Polish side. This may appear as if Poland came out of the settlement worse than Germany, but it has to be remembered not only that the Upper Silesian industrial area was a vital component part of the German industrial system, but also that many persons of Polish nationality voted in favour of Germany rather than Poland because they hoped to enjoy under German sovereignty more stable government and a higher standard of life. For Polish wages are low, and Polish social institutions inchoate, and from the standpoint of the workers the economic considerations often overrode the nationalistic. Similarly, when the plebiscite was taken in the frontier districts of Marienwerder and Allenstein in East Prussia, a predominantly Polish population voted for remaining under Germany rather than for union with the new Polish State.

Apart from Upper Silesia, the chief problem of the Polish frontier in the west is presented by the Polish Corridor leading to the free port of Danzig. The Polish Corridor is a long thin ribbon of territory designed to give Poland a direct outlet to the Baltic. In order to do this it has to cut clean across German territory, dividing the essentially German province of East Prussia from the rest of the German Reich. Across this narrow belt of Polish territory run the main railway lines from east to west, so that German trains passing from East Prussia to other parts of

Germany have to cross the Corridor. This has necessitated a highly complicated arrangement for the transference of goods as well as great difficulties of passenger travel. It would be clearly impossible to subject to the high Polish tariff goods passing in purely internal trade from one part of Germany to another ; but unless all goods could go by sea they must be given the right of free railway passage by the Poles. The problem has been settled none too satisfactorily by the device of allowing free transit in sealed trains ; but trouble is still constantly arising over the movement of both goods and passengers, and the vexatious frontier régime sets up a permanent sense of irritation between Poland and Germany.

Moreover, there is constant trouble over the status and rights of self-government of the free city of Danzig, which, with its surrounding countryside, was formed into an autonomous State under the direct supervision of the League of Nations, but united with Poland for postal and certain other services, and brought within the Polish customs system. Danzig is predominantly a German city, and the complexion of its elected authorities is overwhelmingly German. There has been constant friction between it and the Poles ; and the League of Nations has had none too easy a job, even before the advent of the Nazis, in maintaining at all the precarious settlement reached at the end of the war. Nor is Poland, which wants to make Danzig an integral part of its own territory, by any means content with the present situation. For some time the Poles endeavoured by one device after another to reduce to nullity the nominal freedom of Danzig. When this proved impossible they began the construction of a new port of their own on the Baltic in the near neighbourhood of Danzig, but lying within the territorial area of the Polish Corridor. This port, Gdynia, is now in operation, and threatens Danzig with the loss of an increasing part of its external trade. For the Danzigers, cut off from the main part of Germany by the Polish Corridor, cannot resume their old position in relation to the areas of the west ; and trade with

THE POLISH CORRIDOR

East Prussia also involves considerable difficulties, as it has to be conducted across the artificial political frontier. The situation of Danzig must thus be added to the list of the dangerous and unsolved problems of Poland in the west.

Nor is the position in the Polish Corridor itself at all satisfactory ; for while in the northern part of the Corridor the population is predominantly Polish-speaking, there cuts right across it at its southern end a belt of German-speaking people living along the valley of the Vistula and to the west of Bromberg. Further German *enclaves* are scattered over a large part of the Corridor, and in these circumstances it is most unlikely that the Germans will accept as final a situation which divides their territory into two unequal parts, and leaves the great agricultural province of East Prussia in an impossible position of economic isolation. The two problems of Upper Silesia and the Polish Corridor, with the closely related problem of Danzig, stand as fatal obstacles to the establishment of peaceful or secure relationships between Germany and Poland—all the more now that violent Nationalism is again in power in Germany. Nor can such settlements as the German-Polish Arbitration Treaty of 1925 remove the sense of insecurity which makes the western as well as the eastern frontier of the new Polish State a powerful cause of the continuance of military preparedness in Europe.

Economically, Poland is a country of contrasts. The greater part of its territory is economically undeveloped ; but it includes, especially in Upper Silesia and in the industrial areas of pre-war Austrian Poland, highly developed centres of industry and population which the new frontiers of the Polish State have cut off from their old contacts and assigned to the political control of a Government representing mainly areas far more backward in an economic sense. Taken as a whole, Poland is predominantly an agricultural country. Almost half her whole area consists of arable land, and not far short of a fifth in addition of pasture, most of the remainder being forest. She exports large quantities of agricultural products, especially meat and eggs, and she is also an important exporter of timber. But in addition to her agricultural exports, she is in a position, thanks mainly to the territories annexed from Germany, to export coal and iron in large quantities, and she has also substantial export trades in textile goods and in sugar based on the domestic production of sugar-beet. While Polish exports find from Danzig and Gdynia a substantial and increasing outlet through the Baltic to Western Europe, in the nature of things the most natural market for a large proportion of Polish exports is Germany ; and Germany is also the most natural supplier of the main bulk of Poland's industrial requirements. So urgent is the need for exchange across the newly established frontiers of Poland in the west, that trade is bound to continue on a large scale in spite of acute political animosities. Nevertheless these animosities, combined with the desire of the Poles to build up their own industries behind a high tariff wall, have led to constant friction in the trading relations between Germany and Poland, and since 1925 the two countries have been engaged almost continually in a tariff war, interrupted by periodical attempts to negotiate a satisfactory settlement. The failure of these attempts and the constant measures of economic retaliation on the frontier have been especially disastrous to the German province of East Prussia and to the mixed German-Polish population on both sides of the frontier in Upper Silesia. It is true that in Upper Silesia itself, as far as local trade across the new frontier is concerned, special emergency arrangements have been entered into and for the most part observed, and a limited freedom of movement across the frontier has also been established. Indeed, without this, Upper Silesian industries could hardly carry on at all. But much of the trade of Upper Silesia is concerned with external markets ; and this trade, as well as the efficiency of production, has been continuously hampered by the division of the area and the establishment of quite different economic and social conditions on the two sides of the unnatural frontier.

Poland, we have seen, is for the most part an economically undeveloped country. She has, however, great possibilities of economic growth, for in addition to her resources of coal and iron and timber and her plenty of good agricultural land, she is self-sufficient in her supplies of oil, and possesses a considerable surplus available for export. She is hampered greatly in her development by defective means of communication. Poland has in all only about eleven thousand miles of railway to serve her vast area and rapidly growing population. Whereas Belgium, for example, with little more than one-twelfth of the area of Poland, has one mile of railway for every ten square kilometres, Poland has less than one for every thirty. Nor must it be forgotten that the Polish railway system, such as it is, was developed to serve the needs not of a unified territory, but of areas forming part of three different States. It is therefore ill-adapted to the needs of Poland's present territories, and there is an urgent necessity for the re-planning of existing communications as well as for the building of new lines. If Poland could get the capital she could profitably employ very large sums in the development of her railway system ; for there is little danger of the railways in her extensive territory being rapidly superseded by the growth of road transport. It would be a far costlier business to equip Poland with an adequate road system than to put her railways on a satisfactory footing.

But under present conditions there is little chance of the capital even for the reorganisation of the railways being obtained. The Polish people is far too poor to provide the money out of its own resources and the foreign investor far too shy both of railway finance and of lending to new States as to whose political future he is justifiably uncertain to be willing to risk the large sums that would be required. Poland has therefore to carry on as best she can with her existing railways, supplemented by the comparatively small extensions which she can afford to make out of her own resources and such foreign loans as France, for example, is willing to extend to her mainly for political reasons. Fortunately she has an extensive system of water-ways to help her. But Poland is emphatically to be ranked among those countries which can, at any rate under their present political systems, develop at all fast in an economic sense only if they are in a position to borrow large sums of capital from abroad.

The political situation in Poland is one of considerable confusion. The Seym, the Polish Parliament, is at present dominated by the supporters of Marshal Pilsudski, grouped in a *bloc* under the title of the Non-Party Union with 247 members. Against this pro-Pilsudski majority is arrayed a medley of smaller parties, ranging from the conservative National Democrats with 62 members and the Peasants' Party with 48 members to the separate parties representing the various national minorities and the Communists who, completely suppressed in most areas, still manage to return a tiny handful of members. The official Socialist Party has 24 members, and there are also dissident Labour and Socialist fractions. The position is complicated by the fact that Pilsudski himself was formerly, in his days as a revolutionary agitator, the leader of the Socialists, and that he now occupies an anomalous position between left and right. He is opposed by the extreme conservative elements in the country as well as by the Socialists, and he hovers uncertainly between attempting to dominate the country by means of a parliamentary majority such as he now possesses and the desire to govern by dictatorial methods in face of Parliamentary obstruction. He has recently imprisoned most of the leaders of the opposition parties.

The Polish Constitution, as it was formulated immediately after the war, was a thing of checks and balances designed, while establishing a democratically elected Parliament chosen on the system of proportional representation, to limit the use of parliamentary power by the establishment of special machinery for supervising the activities both of the Seym and of the government. This system, and especially the adoption of proportional representation, prevented in the years after the war the establishment of any strong government, for there arose a maze of parties each representing some particular sectional interest or point of view. This state of things was largely responsible for Pilsudski's *coup d'état* of May 1926, which placed him in a position of dictatorial power. But Pilsudski was not then prepared to become an absolute dictator. He contented himself with insisting on modifications of the Constitution, extending the power of the President and conferring on him the right of legislation by decree in case of national emergency. Thereafter a sort of Parliamentary régime was re-established ; but the alignment of parties was changed by the *coup d'état*, which enabled the friends of Pilsudski to gain a clear parliamentary majority. The Non-Party Union, however, is itself not a unified party following a clearly defined policy, but an aggregation of separate groups often mutually suspicious and inconsistent in their aims, though they all follow Pilsudski's leadership. His prestige as a national liberator for the moment holds the majority elements together ; but the removal of his unifying force would almost certainly be followed by a relapse to the conditions which existed before 1926.

The dissociation of Pilsudski from the Socialist Party has greatly weakened the forces of Socialism in Polish politics, while the virtual suppression of Communism, which had gained largely at the Socialists' expense, has rendered politically inarticulate a large mass of working-class discontent. There have been repeated rumours of the imminence of working-class revolution in Poland under Communist auspices ; but, strong as Communism is among the industrial workers, there are great difficulties in the way of any effective Communist uprising. The great industrial areas of Poland are in Upper Silesia, Teschen and other districts which formed before the war part of the German and Austro-Hungarian Empires. These regions are far distant from Warsaw, and a working-class rising in them would find itself to a great extent isolated from the rest of the country, and above all unable to secure possession of the capital and thus take the authority of government directly into its hands. If the Russians had captured

Warsaw in 1920 Poland would in all probability have gone
over to Communism. But for the present at least there is
little likelihood of a successful Polish revolution organised
from within.

§ 5. ROUMANIA

R u s s i a ' s southernmost neighbour along her western
frontier is the now large and powerful State of Roumania,
which more than doubled both area and population as
a result of the redistribution of territory after the war. Under
the Treaties of Peace Roumania acquired from the Austro-
Hungarian Empire the great upland territory of Trans-
sylvania, and the rich agricultural lands of the Banat and
Bukovina. She further took advantage of her opportunities
during the war to seize the border province of Bessarabia,
which is still in dispute between herself and the U.S.S.R.,
and to complete her possession of the Dobruja, the stretch
of country lying on the Black Sea between Bulgarian Varna
in the south and the mouths of the Danube in the north.
Roumania is thus to-day in population easily the largest of the
countries of South-Eastern Europe, despite the growth of pre-
war Serbia into the new enlarged kingdom of Yugoslavia.

This accession of new territory was not accomplished
without placing considerable racial minorities under the
political sovereignty of the Roumanian State. Roumanians
to-day account for roughly 70 per cent of the population—
nearly thirteen millions out of a total of eighteen. The rest
of the people are divided among a large number of different
nationalities. By far the most numerous group are the
Magyars of Transylvania, whose number has been greatly
swollen by the pushing west of the Roumanian border to
include not only the Transylvanian uplands but the towns
and railway lines at the edge of the plain, which furnish the
principal lines of communication from north to south.
Germans, also mainly in Transylvania, number about a
million, and Jews another million. Russians and Ukrainians
are numerous in the eastern part of the country and

especially in the disputed province of Bessarabia. There are Bulgarians and Turks mainly in the Dobruja and the adjacent regions, while a certain number of Czechs and Slovaks are to be found in the northern part of the country near the Ruthenian border. The Roumanian minorities problem, however, despite its complexity, is not quite as difficult as that of Poland ; for in a serious form it exists mainly in Transylvania and Bessarabia, and the minorities outside this area possess comparatively little coherence or power of common action. The Germans and the Magyars have organised separate national parties of their own within the Roumanian State, and there is also a small party representing the Bulgarians. But the large Ruthenian and Russian minorities have not so far been able to organise themselves along party lines. Nationalist differences are, however, apt to be aggravated because of their coincidence with differences of religious affiliation. The bulk of the people belong to the Russian Orthodox Church ; but the Greeks and the Roman Catholics have each over a million and a half adherents, and the Protestant Church has not far short of this number, while the Jews, as we have seen, number about a million.

The Roumanian State has grown from small beginnings to its present dimensions in comparatively recent times. Its history as a country begins with the recognition of the autonomy, followed shortly by the union, of the two former Turkish provinces of Moldavia and Wallachia which constituted Roumania up to the Balkan Wars of 1912–13. Moldavia and Wallachia, autonomous from 1856 and united in 1861, finally proclaimed their independence of Turkey in 1877, and this independence was recognised in the Berlin Treaty of 1878.

Thereafter Roumania, aided by the richness of her natural resources, grew rapidly in wealth and prosperity, especially after the development of the oil fields near the Transylvanian border. The peasants, however, remained exceedingly poor, and there was a large landless population, more than half the area of the country being held in

large estates by a comparatively small class of rich landowners. These conditions were responsible for the serious
agrarian rising of 1907, and had led to a persistent demand
even before the war for the reform of the system of land-
holding. On the outbreak of the first Balkan War in 1912,
when the remainder of the Balkan countries united to attack
Turkey, the Roumanians kept neutrality, but were prompt
to demand territorial compensation. As a result of the first
Balkan War they obtained from Bulgaria an extension of
their territory to the south in the neighbourhood of the
Dobruja ; and when the victorious Balkan Allies fell out
over the distribution of the spoils of their victory over Turkey,
the Roumanians joined in the coalition against Bulgaria
which took shape in the second Balkan War, immediately
occupied the southern part of the Dobruja, and were successful in retaining it in the Peace Treaty which ensued.

In the Great War Roumania at first remained neutral,
hovering uncertainly between the rival offers of the Allies
and the Central Powers. But in 1916, in return for large
promises, including the acquisition of Transylvania and
the Banat from the Austro-Hungarian Empire, Roumania
joined the Allies, and thus found herself once again at war
with her old antagonist Bulgaria. The Central Powers
promptly met this challenge by invading the country at the
end of 1916, and the whole of Roumania was before long in
their hands, the oil wells being destroyed by the retreating
Allies in order to prevent them from falling into the hands
of the Central Powers. Thus put out of action, Roumania
at the end of 1917 accepted the terms of an armistice with
Germany and Austria-Hungary ; and this was followed by
a dictated peace under which the Roumanians had to agree
to cede important frontier territories to the Central Powers.
Austria-Hungary was to acquire a strip of frontier land
running all round the borders of Transylvania ; Bulgaria
was to regain the territory lost in 1913 ; and the northern
part of the Dobruja was to be left at the subsequent disposal
of the Central Powers. This settlement, however, was
speedily annulled when the armies of Germany and

Austria-Hungary were compelled to evacuate the country in the course of 1918 ; and with the collapse of German resistance the Roumanians were free to put forward claims to a great enlargement of their territory. The question was not, however, settled without further fighting ; for in 1919 war broke out between Roumania and Hungary, and the Roumanians advanced into Hungarian territory and for a time occupied Budapest. This victory over disarmed and dismembered Hungary completed the post-war settlement and left the Roumanians free to turn their attention to the administration of their greatly enlarged territory.

Apart from the problem of national minorities the question most obviously demanding immediate attention was that of the land. Already in 1917 the first steps towards land reform had been taken by the passing of a Land Law for the expropriation with compensation of the great estates ; and this process of agrarian reform was carried further in the years after the conclusion of the war, until the greater part of the country had been divided up into small peasant holdings. Roumania is now essentially a peasant country, dependent above all on the export of cereals, timber, animals and meat, though the export from her oil wells is also an important factor in her trade balance. Of her total territory about 44 per cent is arable, about 14 per cent grass land, and about 25 per cent forest, the richest agricultural areas lying partly in the old provinces of Moldavia and Wallachia and partly in the Banat and the new eastern provinces of Bessarabia and the Dobruja. The Transylvanian uplands are comparatively infertile and sparsely populated, save for a broad belt of territory lying on their western fringe. The Danubian country of Wallachia still forms, especially in the neighbourhood of Bucharest, the most densely populated area of the country ; but the population is also dense and relatively prosperous in the new territories acquired from Austria-Hungary in the north and in the Banat to the west.

Roumanian politics are still dominated to a great extent by the question of the land. Between 1919 and the

establishment of the present dictatorship by the King the
government of the country alternated between the Liberals,
led by Bratianu until his death in 1927, and the Peasant
Parties under the leadership of Dr. Maniu, with an inter-
lude of government by General Averescu at the head of a
coalition dependent on peasant support. But the handling
of the land question and also of the problem of minorities
in Transylvania and elsewhere has been hampered by
dynastic troubles centring round the personality of King
Carol, the last Hohenzollern to retain a European throne.

Post-war politics in Roumania have been throughout
extraordinarily involved and perplexing to the outsider.
The enlargement of the country and the recognised necessity for a large measure of agrarian reform and for the recognition of universal suffrage broke up most of the older parties
and gave rise to the development of numerous fresh political combinations. Of the historical Roumanian parties the
Liberals alone remain in being ; but for a time after the
conclusion of the war they were in opposition and the
government was carried on by a series of coalitions. The
Democratic Coalition of the Transylvanian Vaida-Voevod
soon gave way to the administration of General Averescu,
which was chiefly responsible, under traditional conservative auspices, for carrying through the agrarian reforms
which General Averescu's ambiguous position of authority
among the conservatives combined with great popularity
amongst the peasants put him in the best position to undertake. But no sooner was the land reform an accomplished
fact than the Liberals under Bratianu persuaded the King
to dismiss the Government and reinstate them in power,
and it was under their auspices that the new Constitution
of post-war Roumania was adopted and the country administered on highly dictatorial lines from 1921 to 1926. During
this period the opposition parties for the most part boycotted
Parliament, and there was continual unrest in the country,
including repeated Communist uprisings in Bessarabia.

In 1926 political excitements flared up in consequence of
Prince Carol's dramatic renunciation of his right to the

throne. For the opposition, at loggerheads with the King over the maintenance of the Liberal dictatorship, refused to recognise the situation created by Prince Carol's act. Meanwhile the Liberal Government, in imitation of Fascist models, carried through an extraordinary electoral law, under which any party which received 40 per cent of the votes cast at a general election was to receive 50 per cent of the seats in Parliament over and above its proportion of the other 50 per cent, which were to be distributed in accordance with the voting. This measure, designed to ensure the success of the Government at the forthcoming elections, actually led to the downfall of the Liberal Party. For before the elections were held the state of feeling had become so strong that the King was compelled to dismiss the Liberals and call on General Averescu to form a Government supported by the peasants as well as by the remainder of the opposition parties. In the ensuing election General Averescu's party got four-fifths of the seats in the Chamber and the Liberals were almost wiped out. But in the following year the Averescu conservatives quarrelled with the peasants, and, after an attempt to form a non-party Government, the Liberals came back to power and conducted a new general election in which they in turn wiped out General Averescu's party. The Liberal triumph was, however, short-lived, for after King Ferdinand's death in 1927 the Regency dismissed the Liberal Government, and the peasant leader, Dr. Maniu, formed a new Ministry. The general election which followed pursued the usual course ; the Liberals were overwhelmingly defeated, and the peasants returned with an overwhelming majority, and thereafter, with temporary interruptions due to internal disputes, maintained their hold upon the country until King Carol succeeded, despite his earlier renunciation of the throne, in resuming power with the help of the military, and thereafter made himself virtual dictator in 1931.

These facts are given at some length in order to illustrate the extraordinary working of the Roumanian political system. For even the astonishing electoral law of 1926 is by no means enough to account for the swing over of votes at successive general elections. It is clear on the facts that under present political conditions in Roumania whoever has control of the governmental machine wins the election, and under the electoral system the victorious party is certain of returning with an overwhelming majority. This obviously makes the democratic character of the franchise largely illusory, and adds greatly to the effective power of the Crown. For as the Crown can dismiss the Ministry and put another in its place, and as the Government can be certain of winning the election, this means that the Crown can, under normal conditions, practically dictate the composition of the Parliament. There are doubtless limits to the Crown's power if it seeks to stand out against an overwhelming body of public opinion or to maintain a thoroughly unpopular Government in power ; but short of this, Roumania, as the circumstances of King Carol's return in 1930 and the subsequent government of the country have clearly shown, is far nearer to being an absolute monarchy than a constitutional monarchy in the west European sense.

In external politics, Roumania's attitude is determined mainly by her fears—the fear of Russia in the east and the fear of Hungary in the west. Bulgaria to the south may some day be again regarded as a menace ; but for the time being Bulgaria is too weak to cause the Roumanians serious anxiety. Their fears are centred on Bessarabia and Transylvania, and their desire ever since the war has been to find as broad a basis as possible for alliances designed to preserve the territorial *status quo*. Roumania is joined with Czechoslovakia and Yugoslavia in the Little Entente, which exists mainly in order to maintain the post-war settlement of the Hungarian frontier and to prevent the restoration of the Hapsburg Empire. Shortly after the formation of the Little Entente she set on foot negotiations for broadening it by the inclusion of other border States, especially Poland ; but these negotiations fell through, as the Czechoslovaks and Yugoslavs were by no means willing to become entangled unnecessarily in the problems of the Russian border. Roumania thereupon concluded a separate agreement with Poland, directed evidently against Russia. The dispute over Bessarabia still stands in the way of any final adjustment of her relationships with the U.S.S.R. ; for, though the Russians have followed up their earlier pledges to prevent incursions into Bessarabia from Russian territory by a plain declaration that they will not use force of arms for the recovery of the province, they refuse emphatically to renounce their claims or to recognise Bessarabia as Roumanian territory. In fact, while the U.S.S.R. is pledged not to go to war in order to get Bessarabia back, it is not pledged to refuse to admit Bessarabia to the Soviet Union should it be able by its own efforts to regain its freedom of action.

In the summer of 1933, however, the U.S.S.R. entered with Roumania, as well as with Poland, the other countries of the Little Entente, and a number of other States, into treaties which not only give mutual pledges against aggression but also plainly define the "aggressor" so as to exclude all forms of military action.

§ 6. THE BALKANS

Our study of the States lying along the western frontier of the U.S.S.R. has carried us from Scandinavia in the north to the Balkan countries in South-Eastern Europe. In this region, as well as further north, there has been, as a result of the wholesale redistribution of territory and populations, a pronounced change in the political and economic situation. The expansion of Roumania and Yugoslavia and to a less extent of Greece, the defeat of Bulgaria, and the recreation of Turkey on the basis of her Asiatic possessions under the leadership of Kemal Pasha have changed profoundly the distribution of forces, not only by altering the relative strength of the various Balkan Powers, but also by modifying very greatly their relation to the rest of Europe. Roumania, enlarged almost beyond

Territory gained by Greece from Turkey after Balkan War (1913)

Gained by Greece from Bulgaria after Great War (1919)

THE BALKANS

recognition and brought into close contact with her new and powerful neighbour Poland, ceases to be predominantly a Balkan State and acquires a major interest in the problems of Central rather than of South-Eastern Europe. Yugoslavia, stuck none too securely together out of pre-war Serbia and Montenegro and the Austro-Hungarian provinces of Croatia, Slovenia, Bosnia and Herzegovina, runs up to the Italian boundary on the Adriatic, and is brought by contact with Italy and Vienna into far closer touch with Western Europe. Greece, despite the defeat of her aspirations towards an all-Hellenic Ægean Sea, has gained a considerable accession of territory and an added importance in world trade. Only Bulgaria and Albania remain as purely Balkan States in the old sense of the word ; and Bulgaria, once the leader in Balkan affairs, is now helpless in the midst of her aggrandised and victorious neighbours. For, though her loss of territory during the war was not in itself great, the increase in the size and population of her neighbours has left her easily the smallest of the Balkan States except Albania, and set back indefinitely her pre-war hopes of expansion.

The Balkan Wars.   In considering the post-war situation of the Balkan States, it is essential to remember that these States became involved in the World War immediately after their emergence from two successive regional wars of their own. In the first Balkan War of 1912, Bulgaria, Serbia, Montenegro and Greece were united against the Turk, and succeeded, as long as they were able to maintain their unity, almost to the point of driving the Ottoman Empire clean out of Europe. But the falling out over the spoils of victory which speedily followed this success, and took shape in the second Balkan War of 1913, not only reasserted the power of the Turks in Europe but also resulted for Bulgaria in a serious set-back to her hopes. What the Bulgarians wanted above all was a secure means of access to the Ægean for their commerce, and the possession of the Macedonian lands largely inhabited by peoples akin to themselves, as against the rival claims of the Greeks. After the first Balkan War the first of these aims seemed to have been definitely realised, and it was largely over the second that the victorious Balkan Allies fell out. The second Balkan War lost Bulgaria the Dobruja, which she had held since her recognition as an autonomous principality in 1878, and left her with only a short stretch of coast-line on the Ægean, including the small port of Dedeagatch, instead of the much larger territorial accessions for which she had hoped.

The outbreak of the Great War thus found the Bulgarians in a mood of acute resentment against their immediate Balkan neighbours, and avid to regain what they had lost as a result of the second Balkan War. They had already in 1914 turned towards Germany for financial support in the hour of defeat, and had obtained from the Berlin *Diskonto-gesellschaft* a loan of capital in return for which German finance acquired substantial concessions in the country, especially for the development of coal mines and the improvement of the railway system. It was as natural in the circumstances for Bulgaria to enter the war on the side of the Central Powers as it was for her rival Serbia to be pitted against Austria-Hungary. The Bulgarians thus backed the wrong horse yet again, and the territorial settlement after 1918 cut them off from the Ægean, with only an unsatisfactory promise of special facilities for the building of a railway to Dedeagatch and the establishment of a zone of their own at that none too eligible port. Territorially, Bulgaria was left with no outlet to the sea save on the east, and under the necessity, unless Dedeagatch could be made an effective outlet in face of the political and geographical difficulties, of sending her sea-borne commerce to Western Europe by way of the Straits.

Bulgaria. Bulgaria, with her forty thousand square miles of territory and her six million people, is overwhelmingly an agricultural country. Geographically, the land is divided into two parts by the Balkan mountains, which run right across the country almost to the sea ; while in the south the Rhodope range parts her from the coast lands of the Ægean and from Macedonia and Thrace. Mountainous in the centre and in the south, she possesses large tracts of agricultural land on both sides of the Balkan range. 36 per cent of her land is arable and only about 3 per cent permanent pasture, with roughly 30 per cent of forest country. For the most part, the land is tilled by peasants, who make up 80 per cent of the total population, on very small holdings—small even according to the standards prevailing in South-Eastern Europe. Agricultural methods are very primitive, though there have been considerable attempts at improving them since the war. Before the war wheat was the chief crop, and the mainstay of the export trade. But after the war there was a great development of the cultivation of tobacco, which soon accounted for not far short of half of the total exports, whereas the export trade in wheat shrank considerably for a time, and has only revived during the present slump. The cultivation of tobacco had been extended, especially during the period when Greece and Turkey were largely out of the market owing to disturbed political conditions and to the Greco-Turkish War. With the re-entry of these countries into world trade other forms of agricultural production had to be developed, and the Bulgarians turned more largely to the cultivation of sugar-beet, sesame seed, cotton and maize. But tobacco still predominates ; and this gives the Bulgarians, in common with the Turks and the Greeks, an attitude in economic matters differing substantially from that of their wheat exporting neighbours.

While, however, Bulgaria has suffered less than these other countries from the sharp fall in the world price of raw foodstuffs, she has had great economic difficulties of her own to face. It has been estimated that the immigration of Bulgarian refugees, including Macedonians, from the surrounding territories has increased her population by nearly a million, thus adding to the congestion on her tiny peasant holdings and to the unsatisfied hunger for land.

In these circumstances production per worker engaged in agriculture has fallen off, though it has shown some tendency to rise again during the past few years. In dealing with the refugee problem the Bulgarians have been helped by the League of Nations Refugee Loan of 1926 ; but although something has been done to increase land settlement, the problem has been by no means completely solved, and especially in the south-west part of the country on the borders of Yugoslavia and Greece the disturbed political conditions caused by the strength and lawlessness of the Macedonian revolutionary organisations have been greatly aggravated by the difficulty and persistence of the refugee problem.

Modern Bulgaria, like the rest of the Balkan States, has a comparatively short life as an independent country. The old Bulgarian Empire of the twelfth to fourteenth centuries, after a period of subordination to Serbia, came under Turkish rule in the latter part of the fourteenth century, and thereafter Bulgaria disappeared from the map of Europe until the fruits of the nationalist revival of the early nineteenth century were garnered with Russian help at the close of the Russo-Turkish War in 1878. The Treaty of Berlin established Bulgaria as an autonomous principality, still nominally under Turkish rule, but not including Eastern Rumelia, to which Bulgarian nationalists had laid claim. Eastern Rumelia, however, was occupied in 1885 by a *coup de main* and thereafter administered by the Bulgarian prince as a vassal of Turkey. Not until 1908 did Ferdinand proclaim Bulgarian independence and unite the two areas in a single country, taking the title of Tsar as a sign of Bulgarian pretensions to revive the ancient Empire. Thereafter, as we have seen, Bulgaria speedily became involved in conflict with her neighbours ; for her people, warlike and primitive, were easily roused to a fervour of nationalism, and the existence of large Bulgarian populations beyond the frontiers of the new State gave this nationalism a definite political objective, even though Bulgaria's success in acquiring the territories which she

coveted would only have created fresh problems of irredentism among her neighbours because of the inextricable
mingling of races and nationalities in the disputed areas.

To-day about 80 per cent of the population of the country
are Bulgarians and about 11 per cent Turks. Now that the
Dobruja has been lost, the number of Russians in the
country is comparatively small ; and there are not many
Jews. By religion the mass of the people belong to the
Bulgarian Orthodox Church ; but there is also a substantial
Moslem population, and the Roman Catholics are numer-
ous enough to have some influence.

In the period of re-settlement after the war the agrarian
question dominated Bulgarian politics. The election of
1920 was won by the Agrarians under Stambuliski, who for
the next few years governed the country practically as a
dictator with the support of the left-wing groups and in
face of the strong hostility of the older parties. An Agrarian
Law was at once passed for the division of Church and
Crown lands among the peasants. But there were few large
estates in private possession, and the amount of land available for division was far too small to meet the demand.
In 1923 Stambuliski was overthrown by a *coup d'état*
organised by the conservative elements in the country in
alliance with the discontented Macedonians, with whom
Stambuliski had quarrelled. His murder in the course of
the *coup d'état* left the Agrarians without an effective leader
and brought to an end his dream of a Green International
of peasants to dominate the political situation of South-
Eastern Europe. The *coup d'état* was followed by a situation
not far off civil war, in the course of which the new Tsankoff
Government rigorously suppressed the Communist and
Socialist elements in the country. In 1926 a form of democratic government was restored under Liapchev ; and in the
following year the Constitution was amended to provide
for proportional representation, with the usual results of
multiplying parties and making government by coalitions
inevitable. Communism, suppressed under Tsankoff, revived in the guise of a new Workers' Party which won a

substantial number of seats in the general election of 1931. But after the fall of Stambuliski the prospect of a workers' and peasants' alliance had disappeared ; and the Agrarian Party now joins in governing the country with the *bourgeois* parties of the right, centre and left.

Yugoslavia. Bulgaria's immediate neighbour to the west is Yugoslavia—the new Kingdom of the Serbs, Croats and Slovenes created at the end of the war out of the old kingdoms of Serbia and Montenegro and the neighbouring parts of the Austro-Hungarian Empire inhabited by peoples of Slavonic race and speech. The Serbs, by adding to their pre-war kingdom the Austro-Hungarian provinces of Croatia, Slovenia, Bosnia, Herzegovina and Voyvodina, made themselves dominant partners in a country with a territory of over 94,000 square miles and a population of nearly fourteen million people, whereas pre-war Serbia had a territory of only 34,000 square miles and a population of four and a half millions. But even Serbia as she existed in 1914 was a new country, for she had only just emerged from the Balkan Wars of 1912–14, and in the course of these wars she had nearly doubled her area and added one-third to her previous population. Before there had been any time to devise a new administrative system or to face the problems of government and administration in this enlarged territory, Serbia became involved in a new and greater war during which practically the whole of her territory was conquered and occupied by hostile armies and her national Government forced to retire to alien territory in the island of Corfu, while Austria-Hungary and Bulgaria with their armies of occupation actually governed the country. Thus in 1918, when the Serbian Government was able to resume occupation of the evacuated territory, it was faced simultaneously with the problem of reorganisation within the pre-war area and of uniting the old kingdom with the vast new territories emancipated from the control of Austria-Hungary. Hardly less than for Poland was the creation of Yugoslavia the making of a new State ; and the

GR

fact that there were the already existing Serbian monarchy and Serbian Government and party system to be reckoned with, so far from simplifying the problem, only added to its difficulty.

Even before the new kingdom had been established at all, the struggle had begun between the old Serbs, who wished to make it simply old Serbia writ large, and to govern the new provinces by a centralised system under exclusive Serb dominance, and the National Committees and Assemblies of the emancipated Austro-Hungarian provinces, which demanded a solution based on full equality for all the elements to be included in the new State, and on a considerable measure of regional devolution, if not actual federalism, designed to safeguard the rights of distinct racial and religious groups.

For post-war Yugoslavia, though it is appropriately described as the kingdom of the southern Slavs, is nevertheless a very heterogeneous group of territories. The Serbs themselves form hardly more than a third of the total population ; there are now living in Yugoslav territory over three million Croats, a million Slovenes, half a million Germans, nearly half a million Magyars and almost as many Albanians, and a quarter of a million Roumanian-speaking people. These differences of race and language are deeply complicated by differences of religion ; for whereas the Serbs belong to the Orthodox Church, the Croats are Catholics, and in the total population the Catholics claim 39 per cent as against 47 per cent belonging to the Orthodox Church. Apart from these two major groups there are large numbers of Moslems both in the south of the country and in Bosnia, amounting in all to no less than 11 per cent of the population, while in Voyvodina along the Hungarian border there is a large element of Protestants among the German and Magyar communities. Jews are relatively unimportant, numbering only about 73,000 in the country as a whole.

Nor are the differences which lead to an intense demand for local autonomy racial and religious alone ; they are also to a large extent cultural. The inhabitants of the old Austro-Hungarian provinces, and especially of Croatia, Slovenia and Voyvodina, had assimilated to a great extent the culture of the old Empire, and are in social matters far in advance of the Serbian population further south. In addition, whereas Serbia herself is almost purely agricultural and inhabited almost exclusively by peasants—old Serbia contained no large town with the exception of Belgrade—the people of Croatia are much more urbanised, and there has been a considerable development of mining and manufactures in both Croatia and Slovenia. Yet again, whereas Serbian agriculture is still essentially primitive, in Voyvodina a high level of agricultural technique exists, especially among the Germans and Magyars, who live to a large extent in concentrated communities of their own. Voyvodina is the most closely populated section of the country, with a density of over 180 to the square mile ; Slovenia comes next with about 170, and Croatia not far behind with over 160 ; whereas Serbia has a density of only about 110, and the average for Yugoslavia as a whole is only about 125.

In these circumstances the more advanced peoples of the new northern provinces keenly resent a form of centralised government which has involved in practice the domination of the old Serbs, and an almost complete disregard of the demand for local autonomy and the adaptation of methods of government to the differing needs of the various provinces. This question of centralisation *versus* some degree of local autonomy has dominated Yugoslav politics ever since the creation of the enlarged kingdom.

Nor is it even nearing settlement to-day. It arose, as we have seen, when the constitution of the new State was under consideration at the end of the war. Upon the collapse of the Austro-Hungarian Empire the former Austro-Hungarian provinces at once proclaimed their independence and passed temporarily under the control of provisional administrations, pending a definite settlement concerning their future. They did not feel strong enough to stand alone, and they were ready from the first, on terms, to enter into a new combined State of the southern Slavs. But they were not willing simply to be annexed to Serbia, and to be governed from Belgrade by the old Serbian politicians without any consideration of their special needs. The old Serbs, on the other hand, under the leadership of Pasic, were by no means willing to give up their power or to share it on equal terms with the representatives of the new provinces. They stood for a pan-Serbian policy of unification, and they were acutely suspicious both of the Catholicism and of the more industrialised outlook of the Croatian and Slovenian leaders. Regarding Austria-Hungary as their traditional enemy, they disliked especially the influence of Austro-Hungarian culture in the new provinces ; and they wanted Serbian control of the educational system as well as of the government as a means of Serbianising the country as a whole. It was only after considerable difficulties and long delays that agreement to form a unified State was secured between the provisional bodies in the Austro-Hungarian provinces and the old Serbs ; and this agreement by no means settled the problem of the future government of the country. A temporary coalition was indeed patched up between the old Serbian governmental party, known as the Radicals, and the new Democratic party formed by a fusion of certain sections of the opposition in Serbia with the Liberal groups in Croatia and the other new provinces. This coalition governed the country during the years immediately after the war, in face of a highly mixed opposition consisting on the one hand of a large body of Communists and on the other of the extreme right and the extreme left among the Croatian parties—the Croatian clericals and Radic's Croatian peasant party. In this uneasy coalition the Serbs were successful in retaining their dominance, and in 1921 they pushed through the Constituent Assembly a highly centralised constitution providing for the completely unified government of the whole Yugoslav State. The Croatian peasant opposition, unwisely perhaps, refused to recognise the validity of the Constituent

Assembly and abstained from attendance, and Communist
opposition was effectively got under, first by cancelling
the mandates of the Communist deputies, and then by the
suppression of the party itself after the murder of one of the
Ministers by a Communist fanatic.

The immediate effect of the new constitution was to
strengthen the hand of the old Serbian Radicals. The
coalition was broken up, and a purely Radical Ministry
under Pasic governed the country until 1924. Then at
length the growth of opposition to the Radical policy of
unification, reinforced by the return to Parliament of the
Croatian deputies, compelled Pasic to resign. For a few
months a Democratic Government held office ; but before
long the Democratic groups fell out among themselves,
largely in consequence of the intransigence of Radic and
his Croatian Peasant Party. Pasic returned to power and
followed up his suppression of the Communists by suppressing the Peasant Party as well, and inaugurating a still more
highly centralised régime. There followed a period of
extraordinary confusion. Radic executed a sudden *volte face*
and entered into a coalition with Pasic ; but this soon broke
down, and in 1927 the Radicals coalesced with the Democrats, while Radic resumed his leadership of the opposition.
This was followed in 1928 by the disastrous incident in the
Chamber in which Radic and several of his followers were
shot by a fanatical Radical deputy. The Croatians at once
withdrew in protest from the Chamber, and a period of
complete political confusion ensued, until the King cut
the knot by the *coup d'état* of 1929.

In the course of the *coup d'état* King Alexander made
promises of decentralisation in order to pacify the opposition. In the meantime the Constitution of 1921 was abrogated by royal decree and a purely Democratic Government
installed. All existing political parties were completely
suppressed, and forbidden ever to reform. The country,
which under the previous Constitution had been divided
into a large number of administrative districts carefully
designed to break up the old Austro-Hungarian provinces

and so ensure the success of the policy of centralisation, was redistributed into a smaller number of new areas to be called Banats. Each of these was to be under a Ban appointed by the Crown, with the aid of a provincial Diet. In 1931 a new Constitution was brought into operation by royal decree and the new system of provincial government made definite. This new Constitution presents some extraordinary features. Under it the power of legislation is to be exercised jointly by the Crown and by a National Congress consisting of two Chambers with co-equal powers. If the Chambers disagree the Crown has the power of deciding between them. Of the Upper Chamber one half is elected and the other half appointed directly by the Crown, which has thus the power of controlling almost absolutely its dominant complexion. The popular Chamber, on the other hand, is wholly elected under universal suffrage, but by a system so extraordinary as to reduce to complete impotence all the various provincial minorities. No candidate is allowed to stand for election unless his name is entered on a rational list, and no list is admitted to be valid unless it includes a representative nominated from every electoral division in the country. It follows that no group formed upon a regional basis—e.g. no purely Croatian party—can nominate a candidate at all, unless it can coalesce to form a list with other regional groups in every division—virtually an impossible condition. Indeed, at the elections of 1931 under the new Constitution only one list was able to comply with the required conditions and all the members appearing on this list were accordingly returned without opposition. The Parliament, when it met, thus presented a spectacle of unanimity in singular contrast to the Parliaments elected under the system of proportional representation which prevails over the greater part of Europe. There were no parties, for all the old parties were still prohibited ; but the new members proceeded to remedy this defect by forming themselves into a single party—the Yugoslav Party, to which they all belong. The Yugoslav State has thus been made " safe for democracy " without the disadvantages of an organised opposition. Far more completely even than the Russian system the new Yugoslav Constitution ensures the dominance of a single party in the affairs of State. There has been so far no sign that this dominant party, or the King, who in effect controls it, is prepared to make any real concessions to the demand for local freedom by expanding the autonomous powers of the new Diets formed for each separate administrative area. Yugoslavia exists under a rigid dictatorship : some of the opposition leaders are in prison, and the rest silenced. Revolution threatens in Croatia ; and there is a vast mass of discontent even in old Serbia. Politically, relations with Italy are bad, and the temper of the Government is strongly militarist. It is impossible to believe that Yugoslavia can hold together permanently under anything resembling her present artificial system of centralised dictatorship.

Greece. To the south of Bulgaria and Yugoslavia lies the kingdom of the Hellenes, now including not only the Greek mainland but also the greater part of Macedonia and Thrace to the north of the Ægean Sea, together with Crete and the Ægean islands, except Imbros in the north and Rhodes and the Dodecanese off the south of Asia Minor. Post-war Greece thus, as we have seen, cuts off Bulgaria and Yugoslavia completely from the Ægean Sea ; but the international guarantees in respect of the use of Salonica provide Yugoslavia with an outlet, while Bulgaria, as we saw, has certain rights in the small port of Dedeagatch further east.

In no country were the territorial confusions and readjustments of the post-war period greater than in the Greek lands. In 1919 the Greeks claimed, in addition to the territories which they at present possess, the whole western coast-line of Asia Minor, together with a good slice of the interior and the stretch of territory running eastward from Thrace and the Black Sea, including the command of the Sea of Marmora. This would have brought the Greek lands practically to the gates of Constantinople, and in Asia

Minor would have shut up the Turks far away in the mountainous interior of the country. In addition the Greeks claimed Rhodes and the Dodecanese, still held by Italy, and Cyprus, held by Great Britain.

Even the boundaries granted to Greece by the Allies in 1920 were a good deal more extensive than the territory which she at present holds. For the Allies contemplated the ultimate cession of the Dodecanese, though not of Rhodes, and the transference from Turkey to Greece of Smyrna and a considerable hinterland half way down the coast of Asia Minor. Only the utter defeat of the Greek armies at the hands of the Turks in 1921–22 compelled Greece to retire within the territories which she at present occupies and to leave the coast of Asia Minor under Turkish sovereignty.

Even so, Greece gained substantially in territory and population as a result of the World War ; and these gains were in addition to the considerable accession of territory which came to her as a result of the Balkan Wars of 1912–13. Indeed, the modern Greek State is the result of a gradual growth extending over almost a century. Greek independence was established in the eighteen-twenties in the course of her revolt against the Ottoman Empire ; and the independent existence of the Greek kingdom under the joint guarantee of Great Britain, France, and Russia was definitely recognised in the settlements of 1830 and 1832. The kingdom of Greece at this stage included no more than the Morea, or Peloponnese, together with the lands immediately north of the Gulf of Corinth, and the islands in the western part of the Ægean Sea. The Ionian Islands off the west coast were ceded by Great Britain in 1863 ; and in 1878 the plain of Thessaly was added to the Greek dominions. Thereafter Greek expansion ceased for the generation preceding the Balkan Wars. In 1910 she had an area of about 24,400 square miles, and to this the Balkan Wars added about 21,600 square miles, almost doubling the land surface of the country by the addition of Southern Epirus, the greater part of Macedonia and Western Thrace.

After the Great War the Greeks gained most of the remainder of Thrace and a large territory in Asia Minor ; but of all these gains they retained only about 3,000 square miles, giving the country a total area at the present time of rather under 50,000 square miles, and a population of rather under six and a half millions as against five millions in 1913.

The territorial changes give, however, a very incomplete picture of the change in the Greek State in consequence of the war. For there has been since 1918 a wholesale migration and exchange of populations between the territories now under Greek control and those of Bulgaria and Turkey. In 1913 the Greek population of Macedonia and Thrace was only 40 per cent of the total ; in the area at present under Greek control it is now 90 per cent in Macedonia and about 65 per cent in Thrace, as a result of an organised system of exchange and settlement carried through with the financial assistance of the League of Nations and under the auspices of the International Refugee Settlement Commission set up in 1923. Thus, although Greece failed to make good her claim to those territories in Asia Minor and Eastern Thrace which were largely inhabited by Greeks, the area now under her political control has come to include the great majority of the Greek people, and the alien elements within it have been very greatly reduced. Greek aspirations have not, indeed, been by any means completely or finally satisfied ; for the Greek claim to Cyprus, Rhodes and the Dodecanese holds the same position as the Greek claim to Crete used to hold before the war. The Greeks will not be satisfied until the Italians implement their pledge that the occupation of the Dodecanese should be purely temporary and give up Rhodes, and until Great Britain agrees to the inclusion of Cyprus within the Hellenic State. But as far as Thrace and the mainland of Asia Minor are concerned, exchange of populations seems to have gone far towards achieving a final settlement of the territorial problem.

Every since her achievement of independence in the eighteen-twenties, Greece has had a troubled history. The

Bavarian king donated to her by the Great Powers in 1830 was expelled in 1862 as the result of a military revolt, and thereafter a constitutional monarch was elected and a unicameral system of parliamentary government instituted. But neither Greek monarchism nor Greek parliamentarism ever worked smoothly, and there was constant friction over both internal and external affairs. Greece was and is an exceedingly poor country, and she has been from the first largely in the hands of foreign bondholders, with whom her inability to meet her accumulating burden of debts has led to repeated quarrels. Her financial difficulties have been aggravated again and again by war. Both after the Greco-Turkish War of 1897, in which the Greeks got much the worst of it, and after the Balkan Wars of 1912-13, in which they and their allies were victorious, the national finances were thrown into serious confusion, and the mounting debt burden was already a serious problem before 1914. Moreover the Cretan question was a continuous source of disturbance. In 1897 the Cretans finally secured autonomy under the Ottoman Empire ; but this in no way satisfied their nationalist aspirations towards union with Greece, and in 1908 the Cretans definitely proclaimed themselves a part of the Greek State. The Greek Government, fearful of international complications and possible military defeat, hesitated to endorse the Cretan move, and the consequence was a military revolt in Athens which overthrew the Government and placed the country for a time under the authority of a military league. Under the auspices of this body Eleftherios Venizelos, whose activities form an integral part of all Greece's subsequent history, first came to power. In 1912 the Cretan question was at last solved by the union of Crete and Greece in the course of the first Balkan War. In the following year the assassination of King George brought to the throne King Constantine, who speedily came to be at loggerheads with Venizelos. On the outbreak of the Great War, Venizelos, in the interest of Greek irredentism, proposed that the country should join the Allied Powers ; but the King, who was a partisan of the

Germans, thereupon dismissed him from the ministry, and in 1916 Venizelos seceded to Salonica, then in Allied possession, and set up there a rival Provisional Government. Under pressure of the Allies, who supported Venizelist claims, King Constantine was forced to abdicate in 1917 and was succeeded by his son Alexander, the effective control of affairs passing back into the hands of Venizelos. Under his auspices the convention with the Bulgarians for the exchange of populations between the two countries was arranged in 1919 ; and in the same year, at the request of the Allies, the Greek army landed at Smyrna and occupied the western central part of Asia Minor. But in 1920 King Alexander died, and in the following confusion Constantine was able to return and to expel Venizelos.

This change in Greece's political orientation made the victorious Allies far less sympathetic to Greek aspirations, and the support of the Greek claim to Asia Minor was withdrawn in connection with the repudiation of the Sèvres Treaty between the Allies and Turkey. The Greeks, however, refused to give way, and in 1921–22 suffered complete defeat at the hands of the Turks, who, since the Franco-Turkish agreement of 1921, were receiving the active diplomatic support of France. Smyrna was recaptured by the Turks, and the Greek army evacuated in disorder, and no less than 1,350,000 Greek inhabitants were expelled from Asia Minor by the victorious Turks, while a parallel movement for the removal of Turkish inhabitants from Macedonia and Thrace was organised on the Greek side. In 1922 these mutual expulsions were regulated by a Greco-Turkish convention for the exchange of populations on the lines of the Greco-Bulgarian convention of 1919.

The national defeat in Asia Minor produced powerful reactions in Greece itself. A new revolution broke out and King Constantine was forced again to abdicate. In the heat of the national disgrace the Greek leaders who were supposed to have been responsible for the defeat were executed in spite of protests from other countries. King

George II replaced Constantine, but was speedily compelled to leave the country. In 1924 it was decided by plebiscite to constitute Greece a republic, and the work of drafting a new constitution was begun. For a brief period in 1926 General Pangalos succeeded in establishing a dictatorship, but after his overthrow a new republican constitution was brought into force, and thereafter the country was governed by a bicameral system of the familiar type. The president of the Republic is elected as in France by two Chambers sitting together, and has much the same powers as the French President. The lower Chamber is chosen for four years by manhood suffrage ; but since 1930 women have been granted the municipal vote. Three quarters of the members of the Upper Chamber are also directly elected, and the remaining quarter chosen partly by the two Chambers together and partly by special bodies such as Chambers of Commerce and Universities. But it is doubtful whether parliamentary institutions can be regarded as at all securely established on Greek soil. By far the strongest personality in Greek politics is Venizelos, and political affairs are dominated mainly by the quarrels between his supporters and opponents. At the moment of writing, he has been defeated at a General Election, and an attempt of some of his partisans to make a military revolution has been overthrown.

Economically Greece is mainly an agricultural country. Before the Balkan Wars she had little good agricultural land except in the islands of the Ægean, and she was largely dependent on island produce for essential supplies. Her territorial expansion has now given her excellent agricultural land in Macedonia as well as in the further islands added to her domain. She is not, however, by any means self-sufficient in foodstuffs. Wheat and other cereals have to be largely imported from abroad, while she exports large quantities of currants from her older territories and tobacco from Macedonia. Wheat, oats, barley, maize, vines and olives are cultivated on a substantial scale in addition to currants and tobacco, and there has also been an extension in other types of fruit growing and in the cultivation of cotton in recent years, while some rice is grown in the northern part of the country. There has been some industrialisation since the war under the stimulus of a high protective tariff, but even to-day at least three-quarters of the population live by agriculture, and less than one-third are in urban areas. Greece has consistently both before and since the war had a large adverse visible trade balance ; but to a substantial extent her surplus imports have been covered by emigrant remittances from the United States, to which there used to be a very large emigration of Greek nationals ; to some extent her accumulating financial difficulties of recent years have been due to the fall in these balances on account both of declining emigration and of the world slump.

Greece's financial difficulties have, however, not been by any means wholly due to this cause. The war with Turkey in 1921–22 was financed only by great inflation of the currency, which after the disaster at Smyrna fell to six per cent of its par value in terms of gold. The settlement of refugees, which was accomplished by the breaking up of the great estates as well as by the exchange of peasant holdings, involved heavy additional overseas borrowing in 1924, when Greece had to submit to drastic control by an International Financial Commission in connection with the League of Nations Refugee Loan. An attempt had been made to stabilise the finances and balance the budget by means of a capital levy and of additional taxation levied in 1923, and there was further deflation under the orders of the International Commission in 1924 and 1925 ; but the short-lived dictatorship of General Pangalos in 1926 afforded the opportunity for fresh inflation, and the new Government of 1926 had again to appeal for outside help. This was granted subject to still further foreign control of the Greek finances under the League of Nations Stabilisation Loan of 1928 ; and the United States Government also granted Greece a loan in connection with the settlement of the war debt problem. Thereafter up to the outbreak of the world slump Greek finances appeared to be in a better position, but the slump soon brought to light the instability of the settlement which had been achieved. The great mass of Greek overseas debts are payable in gold, and the fall in the price-level speedily rendered them intolerable and led to a default accompanied by a new quarrel, which is still in progress, with the foreign bondholders. Indeed, ever since 1898 Greece has been without real financial autonomy. She has been compelled to assign a substantial part of her national revenue to meet overseas debt claims, and to submit to the authority of a Financial Commission of delegates representing the leading creditor countries. Since then her burdens have become more and more topheavy ; and so far from succeeding in building up an export surplus, she has continued to import more than she exports. Potentially, Greece, since the acquisition of Macedonia and the Ægean islands, is substantially wealthier than she used to be ; but she is economically undeveloped, and the heavy burden of her existing debts, incurred mainly for non-productive purposes, makes it impossible for her to borrow from abroad on favourable terms the capital needed for the internal development of the country.

Albania.   Bordering upon Greece to the south and upon Yugoslavia to the east and north lies the small independent State of Albania, with a population of well under a million. The Albanians are in general the most primitive of all the European peoples. The greater part of their country is mountainous ; and the narrow belt of flat land along the coast is malarial and for the most part uninhabited. There is only a tiny proportion of arable land in the country, and the population lives mainly by the raising of sheep and goats and to a less extent cattle. There are no large towns and no industries. The standard of life, especially in the southern part of the country, is exceedingly low ; and, although the people live by raising stock, the great majority are vegetarians, and meat, wool and hides form the chief articles of export. To a great extent each household continues to be self-sufficient, producing its own textile goods as well as its own food without recourse to the market. More than two-thirds of the inhabitants are Moslems, a legacy from the long period of Turkish rule; for Albania only became an independent State in 1913. In the north, which is the more civilised part of Albania, Roman Catholicism has some hold, while the Albanian Orthodox Church is active in the southern part of the country. But religious differences are said to count for little among this primitive people, with its civilisation still based more upon the family than upon any larger social group.

Albania gained her independence as a result of the first Balkan War. In 1912 there was a general rising against the Turks; and after an offer of autonomy had been made by the Ottoman Empire the Albanians proclaimed their independence with the support of Italy and Austria-Hungary. In 1913 the Powers recognised Albanian independence and equipped the country with a foreign king, Prince William of Wied, who was never in fact able to establish his position in face of the intrigues of the rival Powers which were scrambling for influence over the country. During the war Albania was occupied from the north by the Allies and from the south by the Greeks, who were anxious to incorporate the southern part of the country with the rest of Epirus in the Hellenic State. In 1915 the partition of Albania was agreed upon in one of the secret treaties made between the Allied Powers; but in the following year the Austrians and Bulgarians succeeded in occupying the country. In 1917, however, the Italians proclaimed an independent Albanian republic under Italian protection; and in 1918, upon the collapse of Austria-Hungary, a Provisional Government was instituted under the auspices of the Allies. This Government was unable to establish its authority in face of the opposition of the people, and in 1920 a revolt broke out and a rival National Government was set up. After some hesitation the Italians decided to recognise the National Government and to evacuate Albania, upon which the Yugoslavs made an incursion from the east and only withdrew when they were stopped firmly by an ultimatum from the Allies. Thereafter until 1924 Ahmed Zogu was at the head of the Government. But in 1924 he was driven to resign and forced to fly from the country by an insurrectionary movement under Monsignor Fan Noli. Zogu thereupon retired to Yugoslavia where, with Yugoslav aid, he organised an army, invaded the country and reassumed power. In 1925 a new constitution was adopted with Zogu as president, and in 1928 he changed his status and became King Zog. At the time of his return Zogu had been inclined to rely upon Yugoslav assistance ; but once established in power he turned to Italy for help, and it was under Italian auspices that the new constitution of 1925 was adopted. Italy provided the resources for establishing the National Bank of Albania and the Corporation for the Economic Development of Albania, which was designed to help in the civilisation of the country. Since then Albania has been for the most part under Italian influence, which has served to keep in check the aspirations of Greece and Yugoslavia for the partitioning of the territory, and at the same time to subdue those irredentist tendencies in Albania itself which look to an extension of its boundaries to include the Albanians still living under Greek and Yugoslav sovereignty.

§ 7. HUNGARY, AUSTRIA, SWITZERLAND

THE PRE-WAR Austro-Hungarian Empire, with its fifty-one million people and its 261,000 square miles of territory, was divided territorially between the two co-equal dominant partners, Austria and Hungary, which had separate Parliaments and, since the re-arrangement of 1867, had been united under the Hapsburgs by a purely personal

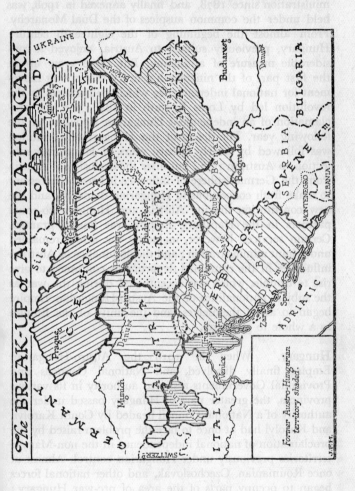

The BREAK-UP of AUSTRIA-HUNGARY

Former Austro-Hungarian territory shaded.

union. Bosnia-Herzegovina, under Austro-Hungarian administration since 1878, and finally annexed in 1908, was held under the common auspices of the Dual Monarchy. From almost the beginning of the eighteenth century Hungary, previously subject to Austria, enjoyed a considerable measure of autonomy. But there grew up in the first part of the nineteenth century that strong movement for national independence which culminated in the revolution led by Louis Kossuth in 1848, and the proclamation of an independent Hungarian Republic in the following year. The defeat of the Hungarian Revolution was followed by nearly twenty years of Hungarian subjection to Austrian rule ; but after the exclusion of Austria from the German sphere of influence it became necessary to make fresh concessions to Hungarian demands, and the new constitution making Austria and Hungary co-equal partners in the Hapsburg Empire was finally granted. Certain services, however, including the army, remained under joint administration ; and the dominance of Austrian influences in the combined departments continued to give rise to trouble, which was accentuated during the war as the subject nationalities of the Austro-Hungarian Empire began to assert themselves, and the unity of the Empire as a whole to give way.

Hungary. When in 1918 the Austro-Hungarian Empire finally dissolved, and National Councils and Provisional Governments assumed authority in its various provinces, the greater part of Hungary passed under the authority of a National Council headed by Count Karolyi, and Karolyi had at once to face the problem raised by the proclamation of national independence in the non-Magyar territories previously under Hungarian control. Almost at once Roumanian, Czechoslovak, and other national forces began to occupy parts of the area of pre-war Hungary ; and even after the armistice the Roumanians were allowed by the Allies to extend considerably their occupation of Hungarian territory. In March 1919 Count Karolyi, unable to sustain his authority in face of aggression from without and Socialist and Communist influences within, resigned office and handed over power to the Socialist and Communist groups, which proceeded to institute a Soviet form of government under Bela Kun. The advent to power of Bela Kun was followed by a fierce internal struggle, particularly in the country districts, as the Communists endeavoured to assert their authority against the land-owners, who had a strong hold over certain sections of the peasantry. But the Hungarians were not left to settle their internal differences alone. In the summer of 1919 the Roumanians resumed their advance into Hungary, and the Bela Kun Government was overthrown. Kun himself fled to Russia, and the Peidl Socialist Government, which attempted to take over authority, was destroyed a week later by a *coup d'état*. The Hapsburg Archduke Joseph thereupon assumed power as Governor ; but the Rou-manians countered by a further advance and occupied Budapest. Under Allied pressure the Archduke was com-pelled to retire, and in November the Roumanians with-drew from Budapest after doing a great deal of damage, and took with them in their withdrawal as much of the movable property and instruments of production of the Hungarians as they were able to lay hands upon. The Allies meanwhile attempted to set up a cabinet representing all the Hungarian parties ; but Admiral Horthy at the head of an irregular force speedily occupied Budapest and assumed the controlling power. The National Assembly elected in 1920 equipped Hungary with a new constitution, to the accompaniment of a White Terror directed against those who had taken part in the Socialist Governments of the previous year. In protest against the slaughter of work-ing class leaders the Labour and Socialist International attempted in June 1920 to organise an international boy-cott of Hungary ; but this was unsuccessful, and the country began to settle down under the new régime with Admiral Horthy as Regent. In 1921 the Archduke Charles twice attempted to return to Hungary and assume the

crown, but on both occasions he was compelled to withdraw by the threats of the Little Entente (Roumania,
Czechoslovakia and Yugoslavia) to invade the country if
any attempt was made to restore the Hapsburgs to the
throne ; for the succession States of Austria-Hungary felt
that a Hapsburg on the Hungarian throne would be a permanent menace to their new-found independence.

Meanwhile in 1920 the Hungarian Government had been
compelled to sign the Trianon Treaty with the Allies, and
to agree to a dictated demarcation of the new frontiers of
the Hungarian State. These frontiers were so drawn as to
confine post-war Hungary within very narrow limits. The
pre-war area of Hungary was 125,000 square miles ; and
of this no less than 90,000 square miles had under the
Treaty of Trianon to be ceded to other States. From a pre-
war population of twenty-one millions Hungary was reduced in 1920 to a population of between eight and nine
millions ; and her new frontiers were so drawn as to leave
in the ceded territories not less than 3,300,000 Magyars, or
nearly a third of the total number of the Magyar nation.
Magyars had constituted 54 per cent of the population of
pre-war Hungary ; in the new post-war State they constituted as much as 90 per cent, the balance being made up of
7 per cent of Germans and a small number of Slav peoples,
chiefly Slovaks. Hungary is thus now a State possessing a
very high degree of national uniformity in its population ;
but the exclusion of nearly one-third of the Magyar people
from its territory serves to keep in being a strong irredentist
spirit and a very great unwillingness to regard as permanent the territorial settlement of 1920. Any map showing the
political and ethnical divisions of post-war Europe will
reveal that only on the west do the territorial frontiers of
post-war Hungary coincide with the frontier drawn according to ethnical divisions. All along the north there is a long
stretch of territory with a Magyar majority that has been
assigned to Czechoslovakia ; down most of the eastern
frontier there is a similar stretch of territory assigned to
Roumania ; in the south large bodies of Magyars in the

lands round the river Tisa are now under Yugoslav rule ; and finally in central Transylvania, cut off from the rest of the Magyars by a broad belt of territory inhabited chiefly by Roumanians, there are considerable *enclaves* of Magyar population under Roumanian rule. Even if Transylvania, with its Magyar *enclaves*, must be regarded as permanently lost to the Hungarian State, it is inevitable that Hungary should look covetously across her restricted frontiers to the immediately contiguous territories in which Magyar populations predominate.

This narrowing of the frontiers of the new Hungary beyond what could possibly be justified on ethnical grounds arose mainly from economic considerations. For example, the boundary between Roumania and Hungary has been so drawn as to include in Roumania the railway lines running along the valley to the west of the Transylvanian uplands, on the ground that these railways form the most natural means of communication between the upland areas. In the north railway communications were also an important factor in determining the new boundaries ; but especially in the east important parts of Hungary's pre-war resources of iron and coal were also taken away and assigned to Czechoslovakia in defiance of national considerations. There was also a strategic element in the drawing of the new boundaries, which, being drawn in accordance with the claims of the new succession States, gave Hungary no natural defences and made her a great plain easily open to invasion from the mountain regions which surround her on almost every side.

Confined to this central plain, post-war Hungary is predominantly an agricultural country engaged in arable cultivation. Sixty per cent of her area consists of arable land, and 18 per cent of meadow and pasture ; and three-quarters of the arable land is normally under cereals. She is an important exporter of wheat and other cereals and also of sugar and to a less extent of animals and meat. Accordingly she has felt very seriously the effects of the agricultural depression, not only because the price of wheat has fallen very low, but also because of the barriers erected against her exports by neighbouring countries for the protection of their own agricultural interests. Industrially postwar Hungary is in a very difficult position. She lost under the Peace Treaty four-fifths of her iron ore and a substantial fraction of her coal ; and she now requires to import most of her coal and a large proportion of the manufactured goods needed for domestic consumption. She retained, indeed, especially in Budapest, the majority of the large factories existing in the country ; but, as these had been cut off from many of the sources from which they used to draw their raw materials, there has been great difficulty in keeping them at work, and Hungary was suffering seriously from unemployment even before the world depression. Nevertheless, she had managed with the aid of her agricultural exports to balance her trade and build up in 1930 a small export surplus. Her chief markets are Austria, Czechoslovakia and Italy ; and the restriction of imports into these countries has since hit her very hard. She has also been hit by the diversion to other routes of a large part of the through traffic which used to go by way of the Hungarian railways ; and ever since the war her financial position has been precarious in the extreme.

Hungary made her first attempt to regulate her own financial situation in 1921, when the Hungarian Government established a new State institution for the issue of bank notes. But in 1923 her financial difficulties compelled her to appeal to the League of Nations for help of the same sort as had been afforded to Austria in the previous year. A guaranteed League loan of the type that had been given to Austria was refused ; but the Hungarians were compelled to accept a large measure of foreign financial control, including the establishment of a new Bank of Issue under foreign advice, and in return for this submission they were allowed to raise a market loan of fifty million dollars subscribed chiefly in Great Britain, the United States, Italy and Switzerland. Thereafter the work of stabilisation went on rapidly, and in 1926 the Special Commissioner appointed by the League of Nations was able to resign on completion of the task assigned to him. But the world crisis of 1929 and the following years soon plunged the finances of Hungary again into chaos, in face of the falling money yield of her exports and the rapidly increasing real burden of her external debts. The League was driven again to intervene, and fresh loans had to be made to help the Hungarians through. The effect of these loans is discussed elsewhere in this book in connection with the measures taken by the League to assist other distressed European countries through the financial crisis.

It is easy to see that Hungary within her new frontiers is very unhappily placed in an economic as well as in a political sense. Budapest, with its million inhabitants, was formerly the capital of a State with twice the population of present-day Hungary and more than three times the area. The industries of Budapest had been built up to supply the needs of this extensive area, and could not well be readjusted without serious difficulties to the contracted internal market of post-war Hungary. Hungarian manufactured products were excluded by high tariffs from the surrounding areas ; and the chief industries—flour milling and sugar refining—suffered especially from the desire of her neighbours to appropriate these food-preparing trades for themselves. The position of Budapest was not quite so difficult as that of Vienna, but it was difficult enough to present a very serious problem. Moreover, Hungary more than any other country suffers from the national enmities of her neighbours as well as from their desire to build up for themselves systems of economic self-sufficiency. The countries of the Little Entente live in perpetual fear of Hungary growing again strong enough to attempt to reassert her pre-war domination. Conscious that the post-war restriction of her territory cannot be justified on nationalistic grounds, they are determined to keep her under by main force ; while among the Hungarian people resentment at national losses mingles with the relics of the pre-war imperialistic temper to maintain nationalist spirit at a dangerous heat. The *status quo* in Hungary is therefore permanently unstable ; and while the country, disarmed under the Treaties of Peace and restricted within largely indefensible military frontiers, is in no position to take the offensive, there remain in the strained relations between the Magyars and their neighbours all the potential seeds of future territorial trouble. No one can reasonably regard the post-war settlement of Hungary as fair, and no one can confidently say that it possesses any of the essential elements of lasting stability.

Austria. Post-war Austria is, like Hungary, a predominantly Catholic country with a population possessing a high degree of national homogeneity. But whereas the Magyars constituted a nationality apart, 97 per cent of the population of post-war Austria are German-speaking, and of the same race and culture as their neighbours across the national frontiers in the German State. For this reason, whereas Hungarian aspirations are centred upon an enlargement of the Hungarian State, a large section among the Austrians, placed in an even more difficult position by the Treaties of Peace, thinks rather in terms of political and economic union with Germany. It was manifest in 1918, and it is manifest to-day, that Austria cannot possibly build up for herself a balanced national life within her restricted frontiers, and especially that Vienna, once the capital of a great Empire and now reduced to the capital of a small and predominantly agrarian State, is doomed to decay and semi-starvation as long as she remains isolated economically on all sides by tariff barriers and other artificial restrictions in the way of international trade and intercourse. The problem of Austria is above all the problem of Vienna, and of the relations of Vienna with the small and infertile agricultural territory which alone was left to her by the Treaties of Peace.

Pre-war Austria, the dominant partner in the Austro-Hungarian Empire, had a population of over thirty millions and a territory of 116,000 square miles. The Peace

Treaties reduced her to a population of six and a half millions and a territory of 32,000 square miles. But even these figures do not completely measure her declension, for Vienna was in effect the banker and Austrian industry to a great extent the supplier of the needs of the pre-war territory of Hungary as well. Moreover, Austria has lost her old access to the sea, and her ports at Trieste and Pola and in Dalmatia, as well as the coast of Bosnia and Herzegovina. Austria is now a purely inland State with a territory mainly mountainous and not permitting of any high degree of cultivation. Over 90 per cent of her total area can be fairly described as mountainous, and nearly 40 per cent consists of forest. Less than a quarter of the total land area is under cultivation in any form. Vienna, with its population approaching two millions, contains not far short of a third of the total population of the country ; and the feeding of this vast urban population involves, in face of the shortage of agricultural land, a large importation of cereals. Austria must therefore export if she is to live. But she has lost in the territories ceded to her neighbours many of the raw materials on which she used to rely. She has little coal within her frontiers, though she has iron ore in plenty, and her abundant timber resources furnish materials for the wood and paper industries that supply an appreciable part of her exports. In the absence of tariff barriers the textile, metal, timber and paper industries might enable Austria to live by exchange at a satisfactory standard of life. But, like Hungary, she is ringed round by a group of countries anxious to sell her their exports and exceedingly reluctant to take her own in exchange. Consequently, despite the most drastic restrictions on imports, Austria has suffered steadily from a large adverse balance of trade, the continuance of which has been rendered possible only by means of repeated borrowing from abroad. In as far as she has been able at all to meet the service of her heavy external debts this has been done only with the aid of fresh loans. Again and again since 1922, when her first appeal for help to the League of Nations was granted and a loan of twenty-five millions provided mainly by Great Britain, France, Italy and Czechoslovakia, she has had to appeal for further help and to submit her finances and her internal policy to rigorous external control under the auspices of the League of Nations. Austria's finances are at present under the control of a League Commissioner ; and she is enabled to carry on at all only with the aid of fresh doles grudgingly accorded by her creditors, who are not willing to face the political consequences of leaving her in the lurch.

As in the case of Hungary, the break-up of the Austro-Hungarian Empire towards the end of the war led to the proclamation of national independence over a large part of pre-war Austrian territory. In Austria itself the National Assembly, which met in 1919, desired to merge what was left of the country with the new German Republic ; and this attempt, promptly vetoed by the Allies, who were unwilling to sanction an extension of German influence into southern and eastern Europe, was renewed with no better success in 1920 and 1921. It was made clear to the Austrians that the Allies, and above all France, would on no account agree to a political union between Austria and Germany, and that the Austrians must reconcile themselves for the time at least to making the best of national independence within their restricted area. A definite renunciation of the policy of union with Germany was made a condition of the League loan of 1922, and thereafter the Austrians had to struggle on as best they could under Allied financial dictation. Their difficulties were made the more acute by the pronounced differences of political complexion between Vienna and the rest of the country. Vienna was, and has remained, a Socialist city, governed by a Socialist municipality which has shown itself, in face of all its troubles, the most enterprising municipal government in Europe. But the impoverished peasants who constitute the main part of the population of Austria outside Vienna are by no means Socialists. They have been so far mainly under the influence of the Catholic Christian Social Party, and disposed to look with extreme jealousy on any sign of Viennese domination. In the period immediately after the war Vienna was almost starved through the refusal of the peasants to send in supplies ; and the constitution of post-war Austria as a federal State, with Vienna as one of its nine largely autonomous provinces, has by no means settled the problem of the hostility between town and country. At first after the war the Socialists were able to control the Government, but subsequently they were driven out except in Vienna ; and the country has been governed by the Christian Socials in alliance with the smaller *bourgeois* parties. More than once Austria has been threatened with an actual Fascist revolution, and in 1927 the country was for some time on the verge of civil war, the strikes among the Socialist workers being broken by military violence with the aid of the peasant population. The Social Democrats have indeed constituted the largest party in the Austrian Assembly, but they have never been able to regain a clear majority over the Christian Socials and the predominantly pan-German Agrarian League.

In 1931 the Austrians, driven to the verge of despair by the effects of the world depression, renewed their attempt to bring about some form of union with Germany, and in agreement with Dr. Brüning's Government in Germany the proposal was brought forward for an Austro-German Customs Union—in other words for complete economic but not political union between the two countries. But this proposal too was promptly vetoed by the French, and pressure was put upon the Germans as well as the Austrians to withdraw it. The question of its consistency with Austria's and Germany's obligations under the Treaties of Peace was finally referred to the Hague Court for settlement ; but it was made clear that whatever the Court said France would not tolerate an economic union which her politicians regarded as the first step towards a political amalgamation. Under Allied pressure the Germans were compelled to renounce the project ; and Austria, in desperate straits financially, was made to give further guarantees of good behaviour as a condition of receiving additional temporary assistance from the League of Nations.

Since then, the position has been further complicated by the rise of an Austrian Nazi movement in close touch with the South German Nazis. Hitler is himself an Austrian by origin ; and the inclusion of Austria in the German Reich has been from the first one of the aims of the Nazi movement. For the present, the path of the Nazis to power is barred by the Christian Social Government of Herr Dollfuss, supported by the irregular force known as the *Heimwehr*, which corresponds to some extent to the German *Stahlhelm*. The Government has imposed a rigid dictatorship, and abrogated the powers of Parliament ; and it has sought to enrol the help of the Pope and of Fascist Italy in resistance to a Nazi revolution. As the western part of Austria is the only obstacle to continuity between Italian and German territory, it might be supposed that the two Fascist Governments would be united in desiring its absorption in Germany. But Mussolini, fearing the complications in Central Europe which a Nazi triumph in Austria might arouse, has so far refused his aid, and has firmly given encouragement to the Dollfuss Government. This, however, holds power only by a precarious tenure ; and it is impossible to foretell the future of Austria even for a few months. In face of a Nazi *coup*, the Austrian Socialists, who are very well organised, might be expected to put up a better resistance than the Germans ; but Herr Dollfuss has disarmed their irregular forces, and it is doubtful if they could maintain themselves in face of their weakness in the country districts.

Switzerland.   Adjoining Austria on the west, with the tiny principality of Liechtenstein[1] tucked in between, lies the Federal Republic of Switzerland, mountainous like her eastern neighbour, but by contrast very highly developed

[1] Before the war, Liechtenstein, while preserving its independence, was associated in customs and other matters with Austria-Hungary. Since the war, without entering into the Swiss Republic, it has handed over to Switzerland the administration of its posts and telegraphs, and has become a part of the Swiss customs area. It has, however, only the tiny population of 10,000, though it ranks as an independent sovereign State.

both industrially and commercially, and suffering from no
such disadvantage as the swollen proportions of the capital
city in relation to the hinterland. Switzerland is indeed,
after Great Britain and Belgium, the most highly industrialised country in Europe. Over 50 per cent of the occupied population are engaged in industry and trade, and
another 7 per cent in the transport services, and only 27
per cent live by agriculture in all its forms. Switzerland is a
considerable importer on balance of cereals and other foodstuffs, which she pays for partly by her exports of manufactured goods and partly with the profits of her important
tourist traffic. The relative magnitude of " tourism " in
furnishing employment to the population of Switzerland
is, however, often exaggerated. 2,700,000 tourists were recorded as visiting Switzerland in 1929, the year before the
world slump began ; but the total number of persons employed in Swiss hotels of all kinds was only 63,000 as against
224,000 employed in the metal and engineering trades
alone. " Tourism " is a vital element in the economic life of
Switzerland, and one great factor in enabling her to import
far more goods than she exports ; but she is primarily an
industrial country and not merely a holiday resort. Her
metallurgical industries are on a large scale and highly advanced, though they are based to a great extent on imported
raw materials. She has an export of cotton goods and of
silks, and also of dyestuffs ; and only of woollen goods does
she import more than she exports. The trade in clocks and
watches also plays an important part in her external commerce, but it is far less important than her metallurgical
and textile industries. Of agricultural products she exports
cheese and condensed milk ; but her imports of all the
staple foodstuffs far exceed her exports.

The league which formed the basis of the Swiss Confederation goes back to the thirteenth century. Switzerland's history is one of gradual expansion through the
inclusion of new areas in the Confederation. In 1815 her
neutrality was jointly guaranteed by Austria, Great Britain,
Prussia and Russia, and with the addition of three new

cantons by the Pact of Zürich modern Switzerland assumed her present form. The year of revolutions, 1848, brought her a new constitution after the internecine conflict of 1847 between the Protestant and the Catholic districts ; and with some amendments, especially in 1874, the constitution of 1848 remains in force to-day. It is based on the principle of federation. Each of the twenty-two Swiss cantons (or rather twenty-five, for three of the cantons are divided) exists in constitutional theory as an independent sovereign State, which has only yielded up to the Confederation certain definite powers of unified government. There remains great jealousy on the part of the independent cantons against any encroachment by the federal power ; but stress of circumstances has led in practice during the past half century to a great increase in the authority of the Confederation, as new services have had to be developed and old services unified under federal control. Up to 1914 the Radical Party, which stood for a centralising tendency, was always in a majority in the Federal Government, but since the war the introduction of proportional representation has destroyed this majority and caused Governments to be based on coalitions of parties. The Radicals still form in 1933 the largest party, but they are followed closely by the Social Democrats, with the Catholics, who stand for the maintenance of local rights, not far behind. The Agrarians have also a substantial representation.

Thus in Switzerland, as in other countries, proportional representation has led to a multiplication of parties, and to the carrying on of government by the balancing of minority forces. In Switzerland, however, the system does not work out in quite the same way as in other countries, owing to the use made of the referendum. Switzerland has applied this method far more largely than any other country ; and in general its influence on her politics has been markedly conservative. Most proposed innovations have been rejected, and the necessity of an appeal to a direct vote of the electorate has restrained Governments from bringing forward proposals for drastic change. Switzerland has thus enjoyed up to now the most stable and unchanging political system of any country in Europe ; but it has been mainly because of her special position that she has been able to maintain her internal tranquillity in face of the inflexibility of her political system. The Swiss constitution is eminently unfriendly to innovation and to political extremes. Of late, however, following upon the growth of Socialism, there has been a considerable swing towards Fascism among the middle classes, which form an important element in the population ; and there has been more than one suggestion of a Nazi revolution in some of the German cantons.

Switzerland has a total population of rather over four millions, predominantly German-speaking. Nineteen of her twenty-five cantons have German-speaking majorities, five French-speaking majorities and one an Italian-speaking majority. In terms of population over two and three-quarter millions of her population speak German, about 800,000 French, under a quarter of a million Italian, and the rest other languages, including the curious Romansch dialect. But it should also be observed that there are over 400,000 foreigners resident in the country, apart from tourists. In religion there is a preponderance of Protestants over Roman Catholics, the Protestants forming about 57 per cent of the total population and the Roman Catholics about 41 per cent. The division between the two groups is largely geographical. The Swiss are thus without either racial or religious unity ; but their long tradition of common government has given them a keen sense of nationality even without these bonds of cohesion. Switzerland's foreign policy has been guided above all by the conception of neutrality. This, as we have seen, was jointly guaranteed by the leading Powers in 1815, and the fear that her neutrality might be prejudiced held Switzerland back from entering the League of Nations immediately after the war. When in 1920 she did enter the League and afford a home for its headquarters, this was done only on the explicit pledge that her neutrality should be in no way prejudiced by her acceptance of the Covenant.

As the headquarters of the League Switzerland has undoubtedly gained in international economic importance. Besides her high degree of industrial development she possesses a very highly organised banking system and has taken a large part in recent years in international financial operations. She has built up for herself a gold reserve very large in relation to the size of the country and of its commerce ; and this gold reserve actually grew in 1931 to five times as large as it had been five years before, through the flight of capital from other countries and the action of the Central Bank in converting its holdings of foreign exchange into gold as a protection against the effects of financial instability. Switzerland is also important economically as the centre of a considerable number of international combines, especially in the metal and engineering industries. Switzerland's metallurgical development would undoubtedly be even greater than it is but for her lack of coal. She has endeavoured to make up for this by a very great development of water power, which is employed largely in her industries as well as in transport. Indeed, the development of electrification in recent years has helped greatly to enhance Switzerland's economic importance, though during the past few years her export trade has been seriously curtailed by the maintenance of the gold standard, and she suffered in the years immediately after the war from the high valuation of her currency in terms of foreign moneys. Accordingly there has been a considerable amount of unemployment in Switzerland, and this has led to a growth of Socialism and working-class unrest, with the consequence, as we have seen, of provoking a counter-growth of Fascism among the middle classes and the peasants.

§ 8. CZECHOSLOVAKIA

CZECHOSLOVAKIA, with her population of nearly fifteen millions and her area of 55,000 square miles, is economically the most important of the new States carved out of the pre-war Empire of Austria-Hungary. In the old Empire Bohemia, Moravia and Silesia formed part of Austria, whereas Slovakia and Ruthenia to the east were in Hungarian territory. The State of the Czechoslovaks was, in fact, born in exile during the Great War ; for from the beginning of the war a triumvirate, led by President Masaryk, set out deliberately to win the favour of the Allied Powers for the creation of a Czechoslovak National State. This triumvirate (Masaryk, Benes and Stefanik) had its headquarters for the most part in Paris ; but throughout the war Masaryk and his colleagues went to and fro from one Allied capital to another seeking support for their essay in the making of a nation. They organised on the Allied side an army composed of exiles and deserters from the Austro-Hungarian forces ; and this Czechoslovak national army saw service on many fronts and especially as an auxiliary to the Tsarist forces in Russia. When Russia went out of the war after the Revolution of 1917, the Czechoslovaks found themselves isolated far from home and cut off from the support of the Allies. The Russians, after the Bolshevik Revolution, fearful of the presence of this potentially hostile army within their territory, attempted to disarm the Czechoslovak troops ; but the Czechoslovaks resisted disarmament and, helped by the Allies with munitions and supplies, held for a time a vast area of Russian territory in Siberia and on the Volga, thus cutting off the new Russian Government, and incidentally the Germans, from the possibility of securing food supplies from the east. The Czechoslovaks thus came to be an important factor in the civil war fought on Russian territory after the conclusion of the Great War, and their final evacuation, by way of the Far East, was long delayed.

Meanwhile in October 1918 the Czechoslovaks in Austro-Hungarian territory had proclaimed their independence ; and with the conclusion of the war, Masaryk and his colleagues were able to return to their own country and set to work upon the formal establishment of the new State, which received prompt recognition from the Allied

Powers. When the new frontiers came to be drawn the Allies were in a mood to be generous to the Czechoslovaks ; and in the territorial adjustments under the Treaties of Peace only very tiny minorities of Czechs or Slovaks were left outside the territory of Czechoslovakia, while near the frontiers substantial elements of other nationalities were included—Germans in the west and north, Magyars along the frontier of Hungary, and Ruthenians in the east. The result was a long narrow land-locked State, extending for 600 miles from east to west, but only 50 miles across from north to south at its narrowest part and 125 miles at its broadest. Czechoslovakia has thus an immensely long land frontier, exceedingly difficult to defend against attack. She borders upon five States—Austria, Hungary, Roumania, Poland and Germany—and only in the case of Poland is there, along the range of the Carpathians, a sharply defined frontier. Czechoslovakia is accordingly most unwilling to stand alone, and her foreign policy ever since the war has been governed largely by the desire to ally herself with powerful enough neighbours to ensure her from attack. Acutely suspicious of the irredentist aspirations of dis-membered Hungary, she has formed part of a *bloc*, known as the Little Entente, in which she is allied with Roumania and Yugoslavia, largely with the object of preserving the territorial settlement laid down in the Peace Treaty with Hungary. With Austria her relations have been far less unfriendly, but, as we have seen, she lives in permanent fear of an attempt to restore the old Austro-Hungarian Empire ; and she was successful in the years immediately following the war in preventing more than once the return of the Hapsburgs to the Hungarian throne.

For a long time the Little Entente has been regarded in Europe as belonging to the *bloc* of Central and East Euro-pean nations under the political influence of France. But of late the growing uncertainty of France's political orienta-tion has tended to make her eastern allies draw more closely together among themselves, and rely more largely upon their own combined resources. Thus in February 1933 the

Little Entente was considerably strengthened by the signing of a new Treaty between the three States concerned. Czechoslovakia, Roumania and Yugoslavia bound themselves to follow a common foreign policy and to enter into no external obligations except by general consent. Under the new arrangement a permanent council consisting of the three Ministers for Foreign Affairs has been set up to direct foreign policy with the assistance of a permanent bureau, one section of which will sit continuously at Geneva. There is to be also a joint economic council of the three countries ; and it is proposed as rapidly as may be to bring the existing political treaties of the three into the greatest possible uniformity. Joint action is to be taken in respect of the navigation of the Danube, the co-ordination of railway, air and postal services, and the adjustment of tariffs on a preferential basis. There is also to be close banking collaboration among the three Central Banks concerned. Czechoslovakia, Roumania and Yugoslavia have thus taken a long step towards the creation of a political confederation, which may turn at a later stage into an economic confederation as well. Whether this close union among three of the succession States can later be broadened out into a confederation wide enough in effect to reconstitute pre-war Austria-Hungary as an economic unit, by the inclusion of the new States of Austria and Hungary within its scope, must remain for the present doubtful ; for the Little Entente has been based so far on a sharp hostility to Hungary which it will take long to overcome, and the Hungarians have by no means renounced their aspirations for a reconsideration of the terms of the Peace Treaty. But undoubtedly, the coming together of the countries of the Little Entente into a much closer and more lasting relationship is the most important step that has yet been taken in Central and Eastern Europe towards overcoming the tendency for economic as well as political nationalism to entrench itself within areas so small as to result inevitably in a strangling of economic activity and a serious lowering of the European standard of life.

Czechoslovakia inherited a very large proportion of the industrial equipment of the old Austro-Hungarian Empire. It has been estimated that no less than four-fifths of the industrial resources of pre-war Austria-Hungary fell to the share of the new Czechoslovak State. Czechoslovakia is therefore by far the most important industrially of the new countries created by the Peace Treaties. Her neighbours to the south and east are mainly agricultural countries which need to export large quantities of foodstuffs in order to pay their debts and meet the cost of necessary imports, whereas Czechoslovakia is a large-scale exporter of coal and manufactured products. In these circumstances it would be natural for her trade to be carried on largely with her agricultural neighbours ; but in fact her closest trading relations have been with Germany, largely owing to the restricted purchasing power of the agricultural countries of Eastern Europe and her own close approach to self-sufficiency in food supply. Nevertheless her trade with Hungary and Roumania and Poland comes next in importance after her trade with Germany, and may be expected to grow rapidly if settled conditions are restored in Eastern Europe. Owing to her position as a purely inland State, Czechoslovakia is dependent for her outlets to the sea upon her share in the navigation of certain important rivers and on her rights at certain ports. The Peace Treaty gave her important rights in the navigation of the Elbe and Oder ; and she is also greatly interested in the navigation of the Danube. Hamburg is the port through which the largest quantity of Czechoslovak goods passes to overseas markets ; but Trieste, Fiume, Stettin and Danzig are also considerable outlets for her commerce.

Thanks to her ability to supply her population with foodstuffs grown at home, Czechoslovakia has been able hitherto to maintain a favourable balance of trade. She needs to import some of her raw materials, especially iron ore from Sweden ; but these imports are far more than balanced by her exports of coal and manufactured goods. She is important as a producer of iron and steel and engineering products. She has large and well-organised textile industries in almost all branches of textile production —cottons, woollen goods, flax and jute, silk and artificial silk. In addition she is a large producer of refined sugar on the basis of her developed agricultural output of sugar beet. Her industries are mainly centred in the Czech end of the country, with Slovakia as an important source of raw materials as well as food, and Ruthenia in the east as a comparatively undeveloped agricultural province. Forty-two per cent of her area is arable, 18 per cent pasture and meadow, and roughly 33 per cent forest ; and her forest area makes her an important producer and exporter of timber and wood products. In common with the other succession States, Czechoslovakia has enacted important land laws breaking up big estates, especially in Slovakia. Under the Act passed by the National Assembly in 1920 something like half a million families were settled in peasant holdings on land previously occupied by great landlords. But, except in Ruthenia, standards of cultivation are relatively high, and agriculture is pursued on fairly scientific lines.

Czechoslovakia, however, counts in the affairs of Europe far more as an industrial than as an agricultural country. As we have seen, she is well equipped with coal and able to export a surplus beyond her own requirements, and she has also abundant water supplies which she has used in recent years as the basis of a rapid development of electrification. In addition to her steel and engineering industries and her textiles, she is growingly important as a producer and exporter of light industrial products. Her glass and porcelain industries command a world market ; and the famous Bata boot factories have a large export trade, especially to the countries of Central Europe. Czechoslovakia thus combines a high degree of self-sufficiency in the matter of supplies with a manufacturing equipment designed essentially for a wide export market. She is therefore deeply interested in the removal of the existing barriers in the way of external trade, especially in manufactured goods ; but

the agricultural element in her population is large enough
to make her unwilling to sacrifice the agricultural interests
in order to expand her industrial exports. This hampers her
in entering into arrangements with the agricultural States
of Eastern Europe for the freer exchange of goods. For
Czechoslovakia is in the position of an industrialised State
which is also, though only to a small extent, a debtor on
international account, and therefore desires to export more
than she imports. She has been able to a substantial extent
to force her way into world markets on a basis of mass
production and low wages ; and the careful administration
of her finances has enabled her to escape from the alternating periods of inflation and deflation through which most
other countries in Europe have had to pass. Czechoslovakia
is potentially a very rich country, but she can hardly hope
to garner her potential wealth until conditions allow her to
raise the standard of living of her inhabitants without
dangerously imperilling her export trade. Her statesmen
are therefore among the influences making most strongly
for stabilisation in European political and economic affairs,
and her foreign policy, continuously in the hands of Dr.
Benes through a long succession of Governments, has been
more consistent, perhaps also more opportunist, than that of
any other important country.

Czechoslovakia has, however, very difficult internal
problems to face. She is a country of greatly mixed nationalities. Of her total population Czechs and Slovaks, between
whom there are important cultural differences, together
constitute about two-thirds ; but Germans are nearly a
quarter, and there are also important minorities—Magyars
5½ per cent, Ruthenians 3½ per cent, Jews 1½ per cent and
Poles ½ per cent. By religion the great mass of the people
are Roman Catholics, more than three-quarters of the
total population belonging to the Roman Church, whereas
only 7 per cent are Protestants, and the remainder divided
among a number of other Churches. National rather than
religious differences therefore present the main problem.
When the new Czechoslovak State was first created the

German minorities refused to recognise the accomplished fact, or to take any share in the government ; and for a long while there was a duplication of party cleavages along both national and economico-political lines. Each of the main parties among the Czechoslovak elements in the population had its counterpart in a corresponding party among the Germans, and in some cases there were also separate Magyar parties. The Communists alone, from the time when they split away from the Social Democrats in 1920, formed a unified party without regard to national differences. Only in 1926 did the German parties belonging to the *bourgeois bloc* agree to enter into coalition with the Czechoslovak parties for the conduct of the government. Since then, although the national parties have maintained their separate existence, the fundamental cleavages have tended to be in terms of economic and political rather than national differences. This is an important sign of the consolidation of the new State within its frontiers as defined by the Treaties of Peace.

There still remain, however, difficult problems of nationality within Czechoslovakia's frontiers. The most difficult problem of all arises out of the position of the Ruthenians in the east of the country, for the Ruthenians, who belong, as we have seen, to the same racial group as the Ukrainians, are peasants living at a low standard of life and culture, and having very little in common with either the Czechoslovaks or the Germans. The Ruthenian National Council voted in 1918 for union with Czechoslovakia, and the Czechoslovaks promised to concede autonomy to the Ruthenians within the new State. But this promise has never been at all completely carried out, though a form of federal administration was finally established in 1927, with some degree of provincial autonomy in local matters. The real reason for uniting Ruthenia with Czechoslovakia had very little to do with nationality : the object was rather to link the Czechoslovak State to Roumania, and thus to make the encirclement of Hungary more effective. It is true that no other State except Russia could have established any better claim than Czechoslovakia to annex Ruthenia; and of course annexation to Russia would not be considered in face of the political alignment of post-war Europe. The Ukrainians of Ruthenia are in fact cut off from Russia, as we have seen earlier, by territories of mixed population assigned to Roumania and Poland. Doubtless union with Czechoslovakia offers the Ruthenians some material compensation, in that union with the industrial part of the country provides an outlet for Ruthenian agricultural produce within a single tariff area, and also means more rapid economic development than would be likely to occur if Ruthenia had become a part of either Poland or Roumania or had remained attached to Hungary. But, short of the adoption of truly federal institutions, the Ruthenians are not likely to settle down contentedly under the new conditions. Nor is Ruthenia the only area in which there is a demand for autonomy; for, while the Czechs and Slovaks are closely allied in race and culture, there are none the less significant differences between them, and there has arisen in recent years a demand for self-government in Slovakia as well. The political problems of the Czechoslovak State cannot be regarded as in any way finally settled by the reforms of 1927, though the forces of disruption are less strong than in most of the other succession States.

In the period immediately after the war Czechoslovakia was governed by a coalition between the Socialists and the Agrarians; and it was under the auspices of this coalition that the new constitution of 1920 was adopted and various advanced measures of social reform instituted, including a levy on capital and a breaking up of the great estates. This coalition, however, was brought to an end by a split among the Socialists. Strong Communist groups arose among the Czechoslovak industrial workers, and in 1920 a split occurred in the ranks of the Social Democratic Party. Before the split the Social Democrats resigned from the Government, and the coalition cabinet was replaced temporarily by a non-party Government of officials. But when the

Social Democratic Party had definitely split into two sections—a Social Democratic majority and a Communist
minority—the majority resumed their place in the Government, though their forces had been considerably weakened
by the quarrel. The third Socialist-Agrarian coalition of
1921 was replaced in 1922 by a predominantly Agrarian
Government kept in office by Socialist support ; and this
Government continued until 1925. The elections of that
year were marked by a serious set-back to the Social
Democrats ; and the Government was then reconstituted
on the basis of an Agrarian-Catholic coalition which was
broadened out in the following year into a general anti-
Socialist *bloc*. This *bloc* retained office until the two major
parties—the Catholics and the Agrarians, quarrelled in
1929. In the general election which followed the Socialists
made considerable gains ; and a new Government was
formed on the basis of a general coalition of Socialist and
non-Socialist parties, with the Communists as the leading
opposition group. This anomalous coalition has since continued to govern Czechoslovakia ; but through all the
changes of the post-war years Czechoslovak policy, especially in international affairs, has in effect maintained a very
high degree of continuity, irrespective of the political complexion of the Government in power.

§ 9. GERMANY

IN OCTOBER 1918 the long sustained military resistance
of the German Empire abruptly collapsed, and the Great
War ended with the Armistice of the following month and
the Allied victory which had been inevitable from the
moment when the United States declared war upon the
Central Powers. For, despite the attitude of President
Wilson, and his famous Fourteen Points, there was not,
from the moment of the American declaration of war, any
real prospect that the Allies would accept a negotiated

peace based on no annexations or indemnities, and thus agree to forgo the anticipated division of the spoils of victory.

The collapse of 1918 brought to an end the great German Empire which had been consolidated in the course of the nineteenth century under Prussian leadership, and involved the establishment of a new Germany, shorn of its colonies and of an important part of its territory in Europe, and equipped with republican institutions, not so much because it had deliberately chosen a republic in preference to a monarchy as because the continued rule of the Hohenzollerns had been made impossible. This Weimar Republic, set up on the morrow of the war, endured until the Nazi *coup* of 1933, when it collapsed no less abruptly than it had come into being, leaving the Nazis to work out, with results which it is impossible to anticipate at present, the structure of a new German State.

We have thus three different Germanies to consider ; for, although both the pre-war German Empire and the Weimar Republic may seem to have passed away, they are both very relevant to any consideration of Germany's future. Was the short-lived German Republic only an episode, and is Germany now heading straight for a restoration of the pre-war imperial system, or is the new Germany which is being born under Nazi rule to be something radically different both from the pre-war Empire and from the post-war Republic ? Or, again, will the Nazi revolution fail to provide a permanent basis for the new German society, and give place to yet another revolution, which will establish a fourth form of German State ?

Before we set out to consider any of these distinct political Germanies, we must say something of the underlying Germany which persists through all the changes in political structure and organisation. For although the economic configuration of the German territories changed with extraordinarily swiftness in the course of the nineteenth century, and the country was transformed from a predominantly agrarian into a great industrial State, there are certain

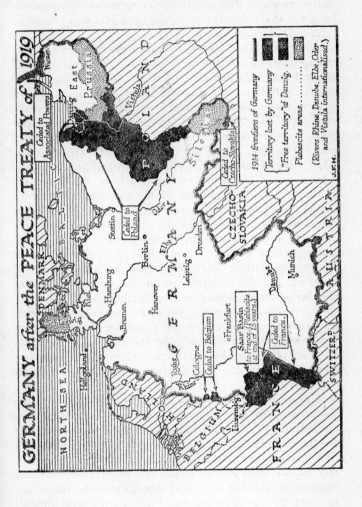

GERMANY after the PEACE TREATY of 1919

1914 frontiers of Germany
Territory lost by Germany
"Free territory" of Danzig.
Plebiscite areas..........
(Rivers Rhine, Danube, Elbe, Oder and Vistula internationalised.)

J.F.H.

Ceded to Associated Powers

Ceded to Poland

Ceded to Czecho-Slovakia

Ceded to Belgium

Saar Basin to France (Plebiscite at end of 15 years)

Ceded to France.

underlying characteristics of the German people and the territories which they inhabit which form the indispensable basis for any judgment upon their political and economic future.

In the first place a very large part of Germany is, from the agricultural point of view, poor soil. There is no great fertile black belt like that of Russia. In the north-east especially the season for agriculture is short, and the cold winters make impossible the forms of cultivation which exist further south and west. In the west, though climatic conditions are more favourable, much of the land is of inferior quality. There are great mountain areas, and a large part of the land surface is covered with forests. The response of nature to the efforts of the cultivator is meagre, until he brings to his aid the resources of modern science. In some respects the most remarkable achievement of Germany in the nineteenth century was her rapid success in improving the yields of the leading crops without losing, through the extension of arable cultivation, her importance as a producer of livestock. In this transformation the emancipation of the serfs, the enclosure and redistribution of the land, the development of the agencies for co-operative credit, the growth and application to agriculture of the chemical industries, and the subsidising of the cultivation of sugar-beet, all played an important part. Germany, in adopting over a large part of her surface intensive systems of agricultural production, and in raising her crop yields per acre to a point well above those secured in countries with far more naturally fertile land, accomplished an astonishing agricultural revolution without which she could certainly not have brought about the great advance of her industries during the latter part of the nineteenth century. But in face of all these achievements the poverty of the land remains an abiding fact ; and this is especially important in those areas in the north-east where agricultural difficulties arise from climate rather than from soil, and can least be overcome by the application of scientific methods.

Of great importance through the history of all the successive Germanies which we shall have to consider is the broad distinction between east and west, with the Elbe as the approximate dividing line. West of the Elbe, and to the south, Germany is for the most part a land of small peasant cultivators, though there are some large estates in the northwest. These peasants till the land themselves with little or no aid from hired labour. Their standard of life is, and has always been, low in relation to that of the urban population ; and their social attitude has much in common with that of peasants in other Western countries, with the difference that, largely under State tutelage, they have far more capacity for co-operative organisation than the peasants of France, or of any other West European country. The Raffeisen system of credit banks goes back to 1849 ; and there are approximately twenty thousand rural credit societies in Germany to-day, in addition to over thirty thousand co-operative societies of other kinds. The German peasants have learnt to act together economically, and they learnt this lesson earlier than the peasants in any other country, even Denmark, though they have not pushed co-operation anything like so far in the field of marketing as the Danes have done in modern times.

On the other hand, eastern Germany is, and has been for centuries, an area of large agricultural estates. This is the home of the Junkers, and of the landless labourers who live by working upon the land of the great proprietors. The country is for the most part poor, and the landlords have always been exorbitant in their claims. The land workers, unorganised and with a quite recent tradition of serfdom behind them, have had little power of self-protection, and their standards of living have remained much below those even of the peasants of western Germany. A little was done under the Weimar Republic to break up some of these great estates and to settle peasant cultivators upon them ; but even to-day the underlying difference between the agricultural economies of eastern and western Germany remains unaltered. The Junkers have not been driven from their strongholds by the Weimar Republic, although economically they have had a bad time, and most of them are heavily in debt, both to the State and to a less extent to private creditors.

Pre-war Germany had an area of about 209 thousand square miles, whereas the Germany of to-day, including the Saar district, has an area of about 182 thousand square miles. Thus, although the German losses as a result of the war were considerable when they are reckoned in terms of economic resources, territorially they lopped off only a small part of the total land surface of the country, certainly not enough to modify from the agricultural point of view the broad generalisations which we have just advanced. We can, therefore, without the risk of making seriously misleading statements, ignore the difference between pre-war and post-war Germany in considering the general agricultural situation of the country. Of the total land surface of post-war Germany, one of the German States, Prussia, alone includes about 62 per cent, and nearly 61 per cent of the total German population lives in Prussian territory. Prussia still occupies, as she has occupied since Germany became more than a geographical expression, the position among the German States of unquestionable predominance in area and population. Of the total area of Germany rather more than a quarter consists of forest land, about half as much again of arable, and about a sixth of pasture and meadow. She has a total population of about 65 millions, and throughout the nineteenth century the birth-rate was exceedingly high ; so that there was strong pressure, despite emigration, which was directed largely to the United States, to improve standards of cultivation. Apart from this, it would have been impossible to maintain and raise the standard of living for the rapidly increasing population, in face of the poverty of the soil and the absence until recently of a developed industrial system by means of which the country could afford to pay for large foreign imports of foodstuffs. But for the rapid rate of agricultural improvement, the situation of the German people would have been throughout the nineteenth century very serious indeed ; and for this reason, as we have seen, the strongest endeavours of the State have been continually directed to the development of scientific methods of cultivation and of the process of agricultural education.

Industrial Germany is not very rich in natural resources, and, as we shall see, is appreciably poorer now than she was before the war. But her great potash deposits, a large part of which she still retains, were a most important factor in enabling her to improve agricultural yields despite the poverty of her soil. Her coal is largely concentrated in the Ruhr area, which produces now nearly four-fifths of the total domestic supply of hard coal, excluding lignite. Iron resources she had in abundance before the war ; but most of these were lost when Alsace-Lorraine, acquired in 1871, was taken back by France in 1918. She has, however, considerable supplies of iron left within her own territories ; and it is upon her resources of coal and iron as well as upon her potash and other mineral deposits that her modern industrial system has been primarily based. Germany needs more now than she did in the nineteenth century to import large quantities of raw materials for the conduct of her manufacturing industries, but she does possess, even shorn of her lost territories, the fundamental requisites for the carrying on of an advanced system of capitalist production centred upon the heavy industries. But in accordance with the concentration of her coal supply her industrial population is highly concentrated upon a few densely populated areas, above all the Ruhr, and to a less extent Upper Silesia and Saxony. Any average figure of the density of population of Germany gives an entirely misleading picture of the real distribution of the people.

Apart from the underlying economic conditions, religious differences are of importance. North Germany is mainly Protestant, though Prussia includes a considerable Catholic minority. Saxony, Brunswick, Thuringia, and the Mecklenburgs are also mainly Protestant. On the other hand, the south, including both Bavaria and the great industrial area of the Rhineland, is mainly Catholic, and so is Upper Silesia. Prussian leadership in the country as a whole has tended to give the German Empire a predominantly Protestant colour ; and this has been one of the factors making against the completion of the process of centralisation. For Catholic Bavaria, insisting strongly upon her autonomy, constituted herself the leader of Catholic opinion in Germany as a whole. German Protestantism is overwhelmingly Lutheran, and the great majority of German Protestants are united in the Evangelical Church Union, over which the Nazis are now making a determined effort to establish a complete control ; but the Protestants, being in a position of predominance, have never needed to unite into any political parties of their own, whereas the Catholics have organised politically as well as culturally, and have been throughout the history of Germany an influential and organised minority taking their own line in political affairs.

Geographically, Germany is essentially a Central European Power, and her contacts with other countries are of importance in north, south, east and west alike. To the north, her frontiers lie along the Baltic, and she is brought into close association with the Scandinavian countries, with whose history that of North Germany is inextricably intertwined. To the west she is the neighbour of France, and along the short coastline looks out across the North Sea towards Great Britain ; and her great ports, and especially Hamburg, have very close commercial and financial associations with London and with the other financial centres of the West. To the south she stretches down to the borders of Austria, once an important member of the predominantly German group of States forming the Holy Roman Empire, and still, in her post-war impotence, the connecting link between Germany and Italy. Since the war, however, Germany meets in the south not one State but many, founded upon the ruins of the Austro-Hungarian Empire. Both economically and politically, and also culturally, her connections with Czechoslovakia as well as Austria are close ; for there is in Czechoslovakia a large German element in the population, and this element until quite recently refused to accept the *fait accompli* of the new Czechoslovak State, and many of its members still continue to think in terms of pan-German unity. To the east pre-war Germany had a long frontier line, marching with that of Russia ; but now she is cut off from direct contact with Russia by Poland and by the new small States bordering upon the Baltic. But, as we have seen in an earlier section, there were never natural frontiers on the eastern side of Germany ; for the great plain stretches right across eastern Germany and Poland far into Russia without any clearly marked geographical differentiation. Moreover, further north, East Prussia, now separated from the rest of Germany by the Polish Corridor, lies far to the east, and Germany's interest in the Baltic brings her near to Russia by sea, despite the disappearance of a common frontier by land.

Thus centrally placed, Germany is bound to be concerned in practically every problem of international importance that arises in Europe. This was the case even before Germany could be said to exist at all as a nation ; for throughout the Middle Ages the Holy Roman Empire, the temporal symbol of the unity of Christendom, was mainly a German Empire, and the Emperors most often had their seats in Austria or in one of the numerous German States. There is thus a long tradition of political association between Germany and Austria and the rest of Southern Europe ; and this tradition still reasserts itself as a living force in the European politics of to-day. Probably the notion of a German hegemony in Central Europe would never have taken the form which it did during the World War had it not been for the existence of this tradition ; and it is certain that, in the new Germany which is being formed now, the traditional connection of the German State with Southern Europe is destined again to assume a position of importance. One aim of the Treaties of Peace was to cut off Germany from contact with the south ; but it is already clear that this is one of the provisions of the Peace Treaty which the movement of irresistible forces will decisively alter.

Pre-War Germany. With these preliminary comments we can turn to consider very briefly the rise of modern Germany and the evolution of that German Empire which collapsed in 1918. It is above all necessary to remember, in considering the development of modern Germany, that she emerged from the Middle Ages far later and far less completely than the other countries of Western Europe. Long after Great Britain had become predominantly a capitalist country, and almost every relic of the medieval system had disappeared, Germany was still a land of serfs and gilds, and of industry and commerce, as well as agriculture, carried on mainly under very primitive conditions. After France had established a régime of personally free peasant cultivators and had developed large-scale industry and commerce and a strongly centralised national State, Germany was still governed, as far as she was governed at all, by an infinity of petty princelings, and only Prussia, under strongly despotic rule, at all resembled a national State in the modern sense. German industry, based on the technique of machine production, grew up almost wholly in the latter half of the nineteenth century ; and even the emancipation of the serfs in a purely personal sense, apart from their freeing from labour dues and inferiority of status as land holders, was deferred until the early years of the nineteenth century. The German Empire did not become a fully accomplished fact until 1870 ; and even the Zollverein, which prepared the way for it, was not effectively in being until 1834.

In the historical evolution of modern Germany the contrast between east and west is again of predominant importance. For, whereas in the west the manorial system decayed and serfs took on gradually the character of free cultivators by stages roughly corresponding to those of the similar evolution in the other countries of Western Europe,

in the east serfdom in the most extreme form was often
positively imposed at a time when in the more advanced
areas of Europe it was being mitigated or abolished. The
imposition of the most extreme form of serfdom in respect
of personal status as well as of labour dues upon the German
population east of the Elbe came about largely in the
sixteenth century, whereas from that time in the west the
severities of serfdom were being at least somewhat relaxed.
The Thirty Years' War in the first half of the seventeenth
century greatly impoverished most parts of Germany, and
was followed by a rapid process of consolidation of large
estates, especially in the east ; and the backwardness of
Germany in both an economic and a political sense was
largely the legacy of this impoverishment. In the middle of
the eighteenth century, Frederick the Great did much, not
only to follow up the work of the Great Elector, Frederick
William, a century earlier, in consolidating the power of
Prussia and bringing his scattered territories under a more
unified administration, but also to promote industrial improvement. But the beginnings of modern Germany in an
economic sense date essentially from the Napoleonic era.
Between the sixteenth century and the eighteenth century
many serfs in the west had been given their personal freedom ; but Napoleon totally abolished serfdom in the
subordinate kingdoms which he set up on German territory
at the height of his power, and though he did not succeed
in making his system permanent, the results of his work both
in breaking down the isolation of the tiny German States
and in sweeping away many of the relics of medievalism
over a large part of Germany left an abiding mark on the
institutions of the whole country.

It was largely under the influence of the French Revolution and the Napoleonic system that the freeing of the Prussian serfs was carried through, and that the status of
serfdom was definitely abolished by the Prussian Edict of
1807. Thereafter one German State after another made an
end of the personal status of serfdom, though in many cases
the requirements of service by the peasant as a condition of

his land-holding survived much longer, and these relics of the old servile status were only got rid of gradually during the nineteenth century, partly by commutation for payments in money and partly by the surrender of an appreciable fraction of the land occupied by the peasants to the nobles. Even in 1914 the peasants in some parts of Germany had not finished paying off the annuities by which they were compelled to redeem the burdens arising out of their past condition of serfdom.

From 1807, however, with Prussia taking the lead, serfdom was being gradually done away with, and the change in the status of the peasant was being followed up by measures for the redistribution and enclosure of the land, and the improvement of the methods of cultivation. Enclosure came in Germany long after the corresponding movement in Great Britain ; and even so its progress in the west was relatively slow owing to the great difficulties encountered in the broken and mountainous country in which many of the holdings lay. At the same time Prussia was taking the lead in a movement for the sweeping away of medieval restrictions on the conduct of industry and trade. Prussia began the process of municipal reform in 1808, and in 1810 the power of the gilds—associations of small masters invested with local monopolies for the conduct of industry and commerce—was drastically curtailed. This process was continued in subsequent enactments, until in 1845 the gild jurisdiction practically lapsed, while the other German States carried on a corresponding process of reform, lagging in many cases some way behind what was done in Prussia. In the eighteenth and early nineteenth centuries, despite the strangling effect of the innumerable separate tariff barriers maintained by the different German States, nothing was done to promote freer trade over Germany as a whole ; and even in Prussia Frederick the Great made no attempt at unification of tariffs. But early in the nineteenth century, first by internal unification within States, then by agreements between particular groups of States, and finally on a wider basis in the Zollverein of 1834, freedom of internal trade over Germany as a whole was gradually achieved. Fresh members one by one joined the Zollverein, which was renewed in 1853 and again in 1865 ; but Austria was kept outside lest her influence might counteract that of Prussia, and so prevent the building up of a unified German State under Prussian leadership. By the 'sixties, under strong State encouragement, largely influenced by the doctrine of economic nationalism preached by List and his followers, German industry was beginning to take on a more modern form, and the coal and iron trades were being strongly developed. The Zollverein, the emancipation of the serfs, and the strengthening of Prussia's hold over the rest of Germany had made the way plain for the creation of the German Empire ; and the Prussian wars of the 1860's completed the preparatory process. With their culmination in the Franco-Prussian War of 1870, Bismarck brought the new German Empire to full achievement.

With the iron fields of Lorraine added to her previous industrial resources, Germany was in a position to advance rapidly to the status of a fully developed industrial power —the more so because the new discoveries of Gilchrist and Thomas in the 1870's made the Lorraine ores a far more satisfactory basis for the producing of steel on competitive terms. From 1865 to the end of the 'seventies the new Germany, largely in imitation of the Free Trade policy which seemed to have been so successful in Great Britain, pursued her economic development under a liberal industrial régime. Internal tariff barriers had been swept away, and external barriers were kept definitely low ; but the onset of the industrial depression of the middle 'seventies altered the situation from the standpoint of industrialists and agriculturists alike, and combined pressure from the Junkers and the great industrialists resulted in the tariff of 1879, under which the industrialists consented to agricultural protection on condition of securing higher protection for their own products. The continued fall of agricultural prices in the 'eighties, and the rapidly increasing competition of cereals from the New World, soon made the protection accorded in 1879 inadequate from the standpoint of the Junker landowners; and in the middle 'eighties they insisted on a sharp rise in the rates of duties on agricultural goods. The industrial tariff still remained low according to post-war notions; and in 1892, with the revival of industrial prosperity, both industrial and agricultural duties were again lowered. But in 1902 Germany finally went over to a system of high protection for industry, combined with a relatively high tariff upon agricultural imports.

Through all this period, under high and low tariffs alike, German industrialism had been advancing at an extraordinarily rapid rate. Between 1871 and 1901 German coal production rose from 32 million to 89 million tons, pig iron production from under 2 million to over $6\frac{1}{2}$ millions, and steel production from an almost negligible amount to 5 million tons. German exports of domestic goods rose in money value by more than 60 per cent over the same period, and the establishment of the gold standard in 1873 definitely signalised Germany's advance to the status of a great industrial country. This advance continued no less rapidly in the early part of the twentieth century. In 1913 Germany produced nearly 190 million tons of coal, about $16\frac{1}{2}$ million tons of pig iron, and over 17 million tons of steel, whereas Great Britain produced 287 million tons of coal, only $10\frac{1}{4}$ million tons of pig iron, and rather over $7\frac{1}{2}$ million tons of steel. In the heavy industries Germany had thus forged ahead at an unprecedentedly rapid pace, and had easily displaced Great Britain from her position as the world's greatest producer of iron and steel, though of course her total output was in 1913 far behind that of the United States.

Politically no less than industrially, Germany was during this period proclaiming with ever-growing insistence her right to be considered as a Great Power; and that rivalry between Germany and Great Britain which, added to the old enmity between Germany and France and the desire of the French to regain the provinces lost in 1871, led up to the Great War, was taking an ever more menacing turn. Germany, late in the field as a Great Power, was at a serious disadvantage in attempting to build up for herself in imitation of her rivals an extensive colonial empire ; and in pursuance of this object, as well as of the status which she desired, she set out to rival Great Britain by sea as well as France by land. The history of this rivalry and of its culmination in the Great War has been told in outline in an earlier section of this book ; and there is no need to repeat it here. It is enough to say that Germany, with a population far exceeding that of either France or Great Britain, and growing at a more rapid rate than either, with a rapidly developing economic system which had already brought her practically to an equality with Great Britain and the United States as an exporting country, and with a political system which still retained from its development out of Prussian autocracy pronounced features of militarism, was in no mood to accept the position of world inferiority which she considered as enforced upon her by the maintenance of the *status quo*, while Great Britain and France regarded with growing misgivings and hostility the rapid development of a power which was felt as a menace to their own established position in Europe and in the world as a whole.

Germany during the War. When war came, the Germans hoped to end it rapidly by taking the offensive. Their entire strategy had been planned upon this basis ; for they recognised that if they were compelled to fight a defensive war against the combination of nations likely to be arrayed against them they would be placed at a serious disadvantage by their dependence on imported foodstuffs and raw materials. They knew that they were not strong enough to command the seas by challenging the combined British and French fleets in open battle ; and this meant that, if the war was to be won rapidly, it must be won on land, by a swift offensive against France before there was time for either Great Britain or Russia to bring their potential land resources into the field. When once this hope of a speedy triumph over the French army had disappeared with the successful checking of the great German advance towards Paris, it became plain that Germany would have to accept the consequences of a defensive struggle, and the war had accordingly to be fought under the disadvantages imposed on Germany by a powerful blockade, which both involved a drastic restriction in the supplies available for the civil population and demanded intense efforts to maintain even the most necessary supplies of munitions and foodstuffs for the armies at the front. That this effort could be sustained over a period of four years, and that it was not broken in the end until the American armies had begun to make their weight felt upon the battlefields of Europe, indicates the intensity of the national effort made by the German Government, and of the sufferings which the highly disciplined German people was prepared to undergo without breaking out into open revolt.

There was indeed much discontent in Germany as the war was prolonged and the promises of victory still made by the military leaders carried less and less conviction among the mass of the people. Autocratic methods of internal government had in 1917 to be to some extent modified, and the forms of civil government which had been largely superseded on the outbreak of war had to be reinstated. In June 1917 the Reichstag adopted the famous resolution in which, while pledging itself to the continued defence of the Fatherland, it declared its desire for a peace based on an accommodation without annexations or indemnities. Despite the failure of the indirect peace negotiations of 1917, the publication in January 1918 of President Wilson's Fourteen Points greatly strengthened the demand for peace within Germany ; and this became more active as the impending collapse of the Austro-Hungarian resistance became more manifest, as the sufferings of the German people increased, and as the intensified submarine campaign failed to produce the anticipated results in stopping the supply of men and munitions to the

Allied armies, or in starving out the civil population of Great Britain. By September 1918 the military leaders had become aware not merely of the inevitability of defeat, but also of the impossibility of continued resistance for more than a very little longer. Their reserves of troops were exhausted, and they realised that at any moment the fighting line might break.

When at the beginning of October Prince Max of Baden was made Chancellor, and the more radical parties hoped that their chance to bring about a negotiated peace had come at last, it was only to be confronted immediately on assuming office with the news from the military leaders that peace must at all costs be made without a day's delay, no matter what the terms enforced on Germany might be. The despairing attempt to lead out the German navy to a pitched battle with the British fleet led immediately to the refusal of the sailors to fight ; for, kept in harbour through the long years of war, the navy even more than the army at the front had developed strong pacifist tendencies and was in no mood to throw its lives away at the call of the military leaders. The naval mutiny at Kiel on October 30th was the real beginning of the German Revolution ; and it is significant that the task of keeping the revolutionaries quiet was instantly entrusted to a leading member of the Social Democratic Party. Noske, who became famous later as the protector of the German Republic against Communist and left-wing Socialist revolts, was sent to Kiel to deal with the situation created by the mutiny.

By this time it was plain that the maintenance intact of the German front in the west could only be a matter of days, and that the break-up of the German forces was bound to come speedily unless an armistice could be concluded. The Kaiser, who had left the capital in panic in order to confer with the military leaders, alternated between desperate hopes of re-establishing his position in Germany by force of arms, and a willingness to listen to the advice of those who were pressing him to abdicate on both internal and external grounds. For it was widely held in Germany that the Allies would never make peace on tolerable terms as long as the Kaiser remained upon the German throne, whereas his abdication might prepare the way for an honourable peace on the lines of President Wilson's Fourteen Points. It was, moreover, held that public opinion in Germany would prove too strong for the existing form of government to be maintained, and accordingly that the abdication of the Kaiser might clear the way for a compromise which would preserve the Hohenzollern succession and save the country from either a plunge into anarchy or the establishment of a Socialist Republic on the Russian model. But the Kaiser was unable to make up his mind ; and finally the Chancellor, Prince Max of Baden, had to proclaim his abdication without receiving his positive consent. By this time matters had gone too far for any constitutional compromise to be possible. Max of Baden realised that his position had become untenable, and resigned power into the hands of the Socialists ; and the Social Democrats, far less because they desired to make a revolution than because they were well aware that, unless they proclaimed the revolution as an accomplished fact, power would speedily pass out of their hands into those of the extremists on their left, finally took the step of proclaiming the birth of the German Republic. By this means they hoped both to re-establish internal order and to put the Allies into a mood to treat with leniency a Germany publicly dissociated from the German Empire which was held responsible for the war. Ebert, accordingly, became the provisional President of the new German State, and Scheidemann the effective leader of a new Provisional Government, which was to be responsible for the conclusion of the Armistice and for settling the outlines of the new German system.

But the Armistice terms, when they were received from the Allies, proved to violate every one of President Wilson's Fourteen Points, and even the Social Democrats toyed for a while with the idea of resuming armed resistance. The

military leaders, however, made it clear that this was out
of the question, and that any terms, no matter how onerous,
had to be accepted if the armed forces were not to break
up in sheer disorder. In these circumstances the Armistice
was signed, and the withdrawal of the German forces was
at once begun. Despite the permeation of the army by
pacifist feeling and acute social unrest, Hindenburg succeeded by a remarkable effort in withdrawing the armed
forces into Germany in good order. He was well aware
that, if discipline were once relaxed, the entire German
fighting machine might break up at a touch into scattered
units beyond any kind of co-ordinated control. But the
Social Democrats were as anxious as he was to avoid disorder, and they accordingly collaborated with him to the
full in carrying through the retreat, and in accomplishing
the subsequent disbandment of the armed forces.

The Weimar Republic.   The German Social Democrats, with power thus thrown upon them, found themselves under the necessity of immediately formulating their
proposals for the constitution of the new German State.
But they were not in a position to act alone ; for they had
to take account of the working-class groupings further to
the left, and of the possibility, if they failed to retain the
leadership of the working-class movement, that the revolution might pass out of their hands and under the control
of the left-wing leaders—which they evidently regarded as
the most terrible thing that could possibly happen.

Before the outbreak of war, German Social Democracy
had formed a united party, but this unity had already
begun to break up in 1914. Karl Liebknecht alone voted
against the war credits in the Reichstag in 1914 ; but in
the private meeting of the Social Democratic Party which
preceded the decision to vote the credits, fourteen members
of the party voted in the minority, and this group formed
the nucleus of an opposition which became more and more
articulate as the war went on. Until 1917 the Socialists
who were definitely opposed to the war remained within

the Social Democratic Party ; but in that year they found continued association with the majority no longer possible, and the Independent Socialist Party was constituted as a separate body. There had been large-scale strikes in the German munition works as early as 1916, and in the spring of 1917 these strikes were renewed on a larger scale. Moreover, in July 1917 the first mutiny broke out in the German navy. In the early months of 1918 there was a still more widespread strike among the German munition workers ; but this, like the earlier movements, was crushed by the opposition of the Majority Socialists and the continued loyalty of the German Trade Union leaders to the cause of the Central Powers. As the year 1918 advanced, and the last reserves were combed out of the factories into the army, unrest at home caused the German Government to endeavour to remove the more active working-class leaders by sending them to the trenches ; but this policy only resulted in spreading unrest to the army, and thus helped greatly to prepare the way for the November Revolution.

When the Revolution broke out, the whole situation was so uncertain that each party was hesitant how to act. The general mass of working-class opinion was undoubtedly in favour of some form of Socialism ; but the working classes were sharply split between the Majority Socialists, the Independents, and the Spartacists under the leadership of Karl Liebknecht and Rosa Luxemburg, who, while they remained still within the Social Democratic Parties, had moved much further to the left, and had taken the lead in stirring up unrest among the workers and soldiers. The Majority Socialists, when control of the State was handed over to them by Prince Max of Baden on the dissolution of the imperial régime, had to decide upon their course in the light of an immediate threat of revolution from the left. Even in the opinion of the *bourgeois* leaders it was at that moment out of the question for anything except a Socialist Government to attempt to govern the country. But the Independent Socialists were unwilling to participate in any Government unless it was clearly laid down that it would seek to establish Socialism in the form of a Socialist Republic largely modelled upon the Russian system, and to this the Majority Socialists, with their belief in constitutional government, were entirely unwilling to agree. The result was a highly unsatisfactory and unstable compromise. The Majority Socialists, under pressure, declared in favour of a " Socialist Republic," and agreed to the formation of an inner Cabinet of Ministers or Council of Commissars—it was not quite clear which—consisting entirely of Socialists. But they insisted on drawing the departmental Ministers from the old official classes ; and the control of the Cabinet over these non-Socialist Ministers was to a large extent nominal in departmental matters. The Cabinet itself consisted of three Majority Socialists and three Independents ; but from the first the Majority Socialists acted coherently together in close consultation with the non-Socialist Ministers, and the Independents found themselves largely excluded from an effective share in the control of policy. Moreover, there arose between the two sections of the Cabinet an immediate quarrel over the question whether a Constituent Assembly should be elected by universal suffrage to decide the form of the new State ; while the Spartacists, under Liebknecht's leadership, passed into more and more open hostility to the Provisional Government, and insisted more and more energetically on the need for a further revolution which would definitely institute a Socialist system.

Before the end of the year the differences between the Majority Socialists and the Independents had become too acute for further collaboration to be possible. The Independent Socialists resigned from the Government, leaving the Majority Socialists a free hand ; and significantly, Noske at this point joined the Cabinet, and shortly afterwards assumed control of the military organisation of Germany. Meanwhile the excluded Independents joined forces with the Spartacists in an attempt to seize power, though some of the more moderate Independents refused to associate themselves with this movement, and from this time began to retrace their steps towards the Majority Socialist Party. After desultory fighting in Berlin and elsewhere the Spartacist attempt was defeated, largely by means of an improvised organisation got together by Noske under the leadership of anti-Socialist officers of the old army ; and in the course of this struggle Liebknecht and Rosa Luxemburg, having been arrested by Noske's reactionaries, were deliberately murdered, though it was publicly put out that they had been killed in the course of an attempt to escape from the authorities. The death of the leaders brought the immediate movement in Berlin to an end, and left the Spartacist forces disorganised. But this was by no means the end of the struggle, and throughout the succeeding months there occurred a series of revolutionary strikes in many parts of Germany—ruthlessly suppressed by Noske and the growingly confident body of reactionaries whom he had called in to aid the Social Democrats in restoring order.

Meanwhile the elections for the Constituent Assembly were carried through under universal suffrage. Of the 421 seats the Majority Socialists with the aid of their powerful organisation secured 163, while the Independents, with no adequate party machine behind them, got only 22. The Spartacists, having boycotted the Assembly, were not candidates, and the combined Socialist parties found themselves in a minority in the Assembly as a whole. Of the remaining seats 42 fell to the Nationalists, the more extreme representatives of the old régime, and 21 to the People's Party, which stood mainly for the great industrialists. Both these parties refused to accept the new Republic as an accomplished fact, and were therefore clearly ineligible for participation in a Government designed to set it up on a permanent basis. Apart from 10 seats which fell to the small fractional parties, this left 163 seats, a number precisely equal to that held by the Majority Socialists, shared between the Centre Party, representing the Catholics, and the Democrats, formed on the basis of a coalition of the more liberal *bourgeois* groups. The Social Democrats, faithful to their principle of parliamentary democracy and insisting

that the time could not be ripe for the establishment of
Socialism until a clear Socialist majority of the electorate
had been secured, immediately proceeded to reconstitute
the Government on the basis of a coalition with the Centre
and Democratic Parties. Ebert remained provisional
President, and the Social Democrat, Scheidemann, became
Chancellor in the new Government; but seats in the
Cabinet were equally shared between the Majority Socialists on the one hand and the combined *bourgeois* parties on
the other, and it was under the auspices of this Coalition
Government that the National Assembly proceeded to the
drafting of the new Weimar Constitution. Weimar, incidentally, was selected as the place of meeting for the
National Assembly largely in order to enable it to get away
from the disturbed conditions prevailing in Berlin and the
other great industrial centres, where it might have been
more under the control of the Soldiers' and Workers'
Councils set up during the revolution.

Moreover, the drafting of the new Constitution was
undertaken not by a Socialist but by Herr Preuss, a well-
known official of the Prussian Ministry of the Interior;
and under his draftsmanship it took the form by no means
of the constitution for a Socialist Republic which the
Independents and the Spartacists desired, but of an eclectic
bourgeois democratic system of government, based on a
mingling of the Parliamentary precedents set by the
Constitutions of Great Britain, France and the United
States. The formation of the new Coalition Government
and the drafting of the Weimar Constitution made perfectly
definite the breach, already implicit in the suppression of
the January insurrection, between the Majority Socialists
and those who wished to turn the collapse of the old order
in Germany into an immediate Socialist revolution.

While the Constitution was being drafted at Weimar, the
Allies at Versailles were elaborating the Treaty of Peace.
When their proposals were presented to the German
Government the Majority Socialists were at first unable to
believe that such terms were really to be forced upon them,

and made an attempt to negotiate for improved conditions by beginning with an indignant refusal. But it was speedily made plain to the German Government that the Allies meant what they said, and were determined upon the imposition of a peace embodying the principle of the " spoils to the victors," and involving the almost complete disarmament of Germany as well as the payment of very heavy, though still unspecified, sums in reparations for war damage. The leader of the Majority Socialists, Scheidemann, having committed himself to an indignant refusal of these terms, refused to change his attitude even when it was made plain that nothing better could be secured, and the Democrats also left the Government, which was then reconstructed in June 1919 under Gustav Bauer—another Majority Socialist and Trade Union leader—as a coalition between the Social Democrats and the Centre Party. This Government signed the Peace Treaty under protest, and instituted the policy of " fulfilment " which came in later years to be chiefly associated with the name of Stresemann.

In the meantime Noske was continuing his work in the active suppression of the left-wing Socialists. In order to give a clear account of his activities it is necessary to retrace our steps and consider what had been happening in Bavaria while the movements already described had been going on in the rest of Germany. The revolution in Munich was among the first in Germany to assume a definite shape, and even before the Armistice had been signed the old royal family had been excluded and a left-wing Socialist Government, under the Independent Socialist, Kurt Eisner, as President, had assumed control. This Government, following the example of the Social Democrats in the Reich, proceeded to the election of a Bavarian Constituent Assembly, with the result that an anti-Socialist majority, based mainly on the Catholic peasantry, was returned. Disputes speedily followed within the Bavarian Socialist Government, and on February 21st Kurt Eisner was assassinated by a reactionary fanatic. There followed a period of utter confusion. The Majority Socialists constructed a new right-wing Socialist Government ; but this was unable to maintain its authority in Munich, where an extremist revolution broke out towards the end of February under an adventurer named Lipp. The rapid overthrow of his Government was followed by the creation of a Communist Government under the leadership of Axelrod. But the Majority Socialists in Bavaria, in combination with the reactionary parties, now invoked the assistance of Noske ; and on May 1st, Reich government troops captured Munich, and the Communists underwent bloody suppression.

At the same time revolutionary movements were being actively suppressed by Noske in other parts of Germany, and by the middle of the year, thanks to Noske's activities, the Workers' Councils had been almost completely suppressed save in a few areas, and the Majority Socialists and their *bourgeois* allies had the situation well in hand.

So matters dragged on through the rest of 1919, with no vital change save that after the signature of the Peace Treaty the Democrats came back into the Government. But in the meantime the forces got together by Noske and the remnants of the old reactionary parties had begun to reassert themselves in political matters. Confident that they had now thoroughly suppressed the extreme Socialist left, they began to bring pressure to bear upon the Social Democrats for a more definitely reactionary policy. On March 10th, 1920, General von Luttwitz and other generals presented an ultimatum to the Social Democratic members of the Government ; and the rejection of this ultimatum was immediately followed by the outbreak of the Kapp Putsch. Under the leadership of Kapp, a Prussian official, the counter-revolutionaries marched on Berlin and captured the city. The coalition Government fled to Stuttgart, and there summoned the National Assembly to meet. They further endeavoured at this moment of danger to invoke against the reactionaries the forces which they had hitherto been endeavouring to suppress. At the orders of the Trade Unions a General Strike was declared, with the participation of almost the whole of the German working class, the

Catholic Trade Unions associated with the Centre Party taking part in it along with the Socialist Unions. With this aid furnished by the workers, the position of the leaders of the Kapp Putsch was speedily made untenable ; and, realising that they had no chance of success, they disbanded their forces and surrendered to the Government. But although the Kapp Putsch thus signally failed it undoubtedly exerted an important influence in weakening still further the hold of the Majority Socialists upon the Government. Immediately after it the Bauer Government resigned, and a new Government based on the same parties as before was formed under another Social Democrat, Müller, solely as an interim administration pledged to the holding of new elections. These elections, held in June, resulted in serious Socialist losses, and immediately afterwards a new coalition Government was formed under the leadership of Fehrenbach of the Centre Party, on the basis of a *bourgeois* coalition from which the Socialists were excluded. In the meantime there had been, in the month following the Kapp Putsch, a serious rising in the Ruhr under Communist leadership—the Spartacists and certain of the Independents having by now united to form the Communist Party. This, like previous movements on a smaller scale, was promptly suppressed by Noske—almost the last act of the Social Democratic Government before its fall. Thus, when the Social Democrats handed over power to a *bourgeois* coalition, they were able to congratulate themselves that they had successfully broken the forces of the revolutionary working-class movement in Germany, and that the country could once more be governed, even by non-Socialists, on strictly constitutional lines.

We have told in some detail the story of the successive phases of the German revolution up to 1920, because an understanding of what happened to Germany during these eighteen months is essential to a realisation of the basis upon which the Weimar Republic rested. The new German Constitution, set up at Weimar, was the work of a coalition of middle parties, Social Democrats, Centre, and Democrats,

carried through in face of a strong opposition from the
adherents of the old régime on the one hand and from the
Independent Socialists, Spartacists, Communists, and
Workers' and Soldiers' Councils on the other. The left-wing
groups wanted to proceed at once to a Socialist republic,
and to leave the election of a Constituent Assembly and the
drawing up of a definitive new Constitution in abeyance
until the Socialists had definitely established their power on
the basis of the Workers' and Soldiers' Councils created
during the November Revolution. They held that the first
step should be to make the power of the Socialist movement
secure in Germany, and that questions of the form of
government could only be considered when the country
had at least to some extent settled down under a definitely
Socialist régime.

The parties of the right and the remnants of the old
official classes and the old army leaders were at bottom no
less hostile than the left-wing Socialists to the Weimar Constitution. But, realising that it was for the time impossible
for them to assume office themselves or to constitute a State
more to their own liking, they threw their weight on the
side of the middle parties and the Social Democrats with the
object of suppressing the left wing, with the mental reservation that when once the left had been sufficiently dealt with
they would be free to resume activities on their own behalf.
The Kapp Putsch, instituted by a number of the more
extreme among the reactionary elements, was clearly pre-
mature, and received no united support even from those
who sympathised wholly with its objects. In 1919 and 1920
the adherents of the old régime were still playing a waiting
game, and using the Social Democrats to do the work of
preventing Socialism which they were not strong enough
to do for themselves.

Between these two extremes stood the two middle
bourgeois parties and the Majority Socialists. The Democrats
were for the most part sincere republicans, desirous of
turning Germany into a constitutional republic on the
model of France or the United States. Largely supported

by the Jews and by the intellectual classes, they were unable at any time to command a really large popular following ; but they were able to give important help to the other middle parties in carrying through the new Constitution and keeping a " moderate " régime securely in power. The Centre Party differed from the Democrats in that it stood predominantly for the interests of the Catholic Church, and was based largely on the votes of the Catholic peasantry and the smaller middle classes in the Catholic parts of Germany, while it had also a large number of adherents among the Catholic Trade Unionists, especially in the Ruhr. Collectively, the Centre Party can hardly have been said to have had on most matters any policy at all. It ranged in social and economic doctrines from right to left, and was held together rather by its common allegiance to Catholicism than by any clear-cut principles of political or economic action. In the circumstances of 1919 and 1920 it wished to create and preserve the Weimar Republic ; for it had no love for the old Empire based on the hegemony of Protestant Prussia, and it was also acutely hostile to any attempt at the establishment of Socialism. With these two parties the Social Democrats were compelled to collaborate if they were determined to base their actions on constitutional and Parliamentary principles ; for only with the aid of the Democrats and Centre were they in a position to command a majority in the Constituent Assembly or to maintain their power at all. The attitude of the Social Democrats was that, while they professed to be, and doubtless believed themselves to be, Socialists, they held that any immediate attempt to establish Socialism would be both contrary to democratic principles and likely to provoke a serious reaction at a later stage. For, in their view, Germany could only become ripe for Socialism when a majority of the German people had been converted to Socialist views. Finding themselves called upon to assume power with only the alternative of handing it over to the extreme left, under circumstances in which this condition was clearly not realised, they refused to go further than to attempt to constitute

a thoroughly democratic *bourgeois* republican State, in
the hope that this would provide a basis on which they
would be able at a later stage to build up Socialism when
the majority had become converted to their point of view.
But in practice this middle policy involved them, as we
have seen, in invoking the aid not only of the *bourgeois*
parties but also of armed reactionary forces for the suppression of their fellow-Socialists further to the left ; and
the more bitter the struggle became the more the Social
Democrats were tempted to depart from their Socialist
principles, and the greater grew the hatred between them
and the left-wing forces, now becoming concentrated in the
Communist Party. For when men have fought with one
another in the streets, when Socialist has killed Socialist
across the barricades, it is no longer much use talking about
Socialist unity ; and in fact the unity of the German working class, broken in the early days of the revolution, has
never been successfully re-established, with the consequence
that the Nazi movement, when its time arrived, was able
to mount rapidly in influence and in the end to scatter the
disunited Socialist forces without their offering any effective resistance. The seeds of the German Socialist collapse
of 1933 were sown in the months immediately following the
November Revolution of 1918.

Between 1920 and 1923 Germany appeared to be
gradually settling down. Governments alternated between
different party groupings. In 1921 Fehrenbach's non-
Socialist Ministry was replaced by a new coalition under
Wirth of the Centre Party, including the Socialists. But by
this time the Socialists, instead of half the seats, had little
more than a third. In 1922, Wirth was replaced by Cuno, at
the head of another Coalition Government of the *bourgeois*
parties, from which the Socialists were again excluded. Then
in 1923 the Socialists returned as members of a Government
under Stresemann of the People's Party, a grand coalition
extending further to the right than any previous Government in which the Socialists had agreed to take part. Towards the end of 1924, when Stresemann gave place to

Marx, the Socialists were again left outside the Government, and did not resume their participation in it until 1928.

These successive changes of Government are closely connected with the movement of events both in Germany itself and in the relations between Germany and the Allied Powers. In January 1921 the total demanded from the Germans in reparations was first fixed—at a fantastic figure which had to be modified out of all recognition in later years. In 1921, too, a further blow was struck at the new German State by the handing over of a considerable area in Upper Silesia to the Poles after the plebiscite conducted under the auspices of the League of Nations. There was a Communist rising in Saxony, easily suppressed, and on the other hand the reactionary Government now in power in Bavaria offered strong resistance to disarmament, and Munich became the chief refuge of the reactionary extremists who had been associated with the Kapp Putsch and with other movements directed against the Weimar Constitution. Erzberger, one of the leaders of the Centre Party, who had been the chief promoter of the Reichstag peace resolution of 1917 and the most active negotiator of the Treaty, was murdered by reactionaries who escaped from the country unpunished ; and the campaign of political assassination was thus extended from the extreme left to members of the middle parties unpopular with the reactionary elements. But the Wirth Government on the whole attempted to pursue a moderate and conciliatory policy in home affairs, and at the same time to improve relations with the Allied Powers. Its outstanding figure, the great Jewish industrialist, Walther Rathenau, was the chief agent of the Treaty signed at Rapallo between Germany and Russia in April 1922, and Rathenau also made heroic efforts to re-establish German prestige abroad by asserting her freedom to follow an independent foreign policy without a positive break with the Allied Powers. But Rathenau, despite the great services which he had performed as the organiser of the German munitions industries during the

war, was desperately unpopular with the extremists of the
right, and in June 1922 he shared the fate of Erzberger and
Liebknecht, being assassinated in Berlin in broad daylight.
The murders of Erzberger and Rathenau were the chief
cause of the formation towards the end of 1922 of the
Reichsbanner, a semi-military organisation of Social Democrats and Centre Party supporters for the defence of the
Republic against reactionary extremists. But the murders
weakened the position of the middle parties, and the
establishment of the Cuno Government in November 1922
with the participation of the People's Party was definitely
a move to the right.

Reparations, the Ruhr, Inflation and Recovery. Mean-
while a serious crisis was developing over the question
of reparations. The Germans maintained that they had
been making every possible effort to fulfil the enormous
demands made upon them by the Allies both for the payment of money and for deliveries in kind ; but towards
the end of 1922 the strain became too great to be borne,
and, after deliveries had fallen definitely behind, the Cuno
Government made a demand for a moratorium, while the
Reparations Commission established under the Peace
Treaty definitely announced that a German default had
taken place. In these circumstances Great Britain was
willing to negotiate for an adjustment of the terms imposed
on Germany ; but the French and Belgians, in a majority
on the Reparations Commission, refused any accommodation, and in January 1923 marched into Germany and
occupied the Ruhr, thus beginning a struggle which lasted
though the greater part of the year. For the Germans, maintaining that the occupation was contrary to the terms of the
Treaty, decided upon a course of passive resistance, and
endeavoured to mobilise the entire forces of the country
behind the movement. A proposal, with this object, once
more to include the Socialists in the Government led to an
ultimatum from Bavaria, now under wholly reactionary
control ; but the proposal was not persisted in at the time,

and for some months longer the situation in Bavaria hung in the balance. Meanwhile passive resistance in the Ruhr, which involved the necessity of supporting a large part of the population out of public funds in view of the suspension of productive activities, placed a tremendous strain on the German public finances, which were already in a bad enough condition owing to the large payments made to the Allies and the disorganisation of German industries in consequence of the war and the subsequent blockade.

There was only one way in which the costs of the Ruhr defence could possibly be met, and this was inflation. During the months for which passive resistance continued— between January and August 1923—internal prices in Germany rose to an unexampled height, and the German mark depreciated still more rapidly in external value. During the previous years the German currency had already become seriously depreciated. In May 1921 the current rate of exchange was 62 marks to the dollar, but by September of that year it had fallen to 105. The Upper Silesia award caused a further serious depreciation, and by the end of November 1921 the mark was at 270 to the dollar, or only $1\frac{1}{2}$ per cent of its par value. There for a time depreciation was arrested ; but in 1922, in face of the effort to make large payments to the Allies, and of the fears caused abroad by the assassination of Rathenau, the mark began again to depreciate heavily. In July 1922 it was at 493 to the dollar, and in August at 1,200. Then, with the beginning of the quarrel with the Allies which led to the Ruhr occupation, it shot up to over 8,000 in the middle of November, and a flight from the German currency by German nationals as well as by foreigners set in.

But even this depreciation was as nothing to that which followed the Ruhr occupation. The mark, which had recovered a little from the low speculative level reached in November 1922, soared in January, the first month of the occupation, to over 40,000 to the dollar. There it was for the moment held again by strong efforts on the part of the German Government and the Reichsbank ; but before long the resources at the disposal of the Germans for maintaining the external value of their currency were exhausted, and between May and November 1923 the mark-dollar exchange reached a fantastic degree of depreciation, until in the latter month a dollar was valued at the astonishing figure of 4,200,000,000,000 marks. In other words, in the course of the Ruhr struggle the external value of the mark to all intents and purposes totally disappeared, and over the same period prices in Germany also reached a level hitherto undreamed of in any country. At the end of the war in 1918 they reached four times the pre-war level ; in 1920 nearly fifteen times, and in 1921 over nineteen times. At that point the real depreciation began. The average for 1922 was 34,000 times that of 1913, and in 1923 price levels became as fantastic as foreign exchange quotations and the official index recorded a figure of 16,620,000,000,000, as compared with 100 in 1913. This process obviously could not go on indefinitely. While it lasted it inflicted tremendous hardship on all those classes whose incomes were relatively fixed, and compelled everyone into whose possession any money came to spend it instantly in the knowledge that if he waited even an hour it was likely to lose a large part of its value. Wage rates had to be recalculated daily in accordance with new price levels ; but by the time they had been paid out price levels had risen much further still. All debtors benefited to the extent that, however large the sums which they had borrowed before the inflation might be, these could soon be paid off with the price of half a dozen eggs or even a postage stamp. Consequently the owners of real capital assets as distinct from money made enormous gains, in that mortgages could be completely written off, and actual goods had come to be the sole recognised economic values. Germans who could sent their money abroad and changed it into foreign currencies, and immense profits as well as losses were made by speculation in marks as the inflation proceeded.

But while some classes profited by the inflation, its continuance soon threatened to bring all business to a stand-still.

For no one could in the circumstances venture to make any forward contract in terms of money, or even to promise to deliver goods at a fixed price in a week's or a day's time. The whole German economic system was accordingly threatened with utter collapse, and when this became too plain to be any longer ignored the passive resistance in the Ruhr had to be abandoned. A new currency, the Rentenmark, based nominally on the value of landed property, was introduced to replace the now valueless mark currency, and Germany reconciled herself to coming to terms with the Allies, and agreeing, as the price of peace, to any terms which she could hope even temporarily to meet.

The Ruhr occupation, while it was disastrous to the German finances, was a burdensome expense to the Allies, and the German resistance, though it had in the end to be given up, had sufficed to show up the absurdity of Poincaré's policy of endeavouring to exact reparations by violence. For it was plain that the ability of Germany to pay reparations must depend on her internal prosperity, and that if in the future she was to be able to pay anything at all her finances must somehow be established on a sounder basis, and the value of her currency restored. Under these circumstances the Allies became willing to come to terms with Germany ; and, after an international expert committee under the presidency of the American General Dawes had reported upon Germany's ability to pay, it became possible to secure general acceptance of the Dawes Plan, under which the Allied claims to reparations were considerably scaled down, and a new loan, to be raised in the Allied countries, was conceded to Germany as the means of re-establishing her financial position. Under this plan, moreover, the temporary Rentenmark was displaced by a new unit of currency, the Reichsmark, based upon gold and possessing the same gold value as the pre-war mark. Prices in terms of the new currency were sharply brought down to somewhere near the pre-war level, and by a method of severe deflation some sort of equilibrium was restored to the German economic system.

From 1924 onwards, Germany entered definitely on a new phase of her post-war history. Under the Governments of Stresemann (August 1923), Marx (November 1924), Lüther (January 1925) and Marx (May 1926), the policy of fulfilment under the conditions laid down by the Dawes Plan was systematically pursued ; while Stresemann, in control for the most part of German foreign policy, helped greatly in rebuilding Germany's international position from a political point of view. To this period belongs the Locarno Treaty of December 1925, which is discussed in another section. Before this, in July 1925, the French and Belgians had evacuated the Ruhr ; and three years later, in 1928, the Armies of Occupation were also withdrawn from the northern Rhineland. At the same time, under the new conditions created by the stabilisation of the mark and the Dawes Loan, it became possible for Germany to embark upon a thorough-going policy of industrial reorganisation, carried out largely with the aid of foreign capital. For the effect of the Dawes Plan and of the Locarno Treaty was to restore the belief of foreign investors, especially in the United States, in Germany's economic future ; and there was, as we shall see in a later section, a tremendous outpouring of American capital into Germany. This was used largely for the reconstruction and rationalisation of the German heavy industries ; but large sums were also borrowed by the German States and municipalities, and applied to the execution of great schemes of public works. At the same time the flight of German capital definitely came to an end with the stabilisation ; and the German people began out of their own resources to supply considerable amounts of new capital for the development of industry.

It has often been suggested that much of this borrowed money which flowed into Germany in an uninterrupted stream between 1924 and 1928 was wastefully used, and that the reorganisation of the German economic system was carried through with quite unnecessary extravagance. This charge is made both in respect of the sums borrowed by the States and municipalities, which imposed a large burden on the German taxpayers, and of the sums applied to industrial development in private hands. But it has to be remembered that in 1924 and the following years the Germans were basing their calculations of what they could afford to borrow on the anticipation that the world would continue to advance rapidly in economic prosperity, and that prices would remain, if not stable, at any rate high enough not to cause serious dislocation, or greatly to exaggerate the burden of current borrowings. Above all they calculated on a continued ability, as long as their own conditions remained stable, to go on borrowing money in the United States until the increase in their productive resources enabled them to supply for themselves the new capital they required, and to meet out of their own resources the necessary payments for interest and sinking fund on what they had borrowed. It was the sharp cutting off of the American investments in Germany in the course of the American boom of 1929 that brought the perilous economic structure of the reconstructed German system crashing down, and made impossible the maintenance of the unstable equilibrium that had existed during the previous four years.

In the light of later events it is clear enough that Germany did over-borrow and was extravagant in the reconstruction of her economic system. But it is difficult to blame the Germans over much for this, as they only shared with other capitalist countries, and above all with their chief creditor, the United States, the belief that the economic difficulties which were the legacy of the war had been successfully overcome, and that industry could rely upon a steadily increasing return for some time to come. Nor is it easy to see how, when the Germans had once accepted the policy of endeavouring to fulfil the Peace Treaty and to meet the revised Allied claims for reparations embodied in the Dawes Plan, they could have managed at all without an amount of borrowing from abroad which was bound to become a top-heavy burden in face of any serious fall in the level of world prices. It is easy to be wise after the event, but it is not at all surprising that Germany borrowed all she could in view of her intense shortage of capital and the great opportunities for industrial activity which seemed to be opening up before her. It is perhaps rather more surprising that the American investors were willing to put so many eggs into the German basket ; but in this case too the explanation lies in the widespread belief that the world had entered on a new phase of advancing productivity which nothing was likely to interrupt.

The new phase in German politics which began with the adoption of the Dawes Plan was also marked for a considerable period by a disappearance of the internal conflicts which had persisted ever since 1918. In 1923, while the struggle in the Ruhr was still going on, there had been a serious quarrel between Bavaria and the Reich, and in Bavaria numerous reactionary plans for a German Revolution had been hatched. In that year Bavaria was under the practically dictatorial rule of von Kahr, who was mainly concerned to preserve the autonomy of Bavaria against interference by the Reich. But there were other forces in Bavaria which were intent on planning a new German counter-revolution ; and Hitler, who had become in 1921 leader of the Nazis and as early as that year had begun planning with General Ludendorff a new march on Berlin, chose the later months of 1923 for an attempt at insurrection in Munich. He succeeded in capturing the Bavarian dictator, von Kahr, who escaped and raised the country against him. The Hitlerite insurrection was suppressed without very much difficulty, and von Kahr resumed his authority. In other parts of Germany, too, there had been in 1923 serious threats of insurrection from both right and left, and, in August, General Gessler had been given dictatorial military powers over the Reich as a whole. A Socialist-Communist coalition under Dr. Zeigner came into power in Saxony, and the Reich Government promptly demanded its resignation. In face of its refusal to give way the Reich forces marched upon Saxony and suppressed the Saxon

Government, installing a right-wing Social Democratic Government in its place. There were similar troubles on a smaller scale in other parts of Germany. General Gessler, however, and his successor, von Seeckt, appointed in November 1923, succeeded in overcoming the forces of unrest, and suppressed by decree both the Communist Party and the Nazis. Thereafter the conclusion of the Ruhr struggle and the acceptance of the Dawes Plan introduced more settled conditions ; and with the revival in industrial activity and the restoration of the price system, Germany settled down to a more tranquil period of internal development. In February 1924 the von Seeckt dictatorship came to an end ; but this adoption of the method of military dictatorship in 1923–24 clearly presaged the resort to extra-constitutional methods of government which has been renewed in later years.

It is unnecessary to follow in detail the revival of German economic prosperity during the years between 1924 and 1929. Despite the slightly falling level of prices, Germany during this period increased the value of her exports from $6\frac{1}{2}$ milliards of Reichsmarks to over $13\frac{1}{2}$ milliards, and turned an unfavourable balance of commodity trade of over $2\frac{1}{2}$ milliards into one of under 400 millions, while there was actually a rising favourable balance during the next two years. It is true that most of this decline in the unfavourable balance came only in 1929, after the falling off of borrowings from abroad, and that in 1927 and 1928 the unfavourable trade balance was larger than it had been in 1924. But this was due to large capital imports from America ; and the really significant figure is that of the rise in the value of German exports. The figures of tonnage for exports are no less significant. In 1924 they were under 16 million metric tons, and in 1929 nearly 55 millions. Obviously the rationalisation of German industry had already produced an enormous effect in increasing German productive capacity and competitive power.

Germany thus seemed after 1924 to be definitely settling down under the new post-war conditions and accommodating

herself to her new position in Europe. The German
Republic seemed to be growing stronger at the expense of
both the extreme right and the extreme left ; and it
seemed reasonable to argue that, as long as economic
prosperity could be maintained, there was no serious threat
of revolution from either side. But this was only the calm
before the renewed storm ; for, with the coming of the
world depression, Germany's economic position speedily
deteriorated in face of the continued claims of the Allies for
reparations and of the large burden of foreign payments
which had to be met.

The position on the eve of these renewed troubles is
fairly well illustrated by the representation of parties after
the Reichstag elections of 1928. Of the parties discussed
earlier in this section, the Independent Socialists had now
disappeared ; some of them had gone over to the Communists, while the right wing had rejoined the Social
Democratic Party, which had become less clearly a reactionary force after the German economy had begun to
settle down. In 1928 the Social Democrats were easily the
strongest party in the Reichstag, with 153 seats out of
a total House of 489 members. They had thus rather less
than one third of the total number of seats. The Communists on the extreme left had 54. The three parties which,
either together with the Social Democrats or without them,
had formed the main support of the successive Governments
of the new German Republic had between them 144 seats,
or, if the Bavarian People's Party, usually allied with the
Catholic Centre, is included, 161. Of these, the Centre
Party had 61 seats and the Bavarian People's Party 17, the
People's Party 45 seats, and the Democratic or State
Party 25. Forty-four seats went to various minor parties,
chiefly representing the Peasant Right, while the Nationalists, still in opposition to the established régime, had 78, and
the Nazis, still at the very beginning of their great growth
under the influence of economic depression, had only 12.
It was thus clear that on the balance of parties there was no
majority either for Socialism or for a right-wing attempt

to overturn the Republic ; for even if the People's Party, which was not republican in theory, be counted in with the Nationalists and certain of the smaller groups, they did not together command as many seats as the Social Democrats alone, and not many more than the Centre, Democrats and Bavarians combined. In these circumstances it was evident that there was a majority in favour of a middle Government, designed to preserve the Republic against both extremes ; and the Majority Socialists were fully prepared, as they had been in the troubled years before 1924, to play their part in maintaining a Government of this type. As the largest party, the Social Democrats were called upon to form a Ministry ; and their leader, Müller, became Chancellor in a mixed Government including the People's Party, the Democrats and one representative of the Centre.

Germany in the World Slump.   Now contrast this position with that which arose in 1930. At the Reichstag election of that year the Social Democrats lost 10 seats and the Communists gained 23. The Centre and the Bavarian People's Party together registered a gain of 10 seats, while the Democrats lost 3. The Nationalists sank by 37, and the People's Party by 15. These losses of the old right-wing parties were the result of the rapid rise of the Nazis, who returned 107 members as against only 12 in the Reichstag of two years before. It should be observed that under the German electoral system there is no fixed number of seats, the number of members returned depending on the total votes cast, so that in 1930 the increased poll resulted in a corresponding increase in the total number of seats to be allotted among the parties.

The explanation of this change is obviously to be found in the earlier effects of the world economic depression, which had strengthened the extreme right and the extreme left at the expense of the parties standing nearest to them, without correspondingly affecting the Catholic Centre. In March 1930 Müller's Government resigned, and a new

Government was formed under Dr. Brüning, and armed with large emergency powers, exercised through the President (Marshal Hindenburg had become President in 1925 on the death of the Socialist, Ebert). This change of Government took place before the General Election of 1930 ; but after the election Brüning formed a new Government, and continued to govern the country with growingly stringent emergency measures as the economic depression deepened.

Now take the third picture—that of the General Election of July 1932, representing the state of feeling at a far more advanced stage of the economic depression. Again the Social Democrats lost seats, sinking by another 10 to 133. Again the Communists gained seats, from 77 to 89. But these changes were relatively small, as were the changes in an opposite direction, in the strength of the Centre Party, which was reinforced by having one of its leading members, Dr. Brüning, in control of the Government. The Centre gained 6 seats, and its Bavarian allies 3, raising them to 75 and 22 respectively. The Democrats were practically wiped out, sinking from 22 to 4. The Nationalists maintained their position, losing one seat only. But the People's Party, which stood nearest to them, almost shared the fate of the Democrats, sinking from 30 to 7. Several of the smaller parties were completely wiped out. But at this election the Nazis returned 230 members as against 107 in 1930 and only 12 in 1928. Clearly economic depression had produced a remarkable revulsion of feeling towards the Nazi movement.

It is true that after this extraordinarily rapid advance the Nazis lost ground at the second election held only a few months later, in November 1932. On that occasion their seats fell from 230 to 196, while the Nationalists rose from 40 to 54, and the People's Party from 7 to 11. But there was no corresponding gain upon the left. The Communists indeed gained 11 seats and returned 100 members ; but the Social Democrats lost 12, the Centre 5, the Bavarians 2, and the Democrats 2 more, reducing their total strength to

only 2 members. It was confidently predicted at the time
that this Nazi setback meant a permanent reverse and the
beginning of the decline of the Nazi movement. But these
predictions were soon to be falsified by the *coup* of January
1933, and by the new elections held under Hitler as Chancellor.

The rise of the Nazi movement is discussed in more detail
in a later section of this book, and no more has been said
about it here than is necessary to explain the immediate
political reactions of the depression in Germany, and to
show the close connection which exists between the rise of
Nazism and the increasing economic troubles of the German
Republic. Nor need we at this stage pursue the history of
the German economy during the depression in any detail.
It is necessary only to single out for treatment those features
which were peculiar to Germany, and involved her in the
taking of special measures differing from those which were
common to most of the countries of Europe.

We shall see elsewhere the tremendous efforts made by
Germany under the Brüning Government to maintain exports and to keep down the volume of imports in order to
meet external claims without going off the gold standard.
Here we are concerned with the effects of this tremendous
strain upon the structure of the German economic system.
In effect it became necessary, in order to prevent a general
collapse of the German economy, for the Reich to extend
enormously the field of its economic control. The collapse
of the *Credit Anstalt* in Austria in May 1931 had serious repercussions upon the position of the German banks. Already
in September 1930 the success of the Nazis at the elections
had been an important factor in causing the withdrawal of
foreign short-term credits from Germany ; and in the
autumn of that year the Reichsbank had to provide nearly
1,000 million Reichsmarks in gold and foreign exchange in
order to meet withdrawals. In the early months of 1931 the
position was for a time somewhat easier, but the collapse
of the *Credit Anstalt* at once caused a new run on the German banks, and in June and the first half of July over 3,000

million Reichsmarks were withdrawn abroad. In spite of the help given by the Reichsbank, one of the leading German banks, the Danat bank, was obliged to suspend payment on July 13th, 1931, and a run on the German banking houses made it indispensable to declare a moratorium. The Government thereupon had to come to the assistance of the German banks, and especially of the Danat bank, and also to negotiate in August the Basle Standstill Agreement, under which the foreign creditors of Germany agreed drastically to limit the withdrawal of money from the country. But it was impossible for State intervention in the affairs of the German banks, having once begun, to stop at that point, and stage by stage, in order to ensure their solvency, the German Government had practically to take over control of them and supply out of its own limited resources enough money to enable them to carry on. Drastic limitations were imposed on the withdrawal of funds, especially for foreign payments ; and the German banking system came after 1931 to be virtually a part of the State machinery of the Reich.

Nor could the Government stop short in the field of banking ; for, in face of the world crisis and of their heavy capital obligations, the leading rationalised German industries were also getting into more and more serious financial difficulties. The Government was compelled to come to their assistance as well ; so that during the past two years an elaborate system of State control has been extended over many of the greater industrial concerns in Germany, and reorganisation, accompanied by a considerable writing down of capital, has been carried through under the direct auspices of the State. It has often been suggested that this means in effect that Germany has now passed over to a virtual system of Socialism conducted under the auspices of anti-Socialists. But there is in reality the greatest possible difference between a Socialism embarked upon voluntarily by people who believe in it and even the most drastic forms of State control imposed unwillingly in consequence of an extreme emergency by a Government which retains an undiminished faith in the merits of private enterprise.

During this period unemployment was rising sharply, and a large part of the huge plants erected during the previous years was laid idle by the impossibility of finding markets abroad, and by the cessation of constructional activity at home. But it is one of the features of large-scale rationalisation that it is economic only if the great plants can be kept running at full speed, in order to spread the high capital costs involved in them over the largest possible quantity of goods. The highly equipped German economic system was therefore even less well able than less highly rationalised industries in other countries to stand up to the conditions of world depression. In a sense, Germany suffered from being too efficient as a producer ; for her calculations of efficiency had left out of account that flaw in the world economic system which prevents it from finding an assured market for all the goods that it is equipped to produce.

In the meantime, under the terms of the Hoover moratorium, the payment of reparations had been definitely suspended for a year in the spring of 1931, and, as we have seen, this suspension had been followed by a series of Standstill Agreements in respect of Germany's short-term foreign debts, though she had still to find the interest on long-term capital invested in Germany, and especially on the Reconstruction Loans carried through in connection with the Dawes and Young Plans. A moratorium in respect of these long-term borrowings was only declared in the summer of 1933 ; and even then payments on the Dawes Loan of 1924 were maintained intact, and interest, as distinct from sinking fund, payments were kept up on the Young Loan of 1930 as well.

The Young Plan of 1929 had been intended further to modify the claims of the Allies for reparations, and to involve a definite advance on the terms embodied in the Dawes Plan of 1924. But, owing to one fatal omission, the Plan of 1929 actually turned out less favourable to Germany than the continuance of the Dawes Plan would have been ;

for, whereas the Dawes Plan had included a provision for scaling down payments in correspondence to any serious fall in the level of world prices, this clause was excluded from the Young Plan. This omission showed extraordinary lack of foresight, in that, when the Young Plan agreements were made, the world depression and the serious fall in prices which accompanied it were already well on the way. It is doubtful whether Germany could in fact have made, under the conditions of the world depression, any payments at all on account of reparations, however drastically these might have been scaled down, if she had at the same time to maintain payments on her commercial borrowings abroad. But in any event the annuities provided for in the Young Plan were obviously far beyond her ability to pay, either under the circumstances of depression or even in the event of a world recovery, except by the old unreal method of borrowing from the United States what she then transferred to the Allies—for them in turn to transfer the most part of it to the United States in payment of war debts. The Young Plan, even more obviously than the Dawes Plan before it, was bound to break down in the long run ; but it broke down far sooner than most people had expected, because of the rapid onset of the world slump.

These conditions had at least one good result ; they compelled the Allies, years after they ought to have done so, at last to face realistically the reparations question, and to recognise that all hope of collecting any substantial sum in reparations from Germany had totally disappeared. It had been possible to get money out of Germany as long as the Americans were prepared to lend it, but it was not possible for a moment longer. It still took some time after the declaration of the Hoover moratorium for the Allies, and especially the French, to become ready to recognise this truth. But by the middle of 1932, when the Hoover year expired, they had been driven to recognise it ; and the Lausanne settlement of July 1932 was utterly different from any settlement that would have stood a chance of acceptance at any earlier date. For, whereas every previous plan had been based on the continued payment by Germany of large annuities over a long period of years, the Lausanne agreement was based on the new principle of accepting a far smaller sum in final payment of all reparations claims ; and the principle, hitherto maintained even by Great Britain, of endeavouring to collect from Germany enough to meet the instalments due on the Allied debts to the United States was definitely abandoned. Before the Lausanne agreement the aggregate instalments due from Germany under the Young Plan amounted to a capital sum of approximately 25,000 million dollars. The Lausanne payments, even if they were exacted in full, could not amount to more than 2,000 million dollars, while there was to be a complete moratorium on all payments for four years. In fact, few people believed after Lausanne that Germany would ever make any further reparations payments at all ; and although the Allies were not prepared to wipe the slate quite clean, those who signed the settlement must have been conscious that this was for all practical purposes what they were doing. To-day, at any rate, no one expects even the Lausanne payments or any part of them actually to be made. The reparations question was thus at last detached in effect from the settlement of the American debt, although it must of course be borne in mind that the agreement reached at Lausanne was in form only conditional on a satisfactory adjustment of war debt claims with America, and that it has not even to-day been ratified by the Allied Powers.

Germany is a country dependent for her prosperity almost as much as Great Britain on her export trade. Moreover, her exports are even more highly concentrated than those of Great Britain upon a comparatively narrow range of industries. Her textile trades are far less important than Great Britain's in the world market, and her exports of coal are relatively small. She depends to a very high degree upon her ability to export steel, engineering and electrical goods, and the products of the chemical trades. This means that the demand for German exports depends very greatly upon world activity in the constructional industries, although she is also to an important extent a producer of minor metal goods and the cheaper luxury goods purchased by the private consumer. This last class of goods, is, however, one against which in any emergency practically every country is likely to adopt the expedient of high protection ; so that in general the dependence of Germany upon her metal, electrical and chemical trades remains the outstanding factor in her economy from the external point of view. This gives her a tremendous economic interest in a revival of world prosperity ; for there is no chance, despite the great effort which she has made in recent years to reduce her dependence on imports, that she can live of her own at a satisfactory standard of life, or establish a balanced economy based on the exchange within her own markets of industrial and agricultural products. To do this would mean producing foodstuffs at exceedingly high costs in relation to world prices, even if it could be done at all ; and it would involve further a complete reconstruction of her industrial system and the sacrifice of a very large part of her existing capital assets. She has thus economically the strongest possible motives for pursuing a policy designed to restore the freedom of international exchange, or at any rate to give her assured markets in foreign countries and especially in Europe, which is by far the most important market for her exports. At the present time this strong interest which the German economic system possesses in creating conditions favourable to the tranquil development of European industrial activity is overlaid by the aggressive nationalism which has swept across the country as a by-product of economic adversity. But it can hardly fail to reassert itself in the long run, under whatever political rule German affairs may be carried on. Even Nazism, if it remains in power, will be bound to accommodate itself to the requirements of the German economic system, since it will be no more able than any other political authority to stand the cost of maintaining a vast mass of unemployed workers, or to forgo the revenues from a large part of the national industrial plant. It may take some time for these underlying economic forces to assert their predominance ; but, failing a world war, it will be impossible for them to be ignored for any long period.

§ 10. SCANDINAVIA

To THE north-west of Europe, and connected with it only by land bridges, lie the three countries which are commonly grouped together under the name of Scandinavia—Norway, Sweden and Denmark. This grouping is based upon a racial and cultural rather than a geographic similarity ; for the three countries show considerable differences of climate, and whereas Denmark is a small, flat, agricultural land supporting a fairly dense population, Norway, at the other extreme, is large and thinly-populated and so mountainous that the major part of its soil is returned as " totally un-productive." The racial unity is, however, very real. The population of all three countries is descended from the Norse-men mentioned in Part One, with very slight admixture. (The Swedes are probably the ethnically purest stock in Europe ; and the problem of minorities is practically non-existent in Scandinavia, apart from Finland and the German minority in Slesvig.) At various times in the history of Europe the three countries, or two of them, have been united under a single crown ; but since the dissolution in 1905 of the union between Norway and Sweden they have been under separate Governments. Scandinavian rule, following the Norse explorations of the ninth and tenth centuries, at one time extended far beyond Scandinavia proper ; but of this empire all that now survives of any importance is the union of Iceland with Denmark under the Danish Crown, Norway's possession of Spitzbergen in the Arctic Ocean, and the rights of Norway and Denmark on the Continent of Greenland, a dispute about which was finally settled in 1933.

The most interesting fact about the Scandinavian Powers

is their development from an adventurous freebooting past to a present of pacifism, high culture and liberal institutions. To the student of history the names of Denmark, Norway and Sweden call up pictures of Viking raids, of Canute's wide empire, of the Stockholm Blood-bath, and of the conquering expeditions of Gustavus Adolphus and Charles XII ; but the observer of the twentieth century is more likely to think of Ibsen's plays, of Nansen exploring the Arctic or directing famine relief for the victims of the European War, of Danish co-operation and Danish high-schools, or of the electoral law or prison system of Norway. All three countries were neutral during the European War, and it seems in the highest degree improbable that any one of them will ever take part in another. One (Denmark) has even declared for total disarmament, and all three have submitted territorial disputes, not only with one another, to international arbitrament. In their case, and in their case only, it appears that the national vigour which formerly went into maritime and military adventures has been able to turn itself, without being weakened or dissipated, into peaceful pursuits.

Norway. Norway, the northernmost of the three countries, is a long mountainous strip of land running through thirteen degrees of latitude and terminating at its northern end well within the Arctic Circle. In the town of Hammerfest the sun, during the summer months, never sinks below the horizon, and much of Norway, owing to the long twilight, has practically no night at all in summer. Though it is so far north, however, the Gulf Stream, which sweeps close around the coast of Norway, keeps the temperature extraordinarily even, especially as the mountains afford protection from the dry continental cold of Russia. This fact, as well as its natural beauties, has brought to Norway a considerable and growing amount of summer tourist traffic.

The average height of Norway above sea-level is 60 per cent greater than the average height of Europe as a whole.

This is not due to the presence of very high mountains, for the highest peaks are only six thousand feet odd, but to the enormous proportion of mountainous over flat land. This feature is continued into the sea, giving the long fiords and the thick flurry of islands which fringes all the coast. The actual coast-line of Norway, with all the indentations included, is roughly six times the length it appears to be on the map. Hence Norway's enormous fishing industry, and her large mercantile marine. The mountain slopes also give rise to many rivers of great speed, which are or will be available for hydro-electric power. It is calculated that there are about twelve millions of horse-power available from Norwegian rivers, of which ten millions are as yet unexploited. This will in due time go far to make up for Norway's deficiency in coal.

This immense mountain area means, of course, that a great deal of the soil of Norway is uninhabitable and useless for economic purposes. The population is nearly three millions, distributed in the ratio of 22½ per square mile—a density lower than that of any European country but Russia. One town only, Oslo, has over a hundred thousand inhabitants. Only 2.5 per cent of the total land area is arable, 24.2 per cent is wood or forest, and 72 per cent is returned as " totally unproductive." A little grain, mostly oats and barley, is grown in Norway, but the principal agricultural crop is potatoes.

It follows that Norway is a heavily importing country. Nearly all her breadstuffs must come from abroad, and she also requires to import a great deal of coal, of which some comes from Spitzbergen, which is an almost uninhabited territory in the Arctic Ocean belonging to Norway. Other Norwegian imports of considerable size are textile manufactures and vehicles ; her mineral imports are mainly coal, as she has a considerable native output of iron and silver. Great Britain and Germany provide the largest share of imports, with the United States a long way behind. Norway pays for her imports by a large export of timber, wood-pulp and paper, and of fish and fish-products, the latter forming 25 per cent of total exports. The canning industry—principally, of course, the canning of fish—has been going ahead rapidly, as have electro-metallurgical industries of various kinds. Great Britain is the chief buyer of Norwegian goods. Norway has also a large carrying trade, which helps to reduce the apparent adverse balance between imports and exports. The Norwegian mercantile marine is enormous in proportion to the population (over four million tons in 1931) ; and when it is remembered that it suffered tremendously severe losses during the submarine campaigns of the war, the figures are all the more remarkable.

Norway's population is very nearly homogeneous, the main exceptions being about 20,000 Lapps, and a few Finns in the extreme north. 97 per cent of the inhabitants are Lutherans ; but religious toleration is universal except for Jesuits. The general level of literacy is very high, and the penal system remarkable for its humaneness.

Vigorous and important during the early Middle Ages, Norway was subsequently for many centuries the weakest of the three Scandinavian countries. After the Union of Kalmar (1397) had united all three under the Danish Crown, Norway, unlike Sweden, remained in subjection to Denmark until the end of the Napoleonic Wars, when the victorious Allies transferred her to Sweden, in order, partly, to punish Denmark for her attitude during the wars. Reviving Norwegian national feeling, however, found this Union more and more irksome, despite large concessions of self-government ; and in 1905, after a long period of disputes centring mainly around the appointment of diplomatic and consular representatives, it was annulled. Since then Norway has been a separate sovereign State ; she was neutral during the European War, and has recently made new trading treaties with various countries, including Great Britain.

Norway is a limited hereditary monarchy, with a Parliament, the *Storting*, elected by proportional representation, everyone over 23 having the right to vote. Norway was one of the first countries to grant the franchise to women (1907). The *Storting* is elected as a whole, but when elected divides into two Chambers, one-fourth of the members forming the *Lagting*, and the other three-fourths the *Odelsting*. The two Chambers meet and discuss separately ; but if they disagree twice the *Storting* meets as a whole to settle the issue. There are 150 members of the *Storting*, elected so that the proportion of town to country representatives is two to one. The members are paid, and must be at least thirty years old. The King has a veto, but it can be overridden. Norwegian local government is unusually free from central control.

The present Norwegian Cabinet is Liberal Left, having succeeded a Peasants' Party Cabinet in 1933. As is common in countries with proportional representation, most Norwegian Governments hold office either in coalition or virtual coalition with other parties. The Norwegian Labour Party, however, does not enter into coalitions. It is remarkable in being the only left-wing Socialist party in Europe with any great Parliamentary strength—it is the largest single party in the *Storting*. It is strongly Marxist in its views, and was for some time affiliated to the Third International, from which it broke away in 1923 ; it remains, however revolutionary in aim, and has not linked up with the Second International. In 1927, for a brief while, the Norwegian Labour Party formed a Socialist Government, which, however, was brought down by a financial panic, Mowinckel, the present Premier, taking its place.

Sweden.   Sweden, the largest of the three Scandinavian countries, has a population of 6 millions, almost all Swedes, distributed in the ratio of 35.4 to the square mile. Stockholm, the capital, has nearly half a million inhabitants, and there are three towns with more than a hundred thousand. Sweden has much less mountain area than Norway, and is more continental in climate ; the Russian winds sweep over it from the east, freezing the Baltic in winter and causing considerable variations of temperature on the

Swedish mainland. Sweden has more productive resources than Norway; 9.3 per cent of the land is cultivated, and over half of the whole area is forest, providing enormous resources for the Swedish timber and paper trades. Large, however, as the forest area is, there are indications of exhaustion, and a policy of afforestation has become necessary.

Sweden is not self-sufficing as regards foodstuffs. Much grain has to be imported, though Sweden is fairly well provided as regards animal products, and does, as a matter of fact, export a certain quantity of butter and bacon. About three-quarters of Swedish farmers own their own land ; there are a good number of small farms, though not nearly so many as in Denmark. Just under one-third of the population lives in the country. Besides foodstuffs, Sweden has to import a great deal of coal, as she has only very limited home supplies. Before the war, coal was imported mainly from Great Britain ; but during the war German coal was largely substituted, and this has still been the position up to the present, though the British Trade Agreement of 1933 is designed to restore British coal to the Swedish markets. Textile manufactures also form a large proportion of Swedish imports.

Swedish imports and exports tend on the whole to balance. The two principal groups of exports are timber products and iron. The timber comes from the great forest areas, and is floated down over the 20,000 miles of inland waterways which Sweden possesses ; it is then sold as timber, or wood-pulp, or paper, or matches. The great Swedish Match Combine, made famous recently by the suicide of Ivar Kreuger, is responsible for a very high proportion of Europe's consumption of matches. As to the iron, Swedish iron has been famous for centuries. The northern mines, in the Lapp region, produce some of the richest-bearing ore in the world, and four-fifths of the product is exported. Swedish production of iron and steel has, however, been declining in recent years. For exports as a whole, Great Britain is Sweden's best customer, but Sweden imports more from Germany.

The Swedes, like the Norwegians, were brought under the Danish Crown in 1397 ; but in the sixteenth century, under the leadership of Gustavus Vasa, they freed themselves, partly by means of the massacre that was known as the Stockholm Blood-bath. Thereafter Sweden grew to the position of a great Baltic Power, and played an important part in European politics, particularly during the seventeenth century. Gustavus Adolphus was one of the leading figures in the Thirty Years' War, and at the end of the century Charles XII made an attempt to turn the Baltic into a completely Swedish lake, and invaded Russia. Like other and later invaders of Russia, he failed, and Sweden lost most of her Baltic possessions, though she retained Finland and part of Pomerania until the end of the Napoleonic Wars, when those districts were given to Russia, Sweden receiving Norway in compensation. During the nineteenth century, partly owing to her small population, Sweden declined in importance as a Power. She maintained neutrality during the European War ; but as one of the principal avenues of entry for goods into Germany, she found this position at times difficult, and the Allied countries were upon more than one occasion inclined to be suspicious. Sweden is bounded by Norway on the western, and Finland on the eastern side. The Norwegian boundary presents few difficulties, though provision has to be made for nomadic Lapps, who know and care nothing for national boundaries, but drive their reindeer impartially to and fro ; as regards Finland, the principal dispute, that concerning the Aaland Islands, was settled in 1921 in favour of the Finns.

Sweden, like Norway, is a limited monarchy, administered under a constitution drawn up in 1809 and amended in 1919, when the franchise was given to women. The Lower Chamber of the Parliament or *Riksdag* consists of 230 members elected for four years by all over twenty-three ; the Upper of 150 members of over thirty-five, elected for eight years by the members of the provincial councils. There is a property qualification for members of the Upper Chamber, and elections to both are conducted by proportional representation. If the two Chambers disagree upon a question of finance they hold a joint session at which decision is reached by a majority vote. Much of the business of the *Riksdag* is, however, transacted through standing committees, which have very wide powers of discussion and amendment.

As in Norway, no party holds a clear majority in the *Riksdag*. The largest single party in both Chambers is the Social Democratic Party, founded in the 'eighties of last century and long led by Hjalmar Branting, which upholds a moderate Socialist policy. There have been several Social Democratic Governments since the war, including the present one, which came into office in September 1932. There is also a Right Wing Party, and an Agrarian Party ; but the Swedish Liberals have split on the question of prohibition.

Prohibition and the liquor trade generally is in fact a bitterly debated question in Sweden, where from 1775 a government monopoly of the trade resulted for a time in a great promotion of drinking, especially spirit-drinking. The Swedes had for long an unenviable reputation for drunkenness. This does not, however, appear to affect adversely the health or culture of the population. The death-rate in Sweden is one of the lowest in Europe, and the level of education among the highest. The enormous number of telephones—1 to every 14 of the population, as against 1 to 40 in Great Britain—is perhaps one indication of a certain level of education. Ninety-nine per cent. of the Swedes are Lutherans ; there are therefore no religious, as there are no racial, minorities to cause difficulties.

Denmark.   Denmark consists of the major part of the peninsula jutting out northwards between the Baltic and the North Sea, together with three islands in the Baltic. The Faroe Islands, north of the Orkneys, are part of the Danish possessions, and the King of Denmark is also King of Iceland, which is now an independent State. In 1920, after a plebiscite had been taken, the Danish-speaking part of Slesvig, which had previously been under German rule, was transferred to Denmark. Apart from the Germans in Slesvig, among whom the German Nazis seem at the moment to be trying to stir up unrest, there are no racial minorities in Denmark. The population is three and a half millions, distributed over an area of 16,576 square miles. Copenhagen is the only large town. The established religion of Denmark is Lutheran. A tiny minority (less than 2 per cent) belong to other communions ; but there is complete religious toleration.

The main interest of Denmark is that it has totally changed its character, as a community, during the past hundred years. Other countries have altered in various ways and have gained or lost in importance ; but Denmark has completely changed. Medieval Denmark was a powerful, fighting, feudal monarchy. In the tenth century Sweyn conquered for his son Canute a vast maritime empire stretching from England to the borders of Poland. This fell to pieces ; but again in 1397, by the Union of Kalmar, Denmark, Norway and Sweden were united under a Danish king, and Denmark was an important Baltic Power for many centuries. In the Napoleonic Wars, Denmark, though officially neutral, was in fact sympathetic to Napoleon ; and Great Britain, fearing lest the Danish fleet should be used against her, demanded its surrender and bombarded Copenhagen. At the Peace of Paris, Denmark was punished by the removal of Norway, which was placed under the Swedish Crown. Thereafter Denmark became less and less important as a European Power. In 1866, after a useless attempt to resist, she was forced to acquiesce in the Prussian occupation of Slesvig-Holstein, though the Powers at the same time agreed to guarantee Danish territory and the Danish Crown. A liberal constitution had been granted in 1849 ; but this had been seriously modified in the direction of giving more power to the landowners, and there was a great deal of unrest.

The great economic change came when the Danish

farmer took to co-operation, in order both to reduce the power of the landlords and middlemen, and to build up Danish agriculture on a new basis so that it should not be ruined by American cereal production.

The first co-operative dairy was started in Jutland in 1882 ; but political and economic education of the Danish people had begun long before, mainly owing to Bishop Grundtvig and his programme of People's High Schools, of which the first was founded as early as 1844. The Danish peasant was thus far better equipped than the average European agricultural producer for understanding the economic purpose of co-operation and for putting it into force.

Danish co-operation, once started, went ahead rapidly. Co-operative dairies are fast ousting the remaining private dairies ; and co-operative societies and dairies have been followed by co-operative factories for pig products and co-operative egg societies. The result of this is that Danish exports of these goods have enormously increased, while at the same time the adoption of intensified methods of production and co-operative purchase have greatly increased the yield of arable land. Denmark, however, though an agricultural country, is not completely self-supporting as regards food ; a considerable quantity of cereals is imported. It should be noted, of course, that Danish agriculture is based upon highly intensive cultivation and stall-fed animals.

Side by side with the growth of co-operative association has gone the division of the land among the people, much speeded up by a law of 1919. There are now hardly any large estates in Denmark ; the land is divided up into small farms (many of them the tiniest possible patches of ground). Tenancy is rapidly disappearing ; nearly 90 per cent of the land is owned outright. Denmark is the only State which has succeeded in making a society of peasant farmers effectively self-governing. This is partly due to the wide understanding and appreciation of the principles underlying voluntary co-operation, and partly to the very high level of education. Elementary education has been compulsory since 1814 ; but the chief feature of the Danish educational system is the " People's High Schools," institutions for the continued education of adults, which are privately run, though in receipt of grant from State funds. These High Schools, together with the many agricultural schools and other institutions—in fact the Danish system of education as a whole—have attracted the interest and admiration of educationalists all over the world.

Denmark is mainly an agricultural country, only about 400,000 persons being employed in shops and factories. Her exports of animal products—butter, cheese, bacon and eggs—enormously exceed all her other exports put together. She imports her other requirements, principally textile goods, coal (of which she has none), metal goods and machinery, and some cereals. There is a mercantile marine of considerable size.

Denmark exports to Great Britain far more than to any other country ; for Danish agriculture has been built up largely for the supply of the British market, above all with dairy produce and bacon. Especially for the latter there is no possible alternative market for exports on anything like the present scale ; for Great Britain is the only really large importer of pig-products in Europe. Accordingly, Denmark is in keen competition with the British Dominions, and especially with New Zealand, in the British market. She went off the gold standard with Great Britain in 1931 ; and when, after the threat to her exports arising out of the Ottawa agreements, New Zealand proceeded to a further devaluation of her currency in order to bring it down to the same value as that of Australia, Denmark was compelled to follow suit with a corresponding further devaluation of the Danish kröne.

Hitherto, Denmark has drawn the largest part of her exports from Germany ; but the new trade agreement negotiated with Great Britain in 1933 is designed, like the similar agreements with the other Scandinavian countries, to increase the proportion of imports—especially coal—

derived from Great Britain ; for Denmark cannot afford to risk her position in the British market by refusing concessions to the British exporters.

The increase in the number of small farmers for many years caused political difficulties, owing to the weight of landowners in the Government ; and the constitution was revised in 1915. Under the present constitution Denmark is a limited monarchy, in which the king appoints the ministers, but cannot make war or peace without the consent of the *Riksdag*. The *Riksdag* is divided into two Chambers, the *Folketing* of 149 members elected by all men and women over twenty-five on the system of proportional representation, and the *Landsting* of 78 members, 56 elected by *Folketing* voters of over thirty-five through electoral colleges, and 19 by the pre-1915 *Landsting*. If the two Chambers disagree and the *Folketing* persists in its views after a fresh election, the *Landsting* may be dissolved. The King's consent to a law is necessary. The largest party in the *Folketing* are the Social Democrats, who represent the town workers, the few agricultural labourers and the smaller peasants ; the present government was formed in 1929 by a coalition of the Social Democrats with the Radical Liberal Party.

Denmark entered the League of Nations, and in 1932 decided to disarm herself entirely.

§ 11. BELGIUM AND HOLLAND

BETWEEN France and Germany, on the north coast of the European Continent, lie the Low Countries, Holland and Belgium, which have the distinction of being the most fought-over area in Europe. Not only does the southern part of this area lie, as students of history have again and again to notice, right athwart the path of any landward expansion of the two great neighbouring Powers ; the Low Countries also contain the mouths of some of the most important rivers of Western Europe. Both of these facts have made for war. Of the famous battlefields of European history, a great many, of which Bouvines, Courtrai, Blenheim, Neerwinden, Waterloo and Ypres may serve as examples, lie on Belgian soil, and the question of the navigation of the Scheldt has troubled Europe almost as much as the question of Alsace-Lorraine.

In the Middle Ages the Low Countries were linked together, but the wars of religion drove them sharply apart, the northern portion achieving independence, while the southern remained under the domination of one or other larger Power until well on in the nineteenth century. For a brief period after the Napoleonic Wars, Belgium was placed under a Dutch king ; but this proved one of the least stable parts of that unstable settlement, and was reversed in 1830–31, since when both countries have been independent States. Both are thickly populated and highly developed, Belgium industrially, Holland more on agricultural lines ; both are too small and too vulnerable by land to be great European Powers ; and both have large colonial possessions, though the great days of Dutch colonial empire are past.

Belgium.   Belgium is the most crowded country in Europe. Its population of 8 millions is distributed in the ratio of 688 to the square mile ; but this general figure minimises the actual density, as the western provinces are comparatively empty, whereas in Brabant, for example, the density rises to 1,325 per square mile. Nor is this due to the existence of enormous towns. Brussels has 850,000 inhabitants, and Antwerp just under 300,000 ; but there are only two other towns with over 100,000. It is the great cluster of smaller towns and hamlets which accounts for the bulk of the population.

As might be expected from the foregoing, Belgium is primarily an industrial country, in fact, one of the oldest industrial countries in Europe. The coal of the Liège region was known in the late Middle Ages, and the iron and steel industry was developing by the end of the eighteenth century ; Napoleon I made great use of Belgium (then in

French hands) as an arsenal for his continental wars, and since that date her industrial development has gone steadily ahead. The most important Belgian products at the present time are coal and iron and steel ; but she also produces zinc, lead, glass and textiles in large quantities, and is one of the main centres of the diamond industry. Being so highly industrialised, she is naturally not self-sufficient in the matter of food production. Over one-half of the land is cultivated (18 per cent is forest), of which 40 per cent is under cereal, and 40 per cent under forage crops ; but under half a million are employed in agriculture, as against over two million in industry and commerce. The main crops are potatoes and sugar-beet, though some wheat and rye are also grown : imports of wheat are very large, and there is also some import of maize and barley. In general, Belgian exports (mainly of manufactured goods, especially steel) tend more or less to balance her imports ; Great Britain is her best customer, and France the chief source of her imports.[1]

Belgium, not altogether through her own fault, has had a chequered and violent history. In the sixteenth century the area of modern Belgium came, along with Holland, into the possession of the Hapsburg Emperor Maximilian, and so to his grandson, Philip II of Spain. The Belgian provinces joined in the revolt against Philip ; but their alliance with the United Provinces—modern Holland—was always uneasy. They were Catholic, and unsympathetic to the Calvinism of the Dutch ; and they eventually broke away, and after the fall of Antwerp in 1585, returned to the yoke of Spain, where they remained, much fought-over in Marlborough's wars, until in 1713 they were handed over to the

[1] The Grand Duchy of Luxembourg, with its population of 300,000, was before the war included in the German Customs Union. In 1919, given the choice between entering the French or the Belgium customs system, it chose the latter ; and Belgium and Luxembourg now form a single customs area. Luxembourg is important industrially as a producer of iron ore, of which it had in 1929 an output of seven and a half million metric tons, and of steel, of which it produces from two to three million tons a year. About a third of the population is engaged in agriculture.

Austrian Hapsburgs. Some measure of autonomy had been secured for Belgium both under Spain and under Austria ; but towards the end of the eighteenth century this was attacked, and there were Belgian revolts against Austria at the time of the French Revolution.

The immediate result of the Revolution was the " freeing " of Belgium, which from 1795 onwards was made part of France, and provided, not entirely to her satisfaction, with French revolutionary institutions ; after the downfall of Napoleon she was removed from France and put under the King of Holland, from whom she successfully revolted in 1830, choosing as King Leopold of Saxe-Coburg. The success of the Belgian revolt was due largely to the friendly attitude of France and England ; but the international status of Belgium was not cleared up until 1839, when by the Treaty of London the principal European Powers guaranteed the inviolability of her territory in time of war. This Treaty was the " scrap of paper " torn up by Germany in 1914. Since the European War, the principal object of Belgium has been to find other means of safeguarding her territory, and her attitude towards international problems and affairs has been governed by this one aim.

By the Versailles Treaty Belgium gained, as well as a populous mandated portion of German East Africa, Ruanda-Urundi, a small area on the German frontier consisting of Malmedy, Eupen, and Moresnet, and containing about 64,000 people. She is not, however, entirely satisfied with her territorial boundaries, particularly as regards the Dutch frontier. She would very much like to possess southern Limburg, and still more the whole of the south bank of the Scheldt, for she regards the Dutch control there as giving the Dutch port of Rotterdam an unfair advantage over Antwerp. More important, however, is Belgium's own internal problem of nationalities.

This cannot be called a problem of minorities, for the Flemings at least equal the French Belgians in numbers, though they are not nearly so influential. The French ascendancy dates mainly from the French revolutionary occupation ; and during the nineteenth century French was the dominant language, and the French-speaking Belgians held all the important posts. The racial difference is only in part a difference of religion ; both sides are Catholic, but the Flemings tend to belong to the old or conservative Catholic tradition. It is, however, partly a class difference ; the Flemings are mainly working-class and "small men." There was great unrest among the Flemings before the war ; and during the war, when the Belgian Government had moved to Havre, a section of the Flemings under Dr. Borms (called " Activists ") planned to establish a Flemish Belgium with German aid. This movement was supposed to have died down after the war ; but it revived, and in 1928 a bye-election returned Dr. Borms, then in prison, with an enormous majority, and rendered necessary the " flamandisation " of the University of Ghent, and some further concessions. The situation, however, is as yet unresolved; the Flemish separatist party (now called the " Front Party ") has 11 seats in the House of Representatives, and 5 in the Senate.

Belgium is a monarchy, with universal voting since 1893, Flemings having been admitted to the franchise in 1898. Women vote in the communal elections, but for the House of Representatives only if they are war-widows or lost sons during the war. The Lower Chamber, the House of Representatives, is elected for four years under P.R., and voting is compulsory ; of the Upper House or Senate, one-third is elected from persons over forty, one-third chosen by the provinces, while one-third is composed of distinguished persons selected by the Senate. From 1884 until the end of the war the Catholic Party was almost continually in the ascendant ; but since then other parties have grown to strength, and the present Government, which took office in 1932, is a Liberal-Catholic coalition. The Belgian Labour Party, which is one of the most moderate Labour Parties in Europe, was revived in the 'eighties. Trade Unionism is strong in Belgium ; the three divisions of the working-class movement—Trade Unionism, Socialism, and Co-operation—are there more closely united than in any other European country but Russia, and Belgium has provided many officials for the various Internationals.

The great overseas possession of Belgium is the Belgian Congo. This, after providing a world scandal of native exploitation in the 'eighties, has been drastically reformed, and is now as good as, if not better than, any European tropical administration.

Holland.   Holland is almost, though not quite, as thickly populated as Belgium. Her population is just under 8 millions, and the density 625.5 per square mile. But a large part of Holland consists of water, and the greatest density is in the provinces of North and South Holland, which, with Zeeland, formed the core of the Dutch State in its early days. The death-rate is low and the birth-rate high, so that the population is rapidly increasing.

The area, and particularly the cultivable area, of Holland, has varied at different dates, according to the encroachment of the sea and the Dutch defences against it. In the Middle Ages, for example, there were great inundations, some of which created the Zuider Zee, and greatly reduced the total area. In modern times, however, there has been much reclamation. The *polder*, or patch of land reclaimed from the sea and then drained so as to make it cultivable, is a characteristic feature of Dutch agriculture, and the largest reclamation scheme in the world—that which proposes to drain a great part of the Zuider Zee—was begun in 1924, and has already advanced some distance. Much of Holland, however, is only protected from inundation by dykes, which can still be cut as they were in the sixteenth century, to check an invader. Holland still relies less on fortresses, of which she has few, than on the help of the sea to defend her.

Rather more than half the population of Holland live in the country. The largest town is Amsterdam, with three-quarters of a million inhabitants ; then come Rotterdam and the Hague, with half a million each. 28 per cent of the land is arable, and 40 per cent is grass and pasture. Holland has very little forest area. Over half the farms are freehold, and nearly all of them small or medium-sized ; there are, however, some large estates in Holland, Zeeland and Gröningen. The production per cultivated acre is remarkably high. As everyone knows, animal products, particularly cheese, butter and eggs, form the chief item in Holland's agricultural production ; she does, however, grow some cereals, of which rye is the chief, and has a large crop of sugar-beet and potatoes. (One-fourth of the potato crop is used for industrial purposes.)

Holland was comparatively slow in taking to industry, the lack of sufficient coal supplies being a handicap. She has now, however, a fair-sized industry, employing in 1920 a million out of a total of $2\frac{3}{4}$ million occupied persons. The textile trades, a large part of whose product is exported, are the most important ; tobacco is manufactured as well, and Holland is also the chief centre of the diamond-cutting industry. But, of course, the great strength of Holland lies, as it has always lain, not in her native industries, but in her commerce. The Dutch carrying trade is not now, as in the seventeenth century, *the* great carrying trade of the world ; but it is still very important. The Dutch mercantile marine was estimated, in 1932, at 4 per cent of the world's total tonnage. In particular, an enormous transit trade with Germany passes through Dutch ports—which fact very seriously disorganised the Dutch economic system during the European war. This carrying trade is the chief factor in balancing Holland's imports and exports ; as regards specific items, she imports wheat, coal and timber in large quantities, and also a certain amount of cattle food such as maize and linseed. She exports a certain quantity of textiles ; but her main standby for exports is animal products of all sorts. (The trade in bulbs, though an interesting item, is of small value in comparison.) The bulk of Dutch trade is done with Germany, but Great Britain eats a large quantity of her butter and cheese.

Holland, as a country, dates from the sixteenth century,

when the fierce Calvinism of the maritime provinces, led, for a time, by William the Silent of Orange, and secretly supported by Elizabeth, held out against all the forces which Spanish fanaticism could bring to bear. Independence of Spain was finally achieved in 1609, and thereafter Holland was a leading Power, in both Europe and the world, for nearly a century. The costs of political strife on the Continent, however, particularly with Louis XIV, proved too heavy for this small country to sustain, even after William III's accession to the English throne had secured her English aid ; and the eighteenth century proved a period of economic decline, aided by political instability in the home government. Many of the Dutch overseas possessions, particularly in the New World and in Africa, were lost ; but she kept the great Malay territories which she had conquered from Portugal in the preceding century. The Dutch East Indies still form a tropical empire many times the size of Holland.

The French Revolution overran Holland as it did Belgium. The Scheldt was opened to navigation in 1792, and from 1795–98 there was a Batavian Republic built on the French model, though the battle of Camperdown (1797) indicated that Holland might not be so easy to hold as Belgium. At the end of the war William I was raised by the Allies to the dignity of King of the Netherlands ; but he had to acquiesce, with what grace he could, in the subsequent revolt of Belgium. Since then, Holland has kept clear of continental entanglements, and she remained neutral, though not without considerable inconvenience, in the European war.

The present constitution of Holland really dates from 1848 ; it was revised in 1917 so as to include universal suffrage. The States-General consists of two Houses, of which the Lower consists of a hundred members elected *en bloc* every four years by proportional representation, and the Upper of fifty members elected by the provinces for six years, half at a time. The eleven provinces have each an assembly of their own, which meets twice annually, a

permanent paid council of administration, and a commissioner appointed by the Crown. There are also communal councils ; but the mayor, who is appointed by the
Crown, controls the communal police, and can, if he
chooses, suspend the sittings of the commune.

There are no racial minorities in Holland. There is
religious toleration ; but there are also religious difficulties.
The Dutch Reformed Church, which is Calvinist and
directly descended from those Reformers who made the
Dutch Republic, represents, to many people's minds, the
religion of the Dutch. Actually it is almost equalled in
numbers by the members of the Roman Catholic Communion, and other Protestant Churches account for half
as many more. There are 115,000 Jews. All these creeds
receive subventions from the national budget according to
their importance ; but their existence confuses political and
economic groupings. The Dutch Trade Union movement,
for example, has long been divided between Christian
(i.e. Catholic) Trade Unions and others ; and the same can
be said, to a certain extent, of political parties. The present
Government, which has held office since 1929, is a coalition of the Catholics with the Right.

§ 12. FRANCE

FRANCE, the traditional home of revolutionary movements since 1789, now seems by contrast the most stably
organised of all the nations of Continental Europe. From
1789 to 1871 France ran the entire gamut of revolutionary
activities, and passed under almost every conceivable kind
of government. Reorganised as a democratic State in
accordance with the principle *des droits de l'homme et du
citoyen* in the years immediately after the revolution of 1789,
she passed over rapidly to Napoleon's military dictatorship,
itself an outstanding revolutionary force in its effects over
the entire Continent of Europe. Then came the Bourbon

restoration of 1815, passing into a more extreme form in the despotism of Charles X. This provoked in turn the revolution of 1830, and the experiment with *bourgeois* monarchy under Louis Philippe. But the *bourgeois* monarch tried to be a monarch as well as a *bourgeois*, and his reign ended with the Radical Revolution of the Year of Revolutions, 1848. The revolutionaries of 1848 were, however, sharply divided in mind and temper. The attempt to turn the 1848 Revolution into a Socialist revolution was crushed in blood, as the Paris and Lyons Socialist risings of 1832 had been at an earlier stage. The uncertainty of the Republican forces gave Napoleon III his opportunity for the *coup d'état* of 1851 and the establishment of the Second Empire. But Napoleon III's Empire went down in ignominious defeat at the hands of Prussia in 1870, and the Third Republic was proclaimed while the Prussian armies were investing Paris. This, however, was not the end ; for the Paris population, given arms in order to resist the Prussians and full of resentment at the ignominious peace, rose and proclaimed the Commune, and thus set up for its short life of a couple of months the first Socialist Government in Europe. The suppression of the Commune of 1871 by Thiers and his mixed following of monarchists and *bourgeois* republicans was even bloodier than that of the Socialist risings of the years 1832 and 1848 ; and, when the monarchist majority accepted the Third Republic in default of a possible candidate for the throne, few supposed that France had settled down to a lasting régime of republican democracy. Nevertheless, the Paris Commune has been, up to the present time, the last French Revolution, and there was less sign in France than in any other European country of a revolutionary temper on the morrow of the Great War. Even to-day, while the French Socialists form a powerful party and French Communism has a considerable following, the *bourgeois* Republic seems more stable in its structure than any other Continental State, and Socialism seems less likely in France than in Great Britain.

France is the outstanding example among European countries of a balanced economy. Among her 41½ million people there is a great diversity of economic activity. Large-scale industries of the most modern kind are to be found within her borders, side by side with a very widespread system of industrial production on a small scale. Industry, large and small, is neatly balanced with agriculture, so as to make the French national economy as a whole relatively self-sufficient—not mainly as a result of artificial measures, but as the outcome of a fairly natural process of growth. Of the occupied population about 50 per cent are engaged in industry and commerce and about 40 per cent in agriculture. France is thus appreciably less industrialised than the other great nations of Western Europe, Great Britain and Germany. Indeed she is industrialised only to about the same extent as Czechoslovakia and the Scandinavian countries, though of course far more than Italy or the countries of Eastern Europe. This balanced character of her economy exerts a profound influence upon her social and political life ; for it means that public opinion in France is also neatly balanced between industrial and agricultural claims. Moreover, the strength and persistence of small-scale industry mean that France's industrialists do not speak with the same voice to anything like the same extent as the industrialists of Great Britain and Germany. There is a divergence of interest and point of view, not only between the agriculturists and industrialists, but also between the representatives of large- and small-scale industry. The *Comité des Forges*, the leading representative of large-scale industrialism in France, has by no means the same attitude as the great mass of small industrial producers scattered all over the country. Moreover, France is a country far more of small towns, near neighbours to the countryside, than of great industrial cities. Paris, with not far short of 3 million inhabitants, is the only really great city ; next to it come Marseilles, with no more than 650,000, and Lyons, with not much more than half a million ; and then there is a considerable gap, the next largest cities being Bordeaux, with a quarter of a million, and Lille, with 200,000 inhabitants. Thus the urban population of France largely retains the characteristic qualities of the small town, and actually as much as half the total population of the country lives not in towns at all but in the rural areas. There is, moreover, in all the towns of France, both large and small, a very considerable *rentier* class, living on small savings at a standard of expenditure very low in relation to that of the British or American middle classes ; and this large class of small capitalists exerts a profound influence on the entire structure of the French political and social system. French politics and French economic policy are bound to reflect this diversity in the population. It is out of the question for France either in economics or in politics to pursue a policy which will outrage the feelings either of the great mass of peasants or of the large bodies of small town dwellers dependent mainly upon small-scale industry and commerce or upon small savings. The great industrialists may be successful in pressing their claims beyond what their relative importance in the national economy would justify ; but there is a point beyond which no French Government can venture to follow them. France is thus, in the modern sense, a far less capitalistic State than either Germany or Great Britain ; and her political system possesses a high degree of stability based on the conservative attitude of the *petite bourgeoisie* in both economic and social questions.

Of those who get their living by the land, the majority own the land which they cultivate or belong at any rate to a land-owning family. The Revolution of 1789 established the class of peasant owners far more firmly in France than it is established in any other great European country. Among those on the land the number of owners greatly exceeds that of agricultural wage-workers, in the proportion of rather more than 5 to 3. Among the agricultural owners and also among the land workers there is a very high proportion of women, partly as a result of the heavy casualties sustained by France during the war, and also partly as a result of the system of land holding and the large measure of recognition accorded to women in the economic though not in the political sphere. Small land holdings are naturally the rule, and there are few big estates left. Strip holdings, scattered over the area of the village land, remain widespread ; and there has been no complete consolidation such as occurred in Great Britain with the disappearance of the peasantry. Agricultural co-operation is strong, and encouraged by the State, which, in 1920, co-ordinated the movement through the formation of a national fund for agricultural credit. This fund is worked through ninety regional agricultural banks and about 5,500 local agricultural banks. Cultivation reaches a high standard, and both agricultural operations and village and small town industries have been greatly helped in recent years by the rapid development of rural electrification. Agricultural progress has also been advanced by the acquisition under the Versailles Treaty of the important potash deposits of Alsace-Lorraine.

Until the coming of the world depression France was short of labour for both agriculture and industry, and there had been during the post-war years a considerable importation of workers from abroad. Thus, until recently there were in France over 800,000 Italians, half a million Belgians, over 400,000 Spaniards, about 350,000 Poles, 140,000 Swiss, and about 90,000 Russians, to say nothing of an appreciable number of labourers imported from North Africa. The shortage of labour arose mainly from the very low rate of increase of the French population. The French birth-rate is one of the lowest in Europe after that of Sweden—about 18 per thousand on the average of recent years as against a death-rate averaging about 17. Such increase as has taken place in the population of late years is therefore mainly the product of immigration. Alsace-Lorraine added about 1,700,000 in 1919 ; but even so the population of France in 1921 was slightly lower, on account of war casualties, than it had been before the war, when it stood at about 39 millions. By 1926 it had reached $40\frac{3}{4}$ millions, and by 1932 about $41\frac{1}{2}$ millions. But there has probably been some fall since then, for the economic depression resulted in a certain amount of repatriation of alien workers ; indeed, by dispensing with some of her imported labour, France was able to get through the earlier stages of the depression without any substantial rise in unemployment, thus transferring the burden of maintaining the displaced workers to their countries of origin.

The re-annexation of Alsace-Lorraine brought to France, in addition to the potash deposits mentioned already, the valuable iron deposits which had provided the basis for a large section of the German steel industry, an appreciable amount of coal, and also a considerable cotton-spinning industry. Alsace-Lorraine added 2½ per cent to the territory and 4 per cent to the population of France, for it is more densely populated than pre-war France taken as a whole. But the re-annexation also brought with it a political problem ; for the attempt to assimilate the government of Alsace-Lorraine wholly to that of France involved opposition from a substantial proportion of the population, and this has more than once given rise to serious troubles, especially those of 1928 which led to the arrest and imprisonment of a number of autonomist leaders. Economically the annexation strengthens the position of large-scale industrialism in France, for the iron and steel works and coal mines taken over from Germany were organised on a basis of large-scale capitalism. France, through the possession of Alsace-Lorraine, advanced to the position of one of the most important European steel producers, and many people predicted in 1919 that there would be a speedy shift over to large-scale industrialism over the country as a whole. But the French economic system, with its tendency to concentrate on supplying local markets or on the production of luxury goods for the world market, has proved strongly resistant to change. French industry depends very greatly on quality and artistic finish in the products which it sells in world markets, and these are more easily secured under a system of small-scale production than within a more rationalised capitalist structure.

In agriculture France meets most of her own needs, but has very little surplus of any important commodity for export. Even in the case of wine, which most people think of as predominantly a French export, the quantities imported are actually ten times as great as those exported from the French vineyards. Imported wine comes, however, largely from Algeria, which forms virtually part of the French productive system. The chief agricultural imports are wheat and maize, and there is also some importation of sugar. For though France grows both wheat and sugar-beet on a large scale—indeed these form, together with oats, her principal crops—she needs to import in most years a considerable quantity of both commodities in order to meet the needs of domestic consumption. In 1931 the imports on which France spent most were first of all coal and coke, secondly cereals, mainly wheat, and third, only a little way behind cereals, wine, whereas her most important exports were chemical products, iron and steel, and silk and cotton textiles, in that order. She was thus mainly an exporter of manufactured goods, and an importer of certain foodstuffs, and of one vital raw material, coal.

In industrial production she is handicapped by her deficiency of coal, despite her accessions in Alsace-Lorraine and her rights since the war over the output of the Saar coalfield. This deficiency makes her important as a market for British coal, and there has been in recent years sharp rivalry between the British, German, Polish and Belgian coal mines in meeting the French demand, complicated at one time by the imposition of special duties on British coal to offset the depreciation of the pound. But although shortage of coal handicaps France industrially, especially in the iron and steel trades, she has done a great deal to make up for her shortage of mineral fuel by the development of electricity based on water power. There has been a rapid increase in the total output of electrical energy in recent years, and nearly a third of the present output is hydro-electric. Electricity supplies to an increasing extent the source of power for the small industries remote from the great northern industrial area round Lille and the Lorraine iron fields.

After chemicals and iron and steel, the two industries for which the acquisition of Alsace-Lorraine has been most important, France depends largely on her textile trades. Her silk goods easily lead the way in the markets of the world, though she is to an increasing extent in competition in this field not only with the cheaper silk goods of Japan, but also with rayon products made in Italy, Germany and Great Britain, and there has been a very sharp fall in her exports of silks during the past two or three years. In the cotton trade, which is only less important than that of silk, she is also largely engaged in quality production, specialising in fancy cotton goods with marketable qualities of artistic design. She also exports clothing on a very large scale, again concentrating mainly upon quality products ; but this trade has suffered even more seriously than any of the others in consequence of the world depression, the export of clothing falling in value from 1,662 million francs in 1930 to 691 millions in 1931. Her production and export of automobiles are also large, and next to them, and to the high quality wines which she sends abroad, comes in her list of exports the trade in soaps and perfumes. Thus the French export trade depends to a very great extent on the demand for luxury goods, and is therefore especially liable to feel the effects of world depression. It is in these circumstances remarkable that France was actually longer in feeling the consequences of the slump than any other leading country. Certain of her most important exports did indeed fall off sharply, creating a considerable amount of local unemployment ; but France's dependence on the world market is on the whole so much less than that of either Germany or Great Britain that she was able to stand up to the loss of a large part of these markets with relatively little disturbance to her economic system, especially as she had abundant resources of money abroad to meet all necessary claims for the purchase of imports. Only as world depression deepened in 1932 did unemployment in France assume really large dimensions ; and even then the comparative smallness of the scale of industry and the comparative nearness of the French population to the land made the amount of suffering involved appreciably less than it would have been in similar circumstances in other industrial countries. For France, unlike Great Britain and Germany, has no system of unemployment insurance, the relief of the unemployed being left to local effort. This has undoubtedly meant that the individual worker who falls out of a job and is not able to go back to his family in the village has suffered more seriously than the unemployed workers in countries where insurance systems exist. But some counterpoise to the advance of unemployment in France was made by the expenditure of considerable sums by the State upon the national programme of economic development laid down in 1926, when, the reconstruction of the devastated areas having been more or less completed, the French Government embarked on a large plan of loan expenditure especially in the field of electrical development for the expansion of the national productive resources. France has not been able in the long run to escape the consequences of the world slump, particularly since growing budgetary difficulties and the exhaustion of the available credits have caused a slowing down in public expenditure on works of development ; but even now her position is less vulnerable than that of other countries because of the strength of her financial situation—though not of her public finance—and the comparatively balanced nature of her national economy.

It was suggested earlier that this balanced national economy was to a great extent natural, and not merely the result of artificial measures ; but it has of course been deliberately preserved by national policy. France is a country with a high tariff on those classes of imports most likely to compete with her domestic industries ; and she has also, at the cost of keeping the price of wheat far above the world level, imposed a stiff system of protection in the interests of her agricultural producers. What is meant, then, by suggesting that the balanced economy which exists in France is natural rather than artificial is not that it would have been able to survive in the absence of a State policy designed to support it, but only that State policy has needed only to maintain an existing balance and not to set up one which had been previously overthrown.

The French tariff system differs from those of other countries in being based far more upon discrimination between products according to their place of origin. The post-war system of tariffs in France has been built up largely not by Parliamentary enactment, but by separate commercial treaties with different countries, made under a general authority conferred upon the executive Government. France negotiates with each country a separate trade treaty laying down the terms on which its imports are to be admitted into the French market; and this results in the existence for many products of a number of distinct rates of duty applying to goods consigned from different countries. The French tariff system also embodies a schedule of general rates of duty applicable in the absence of special treaty arrangements; but these general rates apply in practice only to a fraction of the total imports. It is thus very difficult to measure accurately the height of the French tariff, or to compare it with those in force in other countries. What can be done by way of general measurement will be found set out in a later section of this book.

Politics and Finance.   France since 1918 has had an exceedingly chequered financial history. The war was financed almost exclusively by means of loans without any substantial increase in the level of taxation, which would indeed have been difficult to achieve in view of the grave disturbance to the national economy caused by the foreign occupation of some of the most important industrial districts, and by the calling up of a very high proportion of the able-bodied workers for military service. After the war this process of borrowing continued, and a large part of the French debt to the United States was incurred after 1918.

Since then taxes have been raised to a substantially higher level ; but each increase in the level of taxation has involved acute political controversy, and there is still a very marked reluctance on the part of French Governments to incur the odium of increasing the taxes, and on the part of the French taxpayers to meet the tax-gatherers' demands. Tax evasion has been reduced appreciably by stiffening up the methods of collection in recent years ; but it still goes on to a substantial extent, especially in the case of the tax on incomes, which is exceedingly unpopular with the French tax-paying classes. Largely for this reason, the French raise a high proportion of their total tax revenue in indirect taxation. Thus in recent years, whereas more than half the total tax revenue of Great Britain has been drawn from direct taxation, or as much as 60 per cent if taxes on inheritance are included, France has drawn until quite recently only about one-fifth of her revenue from income tax, and not much more than a third from all direct taxes, including the tax on inheritance, as against 50 per cent from the customs, excise, and business turnover taxes, and a further 14 per cent from registration and stamp duties and similar imposts. Despite the increase in taxation in recent years, the French budget is still by no means balanced. The Daladier Government has recently done what it dares by way of raising taxes and increasing the stringency of collection ; but even so it has been compelled to budget for a substantial deficit in the current year, even after suspending the Sinking Fund on the National Debt.

The French financial situation thus presents the paradox of an inability of the Government to make both ends meet, combined with a very high degree of national strength in the financial sphere. The coffers of the Bank of France are filled to overflowing with gold : and it is hard for the depositors' money to earn a tolerable rate of interest. Money is so plentiful in relation to the opportunities for its use that it seems absurd to suggest that France is unable to meet her debts to the United States. But the idle resources of the Bank of France and the other

banks belong not to the French Government, but to
the French public, and to some extent to foreign depositors ;
and no means has yet been found of extracting them for the
service of the State. For it must be remembered that, despite this appearance of wealth, France taken as a whole remains a poor country in comparison with either Great
Britain or the United States ; and the ability of the great
mass of her people to bear taxation is far lower than the
corresponding ability in these countries. In relation to the
average national income France is already highly taxed,
and it is not easy to tap the surplus wealth which does undoubtedly exist in the hands of a very limited class.

It is the more difficult to place French public finance on a
satisfactory footing because of the experiences through which
the very powerful class of small property owners has passed
since 1914. In the years immediately following the war the
French franc underwent a process of rapid depreciation,
never of course pushed to anything like the same extremes
as the depreciation of the German mark even before the
Ruhr occupation, but sufficient to reduce the gold value of
French money to less than one-fifth of what it had been
before the war, and its purchasing power to an even greater
extent. French wholesale prices stood in 1926 at more than
seven times the pre-war level, and even the cost of living
had risen to more than five times what it was in 1914. When
stabilisation of the franc was at last achieved by the Poincaré Government in 1926–27, the new gold value given to it
was only one-fifth of the pre-war parity, so that in terms of
gold pre-war holders of monetary claims found the value of
their property scaled down by four-fifths. Even at the end of
1932 French wholesale prices were still more than four times
as high as before the war, and French retail prices more than
five times as high, the higher level of retail prices being
largely accounted for by the protection accorded to French
agriculture.

This confiscation of a large part of the pre-war savings
of the French public, including the large body of small
rentiers, has engendered an exceedingly strong suspicion in

France of any policy likely to lead to further depreciation of the value of money. The French public has been prepared to endorse measures of protection designed in the interests of French industry and agriculture, even where these have resulted in some rise in internal prices ; but there has been acute suspicion of any attempt to bring about a concerted rise in the general level of prices throughout the world, on the ground that this might result in a further depreciation in the value of French savings. This has caused the Bank of France and successive French Governments to adopt for the most part a policy of opposition to projects for relieving the world from its present difficulties by any measures partaking of the nature of inflation, though they have been prepared to collaborate in measures, such as those projected at the Stresa Conference, for raising the prices of particular products in the interests of the distressed agricultural countries. For the adoption of the Stresa recommendations for raising the price of wheat would only bring the world price nearer to the price already ruling inside France, and would thus not add to the cost of living of the French people. This whole question of the raising of prices is discussed in a later section, and need not be further developed here.

One marked effect of the experience of inflation during the years between 1918 and 1926 has been to make the French set a very high value on the stability of their currency. Above all other countries they are the devotees of the gold standard. This accounts for the avidity with which they have accumulated in recent years an enormous reserve of gold, even though the maintenance of this large reserve as a non-earning asset involves them in considerable losses in interest upon their capital. In economics as well as in politics French fears customarily outweigh French hopes, and France's currency policy is marked by an extreme caution which stands in the way not only of her co-operation in any scheme of world reflation, but also of a resumption of foreign lending as an outlet for the surplus supply of capital. For the French, having been bitten once in Russia,

are not at all inclined to risk their money in doubtful ventures abroad in an unstable capitalist world. They prefer
to keep it at home, even if for the time being it earns them
next to nothing.

French fears, we have said, tend to outweigh French
hopes. To what an extent this sense of fear has dominated
French foreign policy since the war is analysed in the section of this book dealing with the political problems of
Europe. That French fears seem to be largely justified by
the existing European situation is sufficiently obvious. The
only question is whether the policies which have emerged
from the sense of fear have been such as to remove the
causes of fear, and not to make them more real and urgent.
If France, despite her fears of a German militarist revival,
had in the years immediately after the war collaborated in
the restoration of Germany, and endeavoured to set the
staggering German Republic firmly on its feet, the immediate outlook for Europe might have been far more hopeful
to-day than even the most inveterate optimist can pretend
that it is. But it is easy to understand the French attitude
and to see that many Frenchmen to-day are likely to regard
themselves as abundantly justified by the event. This view
may be, and we think is, fundamentally wrong ; but that
does not prevent it from being in the circumstances a
natural attitude.

For the French, though they succeeded, with British help,
in keeping the Germans out of Paris in 1914, have not forgotten to what an extent German forethought in the strategy
of war had exceeded their own. They had planned all their
military operations in terms of a short offensive and victorious war ; they were ill-equipped with munitions, and
had made no preparations for the carrying on of a prolonged
war of attrition. No wonder they lost confidence in themselves, and no wonder their fears of Germany are deeply
rooted after the experience of four years' occupation of a
large part of their territory. It is true that more than once
since the war the French have made a real attempt at collaboration in the rebuilding of Europe. After the disastrous

Ruhr struggle of 1923-24—disastrous for France as well as for Germany—the advent to power of the Herriot Government in July 1924 did inaugurate a period of greatly improved relations between France and Germany ; and even Herriot's fall in April 1925 did not involve any substantial departure from the foreign policy which he had instituted. Briand carried on this policy under the subsequent Governments. When Poincaré came back to power in 1926 he was a different Poincaré from the Prime Minister who had been responsible for the Ruhr occupation ; for his return to form a new Government of National Union reminiscent of the *Bloc National* of the post-war years was due to the demand for a strong hand in restoring the financial situation rather than to any shift in foreign policy. Poincaré's Government of 1926 included Herriot and other Radicals, until their support was withdrawn under the definite orders of the Radical-Socialist Conference of 1928 ; and this Poincaré Government of National Union was able not only to stabilise the franc but also to carry through the long-postponed process of ratifying the American debt agreement. Only after the withdrawal of the Radicals did the Governments of Poincaré's successors in 1929 and the following years show signs of reverting, especially after Briand's retirement and death, to the strongly anti-German policy of the years before 1924. The Tardieu and Laval Governments of 1929-32 were definitely reactionary ; and when these gave place in 1932 to a new succession of Radical Governments dependent upon Socialist support, the return to a more accommodating attitude in European politics came too late. The Nazi movement in Germany had already passed beyond control, and the hopes based on the simultaneous existence of pacific Governments in London and Paris could no longer be fulfilled ; for the second British Labour Government of 1929 had already fallen a victim to the financial crisis of September 1931. In Great Britain in 1931, as in France six years earlier, finance had been the undoing of a Government of the left. It remains to be seen whether the combination of revived militarism in Germany and growing financial difficulties in France will be too much for the Radical Government of M. Daladier in 1933.

Yet, though France may be in danger of a militarist re-action, there seems to be little present chance of her nation-alism taking the aggressive form associated with it in Ger-many, or even Italy. The French, having recovered Alsace-Lorraine, have no further ambitions of conquest : their militarism, as far as it exists, is defensive and the product of fear and not of the glorification of war. Above all, the French want to be let alone. Regarding themselves, not un-justifiably, as the most highly civilised people in Europe, they want tranquillity to till their soil and develop their social life in their own way. In economic matters they are apt to be strong individualists, as is natural among a people of peasant proprietors and small-scale industrial producers, with a large middle class interested in the maintenance of the *status quo*. But their individualism is tempered in social matters by the high sense of family solidarity ; and the im-portance of the family as a unit of French life and thought cannot easily be exaggerated. Women in France have shown so far little inclination to agitate for political rights ; and this may be, at least in part, because their social rights are already so important and far-reaching. French culture is extraordinarily strong and persistent in its distinctive qualities ; and the strongly established traditions of French family life and of the French agrarian and industrial sys-tems stand formidably in the way, not only of the victory of Socialism, but also of the rise in France of any powerful Fascist or anti-parliamentary movement. France is a Pro-tectionist country ; but she uses her tariffs to forward a domestic policy of social and economic *laissez-faire* in marked contrast to the authoritarian government of the *ancien régime* of Louis XIV.

§ 13. SPAIN AND PORTUGAL

Spain, with an area of over 190,000 square miles, is the third largest of all the States of Europe, being not very much smaller than France and substantially larger than post-war Germany. But in population she is still much behind the other great States of Western Europe. For she has only between 23 and 24 million inhabitants as against over 40 millions in France and 67 millions in Germany. This thinness of population is accounted for partly by the undeveloped character not only of Spanish industry, but also of the methods of agricultural production. But these are closely connected with the nature of the country itself. For Spain consists largely of high upland areas suffering for the most part from a serious deficiency of rainfall ; and the most densely populated districts, which lie round the coast and along the course of the principal rivers, are shut off one from another by mountain ranges which make communications difficult and tend to isolate one region from another in sentiment as well as in economic development. Railway communications are bad over the greater part of the country, and there are large tracts of land which cannot be cultivated effectively until big sums of money have been spent on irrigation and other methods of improvement. If this were done, the country could support a far larger population than it has to-day.

But hitherto both the forms of government and the systems of land tenure have been exceedingly unfavourable to economic improvement. Huge tracts of land were, until the Revolution of 1931, and for the most part are still, in the possession of great landowners, who feel small incentive to provide for any improvement in their cultivation. The masses of the peasantry are ignorant, living at a very low standard of life, and entirely shut off from the means of learning how to improve their agricultural methods ; and successive Governments, though they have made from time to time sporadic attempts at educational reform and at capital expenditure on improving the use of the land, have until the coming of the Revolution of 1931 achieved practically nothing either to educate the peasant population, or to help it improve its standard of life. Since 1931 the revolutionary Governments, based on coalition between the Socialists and the *bourgeois* Republican parties, have begun seriously to introduce a general system of education and to set on foot schemes of agricultural improvement. But there has been no time as yet for these reforms to become effective ; for, although many new schools have been opened since 1931, and the process of redistributing and improving the land has in certain areas been set seriously on foot, it will take time for any tangible improvements to result from measures of this sort. The Agrarian Law which forms the basis of the Republic's attempt to tackle the land problem was only passed in September 1932 ; and the process of actual redistribution of the land is barely more than begun to-day, and has not been applied at all in many districts.

In the meantime the peasants in Spain as elsewhere have suffered seriously from the effects of the world depression ; for Spanish exports, which consist mainly of agricultural products, have fallen heavily in price, and the instability of the Spanish currency has added to the difficulties of the agricultural population in purchasing imported industrial goods. Under any circumstances Spain would be to-day an exceedingly poor country ; but her poverty is the greater and the difficulties of the new Republic are gravely aggravated by the co-existence of the world crisis with the attempt to set the new Republic firmly on its feet.

Spain, we have said, consists largely of upland country, suffering from a severe deficiency of rainfall. Most of the country consists of high plateaux, rising at certain points to considerable mountain ranges. Madrid stands in the centre of a great plateau, shut off from the north by the *Sierra da Guadarrama*. The greater part of the low-lying and more fertile area of the peninsula lies in the south of Portugal ; Spain herself has fertile and low-lying land only in the valley of the Guadalquivir from Linares to Seville and

Sanlucar in the south and along the valley of the Ebro in the north-east, apart from the coastline from Catalonia in the north to Murcia in the south, and a very narrow strip along the north coast and in Galicia in the extreme north-west. Moreover, even a large tract of the more low-lying part of the country is seriously lacking in rainfall. The peninsula as a whole is divided between a humid area consisting of Portugal, Galicia and a strip along the north, and a much larger arid part, covering all central and practically all southern Spain. In these circumstances the chief areas of population, apart from Madrid, are in the south and along the east coast, and there are few towns of any considerable size in the central area, except Saragossa on the Ebro, and Bilbao on the north coast.

Spain is thus a predominantly agricultural country, cultivated for the most part at a very low standard of efficiency and without any attempt, except in the fertile areas in the south and east, to apply scientific methods of agricultural production. Cereals are nevertheless produced on a considerable scale, especially wheat and barley. But Spain has no surplus of these commodities for export, and she needs to import a large quantity of maize. Her agricultural exports, on which she chiefly depends for purchasing the industrial imports which she needs in considerable quantities, are wine, olive oil and fruit ; but she also exports a considerable quantity of raw materials, especially lead and copper, and certain high-grade iron ores. She produces superphosphates, and could develop out of her own resources the means of greatly improving her agricultural standards by the application of chemical manures. She has some iron and steel production of her own, and a large production of cement ; while among other manufactured exports, cotton goods occupy the most important place. But she needs to import most of her coal, and by far the greater part of her machinery, motor-cars, electrical goods and other products of the metal-working industries. She is also a producer of raw silk ; but the silk manufacturing industry is at present undeveloped. On the whole

Spain has had in recent years a small adverse balance of trade ; but this has never reached really large dimensions, and the import of capital in recent years has not been on a large scale. A substantial part of her diversified mineral resources are, however, exploited at present by foreign companies, and this foreign ownership of the Spanish mines stands in the way of the development of native industries, which are further hampered by the absence of any adequate supply of coal.

For some time to come Spain is certain to remain mainly agricultural ; and the great task ahead of her Republican Government is undoubtedly the improvement of the methods of agricultural production, especially in the great central areas which have hitherto been left undeveloped in the hands of the large landowners. In the more fertile parts of the country landed property is more divided, and the standards of cultivation are considerably higher, especially in the southern areas, where oranges and lemons are produced in large quantities, and vineyards and olive groves are intensively developed.

The Spanish land system, as we have seen, has greatly aggravated the natural disadvantages under which the Spanish peasant is compelled to work. When the report of 1928 on the condition of Spanish agriculture was drawn up, over 90 per cent of the land holdings were found to consist of less than 10 hectares, whereas one grandee alone had an estate of 95,000 hectares ; no less than 120,000 kilometres of land belonged to a group of 100,000 owners, while nearly 1¼ million middle-sized owners held between them 60,000 kilometres. The great landlords who held the vast estates for the most part paid very little attention to their cultivation. The peasants, however, depended for their living on the great landowners, and before the Revolution some of them were giving their labour in return for nothing more than their food, while many were working at a wage not exceeding three pesetas a day. The large landowners had put up, and to a great extent are still putting up, a powerful resistance to any measures of agrarian reform ; and it was plain that only a courageous handling of the land question could give the new Republic any chance of settling down upon a firm basis. But for some time after the Revolution it remained highly uncertain whether the Government would be prepared to face the very strong opposition which any large-scale agrarian reforms were bound to provoke, and it was not until the Government of Señor Zamora had been replaced by that of Señor Azaña, in which the Socialists exercised a larger influence, that any real beginning could be made. The fact that during the past year the Government has endeavoured at length seriously to tackle the land question is undoubtedly one of the principal reasons for the intensive efforts which were being made by the opposition during the early months of 1933 to throw out the Socialists and secure instead a Government of Republican concentration likely to be more favourable to the claims of property.

These difficulties, as indeed many other of the difficulties of Republican Spain, have a source far back in history. The natural configuration of Spain, the river-valleys divided by mountain ranges, and the high and separate plateaux, have always made for separation rather than unity ; the caliphate set up by the Moslem invasions very soon fell to pieces, and when the Moslems began to be pressed back the Christian kingdoms which rose to replace them were small and separate. Only at the end of the fifteenth century did the union of Castile and Aragon under Ferdinand and Isabella succeed in creating a kingdom strong enough to bring the whole of Spain under one rule ; and this, as is well known, was the prelude to the most brilliant period of Spanish history. Poverty, however, in spite of the Discoveries and the treasures of the Spanish Main, was close at hand ; the grandee, drawing a monetary tribute but caring nothing for improving the yield of his own estates or the lot of the peasants, dates back to the sixteenth century ; and the development of manufactures, which might have brought prosperity, was prevented by the refusal of the grandee to soil his hands as well as by the religious fanaticism which drove into exile the industrious Jews and Moriscos. Spain, in the seventeenth century, was one of the poorest and worst-governed countries in Europe. Famine was frequent, and the casual traveller could hardly get bed or food. Eighteenth-century attempts at reform did little to mend matters, and though the revolts of 1833, which the Concert of Europe was unable to suppress, inaugurated a rather more liberal régime, the heavy hand of the Spanish Church and the constant dynastic quarrels kept the country at a very low political level.

Before the Revolution of 1931 Spain had existed for eight years under a system of military dictatorship, following upon the Royalist *coup* of General Primo de Rivera in 1923. But even before this Spain, although she possessed in form a constitutional Government, was in fact ruled for the most part autocratically—where she was ruled at all. Alfonso XIII from the moment when he reached his majority and took control of affairs into his own hands made plain his dislike of constitutionalism and his determination to base the government of the country chiefly upon the Church and the Army. Politicians came and went, and Conservative alternated with so-called Liberal Governments ; for Spain, like other countries, possessed her party system, and her politicians bore the appropriate party labels. But in practice the parties were weak, ill-organised, and divided into small fractions under the influence of rival leaders, and their control over affairs was very narrowly limited, not only by the royal power but also by fear of the overriding authority of the Army and the Church. Socialism and Syndicalism acquired a considerable hold on the urban workers in the latter part of the nineteenth century, especially in Catalonia ; and after 1900 they began to spread in some of the rural areas as well, especially in the relatively fertile south. Spanish Socialism has shown from the outset strong tendencies towards Anarchism ; and Syndicalism and Trade Unionism have been until lately more Anarchist than Socialist in their attitude and policy. This is both cause and consequence of the pronounced localism of the Spanish working-class movement, which has made it powerful in holding up industry by sudden strikes in particular areas, but relatively weak as a constructive force operating over the country as a whole.

The political history of Spain during the nineteenth century is indeed largely the history of successive acts of military aggression. When the Army and the Church have been united they have had no difficulty in getting their own way, whatever Constitution might be temporarily in force. But in fact they have not been consistently united, and the Army has appeared on a number of occasions as a force apparently on the side of democracy. Again and again in the century before Primo de Rivera's *coup* some Spanish general had issued a *pronunciamento*, and taken power into his own hands, sometimes for the purpose of overthrowing a nominally liberal Constitution already in force, but also on occasion for the purpose of establishing a more liberal régime. But in practice, generals, whatever their original political allegiance, commonly used their power, while it lasted, for the establishment of some form of personal autocracy; and the extreme instability of Spanish political institutions is explained largely by the rise and fall of a succession of ambitious generals. In the years before Primo de Rivera's *coup*, there had been for some time a lull in the succession of military *pronunciamentos*; but this did not mean that the Army had been inactive in political affairs. Spain was in fact maintaining a very large Army, and the officers of this Army had organised themselves into a series of military juntas which monopolised lucrative positions, dictated conditions of pay to the civil Government, and generally ordered the Government about with a supreme disregard for the Constitution supposed to be in force. The King sided with the Army, and used it, as well as the Church, as an instrument for destroying the Constitution, and establishing his own autocratic authority; and it was primarily to save the Crown from its unpopularity in the country and to make the royal autocracy everywhere effective and complete that Primo de Rivera, then Captain-General of Barcelona, made the military revolution of 1923.

From 1923 to 1929 Primo de Rivera continued to govern the country. The structure of his Government was at first purely military ; but in face of its growing unpopularity he recognised before long the need for giving it a less exclusively military appearance, and in 1925 he restored a civilian Cabinet, which consisted of his own nominees and remained entirely under his own control. In 1927 some further steps were taken to give his administration a more constitutional appearance, without restoring the suspended constitutional guarantees or summoning any sort of Parliament ; and towards the end of his dictatorship Primo de Rivera experimented with an imitation Parliament not elected but nominated from above, and thus totally ineffective as an expression of the real attitude of the country. Primo de Rivera, despite his autocratic methods, seems not to have desired to establish himself as a permanent dictator, but rather to re-introduce some less authoritative form of government as soon as he felt that the position of the Crown, Church and Army had been adequately secured. But his small concessions to the principles of Parliamentarism and civilian government, coupled with his failure to tackle effectively any of the economic problems besetting the country or to prevent a serious depreciation of the Spanish currency, before long made his position increasingly difficult. Even so, he was too liberal for the King ; and, when his growing unpopularity became manifest, the King in 1930 demanded his resignation, and replaced him, not by a constitutional Cabinet, but by another military leader, General Berenguer.

Meanwhile, the growing discontent was assuming a more and more revolutionary form. On the working-class side there were many strikes, mostly sporadic and short-lived, which were suppressed with growing difficulty. But the potential revolutionary forces were still sharply divided among themselves, not only because there was no basis of agreement between Syndicalists and Socialists, Radicals and

Agrarians, discontented elements among the Conservatives
and the other Parliamentary fractions, but also because,
while one section of the revolutionaries wished to create
a united Spanish Republic based on strong centralised
government, another section desired to split up the country
into a number of independent or at least autonomous
States, joined together if at all only by some loose bond of
federal union.

This demand for dismemberment came chiefly from the
advocates of Catalonian independence, for the Catalans,
speaking a language different from that of the greater part
of Spain, and possessing to some extent a culture and
outlook also distinct, have for a long time possessed a
strong nationalist movement of their own. The Catalan
Nationalists, who had their main strength among the
middle classes and the peasants, were in sharp opposition to
the working-class leaders of Barcelona, who desired the
creation of a unified Spanish Republic. But by the middle of
1930 the unpopularity of the dictatorship under General
Berenguer had become so extreme that an agreement for
joint action was reached between the Catalan Nationalists
and the other Radical and revolutionary groups, including
even some of the Conservatives. In face of this alliance it
became plain that the dictatorship could not last. But the
revolt which broke out at the aerodrome of Cuatri Ventos
in December 1930 was successfully repressed, and most of
the Republican leaders were placed under arrest. The
Government meanwhile promised to hold elections in
March 1931, with a view to placing the State once more
upon a semi-constitutional foundation. But the Liberal,
Socialist and Republican parties, knowing that under the
conditions existing in Spain the elections were likely to be
a farce and to result in the return of most of the Government's nominees despite its unpopularity, announced that
they would boycott the elections even if they were held.

Under this threat, King Alfonso was driven in February
1931 to restore the constitutional guarantees, and the
Liberals were by this means persuaded to withdraw their

ban. But their chief leader, Count Romanones, announced, with the support of the Catalans, that he would ask for a Constituent Assembly with power to draw up a new Constitution. Upon this announcement the Government cancelled the elections, and the Cabinet, unable to maintain itself any longer, was compelled to resign. There followed on the King's part a struggle to form a new Government capable of maintaining the dictatorship ; and this was at last done under—for a change—not a general but an admiral, by name Aznar. But this Government had been less than two months in office when at the municipal elections of April 1931 the Republicans won practically everywhere in the towns an overwhelming victory, the immediate consequence of which was the collapse of the dictatorship, and the proclamation on April 14th of a Spanish Republic. King Alfonso fled from the country, announcing at the same time that he refused to abdicate or to give up his rights ; a provisional Government was formed under Don Alcala Zamora ; and a Constituent Cortes was promptly summoned to meet.

The Revolution was practically bloodless, for everywhere before it came the props of the dictatorship had fallen away. The Army equally with the rest of the country had withdrawn its countenance from the successive military dictators, and was in a condition of pronounced unrest. The Church, hitherto regarded as all-powerful in the country districts, and as too strong for its leadership to be effectively challenged over Spain as a whole, crumbled at the instant of the proclamation of the Republic. The head of the Spanish Church fled to Rome, whence he was promptly ordered back by the Pope ; and the immense load of unpopularity which Spanish Catholicism, with the huge drain which it involved upon the very limited national resources, had raised up against itself became manifest in the pronouncedly anti-clerical character which the revolution took from the very start.

The new Cortes speedily got to work upon the drafting of a Constitution. Within the Government, based on a coalition of many parties, from Socialists to dissident Conservatives, there was no agreement at all about the basis on which the new State ought to rest. In these circumstances, instead of drawing up and putting forward a Constitution of its own, the Government handed over the task to a non-political committee of experts, which prepared a draft scheme generally known as the *Anteproyecto*. When this was received, it was handed over by the Government to the Cortes without any recommendation ; and the Cortes thereupon referred it to a committee representative of all the revolutionary parties, which in turn drew up the *Proyecto*, upon which the Constitution was ultimately based. The Socialists were represented upon this committee, but were in a decisive minority, so that the structure of the new Spanish Republic was not that of a Socialist State, but rather of a democratic *bourgeois* Republic like France. Features were, however, borrowed from a number of other Constitutions ; and the Spanish Constitution differs from other *bourgeois* democratic instruments of government both in the far greater stress that it lays on internationalism, and in the more definite and fully worked out statement of public rights and duties which it embodies. In framing these clauses the Socialists did undoubtedly exert a very substantial influence ; but they did not secure any form of government designed to make Spain definitely a Socialist country. They accepted, in fact, the common Social Democratic view that Socialism should be left to evolve through the working of the *bourgeois* parliamentary system. What they did secure was that the new Constitution should be based on an advanced form of parliamentary democracy. Thus the new Spanish Cortes consists of only one Chamber and is elected by universal suffrage, including both men and women. Spain is thus the first Latin country to give women the vote.

The new Constitution was approved in November 1931 ; but before this difficulties had arisen between the various elements forming the revolutionary Government. The unpopularity of the wealthy Spanish religious orders led to an

insistence by the Socialists, with the support of the more
Radical elements in the other parties, on the expulsion of
the Jesuits and the nationalisation of their property. The
approval of this measure by the Cortes in October 1931 led
to the resignation of the first revolutionary Government
and especially of its leader, Zamora, and of the chief Conservative supporter of the Revolution, Maura. The Government was then re-formed under Azaña, with the Socialists
in a somewhat stronger position, but still in a minority ; but
the continued solidarity of the revolutionary forces was
affirmed when the Cortes, immediately after the coming
into force of the new Constitution, elected Zamora as
President of the Republic. At the same time Azaña
re-formed his Government as the first Cabinet working
under the new constitutional system.

Even when the Constitution had been adopted much
remained to be done in providing for the government of
the country. In November the Cortes had adjudged ex-
King Alfonso guilty of high treason and had declared him
an outlaw and confiscated the very large property belonging to the Crown, which, together with the property taken
from the Jesuits, provided at least the nucleus of a supply
of land for distribution among the hard-pressed peasants.
But before the Government could go on seriously to the
task of agrarian reform it had to dispose of the question of
Catalonia ; for the Catalans had been, from the very
outbreak of the Revolution, pressing strongly for the recognition of their complete autonomy within the new Spanish
State, and threatened to proclaim their independence
unless their demands were met. This claim in its extreme
form was explicitly rejected by the Constitution, which
made Spain a unitary State, and conferred wide powers
on the Central Government for dealing with all those
matters which seemed to need uniform treatment over the
whole area. Thus not only foreign relations, including
commercial relations, military affairs and public finance,
but also general legislation on questions of labour, education and social welfare, were placed under the authority of

the Central Government. But in order to placate the Catalonian opposition it was also laid down in the Constitution that the Cortes should proceed at once after its adoption to draw up a series of statutes granting a wide degree of autonomy to the individual provinces of the Spanish Republic. These provinces were to have rights of legislation concurrently with the Central Government, and were to be empowered both to adopt additional laws to meet their own needs and to take over by agreement the administration of specified services from the central body. It was, however, provided that the statutes embodying provincial autonomy should be passed by the Cortes and revocable by it, and should not be embodied in the Constitution so as to become absolute and beyond the reach of amendment. The Catalans, while the extreme Nationalists among them would have liked to go much further than this, were driven to accept the compromise by the existence in Catalonia itself of a strong body of opinion, especially among the workers, hostile to any policy that would have resulted in a weakening of the unified forces of the Spanish Revolution.

Having dealt with the question of Catalonia, the Cortes and the Government found themselves more free to tackle the vital need for economic reform. The Agrarian Law of September 1932 added further to the amount of land readily available for distribution among the peasants, by expropriating without compensation the vast estates belonging to the Spanish grandees, and also the landed property of those monarchists who had been implicated in General Sanjurgo's unsuccessful counter-revolutionary outbreak of August. Apart from these exceptional cases, power was assumed under the Agrarian Law to take over with compensation unused or ill-cultivated lands, lands requiring special measures of irrigation, land in the neighbourhood of towns wherever it was not being cultivated by its owners, and all estates over certain sizes—which were left to be determined province by province at any figure between a hundred and six hundred hectares in accordance with the local conditions and the use made of the land. While compensation was to be paid, its amount was to be strictly limited. Under the old régime the landowners had made, for the purposes of taxation, returns in which they declared the value of their property ; these were now taken as the maximum values in fixing compensation claims : a highly satisfactory arrangement from the stand-point of the State, as the landowners were not likely to have erred in over-estimating the real value of their properties.

The land thus taken was to be available for distribution among the needy peasants either individually or organised in *syndicats* or societies. Peasant co-operation had, in the period before the Revolution, grown up to a certain extent under the auspices of the more radical section of the Catholics as well as of the Socialists ; and the aim of the Socialist Minister of Agriculture was to secure that as far as possible the redistributed lands should pass into col-lective rather than into individual control, as he hoped that this method would be the more effective both in raising the standards of cultivation and in improving the political education of the peasantry. It is too soon yet to say how far this aspiration will be fulfilled, for the process of redistribution is still at an early stage, and no returns are available showing on what basis the land has actually been parcelled out.

At the same time a second Socialist Minister, de los Rios, was actively reforming the Spanish educational system, which had been extremely inefficient, especially at its elementary stage, and almost entirely under the domination of the Church. Something had indeed been done to pro-mote higher education in Spain under the auspices of the Committee for the Defence of Studies, originally estab-lished in 1907 ; and some of the Spanish universities had a high reputation, although their work had been seriously interfered with under the dictatorship, because repeated revolutionary movements among the students had caused Primo de Rivera to spend most of his time alternately closing them and allowing them to be re-opened. But for elementary education practically nothing had been done ; and Spain had and has an extremely high percentage of illiteracy for a European country. The Socialists, even before the war, had been active in endeavouring to promote educational reform, largely under the inspiration of Ferrer, the Anarchist leader, who was executed in the course of the Barcelona revolt of 1909. Many of the Socialist, Syndicalist and Anarchist bodies conducted active educational movements of their own ; but these were of course quite unable to touch the great mass of the people, and were, moreover, subjected to constant persecution at the instigation of the Church. Since 1931 the Government has been spending large sums in the building of new schools in an endeavour to combat Church influence by the establishment of a universal system of secular elementary education. But this too is bound to take time on account both of the poverty of the country and of the shortage of suitable teachers, which has to be remedied by the establishment of special training colleges and other institutions.

In these two fields Socialist influence in the Spanish Government, backed to a large extent by the more extreme groups among the Radicals, has succeeded in making a sound beginning ; and steps have also been taken to equip Spain with at least the rudiments of a code of labour legislation and factory inspection. But all these measures have aroused an increasing amount of opposition among the *bourgeois* elements included in the republican majority in the Spanish Cortes. The old monarchist parties have indeed disappeared ; but the place of these parties, which were swept completely away in the *débâcle* of 1931, has been assumed by those *bourgeois* parties which represent primarily the Spanish industrialists and the more conservative elements in the middle class. These have found in Lerroux's Radical Party a new rallying-point ; and for some time past the followers of Lerroux, with the backing of the entire Right, have been pressing strongly for the exclusion of the Socialists from the Government, and the formation of a purely *bourgeois* coalition. The elections held at the end of April 1933 for the small local authorities throughout rural Spain resulted in the return of a large body of representatives belonging to the opposition parties, though both Socialists and Radicals now gained a foothold for the first time in these backward areas ; and although these authorities do not represent the towns, which provided the main driving force for the Revolution, the elections furnished an immediate excuse for demands that the Government should resign, and give place to a Cabinet more in line with the alleged distribution of opinion in the country.

The Prime Minister, Azaña, met this demand with an offer to compromise. He was prepared, he said, to limit the further legislation to be introduced by the Government to the carrying through of the measures already approved in principle by the Cortes, above all the execution of the land law, and of the measures of educational reform and social legislation already accepted. In return for this concession he asked the Opposition to abandon the tactics of Parliamentary obstruction which they had been pursuing for some time, and to allow the Government to complete its immediate programme, with the implied promise that it would then be prepared to hand over its powers to a new combination based on the real distribution of political opinion—whatever that might prove to be. This offer was, however, promptly rejected by the Opposition, which decided to continue the tactics of obstruction in the hope of forcing the Government's hand. In the summer of 1933, immediately after the passing of the law directed against the Catholic Church, Zamora, a devout Catholic, who was excommunicated for signing the law, dismissed the Azaña Government, and endeavoured to replace it by a new Ministry, including the *bourgeois* Opposition. But this attempt failed ; and the President was forced to recall Azaña, who formed a new Government on practically the same lines as before. The Socialists thus continue for the present in the Ministry, but the outlook, as we write, is exceedingly uncertain ; for it is quite impossible to say how long the present coalition will be able to maintain itself in power in face of the growing *bourgeois* agitation against its continuance.

This agitation does not come entirely from the Right. For there is among the Spanish Socialists themselves a substantial minority which holds that the cause of Socialism is being prejudiced by the policy of compromise involved in maintaining the coalition. At the last Socialist Congress the governmental Socialists had no difficulty in defeating this opposition, but it is undoubtedly gaining strength in the party. The main body of Socialists recognised the need for coalition in order to consolidate the Republic, and to secure that its early legislative measures, including the adoption of the Constitution and the handling of the two great questions of the Church and the land, should be carried through on the most advanced lines that were possible. But many of them hold that, now the Constitution is in force and the main lines of Church and land reform have been laid down, it is more desirable for the Socialists to pass into opposition than to compromise themselves by continued adherence to a partly *bourgeois* Government.

One ground on which this is strongly argued is that continuance in the coalition is seriously prejudicing the propaganda of the Socialists among the workers, who are being induced to follow the lead of the Anarchist-Syndicalists rather than the Socialist Party. The Anarchist-Syndicalists have from the first refused to recognise the new centralised Republic as satisfying even temporarily the demands of the Revolution. They are opposed to centralised Government altogether, and want a localised system of control based on Workers' and Peasants' Syndicates and Councils throughout the country. They, in opposition to the Socialist Trade Unions, have been mainly responsible for the repeated strikes which have broken out during the past year ; and the Socialists, being the Government party, and therefore responsible for the maintenance of order, have necessarily incurred a considerable amount of unpopularity in repressing political strike movements. The Socialist left wing holds that if this state of affairs continues much longer a large proportion of the Spanish workers will drift away from supporting the Socialist Party and the Socialist Trade Unions and will join the Anarchist-Syndicalist forces, with the consequence that the control of the revolution will pass entirely into the hands of those *bourgeois* parties which desire to make France rather than any Socialist system the model for the new Spanish Republic.

For the Anarchist-Syndicalists, however effective they may be as an opposition, seem unlikely to be able to take control into their own hands. Their repudiation of centralised leadership and of strong government makes them largely incapable of acting together, and causes them to dissipate their strength upon a series of local movements with little coherence and little chance of national success. Moreover, the chief strength of the Anarchist-Syndicalists is in Barcelona and the neighbouring towns and in some of the country districts ; they have little strength in the other industrial centres of Spain. This division in the Spanish working-class forces has already made the consolidation of the Socialist elements in the revolution far harder than it would otherwise have been, and the argument of those who wish the Socialists to secede from the Government is that they will do better at this stage by becoming an organised opposition, and thus trying to rally the main part of the working-class forces behind them, than by aggravating the divisions inside the ranks of the working-class movement.

The division between the Socialists and the Anarchist-Syndicalists is reflected in the distribution of Trade Union forces in Spain. The Socialists have behind them the General Union of Workers led by Besteiro and Largo Caballero ; and this body gained ground enormously in the early months after the success of the revolution. From only about a quarter of a million members in 1930 it rose to well over a million in 1932. Meanwhile the rival Anarchist-Syndicalist body, the National Confederation of Labour, lost strength very greatly in consequence of its opposition to the Socialists in the early stages of building up the new Republic. More recently this tendency is said to have been reversed, and the National Confederation of Labour has been profiting by the criticisms levelled at the Socialists for their participation in the Government. But over Spain as a whole the Socialists are the stronger of the two bodies. It seems likely that, as soon as they feel assured that the foundations of land and labour reform and of anti-clerical legislation have been well and truly laid, in opposition, they will be only too glad to leave the Government and devote themselves to the consolidation of the working class as a political force. They are certain, however, to find great difficulties in pursuing this policy ; for Anarchist-Syndicalism has taken deep roots in the Spanish working-class movement and will not be easily defeated. There is in Spain a strong historical tradition of hostility to centralised government, and a strong tendency to split apart and take action on provincial or regional lines ; for centralised government is connected in people's minds with the centralising tendency of the old absolutism, and with the domination of Castile over the other provinces. This Anarchist-Syndicalist tendency makes, of course, against the rise in Spain of any strong Communist party ; for the Communists go further in the direction of centralised control even than the Socialists. At present Anarchist-Syndicalism appears as a force upon the extreme left ; but in the event of any great accession of strength to the Socialists or of the possibility of their gaining full control over Spanish political affairs, it is more than possible that some elements of Anarchist-Syndicalism would appear, as they seem to have done already in Portugal in the spring of 1933, as an influence on the side of Fascism against both Communism and Social Democracy. There is, indeed, no overt sign of this at present ; but it must not be forgotten that Italian Fascism recruited some of its strength from the Anarchist-Syndicalist forces which had previously regarded themselves as the extreme left wing of the Italian working-class movement, while extreme Syndicalism in France under the leadership of Sorel has also flirted with the opposite extreme of monarchist reaction, which has in

France a strongly Fascist tendency, plainest in the *Camelots du Roi*. In these circumstances the interest of the Spanish working class seems clearly to lie in consolidation upon the basis of the Socialist Party and the General Union of Workers ; and this consideration is likely in the long run to take precedence of the attempt to influence the course of legislation by remaining inside a coalition Government with the left-wing *bourgeois* parties. But it would be unreasonable to cast at the Spanish Socialists, because of their continued participation in the Government up to the present time, charges similar to those which have been cast at other Socialist parties for their willingness to enter into coalition with *bourgeois* groups. For the Spaniards had, on the morrow of the Revolution, to deal with a very different situation, in face of the clear necessity in a country as yet industrially undeveloped of consolidating the gains of the Revolution by a frontal attack upon the land system and upon the overweening powers of the Church.

Portugal.   Portugal, that small western portion of the Iberian peninsula, looks at first sight as though it should be part of Spain, and, but for the accidents of history, it would probably have been so. But in the disintegration of the Moorish kingdoms already referred to, Portugal early achieved independence, and, since the twelfth century, with the exception of sixty years' subjugation by Spain, she has maintained, albeit precariously, a separate existence.

Portugal combines a distinguished past history with a highly undistinguished present. First in the fifteenth-century field of exploration, she had at one time an immense colonial empire, but her Eastern possessions have been lost to the Dutch and the British ; her New World influence practically disappeared with the nineteenth-century secession of Brazil ; and all that are now left to her are the African territories of Angola and Mozambique, which enjoy the distinction of being the worst administered African territories except Liberia. In Europe, Portugal, since the Methuen Treaty of 1703, has been practically a dependency of Great Britain ; Wellington's armies in the Peninsula were based on and provisioned from Portugal, and Portugal obediently joined the Allies in the European War.

The occupations of the six and a half million Portuguese —for these purposes Madeira and the Azores are included with the mainland—are mainly agricultural. Eighty-five per cent of the Portuguese live in the country, and the only large towns are Lisbon with half a million and Oporto with a quarter of a million inhabitants. The only manufacturing industry of any size is the textile trade, which employs about 50,000 people; 37.4 per cent of the land is used for pasture and cereal production, 28 per cent is forest, 25 per cent waste, 5.2 per cent vineyard, and 6.2 per cent under fruit of other sorts. Wheat, maize and potatoes are grown, but the standard of cultivation is very low, the average yield for wheat, for example, being less than one-half that of Italy, and lower than that of any country in Europe (including Russia) except Greece. The chief article of export is, of course, wine, though there is also some export of fruit, corks, and fish (mainly sardines). As there is so little manufacture and a very low production of minerals, coal and manufactures have to be imported in large quantities, mainly from Great Britain. There is also a considerable import of cereals, and a heavy adverse trade balance.

The Portuguese peasant lives at a very low standard. The death-rate is high, and the illiteracy rate one of the highest in Europe. The Constitution (drawn up in 1911) is republican and democratic, with universal franchise for males over 21 ; but the government of Portugal is as liable to upheavals as the city of Lisbon is to earthquakes. The Portuguese Chamber is in a chronic condition of suspension. The present Government was formed in July 1932 by a sort of national party known as the *Estudo Novo*, whose programme is mainly support of the British alliance and the initiation of a policy of electrification. So far, however, nothing particular has been heard of the latter.

There are frequent strikes in Portugal, and a small Fascist movement, which the Government has, at the time of writing, just decided to suppress.

§ 14. ITALY

ITALY was the latest of the great countries of pre-war Europe to achieve national unity and independence ; for although the Italian national State was set up ten years before the formal creation of the German Empire, Germany had gone far towards unity under the Zollverein long before the Empire was formally proclaimed. Italian national unity, established in 1860 on the basis of the older kingdom of Sardinia, was not completed until the Franco-Prussian war of 1870 gave the Italians their chance of occupying Rome and so providing their national State with its traditional capital. Emerging thus late as an important Power, Italy was throughout the latter part of the nine-teenth century struggling to achieve a fuller recognition from the other great nations of Western Europe. But she can hardly be said, even up to 1914, to have realised anything like complete equality of status with the three great western Powers, Great Britain, Germany and France, to which she was inferior in population as well as in economic develop-ment.

The war to a great extent gave Italy her opportunity to achieve the desired equality, though she was bitterly dis-appointed with the territorial gains which accrued to her from the Treaty of Versailles. For she had hoped, as a result of her participation on the side of the Allies, to be able to build up a great colonial empire corresponding to those of the other leading Powers. Actually, she was unable to establish her position on the coast of Asia Minor, where she holds only Rhodes and the Dodecanese, the latter to the continued acerbation of Greek national feeling. Her entire colonial empire, which lies mainly in Africa, has a popu-lation of only two millions, and offers relatively poor opportunities for economic development. Italy's Tripoli adventure has been up to the present time an expensive business, from which she has reaped little by way of economic reward. But her colonial empire, relatively poor though it is, counts for much in her eyes as a symbol of national greatness and of imperial claims corresponding to those of Great Britain and France.

Italy is, however, severely handicapped in her endeavour to rank as a great Power side by side with the other leading Powers of the world by the relative poverty of her industrial resources. In an economic sense she is far less developed than any other country with at all equivalent pretensions. Much of her soil is poor ; for a large part of Italy is mountainous and difficult to cultivate, and there are also considerable marsh areas which require a high expenditure of capital before they can be brought into effective use. Moreover, in an industrial sense she is poor in the raw materials required for the characteristic industries of modern capitalism. She has hardly any coal, and only a small supply even of lignite. Her resources in most of the important metals are scanty, and accordingly she has to import very large quantities not only of coal but also of iron for the use of her industries. Such industrial development as she has achieved has therefore been mainly in the lighter industries. In the metal trades she has attained to a large measure of success as a producer of motor-cars, which she exports on a considerable scale. But she has to import large quantities of machinery and finished metal goods as well as of raw materials, and it is mainly upon the textile trades that her position as an industrial exporter depends. Among these the cotton trade at present occupies the leading position, having displaced silk in recent years from its previous pre-eminence. Italy has of course to import raw cotton for the use of her cotton industry ; but she has managed nevertheless not only to supply her home requirements but also to win an important place in the world market for cotton goods. In the silk trade she is of great importance as an exporter, both of silk and of manufactured silk goods ; and, confronted with the competition of artificial silk in recent years, she has also begun to build up an important rayon industry of her own. Her woollen trade, though considerable, is based on small-scale enterprise, and partly dependent on imported raw wool ; for her own wool is deficient in quality. She supplies, however, in these days almost the whole of her home market for woollen goods, though she has not yet built up any very substantial export trade. Among agricultural products she exports on a considerable scale fruit and vegetables, olive oil and cheese. But, although she has made great efforts in recent years to increase her own cereal production, she is still under the necessity of importing wheat and other cereals in order to meet the home demand. Maize, as well as wheat, has to be imported to a considerable extent.

The efforts to increase the area under cereals have met with a substantial amount of success, partly at the expense of other crops, but also in some degree by bringing uncultivated land into use ; and further progress is looked for from the substantial drainage schemes now in progress in the marshy areas with the object of bringing additional land under cultivation. Moreover the Italians have been trying hard to improve the quality of farming as well as the crop area. The Fascist Government has been active in the field of agricultural education, and a National Grain Commission has been specially entrusted with the supply of seeds to the farmers and also with improving the supply of fertilisers, of which the home production has advanced very greatly during the past few years. Italy produces substantially more foodstuffs now than she did a few years ago ; but her production is still not very much above the pre-war standard, for there had been a substantial falling off in the years immediately after the war.

This intensive drive to increase agricultural production is explained largely by the needs of a rapidly expanding population. In recent years the population of Italy has been increasing extraordinarily fast, and the surplus of births

over deaths has been at the rate of about half a million a
year. This fecundity meets with encouragement from the
Fascist State ; for Italy is striving to make up for deficiency
in industrial resources by increasing her man-power, and
is basing her claim to count as a great nation even more
upon the virility of her people than upon her economic
strength. Italians are proud of the fact that their country,
with nearly 43 million people, is now well ahead of France,
which had before the war considerably the larger population.

But the rapid increase of the Italian people in recent
years is not due solely to growing fecundity. Before the war
there was a very large amount of emigration from Italy,
not only to the United States, but also to the Argentine
and other parts of South America, and to France. Between
1901 and 1914 over $8\frac{1}{2}$ million Italians emigrated, and of
these nearly 5 millions went to America, and over $3\frac{1}{2}$ millions to other parts of Europe or to the Mediterranean
littoral. After the war the rate of emigration was very
greatly decreased ; and during the past few years, in consequence of the world depression, it has practically stopped,
so that the Italian population is increasing by the full
amount of the natural surplus of births over deaths. Moreover, there has been some repatriation of Italian labourers
from France since 1930. This rapid increase of population,
welcome though it is from a national point of view, obviously raises for the Italians serious economic problems.
The Italian density of population exceeds 340 per square
mile, although, as we have seen, a considerable part
of the country is unsuitable for cultivation, at least 30 per
cent of the total area being recognised as incapable of
economic development, at any rate without a heavy expenditure of capital. Nevertheless, the Italian Government,
in its anxiety to increase the strength of the country, definitely restricts emigration and encourages the highest possible birth-rate. This is recognised as imposing upon the
Government the necessity for taking measures for the
development of Italian industry as well as agriculture ;

and under the Fascist régime there has been a considerable extension not only of the protective system designed to foster economic self-sufficiency, but also of measures intended to place the resources of the State at the disposal of industry and agriculture.

For Italy is a poor country, and suffers from a serious deficiency of capital. The amount of domestic saving is relatively small, and any rapid advance of industrialisation demands an importation of capital from abroad. But for this Italy is not well equipped to pay, especially as long as the world depression lasts ; for it is difficult for her to stimulate exports beyond the point necessary in order to meet the increasing cost of imports which are urgently needed. Nevertheless, despite increasing population and the bad harvest of 1930, Italy has succeeded in face of the world slump in greatly reducing her adverse balance of trade. This was very considerable in 1928 and 1929, when capital was being to some extent imported from abroad ; but it has been cut down within manageable proportions in the subsequent years, so that it has been possible for the lira to be kept upon the gold standard.

In addition to encouraging the increased cultivation of cereals, Italy has embarked under the Fascist régime on a considerable scheme of afforestation. Previously the Italian forests, which cover not far short of one-fifth of the land area, had been seriously depleted without any attempt being made to replace them ; but in the more mountainous parts of the country afforestation is now proceeding apace, again under the direct auspices of the Fascist State. It cannot be denied that the Fascist Government, despite the poverty of the national resources, has made very great efforts for the economic development of the country, or that economic progress has been far more substantial under Fascism than it was under the Parliamentary régime.

But although one declared object of the Fascist system on coming into power was the improvement of the standard of life and the guarantee of a minimum standard of living for the Italian workers, very little has yet been done to realise this object. Italian industrial wages remain exceedingly low in relation to the standards prevailing not merely in Great Britain, but even in France or Belgium, and cheap labour is still available for Italian industry because of the still lower standard of life among the Italian peasantry. The land, as in France, is in the north divided into very small holdings, and while large estates still exist in many parts of Italy, especially in the south, the standard of cultivation remains low on the whole. There had been before the advent of the Fascist régime a large development of the Co-operative movement ; and this had taken several different forms, including both the co-operation of small individual peasant holders in the purchase of requisites and the marketing of their products and in the collective provision of finance, and also the co-operative farming of large estates by groups of workers, many of whom had also small holdings of their own on which they laboured when their work was not required upon the co-operative farm. The Fascist Government evicted many of the leaders of this older Co-operative movement, which they then took over and reorganised on Fascist lines, in the same way as they took over the Trade Unions of the industrial workers. Co-operation, recognised and encouraged by the Fascist State, exists also in certain branches of industrial production, notably building and road construction. But here too the movement has passed out of the hands of the previous leaders, and under the control of the Fascists.

The Fascist-controlled organisations, Co-operative and Trade Union, offer the workers certain advantages. But they are by no means effective instruments for the preservation of wage standards. Strikes in Fascist Italy are not allowed. Instead, wages are regulated when disputes arise by State authority, and the Fascist Unions are under a leadership amenable to Fascist discipline, and therefore not likely to push matters to extremes. There exists undoubtedly among the Italian workers a large mass of discontent, which is inarticulate only because of the suppression of all independent working-class activity. Nor is

Fascism likely to be able to raise wages in the near future ; for the Italian industrial system works under grave competitive disadvantages, and is able to establish its exports in the world market only with the aid of low labour costs, which depend essentially upon low rates of wages. The maintenance of these exports is essential to the Italian State because of its dependence on imported foodstuffs and raw materials, and accordingly the exigencies of international competition press hard upon the Italian workers, who are to some extent compelled to accept low wage standards in order to force the pace of agricultural development, and thus increase the food supply available for the expanding population. For Fascism is far tenderer to the agricultural than to the industrial sections of the people. It found its main support in the days before its rise to power among the lower middle-classes in the towns and among the agricultural workers, and it is far more inclined to direct its efforts to improving the position of agriculture and of the agricultural population than to raising urban wages. This is the case above all because, whereas improving conditions for the agricultural population involve an expansion of output, the output of Italian industry, which has to be sold to a considerable extent in the world market, is more likely to expand under conditions of low wages than if the industrial standard of living is permitted to rise.

Nevertheless, Fascism has done something to improve the economic condition of the Italian people in the towns as well as in the country. But it has done this rather by the provision of social services than by the raising of industrial wages. There is in Italy no general system of unemployment insurance ; but there has been under Fascism an increasing development of various institutions, especially the *Instituzioni di Dopo Lavoro*, for the promotion of welfare services among the workers. These services have, however, to be kept within bounds set by the need of the Fascist State to live within its somewhat exiguous means, and a large part of the available financial resources is being directed rather to schemes of economic development than to the relief of the unemployed or the provision of social services on the British model. What has been done in this field of industrial development through the various institutions which have been set up for the provision of finance for Italian industry with the aid of the State is briefly discussed in a later section of this book. Italian industrialists have sometimes criticised these activities of the Fascist State as involving a definitely socialistic policy ; and there is no doubt that Fascism is fully prepared, in what it conceives to be the interests of national economic expansion, to interfere largely with the rights of private enterprise. But its interference is always designed rather to provide help for the private employer than to supersede his activities by State action, and Mussolini was probably quite sincere when, in reply to the criticisms of the Italian industrialists, he disclaimed all socialistic intentions in the measures which he had introduced for centralising under State control the provision of capital for Italian industry.

Italian Parliamentarism, which had to grow up in a backward country with a peasant population including a large number of illiterates and working at a very low standard of life, was always a plant of exceedingly tender growth. The Italian Constitution is still based on the Statute of 1848 which granted constitutional government within the kingdom of Sardinia. Up to 1919 the Parliament was still elected under the restricted franchise of 1882, and there were in 1919 only 3 million voters out of a population approaching 40 millions. Universal suffrage and proportional representation, introduced in 1919, did little to give Italian Parliamentarism firm roots in the life of the country. Parties continued to be weak and unrepresentative ; and with the growth of Fascism such strength as Parliamentarism possessed easily melted away. The March on Rome disposed finally of the *bourgeois* Parliamentary State which the Italians had introduced in imitation of the more advanced countries of Western Europe. Such opposition to the Fascist *coup d'état* as did exist came not from the *bourgeois* Parliamentarians, or even from Socialists, wedded to the

Parliamentary system, but from a working class which thought far more readily in Syndicalist and Anarchist than in Social Democratic terms.

Accordingly, having crushed the working-class movement, Mussolini found few obstacles to the building up of the new Fascist State with the support of the Italian upper and middle classes. There was widespread discontent with the working of Parliamentarism and a readiness among these classes to accept an alternative form of political organisation without any feelings of regret at the disappearance of Parliamentary democracy. The growth of Fascism and the changes which it has introduced in the structure and working of the Italian political system are discussed in a later section. Here it is only necessary to emphasise the point that the victory of Fascism in Italy came far more easily and was likely to encounter far less effective challenge than the Nazi *coup d'état* which brought the German Republic to an end. Parliamentary institutions were doubtless weak in Germany as well as in Italy ; but they were far stronger even in the short-lived Weimar Republic than they had ever become among the Italian people, and for this reason Mussolini's successful maintenance of power and crushing out of all effective opposition over a period of twelve years is no indication that the German Nazis will be equally successful in impressing their own peculiar form of dictatorship lastingly upon the German people.

§ 15. GREAT BRITAIN

AMONG the States of Europe, Great Britain stands third in population but only twelfth in area. Highly industrialised except in the northern half of Scotland, she has a dense population. Only two countries in Europe— Belgium and Holland—have their people thicker on the ground, while Italy and Germany come next after Great Britain in terms of density of population. Her total population of 45 millions, or, with Northern Ireland, rather over

46 millions, is well below Germany's 63 millions, and far below the 160 millions of the Soviet Union. But Great Britain is well ahead in population of either France or Italy, which come next on the list ; and in terms of wealth per head she has a long lead over any other European country. Any attempt to estimate national wealth necessarily involves a large amount of uncertainty ; but one recent calculation, made by Professor J. W. Angell in his work on *The Recovery of Germany*, puts British national income in 1924 at 435 dollars a head, as against 231 dollars for Germany in 1928, 223 dollars for Belgium in 1926, 218 dollars for France in 1927, and 140 dollars for Italy in 1925. Ignoring the differences of date, and taking the income for Great Britain as 100, this would give for Germany 53, for Belgium 51, for France 50, and for Italy 32. Professor Angell's comparative figure for the United States works out at 150. Thus on the basis of these figures, which are probably accurate enough for our present purpose, national wealth per head in Germany, France and Belgium has been in recent years about half that in Great Britain, and national wealth per head in Italy about one third.

This high level of national wealth, in comparison with the other countries of Europe, has of course been achieved by means of an intensive process of industrialisation extending over more than two centuries. Great Britain is easily the most highly industrialised country in Europe, not even excluding Belgium. Of her total occupied population seven work in industrial occupations for every one who works in agriculture, whereas for Belgium, which comes next, the proportions are six and a half to two, and for Switzerland and Holland about six to two and a half. Germany, despite the high degree of industrialisation which she has reached, has only two persons in industrial occupations for every one in agriculture, and in France the proportion is five to four.

With this high degree of industrialisation goes naturally a very high degree of dependence on imported foodstuffs. It has been estimated that, on the average of the post-war years up to the beginning of the world depression, Great Britain was importing from abroad over 60 per cent of her total food supply in terms of values as against less than 40 per cent produced at home. Since the world depression the proportion of imports has undoubtedly become greater in volume, though not in relative value. Of the imports from abroad 39 per cent, or almost as much as is produced at home, has been drawn in recent years from foreign countries, and under 22 per cent from countries within the Empire. This dependence on imported foodstuffs is of course very much greater for some commodities than for others. During the post-war period up to the world slump Great Britain was producing at home only about 15 per cent of her wheat, about 44 per cent of her meat, rather less than half her poultry, eggs and dairy produce, about 70 per cent of her vegetables, and about 60 per cent of her fish. Moreover, on the average of the pre-slump years, Great Britain was importing fruit to a value of about £54,000,000 a year as against about £8,500,000 produced at home ; for the most widely consumed fruits are mainly imported products. In the case of sugar only 6 per cent of the raw material used up in domestic consumption was produced at home ; and even this was secured only with the aid of a large subsidy to the growers of sugar-beet. There was also a considerable importation of margarine, and of course the entire supplies of tea, coffee and raw cocoa were imported from abroad.

Great Britain is not only very highly industrialised, but also highly specialised to certain particular groups of industries. She depends to a tremendous extent on her exports of a comparatively narrow range of goods. Foodstuffs in a raw state she practically does not export at all, and her export trade in manufactured foodstuffs is relatively unimportant. Among raw materials, coal is the only really important export ; and the great bulk of her export trade is done in manufactured goods. Among these, even in 1929, the trade in cotton goods, despite the great post-war decrease in exports to the Far East, still stood easily first, accounting for £135,000,000 out of total exports of £729,000,000. Next in order came iron and steel, with £68,000,000, followed by machinery, £54,000,000, woollen goods, £53,000,000, and coal, £49,000,000. These were easily the leading groups; but other textiles and clothing taken together accounted for over £52,000,000, chemicals for £27,000,000, and other manufactures of metal, including electrical goods, for over £40,000,000. There was thus a very high degree of concentration upon the textile and metal industries, with coal standing third and chemicals fourth in the list of exports. These figures, based on exports, do not of course correspond to the relative importance of the various trades in the total productive economy of the country. The textile trades export a far higher proportion of their total product than the others—especially the cotton industry, which has in the past exported over four-fifths of its total output. Exported coal is only a small fraction of the total production; but coal enters largely into the costs of producing exported manufactures, especially iron and steel. In all, it has been estimated that in 1929, of the total number of workers engaged in manufacturing processes in Great Britain, as distinct from transport, distribution and other services, 38½ per cent were engaged in producing for export, whereas in 1930 and subsequently this proportion fell below one-third, or to substantially less than one quarter of the total occupied population, even after an estimate has been made of the number of workers in distribution and transport working for the export trades.

Even one-third or one quarter of the total manufacturing or of the total occupied population is, however, an exceedingly high proportion to be employed in producing for export; and it is clear on the basis of these figures that Great Britain depends to an enormous extent for the maintenance of her present industrial system, as well as for feeding her population, on finding markets for a large quantity of exports overseas. Up to the crisis she had, under her Free Trade system, sought these markets impartially over the whole world, though she has enjoyed since the beginning of the twentieth century a substantial amount of tariff preference both in the self-governing Dominions and in certain of her colonies and protectorates. In 1913 Great Britain sold 37 per cent of her exports within the Empire, and 63 per cent in foreign countries. In 1929 there had been a substantial shifting of the balance in favour of Empire countries, and in that year $44\frac{1}{2}$ per cent of British exports were sold within the Empire as against $55\frac{1}{2}$ per cent in foreign countries. This change was, however, due not to an increase in the volume of Empire trade, but to a severe decline in the volume of trade with foreign countries. In the case of imports, 25 per cent were derived in 1913 from Empire and 75 per cent from foreign sources, whereas, in 1929, 27 per cent came from within the Empire and 73 per cent from abroad. There was thus comparatively little shifting in the sources of British imports in comparison with the pre-war period. Great Britain still continued to depend to an overwhelming extent on imports of both foodstuffs and raw materials from foreign countries ; and, despite the decline in her exports to foreign countries, these still absorbed in the aggregate a substantially larger proportion of her total exports than the Empire.

It is important, however, to bring out not only the relative dependence of the British economic system on Empire and foreign trade respectively, but also the closeness of its connections with Europe. Thus in 1929 Great Britain received nearly 40 per cent of her total imports from European countries and sold them 29 per cent of her exports, whereas all America together accounted for less than 29 per cent of imports and not much more than 16 per cent of exports. Among European countries Great Britain's largest trade was with Germany, which took 5 per cent of her exports and supplied 6 per cent of her imports. Denmark supplied 5 per cent of imports, but took only $1\frac{1}{2}$ per cent of exports. For France both figures were round about $4\frac{1}{2}$ per cent, with a slight surplus on the import side. Next in importance came Holland and Belgium, each with 4 per cent of imports and 3 per cent of exports. No other single European

country except Italy took more than 2 per cent of British exports, and only the U.S.S.R. supplied as much as 2 per cent of British imports. These figures, it should be observed, take no account of the Irish Free State, which supplied 4 per cent of British imports and took 5 per cent of exports. The United States, on the other hand, supplied $16\frac{1}{2}$ per cent of total imports, but took only $6\frac{1}{4}$ per cent of exports in return ; while the Argentine, which came next in importance, supplied $7\frac{1}{4}$ per cent, and took 4 per cent. Of other countries India was by far the most important market of all for British exports, taking $10\frac{3}{4}$ per cent of the total, whereas less than $4\frac{1}{2}$ per cent of British imports came from India. Australia took $7\frac{1}{2}$ per cent and supplied 4 per cent ; Canada took rather under 5 per cent and supplied about 4 per cent, while South Africa took $4\frac{1}{2}$ per cent and supplied 4 per cent, and New Zealand took 3 per cent and supplied rather over $3\frac{1}{2}$ per cent.

Empire Trade. These figures cover enough countries to give a fair idea of the distribution of British exports immediately before the world slump. They show that, despite the rise in the relative importance of exports to Empire countries, Europe was still a market of the most vital importance to British industry, and that any attempt to make the Empire self-supporting on the lines of Empire Free Trade would be bound to involve the most drastic redistribution of industries ; for it is inconceivable that for a very long time to come Empire markets for the types of goods which Great Britain is at present equipped to supply could expand to anything like the extent required to replace the European market. For these reasons, though it may be possible for Great Britain, while other countries are busily engaged in raising their tariffs and placing obstacles in the way of imports, to arrive at preferential arrangements with countries within the Empire and to gain on balance temporarily as a result of these arrangements, it is clearly very much to her interest to do all she can to get the European markets re-opened to her manufactures. This is in the long

run a far more important consideration from the standpoint of her industries than any benefits which they could possibly derive from an extension of Imperial preference. Moreover, certain of the Empire countries, and above all Canada and Australia, are fully determined upon the development of their own industries ; and the discussions at Ottawa in 1932 very plainly showed that the Canadian industrialists especially were by no means prepared to tolerate any lowering of tariff barriers which would be likely to allow British goods to come in on terms damaging to their own position in the Canadian market. They were prepared to give Empire preference only by raising still higher against foreign countries the already high protective duties established in the interests of Canadian industry ; so that the British exporter could at the most only look forward to the prospect of displacing a certain proportion of the imports into Canada from foreign countries, especially the United States, and not to securing the major part of the Canadian market either now or in the future. The same considerations apply with slightly less force to Australia, only because the Australian tariff had already before the Ottawa negotiations been raised to such heights that, quite apart from the question of Imperial preference, there was a wide recognition in Australia of the need for some lowering of barriers in the interests of the consumers.

The Ottawa agreements must therefore be regarded far less as the first step towards the setting up of a self-contained Empire than as temporary arrangements forced on Great Britain by the very high tariffs and other restrictions in the way of trade which have been established in Europe as a consequence of the world slump. This is not to say that Empire preference, once established in Great Britain, can easily be removed. For, even if it could be shown to be clearly contrary to British economic interests to maintain it, there would be considerable political difficulties in the way of its removal now that it has once been established. But, though Imperial preference may remain for some time, it is most unlikely that public opinion in Great Britain will

tolerate any considerable extension of it unless the existing
tariff situation in Europe becomes even more prohibitive
than it is now, or Europe draws together in some sort of
tariff union to the exclusion of Great Britain. That, indeed,
might force upon Great Britain a further attempt to develop
the Empire market by an extension of Imperial preferences
and mutual trading arrangements ; but it would be an
attempt to save something from the wreck of British foreign
trade, and by no means a satisfactory contribution to the
re-establishment of British or of world prosperity. It is far
more to Great Britain's interest as a trading country to
work for a lowering of tariff and similar barriers in Europe
than to enter into any agreements with Empire countries
that might prejudice her position in the European market.

Moreover, it is highly doubtful whether the policy of the
Empire countries, which showed at Ottawa their extreme
reluctance to grant concessions at all corresponding to those
which they expected Great Britain to grant to their own
exports, would justify Great Britain on economic grounds in
granting them additional exclusive advantages. A great
attempt was made by the British Government to represent
the Ottawa agreements as a resounding victory for the
cause of Imperial economic unity ; but everyone knew
that in fact these agreements had shown conclusively
the extreme difficulties in the way of securing any considerable expansion of British exports within the Empire.
Such relative expansion as has taken place of late seems in
fact to be due more to the depreciation in the external
value of sterling in comparison with gold than to the tariff
concessions made by the Empire countries at Ottawa ; and
this remains true despite the " anti-dumping " duties
imposed in Canada.

British Tariff Policy.   It is easy to appreciate the
motives which led Great Britain in the mid-nineteenth
century to adopt Free Trade as the basis of her commercial
policy. She had then over a wide range of industries a great
advantage over all other countries in the efficiency of

production. She needed no protection for her own industries in the home market ; for save in a few cases such as silk, these industries were not in the least afraid of any foreign competition they were likely to encounter. Great Britain let the silk trade go without regret because there were plenty of other trades in which she saw abundant prospects of expansion. She needed, moreover, even at that time, considerable imports of raw materials for the use of her industries ; and it was clearly an uneconomic policy to impose duties on the importation of these materials. In the case of foodstuffs, over which the main battle was fought, there was a case for Protection ; for the British agricultural interest was still numerous and politically powerful, and there was a political as well as an economic case for endeavouring to keep a substantial proportion of the population at work on the land. But in the great Free Trade agitation of the 'thirties and 'forties these arguments of the agriculturists were completely overborne by the manufacturers, who wanted cheap food just as much as they wanted cheap material, in order to keep down the costs of industrial production—for was not cheap food for the workers just as much as cheap material for the factories a raw material of manufacturing industry ? Accordingly, Bright and Cobden and the Anti-Corn Law League carried the day with the support of most of the workers, who saw in Free Trade the prospect both of increased industrial employment and of a lower cost of living. In 1846, when the Corn Laws were repealed, the case for Free Trade in Great Britain was overwhelmingly strong ; and for a long time afterwards the vast majority of the people in Great Britain saw no reason for changing their minds about the wisdom of the step which had been taken.

But as the nineteenth century advanced and new nations entered the race of competitive manufacturing production the situation ceased to be as simple as it had been in 1846. There was almost no revival at first of the demand for agricultural protection ; but with the development of industry on the Continent and especially in Germany, the demand for the protection of manufacturing industry was resumed. Still for a long time the " fair trade " cause made little headway, and it was not until it was reinforced by the sentimental as well as the economic appeal of the new Imperialism that it became formidable. Joseph Chamberlain in the years after 1903 made Tariff Reform a reality in British politics ; and, though his crusade failed and was largely responsible for the overwhelming victory of the Liberals in 1905–6, he did succeed in the long run in committing the Conservative Party to the cause of Protection, and thus prepared the way for the new British tariff policy of 1931 and the following years.

Nevertheless up to 1914 Great Britain did not look at all likely to adopt Protection in the near future ; and even after the war, although there had been some departure from the rigidity of the Free Trade system, the defeat of the Conservatives in 1923 showed that the main bulk of British opinion was still Free Trade in sentiment. By this time, indeed, the arguments in favour of a Protectionist system had become at any rate more plausible, if not really stronger ; for there had been a marked decline in British exports, and German competition, submerged for a time after the war, was again becoming an important factor in world trade. Moreover, the rise in the level of tariffs all over the world and especially in Europe and the United States was giving point to the argument that, whereas Great Britain could afford to maintain a system of Free Trade while the rest of the world kept its tariffs at a moderate level, Free Trade was becoming an unworkable system as tariffs elsewhere became more and more prohibitive. The cry for imperial economic unity was strongly revived, and the Tariff Reformers stood now on the one leg of arguing that Great Britain must aim at building up a self-sufficient Empire, and now on the other that until Great Britain made a loud Protectionist noise at the rest of the world the policy of lowering world tariffs would stand no chance of success. These two arguments were of course in reality

MR

contradictory ; but both of them made their contribution to the conversion of a growing number of the manufacturing and trading classes to the Protectionist cause. Even so, the opportunity to introduce Protection on any considerable scale did not arise until after the world slump and the economic crisis of 1931 ; and when a full-blooded tariff was finally introduced it was necessary for those who introduced it to begin by pretending that it was merely an emergency measure designed to redress the balance of trade, and only when they had got it through by these means to admit that it was meant as a permanent departure in policy.

Even now it is clear that the British attitude remains highly uncertain ; for while some Ministers go about singing hymns in praise of the beauties of the tariff system, and demanding further measures for the establishment of imperial economic unity, others still stress mainly the intention to use the new British tariff as an instrument of commercial bargaining with other nations. Readers must take their choice which Ministers to believe, and must make up their own minds whether Great Britain is in fact heading for a permanent régime of high Protection, or sincere in her willingness to lower her own tariffs as part of a general movement toward lower tariffs in Europe and over the world as a whole.

As we have seen, the new British tariff of 1931–32 was defended largely as an indispensable measure for restoring the balance of trade. There had been, even before the beginning of the world slump, a considerable increase in the adverse balance of British merchandise trade (imports and exports) as compared with the years before the war, and also a decline in the amount of British capital available for investment overseas. Thus in 1913, according to the estimates of the Board of Trade, the adverse balance in respect of merchandise and bullion was £158,000,000, whereas between 1924 and 1929 it was always as much as £350,000,000, and nearer £400,000,000 in both 1925 and 1927. 1926, the year of the coal dispute and the General

Strike, showed an adverse balance of £475,000,000 ; but this was of course quite abnormal.

To set against this adverse balance there were large credit items, including the net revenue derived from British shipping, the income from overseas investment and from financial services performed on behalf of foreigners on the London money market, and certain minor items. After account has been taken of these other sources of income, the Board of Trade figures show for 1913 an approximate credit balance available for overseas investment of over £180,000,000. This figure was never reached in any post-war year. In 1924–25 the available surpluses were £86,000,000 and £54,000,000. After the abnormal year, 1926, in which the credit balance sank to only £9,000,000, there was a rapid improvement to £114,000,000 in 1927 and £137,000,000 in 1928. The year 1929 was already to some extent affected by the world depression, and the balance was reduced to £103,000,000—all these figures being of course, in relation to the level of prices, greatly below the surplus available in 1913. On the advent of the world slump, despite the heavy fall in the prices of the leading British imports, the position became very much worse. Revenue from overseas investment and from shipping services was sharply reduced, and there was also a fall in receipts from financial services. On the other hand, the adverse balance of merchandise trade increased because British exports fell off very sharply indeed. For 1930 as a whole, the credit balance was reduced to only £23,000,000, and in 1931, even after the export of £35,000,000 of gold has been included on the credit side, there is a net adverse balance of £75,000,000, due principally to a further sharp decline in all classes of invisible exports, and to a further fall in exports of merchandise.

It has therefore to be admitted that the economic situation of Great Britain in 1931 was sufficiently serious to call for measures of readjustment, though the financial crisis of September 1931 was directly due, not to the adverse balance of current payments but to a large-scale withdrawal of capital sums from Great Britain on account of an international loss of confidence in the pound. Some people argue that, when Great Britain had gone off the gold standard, the balance of payments could safely be left to right itself, because the effect of the depreciation of the pound sterling would necessarily be to make imports more expensive and exports cheaper until the balance had been automatically righted. But in the first place this view depends for its soundness on the willingness of the British financial authorities to allow the pound to fall in external value without any attempt to control it ; and secondly it assumes that there is so strong a self-acting tendency for the volume of payments to balance that the free movement of the exchanges will speedily bring about an equilibrium by reducing imports and expanding exports. In fact, neither of these things is necessarily true. The pound, after the departure from gold, was not left free to move ; and in the existing state of world confidence the value placed upon it in terms of foreign currencies depends far less on the current payments which need to be made between countries on account of visible and invisible exports than on fluctuations in business confidence affecting the movement of capital sums from one country to another. The depreciation of sterling did undoubtedly stimulate British exports, in the sense that it prevented them from falling as far or as fast as they would have fallen if the pound had been maintained at its previous gold value. But there was little falling off in the volume of imports until protective tariffs reinforced the effects of exchange depreciation. For to go on buying the same quantity of imports as before did not cause the pound to depreciate further in face of the lack of confidence felt by comparison in the financial situation in other countries, and of the preference of their nationals for moving their money to London in spite of the unfixed exchanges. This movement of money prevented the pound from depreciating so as to achieve a balance corresponding to the current balance of visible and invisible imports and exports.

This situation in practice considerably diminished the internal pressure to reduce the British standard of life. Those who held that British wages were too high in relation to wages in other countries believed that the enhanced cost of imports would speedily cause a rise in prices, and thus indirectly bring about a fall in the working-class standard of living, and a redistribution of the real national income. But this did not happen to any appreciable extent in the case of the employed workers ; and there was accordingly a case, in view of the continued adverse balance of payments, for endeavouring to reduce imports by artificial means. This was the case put up by the advocates of the tariff when it was first introduced as an emergency measure in the winter of 1931. For the National Government began, not with a general tariff on a permanent basis such as it has enacted since, but with special measures nominally directed against " abnormal importations." The effect of these measures, combined with the depreciation of the pound sterling, was seen in the figures for the balance of trade and the balance of payments in 1932. The adverse balance of commodity trade (excluding gold bullion movements) fell from £408,000,000 in 1931 to £289,000,000 in 1932 ; and the adverse balance of payments, including the invisible items, but still excluding imports and exports of bullion, was reduced from £104,000,000 to £59,000,000. It is possible to argue that on this ground the British tariff has justified itself as an emergency measure made inevitable by the world slump and by the restrictive policy adopted by other countries ; but it is quite impossible to support on the basis of this argument any permanent change by Great Britain to a protective system. Nor can such special measures as the Wheat Quota—more properly to be called a subsidy— introduced in the interests of English wheat producers, or the similar measures now being brought in under the guise of marketing schemes, logically be defended in one and the same breath as steps rendered necessary by the world slump and the abnormal condition of the trade balance and as permanent measures designed to establish British economic prosperity upon a secure foundation.

In saying this, it is not suggested that Great Britain will or should revert to a Free Trade system in any complete sense, but only that the arguments for a tariff in the present emergency are not necessarily arguments for a permanent tariff when the emergency has passed away. In that matter the future of British policy must depend largely on what happens in other countries, and especially on the extent to which the European countries draw together either unitedly or in distinct groups into customs unions or mutual tariff arrangements. Such developments in Europe might force on Great Britain the maintenance of some sort of Protectionist policy, operated perhaps not by means of tariffs, but rather by means of some system of Import Boards and licenses or quotas. But this, like the continuance of the present system of Empire preference, must be regarded, in view of the special dependence of Great Britain on world markets and particularly on the markets of Europe, rather as a step forced upon her by circumstances beyond her control than as in itself a desirable policy for British capitalism. There is doubtless a case for the regulation of external trade by the State as against the unregulated system of Free Trade ; but this is fundamentally a case for a Socialist system of mutual exchange and barter based on international agreement and not for a protective system designed to aid one country against another in a competitive scramble for markets.

Parties and Politics. We have so far been dealing entirely with the economic situation in Great Britain, as it is affected by her dependence on external trade. We have now to turn to her internal political situation. Before the war Great Britain was ruled alternately by two great political parties both of which went back, though their form had been substantially changed in the meantime, to the eighteenth century. Whigs and Tories, and their successors, Liberals and Conservatives, alternately controlled the government of Great Britain during the whole period of her development as a modern capitalist power up to 1914. Between these two great parties, after their transformation by the Reform Act of 1832, which brought the industrial middle class to a position of supreme political influence, no fundamental division ever arose. However they might differ on secondary issues they were agreed concerning the basis on which social institutions ought to rest, and concerning the form of such vital underlying institutions as those of property and class and the structure of the political system required for sustaining these economic realities. Up to the 'forties the Tories were mainly Protectionist, while the Whigs had more tendencies towards Free Trade ; but it was a Tory Prime Minister who repealed the Corn Laws, and the subsequent distribution of party allegiances showed that there was no fundamental division between the two. In 1867 the urban artisans were given the vote ; but, though on the whole the Whigs had been the party with a greater inclination towards the extension of the franchise, it was a Tory Government that passed the Reform Act of 1867, and in the following years both parties in equal measure adapted their policies and methods to meet the claims of the newly enfranchised class. In the spate of social reform legislation between 1867 and the late 'seventies it is impossible to distinguish any clear difference of policy between the measures passed by Whigs and Tories, or, as it is now more appropriate to call them, Liberals and Conservatives. It is true that in the course of the great depression the reforming zeal of both parties died out as it became both harder to find money for reforms and easier to discount the claims of the working-class voters. But the Liberals, largely because of their close contacts with Nonconformity and industry, and their lesser degree of entanglement with the higher privileged classes, were the more successful in attaching to themselves the working-class voters, and especially those who belonged to the Trade Unions and Co-operative Societies. Labour began to emerge to political importance as a satellite of the Liberal

Party ; and even when, in 1900, the Labour Party declared its independence, it continued in practice to operate as an ally of the Liberals, and remained right up to 1914 far too weak to provide even the nucleus of a Government of its own, and far too closely allied to Liberalism to offer it any effective national challenge.

The war, however, was fatal to the position of the great Liberal Party ; and, as we shall see in a later section, the break-up of Liberalism pitchforked the Labour Party into a position of primary political importance. But it needs to be emphasised that, though Liberalism as a party broke up into a number of quarrelling groups, Liberalism in a non-party sense remained the political creed of a very high proportion of the British people, not only among the lower middle classes—the upper middle classes went over largely to Conservatism—but also among the black-coated workers and even among the more highly paid manual workers. The Labour vote, after the disruption of Liberalism, included an exceedingly high proportion of electors who were far more Liberal than Socialist.

Through the period during which the two great political parties alternately governed Great Britain, there was for the most part fundamental unity in matters of foreign policy as well as in home affairs. In the eighteenth century the dominant factor in British external politics had been the rivalry between Great Britain and France. This disappeared with the fall of Napoleon in 1815, and there was no reason for renewing it when the danger of French domination in Europe had vanished, especially as the development of French industrialism followed so different a course from that of Great Britain as to make the two countries mainly non-competitive in world trade. After 1815 Great Britain shaped her foreign policy so as to avoid as far as possible entanglements in the affairs of Europe. She withheld her effective support from the Holy Alliance and from the European reaction, and as far as possible kept her hands free for developing her economic opportunities over the world as a whole. For a long time no situation developed in Europe of a sort likely to induce her to modify this policy ; for it was not until the rise of Germany in the latter part of the century that any other Power threatened either to make a bid for European domination or to compete really seriously with British exports in the world market. The rise of Germany as a world Power and as an industrial country coincided in time with the advent of Economic Imperialism, based largely on the development of the heavy industries ; and Great Britain, which had come into possession almost by accident of by far the largest colonial Empire in the world, felt herself challenged by the rise of Germany in a political as well as an economic sense. For the Germans naturally wanted, for both economic and political reasons, to build up an Empire of their own, and to secure adequate markets and assured supplies of raw materials in the less developed countries. This rivalry, which prepared the way for the World War, led to a re-entry of Great Britain into European entanglements, culminating in the *Entente Cordiale* with France in 1903–4, and the Triple Entente with France and Russia in 1907.

But, having helped to bring about the defeat of Germany in the World War, Great Britain had for the moment no more to fear from her ; and accordingly her attitude to the Germans rapidly changed, more especially as, in the post-war situation of Europe, a military hegemony of France seemed for a time foreshadowed by the system of alliances which the French were proceeding to build up with the new States of post-war Europe. Accordingly, in the post-war treatment of Germany, Great Britain usually took the side of leniency, though she was not prepared to push her attitude to the point of provoking a quarrel with France. Meanwhile the French, by no means so sure that the German menace was over and done with, missed the opportunity of helping in the successful establishment of the new German Republic, and must bear a large share of the blame for provoking the German militarist reaction in 1933.

In this post-war situation it was impossible for Great Britain, though she tried tentatively to keep out of the affairs of Europe, to avoid commitments. She was a member of the League and thereby committed in general terms to the maintenance of the settlement reached at Versailles and in the other Treaties of Peace. She carefully avoided entering into any further commitments for the preservation of the *status quo* in Eastern Europe, and refused all invitations to become a party to an " Eastern Locarno." But she was led by her recognition of the need for the re-establishment of economic prosperity in Europe, and above all for the rehabilitation of Germany, to sign the Locarno Treaty, which aimed at guaranteeing the permanence of the peace settlement in the West. Moreover, her rulers shared with those of the other European capitalist States an intense hostility to the new Socialist system established in Russia. Great Britain played her part in the fomenting of civil war in Russia in the years immediately after the Russian Revolution ; and, although subsequently her attitude towards Russia alternated with changes of Government, for the most part she could be reckoned as a member of the consortium of capitalist nations designed to resist the spread of Communist ideas.

Ireland. The external political situation of Great Britain in the years after the war was greatly complicated by difficulties within the British Empire. The century-old Irish demand for Home Rule led during the war to the Irish Rebellion of 1916 ; and though this movement was successfully crushed it became impossible after the war for Great Britain to resist any longer the demand for Irish self-government. After an abortive attempt to hold down the Irish by military force Great Britain recognised the inevitable, and in 1921 consented to the establishment of the Irish Free State as a self-governing member of the British Commonwealth of Nations. Ratified in the Irish agreement of 1922, the Constitution of the Irish Free State gave Ireland practically complete autonomy, though causes of dispute remained in the Oath of Allegiance still exacted from the Irish Parliament, and in the provision for the payment of annuities to Great Britain in respect of money supplied in the past for the improvement of the position of the Irish farmers. The right of secession from the Empire was denied to the Irish Free State ; and in 1932 there was a bitter quarrel between the two countries over the re usal of de Valera's Government to keep up payments of the annuities in face of the severe agricultural depression. Great Britain retaliated by imposing heavy tariff duties on imports from Ireland ; and the Irish in their turn declared their intention of resisting British dictation to the last, and set to work under de Valera's influence to turn their country into a self-supporting economic unit based on the principle of economic nationalism.

As the Irish Free State had been accustomed to export, mainly to Great Britain, almost 45 per cent of the products of her agricultural industries, especially livestock, the barring out of a large proportion of her goods from the British market resulted in great economic distress; and the fall in the purchasing power of the farmers also reacted to increase the amount of urban unemployment. Moreover, the Irish Free State, though a large exporter of agricultural produce, is by no means self-sufficient even in respect of food. The Irish farmers grow potatoes and produce large quantities of turnips, mangolds and hay for the feeding of stock; but they produce hardly any wheat and not a very large quantity of any cereal except oats. The total value of the crops averages less than one-third of the value of the output of livestock ; so that if Ireland loses her export trade she loses with it the power to buy necessary foodstuffs as well as imported manufactures.

As we write, no solution has yet been found of the dispute between Great Britain and the Irish Free State, and the economic future of the country remains in these circumstances highly uncertain. Irish Labour, largely on nationalist grounds, has so far given its support to de Valera's policy ; but the Irish workers as well as the farmers are becoming restive under economic adversity, and are making demands for help from the State which the Government finds it difficult to meet out of its diminished resources. Clearly Ireland is not economically strong enough to stand alone without involving herself, at any rate for some time to come, in a serious fall in the standard of living of the people. The mutual trade between Great Britain and the Irish Free State is undoubtedly of economic adv ntage to both countries ; and economic nationalism in I eland has its roots in political passions rather than in any real economic needs. It is to be hoped therefore that the present dispute will be settled, though the attitude of the British Government has so far been one of extreme intransigence, not unprovoked by the fanatical fervour of de Valera's nationalist principles.

India. The second great imperial problem which has troubled Great Britain since the war is that of India. But this falls outside the scope of the present volume ; for it would be impossible to deal adequately with the relations between Great Britain and India without considering other aspects of the Eastern question. It suffices to say that the rise of Indian Nationalism and the still unsolved problems which a new Indian Constitution presents have raised acute issues for the British economic system as well as for the British Empire as a political unit. For India is, as we have seen, the largest market for British exports, and above all for cotton goods. During the war there was a considerable advance of cotton production in India itself ; and since 1918 this advance has continued, and there has also been a considerable import into India of cheap cotton goods produced in Japan. The Indian manufacturers want protection for their own industry against both British and Japanese imports ; and Great Britain has been compelled to concede the principle of tariff autonomy to the Indian Government, which of course she still finally controls, and actually to permit in response to strong pressure from the Indian manufacturers the imposition of protective duties on British goods. Under the Ottawa agreements the Indian Government agreed to give preference to British imports, and the British manufacturer thus enjoys a more favourable position in the Indian market than his Japanese rival ; but the protection accorded to the home manufacturer remains substantial, and there has been strong objection in India to the granting of any preference at all.

Moreover, India, like China, uses the boycott as one of her most powerful political weapons, and there has been from time to time a definite boycott of Lancashire products by the Indian importers, even apart from Gandhi's campaign in favour of the use of Indian cloth produced upon the handloom. Great Britain can obviously ill afford any further contraction in the Indian market. A large part of the trade in cheap cotton goods is already lost, and is most unlikely ever to be recovered ; but there remains a sufficiently large volume of exports to India to exercise an important influence on the political policy of Great Britain in dealing with Indian Nationalist claims. The Diehards in Great Britain wish so to crush the Indian Nationalist movement as to keep the Indian market open to British goods by force ; but the majority of British politicians and the exporters interested in the Indian trade strongly doubt the practicability of this course, and therefore favour more conciliatory methods. It remains to be seen whether the Round Table Conferences and the further discussions now in progress for the elaboration of a new Indian Constitution will result in a working compromise. They may do so ; for the Indians neither possess at present the coherent power required for open rebellion, nor agree in desiring an absolute and immediate withdrawal of the British. The Indians want self-government ; but they are prepared to compromise if Great Britain will meet them half-way, and Indian opinion is so divided, especially over the differences between Mohammedans and Hindus, as to make at least a temporary compromise more likely than an open rupture, unless Great Britain becomes involved in a new European war. Moreover, the position of the Indian princes, who have no desire for democratic institutions to be installed in their territories under the ægis of the

Indian Nationalist movement, strengthens Great Britain in resisting the claims of the more intransigent Indian Nationalists. Nor can it be forgotten that Indian Nationalism is torn asunder by conflicting class interests as well as by racial and religious differences. The Indian Nationalist cotton employers have no desire to unloose among their exceedingly ill-paid workers forces too strong to be controlled ; and this is a further factor making on the side of at least a temporary compromise.

Imperialism and Investment.

With the Imperial problem as a whole this book does not set out to deal ; and the case of India has been mentioned only because of its profound effect upon the internal economic situation in Great Britain. The wider problem of Imperial economic relationships has been dealt with earlier in this section and will recur in the section devoted to European economic problems, where it arises in connection with the project of a European Economic Union, and the difficult situation of Great Britain, which desires to maintain and develop economic connections with both Europe and the Empire. It should, however, be added here that, while the British Empire is by far the oldest of the great colonial Empires of the European Powers, Great Britain has been by no means behindhand in adding to the territory under her political control in recent times. During the last thirty years of the nineteenth century, the British Empire grew in size by over $4\frac{3}{4}$ million square miles, with an estimated population of 88 millions. One-third of the total area of the Empire and one-quarter of its total population were thus acquired during these thirty years alone. This process was continued in the twentieth century, until in 1914 the Empire had an area of $11\frac{1}{4}$ million square miles and an estimated population of 417 millions, of whom 315 millions were in British India, and less than 60 millions were white. The war added further large territories to the Empire under the guise of mandated areas ; and in 1933, including these post-war acquisitions, the Empire has a population of more than

450 millions and a total territory of well over 13,000,000 square miles. It is thus far larger in both extent and population than any of the other colonial Empires, though the French showed tremendous vigour during the thirty years before the outbreak of war in adding to their territories, especially in Africa and Indo-China, and they too acquired after 1918 mandates over a considerable part of the pre-war German Empire.

This growth of Imperialism in Great Britain, even more than in other imperialist countries, has gone side by side with an enormous expansion in the volume of British overseas investment. Overseas investment was indeed no new thing in the last quarter of the nineteenth century. It began on a significant scale immediately after the Napoleonic Wars ; and it has been estimated that by 1875 the total value of British capital invested overseas amounted to about £1,200,000,000. By 1914 this had increased to well over £4,000,000,000, and Great Britain was thus by far the greatest creditor nation, her total overseas investment having been approximately doubled between 1900 and 1914. The French, who came next, had foreign investments valued in all at about £1,800,000,000 ; and the Germans, who had started much later than the French to invest abroad, had already about £1,250,000,000. The United States was on balance still a debtor country, importing capital for the enormously rapid expansion of her own economic system.

Of these foreign holdings of capital, from which Great Britain draws an annual tribute which enables her to meet the cost of a substantial part of her merchandise imports, nearly half was in 1914 invested inside the British Empire. Quite half was in America, including about one-fifth of the total in the United States, and the remainder in Canada and Latin America. Investments in Europe were relatively tiny, amounting to little more than £200,000,000 in all. On the other hand, France had more than sixty per cent of her total investments in European countries, and Germany had also invested far more heavily in Central and

Eastern Europe than elsewhere. There was thus no very great competition in the field of overseas investment between Great Britain and the other leading Continental countries ; and this situation has been largely maintained since the war, in that Great Britain has disposed of the reduced sums available for investment mainly within the Empire and in Latin America, and to a less extent in the Far East, and has not made any considerable long-term loans to Europe. Her debtors in Europe are for the most part short-term debtors, whose obligations arose either out of commercial transactions or from loans by the British banks to the Continental banks, especially those of Germany. As an investor of capital overseas, Great Britain is therefore dependent far more on the prosperity of the Empire and of Latin America than on Europe ; and as the countries in which she has invested most of her resources are primarily agricultural producers the burden of their debts to Great Britain has been enormously enhanced by the fall in agricultural prices.

There has been, however, in respect of fixed-interest bearing obligations remarkably little default despite the long continuance of the depression. There would certainly have been much more had Great Britain remained upon the gold standard ; for the effect of the depreciation of sterling was to relieve to some extent the burden upon the debtors, because most of the loans had been made in terms of sterling, and not of gold or of the currencies of the debtor countries. This of course meant that Great Britain, in allowing sterling to depreciate, forwent some part of her claims upon her external debtors ; but it is probable that she gained more than she lost by doing this, for if default had once started on any serious scale it would have been very difficult to check. It is, however, doubtful how much longer, if the world depression continues, agricultural countries in extreme difficulties will be prepared to go on paying even the present reduced tributes to their creditors in Great Britain ; and the large dependence of Great Britain on her income from overseas investment gives her a very strong interest in the restoration of the prosperity of the agricultural parts of the world. This interest far more than offsets the advantage which she at present gains from the cheap rates at which she is able to purchase many of her imports, though this has of course to be taken into account as a factor tending to give her substantial relief, and largely explaining the reduction in her adverse balance of commodity trade.

§ 16. THE U.S.S.R.

THE UNION OF SOCIALIST SOVIET REPUBLICS is by far the largest country in Europe, even if its European territories only are taken into account. The whole area of the Soviet territories is $8\frac{1}{2}$ million square miles, more than twice the size of the whole of Europe, including European Russia, and considerably larger than the whole of North America. This—its immense size—is the first factor which must be taken into account in any consideration of modern Russia. Though Russia lost more land by the war than any other combatant, all her losses taken together only amounted to 3 per cent of the total.

Within this vast area live 162 million people—rather more than live in North America, but far fewer than live in the rest of Europe. The density of population in Russia is only 18 per square mile, less than that of any European country except Iceland ; but this figure is misleading if it is taken to mean that the population of Russia is spread over the country in that ratio. European Russia is more thickly populated than Asiatic Russia ; there are large tracts of the latter where practically nobody lives. In European Russia, the great cities, Moscow and Leningrad in particular, are more crowded than any other city in the West ; and even in the countryside the Russians live clustered in villages, often with miles of unoccupied country dividing one village from the next. Thus life in many parts of Russia is not nearly as isolated as it would seem to be from these figures ; and the age-old migratory habits of the Russian, agriculturalist as well as pastoral worker, reduce this isolation still further.

This population is divided into many races, speaking an infinity of languages. Over seventy per cent of the population are Slavs of one type or another, speaking Great Russian or tongues resembling it. As under the Tsars Great Russian was the only official language, the only language recognised for publications or taught in the schools, it used to be assumed that practically all the inhabitants of Russia except the vocal minorities were Russians. This the Revolution has shown to be untrue. Of other Indo-European races in Russia the most important are the Germans, of whom there is a large colony on the Volga, and the Armenians in the south, though members of many other nations are to be found there. East of the Volga, and stretching far into Central Asia, are the great groups of mixed Turkish and Tartar peoples, with various types of Mongols to the north of them. Then there are the Georgians in the south, a group of peoples akin to the Finns in the north-west, and smaller race and language units, some of great obscurity, stretching away along the frozen territories into Northern Siberia. It is calculated that in the Institute of the Northern Peoples at Leningrad teaching is given in no less than fifty languages. Finally there are the Jews, heavily persecuted by Tsardom, of whom there are about five millions. Under the Tsars, the Jews were forced to live in an *enclave* or pale which stretched from Poland into Great Russia ; but since the Revolution they have been allowed to move about freely, and in particular large agricultural colonies of Jews have been settled in the Crimea.

The official religion of the Soviet State is atheism. Before the Revolution the majority of the population belonged to the Greek Orthodox Church, with a small Roman Catholic element, particularly in the west, a group of Lutherans in the north, a large group of Moslems, and a sprinkling of Buddhists. Since 1931, the discouragement of religion has been less strong, and adherents of all these five creeds, and of any others, are allowed to practise them, though the numbers are naturally not known.

Russia is thus full of minorities. But the vigorous encouragement given to non-Russian cultures, and the right of secession granted to the constitutent Republics by the Constitution of 1923, has rendered the minority problem in Russia something very different from the same problem, say, in Roumania. It would not be true to say there is no separatist feeling at all ; it can be found in the Ukraine and Georgia, and perhaps elsewhere ; but it is neither strong nor widely diffused.

Russia is predominantly an agricultural country, over 80 per cent of the population making its living off the land. But not by any means all of Russia is cultivated or cultivable. About two-fifths of Russia's whole area—two thousand million acres—is forest, of which a quarter is in European Russia ; and north of the forest, in the extreme Arctic regions, is tundra where not even forest will grow. The cultivated area of Russia is nearly 350 million acres,[1] including the " black earth " belt, and to this must be added, for purposes of food production, the millions of acres of pasturage in the southern steppes, Central Asia, and Siberia. Much of this grassland, particularly in Asia, is, as it has always been, dependent upon fluctuating rainfall, so that estimates of the extent of Russian pasture land would bear little relation to the facts. Of the agricultural land nearly three-quarters is under grain, wheat and rye being the principal crops. Only about a tenth is used for " industrial " crops, of which sunflower, flax, cotton and sugar beet, in the order named, are the most important. The number of livestock is enormous, but has fallen seriously during the past few years.

Of other commodities, the production of timber, oil, hides and fish are the most important. The output of coal and other minerals, though growing, is still small as compared with that of industrial countries. Under twenty million Russians are employed in factory work ; and since

[1] Including pasture in " mixed " farms.

the Five-Year Plan began, attention has been concentrated on heavy rather than on light industry. A certain amount of non-agricultural production is still carried on, as it used to be carried on, by " artels " of villagers ; but very much less than formerly. The external trade of Russia, owing to political obstacles, is still not great ; the main exports are agricultural products and the commodities mentioned at the beginning of this paragraph. The main import is machinery of all types.

It is idle to try and estimate the productive possibilities of Russia, for they are only just being discovered to-day. The mineral wealth of the Urals, for example, has barely been tapped. In some cases, such as that of timber, the approximate extent of the resources is known; but for lack of transport they cannot be utilised. Transport in Russia is bad, partly because of the enormous distances and the poverty of the country. Railways can only, for these reasons, very slowly be made to pay ; and it should be noticed that though the absence of gradients over the enormous plain simplifies in one sense the task of railway engineers in Russia, they have other difficulties to contend with. For instance, much of the bed of the Trans-Siberian Railway had to be blasted out of permanently frozen soil. Western Russia is comparatively well supplied with railways ; but in the east large areas are totally without railway communication.

There is a great deal of navigable waterway, useful for internal communication, but less so for external trade, since the long rivers mostly flow either into the landlocked Caspian, or into seas that are icebound for months in the year. Even the rivers themselves are often partly icebound. The endeavour to gain access to a warm water port has occupied a great deal of the energies of Russian statesmen during the past hundred and fifty years, and accounts partly for the anxiety felt about Vladivostok. Roads are also bad ; there is little stone or even gravel available for road-building, and whereas in winter when the snow is frozen a good deal of sledge travelling is possible, in autumn and spring many of the roads are quite impassable, and in summer full of dust and holes. Some parts of Russia have scarcely got beyond the stage of cameltracks. Aerial transport is beginning, but the traffic is as yet infinitesimal.

It follows that one cannot speak of Russia as self-supporting. It is *potentially* self-supporting, but only if there is sufficient transport available to carry supplies over a wide area. If the crop is good, the black-earth belt has a surplus to send to the northern parts which cannot feed themselves ; but only if transport is available. Similarly, the resources of timber, minerals, cotton, etc., can only be made available if there is capital provided for their development and transport. Until that is done, Russia will be bound to remain at a low standard of life, and liable to recurrent local or general shortages.

One of her greatest assets, however, is her man-power, increasing every year at the rate of two and a half millions, particularly since the Soviet system of child care has so much reduced the rate of infantile mortality.[1] This man-power may not be at the highest grade of skill ; but it is adaptable, mobile and numerous. The great ease with which all rulers of Russia have raised enormous armies—the conscripted soldiers at the time of the fall of the Tsar were said to number fourteen millions—is an illustration.

The salient feature of modern Russia is that it is Communist. To this we shall return in the description of its political institutions ; but we must note that there are certain features of Russian tradition which have facilitated the transition to Communism, hard though it may have been in other respects. " The dictatorship of the proletariat " came easily to a people habituated since the fifteenth century to autocratic government ; nor did the idea that government should concern itself in every department of life seem at all strange to the descendants of those

[1] In 1910 the infantile mortality rate for European Russia was 28.5 per cent ; it had declined by 1927 to 18.4 per cent, and was considerably lower in the large towns.

who had known Peter the Great and Catherine II. On the other hand, the extraordinary gift of the ordinary Russian for communal co-operation has made the Soviet system a natural growth ; and the absence of anything like a trading and manufacturing *bourgeoisie* and its substitution by an " intelligentsia " of writers and State officials who were peculiarly open to the influence of ideas removed at any rate one of the difficulties which confronts every Socialist Party in Western Europe.

Tsarist Russia.   Civilisation, in some parts of Russia, is very old indeed. Kiev was a flourishing city in the ninth century before it was christianised ; Nijni-Novgorod was settled by Scandinavians in the tenth century and became a great trading centre ; and these were only two of many cities. (The ancient caravan ports of Central Asia, such as Bokhara and Samarkand, were at this date part of Asia, not of " Europe.") But this city civilisation was washed under by the Tartar invasions of the thirteenth century, and the modern history of Russia really begins with the establishment in the fifteenth century of a fighting dynasty in Moscow. Ivan III and Ivan IV (the " Terrible ") of that dynasty drove back the Tartars, added large parts of southern and northern Russia to the Russian Empire and began, through expeditions of Cossacks, the settlement of Siberia. But the system of the Russian Tsars was completely autocratic ; after the reduction by Ivan IV of cities such as Pskov and Nijni there was no local autonomy left. There were no representative institutions ; the Duma was an advisory body only ; and there was no check on the power of the Tsar except the ancient " privileges " of the nobles.

Russia's history thereafter, until the Revolution, has two main interests, the spread of the Russian Empire, and the various attempts at Westernisation. Peter the Great conquered the Crimea, and the Swedish possessions on the Baltic, and built St. Petersburg (Leningrad) as a port for the west ; Catherine II seized Russian Poland, and made of Russia a recognised European Power ; the settlement of

1815 added Finland and Bessarabia ; during the nineteenth century the incorporation of Siberia proceeded rapidly ; while between 1864 and 1879 great areas of Central Asia were removed from tribal rule and placed under the Tsar. The conquest of Asiatic Russia was complete by the end of the century, and the Trans-Siberian Railway begun in 1900 ; but an attempt to seize Manchuria failed and led to the Russo-Japanese War—the first serious check to Russian expansion. It is not always realised, however, that the wide growth of the Russian Empire is of comparatively recent date ; Odessa, for example, the great Black Sea port, was only built in 1794.

This vast empire has been the subject of periodic attempts at Westernisation, of which the Soviet industrial policy is only the latest of a series. The first was made by Ivan IV in the sixteenth century when the British Muscovy Company had opened up trading relations. Foreign workers were brought in, a beginning made of education, and an attempt made to reform the alphabet, the coinage, and the Eastern habits of the population. But these reforms did not go deep ; the greatest change which the sixteenth century brought to Russia was the introduction, in 1597, of a serfdom which came much nearer to slavery than the medieval serfdom of the West.

Much more important was the reign of Peter the Great (1685–1725), who set about deliberately to transform Russia into a Western State. Factories and shipbuilding yards were set up, a system of education introduced, and many other reforms, some very much against the grain of Russian habits, enforced by the personal efforts of the Tsar. It should be observed that Peter's reforms, like those of Catherine II after him, were made practically single-handed. What one man could do, he did, not without violent cruelty at times ; but he had hardly any collaborators, and had to wage an unceasing war not merely against corruption and inefficiency, but against definite opposition to the basis of his ideas. " Slavophilism," that school of thought which absolutely denies the value of Western civilisation to Russia, then first made its appearance. It was powerful in the nineteenth century, and the Social Revolutionary Party was largely under its influence ; but it appears to have died down since the Revolution. The recent conflict between Stalin and Trotsky had nothing to do with Slavophilism, but was a dispute about revolutionary tactics.

In spite of these efforts, Russia before 1850 was still an extraordinarily backward country, living largely by barter. The few industrial establishments which existed were either State factories or " estate " factories run by the great nobles, and staffed, in either case, partly by foreign labour and partly by serfs. This low-grade serf labour was commonly housed and fed, after a fashion, entirely by the factory which employed it. The factory kitchen, the factory club, and the factory housing estate are not new ideas in modern Russia, though their administration is new. But in the latter part of the century considerable efforts were made. The serfs were freed in the 'sixties ; and many new developments, of which the most important is Count Witte's immense railway building programme, were set on foot.

All this development, however, had to take place with the aid of foreign capital. Russia was always extremely poor, and could not possibly finance her own works. The external debt became enormous ; and in order to pay the interest, the Russian Government had to export quantities of grain— quantities which had to be increased when in the last quarter of the century the competition of grain from the New World caused a break in prices. (Cf. the events of the years 1930–32.) This export had to be subtracted from the low standard of life of the Russian peasant, already burdened with emancipation dues and unable, under the communal control of the *mir*, or village group, to improve or increase production. The economic situation of the Russian peasant at the end of the nineteenth century was very bad indeed. The condition of the town worker was not much better, and he was forbidden to combine.

The failure of the Russo-Japanese War caused a collapse. Strikes broke out in the large towns, and there were agrarian riots in many parts of the country. In St. Petersburg and other large towns the strikes turned quickly into revolutionary movements, and for a while the Soviet, i.e. the Council of Workers' and Soldiers' Deputies, held the power in St. Petersburg. The Tsar and his advisers appeared to yield, and promised reforms. A Duma, which contained a large membership drawn from the Kadets (=Constitutional-Democrats) and from the various Socialist Parties, was hastily called together ; but when once the danger was over its views were consistently flouted. The revolutionary aspect of the movement was put down ; Stolypin, the Prime Minister, carried out repression with a vigorous hand ; and those Socialists who were not jailed or sent to Siberia for the most part fled abroad.

Such was the situation when the European war broke out : and the war, by straining beyond breaking point the inefficient and wasteful Tsarist system, finally brought about its downfall. Millions of men were put under arms, of whom only about a third were at any time anywhere near the enemy ; and transport broke down so hopelessly that many of them could not be fed, clothed or armed. Before the end of 1916 there was a clamour for bread and peace. In March 1917, a general strike, led by the Soviet of Workers' and Soldiers' Deputies, broke out in Petrograd, and the Tsar's Goverment promptly fell. It was succeeded by a Provisional Government of moderate views, which in May became, by the inclusion of representatives from the Soviets, a Coalition Government under Kerensky.

The Russian Revolution.   The centre of power lay, however, not in the Provisional or the Coalition Government, but in the Soviets which existed or were rapidly formed all over Russia. These however, though preached to by Lenin and other members of the Bolshevik section of the Social Democratic Party, who returned from exile in April, had as yet no definite policy, though they had a Conference and a Central Executive. (A Congress of Peasant Soviets was held at the beginning of June, and elected an Executive which co-operated with the Executive of the town workers.) The hope of all Russian workers was for peace and bread ; but they did not know how to get it.

The unfortunate Kerensky Government was forced by the Allies in June to undertake an offensive which was a complete and disastrous failure, the troops deserting wholesale. In July a strike wave in Petrograd was put down, and gave the Government the opportunity to take reprisals against the Bolsheviks ; though it did not dare to suppress them completely for fear of their influence among the working classes. All through the summer Bolshevik ideas were growing among the Soviet delegates all over the country, a fact which made it possible in the autumn for the Bolsheviks to raise the cry " All Power to the Soviets."

Early in September, while interminable discussions about the policy and methods of summoning a Constituent Assembly were going on, Admiral Kornilov attempted a counter-revolution. This was defeated, almost before it had begun, by the spontaneous efforts of bodies of workers. The result was the formation of the Red Guard. Prices were rising fast, and there were agrarian raids on the great estates in many parts of Russia. In October Lenin recommended the Bolshevik Party to put themselves at the head of an insurrection. They were doubtful ; but within a fortnight revolution came. The Winter Palace fell ; Kerensky fled ; and within ten days, almost without fighting, the revolution was established. Foreign journalists, bred on a tradition of barricades and fierce street fighting, could not really believe that a revolution had taken place. There was not enough blood.

The Bolshevik Party took control of the Revolution because it had secured control of the Red Guard and the Petrograd Soviet (of which Trotsky was the chairman), because it was the party which had opposed the hated offensive, and had been persecuted by the discredited Coalition Government, but most of all because it was the only party which had a clear and definite policy. It could not count on the co-operation of other Socialists ; the

Mensheviks, the other fraction of the old Social Democratic Party, were definitely hostile ; and of the big Social Revolutionary Party, the right wing was hostile, and the left only came over by degrees. But it could count on the town workers, amongst whom Bolshevik ideas had been spreading rapidly, and on the fighting forces, to whom it had promised peace. Through the soldiers, mostly peasant-born, and drifting back in masses to the villages, it could to a certain extent influence the peasants, i.e. the mass of the Russian people ; but the general attitude of the peasants was doubtful. At the end of November, a Congress of Peasant Soviets split, the left half going with the Bolsheviks.

The support of half the peasantry was no good. Accordingly, Lenin, chairman of the Council of People's Commissars (the executive body set up by the Revolution) promulgated on November 8th the famous decree which nationalised all the land of Russia, thus keeping the Socialist framework, but gave it to the peasants to hold. Thus, at one stroke, the support of the bulk of the peasants was assured during all the troubles to come.

These troubles were not long in making their appearance. Immediately upon assuming power, the Bolsheviks issued to all the combatants a suggestion for a general armistice. When that was rejected, they began to negotiate for peace with the German and Austrian Governments. At first the negotiations appeared to be conducted in good faith ; but gradually, it became clear that the Germans, at any rate, intended to treat Russia as a beaten enemy. A renewal of hostilities resulted in the dictated treaty of Brest-Litovsk (March 1918), by which Russia gave up all the border provinces including the Ukraine, and recognised Turkish claims in the Caucasian area. Meanwhile, the opponents of the Revolution were not slow either in taking to arms or in claiming outside support. Kornilov in January raised a White Army in the Don area—his place was later taken by Denikin. In April the British sent an expedition to Murmansk and Archangel ; the Japanese invaded the Far Eastern frontier ; the bandit Petliura began operations from Galicia ; and the Czechoslovak regiments in Siberia and on the Volga were encouraged by the Allies in the disputes which arose between them and the new Russian State. These subsidised attempts at counter-revolution took no heed of the conclusion of European peace ; Wrangel in the Crimea, Yudenich in Estonia, and Kolchak in Siberia (most brutal of all the White Generals) must be added to the list ; in the south the would-be independent republics of Armenia, Georgia and Azerbaijan were hastily recognised by the European Powers ; and the final effort, made after most of the other attempts had failed, was the Polish invasion of 1920. From 1918 to the beginning of 1921 the Russian Government was fighting half a dozen civil wars and invasions at once.

The writings of Winston Churchill, who cannot be supposed to be over-sympathetic to the Communist cause, throw sufficient light upon the political impossibility of these White groups, their hopeless lack of unity and their political incapacity, as is evidenced by Kolchak's violent treatment of Siberian peasants and Denikin's promise to give back seventy-five per cent of the land to its former owners. Taken severally, not one of them had a chance of success ; and gradually they were all defeated, the Poles not without a counter-offensive which all but captured Warsaw. But the price paid was naturally heavy. The first need was an army to defend the Revolution, which Trotsky organised with great success. But the Red Army, and the town workers who had made the Revolution, had to be fed, and fed in a country which economically had collapsed a year before, and to which the European Powers had applied a blockade similar to that employed against the Central Empires in the last years of the war. The only, and the obvious, thing to do was to ration out strictly the supplies, seeing, as far as possible, that those whose services were essential to the defence of the Revolution were first considered. The policy of " War Communism," as enforced between 1918 and 1921, is essentially no more than the policy of rationing and State control which most of the European belligerents had adopted before the end of the war, raised to the nth. The Bolsheviks were not in nearly so much of a hurry to socialise everything as is sometimes supposed ; their first economic controlling body, *Vesyenka*, was set up in December 1917 ; but corn and merchant shipping, those vital points, were not nationalised until the following February, and foreign trade not until June. Various parts of industry were nationalised from time to time ; but the general decree nationalising the whole of industry was not passed until July 1918, and then partly in order to combat sabotage and inefficiency.

For the enthusiasts of the Revolution, assuming that the old régime had gone, and a new system of workers' control was to be instantly inaugurated, had in many cases rushed to seize the factories and put them under the control of " factory committees " whose revolutionary zeal considerably outran their organising capacity. Further, such middle-class technicians as had existed in pre-revolutionary Russia had almost all taken sides against the Revolution, and had either fled the country, or, where they remained, were less inclined to work the new system than to promote its speedy collapse—in which they were cordially encouraged by the outside world. Russia, in the summer of 1918, was full of enthusiastic but incompetent revolutionaries, spies and counter-revolutionary agents of all kinds, as well as many who honestly believed that the Revolution was a hopeless failure. Against these the stern measures of centralised factory control and the reprisals which are associated with the word *Cheka* were put into force. The " Red Terror " did not seriously begin until September 1918 ; it preserved the Revolution by putting to death or banishing or otherwise getting rid of its principal wreckers, but at the price, inevitable under the circumstances, of losing a large proportion of native organisational skill. The Russian worker had to set about learning his industry from the beginning, unhelped.

After 1920–21, however, the external situation eased. The blockade was lifted ; treaties were made with the Baltic

States (1921), with Turkey (1921) after the three southern border States had been absorbed into the Soviet system, with Poland (1921), and with Germany (1922). Furthermore, the States which did not make formal treaties began to admit the existence of Russia as an economic neighbour. The Anglo-Soviet Trade Agreement was signed in March 1921 and lasted until its suspension in April 1933, when negotiations for its renewal were broken off, and Anglo-Russian trade was temporarily suspended by Great Britain as a reprisal against the trial and imprisonment of two British engineers by the Soviet. The embargo ended, and negotiations for a new agreement were resumed in July. At the same time negotiations for American trade credits in Russia were opened in London in connection with the World Economic Conference. Other countries which have recognised Russia, either fully or for trade purposes, include Germany, Austria, Italy, Hungary, France, Japan, the Scandinavian States, Turkey, Persia and Afghanistan.

The establishment of peaceful, if uneasy, relations with the world made it possible for the system of War Communism to be abandoned, as indeed was desirable, for a system of control so stringent in intention could not have been continued. The grain requisitions which were made of the peasantry in order to keep the Red Army and the city workers alive were beginning to be bitterly resented, particularly as the collapse of industrial production meant that the peasant could not be provided with manufactures in exchange for his grain. The chaos of the currency added to the confusion. Lenin's New Economic Policy, therefore, launched in 1921, gave a temporary licence to private traders, thereby enabling the peasant to sell his products for what he could get ; and a beginning was made of stabilising the currency. (The gold *chervonetz* was first issued in 1922.) For a time this considerably eased the situation. But the peasant, stimulated by the high prices which he received immediately from the hungry towns, increased his production sharply ; and as industrial productivity—which requires capital—could not rise so fast, the result was a sharp increase in the price of manufactured goods to the peasants—the " scissors crisis " of 1923–24. This was temporarily met by various measures ; but the root difficulty remained. In January, 1924, Lenin died, of paralysis following attempted assassination ; and his ideas had to be carried out by his successors.

The root difficulty is simply the poverty of Russia. An abundant supply of manufactured goods, which is necessary to raise the standard of life, cannot be produced unless there is plenty of capital and a surplus of food wherewith the workers to be employed in industry can be supported. This surplus must be supplied by the peasant ; but under systems of individualist production he has been for the most part unwilling to do so, because the price of industrial goods (owing to the shortage of production) has been too high to make it worth his while. The position in regard to capital supply is broadly similar. Russia cannot make a substantial advance without the expenditure of large sums on " fixed capital "—railways, manufacturing plant, electrification, and so on. The normal way in which a poor country finances its development is by borrowing abroad ; but Russia has been unable to borrow, mainly because of the strong external prejudice, which showed itself, for instance, in a demand that the Soviet Government should make itself responsible for the enormous burden of Tsarist debt before any fresh money could be lent. In order to obtain the necessary capital resources, therefore, the Soviet Government, unable to borrow abroad, has had to " save " the necessary money out of the very slender resources of its citizens in order to buy the foreigners' goods. This involves the export of foodstuffs as well as oil and timber to pay for them, which again, as in the later years of the nineteenth century, falls upon the peasant.

The Five-Year Plan. In 1928 the Five-Year Plan was begun, which in essence means the adoption of the first of these alternatives. A Western industrial system was to be created, in the main out of Russia's own resources, with the aid of such short-term foreign credits as could be secured. An exhaustive survey of the possibilities had been in hand throughout the preceding year, and a plan was drawn up which laid down the ground which each industry was supposed to cover during the five ensuing years. Naturally, the main stress of the first Five-Year Plan was laid upon the heavy industries, the foundation of an industrial nation. At the same time a drive in the direction of increased production, and particularly socialised production, was to be given in agriculture. The motive for this was partly political. The original granting of the land to the peasants had always been recognised as a temporary measure ; the Communists, and Lenin as much as any, were entirely opposed to the establishment of a society of peasant proprietors in Russia, such as the French Revolution had created in France. At first they hoped, by the setting up of large State farms as examples, to bring the peasantry over to belief in socialised methods ; but this hope was disappointed, and the New Economic Policy had definitely made the peasants less socialistic and intensified the difference between the richer peasants (*kulaki*) and the poorer (*ceredniaki* and *bedniaki*). Accordingly, the Five-Year Plan for agriculture not merely envisaged a great extension of farming on a collective basis, but further aimed at a drive towards equality in the villages by discriminating, and encouraging the villagers to discriminate, heavily between the *kulaki* and their poorer neighbours —in fact, by treating the *kulak* as a criminal.

It may be stated at once that, as far as industry was concerned, the Five-Year Plan succeeded on the whole far more than any observer thought it would. While in some cases the estimated total has not been reached, and while there have been mistakes and the quality of production is still far below the standard of advanced Western nations, nevertheless the measure of achievement has been astonishing. (A Second Five-Year Plan, with greater attention paid to transport and to the lighter industries, was launched at the end of 1932.) With regard to agriculture, the Plan has been less successful. The attempt to socialise the villages, which began at the end of 1929, was too sudden and too vehement, and had to be modified in the spring of 1930, but not before a sort of " stay-in strike " on the part of many peasants had resulted in a lowering of production and a catastrophic slaughter of livestock. At the same time, the collapse of world agricultural prices meant that a much higher export of foodstuffs was necessary to purchase the same quantity of machinery. Many of the State farms or grain factories proved wasteful and impossible to manage ; and though the " collective " farm seems more in keeping with the traditional habits of the peasant, Russian agriculture suffered a serious setback in 1930–33, and it is too soon to say whether a quick recovery is likely.

Meantime, external relations were proceeding none too happily. Trade agreements, as has been said, had been concluded with a number of countries, and a sort of grudging recognition of Russia thereby accorded ; but it was a recognition of the fact, proved in 1919 and 1920, that the Soviet system could not be overthrown by invasion and was unlikely to be overturned at home, and in no sense implied any cordiality, or even any general acceptance of the régime. " Incidents," such as the British Arcos raid of 1926, kept on occurring, produced partly by plain hostility to Russia and partly by resentment at the activities of the Third International. Russia's refusal to ask for admission to the League of Nations seemed to the European Powers impertinent, and though Russian plenipotentiaries have been seen at various international conferences, such as the 1927 Disarmament Conference and the World Economic Conference of the same year, their speeches, based upon an entirely different conception of society, have more than once dismayed and annoyed their fellow-diplomats.

Russian revolutionary propaganda abroad has very much diminished since the early days. At first it was assumed by the Communists that the Revolution in Russia could only succeed as part of a world-wide revolution in which Russia

NR

would merely lead the way ; and the revolutionary out-
breaks which immediately followed the war seemed mo-
mentarily to confirm that view. Accordingly, the Third
International (see p. 683) devoted a great deal of
energy to endeavouring to promote revolution in other
countries. Gradually it became apparent that these
measures were not bringing world revolution any nearer,
and were, on the other hand, tending to lessen the possibility of the peaceful trading relations which Russia so
much needed ; and during the period of the New Economic
Policy, though the language of the Third International
continued as violent as ever, its activities were actually
considerably curtailed. This position aroused the fears of
Trotsky, Zinoviev, and other Communists, who held to the
original view, and maintained, moreover, that the attempt
to carry the Revolution through in Russia alone could only
be done by bribing the peasant, by making him, in fact,
a *bourgeois* proprietor ; and they pointed to the growth of
the *kulak* under the N.E.P. as an illustration. After a long
struggle within the Communist Party, the adherents of
Trotsky were beaten by the adherents of Stalin, its present
secretary, and Trotsky was expelled in 1927. Immediately
afterwards followed the Five-Year Plan, the great attempt
to make Russia self-sufficient, and the drive against the
kulaki, designed partly to guard against the dangers which
Trotsky had pointed out.

Russia, during the last few years, has been definitely set
towards self-sufficiency and peaceful relations with other
Powers ; hence a generally conciliatory attitude towards
such countries as Japan and Poland. But this does not mean
that the Russians have ceased to fear war. They feel that the
capitalist Powers have not abated, only ceased to give rein
to their hostility, that any moment another concerted
attack upon Russia may be made ; and this feeling is increased by the fact that the majority of their European
contacts are made with diplomats who still live in the
atmosphere of international war. Such incidents as the trial,
in April 1933, of the British engineers in Moscow, and the

attitude taken up by the British Press and politicians, with its calm assumption that the prisoners were completely innocent and would certainly not receive a fair trial, do nothing to abate it.

Hence every now and then a wave of war panic overcomes the Government, strengthening the Red Army and the revolutionary defences ; hence, also, the removal of the heavy industry and the munition plants to long distances from the frontiers ; and hence the proposal, made from time to time, that the actual capital itself should be shifted from Moscow to somewhere in the Urals. Russia still is, and feels herself to be, a beleaguered State ; and the present shortage of foodstuffs intensifies this belief. The period of War Communism has not been left very far behind.

The Soviet Constitution.
The U.S.S.R. is a federal republic, made up of seven sovereign republics, the Russian Socialist Federal Soviet Republic (which is much the largest of the members), the White Russian, Ukrainian and Transcaucasian Republics, and the Republics of Turkmenistan, Uzbekistan and Tajikistan. Some of these include in their territories " autonomous republics," such as the German Volga Republic, the Far Eastern Republic and the Tartar Republic in the R.S.F.S.R., and the Republics of Georgia, Armenia and Azerbaijan in Transcaucasia. There are also " autonomous regions " with rather less autonomy. Under the constitution of 1923, the seven republics are sovereign, except where powers have been assigned to the Union ; but the assigned powers are so wide and so numerous, including, for example, foreign trade and foreign relations, defence, the direction of national economic policy and internal trade, taxation and labour legislation, as to give the main controlling direction to the All-Union Government, though there is a great deal of republican autonomy in such matters as public health. In 1932 the question of the demolition of redundant churches was made an affair of the central government.

Civil rights, including the franchise, are enjoyed, broadly

speaking, by all persons of either sex over 18 years of age who earn their own living. The classes debarred from civil rights consist of persons employing hired labour for profit (this includes *kulaki*), or living on unearned income ; monks and priests, imbeciles, and former agents of the Tsarist régime ; but special cases may be considered, and exceptions made, by provincial election commissions. It is commonly estimated that about 8 millions of the population fall into one or other of these classes. Deprivation of civil rights means, in effect, much more than disfranchisement ; it also involves loss of Trade Union membership, ration card, and other essentials. It commonly follows conviction for any serious offence ; and punishments in Russia (except for counter-revolutionary activities) are so light as compared with those of other countries that the loss of civil rights is often felt more heavily than the actual penalty.

The Governmental machine is in form a pyramid, based on the Soviet system and built up by delegation from below. The lowest rank is that of the small town and rural Soviets, including Soviets representative of large factories. (The rural population is considerably more lightly represented than the town workers.) Delegates from these bodies come together to form the *rayon* or district Soviets. Above these is the *Oblast* or provincial Congress of Soviets. This Congress elects an Executive of 451 persons, which meets three or four times in the year, and with the Council of Nationalities (representative of all the republics and autonomous districts) chooses a Presidium of 27. The Presidium, together with the Council of People's Commissars, a body consisting of the heads of the principal State departments and so resembling in composition the British Cabinet, makes up the governing body of Russia. In the early days, when Lenin was its chairman, the Council of Commissars was the most important body ; but under the new constitution it was subordinated in important respects to the Presidium. Under the Council of Commissars is the " Council of Labour and Defence," in effect its Economic Committee, which decides upon the plans for industry and finance submitted to it by the State Planning Department (Gosplan), and below again are many Commissions and Committees for dealing with one or other part of the State activities ; but these are so numerous and also change their name and function so often that it would be impossible to attempt to describe them here.

Such is the constitutional machinery of the Soviet Republic. But a mere description of the machinery is worthless and misleading unless it takes account of two factors of primary importance—the Communist Party and the immense network of tiny groups which may compendiously be called " the collectives."[1]

The Communist Party is the body which in Russia exercises the dictatorship of the proletariat ; but it does this, not by virtue of any special place under the constitution, but by virtue of its past history and its present membership. During the Revolution, as has been stated, the Communists were the only party with a policy ; it was thus necessary, in order to carry the Revolution through, to put Communists in all the positions of strategic importance, and to see that they there carried out the orders of the Party. This position, substantially, still remains. Of the nearly two million members of the Communist Party in Russia, not all, of course, are in positions of importance, and high positions, further, are occupied by Russians who are not Party members ; but the really key places are still held by Communists, and their instructions as to policy and behaviour are given them by the Congress of the Communist Party, or, between Congresses, by its Politburo of nine members, whose secretary is Stalin. It follows that the debates which really influence the direction of Russian policy are those conducted at the Congresses of the Communist Party.

But the Communist Party is more than this ; it is a dedicated Order, to which men and women are only admitted after a searching examination and a period of probation

[1] Not the same as the collective farms.

while their conduct is under close scrutiny by their future fellow-members, and from which they may be expelled if they fail to come up to standard. (During one of the biggest " purges," that which took place in the summer of 1930, 130,000 persons were so expelled.) As far as is humanly possible, the Communist Party does its best to see that both in intellectual understanding and in personal character, its members are fitted for their task of being pivots of the new system. Generally speaking, a member of the Communist Party must be prepared to put himself at the service of the State ; he must be ready to do overtime work and to undertake all sorts of additional activities at the behest of his Party call. The standard of personal service and of personal conduct is high and strictly enforced. Until recently, though this restriction has since been relaxed, the upper limit of salary for a Communist was low. Furthermore, he must obey decisions of the Party on theory and policy when they have been made. Until they have there is enormous latitude of discussion (*vide* all the reports of Communist Party Congresses) ; but when an idea or policy has been definitely rejected, no Communist can continue to hold it.

The Communist Party is thus the driving and directing force of new Russia. Even where Communists are not in direct control, there is Communist influence, as in the famous " Red Triangle," to be found in all factories, whereby a representative of the Communist Party sits with a representative of the factory committee and with the manager to determine factory policy. But it should not be assumed that the only Communists in Russia are the members of the Communist Party. In the first place, there are all the Russians under twenty-four (for whom, it is true, there are Communist youth organisations available) ; in the second place, there is always a large number qualifying for membership ; and thirdly, and most important, there is a vast mass of people who, while heartily agreeing with the Communist policy, either do not want or think they would be unable to pass the stiff tests demanded

of entrants. Some of the most vocal Communist supporters
are not Party members.

Against this discipline and centralised control of the
Communist Party, however, there has to be set an enormous amount of almost spontaneous grouping for self-
government and criticism, which alone could make the
system workable by human beings. The first impression of
many visitors to Russia is not of an iron discipline but of an
endless clatter of tongues, all discussing, making suggestions,
pouring out criticisms of the working of particular parts of
the system, and even modifying it, to an extent which would
and does horrify an English government official, in order
to make it suit local or special conditions. In the administration of justice, for example, there is no country in which
the Mikado's practice of making the punishment fit the
crime is more earnestly followed. Russian laws, except
where they are held to concern the safety of the State, are
not laws so much as general guiding principles ; their
detailed administration in practice is left, not, as in England, to the official of some ministry or other, but to a
" collective," i.e. a local committee, of a factory, for
example, of tenants of a group of flats, of parents of children
in a school, even of prisoners in a prison. Where there is
a Russian, there appears to be a " collective " ; it even
seems difficult to remove a drunk man from the middle of
the highway without an impromptu committee arising to
discuss it.

Further, complaints and criticisms are vigorously encouraged by the central authorities. The newspapers are
full of them ; and there is even a body, called the Workers'
and Peasants' Inspectorate, whose sole duty it is to receive
and investigate complaints, which is independent of any
government department, and which may descend at any
moment in order to see whether a charge, particularly a
charge of inefficiency, corruption, or bureaucracy is well-
founded. Of course, this system is open to abuse ; where
complaints are encouraged there is room for petty spite to
find vent ; and there is undoubtedly too much complaining

in Russia at the present time, and too much nagging at people in responsible posts. Charges of corruption and sabotage are very easily made. The underlying belief is that where consciousness of collaboration in a great and important work is strong enough petty spite will disappear ; and undoubtedly the sense of common purpose, in the towns at any rate, is enormously strong, though the strain of the building of a new society on a low food ration is liable to produce explosions of hysteria and bad temper which do harm. In the meantime, however, the institution is a valuable safety-valve for discontent.

At this point mention must be made of the State Political Department (G.P.U.) Set up in 1922, this body is the direct descendant of the *Cheka*. It is the only police force which operates throughout Russia, the others being simply local forces ; it is also entrusted with the work of defence against counter-revolution from within the State, the Red Army being mainly for external defence. As such, it is responsible for the great State prosecutions for sabotage, espionage, etc. ; it has also very wide powers of secret action ; and it has a large staff, both uniformed and un-uniformed, the latter being employed, often unknown to their fellows, in ordinary employment. It is not an institution which sounds pleasant to English ears, though Continental countries are more accustomed to the use of secret police ; it should, however, be mentioned that it performs many other functions which are more positively social. For instance, the entire organisation for the reclamation of the " homeless children "—a splendid piece of imaginative work—was initiated and carried out by the G.P.U.

Even a description of the working of her political institutions does not, however, adequately describe Russia to-day ; the complete social changes involved in the abolition of private property, the institution of State planning and the exaltation of the productive worker over the recipient of unearned increment go so deep that only a book would suffice to expound them. The visitor to Russia is continually receiving shocks, continually being reminded that he is in a topsy-turvy country, a country where the ideals which are accepted over the whole of the rest of Europe and America are simply rejected, and a new set of ideals is in force. Russia may not be a Socialist country, and her present rulers would certainly admit that she is not ; but her face is set towards Socialism, and that involves a re-orientation of the whole of life and a denial of the values upon which capitalist civilisation is based.

Furthermore, this drive towards Socialism is based upon the conscious and passionate co-operation of millions of Russian citizens. Citizenship, in Russia, means far more than the passive casting of a vote at intervals ; it involves a continuous participation in the task of building up, as rapidly as may be, the Socialist State of the future. Opinions differ as to the extent to which a knowledge and understanding of the aims of the Soviet State is diffused among its citizens ; but, leaving on one side the minority who are treated as social enemies (and who will continue to be so treated as long as Russia feels herself a beleaguered city) there is no doubt that wide and deep among her citizens, and particularly among the young persons and the children, this " State-consciousness " is alive and active. Russia alone, of all States in the world to-day, has succeeded in re-creating some of the spirit which was to be found among the citizens of ancient Athens ; and the contrast between this spirit, and the dull and dead apathy, alternating with moods of blind and violent revolt, which is to be found among the populations of Central and Eastern Europe—who live, for the most part, actually at a higher standard than the majority of Russians —has struck observers who cannot be accused of any sympathy with Communism.

The fight against illiteracy, and the clamour of the Russian proletariat for education, which makes it almost impossible to buy a book or a newspaper in spite of the tremendous increase in the production of both since the Revolution, is only one aspect of this enthusiasm. So also is the enlistment of millions of Russian women, on equal terms with men, in productive industry and government service, although the social effects and implications of the sex equality introduced by the Revolution go far beyond a mere drive for increased production. The treatment of children, on the other hand, must be admitted to be far more Socialist than productive in intention. The Soviet laws relating to child-life and labour are, in intention, the most generous in the world ; and one great aim of Soviet policy is to secure that the new industrial State of Russia shall not be built, as the European industrial system was built, at the expense of the growing generation. Whether the resources of the Union will be consistently adequate to maintain the high initial standard of child-care and education which has been set, depends of course in the last resort upon the economic progress of the Union as a whole ; of the effort and intention, however, there is no doubt.

PART III: ECONOMIC CONDITIONS IN EUROPE

1. The Economic Situation After the War
2. The World Slump
3. The Situation of European Agriculture
4. The Debtor Countries of Europe
5. The European Monetary Problem
6. Proposals for Raising the Price-Level
7. Proposals for Restoring the Gold Standard
8. The Slump in European Industry
9. The Great Industrial Countries
10. The Strangling of European Trade
11. Wages in Europe

§ 1. THE ECONOMIC SITUATION AFTER THE WAR

In the minds of many people who lived through the war as civilians in Great Britain or the United States the years between 1914 and 1918 are connected above all with memories of an unwonted economic plenty. For during the war, though an immense part of the man power in all the belligerent countries was away fighting and a large fraction of those who remained were producing not commodities for the satisfaction of normal human needs but munitions of war to be shot away or trodden into mud on one or another of the long fighting fronts, on the whole in both Great Britain and the United States the populations that were left behind lived better than they had ever lived before. Prices were high, and rose higher ; but earnings rose too, and there was no unemployment to depress the standard of living. Of some things there was indeed a shortage ; and in Great Britain rationing schemes had to be introduced and became more severe during the last period of the war in consequence of the intensified submarine campaign and the scarcity of tonnage. But, when all allowance has been made for rationing and the limitations imposed by it on the consumer's range of choice, the fact remains that in both Great Britain and America the years of war were from the standpoint of the ordinary consumer years of prosperity—years to which men look back with wonder now that they have experienced the pinch of peace.

While this is true to a great extent of the civil populations of Great Britain and the United States, it is certainly not true of the populations of most of the belligerent countries of Continental Europe. Russians, Germans, Belgians, Poles, Austrians, Serbs and Hungarians have certainly no cause to look back on the experience of the years of war with any sense of economic regret. In Russia the comparatively undeveloped and highly inefficient organisation of industry and transport broke down completely under the strain of warfare. Town dwellers suffered acutely ; and the peasants were largely cut off from supplies of industrial goods, while the market even for their produce became more and more disorganised as the war advanced, and larger and larger masses of men were enrolled in military service. Germany, experiencing the rigid blockade of her frontiers, went shorter and shorter even of the elementary needs of life as the struggle continued ; and the disastrous reactions on the physical welfare of the German people have by no means yet been overcome. Belgium under German occupation went through the same experience of acute shortage and under-nourishment ; and the same fate befell the territories further east which were under the occupation of the Central Powers. In the actual theatres of war production became impossible, and the means of living of millions of people were ruthlessly destroyed. In Great Britain or the United

States one can sometimes hear men only half in jest asking for another war as a means of curing unemployment, stopping wage reductions, and ushering in a new period of economic prosperity. But over the greater part of Europe men cherish no such illusions. If they are in a mood to go to war again, it is not because they think of the last war as an automatic dispenser of economic prosperity.

Continental Europe, taken as a whole, emerged from the war far less productive than it had been in 1914. There had been indeed in all the belligerent countries a great development of those industries which minister directly to the needs of war ; but this development had been forced artificially and was dependent upon military demand, so that much of the productive plant which had been built between 1914 and 1918 was not readily adaptable to meeting the needs of communities endeavouring to " return to normal conditions." Such stimulation as the war had applied to particular industries was far more than offset by the general deterioration of the industrial machine and by the disproportion between producing capacity in different branches of industry. Moreover, the land had suffered, not only in the devastated areas, but also to some extent elsewhere, as a result of the shortage of men and of manures. There had been in many areas much slaughtering of beasts, and over large parts of Europe the old agrarian systems were manifestly breaking down ; while in the new States that were being set up on the ruins of the pre-war Russian and Austro-Hungarian Empires, the basic questions of land ownership and the rights of cultivation were still unsettled, and secure conditions for the productive use of the land were still to seek.

Immediately after the conclusion of hostilities, many people thought that the broken-down economy of Continental Europe stood in such obvious need of wholesale rebuilding as to ensure for years to come a large sustained demand for the products which the more fortunate countries were able to supply, and a complete immunity from unemployment while the necessary work of reconstruction was being carried through. These hopes, however, speedily faded away. There was indeed the short-lived hectic post-war boom of 1919 and the first half of 1920, during which prices soared far above the highest points which they had reached during the years of war, and huge fortunes were made by businesses which were able to supply both the capital goods and the consumers' goods that were most urgently required both by the stricken nations for the rebuilding of their shattered resources, and by the new States for the construction of the necessary equipment for national economic life. The post-war boom, however, was even at its height never a boom in the sense in which a boom implies a real accession of prosperity. It was a boom in prices and not in production. Huge fortunes were made not by selling large quantities of goods but rather by charging fantastically high prices for an exceedingly short supply. The illusory prosperity of 1919 and 1920 was based on scarcity, and not on plenty, and its collapse was inevitable as soon as men began to realise that in face of the real scarcity there existed in the nations which stood most urgently in need of supplies no real and present capacity to pay.

During this short-lived boom output in relation to the number of men employed remained at a very low level ; there was a scarcity of up-to-date plant adapted to meeting the needs of the post-war world, and neither employers nor workers were in a mood to give really efficient service. The employer, finding money come easy as prices rose—for in those days only the veriest fool could avoid making high profits—was under no compulsion to exert himself in cutting down the costs of production or in making his methods more efficient. If, as was often the case, he had worked at high pressure during the war, he wanted a rest, and he took the easy conditions of money-making as they came without much thought for the future, even where he did not plunge into orgies of financial speculation based on the unreal expectation of a continuance of demand at steadily rising prices. The workman, for his part, had also been at a strain either in the workshops or in the trenches during the years of war ; and he too was inclined to take things easy as long as the boom lasted. Trade Unions were powerful then, and there was in most industries little fear of the sack to keep men up to the mark. The idea that everything would come right on the morrow of the war had been dinned into the ears of all classes in all the belligerent nations, and in the Allied countries it was difficult to destroy quickly the expectations which patriotic statesmen had aroused in the course of war propaganda.

In the defeated countries the situation was in this respect very different. There too the peoples had been led to expect an epoch of abounding prosperity after the war ; but this expectation had been based on the assurance of victory, and in Germany and Austria men, facing the knowledge of defeat, sank deeper and deeper into despair as the news came through of more and more onerous terms being imposed by the victorious Allies. Moreover, in these countries the physical vigour of the workers as well as their morale had been seriously impaired by the long struggle, and the industrial equipment had been much more seriously damaged than that of the victorious Powers. Low production was in their case inevitable, quite apart from the psychological causes which tended to bring it about in the victorious countries.

In the latter part of 1920 the illusory post-war boom definitely broke. Prices in terms of gold fell with unparalleled sharpness, so that in all the countries which either remained upon or were intent on returning to the gold standard a rapid and destructive process of deflation set in. This deflation, wherever it occurred, intensified the difficulties of the economically weaker countries, and led in their case to a precisely contrary tendency. In the new States of Europe, in Germany, and before long in France and Italy as well, the machinery of government could be kept at work only by printing the money required to meet the immediate expenses of the State ; and the inflationary process thus begun speedily communicated itself to the operations of industry, causing a wave of speculative activity in both internal and international business dealings. Thus prices in different countries pursued an erratic and dissimilar course, as some followed the path of deflation on their way back to the gold standard, while others hovered between attempts at stabilising their currencies at varying levels of exchange, and renewed plunges into inflation as their difficulties began again to accumulate.

Post-War Recovery.

From the standpoint of Europe as a whole the period since the war can be divided roughly into four distinct phases. There comes first the short-lived and deceptive boom of 1919 and 1920, during which something was done to meet the most urgent needs of reconstruction, but done without much attempt to count the cost, or to place the economic systems of the European States on a sound or permanent footing. The second phase extends from the collapse of the boom in 1920 to about 1923. These were years of depression, unemployment, unrest and falling standards of life, accompanied, as we have seen, in most of the countries of Continental Europe by great instability of the currency and great uncertainty as to the economic future. But from 1924 onwards Europe was recovering in an economic sense ; production was increasing fast, and one currency after another was being at least provisionally stabilised, although there were still to be many set-backs, and in some cases currencies were stabilised only to be upset and re-stabilised several times over. Trade as well as production was increasing as the States of Europe began to settle down within their new frontiers, and to build up the new relationships based on the changed political divisions of the post-war world. This period of real reconstruction, as contrasted with the unreal reconstruction of 1919 and 1920, lasted at least in appearance until the coming in 1929 of the great slump under which Europe is still prostrate.

Some measure of the situation which existed in Europe on the eve of the period of recovery between 1924 and 1929

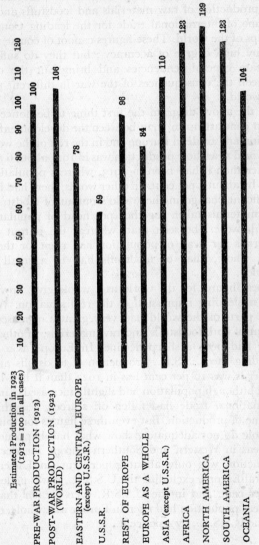

THE EFFECT OF THE WAR ON EUROPEAN AND WORLD PRODUCTION

Estimated Production in 1923
(1913 = 100 in all cases)

PRE-WAR PRODUCTION (1913)	100
POST-WAR PRODUCTION (1923) (WORLD)	106
EASTERN AND CENTRAL EUROPE (except U.S.S.R.)	78
U.S.S.R.	59
REST OF EUROPE	96
EUROPE AS A WHOLE	84
ASIA (except U.S.S.R.)	110
AFRICA	123
NORTH AMERICA	129
SOUTH AMERICA	123
OCEANIA	104

For the remaining area, the Caribbean, the figure for 1923 is as high as 164.
The figures, except for the U.S.S.R., are from the League of Nations' Memoranda on Production and Trade. The U.S.S.R. figure is from official Russian sources.

can be secured by looking at the figures published by the League of Nations showing roughly the movements in the production of raw materials and foodstuffs and in the volume of international trade for the leading Continental groups of the world. These figures cannot of course pretend to any high degree of accuracy ; but they do sufficiently indicate general tendencies and bring out the contrast between the consequences of the war in different parts of the world.

In the above diagram the first thing to be noticed is the sharp contrast up to 1923 between the development of production and trade in Europe and in the rest of the world. In the world as a whole production was in 1923 about 6 per cent greater than it had been in 1913, whereas population had risen by about 5 per cent. In other words, there had been no significant change in the world's output of foodstuffs and raw materials taken together per head of population. It will, however, be seen that, whereas the output of raw materials per head of population had risen for the world as a whole, that of foodstuffs had to a small extent declined.

These figures for the world as a whole give, however, a very misleading impression of the real situation. Whereas some parts of the world had very greatly increased their output of both foodstuffs and raw materials, in other areas there had been a sharp decline. In Europe as a whole, including the U.S.S.R., production of foodstuffs and raw materials was 16 per cent less in 1923 than it had been in 1913, although population had slightly increased. European international trade had fallen off scarcely less than the volume of production. But even these figures for Europe as a whole do not adequately show what had happened ; for whereas in Western and Southern Europe the decline in production was only about 4 per cent, in Eastern and Central Europe, excluding the U.S.S.R., it was no less than 22 per cent, and in the U.S.S.R. even greater than this, whereas population had risen in Europe as a whole, excluding the U.S.S.R., by 4 per cent.

GENERAL INDICES OF PRIMARY PRODUCTION, 1925–1931

Weighted by values of 1930. Base=Average of 1925-9 = 100. From League of Nations Review of World Production, 1925-1931.

	1925	1926	1927	1928	1929	1930	1931
Europe, without U.S.S.R.	95	89	100	104	112	103	98
Europe, with U.S.S.R.	94	92	100	103	110	104	100
North America	96	100	98	103	102	93	88
Latin America	96	96	101	103	104	102	97
Africa	95	95	98	103	108	106	104
Asia, without U.S.S.R.	97	97	99	102	105	108	102
Oceania	93	101	99	105	102	110	108
World	95	96	99	103	106	101	96
*Industrial Production (12 countries, without U.S.S.R.)	91	92	100	105	112	97	84
†Industrial Production (10 countries, including U.S.S.R.)	93	93	99	104	112	101	86

*League of Nations estimate.

†Estimate of German Institut für Konjunktur-forschung.

These figures serve to reveal the very real poverty of the European countries, and especially of Eastern and Central Europe, in the years immediately after the war ; and this fundamental fact of poverty is seen still more clearly when the figures for Europe are contrasted with those for other Continents. Thus in North America production had risen by 29 per cent and population by 19 per cent, while in Central America, as against a rise of only 7 per cent in population, production was actually up by 64 per cent on the pre-war figures. Even Asia showed a rise of 10 per cent in production as against 5 per cent in population.

It is unfortunately not possible to give any corresponding figures showing what had happened between 1913 and 1923 to the output of manufactured goods ; but there is good reason to suppose that the course of manufacturing production had been over this period much the same as that of the production of foodstuffs and raw materials ; for although there has been in recent years a considerable economy in the quantity of materials needed to produce a given output of finished commodities, it is practically certain that the greater part of this economy was achieved after 1923. It can therefore be taken as at any rate a fair approximation to the truth that in Europe as a whole the standard of wealth had fallen by at least 15 per cent in the decade which ended in 1923, and that in Eastern and Central Europe the fall in the standard of wealth was probably as much as 25 per cent—a truly desperate situation in view of the pre-war poverty of most of the countries concerned.

At the same time the figures given above show that after 1923 a rapid recovery did set in ; and this is made even clearer by the table on p. 403 which carries on the record on a somewhat different basis past the coming of the slump in 1929.

On the basis of these further figures it will be seen that between 1925 and 1929 the production of foodstuffs and raw materials rose in the world as a whole by about 12 per cent, whereas in Europe the rise was no less than 18 per cent. Taking foodstuffs alone, world production rose between these years by 6 per cent, and European production by 12 per cent, while for raw materials the rise was in both cases very much greater, amounting in the world as a whole to 21 per cent, and in Europe to no less than 30 per cent. It is a significant fact that during these years, despite all that was said about the tremendous wave of prosperity in the United States, the actual rise of production was considerably slower in North America than in Europe, so that as against the rise of 18 per cent in total production in Europe, North America showed a rise of only 6 per cent. This discrepancy was partly due to the bad harvests in America in 1929 ; but even if we take the figures for raw materials alone, the advance in the United States between 1925 and 1929 was only 15 per cent, or half the advance recorded in Europe for the same period. Even in 1928, despite the large harvests in the New World, the production of foodstuffs in North America was only 8 per cent greater than in 1925. It is thus clear that in the years immediately before the world slump Europe had not only regained and surpassed as a whole the pre-war standard of production, but was also advancing at a substantially faster rate than the rest of the world, though in comparison with the pre-war situation the advance in production in Europe was still very much less than the advance in the world as a whole. On this point no figures are available as a basis for direct comparison between 1913 and 1929, but a comparison can be made between 1913 and 1928. On this basis, in the world as a whole population had risen by 10 per cent, and production by 25 per cent, made up of a rise of 16 per cent in the output of foodstuffs and of 40 per cent in that of raw materials. For Europe, excluding the U.S.S.R., the increase of population was 6 per cent and that of production 11 per cent, or, including the U.S.S.R., 8 per cent in population and 10 per cent in production. On the other hand, in North America population had risen by 26 per cent, and production by 35 per cent. In Asia, the corresponding figures are 7 per cent and 24 per cent, and in South America 43 per cent and 56 per cent. Europe in fact had made up

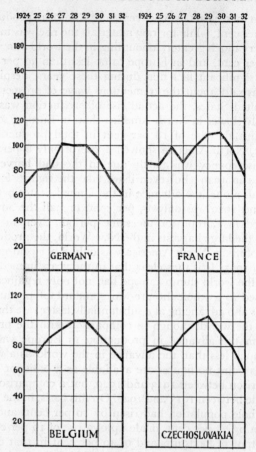

THE RISE AND FALL OF EUROPEAN

Official Production Indices of the various

	1924	1925	1926	1927	1928	1929	1930	1931	1932
Germany	69	80	81	101	100	100	90	74	61
France	86	85	99	87	100	109	110	98	76
Gt. Britain	95	—	—	101	100	106	98	89	88
U.S.S.R.	30	50	70	82	100	124	156	189	200
Belgium	77	75	86	94	100	100	90	79	68

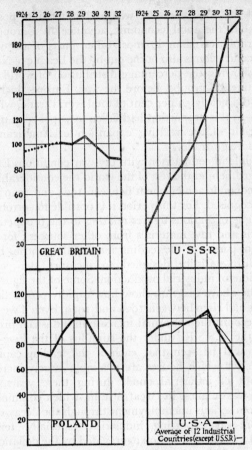

INDUSTRIAL PRODUCTION, 1924–1932

Countries (Production in 1928 = 100)

	1924	1925	1926	1927	1928	1929	1930	1931	1932
Czechoslovakia	74	79	77	90	100	104	91	81	59
Poland	—	73	71	88	100	100	82	69	54
U.S.A.	86	94	97	96	100	107	87	73	58
12 Industrial Countries	—	87	88	95	100	108	93	80	—

some of the leeway of the war and immediate post-war years ; but the total economic advance in Europe was considerably less than in most other parts of the world.

This conclusion is also borne out by the League of Nations figures showing the percentage distribution of world trade by Continental groups. Before the war, Europe, including Russia, did nearly 59 per cent of total world trade, whereas in 1928–29 this proportion had fallen to 52 per cent, mainly as a result of the relative expansion of American and Asiatic foreign trade.

But while in comparison with pre-war conditions Europe still lagged behind the rest of the world the considerableness of her economic achievement between 1924 and 1929 needs to be recognised. For this period it is possible to corroborate the League of Nations figures relating to the production of foodstuffs and raw materials from other sources ; for from about 1924 most of the leading industrial countries began to publish statistics designed to measure the general fluctuations of industrial production. Some of the figures set out in the above diagram show how rapidly production in industry had risen between 1924 and 1929. Even if we leave out of account the abnormal increase in industrial production in the U.S.S.R. under the stimulus of the Five-Year Plan, it will be seen that each of the leading capitalist countries for which figures are available largely increased its output of industrial goods during these years. The increase was smallest in Great Britain, which continued to suffer from serious unemployment through the decay of the great pre-war exporting industries, especially textiles, coal and metals—a situation aggravated by the deflationary policy pursued by successive Governments and by the Bank of England, in connection with the return to the gold standard at the pre-war basis of parity between the pound sterling and the United States dollar. But even in Great Britain industrial production rose by 12 per cent between 1924 and 1929 ; while in Germany, under the influence of the great influx of foreign capital in the five years following the Dawes Plan of 1924, the increase actually amounted to nearly 48 per cent, accompanied by a still greater expansion in the volume and value of German industrial exports.

Agriculture and Industry. It is beyond doubt that during these years there was not only a sharp increase in total European production, but also a really considerable advance in industrial efficiency. The years between 1924 and 1929 were in Europe as a whole a time of great activity in the constructional trades, and the heavy industries especially were largely re-equipped on a basis of increasing mechanisation which greatly increased the output per worker employed. This process was going on all over the world, and was probably proceeding at a substantially more rapid rate in the United States than in Europe, despite the larger advance during the period in total European production. For in the United States an unemployment problem, concealed by the absence of any statistics or any system of unemployment relief, was already coming into existence even during the period of the greatest apparent economic prosperity. Nor was the development of mechanisation and of the rationalisation of economic processes confined to the manufacturing and extractive industries. It was going on with at least equal speed in agriculture in the countries of the New World, where farming was being carried on with a rapidly increasing use of mechanical appliances and economy in the employment of labour. This, however, was not the case over the greater part of Europe. For in most of the European countries and especially in the new States, there had arisen after the war from the peasants and land-workers an irresistible demand for the division of the land ; and this had led in one country after another to the passing of new land laws under which a great many of the large estates were broken up into small peasant holdings.

This process of breaking up the great estates, whatever may be thought of its social consequences, undoubtedly reacted for the time adversely on agricultural production ; for peasant cultivation is in a technical sense usually very backward, and there was little opportunity on the new peasant holdings for the adoption of those labour-saving devices which were rapidly increasing the productivity of agriculture in the New World. In most of the States of Central and Eastern Europe there was a decline in the average production per acre, accompanied by a larger use of labour on the land—in other words by an increase in the real though not necessarily in the money costs of agricultural production. This decrease in agricultural productivity over a large part of Europe, occurring simultaneously with a great rise in productivity in the New World, made conditions inevitably difficult for the small peasant farmer ; and the position was further aggravated by the burden of debt by which many of the European peasant populations were weighed down. This burden was heaviest where the terms on which the peasants got the land involved the payment of large sums in compensation to the former owners, as in Tsarist Russia ; but even apart from this the peasants were mostly burdened with debts incurred at a time when capital was scarce and commanded an abnormally high rate of interest, and on a basis of agricultural prices which could no longer be sustained under competitive international conditions in face of the growing productivity of the large-scale agriculture of the New World. These conditions, as we shall see, led to the adoption in one country after another, in the hope of enabling the peasants to go on paying their debt charges without facing absolute starvation, of measures of high agricultural Protection designed to keep up the domestic price of agricultural produce even in face of the sharp fall in the world prices of the leading agricultural goods. But of course no merely domestic measures of Protection could help those peasants who were compelled to look to foreign markets to absorb a considerable proportion of their supplies. Indeed, the growth of agricultural Protectionism in Europe steadily worsened the position of the peasants in the food-exporting countries, and led, not only to desperate financial measures designed to save these countries from complete economic collapse,

THE FALL IN AGRICULTURAL PRICES, 1924–1932

End of Year	1924	1925	1926	1927	1928	1929	1930	1931	1932	
Wheat, No. 2 N. Manitoba	73/-	66/-	56/6	58/-	49/3	55/6	24/6	30/9	25/3	per qr.
Wheat, English Gazette, average	12/2	12/5	11/10	9/10	9/6	9/6	6/-	6/1	5/4	per cwt.
Barley ,, ,,	14/5	10/6	10/7	11/4	10/2	8/8	8/3	8/3	6/11	,,
Oats ,, ,,	9/6	9/3	8/2	9/3	8/11	7/-	5/6	6/8	5/9	,,
Maize, La Plata, landed	48/-	38/3	32/-	38/-	42/3	31/-	17/9	18/6	19/-	per qr.
Beef, English sides, shillings	6.2	5.7	4.8	4.7	5.3	5.7	5.3	4.5	4.5	per 8lbs.
Beef, Argentine, chilled hindquarters, shillings	5.0	3.9	4.0	4.2	4.2	5.2	4.7	3.8	3.8	,,
Mutton, English Wethers, shillings	8.8	6.5	7.8	6.7	7.0	7.0	6.8	5.2	4.8	,,
Mutton, No. 2, frozen, shillings	5.8	4.8	4.3	4.8	5.0	4.8	3.9	2.8	2.9	,,
Bacon, Danish	113/-	129/6	88/-	79/6	98/-	105/-	61/6	45/-	65/-	per cwt.
Butter, Danish	244/6	173/-	185/-	181/-	200/-	180/-	142/-	136/-	122/-	,,
Cheese, Canadian	100/-	104/-	94/-	101/-	105/-	97/-	76/-	65/-	64/-	,,
Wool, English Southdown, washed	3/1	2/-	1/9	2/4½	2/3½	1/11	1/1½	1/1½	10d.	per lb.

but also to dictatorships of increasing severity directed against the hunger movements and economic unrest among the impoverished peasants.

The extent to which agricultural prices were already falling in the years before the coming of the world slump can be shown by selecting from the available British statistics a few outstanding instances. Thus, if we compare prices in 1924 with prices in 1929 we find that Canadian wheat (Number 2, North Manitoba) had fallen from 73s. a quarter in December 1924 to 55s. 6d. in December 1929. English wheat, meanwhile, had fallen from 12s. 2d. to 9s. 6d. a hundredweight, English barley from 14s. 5d. to 8s. 8d., and English oats from 9s. 6d. to 7s. Meanwhile, the price of maize landed in England had fallen from 48s. a quarter to 31s. Danish butter was down from 244s. 6d. a hundredweight to 180s., and Danish bacon from 113s. to 105s. In the case of meat, however, the fall was in general far less severe than in that of cereals. English beef had fallen only from 6·2s. per 8 lbs. to 5·7s., and Argentine chilled beef had actually risen slightly in price. But English mutton was down from 8·8s. per 8 lbs. to 7s., and New Zealand frozen mutton from 5·8s. to 4·8s. In cheese there had been relatively little decline ; in the case of Canadian Cheddar from 100s. per cwt. to 97s. But wool prices (English Southdown) had fallen tremendously—from 3s. 1d. per lb. at the end of 1924 to 1s. 11d. at the end of 1929.

In the meantime there had been a sharp increase in the stocks of such agricultural commodities as are capable of being stored. On 1st August 1926 the stock of wheat in the world was estimated at under 6½ million metric tons ; by August 1929 it had risen to over 15 million metric tons, and these figures in both cases under-estimate the accumulation, as they include only stocks in four countries—Canada, the United States, the Argentine and Australia.

There had been a similar sharp fall in the years between 1924 and 1929 in the prices of many of the leading raw materials. Thus American middling cotton had fallen from 13·6 pence per lb. at the end of 1924 to 9·4 pence at the end of 1929 ; and Egyptian cotton even more sensationally from nearly 30 pence to 14·2 pence. Italian silk was down from 28s. a lb. in 1924 to 18·9s. at the end of 1929, and Livonian flax from £121 a ton to £58. Cleveland pig iron fell from 81·5s. a ton to 72·5s., and Welsh Admiralty Steam coal from 27s. to a little over 20s. Durham coal descended from 22s. to 16s. 9d., and Sheffield house coal from 27s. to 21s. a ton. Portland cement was down from 60s. 9d. a ton to 47s. Certain of the lesser metals showed an even more considerable fall. Tin fell from £267 a ton in 1924 and over £300 a ton in 1926 to £178 at the end of 1929 ; and lead, from £45 in 1924 to £23 in 1929. Copper, on the other hand, owing to strong combination among the producers, was actually a fraction higher—£68 as against £67—in 1929 than in 1924.

There had been no corresponding fall in the prices of finished industrial goods, though these too had shown in certain cases a downward tendency. In the case of cotton goods there had been a very sharp fall indeed. The price of cotton yarn, for example (32 twist), fell from 24·5 pence at the end of 1924 to 13·9 pence at the end of 1929 ; and cotton cloth (39 inch shirtings) fell from 18s. a piece to 13s. Everywhere, manufactured goods had become much dearer than before the war in relation to both foodstuffs and raw materials, as the accompanying table very plainly shows.

In face of this situation there was developing during the years of advancing prosperity which immediately preceded the world slump a serious disequilibrium between the prices of manufactured commodities and those of foodstuffs and raw materials, as well as a further discrepancy between the factory prices of finished goods and the prices of the same goods passing into the hands of the consumer by way of retail trade. It is a familiar fact that in periods of falling prices the wholesale prices of commodities usually fall faster than the retail prices which measure the main elements in the cost of living, and that there also tends to be a lag between the fall in the prices of manufactured goods at

THE FALL OF INDUSTRIAL PRICES IN GREAT BRITAIN, 1924–1932

End of year	1924	1926 General Strike year	1928	1929	1930	1931 Off gold standard	1932
Cotton, American Middling, *d.* per lb.	13·6	6.9	10.6	9.4	5·3	5·3	5·1
Cotton, Egyptian Sak. *d.* per lb.	29.9	14.0	19.5	14.2	7·7	7·1	7·2
Cotton Yarn, 32's Twist, *d.* per lb.	24.5	12·4	15.5	13.9	9.0	9·1	9.0
Cotton Cloth, 39in. Shirtings, shillings per piece	18/-	12/-	14/-	13/-	10/1½	9/9	9/2
Wool Tops, 64's, *d.* per lb.	82	45	46	31	22	23½	23
Silk, Raw Italian, shillings per lb.	28/-	26/3	22/6	18/9	10/9	11/9	9/-
Pig Iron, Cleveland G.M.B. No. 3, shillings per ton	81.5	87·5	66.0	72.5	63.5	58.5	58.5
Iron Bars, Middlesbro', £ per ton	12.0	12.25	10.25	10.75	10.75	10.0	9.75
Steel Rails, Middlesbro', £ per ton	9.0	8.5	8.5	8.5	8.5	8.5	8.5
Tinplates, S. Wales, shillings per box	23/6	21/9	18/-	18/9	15/6	14/6	16/-
Coal, Welsh, Best Admiralty, shillings per ton	27/-	29/3	19/4½	20/1½	20/-	19/6	19/6
Coal, Durham, Best Gas, shillings per ton	22/-	23/-	14/9	16/9	15/3	14/7½	14/6
Coal, Sheffield, Best House, shillings per ton	27/-	30/-	21/-	21/-	23/-	23/-	23/6
Cement, Best Portland, shillings per ton	60/9	60/9	47/-	47/-	47/-	43/-	43/-
Timber, Swedish U/s 2½ x 7, £ per standard	21	19	19	19	18	16	15
Copper, Standard, £ per ton	67·4	56.2	74.0	68.0	46.5	38.5	28.6
Tin, Standard, £ per ton	267	300	226	178	117	141	148
Lead, English Pig, £ per ton	45.0	30.25	22.25	23.25	16.25	17.0	12.5

COMPARATIVE DECLINE IN PRICES OF VARIOUS KINDS OF GOODS FROM JANUARY 1929 TO JANUARY 1932

Percentage decline in prices of

	Agricultural Goods	Raw Materials	Manufactures	Imports Average of 1929 to Average of 1931	Exports Average of 1929 to Average of 1931	Cartellised Goods	Competitive Goods	General Wholesale Index	Cost of Living
U.S.A. .	50	39	26					31	17
Canada .	52	38	22					27	15
Germany .	30	31	21	33	18	20	50	28	19
Italy .	35	44	30	31				31	
Great Britain .	19			31	14			23	11
Poland .	42								
Jan. 1929 to Jan. 1932.									
Czechoslovakia				35	22			27	7
France .				59	25			36	0
Sweden .				37 (Sept. 1931)	22			28	19

wholesale, and those of raw materials, which are the first to feel the full effects of adverse trade conditions. But in the present case to these familiar phenomena of a falling price-level there was added a wholly abnormal fall in the relative purchasing power of the agricultural section of almost every community in the world, owing to the exceptional severity of the fall in the prices of primary foodstuffs as well as agricultural raw materials. The important point is not that the agricultural populations of the world suffered most as a consequence of the world slump of 1929 and the following years, but that the disproportion between their purchasing power and that of the industrial population had already begun to make itself manifest during the preceding years of apparent industrial prosperity.

In some quarters this fall in the relative prices of farm goods has been attributed to agricultural over-production, and the enormous increase in the cultivation of wheat in Canada has been cited as an outstanding example of this tendency. But, as we have seen earlier, the production of foodstuffs in the world as a whole was actually advancing at a considerably less rapid rate than that of raw materials destined for use in industry. Some of these raw materials are of course of agricultural origin, so that the prosperity of the agriculturists depends on the demand for industrial raw materials as well as on the demand for foodstuffs. But even when this is taken into account there is certainly no evidence that the output of agricultural commodities was expanding faster than the output of raw materials not derived from the cultivation of the land. The explanation of the decline cannot therefore be found in an expansion of agricultural output beyond the general average of the expansion of output of primary commodities of all kinds.

It is, however, suggested that as the world's standard of living rises the relative demand for foodstuffs tends to contract, as people spend a smaller proportion of their incomes on the elementary needs of life, and have a larger amount left to spend on more diversified classes of goods and services largely derived from industrial production.

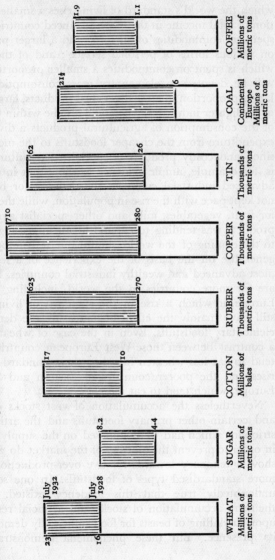

ESTIMATED WORLD STOCKS OF CERTAIN COMMODITIES

White areas represent stocks in July, 1929; shaded areas addition to stocks at July, 1932

COFFEE
Millions of
metric tons
1.9
1.1

COAL
Continental
Europe
Millions of
metric tons
21½
6

TIN
Thousands of
metric tons
62
26

COPPER
Thousands of
metric tons
710
280

RUBBER
Thousands of
metric tons
625
270

COTTON
Millions of
bales
17
10

SUGAR
Millions of
metric tons
8.2
4.4

WHEAT
Millions of
metric tons
July 1932
July 1928
23
16

Or

Undoubtedly this is to some extent true. To the extent to which the world's standard of living rises a smaller proportion of total income in the more advanced countries will be spent on commodities of all sorts, and a larger proportion on various forms of personal service ; and of the income which is spent on commodities a smaller proportion again will be devoted to elementary mass consumption and a larger proportion to more diversified products, largely those of the lighter industries. There will also be within the range of the consumption of agricultural products a diversion of expenditure from the cheaper foodstuffs to the more diversified and costly products of specialist agriculture. There is, for example, ample evidence to show that in the more advanced industrial countries the demand for bread has not kept pace with the rise in population, while the demand for fruit, vegetables, milk and other specialist agricultural products was tending to expand at an increasing rate up to the coming of the world slump. But it is impossible to generalise on the basis of the experience of a few of the most advanced and wealthy industrial countries. For there are far more countries in the world, including many in Europe, in which a rise in the standard of living would still have mainly the effect of increasing the demand for elementary foodstuffs. Even in the case of wheat there is a contrast between those West European countries which tend to eat less wheaten bread as their standard of living rises and the poorer countries of Eastern and Southern Europe, which tend to eat more.

Nevertheless the accumulation of vast stocks of wheat and certain other primary foodstuffs and the artificial restrictions which had to be imposed on the supply of meat in order to prevent the glutting of the market do appear to show a tendency towards relative over-production of the more standardised types of foodstuffs. In one sense it is undoubtedly true that this tendency existed. Indeed, the mere accumulation of stocks and artificial restrictions upon the killing of beasts for food sufficiently demonstrated its presence. But these phenomena demonstrated the existence of over-production only in a purely market sense, that is to say in relation to the amounts that could actually be sold at prices at which the holders were prepared to dispose of them. When we ask why the market was thus limited we are driven back again on the absence of adequate purchasing power in those countries in which the rise in the standard of life might still be expected to cause an increase in the demand for standard foodstuffs. The peoples of these countries were so impoverished that they could not afford to buy more, and by buying more to offset the declining tendency of demand per head of population in the more advanced countries. But why did their demand fail to expand ? Largely because the inflated burden of debt at the declining level of general prices caused a curtailment in the purchasing power both of the agriculturists and of the industrial workers in the poorer countries. Thus, when once the demand for elementary foodstuffs failed to expand at an adequate rate in the advanced countries which had a sufficiency of purchasing power, the fall in prices caused by this failure reacted upon the position of the less wealthy countries, and so decreased their purchasing power as to exaggerate the falling tendency of prices and make their situation worse.

In face of these conditions the economic situation of the world was essentially unstable, even before the coming of the world slump in 1929. Nor was the worsening position of the agriculturists the only prominent cause of disequilibrium in the world's economic affairs. As we have seen during the period from 1924 to 1929 production in Europe was expanding substantially faster than production in the United States, despite the boom conditions prevailing on Wall Street and in the real estate market, and the widespread " prosperity psychology " among the American people. The American level of money wages was expanding but slowly, while prices were being held steady by the monetary policy of the Federal Reserve System. At the same time the farmers' purchasing power was falling off sharply ; and the number of workers employed in both industry and agriculture was declining as a result of economies in the methods of production. It is certain that the pay roll of American agriculture was substantially lower in 1929 than it had been some years before, and hardly less certain that the total sum distributed in industrial wages was quite failing to keep pace with the increase in productive capacity. The enormous speculative gains made in the United States boom by the purchase and re-sale of securities and real estate were based not on any corresponding expansion in the output of industrial goods, much less in the available market for them, but on a false anticipation of the future course of American prosperity, which ignored the real limitation of the market for mass-produced goods resulting from the decline in the total purchasing power of farmers and industrial workers alike. Instalment purchase pressed to prodigious lengths did something to cover up the deficiency in effective demand out of income ; but despite this artificial infusion of additional consuming power American production had begun to sag some time before the crisis on Wall Street occurred.

The utterly fictitious character of the valuations placed on securities and real estate during the boom could be seen even at the time in the absurd discrepancy between the market prices of industrial stocks and shares and the income yield from these same stocks and shares even under the prevailing boom conditions. American stock market and real estate prices were discounting in advance an assumed increase of national prosperity far beyond what had been actually achieved at the height of the boom. They were based on a complete ignoring of the real conditions of production and consumption, and an entire failure to realise that the prosperity of industry is bound up with the distribution to the main body of working-class and agricultural consumers of a sufficient volume of purchasing power to enable the rapidly increasing output of commodities to be sold at a remunerative price. The policy of maintaining the general level of prices stable in face of rapidly declining real costs of production in both industry

and agriculture could only have worked at all if means
had been found of placing the additional purchasing power
brought into existence by the inflationary action of the
banks in the hands of those classes of consumers who would
have used it to buy the increasing supply of goods which
industry and agriculture were in a position to produce. As
this was not done, partly because less men were being employed, and partly because of the declining purchasing
power of the agriculturists, the new money issued in the
form of additional credits through the banking system inevitably lapped over into speculation in the hands of the
richer sections of the community, and this prepared the way
for an inevitable smash as soon as the disproportion between
the power to produce and the disposition to buy had become manifest.

§ 2. THE WORLD SLUMP

I T H A S been necessary, in a book dealing primarily with
European conditions, to discuss the situation in America
during the boom of 1928–29 because the American boom
and the slump which followed inevitably upon it had such
tremendous reactions upon the situation in Europe. Both
the boom and the slump reacted adversely on the European
economic situation ; and, if now men are more disposed to
blame the slump because its consequences are nearer to
them and more obvious, it is still necessary to remember
that Europe's troubles began with the boom and were
serious in certain cases even before the coming of the Wall
Street crash.

The American boom reacted on the situation in Europe
chiefly by causing both a precipitate withdrawal of American capital from investment in Europe, and also to some
extent a diversion of European capital to the United States
in the hope of a share in the extravagant profits of American
speculation. How this happened can be seen at a glance
by studying the figures published by the League of Nations

to show the approximate magnitude of the exports of capital
from the principal creditor countries and the imports o
capital into the principal debtor countries during the years
between 1924 and 1929. In the five years from 1924 to
1928 the United States exported to foreign countries well
over 3,000 million dollars of capital, and well over 1,000
million dollars were exported in the one year 1928. In the
following year, 1929, the export of American capital fell
sharply from 1,100 million dollars to a little over 200
million dollars, thus creating a sudden void in the supply
of capital on which Europe had been basing the expansion
of its industrial production.

The effects of this withdrawal of American capital can
be seen in the figures showing the import of capital into
the leading European countries. In this connection by far
the greatest significance attaches to the situation in Germany. In the five years from 1924 to 1928 the total import
of capital into Germany is estimated to have amounted to
over 3,500 million dollars, of which over 1,000 million
dollars was imported in each of the years 1927 and 1928.
In 1929 the import of capital into Germany fell sharply
to 550 million dollars, and in 1930 to less than 150 million
dollars, thus bringing the movement of German rationalisation abruptly to an end, and creating the conditions
which led a little later to the complete suspension of reparation payments and the freezing of ordinary commercial
debts. These reactions were inevitable, in spite of the
tremendous efforts which the German Government made
to curtail imports while expanding exports at an unprecedented rate, in both cases at the expense of a severe fall
in the standard of living of the German people. In the same
way the import of capital into Hungary fell from 91 million
dollars in 1928 to 38 million in 1929 and 24 million in
1930 ; and the import of capital into Poland from 124
million dollars in 1928 to 67 million in 1929 ; while Yugoslavia, which had imported 27 million dollars in 1928,
actually turned in the following year into a net exporter
of capital. There was a similar fall in the imports of capital

into many of the non-European borrowing countries ; thus the Argentine, which had imported 181 million dollars in 1928, practically ceased in 1929 to import capital at all ; and Japan, which had imported 80 million dollars in 1928, became a small net exporter of capital in the following year.

The devastating effects on Europe of this sharp falling off in the importation of capital, a large part of which had been drawn in the preceding years from the United States, was only gradually felt, for to some extent the gap caused by the cessation of long-term loans and commercial advances from America was made good for the time being by the diversion of British lending to Europe and by the straining of the resources of the European banking system in the attempt to provide extended credits for industries left in the lurch. But these attempts to maintain the supply of credit in face of the tremendous fall in the volume of American lending, while they staved off trouble for a time, only served to aggravate the collapse when it did come. The banks which had granted credit for short periods found the money which they had advanced irrecoverable, and were compelled to resort to various forms of standstills and moratoria as the alternatives to complete and open collapse. It was gradually realised to what an extent Europe in general and Germany in particular had been living during the years before 1929 on American loans, and what disastrous consequences the withdrawal of these loans was, under the existing conditions of international relationships, bound to have upon the economic structure of the European Continent.

For the withdrawal of American lenders from Europe brought to light the inherent absurdity of the situation which had existed even during the period of apparent prosperity before the world slump. Europe taken as a whole imported from the United States far more goods than the United States, behind a high tariff wall, was willing to receive in exchange. And although the difference was to some extent decreased by third-party trade—that is to say, by American imports from non-European countries paid for by European exports to these countries—as well as by tourist expenditure and immigrant remittances, there remained, even after making allowance for these factors, a heavy adverse balance against the European importing countries. But at the same time these countries were due to pay to the United States, not only interest at high rates on the large and accumulating loans of American capital which had been made during the post-war years, but in addition claims to debt interest and repayment of principal arising out of public loans made by the United States to European countries in connection with the World War. The balance of trade being what it was, there was clearly no possibility that Europe could meet these enormous American claims. In the attempt to meet them gold was exported from many of the European bank reserves to the United States ; and the gold reserve of the American Federal Reserve System mounted up by leaps and bounds. This increase in the American stock of gold would have been far greater had it not been for the special position of France. For the French, especially during the period of the flight from the franc in consequence of inflation, had built up large private balances in the United States, and the repatriation of these balances set up a reverse flow of gold from the United States into the cellars of the Bank of France. For the most part, however, this reverse flow came later, after the onset of the world slump ; and the immediate effect of the withdrawal of American capital from investment in Europe was a great accumulation of gold stocks in America, accompanied by a decline in the gold resources of most of the European countries.

In these circumstances far more people began to realise— what had been apparent previously only to a few—that Europe had been living economically during the post-war years in a quite unreal world. To all appearances Germany had been paying reparations, and European countries had been meeting, mainly out of the sums paid as reparations, American claims to debt interest and interest on commercial loans. But it now became clear that Germany had only paid reparations at all to the extent that she had borrowed from America the wherewithal to pay, and that in effect the payments made by Europe as a whole to America had been nothing more than a handing back of a part of the sum simultaneously lent by the American investors to a variety of European borrowers, both public and private. It became apparent that America could only receive payment of the sums which she claimed from Europe as long as she was prepared to go on lending to Europe the money with which to pay, and thereby to swell year by year the total of the claims which would have to be met in future. The Americans could have their money *on paper*—on the express condition that they never received any of it, but rather continued to lend Europe each year substantially more than European debtors were even supposed to repay. For there was also the large adverse balance of commodity trade against Europe to be taken into account.

Unless the Americans were willing to sacrifice not only their claims in respect of war debts but also a substantial part of the capital which they had invested in Europe since the war, there was only one way out of this difficulty. They would have so to lower their tariffs as to admit into their markets an enormously increased quantity of European goods. But this American big business, supported by a large body of opinion among both investors and workers, was wholly unwilling to do ; for it appeared to menace the profits of the most securely entrenched American manufacturing industries, and also the vaunted " American standard of life " of the workers employed in these industries. Accordingly, the Americans, willing neither to modify their trade policy nor to give up their claims, were driven into the same expedients of moratoria and standstill arrangements as were arising in the European countries.

These realities existed just as much before the Wall Street crash of 1929 as after it ; but until the crash had actually occurred comparatively few people realised how momentous for Europe the consequences of the contraction of American overseas investment had already been. It was hoped that the interruption of American lending was only temporary, and that some sort of equilibrium would be speedily restored ; and few economists and still fewer statesmen or business men were prepared at that stage to look squarely at the realities of the situation. Only in Germany, on which the full brunt of the disaster fell, was there an early awakening to the full gravity of the crisis which was facing Europe ; for the Germans could hardly help being aware that their ability to fulfil the terms of the Versailles Treaty was dependent entirely on the maintenance of the large-scale borrowing in which they had been engaged continually since the adoption of the Dawes Plan in 1924. But even the Germans, making an intensive effort at fulfilment for the time being in the hope that political conditions would so change as to make possible a clearer appreciation of economic realities, were not concerned to pull the underlying facts out into the light of day. They were still following up the policy of Herr Stresemann, still endeavouring to fulfil their Treaty obligations, not with any expectation that these could in the long run be fulfilled, but in the hope that a few years of fulfilment at whatever cost would so re-establish Germany's position and confirm the security of post-war Europe as to make possible rational reconsideration of the Versailles Treaty.

So matters stood when, in the autumn of 1929, the American boom collapsed in the sensational panic on Wall Street, and the artificially inflated values of American securities and real estate began to be written down at the rate of many millions of dollars a day. Of the speculators, American and foreign, who had been active in the stock markets on the eve of the collapse, a very few got out while the going was good, and a substantially larger number, mistrustful of the confident prophecies that the collapse would be of short duration and the boom be resumed before long, cut their losses and escaped, damaged but not completely wrecked by their experiences. But many others held on, to incur further huge losses, as, after a brief and partial recovery of prices in the early months of 1930, the slump deepened and deepened during the following years. Among those who made heavy losses on the American stock markets in 1929 and 1930 were many European speculators ; and their losses further aggravated the difficulties of European industry and commerce in the following months. But far more serious than the losses of the speculators were the collapse of the American market for European exports and the reactions of this collapse on the demand for European goods in those non-European countries which had largely paid for their manufacturing imports by exporting raw materials to the United States. There was everywhere on the morrow of the American collapse an immense contraction in the volume of transactions in raw materials ; and there followed before long a sharp fall in the sales of manufactured goods all over the world. But in addition to the decline in the volume of world trade which came hard on the heels of the American collapse, there was also a sharp fall in the level of prices of practically every type of commodity, except those which were temporarily protected by the policy of powerful combines or by the holding up of prices of particular goods in certain home markets with the aid of high tariffs and other restrictions on the freedom of importation.

The extent of the decline of world trade cannot unfortunately be measured effectively in terms of actual volume except for a very few commodities ; for the tonnage figures of imports and exports published by a number of countries in fact convey very little information. It is therefore necessary to fall back upon the statistics of prices, though of course in using these it has to be remembered that the decline in the volume of world trade was far less than the decline in monetary values, owing to the sharp fall in prices which was both cause and consequence of the decline. In comparing values it is necessary to adopt some common currency unit for measuring the movements of trade in different countries, and it is best here to follow the statistics compiled by the League of Nations which measure the trade of the world in terms of gold dollars. From the accompanying table it will be seen that if the year 1928 is compared with the year 1932 the value of world trade has fallen in all by over 60 per cent in these four years. But this decline was very unevenly spread among different countries, and in the case of particular countries between imports and exports. Thus in Europe the heaviest decline in the value of exports was in the case of Poland, reaching 75 per cent, followed by Austria and Estonia with 66 per cent, Czechoslovakia and Spain with 65 per cent, and Great Britain with 64 per cent (U.S.A. 68 per cent); but whereas Spain's and Estonia's imports declined quite as heavily as their exports, in the case of Great Britain the decline in imports was only 56 per cent as against 64 per cent for exports. In the case of imports, four European countries—Hungary, Finland, Estonia and Latvia—contracted their purchases in terms of gold dollars by more than 70 per cent between 1928 and 1932; and eight others, including Germany, Italy and Czechoslovakia, by more than 60 per cent. Most of these were agricultural countries; but Germany's imports fell by 67 per cent as against a decline of 55 per cent in exports—yet another sign of the intensive effort made by the Germans to maintain their precarious position in face of the withdrawal of American capital from investment in Germany. Among other developed countries, Italy reduced her imports by nearly two-thirds as against a fall of 56 per cent in exports, while Czechoslovakia and Austria both suffered a fall of two-thirds. At the other end of the scale stands the Soviet Union, which experienced a decline of only 30 per cent in exports, and 27 per cent in imports. France, on the other hand, contracted her imports by 44 per cent as against a fall of 62 per cent in the value of her exports. Over Europe as a whole, the gold value of exports fell in these years by 58 per cent, and that of imports by 56 per cent.

It is interesting to compare these figures with the experience of the United States over the same four years. As we have seen, in the world as a whole the gold value of

THE PERCENTAGE FALL OF IMPORT AND EXPORT VALUES, 1928–1932

	Exports	Imports	Balance of Commodity Trade in millions of dollars*	
			1928	1932
Europe . .	58	56	− 325	− 163
Great Britain .	64	56	− 143	− 83
Germany . .	55	67	− 28	20
France . .	62	44	− 5	− 23
Italy . .	56	64	− 32	− 6
Belgium . .	52	49	− 3	− 4
Holland . .	57	56	− 23	− 15
Czechoslovakia .	65	61	5	—
Denmark . .	51	54	− 2	—
Poland . .	75	57	− 8	2
Roumania .	37	64	− 3	2
Spain . .	65	68	− 14	− 22
Sweden . .	59	54	− 3	− 3
Switzerland .	63	33	− 8	− 16
U.S.S.R. . .	30	27	− 6	− 6
Norway . .	44	55	− 8	− 2
Finland . .	54	74	− 4	2
Yugoslavia .	57	66	− 2	—
Bulgaria . .	46	51	− ½	—
Austria . .	66	57	− 12	− 7
Hungary . .	60	72	− 6	—
Greece . .	56	60	− 7	− 3
Turkey . .	45	64	− 2	½
Latvia . .	63	72	− ½	—
Estonia . .	66	78	—	—
Lithuania .	27	43	—	—
Portugal . .	45	51	− 6	− 3
U.S.A. . .	68	68	79	25
World . .	62	60	− 186	− 112

* Monthly averages

import and export trade fell by something over 60 per cent. In the case of the United States the fall was substantially larger, reaching considerably over 68 per cent on both sides of the account—the same figure for both imports and exports. But whereas the United States exports in all only a small fraction of its total output—about 10 per cent in normal times—and therefore the direct effect of even a fall of two-thirds in the value of exports need not have been very considerable if conditions had been maintained in the home market—which of course they were not—it is easy to see how catastrophic must be the effect of a fall of over two-thirds in the value of the United States purchases from abroad. For America is, or rather was before the slump, the world's greatest market for raw materials, the second largest market—only a little behind Great Britain—for manufactured goods, and the third largest market for imports of foodstuffs. In 1928 the United States imported 4,078 million dollars' worth of goods, but in 1932 this total had fallen to 1,322 million dollars ; meanwhile, in face of all the restrictions in force in Europe, the corresponding contraction of European imports was from 19,455 million dollars to 8,466 millions. Nevertheless, so great was the fall in United States exports over the same period that the favourable trade balance due to America had shrunk from over 950 million dollars in 1928 to under 300 millions in 1932.

The extraordinary changes effected by the world slump in the trading position of the leading European countries can be further illustrated by its reactions on the commodity balance of trade. In 1928, before the withdrawal of American capital, Germany had an adverse visible trade balance of over 3,300 million Reichsmarks. This adverse balance shrank to about 360 million Reichsmarks in 1929. In 1930 there was actually a favourable balance of nearly 1,000 million Reichsmarks, and in 1931 this favourable balance had risen to nearly 3,500 millions. But in 1932 the fall in exports reduced it to about 1,070 millions. France, on the other hand, had in 1927 a favourable balance of over

THE FALL IN WHOLESALE PRICES
(1929 = 100)

	1930	1931	1932	March 1933
A. GOLD STANDARD COUNTRIES				
France	88	80	68	62
Belgium	87	74	63	59
Switzerland	90	78	68	64
Holland	82	68	56	51
Unweighted average of above	87	75	64	59
B. RESTRICTED GOLD STANDARD COUNTRIES				
Germany	91	81	70	66
Czechoslovakia . . .	87	79	73	70
Italy	86	74	68	63
Poland	86	74	65	61
Yugoslavia	86	73	65	67
Bulgaria	81	68	60	53
Estonia	87	78	71	68
Latvia	85	71	72	70
Unweighted average of above	86	75	68	65
C.				
U.S.A.	91	77	68	63
Canada	91	75	70	67
D. STERLING COUNTRIES				
Great Britain . . .	88	76	74	71
Denmark	87	76	78	82
Norway	92	82	82	81
Sweden	87	79	78	75
Finland	92	86	92	91
E. OTHER COUNTRIES				
Austria	90	84	86	82
Hungary	79	78	76	68
Greece	91	81	98	111
Spain	101	102	101	99

1,700 million francs ; by 1929 this had turned into an adverse balance of over 8,000 millions, and by 1931 the adverse balance had risen to over 22,000 millions—to fall again to about 10,000 millions in 1932. Italy, on the other hand, had reduced her unfavourable balance from nearly 7,400 million lire in 1928 to 1,440 millions in 1932.

In order to relate these figures showing the fall in the value of trade to the volumes of commodities passing between countries, it is necessary to take account of the change in the level of prices over the four years covered by the statistics. On the average, world wholesale prices fell during these four years by about one-third in terms of gold currencies, the fall being about 33 per cent in the United States and 34 per cent in France, as against as much as 25 per cent in Great Britain, despite the depreciation of sterling. These figures of course measure the general move-ment of wholesale prices and thus lay the main stress on those foodstuffs, raw materials and semi-manufactured articles whose values most readily admit of comparative measurement. The fall in the prices of manufactured goods was substantially less than this, and the fall in food-stuffs and raw materials slightly greater and, in the case of certain commodities of vital importance to particular countries, considerably greater. In the case of agricultural prices, the magnitude of the fall up to the end of 1932 can be measured by the accompanying table giving selected British quotations for the prices of a number of leading commodities.

The separate index numbers of prices compiled by a limited number of countries for raw materials and manu-factured goods make it possible for the relative magnitude of the fall in prices to be at least approximately estimated. Thus in Germany between the beginning of 1929 and the *beginning* of 1932 agricultural prices fell by 30 per cent, prices of raw materials by 31 per cent and prices of manu-factured goods by only 21 per cent, whereas in the United States the corresponding figures are 50 per cent for agri-cultural goods, 39 per cent for raw materials and 26 per cent

	Fall in Wholesale Prices per cent From average of 1929 to March, 1933	Fall in Cost of Living per cent 1933	Currency Depreciation in relation to Gold per cent March 1933	Date of Suspension of Gold Standard	Date of Imposition of Foreign Exchange Control	Central Bank Rate March 1933	Increase or decrease of Gold and Foreign Exchange Reserves 1929 Average to March 1933	New Capital Issues Percentage Fall, 1932	Industrial Share Values Percentage Fall 1929–1932
A. GOLD STANDARD GROUP									
France	38	6	—	—	—	2¼	+25	−59	−53
Belgium	41	17	—	—	—	3½	+49	−92	−66
Holland	49	18	—	—	—	2½	+53	+7	−72
Switzerland	36	18	—	—	—	2	+168	−1	−47
Italy	37	19	2	—	—	4	−27	−50	—
Poland	40	27	—	—	—	6	−50	−44	−72
B. RESTRICTED GOLD STANDARD GROUP									
Germany	34	24	—	7/31	7/31	4	−69	−85	−60
Czechoslovakia	30	7	—	9/31	9/31	3½	−23	−51	−48
Hungary	32	21	—	7/31	7/31	4½	−45	—	−43
Bulgaria	47	41	—	10/31	10/31	8	−38	—	—
Latvia	30	25	—	10/31	10/31	5½	−41	—	—
Estonia	32	25	—	11/31	11/31	5½	−26	−25	—
C. STERLING GROUP									
Great Britain	28	16	29	9/31	—	2	+17 [1]	−55	−40
Sweden	25	10	32	9/31	—	3½	+6	−52	−63
Norway	19	11	34	9/31	—	4	−13	−28	−35
Denmark	18	9	43	9/31	11/31	3½	−60	—	−25
Finland	9	19	40	10/31	—	6	+44	−25	—
D. OTHERS									
Austria	18	6	23	4/33	10/31	5	−74	−42	−34
Yugoslavia	33	31	22	—	10/31	7½	+84	—	—
Greece	+11	1	56	4/32	9/31	9	−34	—	—
Spain	19	1	56	Never restored	5/31	6	−5	—	—
U.S.A.	37	28	—	3/33	3/33	3½	0	−88	−76

[1] Gold only.

for manufactured goods. These changes in the relative prices of different classes of commodities are further reflected in the difference between the decline experienced by particular countries in the values of the goods which they import and export. Thus from 1929 to 1931 the average value of German imports declined by 33 per cent, and that of German exports by only 18 per cent ; and in the case of the United Kingdom import prices fell by 31 per cent and export prices by only 14 per cent, whereas in Yugoslavia export prices fell by 45 per cent and import prices by 32 per cent, and in Latvia export prices by 35 per cent and import prices by 24 per cent. Again in Germany the prices of imported raw materials fell between 1929 and January 1932 by 48 per cent, and the prices of raw materials manufactured at home by only 17 per cent, while in Czechoslovakia the general price level of imports fell by 35 per cent, and that of home-produced goods by only 22 per cent. For France the corresponding falls were 59 per cent for imports and 25 per cent for home-produced goods. These differences of course reflect to a considerable extent the protective measures adopted to shelter home markets from the competition of cheap imports from abroad. That the same result can be secured by industrial combination within a particular country is shown by the official German statistics dealing with the relative prices of goods subject to the control of cartels and those still sold under relatively competitive conditions. Between January 1929 and January 1932 the prices of non-cartelised goods in Germany fell by one half, whereas the prices of goods subject to the control of cartels fell by only one-fifth.

Differences in national policy in meeting the slump resulted naturally in corresponding differences in the internal price movements in the various countries. Practically everywhere the fall in wholesale prices was very much larger than the fall in the cost of living, though in one or two predominantly agricultural countries the difference between the two figures was not very great. Latvia and Estonia are examples of a fairly uniform rate of fall, while in Finland, owing to currency depreciation, the cost of living has actually fallen substantially more than the level of wholesale prices.

These, however, are exceptional cases, as the accompanying table clearly shows. Thus in France the fall in wholesale prices has been almost five times as great as the fall in the cost of living, owing to the effect of measures of domestic Protection. In Switzerland and Italy wholesale prices have fallen twice as much as the cost of living, and in Holland nearly three times as much ; while in Great Britain and Denmark also the reduction in wholesale prices is about twice the fall in living costs ; and in Czechoslovakia actually eight times as great. As these figures are to some extent affected by the depreciation of certain currencies in 1932 after the abandonment of the gold standard a column has been added to the table showing for January 1933 the approximate percentage of currency depreciation in the countries affected by this factor.

These differences between the movements of wholesale and retail prices must not of course be taken as measuring the changes in the ability of industry to pay wages or make profits in the process of production ; for the wholesale price figures refer, as we have seen, chiefly to raw materials, raw foodstuffs and some semi-manufactures, and must not be taken as an indication of the prices charged by the producer for manufactured goods leaving the factory. The fall in the prices of manufactured goods lies at a point intermediate between the fall in retail prices and that of the cost of living, with great differences between one industry and another in the extent to which manufacturers have found it possible to maintain prices by means of combination, with or without the aid of tariffs and other measures of Protection. The difficulty of the manufacturers has been that they have had to choose between lowering their prices and attempting to maintain them in a falling market. The latter policy could be pursued only at the cost of a severe contraction in the demand for their goods, so that a policy of high prices has resulted in much less being sold ;

whereas a policy of lower prices has been exceedingly difficult to carry into effect in face of the determination of the wage-earners to maintain money rates of payment with as little diminution as possible, and even more in face of the immense burden of debt arising out of money borrowed and expended at a time when prices were at a far higher level and rates of interest were ruling high. Inevitably the assets bought with this borrowed money have depreciated very seriously in value in consequence of the slump, while the rates of interest which business men undertook to pay before the coming of the slump are now out of all relation to the current value of borrowed money. In the case of purely short-term borrowings it has been possible in some cases for businesses to pay off their existing obligations and replace them by new money borrowed at a substantially lower rate of interest. But this has not been possible in the countries which have been suffering from a severe shortage of working capital and seriously menaced by the instability of their economic systems in face of large external debt burdens and of a sharp fall both in the prices of their exports and in their ability to find markets for them. Consequently, the more distressed a country has been, the heavier have been the debt burdens under which it has been compelled to stagger. Even, however, if it had been possible to reduce interest to substantially lower rates this would not really have cured the difficulty. For it would have remained true that the capital assets created by means of the borrowed money no longer possessed anything like the value originally invested in them, so that the payments due on the debts had become an almost unbearable burden. Something has been done, by way of standstill agreements, moratoria and similar methods of deferring payment, to ease the immediate burden of the excessive interest charges ; but these measures, which have at most only been pressed far enough to tide the distressed countries over their immediate difficulties, cannot in any case, unless there is a sharp recovery in the level of world prices, affect the larger question of the disproportion between the sums owing by businesses in

respect of their past borrowings and the current value of
the assets which provide the sole means of off-setting these
charges. Standstills and moratoria can only be conceivably
of any use in dealing with a purely temporary emergency.
They are based on the assumption of a speedy recovery,
not only of world trade but in the prices at which world
trade is done, to a level corresponding far more closely to
the levels at which capital debts were originally incurred.
Failing a very considerable rise in the level of world prices,
cancellation or repudiation of pre-slump debts is bound to
occur on a very large scale over by far the greater part of
Europe ; and this applies no less to commercial debts than
to the international and domestic debts of States and other
public bodies.

§ 3. THE SITUATION OF EUROPEAN AGRICULTURE

NATURALLY, apart from the complicating factor of external debts, which has been of outstanding importance
especially in the case of Germany, the countries which have
suffered most acutely as a result of the world slump have
been those which rely for the means of paying for their
imports on the sale of the agricultural goods and raw
materials which have declined most sharply in value. Of
all commodities that which affects the largest number of
countries is wheat ; and it is on wheat above all other
classes of goods that attention has been concentrated in the
attempt to restore the position of certain of the struggling
countries of Eastern Europe.

Of the twenty-four European countries which are of
importance to the trade in wheat as either importers or
exporters, only seven are normally exporting countries, as
against fifteen countries which normally require a net
import of wheat. By far the largest wheat exporter of
Europe is the Soviet Union, followed at a long distance by

Roumania, Hungary, Czechoslovakia and Bulgaria. Poland and Lithuania both export wheat in some years, but only to a quite small extent. The Soviet Union, before the war of overwhelming importance in the wheat market of Europe, practically dropped out during and immediately after the war, and even on the average of the years 1923–27 was only exporting about $5\frac{1}{2}$ million quintals a year out of a total domestic wheat production of about 189 million quintals ; but by 1930 production in the Soviet Union had risen to nearly 270 million quintals, and exports in this and again in the following year reached 25 million quintals. As compared with these totals the six other wheat exporting countries of Europe together exported on the average of the years 1923–27 under $5\frac{1}{2}$ million quintals, or about the same as the Soviet Union during the same years. In 1931, thanks to a bumper harvest in Roumania, the exports of these other six countries rose to nearly 20 million quintals ; but even so their total exports were well below the total exports of the Soviet Union. Including Russia, European countries had on the average of 1923–27 under 11 million quintals of wheat available for export, and in 1931 under 45 million quintals.

On the other hand, Great Britain alone imported on the average of 1923–27 over $52\frac{1}{2}$ million quintals, and in 1931 nearly $60\frac{1}{2}$ million ; so that, if Great Britain had set out to meet her needs for wheat from the European rather than from Empire markets, she could have absorbed and could still absorb the entire European surplus. The four next largest wheat importers—Italy, Germany, France and Belgium—together imported on the average of 1923–27 about 62 million quintals, and in 1931 $56\frac{1}{2}$ millions, the fall being accounted for mainly by the reduction of German wheat imports from 14 million quintals to 5 millions, and the Italian from 23 millions to 15, as against an expansion of the French imports from $13\frac{1}{2}$ millions to $23\frac{1}{2}$ millions. Thus, even if Great Britain were out of the European market as a buyer of wheat, Italy, Germany, France and Belgium could together absorb the entire European surplus

PRINCIPAL WHEAT EXPORTING COUNTRIES OF EUROPE

	Average of 1923-27			1931		
	Production million quintals	Net Exports million quintals	Yield per Hectare quintals	Net Exports million quintals	Production million quintals	Yield per Hectare quintals
U.S.S.R.	188.9	5.4	7.5	25.0 (1931)	269.2 (1930)	8.3 (1930)
Hungary	18.7	2.3	12.8	3.6	19.7	12.2
Yugoslavia	17.7	1.5	10.4	3.1	26.9	12.6
Roumania	26.4	1.2	8.5	9.9	36.8	10.6
Bulgaria	9.5	0.3	9.2	2.4	16.7	13.9
Poland	14.7	—	11.4	0.4	22.6	12.5
Lithuania	1.1	.1	11.0	0.2	2.3	11.7

PRINCIPAL WHEAT IMPORTING COUNTRIES OF EUROPE

	Average of 1923-27			1931		
	Production million quintals	Net Imports million quintals	Yield per Hectare quintals	Net Imports million quintals	Production million quintals	Yield per Hectare quintals
Great Britain	14.8	52.6	22.0	60.4	10.3	20.3
Italy	57.3	23.2	12.0	14.9	66.6	13.9
Germany	28.8	14.1	18.4	5.1	42.3	19.5
France	75.9	13.4	14.0	23.6	71.9	13.8
Belgium	3.8	11.2	26.2	12.9	3.8	24.4
Holland	1.5	5.9	27.3	7.4	1.8	23.6
Switzerland	1.0	4.3	21.7	5.6	1.1	20.3
Greece	2.9	3.7	6.1	6.6	3.1	5.0
Ireland	0.3	2.9	24.1	2.9	0.2	25.2
Sweden	3.2	2.3	19.8	1.2	4.9	17.8
Austria	2.7	2.0	13.6	3.0	3.0	14.3
Czechoslovakia	11.6	2.0	16.0	4.2	11.2	13.5
Denmark	2.3	1.4	26.6	3.9	2.7	26.1
Portugal	3.1	1.4	7.3	0.8	3.5	6.9
Norway	0.2	0.9	16.1	1.3	0.2	13.9

without making any allowance for the imports of the smaller countries. In all, the European import market amounted on the average of 1923–27 to 137 million quintals a year, and in 1931 to 135 million quintals, or more than three times the total quantity available for export from the European countries possessing a surplus, even including the U.S.S.R. Even if Great Britain is excluded from the calculation, owing to her relation to the wheat market in America and Australia, there still remains in the rest of Europe a sufficient net demand for wheat to absorb the entire output of the European exporting countries and then buy nearly as much again from the producing countries outside Europe.

In these circumstances there has been strong pressure from the countries chiefly concerned in the export of wheat to secure a preferential outlet for their surplus in the European markets. These countries want of course not merely a market for their exportable supplies of wheat, but a market at a price substantially above that ruling over the world as a whole. For this price, determined partly by the more favourable conditions of production in the New World, and still more of late by the existence of large stocks of unsold wheat which have hung continuously over the market with a permanently depressing effect upon prices, is far too low to enable the peasant cultivators of the European producing countries to exist at a tolerable standard of living, above all in face of the heavy burdens of debt by which they are weighed down. The project of securing a guaranteed market for the exportable surplus of wheat from the countries of Eastern Europe has come up during the past two years at a whole series of conferences, beginning with consultative action by certain of the exporting countries without the U.S.S.R., and broadening out into an attempt to tackle the wheat problem on European lines through the Special Committee on European Union formed under the auspices of the League of Nations as the outcome of Briand's proposal for a tentative advance towards a United States of Europe.

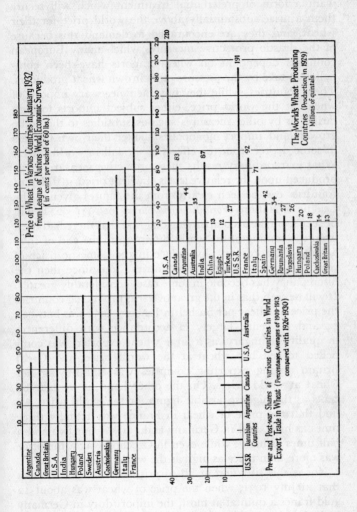

Price of Wheat in Various Countries in January 1932
from League of Nations World Economic Survey
(in cents per bushel of 60 lbs.)

Argentine
Canada
Great Britain
U.S.A.
India
Hungary
Poland
Sweden
Austria
Czechoslakia
Germany
Italy
France

The World's Wheat Producing
Countries (Production in 1929)
Millions of quintals

U.S.A	
Canada	83
Argentine	44
Australia	35
India	67
China	13
Egypt	12
Turkey	27
U.S.S.R.	191
France	92
Italy	71
Spain	42
Germany	34
Roumania	27
Yugoslavia	26
Hungary	20
Poland	18
Czechoslakia	14
Great Britain	13

Pre-war and Post-war Shares of various Countries in World
Export Trade in Wheat (Percentages, Averages of 1909-1913
compared with 1926-1930)

U.S.S.R   Danubian   Argentine   Canada   U.S.A   Australia
Countries

The wheat exporting countries included in the League want a form of preferential treatment which will secure them a price substantially above the world price for their wheat, and they are encouraged to demand this because of the drastic protective measures which many European countries dependent on wheat imports have been compelled to take by the pressure of their own wheat producers. These countries, while they buy their necessary imports of wheat at the world price, either subject imports to high tariffs, or by other measures such as subsidies to the home growers and import monopolies shelter their own farmers in some degree from the effects of the fall in world prices. What extraordinary results these protective measures have produced upon the relative levels of wheat prices in different countries can be seen clearly from the figures given in the League of Nations *World Economic Survey* for 1931–32. It will be seen from the accompanying diagram that there had been from the coming of the world slump up to the end of 1931 a quite extraordinary divergence in the domestic price of wheat in various European countries ; and since then the discrepancy has become in some cases considerably greater. It will be seen that in the great overseas producing countries the price of wheat per bushel in January 1932 was between 44 and 60 cents, largely in accordance with differences in quality. Hungary, as a large wheat exporter, was compelled to sell her wheat at the world price, and Great Britain among exporting countries was still buying her wheat at world prices. On the other hand, if we take 60 cents as the highest possible figure for the world price, we find that the price of wheat in France was actually three times as high, and in Germany and Italy about two and a half times as high ; while even in Czechoslovakia the price was more than twice as high as the world price.

Nor is this situation at all surprising in face of the fact that in July 1931, when the price of wheat was about 12 gold francs a quintal at most, the import duty in Germany had already reached nearly 31 gold francs a quintal. In fact, in those States where domestic wheat growing is important but not on a sufficient scale to meet the entire demand, the home consumers are being compelled in the interests of farmers threatened with ruin to pay exceedingly high prices for the absolute necessaries of life.

In these circumstances it seemed to the wheat-exporting countries, especially in view of the smallness of their available surplus in relation to the volume of European demand, by no means out of the question to claim preferential treatment for their exports to those European countries to which they were most nearly allied by their political interests. The Stresa Conference of 1932 worked out a scheme for a European effort to raise the price of wheat by means of a Guarantee Fund, and with the aid of a preferential system for European imports. But Great Britain, relatively little interested in wheat from the standpoint of domestic production, and finding substantial relief to the strain on her balance of payments from the abnormally low price at which she was able to buy wheat from overseas, was not at all likely to go into a European agreement designed to raise prices in the interests of the peasant cultivators of Eastern Europe. She had indeed, owing to her long- and short-term investments abroad, an interest in saving some of these countries from financial collapse ; but it was most unlikely that this interest would outweigh her interest in buying her wheat supplies at the cheapest possible rate, especially as she was proposing, in connection with the Imperial Economic Conference at Ottawa, to offer such preferences in the wheat trade as she was prepared to give at all to those Empire countries which had far larger surpluses than Europe to dispose of. She had, of course, already protected the domestic growers by means of a subsidy disguised as a quota scheme.

The European wheat exporting countries associated with the League of Nations had in their minds in endeavouring to secure preferential arrangements on a European basis not only the competition of wheat from the New World, but to at least an equal extent the increasing re-entry of the Soviet Union into the world market for wheat. As we have seen, Russia was before the war by far the largest European wheat exporter ; and even after the war she speedily recovered the first place in European exports, though the quantities which she was able to export still remained far below the pre-war volume. In the meantime, her place as an exporter had been supplied by the enormous growth of wheat output in the New World, and especially in Canada, so that the sudden re-entry of the Soviet Union on a large scale into the world trade in wheat in 1930 and 1931 raised an acute problem for those exporters who had regarded her disappearance as permanent. The Russians, for their part, stood in sore need of industrial imports required for the purposes of the Five Year Plan ; and apart from oil and timber there was no commodity except wheat which they could export on a large scale in payment for their imports. They had therefore the strongest possible incentive to increase the production and export of wheat from Russia, despite the unfavourable conditions prevailing in the world wheat market. For Russian external trade, carried on by means of a State monopoly, is not quite in the same position as the external trade of other countries. The Russians were in a position to sell their wheat for what they could get for it irrespective of its cost of production in Russian money. The less they received for it the less imports they were in a position to buy, and the higher was the price at which these imported goods had to be sold in Russia or accounted for by the Russian industries to which they were consigned.

The Russians, even more than the peasant cultivators of the other exporting States, were therefore in a situation in which the lower the price they could get for their wheat the stronger became their incentive to sell an increased quantity. Only the difficulties experienced as a consequence of the too-hasty collectivisation of a large part of Russian agriculture and the deficiency of the 1932 Russian harvest temporarily eased the situation created in the world market by the revivial of Russian competition.

The other exporting countries of Eastern Europe want,

then, to keep Russian as well as overseas wheat out of the markets of the European importing countries, which they hope to be able to influence until their own surpluses have been absorbed at a satisfactory price. But the divergence of interests among the European States has so far been too great for the wheat exporting countries to gain their point ; and, although France has been sympathetic to their claims, there has been no readiness to act upon the suggestions of the Stresa Conference for an inclusive European wheat pact at the expense of the U.S.S.R. and the New World. The project will doubtless come up again ; but the growing acuteness of political differences among the European States makes the likelihood of any effective action being taken upon it even more remote than it seemed when it was first put forward two years ago.

Meanwhile, at the World Economic Conference, an attempt has been made to secure an agreement between the four leading non-European wheat producing countries to restrict their acreage, as the first step towards a general attempt to raise prices by the restriction of supply. It is, however, difficult to believe that, save perhaps in the United States, such restriction can be successful, even if it was desirable ; for if the Canadian farmer or the European peasant is forbidden to grow wheat, what is he to grow instead, and who is to compensate him if he has to leave his land untilled ? As we write, the recovery of wheat prices in the U.S.A. under the influence of reflation, is cooling the ardour of the wheat interests elsewhere for restriction schemes ; and it is to be hoped that the idea will have been dropped before this book appears.

Wheat is not the only cereal which is of importance to the agricultural countries of Europe. Barley, oats, rye, and maize also play an important part in the agricultural economy of Eastern Europe. Thus in the case of barley, five countries besides the U.S.S.R. export considerable quantities, and there has been a sharp increase in the total European exports during the past few years. On the average of 1923–27 Roumania, Czechoslovakia, Poland, Hungary and Bulgaria together exported nearly 8 million quintals of barley, and this total rose in 1931 to nearly 13 million quintals. Corresponding figures for the U.S.S.R. at the two dates are $3\frac{1}{2}$ millions and $9\frac{1}{2}$ millions. The total net imports of barley into Europe amounted for these two dates to 20 million quintals and 24 million quintals respectively, so that if the U.S.S.R. is excluded, European exporters supplied only about half the total demand of the European importers, and even with the inclusion of the U.S.S.R. at the relatively high level reached in 1931 Europe was not self-sufficient in its supply.

In the case of oats, the international trade between European countries is of considerably less magnitude. On the average of 1923–27 only five countries, including the U.S.S.R., exported oats on any considerable scale, and the total exports of these countries came to only 2.3 million quintals, of which 600,000 quintals came from the U.S.S.R. In 1931 the total exportation was larger, amounting to 4.4 million quintals, but of this total no less than 3.9 millions came from the U.S.S.R. As against these total exports the net total import into Europe amounted on the average of the earlier years to over 11 million quintals, and in 1931 to nearly $13\frac{1}{2}$ million quintals. The position is different in the case of rye, of which Europe is by far the most important producer. Total imports of rye amounted on the average of 1923–27 to 2.4 million quintals from Bulgaria, Hungary, Poland, Roumania, and Yugoslavia taken together, and 4.8 millions from the U.S.S.R., and in 1931 to 3.7 millions from the same group of countries and over 11 millions from the U.S.S.R., making Europe more than self-sufficient in this cereal. On the other hand, in the case of maize, there is a very large net import into Europe from the New World, the net European importation averaging nearly 54 million quintals between 1923 and 1927, and no less than 93 millions in 1931. The chief European exporters of maize are Roumania, Yugoslavia, Bulgaria and Hungary, Roumania having by far the largest export. These four countries together exported nearly 16 million quintals

EUROPEAN AND WORLD PRODUCTION OF CERTAIN AGRICULTURAL PRODUCTS AND EUROPEAN IMPORTS AND EXPORTS IN 1930

	World Production	European Production	American Production	Asiatic Production	African Production	Oceanian Production	European Imports (+) or Exports (−)	World Production Average 1923-7	European Production Average 1923-7	Index of World Production 1930 (1925-9=100)	European Index of World Production 1930 (1925-9=100)	Index of World Production 1931 (1925-9=100)
Wheat	1,319	640	425	162	31	60	+108	1,137	527	111	111	103
Barley	426	233	101	69	21	2	+10	345	193	113		97
Oats	687	415	260	4	4	4	+5	653	386	102		95
Rye	492	470	18	3	—	—	−2	462	443	100		91
Maize	1,021	182	711	75	51	2	+52	1,143	180	90		97
Potatoes	2,018	1,848	142	19	3	5	—	1,707	1,546	111		111
Sugar-Beet	781	689	88	3	—	—	⎰ Sugar +12	545	473	99	Beet-sugar 133	99
Sugar-cane (incomplete)	1,244	3	686	335	95	125	⎱	1,100	1	100	Cane-sugar 99	100
Wine (hecto-litres) (incomplete)	159	133	10	—	15	1	+10	167	148	93		96
Olive Oil	4.6	3.6	—	0.5	0.5	—	−0.7	7.5	6.6	52		104
Citrus Fruits	67	21	30	6	1	9	+2	45	19	—		—
Tobacco	24.0	4.4	9.7	9.4	0.6	—		21.6	4.4	109		—
Linseed	40.9	8.8	27.9	3.9	—	—	+11	37.4	7.4	103		102
Cotton	56.3	3.5	31.6	15.5	4.7	—	+19.6	54.1	1.5	97		127
Flax	6.0	6.0	—	—	—	—	+0.3	5.3	5.2	115		—
Wool (metric tons, 000)	1,630	359	462	116	175	518		1,516	367	100		105
Raw Silk ,, ,,	60	7.3	—	52.3	—	—		49	6.0	110		156
Art Silk ,, ,, (for comparison)	200	131	53	16	—	—		89	62	140		

Figures in millions of quintals except where otherwise stated.

on the average of 1923–27 and 13 million quintals in
1931. The U.S.S.R. is comparatively unimportant as an
exporter of maize, averaging only 1½ million quintals in
1923–27 and 1 million quintals in 1931.

It was proposed at the Stresa Conference to provide
guaranteed markets for all these cereals in the European
importing countries. The proposed convention was based on
the granting by the importing countries of special facilities
for the import of cereals up to an aggregate tonnage equal
to the average exports of the exporting countries between
1929 and 1931. This would have given a total of 18 million
quintals of barley, 16 million quintals of wheat, 13½ million quintals of maize, 4 million quintals of rye and 1
million quintals of oats. It was proposed that all, or nearly
all, European countries should participate in the convention by making a financial contribution in aid of the re-
establishment of agricultural conditions in the exporting
areas. This contribution was to amount to 75 million gold
francs a year, to be devoted to the revalorisation of cereals,
the contributions made by the various States being subject to reduction " in proportion to the effective operation
of the advantages granted to the selling countries under
bilateral treaties for the importation of the above-mentioned
cereals." The fund was to be administered by an International Committee representing both the importing and the
exporting countries, and this Committee was to have some
power to supervise the use made by the agricultural States
of the sums received from the fund. But as we have seen,
there appears to be little chance of any proposal on these
lines being accepted by a sufficient number of the importing countries to allow it to become operative. Nor is it by
any means clear how it would in fact work, or what reactions the attempt to close the European cereal market as a
whole to supplies from abroad, except to meet the combined needs of Europe after absorbing the exportable
surplus of the East European countries, would be likely
to set up. It is at any rate highly unlikely that Great Britain,
in view of her commitments at Ottawa to her own

Dominions, would agree to participate in any scheme giving preferential treatment to cereal imports from Continental Europe ; while it is clear that the adoption of the proposed convention would have serious consequences for the U.S.S.R., which is bound to depend largely on the export of cereals for the purchase of necessary imports.

The plan elaborated at the Stresa Conference dealt only with imports of cereals from the countries of Central and Eastern Europe, and did not attempt to provide any special assistance for the producers of other types of agricultural goods. Of these other types of goods the most important from the European standpoint are meat, butter and cheese. In these cases too there has been during the world slump a very sharp fall in prices, following in most cases on a gradual decline during the preceding years. Thus in the case of beef the average end of the year British price fell from 5·7s. per 8 lbs. in 1929 to 4·5s. in 1932. Argentine chilled beef actually rose in price between 1924 and 1929, largely owing to the successful operations of a ring, but after 1929 there was a sharp fall from 5·2s. per 8 lbs. to 3·8s. In the case of English mutton the fall in price was even more severe—from 7s. in 1929 to 4·8s. in 1932, while New Zealand mutton fell from 4·8s. to 2·9s. Danish bacon was 129s. 6d. in 1925, but fell to 79s. 6d. in 1927, and then, after a rise in 1929 to 105s., to only 65s. in 1932. Meanwhile Danish butter fell from 180s. a cwt. in 1929 to 122s. in 1932. And there was also a sharp fall, though not quite of the same steepness, in the prices of the various types of cheese.

These declines in prices, though they were by no means uniform in the different European countries, everywhere exposed the countries exporting meat and dairy produce to serious financial difficulties. The country in Europe which possesses by far the largest number of livestock is the U.S.S.R., which is far ahead of all other countries in the number of horses, cattle, sheep and goats, and second only to Germany in pigs. The socialisation of Russian agriculture is said to have caused a very large fall in the number of livestock, on account of slaughtering by the

PR

EUROPE'S TRADE IN BUTTER, CHEESE AND EGGS, FRUITS, WINE AND OLIVE OIL, 1931

NET IMPORTS AND EXPORTS

	Butter		Cheese		Eggs		(a) Citrus Fruits (b) Grapes and Raisins		Wine Hectolitres 000		Olive Oil	
	Imports	Exports	Imports	Exports	Imports	Exports	Imports	Exports	Imports	Exports	Imports	Exports
Great Britain	3,918	—	1,432	—	3,092	—	(a) 6,198 (b) 1,604	—	646	—	88	—
Germany	1,001	—	513	—	1,430	—	(a) 3,531 (b) 1,113	—	634	—	13	—
France	135	—	225	—	238	—	(a) 2,329 (b) 13	—	—	15,112	130	—
Belgium	176	—	221	—	349	—	(a) 715 (b) 46	—	345	—	5	—
Italy	22	—	—	358	—	157	—	(a) 3,843 (b) 400	—	1,654	—	131
Austria	—	6	4	—	164	—	(a) 347 (b) 153	—	281	—	—	—
Switzerland	106	—	—	208	156	—	(a) 325 (b) 143	—	1,155	—	62	—
Greece	9	—	17	—	30	—	(a) 62	(b) 857	—	452	—	73
Spain	—	—	16	—	—	227	—	(a) 8,691 (b) 602	—	3,351	—	939
Portugal	1	—	3	—	—	227	—	(b) 42	—	756	—	14
Czechoslovakia	16	—	—	35	74	—	(a) 476 (b) 59	—	148	—	5	—
Denmark	—	1,709	40	—	—	974	(a) 125 (b) 41	—	57	—	1	—

							(a)	(b)					
Sweden	195	7	—	—	16	(a)	305	—	—	67	—	3	—
Norway	6	—	11	—	7	(a) 47	(b) 178	—	46	—	13	—	—
Ireland	177	11	—	—	515	(a) 39	(b) 132	—	25	269	—	—	—
Hungary	18	—	2	—	119	(a) 73	(b) 185	—	—	178	1	—	—
Yugoslavia	3	—	18	—	263	(a)	138	179	—	1	2	—	—
Roumania	1	—	1	—	129	(a)	147	13	—	—	5	—	—
Poland	124	—	10	—	481	(a)	178	28	—	—	4	—	—
Bulgaria	1	—	14	—	224	(a)	73	—	2	—	2	—	—
Albania	—	—	7	—	15	(a)	17	31	1	—	—	—	3
Finland	174	—	26	—	19	(a)	43	—	—	—	1	—	—
Lithuania	87	—	11	—	33	(a)	14	—	—	—	—	—	—
Latvia	187	—	—	7	—	(a)	26	—	—	—	—	—	—
Estonia	144	—	—	—	14	(a) 9	(b) 9	—	—	—	—	—	—
Holland	289	—	858	—	859	(a) 668	(b) 149	—	116	—	1	—	—
U.S.S.R.	309	—	1	—	204	(a)	74	5	—	84	1	—	—

Figures in thousands of quintals, except as stated.

EUROPE'S TRADE IN MEAT, 1931

NET IMPORTS AND EXPORTS

Thousands of quintals

		(a) Cattle and (b) Pigs		Beef		Mutton		Pork		Bacon		Total excluding Cattle and Pigs	
		Imports	Exports	Imports	Exports	Imports	Exports	Imports	Exports	Imports	Exports	Imports	Exports
Great Britain	(a)	794	—	6,028	—	3,630	—	482	—	5,847	—	15,987	—
	(b)	475	—										
Germany	(a)	53	—	65	—		5	164	—	—	4	220	—
	(b)	—	141										
France	(a)	174	—	685	—	188	—	244	—	32	—	1,149	—
	(b)	513	—										
Belgium	(a)	60	—	389	—	19	—	—	167	—	—	241	—
	(b)	—	26										
Italy	(a)	98	—	494	—	—	—	—	49	—	9	436	—
	(b)	—	226										
Austria	(a)	54	—	148	—	—	—	101	—	1	—	250	—
	(b)	735	—										
Switzerland	(a)	23	—	28	—	—	—	1	—	9	—	38	—
	(b)	14	—										
Greece	(a)	70	—	1	—	—	—	—	—	1	—	2	—
	(b)	3	—										
Spain	(a)	1	—	2	—	—	—	—	15	—	3	—	16
	(b)	—	2										
Portugal	(a)	4	—	1	—	—	—	—	4	—	—	—	3
	(b)	—	—										
Czechoslovakia	(a)	19	—	6	—	—	—	46	—	11	—	82	—
	(b)	187	—										
Denmark	(a)	—	124	219	—	12	—	42	—	—	2,710	—	4,002

Sweden . .	(a)	—	1	—	1	6	—	—	270	—	—	—	271
	(b)	—	49										
Norway . .	(a)	1	—	12	—	16	—	4	—	—	—	32	—
	(b)	—	1										
Ireland . .	(a)	—	756	—	1	—	12	—	187	52	—	—	148
	(b)	—	472										
Hungary . .	(a)	—	101	—	20	—	12	—	10	—	—	—	42
	(b)	—	105										
Yugoslavia . .	(a)	—	109	—	37	—	—	—	20	—	—	—	57
	(b)	—	273										
Roumania . .	(a)	—	96	—	39	—	—	—	4	—	—	—	43
	(b)	—	203										
Poland . .	(a)	—	21	—	98	—	12	—	121	—	609	—	840
	(b)	—	351										
Bulgaria . .	(a)	—	8	—	—	—	—	—	—	—	—	—	—
	(b)	—	1										
Albania . .	(a)	—	1	—	—	—	—	—	—	—	—	—	—
	(b)	—	—										
Finland . .	(a)	—	—	—	6	—	—	—	1	—	11	—	18
	(b)	—	—										
Lithuania . .	(a)	—	20	—	52	—	—	—	50	—	182	—	284
	(b)	—	109										
Latvia . .	(a)	—	—	—	1	—	—	—	—	—	18	—	19
	(b)	—	15										
Estonia . .	(a)	—	1	—	3	—	3	—	—	—	7	—	13
	(b)	—	9										
Holland . .	(a)	—	21	134	—	—	51	—	361	—	655	—	933
	(b)	—	17										
U.S.S.R. . .	(a)	141	—	16	—	—	—	—	—	—	18	—	2
	(b)	83	—										

peasants during the collectivisation campaign ; but Russia remains even so by far the largest livestock producer. She is, however, quite unimportant in the trade in either cattle or meat, though she exports butter on a considerable scale. Next to Russia the chief countries in terms of numbers of livestock are Germany and France for cattle, Great Britain, Spain and Roumania for sheep, Germany, France, Poland, Denmark and Spain for pigs, and Greece and Spain for goats.

But these figures by no means correspond to the relative importance of the various countries in external trade. For example, by far the largest cattle exporter of Europe is the Irish Free State, which sent, until the recent dispute over the land annuities, most of her cattle to the British market. Next, but a long way behind, comes Denmark, which is also, unlike Ireland, a large exporter of beef. Then, after a considerable gap, come Yugoslavia, Poland, and Roumania, exporting both beef and cattle, and after them Lithuania and Hungary, also concerned with the export of both live cattle and meat, and Bulgaria as an exporter of cattle alone. By far the largest importer of both cattle and meat is Great Britain, followed at a long distance by Germany and France. Italy and Belgium are also fairly important importers, and the U.S.S.R. has been importing cattle in recent years for the improvement of her native breeds, and for the replacement of recent losses. Mutton is of relatively little importance in the trade of most of the European countries, only Poland having any considerable exports, while in the export of pigs and bacon Denmark takes easily the leading place with her great bacon exports, followed at a long distance by Holland and Poland as exporters of bacon, and by Poland, Roumania, Yugoslavia, Ireland and Italy as exporters of pigs. Great Britain is the only considerable importer of bacon, but Germany and France as well as Great Britain import pigs upon a substantial scale.

In the export of butter, the leading place is easily held by Denmark. In most recent years Holland has occupied the second place, but her exports are seldom more than a quarter of the Danish. Recently there has been a large increase in the exports of butter from the U.S.S.R., which in 1931 exceeded Holland's. Other exporters of some importance include Sweden, Latvia, Ireland, Finland, Estonia, Poland, and Lithuania, while Holland is the principal exporter of cheese, followed at a long distance by Italy and Switzerland. For both butter and cheese, by far the most considerable importer is once more Great Britain, followed by Germany at a long interval, and then, again at a considerable distance, by Belgium, France, and Switzerland.

There is of course no question of the power of the European market to absorb, if it is prepared to grant preferential treatment, the entire available supply of meat produced in Europe. In the case of cattle and beef, even if the entire British market, which is much larger than all the rest of the European market put together, is left out of account, the requirements of the importing countries of Europe were in 1931 many times as great as the total exports of the exporting countries. In mutton both the import and the export trade are, apart from Great Britain, on a quite small scale in relation to the total consumption ; but in this case too there is a net import into Continental Europe. In the case of bacon alone Great Britain is the only substantial importer, and it would be impossible for the Continental market to make itself self-sufficient apart from the British demand. Denmark and Holland, and to a less extent Poland and Lithuania, must sell their bacon in the British market or outside Europe if they are to maintain their present position. Denmark, for example, would lose the entire basis on which her present economic system has been built up if she were to be shut out from the British bacon market ; for it would be utterly impossible for her to find in Continental Europe an alternative market for even a tiny percentage of the displaced supplies. Denmark's economic fortunes are therefore intimately bound up with her position in the British market, and any preferential system which threatens to expand British imports from

Empire countries such as New Zealand, or any attempt to make Great Britain herself more self-sufficient in her bacon supply, constitutes a desperately serious threat to Danish prosperity. This applies to butter as well ; for here too Danish exports are on a scale for which it would be impossible to find an outlet if the British market were closed or seriously restricted. In 1931, for example, no European country except Germany imported even one-tenth of the quantities exported by Denmark, and the entire German market would only absorb a little over half the Danish exports.

If any European agreement on the lines of the Stresa project were to be attempted for the marketing of meat supplies and dairy produce as well as cereals, it is clear that Denmark could not be a party to it except in the very unlikely event of Great Britain also agreeing to come in. Any such agreement, in order to be of use to the States of Eastern and Central Europe, would have to apply primarily to the trade in cattle and beef. For it seems unlikely, in view of the preponderant importance of Denmark and Holland, that any agreement could be even projected in the case of either butter or cheese. Probably the realisation of the extreme difficulties standing in the way of such an agreement, even in the case of cattle and beef, prevented the Stresa Conference or subsequent meetings of the Central and East European countries from putting forward any proposal for a guaranteed market for the European cattle-raising industries. If, however, the Stresa proposals in relation to cereals were actually carried out, their success would probably be followed up by an attempt to raise the question of meat and dairy supplies as well.

§ 4. THE DEBTOR COUNTRIES OF EUROPE

THE PLAN for the revalorisation of cereals was only a part of the project elaborated at Stresa for the rendering of assistance to the distressed countries of Central, Eastern and Southern Europe. The Stresa Conference was concerned chiefly with the position of eight countries—Austria, Bulgaria, Czechoslovakia, Greece, Hungary, Poland, Roumania, and Yugoslavia—though some consideration was also given to the position of Turkey. These eight countries, according to the reports presented to the Conference, had, taken together, an external debt, including both public and private and both long- and short-term obligations, of well over 24,000 million Swiss francs, involving an annual payment of over 1,300 million Swiss francs. But this debt was very unequally divided between the eight countries concerned. The largest aggregate sums were owed by Roumania and Poland, followed by Yugoslavia and Hungary, and then at a further distance by Greece, Austria and Czechoslovakia ; the Bulgarian external debt was relatively small. But if these debts are considered not as absolute amounts, but in relation to the abilities of the various countries to pay, the position appears in a rather different light. The most useful way of measuring the debt in relation to ability to pay is to consider the relation which the debt service bears to the value of the exports of the countries concerned. On this basis both Greece and Hungary had in 1931 external obligations which swallowed up almost half the total sums due to them in payment for their exports, and Yugoslavia and Roumania nearly 30 per cent. For Poland the corresponding figure was 24 per cent, and for Austria 22 per cent, for Bulgaria 16 per cent, and for Czechoslovakia only 5 per cent. Clearly the burden upon Czechoslovakia as a developed industrial country is by no means excessive ; but all the other countries, and especially Greece, Hungary, Yugoslavia, and Roumania, have plainly been placed in a position that cannot be sustained in face of the sharp fall in prices and above all in the prices of those goods which they principally export. Moreover, their position in 1932 is very much worse than it was a year before, owing to the further fall in the value of their exports.

If we turn now to the actual state of trade in these countries in relation to the balance existing between their imports and exports, we shall find still further reason for understanding the impossibility for them of maintaining the payments upon their external debts. Thus Greece has not only an exceedingly heavy net burden of debt, but also a heavy adverse balance of commodity trade. In 1929 this adverse balance—that is to say, the excess of imports over exports—amounted to no less than 428 million Swiss francs, or three times the total burden of the external debt. In 1931 this adverse balance had been reduced to 259 million Swiss francs ; but clearly Greece, as a debtor on trading account, had no resources for the meeting of debt claims save as a result of fresh borrowing. Austria was in an even worse position. In 1929 she had an adverse balance of commodity trade amounting to 782 million Swiss francs, and even in 1931 this had only been reduced to 622 millions, or again nearly three times as much as the total sum required for the service of the external debt. Austria, as a country requiring to import foodstuffs and faced with countless obstructions in the way of her exports of industrial goods, is in an even worse position than Greece for the re-establishment of her economy. Even the disappearance of her entire external debt would by no means enable her to make her accounts balance, though she still derives some relief from the financial services which she continues to perform, albeit to a far less extent than in the days of the Austro-Hungarian Empire, for other parts of Southern and Eastern Europe.

Greece and Austria are the two extreme cases ; but the position is serious in several other countries as well. Thus in the case of Yugoslavia, imports and exports about balanced in both 1929 and 1931, but this left no funds available for the payment of external debts. Hungary had a small adverse trade balance in 1929 and a very small favourable balance in 1931 ; but this favourable balance was only one-fifteenth of the sum required for the service of the external debt. Poland, which had an adverse balance of trade of 176 million Swiss francs in 1929, had converted this by 1931 into a favourable balance of 242 millions ;

THE DEBTOR COUNTRIES OF SOUTHERN AND EASTERN EUROPE

Figures in millions of Swiss francs. (From Report of Stresa Conference, 1932)

	Balance of Commodity Trade		Foreign Debt Charge 1931	Debt Charge as percentage of Value of Exports in 1931	Fall in Value of Imports % (1929 = 100)	Value of Exports %	Budget Deficits or Surpluses	
	1929	1931	1931				1929	1931
Austria .	−782	−622	−214	22	44	40	+15	−234
Bulgaria .	−69	+47	−35	16	43	7	−11	−34
Greece .	−428	−309	−140	49	34	40	+51	−16
Hungary .	−23	+16	−248	48	48	45	−75	−114
Poland .	−176	+242	−268	24	53	33	+21	−118
Roumania .	−14	+192	−203	28	46	24	+47	−197
Yugoslavia .	+25	0	−124	30	37	40	—	—
Czechoslovakia	+78	+213	−105	5	41	36	+27	+1
	−1389	−221	−1337					

but even this amount was less by 26 millions than the sum required to meet the debt service. Roumania again had a small unfavourable balance in 1929 and a favourable balance of 192 million Swiss francs in 1931 ; but this balance fell 11 millions behind the sum required for the service of the debt, and in 1932 the favourable balance of trade was very greatly reduced without any corresponding diminution in the volume of debt. Bulgaria was in a better position. She had converted an unfavourable balance of 69 million Swiss francs in 1929 into a favourable balance of 47 millions—12 millions more than the cost of her debt service—in 1931. But in 1932 this favourable balance was not sustained, and the country was again plunged into serious difficulties. Czechoslavakia alone of the countries under discussion has had throughout a favourable trade balance. This amounted to 78 million Swiss francs in 1929, and 213 millions in 1931, so that in the latter year the service of the external debt was covered more than twice by the balance of exports.

Even these figures do not present by any means an adequate picture of the difficulties which are being experienced by the agricultural countries of Eastern Europe, for the improvement which they have brought about in their trade balances has been achieved only by the most drastic curtailment of imports, necessarily at the expense both of the equipment of industry and agriculture, and still more of the standard of life of their populations. Thus Hungary practically halved the value of her imports between 1929 and 1931, and reduced them in 1932 to a third of what they had been in 1929. Poland curtailed her imports to an even greater extent than Hungary. Bulgaria almost halved hers, and even Czechoslovakia reduced imports from well over 3,000 million Swiss francs in 1929 to 1,800 millions in 1931, with a further sharp fall in 1932. Roumanian imports fell from over 900 millions in 1929 to well under 500 millions in 1931, with a further sharp fall in 1932, and Yugoslavian imports fell from 700 millions to 435 millions. Even Austria, which was in the worst position for curtailing imports owing to her dependence on imported foodstuffs, reduced their value from 2,380 millions in 1929 to 1,580 millions in 1931, and this was followed by sharp further curtailment in 1932.

The position of the countries which we have been discussing in relation to the rest of the world can be visualised even more plainly if their trade one with another is eliminated, and the total balance of their trade with the rest of the world considered in relation to the magnitude of their external debts, and of the annual debt service. In 1929 this group of countries taken together imported 7,474 million Swiss francs' worth from other countries, and exported to other countries 6,103 millions—a total adverse balance of 1,378 millions. In 1931 their combined imports from other countries had fallen to 4,442 million Swiss francs, and their combined exports to 4,286 millions. The adverse balance had thus been reduced to 136 million Swiss francs, or less than one-tenth of what it had been two years before. But the service of the external debt for the same countries taken as a group amounted in 1931–32 to 1,337 million Swiss francs and the total amount of their public and private external debts to 24,360 millions. In other words, under pressure of the sums due to other countries, these debtor States had stopped buying from abroad everything with which they could possibly dispense, with disastrous results on the exports of the industrial countries. But even so they had not succeeded in establishing a favourable balance of trade, or in providing any sum of money derived from exports for meeting the enormous requirements of their foreign debts.

Under these circumstances, when the inflow of foreign capital, which had up to 1928 preserved an apparent ability to pay, ceased abruptly in 1929 and the following years, a crisis was certain to occur, and either there was bound to be currency depreciation of a most alarming sort, or steps would have to be taken both to restrict dealings in foreign exchange and to suspend to some extent the payments due upon the external debts. If the exchanges had been left free and the currencies of these countries allowed to depreciate, this could not possibly have been a means of straightening out their finances ; for every fall in the external value of their currencies would have been accompanied by a sharp rise in the effective debt burden falling upon their populations. In view of the magnitude of their external debts it was inevitable that they should make every possible effort to remain upon the gold standard at whatever external sacrifice in order to avoid this multiplication of their debts. Accordingly they were driven one after another to impose drastic restrictions on foreign exchange, in addition to limiting imports by means not only of tariffs, but also of quotas and embargoes of the most far-reaching character. Thus, Austria, after a prolonged attempt, with the aid of the Central Banks of other countries, to avoid exchange restrictions, had finally to restrict dealings in October 1931. In the same month Bulgaria made foreign exchange dealings an absolute monopoly of the National Bank, and introduced a drastic system of control over imports by this means. Greece restricted foreign exchange in September 1931 ; and in the following months her system of control became more and more drastic, until foreign exchange was granted solely for the purchase of absolutely indispensable food imports. But even this method was not effective, and in April 1932 Greece was driven off the gold standard despite the disastrous effects of a depreciation of the drachma on the domestic burden of her foreign debts. Hungary restricted foreign exchange in July 1931, and Roumania in February 1932, and more drastically in May 1932. Yugoslavia, which only stabilised her currency early in 1931, and only then abandoned her earlier restrictions on foreign exchange, had to reintroduce restrictions in October 1931, and to establish direct State control over certain classes of imports at the beginning of 1932. Of the countries under consideration Poland alone had not up to the date of the Stresa Conference imposed any restrictions on foreign dealings.

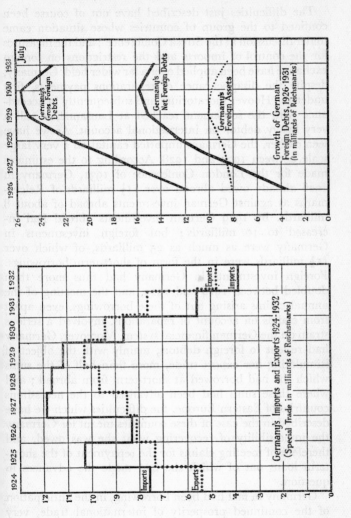

Growth of German
Foreign Debts, 1926-1931
(in milliards of Reichsmarks)

Germany's
Gross Foreign
Debts

Germany's
Net Foreign Debts

Germany's
Foreign Assets

Germany's Imports and Exports 1924-1932
(Special Trade in milliards of Reichsmarks)

Imports

Exports

The difficulties just described have not of course been confined to the group of countries whose situation came under discussion at the Stresa Conference ; and the measures for the control of imports and the restrictions on foreign exchange have been applied over a far wider field. Germany, despite the disappearance of reparations payments, first under the Hoover moratorium and subsequently in accordance with the settlement reached at Lausanne, is still a very heavy debtor on international account. As we have seen earlier, the Germans imported capital on a very large scale between 1924 and 1928. According to the estimates made for the London Conference of 1931, Germany in 1926 already owed abroad over 11½ milliards of Reichsmarks as against German investments abroad of about 8 milliards. By 1929 German investments abroad had increased to 10 milliards ; but foreign investments in Germany were as much as 25 milliards, of which over 11½ milliards were in the form of short-term borrowings. Foreign investments in Germany had thus more than doubled between 1926 and 1929, and the meeting of the annual claims arising out of these borrowings, even apart from claims on account of reparations, involved a serious strain on the German financial system. Moreover, Germany had re-lent to foreign debtors, mainly with the object of stimulating her export trade, more than half of the sums which she had borrowed at short-term from abroad ; and where these sums had been advanced to the necessitous countries of Eastern Europe, the difficulties which we have described in the case of these countries meant for Germany the impossibility of recovering what she was owed, and therefore of meeting claims for the repayment of the short-term loans out of which she had made the advances in question.

Germany in fact had been borrowing, in the anticipation of the continued prosperity of international trade, very heavily at both long and short term ; and when to the withdrawal of American capital was added the world slump, it was impossible for her, despite the most intensive efforts, to keep up her international payments. She had, however, like the countries of Eastern Europe, a very strong incentive for remaining upon the gold standard, in order to avoid increasing still further the burden of her external debts, and she had accordingly, no less than the countries of Eastern Europe, to resort to the most drastic measures for improving her balance of trade, and for restricting the movement of money out of the country. If this had not been done, there would have been added to the heavy burden of the current claims upon her a growing attempt by foreign creditors to withdraw their resources as her financial position became more and more unstable, and almost certainly a flight from the mark by German owners of capital.

Germany, as we have seen, made a tremendous effort to meet the situation at least in part by the stimulation of exports. In 1929 total German exports were valued at 968 million Reichsmarks a month, and in 1930, despite the slump, the monthly average was actually increased to 1,055 millions. Even in 1931, despite the sharp further fall in prices and in the total of world trade, Germany still succeeded in exporting over 767,000 million Reichsmarks' worth of goods, and it was not until 1932 that this intensive effort failed, in face of the intensification of the world slump, and the total of German exports fell to a monthly average of 478 million Reichsmarks. In the meantime imports had been curtailed to a quite extraordinary extent ; in 1928 they were valued at a monthly average of 1,167 million Reichsmarks, but by 1931 this total had been reduced to under 561 millions, and in 1932 to under 389 millions. Germany thus converted an unfavourable visible trade balance of 200 million Reichsmarks a month in 1928 into a favourable trade balance of over 200 millions a month in 1931. But in 1932 this favourable balance, despite all her efforts, fell to 89 millions a month, and in the opening months of 1933 fell catastrophically to under 25 millions, recovering to about 60 millions in the spring. In the meantime she succeeded in paying off a part of her short-term foreign debt, and in converting a further part of it from short to long term. But her total indebtedness remained at the end of 1931 in the neighbourhood of 23 milliards of Reichsmarks as against 25 milliards in 1929, while there had been a fall in her own investments abroad practically equivalent to the reduction in her foreign debt, so that her net position was hardly any better, in spite of all the privations which her people had been forced to suffer. In 1933, Germany still owed creditors in the United States over £400,000,000, in Holland over £170,000,000, in Switzerland £135,000,000, and in Great Britain about £111,000,000, apart from smaller debts to creditors elsewhere. In these circumstances the Germans were forced, in the summer of 1933, to declare a moratorium on their foreign debt payments at long as well as short term.

Germany, in addition to intensive measures to expand exports and to the raising of tariffs to a very high level in order to exclude imports, was compelled to resort to the control of foreign exchange. All transactions in foreign exchange were centralised in the hands of the Reichsbank, and all persons becoming possessed of foreign exchange, whether in payment for exports or in any other way, were compelled to hand over their holdings to the Reichsbank. Foreign owners of securities who attempted to sell them in the German market were no longer able to take the proceeds out of the country ; nor could short-term creditors recover the sums due to them, as withdrawals were strictly regulated under the provisions of the Standstill Agreements, which have been regularly renewed since their conclusion at the time of the Hoover moratorium. At the same time, owing to the difficulties of the German banks, the Government of the Reich has been compelled both to regulate their operations by drastic Government measures, and largely to accept responsibility for the security of their deposits and to invest fresh capital in them in order to enable them to carry on, and so avert a complete collapse of the internal economic system.

§ 5. THE EUROPEAN MONETARY PROBLEM

DRASTIC interferences with the free movement of goods and money across national frontiers have, however, not been limited to the debtor countries. Practically every country has in the course of the world slump repeatedly raised its tariff rates either generally or on particular classes of goods, and a number of countries, including France (which remains upon the gold standard), have added to their ordinary rates of duty special discriminating duties against imports from countries whose currencies have fallen in international value. Again, a very large number of countries, including creditor as well as debtor States, have adopted quota or licence systems for the restriction of wide classes of imports. Belgium has done this for wheat, coal, and a number of other commodities ; Czechoslovakia for meat, butter, and other food products and for all classes of luxury goods ; France for wheat, meat, and other food products, and also for coal, iron and steel, machinery, and a number of other manufactured imports ; Holland for meat, clothing, and luxury goods ; Sweden for wheat and sugar ; Switzerland for wheat ; and so on, for the list could be considerably prolonged. In effect, all over Europe even the most drastic raising of tariffs has been found inadequate for the protection of the national economy of each country against the consequences of the world slump, and resort has been had to all manner of other devices designed both to improve the balance of trade and to shelter the home producers of a wide range of goods against the consequences of the fall in world prices.

But of course each of these measures, while it may do something immediately to improve the trade balance or the position of a particular group of producers in whose interests it is carried out, is bound to react so as to worsen the world situation as a whole, and by provoking measures of retaliation and counter-protection in the long run to cause a further decline in the general trading position of the countries which resort to it. It may be possible by these means for some countries to improve their trade balances at the expense of others, and to increase the volume of employment in certain special industries to which they give a large measure of protection ; but this can be done only at the expense of a declining total of world trade, and of raising the average costs of production of commodities by promoting artificially their production under less favourable conditions than could be secured if trade remained even as open as it was three or four years ago.

In certain instances a country may be justified in desiring at all costs to maintain a particular branch of production within its national frontiers, even if this involves a higher cost of the commodity to the home consumer. In a larger number of instances it was impossible to expect that countries faced with the closing of their traditional markets would refrain from an endeavour to protect themselves by retaliatory measures ; and it can be argued that in the existing circumstances the drastic restrictions imposed on international commerce were inevitable from the standpoint of each country which put them into force. But it cannot possibly be argued that their total effect on the world as a whole and on every country individually has been anything except disastrous. For whatever has been done to help particular interests or for the improvement of one country's balance of trade as against another's has been far more than offset by the general decline in production and employment which has necessarily resulted from the restrictive systems now in force over practically the whole of the world.

The debtor countries, as we have seen, have had under the circumstances of the past few years very strong reasons for remaining upon the gold standard, even where this could be done only by imposing the most drastic restrictions on foreign exchange. For, if they had attempted to re-establish their trade balances by allowing the external value of their currencies to fall, any advantage which they could have secured by this method would have been far more than counteracted by the sharp rise which would have taken place in their foreign indebtedness. Thus, in addition to France, Belgium, Holland and Switzerland, which have remained upon the gold standard by virtue of the strength of their international financial position, the great majority of the States of Central and Eastern Europe have also preserved the nominal parity of their currencies, even where this has been done only by foreign exchange control of the most drastic kind through their Central Banks, and sometimes at the cost of causing transactions on what is called the "Black Bourse" at rates very different from those nominally in force.

From the standpoint of the status of their national currencies, European countries can now be divided roughly into four groups. First come the real gold standard countries, mentioned above, to which should be added Italy, and doubtfully, Poland ; second comes the group of countries which have followed Great Britain off the gold standard, and pegged the values of their currencies more or less in relation to the pound sterling. This group includes the Scandinavian countries, Denmark, Norway and Sweden, together with Finland—though there the amount of depreciation is somewhat greater—and also Portugal ; thirdly, there is the group which remains nominally on the gold standard, but under a system of drastic exchange control ; besides Germany this group includes Bulgaria, Estonia, Hungary, Latvia, Lithuania, Roumania, Czechoslovakia, and in effect Turkey, for although the Turkish currency is heavily depreciated in terms of gold, the depreciation is no greater now than it was in 1929. Fourthly, we have the group of countries which, after endeavouring for some time during the slump to remain at least nominally upon gold, have been driven to measures of currency depreciation. This group includes Greece and Yugoslavia, and in effect Austria, and with it must be classed Spain, which can alternatively be treated as standing by itself, in that the Spanish currency has fallen between 1929 and 1933 from a nominal depreciation in terms of gold of 24 per cent to one of 57 per cent. It is clear that if the slump continues much longer the number of countries in group three is bound to decrease as other States find themselves compelled to follow the example set by Greece and Yugo-slavia in 1932 and to allow their currencies to depreciate in external value.

This instability of European currency systems introduced, even before the sudden abandonment of the gold standard by the United States, considerable complications into the working of international trade. The present situation means in effect that, largely on account of the enormous burden of European debts, currencies are being pegged by exchange control at purely artificial values, which could not possibly be sustained if the free movement of money from country to country were to be again allowed. For despite the main-tenance of a nominal parity of exchange, there exists no real balance in the international economy of the countries concerned, so that the freeing of the exchanges would be certain to result immediately in heavy depreciation. This, of course, could not occur if these countries were really, as they still pretend to be, on the gold standard—that is, if they were really prepared to give gold in exchange for national currency at a fixed value. But this is altogether outside the bounds of possibility. For most of the countries in question have already lost the greater part of their gold in their attempts to maintain gold payments during the earlier stages of the slump, and not one of them has resources in any way sufficient to meet even a tithe of the claims that would be made upon them if they attempted to resume gold payments under the existing conditions. As we have seen, they have no real balance of exports out of which to meet the claims of their external creditors.

Nor have they for the most part any large invisible imports to set against these claims. Certain of the debtor countries of Southern and Eastern Europe used indeed to have large invisible imports in the form of remittances sent home by emigrants who had settled abroad, chiefly in the United States. But although these remittances are still

CURRENCY STABILISATION AFTER THE WAR

	Degree of Depreciation at Most. Annual Average. Par value with dollar = 100	Year of Maximum Depreciation	Year when de facto Stabilisation became effective	De Jure Stabilisation or New Currency	Degree of Depreciation % in Jan. 1933
Great Britain	133	1920	1925	1925	30.9
France	594	1926	1927	1928	0.4
Belgium	589	1926	1927	1927	0.3
Italy	496	1926	1928	1928	2.8
Germany	incalculable	1923	1924	1924	0.2
Austria	1,450,000	1924	1924	1924	0.7
Hungary	1,450,000	1925	1926	1926	0.4
Czechoslovakia	1,612	1921	1923	1929	—
Poland	17,000,000	1923	1924, 1927	1924, 1927	0.3
Roumania	4,176	1926	1929	1929	0.2
Yugoslavia	1,800	1923	1926	1931	23.0
Bulgaria	2,804	1922	1929	1929	0.4
Greece	1,532	1926	1928	1928	53.5
Finland	892	1921	1926	1926	42.1
Estonia	8,861	1925–6	1927	1927	0.3
Sweden	131	1920	1923–4	1924	31.7
Norway	192	1924	1928	1928	35.5
Denmark	170	1920	1927	1927	36.9
Holland	119	1921	1925	1925	—
Switzerland	114	1920	1925	1925	—
Spain	202	1931	—	—	57.6
Portugal	3,192	1924	1931	1931	31.4

maintained to a certain extent, the American slump has caused an exceedingly sharp fall in their total amount ; and this factor has been added to the withdrawal of American capital from Europe, and has caused a further discrepancy in the balance of payments between European countries and the United States. Some of the debtor countries have also been able in the past to derive a certain revenue in invisible imports from tourist traffic ; but this too has declined very greatly in consequence of the slump, so that their unfavourable trading position taken in relation to the volume of their external debts gives by no means a misleading impression of their total ability to pay. In present circumstances any effective restoration of the gold standard in any of these countries is, by itself, totally out of the question. Some of them may succeed in remaining nominally on gold for some time to come, because it seems better to them to do this than to run the risks of a currency depreciation to which they can see no limit. But they can only remain even nominally upon gold at the cost of a continuation of the existing high tariffs, of the quotas and embargoes and of the exchange restrictions which are more and more strangling world trade as the slump becomes intensified. And it is even more doubtful whether they can keep their exchanges pegged at all now that the United States has deliberately allowed the gold value of the dollar to fall.

Nevertheless it is constantly being argued that the world ought to make a combined effort to return to the gold standard. This insistence on the necessity for a return to gold is based on the belief that the stability of the international value of national currencies is essential for the carrying on of world trade, in that the instability of currencies in terms one of another necessarily introduces into all international transactions an element of uncertainty which converts ordinary trading operations into highly speculative affairs. There must, it is urged, be some international standard in terms of which all national currencies can be stably measured ; and although many suggestions have been put forward for some other international standard as an alternative to gold, there exists at present no other standard likely to command any sufficient measure of general consent to secure its international adoption, or likely to work well or smoothly even if the nations of the world could be persuaded to adopt it.

These arguments in favour of a return to the gold standard raise a number of distinct considerations. In the first place, as we have seen, whatever may be thought about the desirability of a general return to the gold standard, no such return is at present possible in any real sense for the great majority of countries. Let us suppose for the moment that all countries are agreed upon the desirability of going back to the gold standard, as they were in effect agreed, as far as the politicians and bankers were concerned, in the period immediately before the world slump. What, then, would be the difficulties standing in the way of a general return ? The first fundamental difficulty would be that, at the present levels of world prices, debt burdens are alto- gether out of proportion to national ability to pay, so that any attempt to return to the gold standard would involve heavy and continued external payments by a large number of debtor countries which could not possibly hope, at present price-levels, to meet their debt claims out of a surplus of exports. Even if these countries, which at present have for the most part hardly any gold reserves, were equipped somehow with a fresh supply of gold sufficient to enable them to meet external claims for a year or two to come, this would in no way meet the difficulty ; for there is no reason to suppose that in a year or two's time they would not again have lost the new gold supplied to them, and be once more unable to meet external claims arising out of their adverse balances of payments. But in these circumstances who is going to supply them with the gold, or alternatively with the foreign exchange as a substitute for gold, which they would need in order to return even temporarily to the gold standard ? The answer is that no one in his senses is going to supply them on these terms ;

for to do so would be only to reproduce on an infinitely larger scale the situation which has existed for some time past in Austria, which has been provided with new credits under the auspices of the League on a scale just sufficient to prevent default on her existing obligations, without any result in improving her ability to meet in future years the undiminished volume of claims still outstanding.

It is clear in these circumstances that no effective return to gold is possible for most of the debtor countries unless either or both of two conditions can be satisfied. Either existing debts must be cancelled, or so drastically scaled down as to come again within the ability of the debtors to pay without fresh capital borrowing for the purpose of payment ; or prices must be so raised that the existing debts come to represent a greatly reduced quantity of goods of those kinds which the debtors are in a position to export. This second condition would not necessarily be satisfied by a general rise in the level of world prices unless this rise were very considerable indeed. For what most of the debtor countries—Germany is in this case an exception—need most of all is a sharp rise in the prices of agricultural products, and to a less extent other raw materials ; and a moderate rise in the general level of prices would not have nearly enough effect materially to increase their ability to make external payments unless it were so distributed as to increase the purchasing power of their exports not only generally but also specifically in terms of industrial imports.

What seems to be needed from the standpoint of these countries is not only an absolute rise in the price level, but at least equally a rise in the prices of agricultural goods in relation to those of the manufactures which they chiefly require to import. To achieve this was of course the principal object of the proposals for the revalorisation of cereals put forward at the Stresa Conference—at which, incidentally, Turkey, Greece and Bulgaria also urged the claims of tobacco for inclusion in the scheme. But if, as the Stresa proposals involved, this revalorisation were to be accomplished by a mere discrimination in favour of the exports of the agricultural countries of Eastern and Southern Europe, excluding the U.S.S.R., and not by a rise in the world level of prices for cereals and other agricultural products and raw materials, the advantages secured by it would necessarily be conditional on the maintenance of the system of high tariffs and import quotas and embargoes which is widely regarded as a powerful obstacle in the way of any general recovery of world trade as a whole. Any advantages secured by the countries of Eastern Europe by this method would therefore, from the standpoint of the world, and even of Europe as a whole, be purchased only at a very high cost, and at the expense of perpetuating conditions which must be swept away if there is to be any general recovery under the capitalist system.

It follows that, if an escape from the existing difficulties is to be sought under the capitalist system by way of a recovery in prices, this recovery must be brought about not by an artificial raising of the prices of certain particular classes of goods through preferential tariffs or similar devices, but by some method compatible with the recovery of a greater degree of freedom in international exchange. This clearly involves in the first instance an attempt to raise prices generally by monetary means, as the only possible alternative to widespread bankruptcy and default on the part of the debtor countries.

The alternative in whole or in part to action designed to raise prices is the writing off of a very large part of the existing debts, including not only external debts, but also those internal debts which, at the lower prices now prevailing, are out of all relation to the ability of the debtors to pay. But hardly a beginning has yet been made towards a constructive solution of this problem. For it appears to have been conceived throughout from the standpoint of the creditors rather than the debtors, and with the object of preserving as far as possible the existing structure of debt, on the ground that any widespread departure from it would be a serious blow at the whole conception of the sanctity of contract. It is repeatedly stressed that " respect for undertakings entered into is an essential factor " in the return of confidence, and that such readjustments of debt as are required ought to be effected not by any general scaling down over the whole field but only by separate arrangements entered into directly between the parties to each contract in accordance with the ability of the debtors to pay. But it seems altogether utopian to suppose that the method of separate negotiations could bring about any scaling down of the kind required, save as a result of widespread default on the part of the debtors spread over a considerable period of time. In effect, if this is to be the method of settlement, it is likely to come about only at the end of a considerable period of further deflation, and rather as a recognition of accomplished bankruptcy than as a means of re-establishing the prosperity of the world.

§ 6. PROPOSALS FOR RAISING THE PRICE-LEVEL

THE QUESTION then is whether there is a real chance both of devising measures likely to be effective in raising general price-levels throughout the world and of persuading a sufficient number of nations to put these measures into force. Let us confine ourselves for the moment to the question whether such measures can be devised, without raising the further question whether, even if satisfactory action along these lines is possible in theory, it stands any considerable chance of acceptance in the near future. A large number of different schemes have been put forward by economists in the various countries during the past two or three years. At one extreme we have those economists who believe that, if the Central Banks in the leading countries were simultaneously to pursue, by means of open market operations on a very large scale, the expansion of the basis of credit, and if the currency laws of the countries concerned were to be so modified as to make this possible, the mere increase in the supply of money would, without any further action, be effective in raising prices, so that it would only be necessary to secure that the expansion of the basis of credit should take place at the right relative rates in the different countries. It is very difficult to believe in the probable efficacy of this method under the existing circumstances. Even if it is not disputed that the expansion of the basis of credit can by itself raise prices at a time when trade and industry are either pursuing a normal course or are definitely on the up grade, there is no reason whatever for believing that in a period of intense slump and lack of confidence among business men a similar effect is at all likely to follow. On the contrary such a method is certain to fail both for lack of the willingness to borrow among business men and because the banks as lenders will have under it no greater reason to believe in the solvency of potential borrowers than they have at present. If, for some quite other reason, the confidence of business men were on the increase the infusion of an additional supply of available credit might be effective in stimulating business activity ; but it is quite irrational to hold that a mere announcement of the readiness of Governments and Central Banks in the leading countries to broaden the basis of credit would by itself suffice to bring this increased confidence into being, especially in the existing disturbed political as well as economic conditions.

An expansion in the basis of credit need not mean any expansion at all in the volume of credit actually being used. Of course, if the basis of credit is expanded without the additional supplies of money finding an outlet, this creates an awkward situation for the banks, which find themselves with a supply of unusable money on their hands, and therefore unable to earn profits at the levels to which they have become accustomed. But it does not follow that the consequent pressure upon the banks to expand their loans will achieve any substantial result unless there are willing and solvent borrowers ready to take up the money. The only result that is likely to follow from such a situation is a pressure of money into the markets for gilt-edged securities, the prices of which will be forced up by the competition to buy, so that the rates of long-term interest will tend to fall, as has happened in Great Britain very notably during the past year or so. This will facilitate conversion operations in those countries whose financial standing is still relatively good ; and it will accordingly to some extent ease the burden of public debts, especially where there are large masses of war debts available for conversion. It will also enable a certain number of business men to replace borrow-ings at a high rate by money at a lower rate of interest, and will thus do something to reduce business losses, or even to increase profits. But its effects in this latter field are likely to be very limited, and are most unlikely to result in any expansion of business activity, as the new money will pass chiefly into the hands of banks and financial institutions or of the owners of capital, and will not necessarily be transferred to the public for increased spending.

It is therefore necessary to reject the idea that under present conditions world prices can be raised or world business activity increased by the mere broadening of the basis of credit in the leading industrial countries through the action of their Central Banks, unless this broadening of the basis of credit is accompanied by deliberate measures designed to increase the demand for actual credits to be applied to the purposes of production. If this further requirement can be satisfied, no doubt monetary expansion can be made to serve a very useful purpose in raising the levels of prices. But the satisfaction of it involves a con-siderable increase in the willingness of Governments to spend both on capital account and upon current services. Such a policy of expanded Government spending is obviously inconsistent with the " economy " policies which practically all Governments have been pursuing to an increasing extent each year since the coming of the world slump. In practically every field of public expenditure, with the exception of expenditure upon armaments, there has been throughout the world and above all in Europe a determined attempt to cut down outgoings in the hope of balancing budgets heavily unbalanced on account of the decreased yield of taxation and the increase in the cost of maintaining the unemployed. The salaries of public employees have been reduced ; normal programmes of expansion in the services of health and education have been indefinitely postponed, and even the existing forms of provision have been pared to the bone in the attempt to save money. At the same time housing schemes have been drastically curtailed, and there has been a check to the expenditure upon road construction and road improvement, which had been rising rapidly during the years immediately before the slump. Even schemes of long-term capital development such as afforestation and the development of electrical power resources, or in Great Britain the electrification of the main line railways, have been abandoned or postponed on the plea that the States concerned clearly cannot afford them. All these measures have resulted together in a sharp decrease in the volume of consumers' demand ; for they have both thrown people out of work in large numbers and decreased the purchasing power of those who have remained in employment. They have furthermore, as far as abandoned schemes of capital development are concerned, reacted indirectly to cause additional unemployment and business losses in the industries in which activity would have been stimulated by the execution of Government works.

It has been attempted in all countries to justify these measures of "economy" on the plea that taxation is already far too high, and that high taxation is strangling enterprise. It has been suggested that, if States will but push their economies far enough, the benefits of the tax reductions which they will be able to allow will bring about a revival of industrial activity. It is of course quite true that taxes are at present, in relation to the tax levels to which countries have been used in the past, exceedingly high, and that high taxation is bound to have at least some discouraging effect on business enterprise, though this effect is often greatly exaggerated by business men. For the chief adverse consequence of high taxation on business enterprise arises through its tendency to discourage fresh investment of capital in industry. But at a time of slump investment has already reached so low a level that not much further discouragement is possible as a result of the height of taxes. High taxation is in fact far more likely to slow down the rate of industrial activity in times of boom, when such a slowing down is far less open to objection, than at a time of slump. The fact of course remains that during a slump the ability of the community to bear taxation without hardship is less ; and this applies especially where States raise a large part of their revenue by indirect taxes. The pressure to get taxes reduced is therefore perfectly natural ; but it is quite mistaken to suppose that any reduction in taxation that is likely to be brought about by economies of the kinds at present contemplated can have any material effect in stimulating industry. Indeed, if the lowering of taxes is accomplished by way of economies in the social services and in public capital expenditure, its effect on industry is likely on balance to be markedly adverse.

When Governments decide on measures of economy and look round for means of making their decision effective, they are always apt to single out the social services for special attention. Attempts to reduce military expenditure meet always with strong resistance, and to-day encounter exceptionally strong opposition because of the increasingly disturbed political state of Europe. There remain as possible fields for economy only the social services and the service of the public debt. But although something can be done— as it has been done with marked success in Great Britain during the past year or so—to reduce debt charges by means of conversion operations, and although a substantial further saving is automatically achieved by the low rates of interest possible on the short-term debt at a time when there is little demand except from the Government for short-term funds, by far the greater part of the debt is not open to these forms of treatment, since it consists of relatively long-term obligations not immediately open to conversion.

This part of the debt can be made less onerous only if the Government is prepared to break the contractual obligations into which it has entered with the bondholders ; and this capitalist Governments are exceedingly reluctant to do, except when they are driven right up against the wall, as Australia was in her recent financial crisis. A capital levy being virtually impossible at the bottom of a tremendous slump, the contractual debt burden could be reduced only by legislative measures lowering the rates of interest in breach of the existing contracts. This lowering of rates would, in the opinion of many people, be amply justified on the ground that the real interest payable on the debt has risen to an enormous extent during the past few years, as a consequence of the fall in prices. But any attempt at compulsory reduction of interest rates would be certain to meet with very strong resistance from the monied classes, who would be backed up in their opposition by a very large number of small debtholders, unless it were proposed to discriminate between large and small owners, and also to continue payment in full of the interest on blocks of debt held by such bodies as Friendly Societies, and other collective institutions standing mainly for the interests of relatively poor people. No capitalist Government, until it is driven near to desperation by the magnitude of its financial burdens, is therefore likely to be willing to adopt this remedy.

Consequently, when economies are made by Governments in difficulty, the social services have usually to bear the brunt. But it is difficult in practice to achieve large net economies in this field because, even if expenditure on health and education is drastically curtailed, the growing burden of unemployment is bound to involve a heavy additional cost to the State in one form or another, even after the sums paid in relief to those out of work have been cut down as far as public opinion will allow. One Government after another starts out with promises of very large net "economies," only to find that it can in practice do little more than prevent expenditure from rising higher as unemployment grows. If, however, the effect of its supposed "economies" is to make unemployment grow still faster, it may well be that there is in fact no net decrease at all in what the Government spends. It has merely ceased to spend money in a more desirable so as to be compelled to spend it in a less desirable way.

It has of course to be admitted that it would be difficult at the present time for any Government to extend to any significant extent its spending out of revenue. If Governments are to spend more in an effort to stimulate trade revival, this additional spending must be done, unless there is to be direct inflation on Government account, mainly in the form of additional expenditure out of borrowed money. The State must go into the market, or to the banks, and borrow additional capital resources, which it will then employ in setting men to work directly, and in placing with contractors orders which will result in their setting additional men to work. The spending power thus placed in the hands of workers at present unemployed will be in part offset by decreased expenditure in unemployment relief, and this will of course relieve the budget as far as relief expenditure falls at present upon national funds. But men in work will be receiving larger incomes than the unemployed, and there will accordingly be a net increase in the amount of spending power distributed in the community. The direct expenditure incurred by the Government will thus be passed on through its immediate recipients into other hands, and the stimulus originally applied to the industries to which the Government gives out its orders will be diffused through the entire community, with the effect of increasing business activity over a wide field.

It is often suggested that this policy is bound to result in a rise in prices ; and indeed, to achieve a rise in prices is under existing conditions one of its principal objects. But it is probable that the increase in Government spending would have to be pushed to considerable lengths before it would in fact result in any material rise in the price level, on account of the large mass of productive resources now lying unused. For this reason it is entirely within the power of a single Government in a financially strong country to carry a policy of reflation by increased Government spending to considerable lengths without fear of any adverse reactions on the external value of the national currency. For these reactions could come into being only if the policy did lead to a rise in prices within one country, unaccompanied by a corresponding rise elsewhere. A national policy of reflation, accompanied by the necessary increase in Government expenditure, can therefore be used to a certain extent even by a single country acting alone as a means of reducing unemployment and stimulating industrial activity within its own borders. But while the pursuit of such a policy by the Government even of one only of the leading countries in world trade would have some stimulating effect on conditions elsewhere and so help towards the re-establishment of confidence, it is unlikely that it could have any material result in raising the level of world prices unless the same policy were being pursued by other leading countries as well.

If, therefore, the policy which we have just been discussing is to be used as an instrument for raising world prices, it must be pursued internationally by agreement among the leading Governments ; and this agreement must include not only the broadening of the basis of credit by means of the Central Banks, but also the initiation by all the Governments concerned of a policy of public spending, and a reversal of the " economy " measures at present in force. If this were done by the Governments of the leading countries acting together, there is every reason to believe that it could be effective in bringing about a rise in world prices.

It will, however, be urged that, while the leading creditor countries are in a position to institute a policy of this sort, the same conditions do not apply to the debtor countries, since these countries are compelled, in their intensive efforts to arrest national bankruptcy, to impose drastic restrictions on imports, whereas the policy of national expansion obviously involves in all countries which are not fairly self-sufficient in raw materials and machinery the admission of additional imports of these classes. It must be agreed that the debtor countries, now held firmly in the grip of their respective bondholders, are not in a position to embark upon measures of reflation ; and yet it may be held that if the leading industrial countries did seriously carry out the policy suggested above, the effect would be so to improve the position of the debtor countries as exporters, both through the rise in prices which would follow its adoption and through the increased demand for their goods, as greatly to improve their position and increase their ability to meet their debts. But it is highly questionable whether the debtor countries can be expected, if a policy of reflation is carried through on these terms, to consent to the benefit of it being transferred almost wholly to the foreign bondholders at the expense of a continuance of poverty for their own populations. They could only be expected to agree willingly—though it is true they might be coerced against their will on other terms—if, side by side with the proposed measures of reflation and Government spending, an international agreement were reached for the scaling down of their external debts to a figure well within their re-established capacity to pay.

But can the nations of the world be persuaded to accept an international scheme for the raising of prices, even if such a scheme can be devised on sound working principles ? On this point there is bound to be grave doubt. For the entire idea is workable only on the assumption that there is general agreement among a sufficient number of the leading countries that world prices ought to be raised if it is possible to raise them. But there are still in a number of countries powerful forces which are opposed to any such attempt, however feasible it may be ; and these forces have up to the present been especially powerful in France, though the French attitude has of late, under a more Radical Government, shown some sign of weakening.

Broadly the contention of those who are hostile to an attempt to raise world prices is that, unpleasing as the prospect may be, the only way to recover from the present slump lies through a drastic scaling down of costs so as to bring them into conformity with the prices at present ruling, or even with the lower prices which are certain to come into being if this deflationary policy is ruthlessly pursued to the end. These critics of reflation hold above all that the existing world levels of wages are far too high, and that there can be no recovery of prosperity until wages have been brought down in correspondence with the fall in the level of wholesale prices in recent years. They hold obstinately to this view despite the fact that the world has at present a vast unused surplus of productive power which appears to most people to require not a scaling down of wages but rather a larger and more generous distribution of consuming power to the great mass of the people. Their answer to this criticism is that, if wages are sufficiently reduced, there will be an increase in the volume of employment—so that more money will be distributed in wages at the new lower rates than is being distributed at the high rates now prevailing—and further that the purchasing value of the wages will increase as prices fall, and as the margin between wholesale and retail prices is reduced on account of the fall in interest rates as well as in the wages paid in distribution.

This argument is highly questionable, for it is improbable that any reductions in wages which could be achieved without tremendous friction in almost every country would result in any considerable expansion in the volume of employment. Moreover, the trades in which it is easiest to reduce wages are precisely those in which wages have already fallen most severely, and the resisting power to wage decreases differs very greatly from trade to trade, so that the attempt to re-establish equilibrium by these means would be likely to result in practice in making the existing disequilibrium even worse. Apart from this, the process of scaling down costs so as to adjust them to existing price-levels, or rather to the still lower price-levels which the pursuit of such a deflationary policy would certainly involve, would be bound to take a very long time, and would in the interval condemn the world to a continuance and intensification of the existing depression. Even if theoretically this method could succeed in the long run, it is most unlikely that it could succeed in practice ; for long before it could have produced the required effects European civilisation would almost certainly have crumbled into ruins.

Nevertheless the hostility to the attempt to raise prices by international action finds influential support, not only among deflationary economists but also among certain sections of the public in each country. Co-operators, for example, wedded to the consumer's point of view, are exceedingly apt to oppose the suggestion that Governments should do anything to raise prices ; and, especially in France, there is a very powerful and quite intelligible sentiment of opposition amongst the large body of small *rentiers* who form one of the most influential sections of French public opinion. These small *rentiers* have already passed through one period of inflation, as a result of which a large part of their savings has been in effect taken away from them. They regard the stabilisation of the franc at one-fifth of its pre-war gold value as meaning in effect that someone has stolen four-fifths of their savings ; and they are determined to hang on desperately to the one-fifth that they feel to be left them, and accordingly to oppose any measures that savour of renewed inflation or attempt by raising prices to decrease the purchasing value of their money. These small *rentiers* have, to be sure, gained considerably in purchasing power during the past few years as a result of the fall in world prices, though their gains from this source have been reduced by the protectionist measures adopted in the interests of the French producers. They might be reconciled to an attempt to raise the level of international prices if they thought that it would be accompanied by an at least equivalent fall in those French prices which are at present artificially raised by protective measures ; but without some such guarantee as this they are likely to remain suspicious of any effort to raise prices by means of international reflation.

Until quite recently the influence of the bondholders seemed likely to be decisive in determining French financial policy ; and as long as France remained relatively immune from the consequences of the world slump there was little chance of persuading any French Government to act in any way inconsistent with the bondholders' point of view. But during the past year France has discovered that her comparative immunity from the consequences of world depression cannot be maintained in face of the prolongation and intensification of the slump throughout Europe. The worsening of economic conditions in France has already produced some change of attitude. It is, however, very doubtful whether even to-day France could be persuaded to come wholeheartedly into any scheme of the kind suggested. She would almost certainly, even if she agreed to come in at all, seek to make her participation conditional on the scheme being accompanied by special measures in the interests of the smaller countries of Central and Eastern Europe with which she has been so largely associated in a political sense. In other words, she would probably try to make the adoption of the Stresa scheme for revalorisation of cereals a *quid pro quo* for her participation in any world monetary agreement having a reflationary object. Even this implies a great modification of her present attitude, which is still based on a fanatical adhesion to the gold standard, and a faith in the efficacy of plans for raising commodity prices by the artificial restriction of output.

Could then Great Britain and the United States, even in the absence of French co-operation, carry out a modified scheme on the lines of that which has been discussed above ? It might be possible for Great Britain and the United States, acting together, to set going measures of international reflation through an expansion in the basis of credit in their own countries, and so to stimulate activity in the rest of the world ; but it would not be possible without French collaboration to place adequate resources at the disposal of the debtor countries.

§ 7. PROPOSALS FOR RESTORING THE GOLD STANDARD

PRACTICALLY all the schemes which are now being put forward in responsible quarters for the restoration of prosperity by international action involve the ultimate restoration of the gold standard, if not in its old form, at any rate in some form guaranteed to restore stability to the international exchanges. But it is by no means clear that those who demand this return to gold have for the most part envisaged clearly the differences between the pre-war situation and that of to-day. For in effect the gold standard as it existed in the nineteenth century and before the war was to a very great extent a sterling standard as well. London occupied a position of such predominance in the world's financial system as a clearing-house for international transactions of any and every sort that the gold standard was in effect operated from London and in accordance with the needs of London as a financial centre, though by no means always in accordance with the needs of British industry. There was little criticism of the gold standard as long as it was worked in this way ; for London's predominance secured in effect its management under the auspices of a single authority with sufficient power in its hands to control the situation. But since the war these conditions no longer exist. The control of the world's financial affairs is divided between a number of great financial centres ; and, although London has continued to hold its position of preponderance in the market for trade bills, it has lost its old position in the market for new capital issues, and is no longer the great reservoir of money for supplying the needs of the whole world.

In these changed circumstances no one country can

control the gold standard. The attempt has been made to control it by creating in each country a Central Bank on an approximately uniform basis, and bringing together the leading personalities of these Central Banks by means of regular consultations, as well as through the Bank for International Settlements, which has, however, hitherto, occupied a position of relatively minor importance. This system of consultation among independent Central Banks has never worked well or smoothly, and cannot be expected to work well in face of the very difficult problems which the post-war economic situation has presented to those responsible for the world's monetary management. There have been at work forces upsetting the monetary equilibrium of each separate country and of the world as a whole. There has been no real balance in the volume of payments due to and from country and country. War debts and reparations have again and again upset the normal working of the financial system. There has been a mass of migratory money moving from one financial centre to another in search now of a higher return, and now not of any return in the form of interest or profits but only of security against loss. The successful management of the world's money under these conditions has demanded a quite different administration of the gold standard from that which existed before the war, and has called for far stronger and more unified control if the standard is to work smoothly in accordance with the pre-war rules. But it was out of the question to create any international agency strong enough to exercise this control, for no great country was prepared to let the control of its monetary affairs pass out of its hands. Accordingly, what we have got has been neither strong and effective national management nor strong and effective international management, but rather weak national management complicated by ineffective international consultation.

It is, however, so important for the carrying through of international transactions that there should be a common standard linking together the different national currencies that we cannot, on account of the very real difficulties in the way, agree permanently to abandon the gold standard unless and until we can find some satisfactory international alternative. For a world in which the relative value of different national currencies is liable to constant fluctuation is a world in which every transaction involving international payments is bound to contain a very large speculative element, and one in which financiers and traders, in their attempts to protect themselves against these speculative risks, try to safeguard their transactions by methods (e.g. the gold clause in many American contracts) which are apt to become extremely oppressive in their working, and to throttle trade instead of giving it air to breathe. If, then, we are to have an international standard, and there is in practice no alternative to gold as a basis for this standard, the question we have to consider is whether the gold standard can be so modified as to avoid the overwhelming difficulties which have arisen in its working since the war.

In the first place, it is clear that a return to the gold standard by any country which has been driven off it during the present crisis does not at all imply a return to the previous parity. There is no reason at all why, if Great Britain or Scandinavia goes back to the gold standard, they should go back on the basis of equating the pound sterling or the crown to the same amount of gold as these currencies represented before September 1931. It is perfectly open to any country to return to the gold standard at a quite different parity—for example, by stabilising its currency at the parity now existing between it and those currencies which are still based really as well as nominally upon gold—in relation to the franc value of the pound sterling, for example. It would indeed be madness even to consider a return to the gold standard under present conditions in any other sense than this ; for an attempt to write up the value of the pound to what it was worth in terms of gold before 1931 would be a repetition—far more disastrous and far-reaching in its effects—of the profound mistake which

Great Britain made in the terms of the return to the gold standard in 1925. Let us assume therefore that if the world is to return to gold at all the return will be made on a basis of a substantial devaluation of the pound sterling and of the currencies of those other countries which have gone off gold since the beginning of the crisis—even including the United States. For, though the U.S.A. was not driven off gold by any adverse balance of international payments, she may well desire to write down permanently the gold value of the dollar in order to raise her internal prices and reduce the real burden of farm mortgages and other internal debts.

On this basis, a return to the gold standard is practicable without disaster, provided certain other conditions are satisfied. These conditions are of two kinds ; some of them are conditions which must be met before the return to gold can be safely carried into effect, while others are conditions for the subsequent working of the gold standard under the changed circumstances of world economy. Let us take this second set of conditions first. Hitherto it has been assumed that the adoption of the gold standard involves the keeping of a large reserve of gold against the internal issue of currency, and accordingly that the basis of the national issue of credit must fluctuate in accordance with the supply of gold in the possession of the Central Bank of the country concerned. It has further been assumed that the value of the national currency in terms of gold must be fixed definitely once and for all, and that no provision must be made for changing this value under any conditions. If we are to restore the gold standard both these assumptions ought to be definitely given up.

In the first place there is clearly no real need for keeping a reserve of gold against the purely internal issue of currency, or for maintaining any fixed relation or proportion between the volume of currency issued for internal use and the supply of gold in the possession of the Central Banks. It is imagined that such an internal reserve is necessary only because paper money has been evolved gradually as a substitute for the direct use of coined gold as a medium of exchange, and there is still felt to be something wrong in treating paper money as having a value of its own unless it is definitely representative of a stock of gold lying somewhere for which it can, at least in theory, be exchanged. The existence of this supply of gold and of a definite statutory requirement that the issue of currency shall bear a fixed maximum proportion or relation to it is further felt to be a safeguard against the manipulation of the national money by a Government which desires to inflate. But no one suggests that the reserve of gold held against the internal issue of currency is of any real use except as a means of giving people confidence in the currency, and of acting as a barrier in the way of inflation.

The first of these arguments is now obsolete. The existence of a stock of gold serving nominally as a basis for the internal issue of currency is no longer the necessary foundation for confidence in the national issue of money or any real foundation at all. For it has been amply demonstrated that the existence of a stock of gold is no guarantee that if a crisis really arises—and it is only in a crisis that men are likely to " go for gold " in preference to paper—the holders of paper money will be actually allowed to change it into gold, or that the previously existing parity of the paper money with gold will be even nominally preserved. Countries will go off the gold standard, however they may be committed to it by legislation, if they find themselves unable to maintain it without disaster.

Under modern conditions a country needs a stock of gold only for the purpose of meeting the normal requirements for export—that is to say, for settling such balances as cannot be settled in other ways, and for correcting when occasion arises the tendency towards undesirable minor fluctuations in the external value of the national money. It is impossible to use gold for the purpose of preventing major fluctuations ; for, as the history of the world during the past few years has amply demonstrated, it is quite beyond the power of the great majority of countries to carry a stock of gold sufficient to meet a real financial crisis without a suspension of the right to export it. Gold as a means of settling international balances can only be used provided that these balances are manageable in size and arise out of temporary and not permanent disequilibria in the financial relations between countries.

Accordingly, a country needs only enough gold to meet potential demands for gold export, excluding such abnormal demands as are liable to arise in connection with any serious international crisis. To hold a stock of gold larger than this requirement dictates is wasteful ; for it means locking up resources in the holding of non-earning assets. Given a stock of gold adequate within these limits, there is no reason why the internal issue of currency should not be wholly divorced from any quantitative relation to the stock of gold—in other words, why countries should not adopt in their internal issues of currency and credit a policy of pure monetary management. This does not mean that a country would be free to inflate *ad lib.*; for it would still be governed in its internal monetary policy by its adhesion to the international gold standard in terms of the parity laid down for the time being by its Central Bank, and it would be under the necessity of so regulating its internal issues of currency as to keep its internal levels of prices in equilibrium with the price-levels of other countries adhering to the common standard, in order to avoid the possibility of a drain of gold. What is suggested is, not that countries should be set free to inflate as much as they like, but that their policy in the issue of currency and credit should be related to the need for preserving the established parity of their money and preventing a drain of gold, and not by means of a definite statutory relationship between the total quantity of gold held and the amount of currency erected upon it.

But it is here necessary to propose a further modification in the international gold standard as it has been hitherto conceived. It is desirable in the interests of international trade to establish short-term stability in the relative values of different national currencies ; but there is no reason why the gold parity of any currency, or accordingly its external value, should be fixed definitely for all time. It would be far better to give the Central Bank the same power as it now possesses in varying the rate of discount and re-discount to regulate the gold value of the national currency by changing from time to time its buying and selling prices for gold. It would indeed be highly undesirable to make frequent changes in the gold parity of the national currency, or to use the power to alter this parity except in accordance with long-run changes in the economic structures of the different countries. But, provided that the short-term stability of the external value of a currency were sufficiently guaranteed, there would be no handicap to external trade in recognising the possibility of rare changes in the gold parity as the alternative to financial crises accompanied by the suspension of the gold standard. It would be far better for the trader to know that the Central Bank, in consultation with the Government, had the power of varying the rate of parity and so preventing a crisis than to pass once again through the experience which he underwent in 1931.

In other words, we must not expect too much of the gold standard, or be prepared to put in it an absolute and unqualified trust. We must use it, if we use it at all, as an instrument of which we recognise the fallibility ; and we must not be so scared of the fallibility of bankers and Governments as to fly from our fear of their mistakes to an absolute reliance upon an automatic standard which has of late served us exceedingly ill.

These are the two conditions which should be laid down for the working of the gold standard in the future, if it is to be restored as a basis for international monetary transactions. Let us be sure that we have them clear in our minds. They are, first, that countries should cease to regulate their internal issues of currency and credit in any definite proportion or relation to the stocks of gold in the possession of their Central Banks, and should aim at keeping gold reserves sufficient only to meet normal demands for export. And secondly, that the gold parity of each national currency, or in other words, each Central Bank's buying and selling prices for gold, should be fixed in future not absolutely and for all time, but subject to modification at long intervals in order to adjust the relative values of national currencies to long-term changes in the national economies of the different countries.

There are, however, as we have seen, other conditions than these which have to be satisfied before any return even to such a modified gold standard can safely be made by the countries which have departed from it during the past few years. No gold standard, however modified, can possibly work if there are in the economic relations between countries such permanent disequilibria as are bound to set up a drift of gold from one group of countries to another group, or in the absence of free movement of gold certain to cause a permanent disequilibrium in the balance of payments due from country to country. Such disequilibria are, however, bound to exist as long as prices remain at anything like their present levels, and further as long as huge masses of international debt not representative of real productive assets have still to be met. In other words, any effective return even to a modified gold standard pre-supposes either a rise in prices so substantial as to make present debt burdens nugatory—and this for many and sufficient reasons no one is likely to contemplate—or, in the alternative, some rise in prices combined with a drastic scaling down of existing international debts both public and private. It is not possible in this matter to isolate war debts, or to claim that when once war debts and reparations have been got safely out of the way matters will speedily right themselves without further readjustment. For even if these aggravations of the trouble disappeared there would remain commercial debt burdens which are impossibly heavy either at present prices or at any level of prices which is at all likely to be established by international action of the kind discussed earlier in this section.

If these prior conditions could be satisfied, there would be a great deal to be said for an attempt to work a modified gold standard. For all sensible people want the countries of the world to be drawn economically more closely together, and to weaken the forces of economic nationalism which have grown so strong in recent years. And most people realise that the absence over the whole world during most of the period since the war of an effective international monetary system has been one of the principal causes leading to the rise of nationalism in the economic field. If we can get a workable international monetary standard, we shall by doing this be erecting a framework within which it will be far easier than it can be at present for a system of international economic co-operation to be built up. Even those who have no love at all for the gold standard in the forms in which the world has known it hitherto may well see very strong reasons against adding to the existing potency of nationalism in the world the reinforcement of a purely nationalist monetary policy in each country.

To this some people would reply that the case for the gold standard is sufficiently answered by the obvious fact that the available world supply of gold, even apart from its existing mal-distribution, is inadequate to serve as the basis for the exchange, even at the present prices, of the greatly increased emission of goods and services which is possible with the aid of our rapidly expanding productive resources. But there is no real reason for supposing that the supply of gold in the world is inadequate, provided that this supply is rightly used. Changes in the working of the gold standard, such as a drastic reduction in the quantities of gold which the laws of the various countries compel Central Banks to keep as reserve against currency, would in themselves result in very large economies in the total world demand for monetary gold ; and there is no reason why these economies should not be pushed further and further as the world gets more used to the working of the new system. Moreover, there is no reason at all why the supply of gold should not be reinforced to any extent that may be needed either, as has been suggested, by the creation of a new international paper currency which countries will agree to treat as the equivalent of gold, or by the use of silver, or in a variety of other ways. Any required expansion in the gold basis of the world's credit economy could be made by these methods without interfering at all with the operation of the gold standard.

It is, however, sometimes urged that, if the world does go back to gold, its demand for the actual metal will be found to be not less but greater than it was before the crisis of 1931. For up to 1931 a number of the smaller countries kept a large part of their resources, not in the form of actual gold in the cellars of their Central Banks but in gold exchange—that is to say, in the form of deposits of money in the gold standard countries. This system, it is said, economised considerably in the use of gold, because it meant in effect that the same gold reserve was being used to back the issues of currency and credit both in the country which actually had the gold and in the countries which adopted the " gold exchange " method of working the gold standard. But, it is said, after the experiences of 1931, countries will never again be persuaded to treat gold exchange as the equivalent of gold. Each country will want to pile up its own gold reserve, as Switzerland, Holland and Belgium as well as France have piled up their reserves since 1929. For, if a country holds its reserve not in gold but in foreign exchange, it stands to lose if the country in which the whole or part of its reserve is held goes off gold, or under the proposed new gold standard system decides to modify the gold value of its currency. This is, of course, true enough. But the objection would not apply if the smaller countries were prepared definitely to peg their own currencies to those of one or another of the leading financial nations. For example, if Scandinavia and certain of the countries within the British Empire were to agree to enter a sterling area, they could continue to operate the gold exchange standard, provided they kept their balances in London or in some other centre falling within the area. Similarly, some of the smaller European countries could, if they so desired, peg their currencies to the French franc, and some of the South American countries could peg theirs to the American dollar. It is, however, true that the gold exchange standard is not likely to work in future unless there is either a general return to the gold standard by the leading nations on the old pre-crisis terms (which seems both unlikely and undesirable) or a definite linking by certain of the smaller countries of the fortunes of their currencies to the currency of one of the great financial nations. A third alternative would of course be the creation of a consortium of the smaller countries to manage a combined currency of their own on the basis of a common gold reserve. This might, for example, work in the case of Scandinavia, but it is certainly unworkable amid the existing antagonisms of the countries of Central and Eastern Europe.

§ 8. THE SLUMP IN EUROPEAN INDUSTRY

IT IS NOW time to turn from the predominantly agricultural countries of Southern and Eastern Europe to the industrial nations of the west, and to see how these countries have fared during the world depression and what are their economic problems to-day. In predominantly agricultural countries the onset of depression makes itself felt directly in a fall in the standard of living among the general mass of the population. The peasant finds himself able to buy less industrial goods ; and as these goods are chiefly imported from abroad, imports fall off, and the whole country readjusts itself to a lower standard of living. Unemployment does of course arise in such industries as exist within the national frontiers ; but where a substantial part of the industrial products used in the country is normally imported from abroad, this unemployment can be to some extent kept down by the imposition of high protective tariffs and restrictions, which secure a larger share of the domestic market for the home producers. Under these circumstances, the effects of adversity are widely spread among the mass of the population. Where the general body of the peasants is heavily burdened with debts contracted at a higher level of prices, the slump of course hits the peasant population exceptionally hard, and reacts less, and indeed may not react at all, on the standard of living of the creditor classes within the country. How it will react upon the industrial workers will depend largely on the question whether the national industries are producing exclusively for the home market, and can therefore be effectively protected, or are working also for export, and therefore subject to strong pressure from employers to accept reduced wages in the interests of more effective international competition. Trade Unions in these agricultural countries are usually too weak to resist demands for wage reductions if they are seriously pressed, and there is usually no form of public provision for the unemployed ; and where industrial workers are recruited from a much larger mass of peasants, who are themselves suffering from severe impoverishment on account of the slump, there is usually a huge reserve of blacklegs on whom the employers can draw if the workers attempt to resist their claims. Wages in industry are therefore likely to be pressed down to a very low level wherever the national manufacturing industries are working under conditions of international competition. Where, however, the protective system is such as to afford complete shelter to native industries, and production no more than suffices to meet the restricted demand of the home market, this may not occur ; and in this event the industrial workers will only suffer as a result of the increase in the cost of living which is certain to follow the adoption of a high protective policy.

On the other hand, in the industrial countries the effects of a slump make themselves manifest first of all not in a fall in the general standard of living of the population but rather in an increase of unemployment. Industrialists, finding the demand for their products restricted, cut down output more readily than they reduce selling prices, and are indeed apt to find that even a willingness to reduce prices to a considerable extent produces relatively little expansion in the demand for their goods in the overseas markets on which they have been accustomed to rely. For the further the depression goes the more the overseas countries shut themselves up behind high tariff walls erected in the interests of the home producers, and for the improvement of their national balances of payments. Unemployment on a large scale is therefore the habitual accompaniment of industrial depression in the more advanced countries. In these countries, moreover, Trade Unions are usually powerful enough, save in the industries most exposed to foreign competition, and most adversely affected by the slump, to put up a strong resistance to the attempt to cut wages drastically ; and even if the Unions are compelled in the end to accept substantial wage reductions, there is almost always a lag between the incidence of the depression and the acceptance of the reduced rates. The workers who are able to retain full-time employment in the advanced countries may even gain in purchasing power as a result of the depression, and this applies especially to those trades which are least subject to fluctuation in the demand for their products. The so-called " sheltered " industries, in which the demand is as a rule relatively well maintained, therefore tend to gain at the expense of the unsheltered, and the greater part of the economic loss, as far as it falls upon the workers, is transferred to those employed in the unsheltered industries, and to those workers in other industries who either retain only part-time employment or are thrown completely out of work.

Most of the advanced countries have some form of public provision for the maintenance of the unemployed, either through a national system of unemployment insurance— which may or may not extend over the whole industrial population—or by some locally organised system of relief.

As the numbers unemployed or under-employed increase in the course of a depression, the burden falling upon the State or upon the local authorities, in as far as they are responsible for the maintenance of the unemployed, rises very greatly. This increase may be concealed where the charge, or a large part of it, is met out of a separate unemployment fund contributed to by employers and workers as well as by the State. In such cases something may be done to meet the increased charge for the maintenance of the unemployed by raising the contributions levied upon workers and employers, and this at the same time reduces indirectly the wages of those still in employment, and places an additional part of the cost of maintaining the unemployed as a charge upon the productive system. Germany, for example, which has an inclusive scheme of unemployment insurance, pursued this policy during the early years of the slump to the fullest possible extent, raising the contributions of employers and workmen to the unemployment fund very greatly indeed, and provoking thereby strong protests from both sides against the unfairness of the impost. But even Germany reached before long, as unemployment continued to grow, the limits of the resources which could be raised by this method, and was compelled to accept a greatly increased budgetary charge for keeping the unemployed from starvation.

In Great Britain, which has also a fairly inclusive scheme of unemployment insurance, something was done by way of raising contributions, but for a long time the increased cost was mainly borne by according permission for the unemployment fund to borrow money in anticipation of a coming recovery of trade, which would reduce the number of the unemployed not only within the current ability of the fund to meet the cost, but to such an extent as would enable it to repay the debts incurred during the depression. This method relieved the budget of an additional charge, but did this only at the cost of placing upon the unemployment fund a debt which was never in fact likely to be repaid ; so that in the end Great Britain, like Germany, was compelled to accept the greater part of the charge as a budgetary burden.

In both these countries this burden became, as the slump continued, so heavy as to cause a great outcry among the richer tax-payers. It was said that many people were getting relief without having any real right to it, on the ground that they were " not genuinely seeking work," that unemployment benefit was on an unnecessarily generous scale in view of the fall in the cost of living, and above all that the existence of unemployment benefits to which the workless were entitled as of right was a most powerful cause in preventing the readjustment of wages to the changed levels required by the world depression, because it prevented a stampede for work at any price from breaking down the established Trade Union conditions and the bargaining strength of the Trade Union movement.

Germany, in far greater financial difficulties than Great Britain, and confronted with an unbalanced budget at a time when extensive State borrowing was virtually impossible owing to financial stringency, had by far the strongest inducement for making all possible " economies " at the expense of the unemployed ; and as the crisis advanced, the scaling down of benefits, the weeding out of those whose claims were open to question, and the transference of the chronically unemployed to a different form of relief at a much lower scale of payment proceeded apace. But Great Britain was not long in following Germany's example. Even before the financial crisis of 1931 the Labour Government of Great Britain had so far responded to the attacks of the newspapers upon the unemployment insurance scheme as to pass an Anomalies Act, designed to weed out undeserving applicants and to revise the conditions of relief so as to exclude a substantial number of claimants who were legally entitled to it as the scheme stood. This measure effected a financial saving, especially at the expense of women, above all married women, who were adjudged to be no longer genuinely seeking work. But after the financial crisis of 1931 and the fall

of the Labour Government, far more drastic " economies "
at the expense of the unemployed were speedily introduced.
The system under which unemployed workers had been
entitled, practically without limitation of period, to benefit
at a standard rate, was swept away, and on the German
model a differential system of relief, subject to a " means
test," was introduced for those whose idleness had extended
over a protracted period. By this measure, which created
widespread resentment in the industrial districts, a substantial saving in budgetary expenditure on the unemployed was brought about, though some part of the charge
repudiated by the State had to be taken over by the local
authorities, which found themselves compelled more and
more to relieve the sheer necessities of workers whom the
State either declined to maintain at all or relieved on an
obviously inadequate scale. Undoubtedly a further effect
of the " means test," besides the privation which it caused
to large masses of workers who had been for a long time
out of a job, was to weaken the power of the Trade Unions
in resisting wage reductions, by making available a large
mass of labour which was prepared to take a job at practically any wage. A similar result followed to an even
greater extent the " reforms " introduced into the German
system of unemployment insurance.

In the countries which have no general system of public
maintenance for the unemployed an increase of unemployment is bound to result immediately in a far larger amount
of economic distress. In these countries, though there may
be, as in France, some system of local relief, the unemployed worker is left without any assured income at all,
and any relief accorded to him through public or private
agencies is generally at best only on the poorest subsistence
scale. He begins by using up any savings he may possess,
and by getting such assistance as he can from relatives or
friends ; but when these resources are exhausted he has
nothing to fall back upon except the soup kitchen and the
meagre help extended to him out of local funds. In countries in which, though they are considerably industrialised,

there remains in being a large peasant population, a certain fraction of the unemployed industrial workers is usually able to go back to the land, and share in the reduced standard of living available for the peasant population in face of the depression. This to some extent relieves the pressure of indigent populations in the industrial centres ; but those who are unable to return to the country usually suffer in such countries the most desperate privations of all. They are not numerous enough to be able to force redress for their grievances, and they are left to live in a condition close to sheer destitution by picking up such scraps as they can. Most of the larger industrial towns in the less industrialised countries of Europe have thousands of people living in them to-day on the very verge of starvation, miserably clothed and housed, and deteriorating further and further, men, women and children alike, in health and physical efficiency as the slump drags on. These unfortunates are strong enough at times to make a riot, but they are far too weak to secure any effective redress. They are ready to turn to anyone who will offer them food and shelter, and they can accordingly be found allying themselves now with Communism and now with the extremest sort of Fascism, according to the hopes which are held out to them from either left or right. They are too far " down and out " to afford the luxury of real political or economic convictions ; all they are looking for is some way, they care not what, out of the desperate situation in which they are compelled to live.

The more advanced industrial countries have no such pockets of utter misery as these in their midst. But even in their case the position becomes sufficiently serious when over a prolonged period a large part of their industries is shut down. The situation would not be quite so bad if the unemployment were fairly evenly spread over industry as a whole ; for in that case it would probably take the form of spells of unemployment between jobs for a large proportion of the total body of workers rather than of chronic unemployment year in and year out for a more limited number. What happens in fact is that unemployment, falling very unevenly upon different industries, also bears very differently upon different areas ; for the heavy industries, in which for the most part unemployment has been most severe, are usually localised in particular districts especially round the coalfields and the iron deposits, and in both Great Britain and Germany there are many almost derelict areas in which the greater part of the population has been unemployed for years on end.

Both in areas of this sort and elsewhere the privations of the German workers have been far worse than those of the British, both because German wage levels have fallen more sharply and because the pressure on the German economic system has caused a more drastic curtailment of benefits and relief. But even in some parts of Great Britain the position is bad enough. In South Wales, in Durham, and in some areas in Lancashire, there are industrial centres in which practically the whole population is living on some form of public relief which barely suffices to keep families fed and housed, without providing any surplus for the purchasing of new clothing, much less for any of the ordinary amenities of life. These conditions have caused in more than one country dangerous divergences of point of view, and even antagonisms, to develop between the employed and the chronically unemployed sections of the working class. The latter have been driven, in despair, either towards Communism or towards Fascism, whereas the employed have for the most part remained within the ranks of the older parties.

It is often urged by industrialists and even by some economists that the provision of unemployment benefit on anything like a living scale serves to exaggerate depression because of the high taxation which it involves at a time when profits, and accordingly the ability of the rich to meet taxes, are low. But against this contention must be set the fact that the distribution of a large mass of purchasing power among the unemployed is a most important factor in maintaining the domestic demand for consumers' goods, and therefore in checking depression in the industries producing these goods. If the sums levied in taxation for the maintenance of the unemployed were left in the pockets of their original recipients it is exceedingly likely that a substantial part of them would, under the prevailing conditions of depression, not be spent at all either on consumers' goods or by way of investment as new capital in industry. The money, or a large part of it, might be accumulated instead in idle bank balances or in some other way diverted from any use which would serve as a stimulus to industry and employment. It is, on the other hand, certain that its distribution in the form of unemployment benefit will cause most of it to be spent immediately on the purchase of necessary products, and that the money so spent will thereby be made to circulate among the general body of the community, stimulating further demand in the course of its circulation. It is surely evident that the economic position in Great Britain would be a great deal worse than it is but for the existence of a general system of maintenance of the unemployed, and that the " economies " made in this maintenance by the National Government in 1931, so far from improving the economic situation, tended to make it worse. It is at any rate a fact that most people have been surprised at the success with which demand in the British home market has been maintained during the worst period of the depression ; and it is difficult to find for this any sufficient cause apart from the partial preservation of the purchasing power of the unemployed which the system of compulsory State insurance has brought about.

This assertion of the beneficent influence of a system of adequate maintenance for the unemployed still seems to fill many people with surprise. But why should it ? It is obvious that the present world crisis is not the result of any shortage in the world's means of producing wealth. The poverty and unemployment which the crisis has brought into being co-exist with a productive power far more abundant than the world has possessed at any previous time.

There is no lack of physical or of human resources for the achieving of a higher standard of living for everybody. The flaw in our present economic system lies in its failure to find means of creating an adequate demand for the goods which it is well able to produce. In these circumstances it is not at all surprising that a distribution of purchasing power in a form in which it is certain to result in an increased demand for the products of industry, so far from worsening the economic situation of the country which adopts it, should help to preserve that country from the worst consequences of the slump.

It is not of course suggested that the mere adoption of a system of provision for the unemployed even on the most adequate scale can be a remedy for trade depression. For the existence of unemployment implies a fall in the real income of the community below what its productive resources are sufficient to create. Even if purchasing power over consumable goods is maintained by adequate grants for maintenance, the money required for these grants, in as far as it is raised by taxation, comes out of someone's pocket and subtracts from the purchasing power of one section of the community what it adds to the purchasing power of another section. In the circumstances of a trade depression this will probably result in an increase in the amount actually being spent, and so prevent the depression from going as far as it otherwise would. But it will not avail to turn a depression into prosperity ; for this involves not merely a diversion of purchasing power from one section of the community to another, but an increase in the aggregate amount of purchasing power, combined with a fuller utilisation of the available resources of production.

Let us now look at the actual situation of the leading industrial countries of Europe from the standpoint of the effects of the slump upon the volume of employment and production. There are unfortunately no complete statistics available of the unemployment existing even in the industrial countries of Europe. For whereas Great Britain and Germany have fairly adequate, though not complete, figures, France has no records covering more than a fraction of the unemployed, while some of the smaller countries have either no statistics at all or only very incomplete figures. But some idea of the effect of the world depression on the volume of unemployment in Europe can be gathered from such statistics as are available. The combined figures for 22 countries for which statistics, complete or incomplete, can be secured, show that the average number recorded as unemployed in 1928 for all these countries taken together was well under $3\frac{1}{2}$ millions; and of this total Great Britain and Germany together accounted for about $2\frac{1}{2}$ millions. As against this at the end of 1932 the total numbers registered as unemployed in the same group of countries had risen to over $13\frac{1}{2}$ millions. Germany alone had over 6 millions and Great Britain nearly 3 millions out of this total, while Italy had over 1,200,000. Unemployment, as far as it is revealed by the European statistics, had thus risen fourfold as a consequence of the world slump, and almost every country had recorded a very large increase in the numbers out of work. In Great Britain the number of registered unemployed had been multiplied by two and a half and in Germany and Italy and Sweden by four; while in Belgium, France, Holland and Czechoslovakia the percentage increase was many times as great as in any of these countries.

It is not of course suggested that a large percentage increase necessarily indicates an exceptional severity of unemployment, for that depends on the level from which the figures start. But a glance at the accompanying table will suffice to show that almost every country engaged in industrial production was suffering from unemployment at a level which implied a severe restriction in the quantity of the national production and a considerable strain on the financial resources of the community where any system of public provision for the unemployed was in force. Unemployment is most spectacular in Germany, but in relation to some of the other countries the smaller totals recorded as unemployed represent an even greater loss in production

UNEMPLOYMENT DURING THE DEPRESSION

Average Numbers (ooo's omitted) Registered as Unemployed during

	1928	1929	1930	1931	1932	1933 (January)
Great Britain	1,290	1,262	1,994	2,717	2,846	2,955
Germany	1,200 (estimated)	1,679	3,145	4,573	5,580	6,014
Italy	324	301	425	734	1,006	1,225
Belgium	28	27	74	201	337	403
Holland	22*	28*	41*	88*	271	399
Denmark	52	45	41	59	126	187
Sweden	30	33	42	65	90	120
Czechoslovakia	39	42	105	291	554	873
Poland	126	132	227	300	256	267
France	15*	10*	14*	75*	306*	352*
Austria	182	192	243	300	378	397
Hungary	15	15	44	52	66	78
Irish Free State	23	21	22	25	60	96
Switzerland	3·2%	3·5%	11%	18%	21%	28%
Other European Countries	49	67	95	144	182	244
Total (excluding Switzerland)	3,395	3,854	6,512	9,624	12,058	13,610

* Incomplete.

and an even more serious decline in national purchasing power. The 1,225,000 unemployed in Italy, the 873,000 in Czechoslovakia, the 403,000 in Belgium, the 397,000 in Austria, the 351,000 in Holland, to say nothing of the smaller totals for countries with relatively tiny industrial populations, reveal the intensity of the economic crisis through which European industry as well as European agriculture has been passing. The 352,000 unemployed recorded for France represent only a relatively small proportion of the total numbers out of work in that country; but it is unfortunately not possible to make any inclusive estimate. Some idea, however, of the magnitude of French unemployment can be secured from the fact that in 1931, when the number recorded as unemployed was only 75,000, a writer in the *Economist* estimated that the real number out of work was already well over a million.

Unemployment on this scale obviously implies a considerable fall in the volume of production, and the existence of such a fall is borne out by the indices of industrial production published by a number of the leading countries. We have already seen to what an extent these indices had shown a rising tendency in the European countries in the years immediately before the slump, and we have now to study their decline during the past few years. If we take the position in the last quarter of 1932, or the nearest available figure, we see that production in Germany had fallen since 1928 by nearly 40 per cent, and production in Poland by as much as 46 per cent. For Austria the fall is as much as a third, and for Belgium and Hungary nearly a third. For France and Sweden it is a quarter; and Great Britain is the only country for which figures are available where the decline is relatively moderate, amounting to no more than 10 per cent in spite of the serious falling off in British exports.

These figures relate to the general volume of industrial production, including all those industries for which it is possible to compile adequate figures. It is perhaps worth while to set beside them the separate indices for two highly

EUROPEAN INDUSTRIAL PRODUCTION, 1929 AND 1932

	Coal Production Monthly Average in metric tons millions		Pig Iron Production Monthly Average of metric tons		Steel Production Monthly Average Millions of metric tons		Machine Production Index Number 1928=100		Textile Production Index Number 1928=100		Industrial Production General Index 1928=100	
	1929	1932	1929	1932	1929	1932	1929	1932	1929	1932	1929	1932
Great Britain	21.8	17.7	.64	.30	.82	.45	107	78	99	85	106	88
Germany	12.6	8.7	1.10	.33	1.35	.48	101	38	92	80	100	61
France	4.5	3.9	.86	.46	.81	.47	114	70	93	61	109	76
Belgium	2.2	1.8	.34	.23	.34	.23	—		95	58	100	68
Poland	3.9	2.4	.06	.02	.12	.05	101	44	91	58	100	54
Czechoslovakia	1.4	0.9	.14	.04	.18	.06	—		101	67	104	59
U.S.S.R.	3.5	5.2	.36	.50	.41	.48	—		—		124	205 (9 months)
Holland	1.0	1.1	—		—		—		—		—	
Saar	1.1	0.9	.18	.11	.18	.12	—		—		—	
Luxembourg	—		.24	.16	.23	.16	—		—		—	
Sweden	—		.04	.02	.06	.05	—		—		106	84
Austria	—		—		—		—		—		103	66
Hungary	—		—		—		—		—		98	61
U.S.A.	46.0	26.8	3.6	0.7	4.6	1.1	*	*	108	77	107	58
Japan	2.9	2.2	0.1	0.1	0.2	0.2	*	*	114	115	111	108

* No figures available.

important classes of manufactured goods—textiles and machinery. In the case of textiles, output in both Germany and Great Britain had been relatively well maintained but it has of course to be remembered that in Great Britain employment and production in the textile trades were already at a low level before the world slump began, and it should be further noted that there was a sharp recovery in the volume of British textile production from 1931 to 1932, almost wholly as a result of the bonus to British exports which followed the departure from the gold standard The French textile industries, supplying to a large extent luxury goods, fell off much more than the German or the British ; and the decline was still more serious in the textile trades of Poland and Czechoslovakia, these falls reflecting the decreased purchasing power of the consumers in Eastern and Central Europe.

In the case of machinery, indices are available for four countries only. But the figures for these countries are of the highest significance. Again it is Great Britain which shows the smallest aggregate fall—24 per cent ; but in this case the maintenance of output cannot be attributed mainly to the departure from the gold standard or to the new tariff policy inaugurated in 1931–32, as the figures for 1932 are substantially below those for 1931 and the previous years. The explanation is to be found partly in activity in the British electrical industry in connection with the construction of the new " grid " system, partly in the relative success of the British motor trade in standing up against depression, and partly again in the effects of the maintenance of the general volume of consumers' demand in keeping the demand for machinery and miscellaneous metal goods at a not unsatisfactory level. But here again it must be remembered that Great Britain had a large volume of unemployment in the machine-making industries before 1929.

France, with a fall of nearly a third in the volume of machine production, stands next to Great Britain in her success in resisting the slump ; but again a study of the figures shows that in France demand was well maintained up to 1931 and then showed a very sharp falling off, which was still continuing in 1933. The two remaining countries, Germany and Poland, both show an appallingly heavy decline in the volume of machine construction. Polish machine output has fallen since 1928 by 56 per cent, and German by no less than 62 per cent. These figures of course reflect directly the cessation of the great movement of rationalisation and re-equipment with the aid of borrowed capital which was taking place in Germany and to a less extend in Poland before the withdrawal of America from the European capital market.

It is unfortunately not possible to present corresponding figures for other manufacturing industries ; but it is worth while to set beside the above figures the statistics showing the production of two commodities which are both vital to the economy of the developed nations of Western Europe. It will be seen from the accompanying table that the output of coal in Europe stood at a monthly average of about 46 million tons for the eight chief producing areas in 1928, and that in 1932 this monthly average had fallen to rather under 37½ million tons. This decline is considerably less in most countries than the decline in the general volume of industrial production, the difference being largely due to the maintenance at a relatively high level of the demand for household coal and coal used in transport and public utility services, and also in certain of the industries producing consumers' goods. It will be seen that in this case too the decline is considerably greater in Germany than in either the United Kingdom or France ; for in Germany there has been both a heavy falling off in the coal-using industries and a serious decline in consumers' demand.

The figures for steel naturally show a considerably larger reduction than those for coal, in that a large proportion of the output of steel is designed for use in the constructional trades, which are always the most seriously affected by an industrial depression. Taking together the eleven leading steel-producing countries in Europe, with

Rr

the exception of the U.S.S.R., we find that in 1928 their
average monthly production of steel was just under 4
million tons. In 1932 this average monthly production had
fallen to less than $2\frac{1}{4}$ million tons, though there was a small
rise in the final quarter of the year. Again the fall in output
was more serious in Germany than in any of the other
leading countries, as the table on page 511 shows. But
among the smaller producing countries, Poland and
Czechoslovakia showed a decline comparable in severity
with that which occurred in Germany. The paralysis in
the constructional industries of Central and Eastern Europe
is thus abundantly illustrated.

It is interesting to compare the incidence of the world
slump on European production, as measured by these
statistics, with the experience of the United States. In the
United States the index of general industrial production
fell between 1928 and the last quarter of 1932 by 41 per
cent—a larger fall than occurred in any of the European
countries with the exception of Poland. On the other hand,
in the case of textiles the fall in America between the same
dates was only 12 per cent ; but this was the result of a
sharp recovery in American textile output in the later part
of 1932, and for the year as a whole the fall in textile production was 23 per cent. Even this last figure, however,
shows American textile output to have been maintained
better than that of any of the European countries with the
exception of Germany and the United Kingdom.

In the case of machinery, there is unfortunately no
comparable index available for the United States ; but the
American figures of coal and iron production tell with
sufficient clearness the tale of prostration in the heavy industries. In 1928 the average monthly production of coal
in the United States was over $46\frac{1}{2}$ million tons, but it fell in
1932 to under 27 million tons ; while for steel the fall was
enormously greater, from nearly $3\frac{1}{4}$ million tons in 1928
and over $3\frac{1}{2}$ millions in 1929 to under three-quarters of a
million tons in 1932. Europe had thus fared in the heavy
industries infinitely better than America, and had also done

appreciably better on the whole in the maintenance of the general volume of industrial production.

The above statistics have throughout excluded the experience of the U.S.S.R., as this runs directly counter to that of the capitalist countries, at any rate up to the final quarter of 1932. Thus, between 1928 and 1931 industrial production in the U.S.S.R. rose, according to the published figures, by no less than 89 per cent ; and by the third quarter of 1932 the rise exceeded 100 per cent. Since then there is known to have been a falling off; but the figures for the last quarter of 1932 are not yet available. Similarly in the case of coal a monthly output of three million tons in 1928 rose to one of over $5\frac{1}{4}$ millions in 1932, and the monthly output of steel from 354,000 tons in 1928 to 482,000 tons on the average of the first ten months of 1932. Of course these figures reflect the intensive effort made by the U.S.S.R. to carry through the rapid industrialisation of the country under the first Five-Year Plan ; and Russia, starting from a very low level of industrial production, was naturally able, by applying all her energies to the increase of production, to record a very large percentage increase. But the fact remains that for several years in which production over the rest of the world was falling at an unexampled rate, the U.S.S.R. alone was able to go forward rapidly on the basis of a planned economy under Socialist control.

Even if in 1933 the process of Russian industrialisation appeared to be suffering a setback, it is clear that this tendency arose from quite different causes from those operating in other countries ; for there can never be under the Russian system any question of the lack of an adequate demand for all the goods that Russian man-power can produce, though it is of course possible for the Russians to make mistakes by applying a disproportionate part of their limited resources to certain kinds of capital equipment, and it is arguable that they have done this in recent years in the giant power-stations which they have installed. A Russian, however, would probably reply that, even if provision has been made for the generation of electricity on a scale far exceeding present or immediately prospective requirements, this is only reasonable foresight designed to avoid the necessity for the reconstruction of plants in the near future as industrialisation continues its rapid advance. This argument may be open to question, or it may be held that it has been pushed too far in practice ; and there has undoubtedly been some setback in Russia at the beginning of the second Five-Year Plan. But the point is not that all is going well in Russia, but that in as far as things go ill the cause is to be found not in lack of markets but in lack of skill and power to organise production under the totally new conditions which the Russians have set themselves to master at a prodigious pace.

It is possible to get some further light on the effects of the slump in Europe by considering the amount of freight traffic being carried over the various European railway systems. This is shown in the accompanying table, which again brings out, despite the serious financial plight even of the British railways, the relative immunity of Great Britain from the most serious consequences of the slump in depressing the volume of internal trade. For here again the decline is far more serious in Germany than in most of the other countries for which statistics are available. Roumania, thanks to the construction of new lines, shows an advance in total freight traffic over the figures for 1928. But everywhere else the decline is very serious indeed, reflecting directly both the fall in the volume of external trade and the decline in the internal demand for commodities and therefore in the standard of living of the people. The figures of shipping clearances tell for the most part the same story. It is unfortunate that comparable figures are not available for Germany for 1928 and 1932. It is, however, possible to get comparable figures for 1930 and 1932 ; and these show an exceedingly heavy rate of decline, from 2,409,000 tons in 1930 to under 2 million tons in 1932. The figures showing the amount and proportion of tonnage laid up idle in the leading countries in the latter part of 1932 tell the same tale. France and United States had about

TRADE DURING THE DEPRESSION

	Net Imports Tonnage 000 metric tons		Net Exports Tonnage 000 metric tons		Net Imports Value million dollars		Net Exports Value million dollars		Shipping Clearances with cargo only*, with cargo and ballast † thousand tons		Railway Freight Traffic, millions of ton-kilometres	
	1929	1932	1929	1932	1929	1932	1929	1932	1929	1932	1929	1932
Great Britain	5,565	2,792	—	—	451	190	295	107	5,723*	4,449*	2,570	2,028
Germany	—	—	4,564	3,576	267	92	252	112	2,409* (1930)	1,996*	5,745	3,242
France	4,955	3,962	3,326	1,933	190	98	163	64	4,099*	3,708*	—	—
Belgium	3,746	2,615	2,148	1,630	82	38	75	34	2,469†	2,021†	699	378
Holland	2,582	2,049	1,358	1,166	92	44	67	28	1,824*	1,116*	—	—
Denmark	—	—	—	—	38	17	36	17	—	—	—	—
Sweden	—	—	—	—	40	18	40	14	1,292*	955*	—	—
Switzerland	726	728	87	38	45	29	34	13	—	—	—	—
Czechoslovakia	836 (1931)	698 (1931)	1,123	722 (1931)	49	18	50	18	—	—	911	581
Poland	424	149	1,753	1,125	29	8	26	10	447† (with Danzig)	468†	2,160	1,279
Italy	2,290	1,474	399	305	95	35	65	29	1,777†	1,593†	1,017	790
Spain	594	428	961	484	44	16	34	12	2,277*	1,932*	—	—
U.S.S.R.	161	192	1,179	1,462	38	30	40	24	—	—	—	—
Austria	856	507	342	156	38	16	25	9	—	—	379	221
All Europe	—	—	—	—	1,640	706	1,318	543	5,421*	4,219*	59,897	31,508
U.S.A.	—	—	—	—	362	110	430	135	—	—	—	—

30 per cent of their total tonnage laid up at these dates, Poland 26 per cent, and Germany 22 per cent, as against 16 per cent in the case of the United Kingdom, although even the British position was serious enough, with a total of over 3 million gross tons out of use.

Enough has been said to show clearly the disastrous effects which the world slump has had on the industries of the leading European countries. This decline in industry has of course reflected itself, as the corresponding decline in agriculture has reflected itself in Eastern Europe, in serious budgetary difficulties in all the industrial States. For declining production at falling prices has meant everywhere a narrowing of profit margins and therefore a decreased yield of existing taxes, and especially of taxes levied upon the incomes derived from profits. In the case of taxes falling upon the *rentier* classes the position is somewhat different, since the proportion of the national income falling to these classes has considerably increased as a result of the drop in prices. *Rentier* incomes as a whole have been comparatively well maintained ; for, despite the widespread difficulties of the debtor countries, the amount of absolute default on existing debts has been in most of the industrial countries kept within fairly narrow limits, and even the needy agricultural States have to a large extent kept up their interest payments on their external debts. *Rentier* incomes have indeed been reduced to a certain degree by conversion operations carried through by Finance Ministers under the favourable conditions created by the fall in interest rates ; and the same result has been secured by reborrowing at lower rates on short-dated commercial debentures and other loans. But these reductions in *rentier* incomes have been by no means sufficient to offset the relative advantages which *rentiers* have gained as a result of the fall in prices. Accordingly, *rentier* incomes have become for most countries an increasingly important source of tax revenue, though there has been surprisingly little attempt to impose any special taxation upon them, despite the relative improvement in

their ability to pay. The special position of wage incomes
will be discussed later in this Part. It suffices to say here
that, while particular groups of wage-earners have doubtless gained as a result of the fall in prices, the general effect
of this fall upon wage incomes has been fully offset and in
some countries much more than offset by the extension of
unemployment and short time. It has therefore not been
possible, even apart from the resistance certain to be
offered by the wage-earners to attempts either to tax them
directly or to increase heavily the burden of indirect
taxation, to make budgets balance by additional taxation
levied either upon wage-earners or upon commodities of
necessary consumption, though the effect of rising tariffs
throughout Europe has undoubtedly been to transfer to
the general mass of consumers a considerable part of the
costs of the depression.

§ 9. THE GREAT INDUSTRIAL
COUNTRIES

So far we have been considering the effects of the
world slump upon the industrial countries, but it is clearly
necessary, apart from this, to attempt to give some sort of
picture of the industrial situation in Europe apart from the
abnormal influences exerted upon it by the world crisis.
For we are concerned with the economic situation in
Europe not only as it exists to-day at the bottom of the
depression, but as it existed in 1914 and as it might be
expected to exist again if the efforts of the world to bring
the depression to an end met with some real measure of
success. We must, then, look at the position of the leading
industrial countries of Europe on the eve of the world
slump, when, as we have seen, most of them had settled
down or appeared to have settled down on a basis of
stabilised currencies, and to be going forward with an
increase of productive activity corresponding to the
changed economic conditions of post-war Europe. The

leading industrial countries which it seems necessary to consider in this connection are Great Britain, Germany, France, Belgium, Holland, Italy, and for some purposes Czechoslovakia. The first six of these countries, excluding Czechoslovakia, for which no pre-war figures are of course available, were responsible in 1913 for 45 per cent of the total export trade of the world, and for over 50 per cent of the world's net imports. In 1929, on the eve of the world slump, their share in the world's exports had fallen to about 35 per cent, while their share in imports was about 41 per cent. In the meantime the United States had increased its share of world exports from $12\frac{1}{2}$ to nearly 16 per cent, and of net imports from $8\frac{1}{2}$ to 12 per cent, while the rest of Europe, excluding the U.S.S.R., had advanced from a share of 10 per cent to one of 13 per cent in exports, and from 12 per cent to 14 per cent in net imports. Meanwhile the share of the U.S.S.R. had fallen from 4 per cent to less than $1\frac{1}{2}$ per cent in net exports, and from $3\frac{1}{2}$ per cent to not much more than 1 per cent in net imports.

Among the leading countries there had been considerable shifts in relative importance. Thus Great Britain had actually increased her proportion of net imports from 15 to over 16 per cent of the world total, but if trade with the Irish Free State is excluded, her proportion remained about the same. On the other hand, her share in net exports had fallen from 13 per cent to under 12 per cent, or, excluding trade with the Irish Free State, to less than 11 per cent.[1] Germany had suffered a decline in her share of both imports and exports, from 12.3 per cent to 9 per cent in the case of imports and from 12.4 per cent to just under 10 per cent in the case of exports. France too had lost, despite her increased territory, with a fall roughly from $7\frac{1}{2}$ per cent to 6 per cent of the world total of imports, and 7 to 6 per cent of world exports. Italy retained her share of both imports and exports practically unchanged, while Belgium and

[1] Trade between Great Britain and the Irish Free State did not count as external trade before the war, and the foreign imports and exports of the Irish Free State were then included in the United Kingdom totals.

Holland had both suffered considerable declines ; but most of the countries registering a decline in their external trade had been to some extent regaining their position during the years immediately before the world slump.

If we analyse somewhat more in detail the composition of the export trade of the leading European countries, the immense dependence of most of the leading countries on exports of manufactures at once becomes plain. Thus in 1929, of total British exports amounting to £729 million, £563 million were accounted for by manufactured goods as against £118 million for raw materials (largely coal) and only £46 million for food and drink. Germany, out of total exports valued at £660 million, exported £481 million's worth of manufactures as against £143 million's worth of raw materials and only £34 million's worth of food and drink. France's total exports were valued at £403 million, and these included £273 millions' worth of manufactured goods, £79 million's worth of raw materials, and £48 million's worth of food and drink. Italy exported in all £161 million's worth of commodities, and of these over £100 million's worth were manufactures, £40 million's worth food and drink, and £20 million's worth raw materials. Czechoslovakia exported £89 million's worth of manufactures out of total exports of £124 million, and only £14 million's worth of food and drink and £21 million's worth of raw materials.

These figures show to what an extent the more industrialised countries depend on the sale abroad of manufactured goods, whereas their imports consist to a very large extent of foodstuffs in a raw state and of materials, including some semi-manufactures, necessary for the carrying on of their industries. It used to be held that, especially under Free Trade conditions, each country would tend to develop a range of industries corresponding to its special productive opportunities, and that accordingly world trade would tend to benefit buyers and sellers alike by promoting the production in each country of those goods for which it enjoyed the maximum comparative advantage. Tariffs, of course, interfere to a considerable extent with these desirable forms of specialisation ; but even apart from tariffs it is a marked characteristic of the modern productive system that each country which advances to the possession of a developed industrial system tends to direct its efforts largely to the manufacture of the same types of commodities, so that each of the highly industrialised countries is in fact trying to sell in the world market very largely the same classes of goods, and not different goods according to the different productive advantages which it possesses. Each advanced country depends in a high degree for the maintenance of its exports on a comparatively narrow range of industries—iron and steel, engineering, and textiles above all others—and there is growingly keen competition to sell the products of these industries in the less industrialised parts of the world, as well as a tendency for each country to protect its home market against the products of its rivals.

It is of course true that within this broad grouping of industries there is room for a large amount of specialisation upon particular products. It does not follow, because Great Britain and Germany and Belgium are all trying to export steel, that they are all producing exactly the same kinds of steel ; and especially in the higher qualities of production a considerable degree of specialisation does exist between one country and another. But over an increasingly wide range of products there is competition in the production and marketing abroad of exactly the same types of goods ; for any country which desires to carry through a process of advanced industrialisation necessarily sets itself to develop many of the same products, and the differential advantages which in the nineteenth century were held to count for so much in determining the forms of national specialisation are in practice nowadays of a good deal less account than they once were. For it is often possible artificially to reproduce, as in the case of the cotton industry, the atmospheric conditions which once gave predominance to a particular area, while the evolution of machine technique and the development of supplies of raw materials unworked in the

THE COMPETITION FOR EXPORTS

Rough classification of the export of certain leading countries under broad groups of commodities (based on exports of 1930)

Per cent of total exports	Great Britain	Germany	France	Belgium	Italy	Czecho-slovakia	Poland	U.S.A.
Coal and Coke	9	6		4		2½	14	2
Metals and Metal Goods	29	40	20	34	7	16	12	31
Chemicals and Drugs	6	10	9	5	2	3½		2
Textile and Clothing	30	15	28	20	39	27	6	4
Leather and Skins	1	5	5	4	2	4		2
Rubber and Rubber Goods	1	1	1	2		2		1½
Paper and Paper Goods	1½	4	2	2		1		1½
Glass and Pottery	2	3	1	5		?		
Timber and Woodwork			1			1½		
Cement and other Minerals				1				3
Mineral Oils			2		5	2½		
Precious Stones								12½
Food and Drink	8	4	14	3	24	24	38	14
Tobacco	1½					2		4
Raw Cotton								13
Other	11	12	16	13	20	14	15	11½

nineteenth century have combined with the improvement of transport to make it easier to carry on a wide range of industrial production in almost any country which possesses a seaboard and adequate supplies of a few primary materials in reasonable proximity to the sea.

In these circumstances, international competition between the industrial countries necessarily becomes more acute, and the differences between them tend to disappear, or at least are narrowed, while the contrast between their position and that of the primary agricultural countries becomes sharper with the advance of industrialisation. The truth of this can be seen in broad outline by comparing the position in production and export of certain of the leading commodities of the great industrial nations of Western and Central Europe. Take first the case of iron and steel. Germany, France, and Great Britain are all important steel-producing countries, and of the lesser Powers, Belgium also occupies an important position in this trade. Every highly industrialised country in the modern world inevitably desires to produce steel on a substantial scale, although some countries are unable to do so on a sound economic basis owing to the lack of the necessary materials —especially coal. France, before 1918, was fatally hampered in this respect by lack of both coal and iron ore ; but the acquisition of Alsace-Lorraine, and temporarily of the Saar coalfield, has raised her to a position of practical equality in the world steel trade with her pre-war rivals. These four countries—the United Kingdom, Germany, France, and Belgium (with which Luxembourg must now be included in view of the Customs Union concluded at the end of the war) are in sharp competition in the steel markets of the world. Three of them consume at home the greater part of the steel which they produce ; but the fourth, Belgium, is under the necessity of exporting the greater part of her output owing to the narrow limitations of her own home market. In 1929 these four countries shared among them in not unequal proportion the greater part of the steel trade of the world ; for, although the United States produced almost as much steel as all Europe put together, by far the greater part of this steel was consumed at home, and America was of relatively little importance in the export market.

In 1929 Germany led the way in European steel output with an export of over 5 million tons. Belgium came next with $4\frac{1}{2}$ millions, and France and the United Kingdom had both over $4\frac{1}{4}$ millions, as against less than $2\frac{1}{2}$ million tons exported by the United States. These four countries were largely producing the same types of commodities and attempting to sell them in acute rivalry in the markets of the world. Three of them, Germany, France, and Belgium, belonged to the Continental Steel Cartel, and had entered into an agreement among themselves and with certain of the smaller producing countries for a limitation of the total quantities produced in accordance with a quota system, allotting a definite maximum output to each national group, with fines for exceeding the permitted quantities. Great Britain remained outside the Cartel, not so much as a matter of principle as because the British manufacturers had been unable to reach any satisfactory agreement with their Continental rivals concerning the quota which ought to be allowed them. The British manufacturers claimed a virtual monopoly of the Empire markets, but wished to be free to export a considerable quantity of steel to Europe as well, whereas the Continental manufacturers, while they were prepared to grant Great Britain her predominant position in the British Empire, wished drastically to limit the quantities of British steel which could be exported to the markets of Europe. In all these countries productive capacity was in 1929 considerably ahead of actual output, for the steel industry was among those most expanded in each country as a result of the war, and the territorial readjustments after 1918 had the effect of inducing each country to try to build up within its own territories an extensive and self-sufficing steel industry of its own. This applies especially to Germany, which, finding herself deprived of a large part of her pre-war resources in the iron and steel trades, set to work to create a new industry with the aid of the most modern processes of production on a scale fully commensurate with that which had existed within her pre-war territories.

This redundancy of productive capacity naturally accentuated the competitive struggle between Great Britain and the groups belonging to the Continental Cartel, and in this struggle the lower wage rates prevailing on the Continent, and especially in Belgium and France, acted to the detriment of the British producers, especially as post-war developments of technique had tended to reduce the qualitative advantage previously possessed by the general mass of British steel over the Continental product. Great Britain still retained to a large extent her supremacy in the manufacture of the most highly priced special steels ; for in these her qualitative advantage remained almost intact. But in the cheaper types of steel she was definitely losing ground, especially in relation to Belgium. Before the war, in 1913, Belgian exports of steel, not including those from Luxembourg, for which no separate figures are available, only amounted to $1\frac{1}{2}$ million tons against the $4\frac{1}{2}$ millions of 1929, whereas the British exports had fallen from almost 5 million tons in 1913 to 4,380,000 in 1929.

There was keen competition between the leading industrial countries, not only in the various branches of iron and steel manufacture, but to an equal extent in the machine-making trades which use steel as their principal material. In this field, too, the advance of modern technique has tended to reduce the differential advantage possessed by this or that country for the manufacture of particular types of product, and international competition to sell the same classes of goods has become more intense. In 1929, Germany, Great Britain, and France were the leading exporters of machinery, with Belgium, Sweden, and Holland coming next, but a long way behind. The German export of machinery, other than electrical machinery, reached in 1929 a total of 700,000 tons. Great Britain came next with over half a million tons, and France third with over

200,000. Belgium and Luxembourg exported over 80,000 tons, Sweden 58,000, and Holland 54,000. In electrical machinery Great Britain occupied the leading position, closely followed by Germany, with Sweden and Switzerland next, then France and then Belgium. Great Britain's export in 1929 was not far short of 40,000 tons, Germany's about 35,000, that of Sweden and Switzerland about 11,000 in each case, France's 6,500 and Belgium's 3,000. Once again, while each country had to some extent its own specialities, these exports were directly competitive over a very wide range of goods, and the same considerations as in the case of steel largely applied, in that Great Britain's comparative advantage was tending to some extent to disappear except in the range of the highest quality products.

Or take again motor-cars, a field in which the entire European output is dwarfed by that of the United States, and European exports are exceedingly small even in relation to the volume of European production. As a producer, France in 1929 led the way among the European countries, closely followed by Great Britain, with Germany a bad third and Italy a long way behind. In exports, France also took the leading place, followed fairly closely by Great Britain, with Italy third at a considerable distance and Germany relatively unimportant. In all these cases by far the greater part of the output was actually marketed within the country of origin, and British sales for export were very small indeed in the European market, which was mainly filled by the United States, France, and Italy.

The chemical industry was a further field of intense competitition between the leading European Powers. In this case there seem to be no satisfactory figures on a comparable basis for any year later than 1925. In that year Germany had the largest share in the world trade in chemical products—23 per cent of total world trade as against 28 per cent before the war, whereas her share of world production had fallen from 24 per cent to 17 per cent. The United States came next with 16 per cent of world exports as against only 10 per cent before the war ; and the United States share in world production had actually risen from about a third to almost half of the total. Great Britain stood third with 14 per cent of total exports as against 16 per cent before the war, but France was only a very little behind with an export percentage of 13 as against 10 per cent in 1913. It will be seen that the British share in world exports, like the German, had actually fallen ; but this fall had been accompanied by a substantial improvement in the British position in the matter of dye-stuffs. Before the war, Germany had more than four-fifths of the total production of aniline dyes, whereas in 1925 her share was less than one half. Great Britain had meanwhile increased her percentage of the world total from 5 to 12, and France hers from 1 per cent to 9 per cent. In view of the increasing importance of the chemical industries from both an industrial and a military standpoint there has naturally been keen rivalry to develop them within each national area ; and special measures of protection, of which the British Dyestuffs Act is an example, have been instituted with this object. In the sphere of chemical as well as in that of metal goods, productive capacity is a long way ahead of world consumption, so that in this field too the various countries which are largely producing the same types of products are in keen competition one with another.

So much for the group of trades usually known as the heavy industries. Let us now turn to the textile trades, as the outstanding example of international competition in the sphere of consumers' goods. The textile trades have declined in relative importance in the economy of the leading industrial nations since the rise of the metal industries during the past half century ; but they still occupy a position of very great prominence, and despite the sharp fall in British exports of cotton goods, these are still by far the largest single item in the total of British exports. Before the war Great Britain occupied a position of practically undisputed pre-eminence in the world trade in cotton piece goods, her exports of which far exceeded those of all the other European countries put together. Even in 1929 she retained,

though to a reduced extent, her position of supremacy, with an export of over 8,000 million square yards
of piece goods as against 1,000 millions each exported by
Italy and France, her two nearest rivals. But there had
been a sharp reduction in the total volume of British exports. This was due to a considerable extent to the rise of
cotton production in the Far East, and especially in Japan.
During the war the British cotton trade was largely shut
down, owing to the impossibility of affording tonnage
either for the supply of necessary raw materials or for exports on the old scale, and also on account of shortage of
labour. During this temporary absence of British exporters
from the Far Eastern market, the production of cotton
goods for domestic use was extended very greatly in both
India and China ; and Japan not only equipped herself
for supplying most of her own requirements, but also embarked upon an active policy for the expansion of her
exports. Consequently, when the British producers attempted to re-enter the markets which they had lost, they
found themseves confronted with the competition of Far
Eastern production, based on exceedingly ill-paid labour
working with the aid of the most up-to-date technical
machinery. Man for man, the British cotton operative remained more productive than his Far Eastern rival ; but
in the cheaper classes of goods the superiority of Great
Britain in terms of costs had been so narrowed as to make
it increasingly difficult to compete with the low-wage products of the Far Eastern countries, especially when, as in
Japan, exporters received the active aid of the Government. Under these changed conditions a substantial part
of the pre-war market could not be regained, and in the
years after the war the continued expansion of Far Eastern production menaced the Lancashire cotton trade to
an ever-increasing extent. At the same time, European
countries, intent on expanding their production, raised
their protective duties in the interests of home manufactures ; and this rendered more difficult the access of
British goods to the Continental markets, while production

in the United States was also increasing fast, mainly for the fulfilment of domestic needs, for even in 1929 the United States remained quite unimportant as an exporter of cotton goods.

The raising of tariffs in Europe was, however, far more important in relation to the wool and worsted trades than to the trade in cotton goods ; for the great bulk markets for cotton piece goods lie outside Europe, whereas in the case of woollens the European market is of primary importance. Great Britain remained in 1929 the principal country in the export trade for the leading types of woollen goods. In the sphere of woven goods of wool and worsted her exports were considerably more than twice as large as those of any other country, with Germany and France as her nearest rivals, and Italy and Czechoslovakia some further distance behind. But in the trade in semi-finished materials, wool tops and yarn, though Great Britain occupied the leading position, France was not far behind her, and Germany and Czechoslovakia were also of substantial importance. All these countries, as well as the smaller European producers, had adopted systems of tariff protection in the interests of their own industries, and they were all in keen competition to export their goods to the markets of the agricultural countries. The exports of the different countries were not indeed entirely competitive, both France and Great Britain concentrating to a considerable extent on the finer qualities, whereas Germany and Czechoslovakia were more concerned with the trade in the cheaper classes of goods. In the artificial silk trade, there was also sharp rivalry among much the same group of countries, Great Britain, Italy, France, and Germany all competing for a share in the European as well as in the world market in this growingly important form of textile production.

The purpose of this analysis of certain of the major industries of Europe has been to bring out the growingly competitive tendency of modern industrial countries. Internally the tendency in each country has been away from

unregulated competition and towards closer forms of combination among the different producers, with the object of
regulating both output and prices ; but, in the international
field, competition has become more intense as each country,
on reaching an advanced stage of industrial development,
has equipped itself with much the same range of industries
and entered into the world market with directly competitive goods for sale. It is perfectly true that this intensification of international competition has led in a number of
trades, notably steel, to the development of international
cartels between rival national groups of producers, and that
sometimes large combines have been created directly upon
an international basis, with affiliated organisations in
each country for the exploitation of that particular market.
This tendency may in the long run considerably limit the
competitive character of international capitalism. But it
is quite a mistake to suppose that international capitalist
combination has yet in most industries reached such a
point as seriously to limit national rivalries or competition
between rival national groups of producers in the world
market. Despite the counter-tendency towards international
combination, the general movement has been in the direction of intensified competition on a national basis, with an
increasing element of support from each national State
for its own producers. Indeed, the tendency towards international combination has arisen only because of the
adverse effect on the profits of the various national groups
of unregulated competition in the world market. It is
therefore a sign of the strength of the competitive tendency
and a reaction to it, and by no means a sign that Capitalism
is of itself becoming progressively more international.

How, indeed, could competition fail to be intensified in
face of the influence of technical invention on the industrial
systems of the leading countries ? If each country sets out to
produce much the same classes of goods, and if the improvement of technique over the world as a whole is such as
to give a great advantage in respect of cost to large-scale
production and to make possible the creation of huge

producing plants with a capacity considerably ahead of the total consuming power of the world market, it is inevitable that the national groups of producers, each desirous of taking the fullest possible advantage of these productive opportunities, should compete more and more aggressively one with another—at least up to the point at which they find that a continuance of competition is likely to drive prices down to a ruinous level, even in face of the economies that they have been able to achieve by the application of the newest productive methods. For it is characteristic of these new methods of large-scale production that, while the new factories can produce far more cheaply than their older rivals as long as they can be kept working up to their full capacity, as soon as they fall below this capacity costs of production in them rapidly increase. This happens largely because modern plants are designed in relation to a definite optimum output, so that if they produce either more or less than this some of the advantages of their efficiency are lost ; and it is also because their equipment with heavy machinery of a very expensive sort makes the capital costs of constructing them very great. These capital costs have to be met out of the selling price of the product ; and they can be kept down only if they can be spread over a very large quantity of output. If, then, in the producing countries taken together, the total productive capacity is considerably ahead of the total world demand at the prevailing prices, and if, further, efficiency does not differ very greatly from one country to another, it follows that, in default of agreement, the trade is likely to be so shared out as to keep the industry of each country working at an uneconomic level—unless indeed the producers in a particular country are able so to press down the wages of their employees as to gain a comparative advantage in terms of costs, even if they have no real superiority in efficiency.

Under these circumstances strong inducements arise for the rival national groups of producers to get together and try to reach some sort of accommodation. But even the case of steel, in which this has been done, serves to illustrate the extreme difficulty of making a durable working agreement of this sort. There is almost certain to be continual quarrelling over quotas and allocation of markets, even in so comparatively simple a case as that of steel, while in most industries the far greater diversity of the products renders it much harder to draw up and apply any system of quotas at all. Consequently in most industries competition between national groups of producers and exporters remains in force, comparatively little affected by those tendencies towards international cartels or agreements which have manifested themselves in those branches of the heavy industries where products are most standardised, and output most easily measurable.

In default of international combination among the national groups of producers, it becomes highly important to each national group to retain to the fullest possible extent a monopoly in its own home market ; and the very difficulty of arriving at international agreement is therefore one of the factors which tend to increase the pressure for protective tariffs in the interests of the home manufacturers. But protective tariffs, while they may be of considerable advantage to industries whose home markets are able to absorb a high proportion of their total output of a particular class of goods, can do little for industries, like the British cotton trade, which have been accustomed to sell the greater part of their total output in foreign markets. Under these circumstances industries highly developed for purposes of export, and countries largely dependent upon such industries, suffer relatively to those which have not pushed industrial specialisation to so advanced a point.

In view of what has been said about the similarity of the productive systems and of the exports of the leading industrial countries, it is perhaps worth while to set out by way of a table a very rough statement of the composition of the export trade of certain of the leading countries according to the values of 1930. The figures given on page 523 show the values of certain of the main classes of exports as a percentage of the total value of each country's exports in that year. It will be seen that in Great Britain, Germany, France and Belgium—that is to say, in the four most industrialised countries—the two groups of metals and textiles occupied a predominant position, but there is some difference in their relative importance in the various countries. Thus, in Great Britain metals and textiles stand about on an equality, whereas in Germany and Belgium metals are much more important than textiles, and in France, as also in Italy and Czechoslovakia, this position is reversed. Next in importance comes in the leading countries the chemical group. This is most important in Germany and France, but substantial in Great Britain and Belgium as well, whereas in the industrially less developed countries, Italy and Czechoslovakia, this group of exports is of smaller relative importance. In the case of Poland, which is industrialised only in a very minor degree, metals stand first among the manufactured exports, and textiles second. But both these groups are still small in relation to the exports of coal and agricultural products. Figures for the United States, given for purposes of comparison, show that there too the metal group now stands easily first ; but after metals, the most important exports of the United States are foodstuffs, raw cotton and oil, and American manufactured exports are still of relatively little importance save in the metal and engineering industries.

Naturally, all the most highly industrialised countries, with the exception of Germany, show an excess of imports over exports ; for these are the countries which have had time to grow wealthy on a basis of industrialisation, and to build up for themselves by the export of capital claims to an annual revenue from abroad. Such a situation normally expresses itself in what is sometimes called an " adverse " balance of trade. Germany alone among the advanced countries of Europe has built up for herself in recent years a surplus of exports ; and, as we have seen earlier, she has achieved this only by means of a drastic curtailment of imports at the expense of her domestic standard of life—

a measure forced upon her partly by the exaction of
reparations, but to an even greater extent by the loss of her
pre-war foreign holdings of capital and the magnitude of
her post-war borrowings for purposes of economic reconstruction. Of the remaining countries Great Britain has by
far the greatest excess of imports—five times as great in
1929 as that of any other European country. Great Britain
was able, up to the coming of the world slump, to sustain
this enormous excess of imports partly because she had by
far the largest holdings of capital abroad, and partly
because she derived a large net revenue annually from her
mercantile marine, and from the services performed by the
City of London in the financing of world trade. Italy,
which had the next largest excess of imports in 1921, was
only able to balance her payments by a considerable net
import of capital, while France and Holland, which stood
next in excess of imports, were both countries owning a
large amount of capital abroad. In the case of France, the
excess of imports was far less than the actual balance of
current payments would have allowed ; and the account
was being squared by the deposit of considerable sums of
French money abroad, and also by the accumulation of
gold in the Bank of France. Apart from Germany, the only
country at all advanced in industrialisation which possessed a surplus of exports was Czechoslovakia, and in this
case the export surplus was so small as to be of little significance. Czechoslovakia had roughly a balanced industrial
system in respect of her external claims and payments. The
U.S.S.R. which, owing to large exports of wheat and
timber, had in 1929 a small export surplus, had converted
this by 1931 through short-term foreign credits into a
considerable surplus of imports. But it is also noticeable that
several of the less developed countries which had in 1929
a surplus of imports had by 1931 so reversed the position as
to have an export surplus instead. This applies to Poland
and to the group of less advanced countries in South-
Eastern Europe.

§ 10. THE STRANGLING OF EUROPEAN TRADE

MUCH ATTENTION has been drawn to the disastrous effects of the tangle of restrictions on trade which country after country has built up in the years since 1929, and more especially during the past two years. This restrictive policy has been in the circumstances practically inevitable, in that each country has found itself faced with a set of circumstances in which there has seemed to be no alternative to a purely nationalist policy of *sauve qui peut*. It is of course quite true that the world was seriously afflicted by economic nationalism even before the coming of the world slump. When the first World Economic Conference met in 1927 the chief object before it was that of removing or reducing restrictions on world trade which had already risen to heights unparalleled in pre-war times. Even then, European tariffs were in most cases far above the tariffs which existed before the war, and many countries were operating side by side with their tariffs systems of import control and regulation designed both to protect their domestic industries and to improve the balance of trade, or even, in certain instances, to discriminate against the products of countries with which they were on bad terms.

But in 1927 most of the delegates to the World Economic Conference regarded these restrictions rather as signs of the continued dislocation arising out of the war than as indicative of the considered policy of post-war Europe. The process of returning to the gold standard and of stabilising the currencies of the post-war nations was not yet complete ; and as long as currencies remained unstable the work of building up the post-war system of international economic relationships could hardly be carried through to a satisfactory conclusion. The World Economic Conference of 1927 was conceived as the direct successor to the Genoa Conference, which had dealt with the stabilisation of currencies and the return to the gold standard. It was to be an important stepping-stone towards the re-establishment of normal trading relations between the nations of the world on the basis of the work already done for the re-establishment of normal financial relationships. The various quotas, restrictions and embargoes which then existed were thought of as in process of disappearance as European conditions became more stable, and the Conference actually adopted a draft convention aiming at the complete abolition of all restrictions and embargoes on the import and export of goods except by way of tariff duties and in the exceptional case of State monopolies. This convention was in fact never brought into force ; for it failed to secure the required number of ratifications. But most people supposed in 1927 that even if embargoes and quotas could not be at once altogether swept away they were destined for the most part to disappear before long.

Moreover, the World Economic Conference of 1927 strongly recommended an international effort for the reduction of tariffs, and the Tariff Truce negotiations initiated by the British Labour Government in 1929 followed logically upon the work of the Conference in this field. Between 1927 and 1929 the actual accomplishment in the reduction of tariffs was almost nil ; but it is probable that the effect of the Conference of 1927 was to slow down the growth of economic nationalism by preventing tariffs from rising during the next two years as fast as they would have risen if it had not been held. Even as late as 1929 most people thought that, currency stabilisation having now been virtually completed by the adhesion *de jure* or *de facto* of practically all the important trading nations except China to the gold standard, most countries would speedily go on to the establishment of more liberal trading relationships on the stable financial basis thus ensured.

The coming of the world slump swept away all these hopes of a re-establishment of world Capitalism on the basis of an economic liberalism approximating to that of the nineteenth century. Very soon after the Wall Street crash of 1929 tariffs began again to rise sharply, and the new development was most marked in the case not of manufactured goods but of agricultural products. For the distress of the agriculturists led in one country after another to special measures designed to raise the domestic prices of cereals and other foodstuffs beyond the world level, which was set by conditions in the exporting countries of the New World. Before long, tariffs on manufactures also began to rise again ; and as the crisis deepened, especially in 1931, tariffs began to be used in a new way and to be reinforced, as we have seen earlier, by all manner of new restrictions on the importation of goods. After September 1931, when the world had ceased to have any effective common monetary standard, there was added to high tariffs and restrictive embargoes on trade the new factor of a far more drastic control of foreign exchange, through the centralisation in many countries of practically all foreign exchange transactions in the hands of the Central Banks.

All these measures, from tariffs to the control of foreign exchange, were deliberately used by countries with the object of sheltering themselves from the effects of the world depression, and more specifically of improving their balances of payments in relation to other countries. Normally, a protective tariff, or any substitute for it in the form of a regulation of imports by licence or quota, is designed to foster the production in a country of goods that would otherwise be imported from abroad. But under the new conditions this object became for many countries secondary, and was replaced, or rather complemented, by the quite different object of preventing imports, irrespective of the possibility of manufacturing the goods in question at home. The object was now to sell more exports and to buy less imports in order to have a balance available for meeting external claims, above all the service of the growing burdensome external debts, as well as to protect home producers against the consequences of sharply falling world prices. Of course in practice these two essentially different objects could not be kept distinct, in that a protective tariff may tend to restrict imports more than exports and thereby to improve the trade balance, while a tariff designed to keep out imports in the interests of the trade balance may also stimulate to some extent production of the excluded goods at home. But, though the two aims of the policy pursued during the crisis intermingle, it is important to keep the distinction between them in mind. Protectionism became Protectionism run mad because its objects were no longer merely Protectionist in the familiar sense of the term.

It is unfortunately quite impossible to make any quantitative measurement of the new restrictions on trade which have developed since the beginning of the world slump. In 1927, for the purpose of the World Economic Conference, an approximate measurement was made of the changes in tariffs which had taken place between 1913 and 1925. This showed that in some countries the *ad valorem* incidence of the general rates of duty in force was substantially lower than before the war, largely as a consequence of the higher prices prevailing for goods on which the duty was levied at a fixed money rate. Thus both France and Denmark had in 1929 tariff levels lower by 30 per cent on the average of their *ad valorem* incidence than the tariffs in force before the war, while in Sweden there was a fall of 20 per cent, and in Austria one of 35 per cent. On the other hand, the German tariff was up by 25 per cent, the Dutch, Hungarian, and Spanish tariffs by 30 per cent, the Belgian tariff by 35 per cent, and the Swiss tariff by no less than 70 per cent. These percentages of course do not indicate the absolute height of the tariff barriers imposed by the countries mentioned. For a comparatively small increase in tariff rates means a large percentage increase in the rates of low tariff countries such as Switzerland. Absolutely, the highest tariff in 1925 was that of Spain, which was estimated at 44 per cent *ad valorem* on the average of all classes of imports. As against this, the French and Austrian tariffs were only 12 per cent, and the German 15 per cent, while the Danish tariff was as low as 6 per cent, and the Dutch and British only 4 per cent, the latter of course then consisting of relatively high duties on a narrow range of goods. The tendency towards high tariffs in the new countries of Southern and Eastern Europe can, however, be seen from the fact that the tariff levels of Hungary, Poland, and Yugoslavia were all estimated as averaging 23 per cent *ad valorem*, and that of Czechoslovakia as averaging 19 per cent. Italy, with a 17 per cent tariff, had maintained the average *ad valorem* incidence unaltered from what it had been before the war. It should, however, be borne in mind in considering these figures, which relate to 1925, that in 1926 the French tariff was raised by two increases, each of 30 per cent, in view of the depreciation of the franc.

Up to 1925, and indeed for some time afterwards, the increase in tariff rates had been mainly applicable to manufactured goods. If the average *ad valorem* rates for manufactures alone are considered, instead of the rates averaged over all classes of imports, both the post-war tariffs of Europe and the increase in relation to the pre-war levels work out a good deal higher. Thus for Germany, whereas the general rate of increase was only 25 per cent, the rate for manufactured goods only was higher by 54 per cent than before the war. For France, duties on manufactured goods were higher by 5 per cent, as compared with a fall of 30 per cent in the duties on all classes of goods, even before the additional increases of 1926. In Belgium the rise was 67 per cent for manufactures as against 35 per cent for goods of all sorts ; while Hungary was taxing manufactures at a rate 50 per cent above that of 1913 compared with 30 per cent for all goods, and Italy had raised her rates on manufactures by 22 per cent, while admitting foodstuffs and raw materials at lower rates than before the war.

Between 1925 and 1929 a substantial further rise occurred. Holland and Great Britain, both starting from a very low level, more than doubled their average rates of duty on goods of all classes. Denmark raised rates by more than two-thirds, and Belgium by one half. The French rates rose by more than a third, and the German by nearly a third, and Switzerland and Sweden also showed small increases.

On the other hand, the Italian, Polish, Yugoslav, Czecho-slovak, and Hungarian tariffs all fell to some extent, and the Spanish tariff was nominally reduced to a considerable extent ; but in this case the reduction was in fact offset by special additional charges of various kinds. It is not possible for the years between 1925 and 1929 to calculate accurately the relation between the general rise in tariff levels and the rise on manufactured goods taken alone. But it seems clear that during these years the upward movement of agricultural tariffs was even more marked than the rise in the rates charged on other classes of commodities.

After 1929, as we have seen, tariffs rose faster still. But it is neither possible, nor would it be of much use, to measure their rise by any attempt to continue to the present time the tariff level indices compiled for the use of the World Economic Conference of 1927. For after 1929 the absolute height of a country's tariff or the change in its tariff rates no longer measures with any degree of accuracy the extent of the barriers which it places in the way of imports. Especially after the abandonment of the gold standard by a considerable group of countries, the rates payable on imports were in many cases subject to additions designed to offset the effects of currency depreciation in the exporting countries ; while direct restrictions and embargoes, and even more in the countries of Central and Eastern Europe the control of foreign exchange, came to be instruments of restriction far exceeding in their effects even the high tariff rates which were now in force. There was in addition a growing tendency towards tariff discrimination according to the origin of the imported products, though this tendency was kept in check to a great extent by the operation of the Most Favoured Nation Clause, which appears in a very large number of commercial treaties, including practically all the treaties concluded by Great Britain and the United States. For the Most Favoured Nation Clause secures that any concession made to a particular country shall be ex-tended, if it takes the form of a tariff preference, to all countries which have commercial treaties including the

Clause with the country granting the preference. This of course does not prevent discrimination in the form of a higher rate of duty at the expense of a country with which there is no commercial treaty, or none embodying the Most Favoured Nation Clause ; but it has served to limit the extent to which discrimination can be carried.

It is, however, highly questionable whether, in the circumstances of Europe to-day, this check on the power to discriminate has in practice been a good thing. For, while the Most Favoured Nation Clause has a liberalising influence in extending to a wider range of countries any concession made in a particular bilateral treaty by one country to another, the mere fact that this is so may prevent countries from making actual tariff concessions which they would be prepared to make if these concessions could be confined exclusively to their mutual relations. Again and again it has been suggested that the best hope of escape from the existing régime of high tariffs in Europe lies not in an attempt to get countries to reduce their general tariff rates for the benefit of all nations, but rather in the conclusion of bilateral or multilateral commercial treaties between neighbouring countries which have a great deal to gain from freeing their mutual economic intercourse. This applies especially to the new States created by the Peace Treaties ; for in many cases the frontiers of these States, drawn primarily in relation to ethnical factors, cut clean across previously unified economic areas, and the pursuit of purely nationalist tariff policies by the separate countries results in serious economic loss through the dislocation of established industries and the added costs of production where raw materials or semi-manufactured goods have to pay duty on passing across a national frontier. If, for example, the Danubian States, or some of them, could be induced to modify their existing tariffs so as to encourage trade among themselves, even perhaps ultimately to the point of constituting a complete Customs Union, this would obviously minister to their collective prosperity and increase their collective power in the

European economic system. Or if, again, the Scandinavian countries, or any other neighbouring groups, could agree to modify their internal tariffs, even without altering the degree of Protection accorded to their combined industries in relation to the outside world, this could be made the means of improving the economic condition of their own peoples to the advantage of the world as a whole.

In practice, however, any attempt to negotiate a bilateral or multilateral arrangement on these lines between a group of countries at once leads to objection on the part of those countries which use the Most Favoured Nation Clause as an instrument of international economic bargaining. During the past few years several promising attempts at mutual tariff reduction, or at the conclusion of arrangements designed to facilitate the exchange of goods between neighbouring countries, have been brought to nothing by the objection of other powers to any departure from the strict letter of the Most Favoured Nation Clause. Great Britain has taken a prominent part in the raising of objections on this ground ; for the traditional bargaining asset of British commercial policy has for a long time been the negotiation of commercial treaties based on Most Favoured Nation treatment. As long as Great Britain was, to all intents and purposes, a Free Trade country, she had a strong claim to demand the admission of her goods into all markets on the most favourable terms consistent with the national attitude of the importing country—that is to say with its determination to protect any or all of its own industries. But when Great Britain became not merely a Protectionist country, but a country with a high protective tariff based on preferential treatment for her own Dominions and Colonies, the force of her old arguments for Most Favoured Nation treatment largely disappeared, and the sole ground on which she could base a continued claim for such treatment came to be her economic power in the world market.

It seems clear that under these conditions no Protectionist country can reasonably stand in the way of those neighbouring countries which are prepared to conclude bilateral or multilateral treaties among themselves. The Most Favoured Nation Clause is bound in the near future to be modified ; and there is much to be said for the view that the agreement to modify it is much the most effective step that can be taken towards the reduction of world tariffs.

For, with Europe in its present condition, any frontal attack upon high tariffs, or for that matter upon the other forms of restriction which stand even more than tariffs in the way of an expansion of world trade, is practically certain to fail, whereas there might be a real chance for the conclusion of arrangements for the freer movement of goods between neighbouring countries. The past two years have, however, afforded ample evidence of the difficulties in the way of making effective progress along these lines. First the attempt of the Scandinavian countries to negotiate mutual arrangements among themselves for economic consolidation and a mutual basis for tariff relations reached towards the end of 1930 the favourable point of a positive though limited agreement, and a convention was signed at Oslo by the representatives of Denmark, Holland, Norway, Sweden and Belgium, which both stabilised mutual tariff relationships and provided for the notification of any suggested changes in tariffs in the future by each of the signatories to the rest. This seemed to be a favourable beginning for the attempt to build up a system of multi-lateral arrangements between particular countries. But the next stages of the process afford far less ground for satisfaction.

With the encouragement of France, the mainly agri-cultural countries of Eastern Europe set about considering the possibility of mutual trade arrangements designed to enable goods to pass more freely within their combined frontiers. But at an early stage very serious difficulties arose. Of the States of Central and Eastern Europe which have to be considered in connection with any proposal for mutual tariff arrangements on a basis of multilateral treaties, the great majority are agricultural countries. But two—Austria and Czechoslovakia—are also industrial producers on a considerable scale. The agricultural countries want an outlet for their goods in the markets of the industrial countries ; but even if both Austria and Czechoslovakia were to supply their total demand for agricultural imports from inside this group of countries, there would still remain a considerable surplus of agricultural goods to be marketed elsewhere. The agricultural States want to secure preferential arrangements for the marketing of this surplus in other importing countries, for example, in Italy and Germany. But these countries will obviously not consent to give the required preferential treatment except in return for similar treatment for their own industrial exports. On the other hand, Czechoslovakia is only prepared to consider a closer customs relationship with her agricultural neighbours because she hopes thereby to secure a preferential outlet for the products of her industries ; and if the more strongly organised industries of Germany were to be given the same treatment as her own the value of the preference would be from her standpoint largely nullified. Czechoslovakia, therefore, is willing to consider multilateral arrangements with her agricultural neighbours, but is not prepared to consider any wider tariff union or system of preference which would include Germany or any other highly industrialised nation. On the other hand, the Great Powers have no desire to see mutual tariff arrangements which might be the precursors of a complete customs union between the countries of Central and Eastern Europe on any terms which might involve the exclusion of their industrial products from these markets, or build up these countries into a powerful political *bloc* not susceptible to their respective influences. The Italians would by no means allow such a *bloc* to arise under conditions which might bring it within the German sphere of influence, nor would the Germans tolerate it on terms which might strengthen the hand of Italy or France.

In these circumstances, the attempt to make an approach to a customs union, or at any rate to a preferential tariff convention, among the Danubian countries and their agricultural neighbours broke down, both because of the internal differences and hostilities of the countries directly concerned, and because of the mutual suspicions of the Great Powers, which insisted that no scheme must be drawn up without regard to their political and industrial interests in the Danubian and Balkan areas. In addition, any chance that the project of a Danubian customs union might have had was almost completely wrecked when Austria and Germany, in the midst of the discussions, announced the decision to create an Austro-German Customs Union ; for this project, the alternative for Austria to inclusion in some sort of Danubian economic union, was regarded by the French as a first move in the direction of the political absorption of Austria into Germany, and as a violation both of the terms of the Peace Treaty and of the undertaking entered into by Austria in return for the financial assistance given to her under the auspices of the League of Nations. The announcement of the projected Austro-German Customs Union therefore caused an international political crisis. It was made clear to the Austrians that they could no longer expect any help from the League if they persisted in the project, and to the Germans that persistence on their side would involve the disappearance of any hope of an accommodating disposition on the part of the Allied signatories to the Peace Treaty in the matter of reparations and Treaty revision. In these circumstances both Germany and Austria were coerced into the abandonment of the projected Union, which was subsequently declared by the Hague Court to be inadmissible on the ground of undertakings previously entered into by the Austrian Government.

This question of the Austro-German Customs Union, coming in the middle of the negotiations for a mutual economic arrangement among the Danubian and Balkan countries, further emphasised the interrelation of political and economic forces in the precarious post-war settlement of Europe. Germany, Italy and France had taken up divergent attitudes in the Danubian negotiations, and Germany and France again fell foul of each other over the Austro-German Customs Union. It soon became clear that progress along these lines was to all intents and purposes hopeless for the present ; and even if the intensification of the world economic crisis in 1931 had not further prejudiced the position, it is clear that the attempt to promote any sort of economic unification among the Danubian States would have been bound to break down. In the event, the intensification of the crisis after the collapse of the *Credit Anstalt* in Austria, the subsequent difficulties of the German banks, and the run on the pound and the suspension of the gold standard in Great Britain, so added to the economic difficulties of each of the countries directly concerned as to make them more intent on the erection of further trade restrictions designed to safeguard their respective balances of payments than on attempting to build up any wider union favourable to the re-establishment of international trade.

During this period, side by side with the attempt to build up closer economic relationships between particular groups of countries, the League of Nations, and its auxiliary, the Committee for European Union, were discussing the proposal originally put forward by Briand in 1930 for a closer political relationship among all the States of Europe belonging to the League. At the outset, the Committee for European Union, which met for the first time in January 1931, was concerned largely with discussing the special difficulties of the agricultural countries in Eastern Europe. But later, when the difficulties in the way of success in this field had become manifest, the discussions of the Committee turned largely on the pact of economic non-aggression suggested by M. Litvinov on behalf of the Soviet Union. This project had no better fate, though the policy which lay behind it did result in the negotiation of a substantial number of political non-aggression pacts, accompanied in some cases by commercial treaties between the Soviet Union and other European countries, and in particular in a substantial improvement in the relations between Poland

and the U.S.S.R. Apart from this, the Committee for European Union accomplished nothing. In May 1931 sixteen States did sign a draft scheme for the establishment of an international agricultural credit association, designed to ease the financial difficulties of agricultural producers in Eastern Europe ; but this scheme was also submerged, before it had ever become effective, in the intensified economic crisis of the latter part of the year. The Committee for European Union continues to meet and to discuss, but it has shown no signs as yet of any ability to grapple with the difficult situations which confront it.

It is indeed doubtful whether in the present condition of Europe any body which attempts to negotiate inclusive economic pacts for the whole of the Continent stands any chance of success. The political conditions of stability which are indispensable as the basis for such pacts simply do not exist, and it is beyond the power of the Committee for European Union to call them into being. In its political aspects, Briand's project for a United States of Europe involved the assumption that the existing States of Europe could be taken as stable entities, strong enough and settled enough in their established constitutions and within their existing frontiers, to become the units of a permanent federal organisation. In other words, Briand's proposal for a federal Europe rested on the assumption that the settlement of European sovereignties imposed by the Treaties of Peace would endure, and that countries could be persuaded to reach mutual arrangements based on the recognition of the permanence and inviolability of the existing frontiers. At the time when the project was originally put forward, there appeared, superficially at least, to be some warrant for this view ; but subsequent events in Europe have largely knocked away the foundations on which it rested, and revealed the insecurity of the political as well as the economic structure of the European States.

All the negotiations of the past few years have therefore produced no real effect in removing the barriers in the way of international intercourse, which have on the contrary

become more and more obstructive and difficult to sur-
mount as the economic crisis has deepened, and as political
suspicions have become more intense. Vainly has one
conference after another, and one expert committee after
another, proclaimed by universal consent the desirability
of resuming more normal international economic relations
and of sweeping away a large number of the restrictions
which at present exist. These aspirations have remained
wholly ineffective in influencing the actual policy of the
European States. They were nevertheless repeated almost
without modification in the Report of the Preparatory
Committee for the World Economic Conference, and the
States of Europe were once more adjured to declare in
favour of the things they have declared in favour of on at
least a dozen occasions already. But it is surely obvious
that the restrictive system which now exists is a symptom
of the world's disease, and that accordingly there is no
hope of removing it unless the causes which underlie it
cease to operate. These causes are two-fold—economic and
political. Economically, the outstanding causes are those
which we have discussed already in this book—the sharp
and unequal fall in world prices, and the existence of fundamental disequilibria in the balances of payments due from
country to country and in an altogether top-heavy burden
of both internal and international debts. Politically, the
causes are to be found in the growingly articulate and open
dissatisfaction with the settlement reached at the conclusion
of the war, and the increasing determination of the defeated
countries to reassert themselves in European affairs, and to
reverse at least in part the sentence passed upon them in the
hour of defeat.

These political causes are doubtless largely aggravated by
economic factors. If Europe had been prosperous and advancing in wealth and economic prosperity, far less would
have been heard of the demand for Treaty revision, and
militaristic nationalism would have far less room for
growth. Nazism in Germany would never have risen to
power had there not been a vast mass of economic distress

and discontent on which it was able to work. The Balkan countries would probably never have passed under largely military dictatorships if they had not been plunged into economic difficulties by the world crisis. Even Hungary, which has most cause, on purely nationalist grounds, to resent the Peace settlement and to demand territorial redress, would probably have stayed quiet if there had not been a marked recrudescence of militarism over Europe. When the economic foundations of society are utterly insecure, and men are in despair of finding remedies for their economic troubles, they are apt to turn to militarism and nationalism as a way of escape from sheer wretchedness, and to make political conditions the scapegoats of economic adversity.

The moral is that if Europe is to be lifted out of the present depression, and some greater measure of freedom restored to international trade, this cannot possibly be accomplished by a direct attack on tariffs, embargoes, exchange restrictions and the other secondary phenomena of national distress, but only by a courageous attempt to remove the underlying economic causes of the trouble. Nothing will be achieved by international economic action until countries are prepared to concentrate their attention mainly upon an attempt to raise world prices, and to provide a more satisfactory basis for the issue of currency and credit, with the object of promoting in each country effective national action to stimulate demand and set the productive system once more at work, to raise the standard of living of the employed population, and to bring the unemployed back into useful economic activity. Unless this can be done, we must expect a continuance of the existing restrictions on trade and commerce, and even a further intensification of them as lesser measures fail to achieve their purpose. A little may indeed be done by bilateral negotiations between particular countries, such as the mutual arrangement for the gradual reduction of tariffs arrived at between Belgium and Holland in 1932 ; but there seems to be little hope that measures of this sort will in the existing conditions be adopted by most of the States which are in the worst economic situation, most exposed to the interplay of political and economic causes of friction, and most at the mercy of the jealousies and antagonisms of the Great Powers.

§ 11. WAGES IN EUROPE

SOME REFERENCE has been made in the foregoing sections to the importance of relative wage-levels in their effects upon the competition between the leading industrial countries of Europe. The purpose of the present section is both to throw what light can be thrown upon the relative levels of wages in these countries, and to say something about the movements of wages during the world slump. Unfortunately, it is exceedingly difficult to make any reliable comparisons between either the money wages paid in the various countries or the real value of these wages in terms of purchasing power ; and it is still harder to compare wages in the different countries as elements in the cost of production. These difficulties arise partly from the absence of the necessary statistics, and partly from the fact that international statistical measurement of wages and of their purchasing power is a problem of extreme complexity even where figures are available.

There seem to be no reliable figures by means of which the general levels of money wages in the various European countries before the war can be compared. The only comparisons that seem to be available are in terms of real wages, and not of money. The Ministry of Labour in Great Britain has attempted a rough comparison of the real wage levels existing in 1914. According to these figures, real wages in Berlin were rather more than four-fifths of real wages in London, while real wages in Paris were rather less than three-quarters of the London rates. Provincial rates in France were a long way below the Paris rates. Belgian real wages were appreciably lower, at about three-fifths of the British level, real wages in Scandinavia a little higher than in France, while real wages in Italy were little more than half the London rates, and in Spain substantially less than half. On the other hand, industrial wages in the United States and Canada were between 80 and 90 per cent higher than the corresponding rates in Great Britain.

For the post-war period a somewhat more authoritative comparison is available from the figures compiled by the International Labour Office. These figures are based on taking the actual money wages in the various countries, and then assessing their purchasing power by a somewhat complicated process in terms of the cost of a standard basket of commodities, making allowance for the different standards of consumption in the various countries. According to these figures, in the middle of 1929 German wages were about 70 per cent of the British, and French wages about 53 per cent, while wages in Spain and Austria were only about 45 per cent of the British level, and wages in Italy only 42 per cent. On the other hand, the Dutch level was 85 per cent of the British, and wages in Scandinavian countries, calculated on a somewhat different basis, since the original figures represent earnings and not rates of wages, were as high as wages in Great Britain. Thus, since 1914 real wages in Germany, France and Italy had all fallen substantially in relation to real wages in Great Britain. In the meantime the relative levels of real wages in Great Britain and the United States had undergone little change, American wages being in 1929 rather more than 90 per cent higher than British wages in terms of purchasing power.

Let us turn now from real wages reckoned in relation to the cost of living to the actual money wages paid in the various countries. Again let us take 1928 as the most convenient date for studying the wage position before the coming of the world slump. In that year wages in Great Britain, according to the calculations of the Ministry of Labour, were from 70 to 74 per cent higher than pre-war

APPROXIMATE MOVEMENT OF MONEY AND REAL WAGES BEFORE AND AFTER THE DEPRESSION (YEARLY AVERAGES)

	MONEY WAGES				REAL WAGES				
	1926	1929	1931	1932	1926	1929	1931	1932	
Great Britain	102	100	98	96	97	100	109	110	weekly rates
Czechoslovakia	92	100	103	103	96	100	107	109	,,
U.S.A. (skilled men)	97	100	101	88	93	100	105	113	,,
U.S.A. (general)	96	100	100	60	93	100	92	79	weekly earnings
Ireland	102	100	100	95	97	100	106	107	,,
France	85	100	108	103	93	100	106	108	daily rates
Poland	68	100	94	84 (Sept.)	82	100	111	109 (Sept.)	,,
Switzerland (men)	99	100	101	—	98	100	109	—	daily earnings
Sweden	97	100	103	—	95	100	110	—	,,
Norway (men)	121	100	95	—	98	100	103	—	,,
Germany	83	100	97	83	90	100	110	105	hourly rates
Italy	—	100	89	85	—	100	102	102	hourly earnings
Denmark	106	100	102	101	99	100	114	114	,,
Estonia	87	100	100	94	96	100	117	116	,,
Roumania	90	100	86	69 (June)	107	100	119	119	monthly earnings
U.S.S.R.	83 (1927)	100	120	136 (March)	—	100	—	—	,,
Hungary	87	100	88	—	100	100	102	—	yearly earnings
Finland	93	100	85	—	96	100	100	—	,,

wages ; wages in Germany were from 50 to 60 per cent higher ; and in France the rise was from 25 to 35 per cent, after allowance has been made for the fall in the gold value of the franc. In Switzerland, wages had rather more than doubled, and in Sweden substantially more than doubled ; while in Denmark, where the figures are based on hourly earnings, and therefore exaggerate the increase, the rise was over 150 per cent. Unfortunately no particulars are available for Italy or for most of the smaller European countries ; but in the United States the various published indices show that wage rates had on the average rather more than doubled between 1914 and 1928. Thus the rise in money rates of wages was higher in the United Kingdom than in Germany or France, but in both Scandinavia and the United States money wages had advanced at a substantially more rapid rate than in Great Britain.

For one trade only is it possible, as the result of a special investigation, to present an estimate of the relative wages paid in each of the chief producing countries. These figures are taken from a *Report on the Conditions of the Steel Trade in Continental Europe*, made by a British mission of investigation in 1930. In that year the average wages of steel workers of all grades in Great Britain were about 60s. a week, in Germany about 51s., in France about 37s., in Belgium and Luxemburg from 35s. 6d. to 36s. 6d., and in Czechoslovakia only 30s. 6d. These figures illustrate the amount of leeway which the British steel industry had to make up by means of higher efficiency in order to offset the lower wages paid in the various Continental countries. It should, however, be observed that the chief competition with British steel in foreign markets, except for the cheapest grades, came not from the countries with the lowest wages, but from Germany, where the rates most nearly approached those in force in Great Britain. This fact illustrates the impossibility of measuring wage-costs—i.e. the amount of wages involved in producing each unit of product—by the sum paid out in money wages per hour or per week to each worker employed. For wage-costs depend not only on the efficiency of the workers, but also to a large extent on that of the plant upon which they are employed, and of the management in all its aspects. High wages are not necessarily a handicap if they go with high personal efficiency on the part of the workers, and a high level of plant equipment and administrative capacity on the managerial side.

A similar conclusion arises from the figures published by the International Labour Office showing for the coal industries of the various European countries both the relative wage-levels, in terms of a common currency, and the labour-cost per ton of coal extracted. The figures, which relate to 1929, bring out the wide disparity between the labour-costs per ton and the relative daily earnings of the miners.

	Daily earnings	Labour-cost per ton
Great Britain	100	100
Ruhr	94	91
Upper Silesia	73	64
Saar	81	112
France	64	107
Belgium	61	119
Holland	100	95
Poland	52	46
Czechoslovakia	62	70

This comparison, of course, takes no account of the quality of the coal produced or of the ease of production as distinct from the efficiency of the industry. Nor does it take any account of the differences in working hours.

Let us now turn to the movement of wages during the world slump. It is unfortunately impossible in this field to present really up-to-date comparable particulars, and no attempt has been made to carry the comparison beyond the third quarter of 1932, or to take account of the serious wage reductions which have been made since then in certain countries, notably in Germany and the United States. Using as a basis the wages paid in 1928, which we took as representative of the wage levels existing on the eve of the world slump, we find that in the summer of 1932 there were two countries in which, despite the fall in the

level of world prices, money wages were slightly higher in
1932 than they had been four years before. These two
countries were Czechoslovakia and Denmark. In all the
other countries for which particulars are available there
had been a fall in money wages ; but the fall was very
different in the various countries. In the United Kingdom
it was only 4 per cent, whereas in Germany it was already
15 per cent, and in Italy 13 per cent. In the case of the
United States the fall in weekly wage rates was only about
12 per cent ; but the figures of weekly earnings showed a
reduction, in comparison with the earnings of 1928, of no
less than 42 per cent, largely as a result of widespread
short-time working. In the case of France no particulars
seem to be available.

If, however, we consider the movement of wages during
the world slump in terms, not of the amount of money paid
out or of the weekly rates of money wages, but of the purchasing power of these wages, we get a very different situation ; for in all the countries for which particulars are
available real wages for full-time work as distinct from
money wages were higher in 1932 than in 1928. The rise
was highest in Denmark, where it amounted to 15 per
cent ; but Czechoslovakia with 13 per cent and Great
Britain with 12 per cent were not far behind. Poland, for
which statistics are available only in terms of real wages,
showed a rise of 19 per cent, on account of the very heavy
fall in prices, and was thus actually ahead of Denmark and
Czechoslovakia. In the case of the United States, figures
are available only for earnings. Weekly earnings had fallen
by 23 per cent owing to short-time working, but hourly
earnings had risen by 8 per cent. Thus in all countries the
workers, to the extent to which they were able to find
regular employment, had benefited between 1928 and 1932
by the fall in the cost of living. But for the working
class as a whole this benefit was more than counteracted
by the great increase in unemployment and under-
employment.

On the basis of these figures it is possible for employers to argue that wages have remained too high in face of the fall in prices, so that wages costs are now disproportionate to the selling prices of goods, and are a cause of maintaining the prices of finished commodities and goods at retail too far above the prices of raw and semi-manufactured commodities. According to this view, wage-rates ought to be reduced at least in proportion to the fall in the cost of living, if not actually in proportion to the much greater fall in the level of wholesale prices. Many employers and some economists contend that, if this were done, the effect would be to cause an expansion of employment, by making it profitable for firms to carry on production where they are at present unable to produce at a profit. It cannot of course be disputed that if, in a particular country which exports a substantial proportion of its products, wage-rates are reduced without corresponding falls in wages in other countries, the country which reduces its wages will be in a position, other things being equal, to capture some trade from its rivals in the markets of the world. But this " advantage " to the country which reduces its wages is conditional upon other countries not following its example, whereas in practice a fall in wages beginning in the exporting industries of one country will usually be communicated before long to the competitive industries of other countries, so as to restore something like the old relation between the cost-levels of the two groups of employers.

When this has happened there is no reason to suppose that any country will benefit as a result of the reduction of wages ; for any tendency for more goods to be sold when the fall in wages is passed on to the consumers in the form of lower prices will, if the change in wage rates is generalised over industry as a whole, be likely to destroy so much purchasing power in the hands of the main body of consumers as to leave the total demand for the products of most industries no higher at the lower prices than it was when both prices and incomes were at a higher level. Indeed, this is an understatement ; for, as we have seen in our discussion of the effects of unemployment insurance, one highly desirable result of the provision of adequate maintenance for the unemployed is to keep up consuming power in the domestic market, and this advantage applies fully as much to the maintenance of wage-rates as to the provision of unemployment benefits. This desirability of maintaining wages during a slump holds with especial force in those countries, such as the United States, which rely on their home markets for the sale of a high proportion of their output. Its force is somewhat less in the case of the exporting countries, at any rate where there is a real prospect that they will be able to reduce wage-rates faster than their rivals. But any gain secured to an exporting country by the application of this policy will clearly be secured only at some other country's expense, and so far from helping towards the recovery of world trade as a whole will be likely to intensify the general depression. Low wages are assuredly no cure for business depression ; for their effect is to diminish demand, whereas what is needed is a stimulus to additional production and employment.

This argument would lose some of its force if in fact reductions of wages were accompanied by a corresponding fall in the prices of consumers' goods. But this is practically never the case. Even if prices at the factory were to be reduced by the whole amount of the wage reduction—itself a most unlikely supposition when wage reductions are made on the plea that industry is becoming unprofitable—this fall in factory prices would practically never be reflected in a corresponding fall in the prices of goods to the retail consumer. There is always a lag between the fall of wholesale and that of retail prices ; and even after this lag retail prices never rise so much as wholesale prices during a boom, or sink so much in the course of a slump, owing to the many fixed charges which have to be met in the course of the passage of goods from the factory to the consumer. Accordingly a reduction in wages tends to reduce the funds available in the hands of consumers for the purchase of finished commodities by more than it tends to decrease the unit cost of these commodities to the consumers ; and it thus usually brings about a net decrease in the real volume of demand for consumers' goods.

Nevertheless, it has of course to be admitted that, while countries continue to rely on the incentive of profit for getting production carried on at all, it is impossible for them in the long run to sustain a level of wages which makes production unprofitable. But the remedy is to be sought not in reducing wages and so destroying yet more purchasing power, but rather in so stimulating demand as to provide fuller employment for industry, and make possible a reduction in the costs of producing goods by enabling employers to spread their overhead charges over a larger volume of output. If this is not sufficient, then it is far better to allow factory prices to rise to a somewhat higher level through the stimulation of demand than to attempt to accommodate wage incomes to a level of prices which is unduly low.

Under conditions of modern technological development in industry all the more advanced industrial countries in Europe have of late years been achieving very large economies in the use of manual labour. Each successive census in these advanced countries shows a diminishing proportion of the total population engaged directly in productive industry, and a higher proportion occupied in the various auxiliary services, such as transport and distribution, and in professional, administrative and technical occupations. At the same time, the proportion of the national income paid out in salaries tends to rise, while the proportion paid in wages, despite the increase in average wage-rates, remains practically constant. These are the inevitable results of the process of rationalisation, which to an increasing extent substitutes machinery for human labour in the carrying out of standardised productive operations and also results in the elimination of waste labour through the more scientific organisation of industry. It is a question much disputed how far the present height of unemployment in the world is the consequence, not only of the slump conditions at present prevailing, but also of what is called " technological " unemployment—that is to say, of the supersession of human labour by machines and by more scientific industrial organisation. Undoubtedly, there existed even at the height of the boom in the United States a considerable amount of industrial as well as agricultural unemployment. Great Britain and Germany both had serious unemployment problems even before the coming of the world slump ; and while a large part of the British unemployment was undoubtedly due to the decline in the great British export industries, a substantial part of the unemployment in Germany seems to have been the result of the intensive campaign of technical rationalisation which was carried through in the German coal mines and heavy industries between 1924 and 1929.

Indeed, it stands to reason that if widespread substitution of machinery for labour occurs in the industries which have hitherto employed the largest quantity of labour, considerable unemployment will result. For, even if it is possible ultimately to re-employ the displaced operatives in other rising industries, and to receive into these industries the fresh recruits who leave school each year, there is bound to be a considerable interval of dislocation while the necessary readjustments in the economic system are being made. This interval is likely to be longest where the industrial system is carried on at haphazard and not in accordance with any co-ordinated national plan for directing the available resources into the right channels. Above all, under these conditions a large amount of unemployment of an obstinately prolonged character is likely to arise in those areas which have in the past specialised chiefly in the trades whose demand for labour is falling off. Obvious examples are the areas in which coal mines, iron and steel manufacture and the cotton industry are chiefly carried on. Moreover, during this period of dislocation there will be a marked tendency to displace from industry the older workers ; so that when men or women of middle age once lose a job it is exceedingly difficult for them to find alternative employment. The new industries tend to recruit chiefly the younger workers, and the older workers find it harder to sacrifice their acquired skill and adapt themselves to totally new methods of production.

In these circumstances, the registers of unemployment in the advanced industrial countries come to include a large number of older workers who are not likely to find jobs at all ; and it has repeatedly been urged, with obvious justice, that the right way of dealing with these older workers is to take them off the unemployment registers, and provide them, at the expense either of industry or of the community as a whole, with adequate pensions. It is, however, usually impossible to place this charge directly upon the industries in which the displacement of workers chiefly arises, because these industries include many which, owing to the decline in the demand for their products, lack the ability to meet any additional charges. Accordingly, the greater part of the burden has to be shouldered by the community as a whole.

The existence of a large mass of unemployed workers eager to find jobs is in itself a factor likely to result in the depression of wage-rates. This is especially the case where the State does not make adequate provision for the maintenance of the unemployed ; whereas, as we have seen, the effect of an adequate system of maintenance for those out of work helps the Trade Unions, where they are well organised, to maintain wages even under adverse conditions. Accordingly, in periods of depression wages tend to fall fastest in those countries which (a) are most subjected to competitive pressure in the marketing of their products, (b) have the weakest Trade Union movements, and (c) make least provision for the public maintenance of the unemployed. Not all these conditions need to be satisfied at once ; in the United States, for example, international competition is a relatively unimportant factor, but Trade Unionism is weak in most trades, and there is no system of public maintenance for the unemployed. In Germany, because of the exceptional financial situation, which compelled the forcing of exports on the world market at any price, the existence of strong Trade Unions and a system of unemployment insurance have not availed in the long run to protect wages, though they did considerably delay the fall, which only began in 1931 and became really serious in 1932. In Great Britain and in Scandinavia wages have been relatively well maintained, despite competitive stringency, because Trade Unionism and public provision for the unemployed have combined to strengthen the workers' power of resistance.

The tendency towards rationalisation and the displacement of productive labour in the industries of the most advanced countries has highly significant effects upon the class structure of these countries. It increases the numbers of salary earners, including not only clerks, but also the more highly paid technical and administrative staffs attached to the various forms of industry and service. At the same time the relative decline in the old basic industries and the rise of newer industries of a highly mechanised type gradually undermine the strength of the older Trade Unions, which have grown up principally in the basic industries. The strongholds of Trade Unionism in all the advanced countries of Europe are in the coal-mines, the iron and steel works, and the engineering and textile factories ; and the relative weakening of the position of these industries inevitably affects Trade Union bargaining power. Meanwhile the newer industries grow up largely in areas remote from the older centres of Trade Union strength. They employ a much smaller proportion of highly skilled labour, and rely largely on the services of semi-skilled machine-minders, including a higher proportion of women. These workers are less readily susceptible to Trade Union influence. A high proportion of the women do not expect to remain permanently in industry, and have therefore not the same abiding interest in their industrial conditions as the male workers, while even among the men the smaller proportion of highly skilled workers to the total number employed tends to make Trade Union organisation less stable ; for it is among the skilled craftsmen that the strongest Trade Unions have for the most part hitherto been built up.

The Trade Union movement may in process of time be able to overcome these difficulties and adapt its methods and organisation to the needs of the new industrialism. But it is already evident that considerable adaptation will be required if Trade Unionism is not permanently to lose strength as a result of the modern changes in industrial technique. Above all it seems clear that the Trade Unions, in order to retain their power, will have to organise in future far less on exclusive craft lines, and far more in such a way as to bring together in one closely knit organisation the whole mass of workers, skilled and unskilled, employed in a particular industry, as well as to co-ordinate the Unions in the various industries for closer common action. It is also clear that under these changed circumstances Trade Unionism is bound to become far more political, in the sense of seeking the realisation of its objects to a greater extent than in the past by securing protective industrial legislation. This has already become manifest in the strengthening of the movement for the passing both of minimum wage laws and of laws limiting the duration of the working day. But it goes further than this ; for under modern conditions, wage-rates and the treatment of the unemployed come to be inseparably connected problems, and Trade Unionists come more and more to realise that they cannot hope to secure their position unless they are able to exercise political as well as economic pressure. Trade Unionism thus becomes to an increasing extent a political force, and industrial disputes take on more and more the added character of political conflicts. This was seen in the highest degree in the British General Strike of 1926 ; but it also appeared very clearly in the relation of the German Trade Unions to the successive Republican Governments up to the date of the Hitler *coup*. For it was by using the State as an instrument for the enforcement of wage rates rather than by their unaided industrial strength that the German Trade Unions were able to maintain wage rates through 1930 and 1931. Fascism, in its special aspect of a movement directed against the independence of the Trade Unions, and helped with this end in view by the great industrialists, is among other things an attempt to defeat these claims of the Trade Unions to political power as a necessary instrument of industrial protection. And it is already clear from the experience of Italy during the past ten years that the tame Fascist Unions created within the structure of the Corporative State are highly ineffective, and indeed are meant to be highly ineffective, instruments for the preservation of the workers' standard of life.

Part IV: EUROPEAN POLITICAL SYSTEMS

§ 1. THE NEW CONSTITUTIONS OF POST-WAR EUROPE

POST-WAR EUROPE has been a laboratory of new experiments in the art of politics. Before the war ended, Russia had led the way, passing in her two Revolutions of 1917 swiftly from Tsarist autocracy to the dictatorship of the proletariat. In Germany, the Bismarckian system had begun to crumble some time before the military collapse ; and there had been concessions to popular sentiment which helped to prepare the way for the new order. The complicated political adjustments of the Austro-Hungarian Empire had lost their perilous balance long before 1918. And finally the German occupation of Poland and the confusion in the other territories severed from Russia under the Treaty of Brest-Litovsk had already raised in an acute form the question of constitution-making for brand-new States, mostly of uncertain boundary and highly doubtful political complexion. During the last year of the struggle between the Allies and the Central Powers civil war went on side by

GOVERNMENTS AND PARTIES IN EUROPE

Country	Complexion of Government	Number of Seats in Popular Chamber	Representation of Leading non-Socialist Parties	Representation of Socialist Parties	Representation of Communist Parties
Albania	N.-P.	59	—		
Austria	Chr. Soc., Agr., Heimwehr	165	Chr. Soc. 66, Agr. 10	72	—
Belgium	Cath. Lib.	187	Cath. 79, Lib. 24	73	3
Bulgaria	Nat.	274	Nat. 155, Dem. 62	5	31 (Labour)
Czechoslovakia	Coal. (incl. Soc.)	300	Agr. 62, Cath. 44	Soc. Dem. 64, Nat. Soc. 33	28
Denmark	Soc. Rad. Coal.	149	Lib. 39, Cons. 27	62	2
Estonia	Coal.	100	Agr. 42, Centre 23	22	—
Finland	Coal.	200	Agr. 52, Nat. 32	79	—
France	Rad. Soc.	614	Rad. Soc. 160	128	10
Germany	Nazi	647	Nazi 288, Cath. 92, Nat. 52	120*	81*
Great Britain	Nat. Coal.	615	Cons. 470, Lib.-Nat. 35, Lib. 33	50	5 (I.L.P.)
Greece	Popular	250	Pop. 135, Lib. 111	—	—
Hungary	United	245	United 148, Chr. Soc. 27	14	—
Iceland	Coal.	42	Prog. 23, Nat. 15	4	—
Irish Free State	Fianna Fail	153	Fianna Fail 70, Cumann na nGaedhael 54	7	—
Italy	Fascist	400	Fascist 400	—	—

...le with reconstruction war, and civil war raised everywhere the problem of the organisation of possession.

Europe plunged into a chaos of political experiment, when most men—even most statesmen—had no clear vision of the needs of the situation of the countries for whose political future they were asked to provide. Except in Russia, where the break-up of the old regime...

Latvia	Coal.	Agr. 14	100	21	
Lithuania	Coal.	People's 22, Chr. Dem. 14	85	15	
Luxembourg	Coal.	Cath. 25	54	14	
Holland	Coal.	Cath. 28	100	22	4
Norway	Agr.	Cons. 41, Rad. 33, Agr. 25	150	47	
Poland	Non-Party Union	N.-P. U. 247, Nat. 63, Agr. 42	444	24	
Portugal	N.P. Directory	Mod. Dem. 85, Nat. 25	163	2	
Roumania	Nat. Agr.	Nat. Agr. 274, Nat. Lib. 28	387	7	
Spain	Soc. Rad. Soc. Coal.	Rad. 89, Rad. Soc. 54, Catalans 43	466	114	
Sweden	Soc.	Cons. 58, Agr. 36	230	104	8
Switzerland	Coal.	Rad. Dem. 52, Cath. Cons. 44	187	49	3
Turkey	People's	People's 304	317	—	?
U.S.S.R.	Communist		472	—	
Yugoslavia	Nat.	Nat. 305	305	?	

Agr. = Agrarian, Cath. = Catholic, Chr. Soc. = Christian Social, Coal. = Coalition, Cons. = Conservative, Dem. = Democratic, Lib. = Liberal, Mod. = Moderate, Nat. = National, N.P. = Non-Party, Prog. = Progressive, Rad. = Radical.

* Unseated.

side with international war ; and civil war raised everywhere the problem of the organisation of government.

Europe plunged into an orgy of constitution-making when most men—even most statesmen—had no clear vision of the needs or situation of the countries for whose political future they were called upon to provide. Except in Russia, where the break with the past was as complete as it could be made, and Lenin and his associates were setting to work to apply a definite theory, statesmen as a rule continued to think of the problem of the constitution in terms of pre-war ideas and policies. The established countries were only adapting their pre-war constitutions in various secondary ways—by wide extensions of the franchise, for example ; and even Germany, though she did make a brand-new constitution for herself, built largely on the foundations of the German Empire, and almost wholly on ideas and programmes of pre-war vintage. In the new States— Czechoslovakia, Austria, Hungary, the Baltic countries— the problem of constitution-making was envisaged mainly as that of imitating the familiar features of the State-systems already existing in the established political societies of Western Europe and in the United States—on the basis of an eclectic choice of methods and machinery from among the repertory of these societies, with only secondary additions or adaptations ; and even those were taken from pre-war programmes of constitutional reformers. Proportional representation, adopted almost universally by the new and reconstructed States, was the chief innovation upon the older parliamentary models ; and there was assuredly nothing novel about the idea of P.R.

In these circumstances, the constitution-making of the post-war settlement showed in most countries a singular lack of originality. The Germans used the opportunity of defeat, carrying with it the collapse of Kaiserdom, to realise, at any rate on paper, the pre-war programmes of the democratic parliamentary parties ; and statesmen in the new States, eager to secure recognition from the Great Powers and to keep Bolshevism beyond the pale, saw the safest hall-mark of national respectability in the traditional parliamentary régime. They set up in business as good *bourgeois* ; and if they often succeeded in equipping themselves with parliamentary institutions based rather on the academic theory than on the political practice of pre-war Parliamentarism, this was hardly their fault. For the parliamentary institutions of Great Britain, France, Holland, Belgium, Scandinavia, and Switzerland have grown, and not been made in a few months by a convention of professors and politicians ; and often the most vital elements in them appear least in their formal structure.

Except in the case of Russia, the really interesting features of post-war political experiment occurred, not when States were re-making their constitutions in 1918 and 1919, but later, when they had had some experience of the conditions of the new world into which they had been born. Even then the originality came mainly, not from the new States set up on the basis of the Peace Treaties, but from older States which found their established constitutions unsatisfactory or inefficient. Fascism came first in Italy, and not in any of the new States, or in Germany. Another sort of dictatorship invaded Spain, the last stronghold of an obsolete feudal and religious autocracy. The example of dictatorship no doubt became contagious ; but the minor dictatorships of Southern and Eastern Europe furnished no fresh enlightenment in the art of governing.

To the observer who set out to sum up, in the immediate post-war years, the consequences of the struggle in terms of constitutional structure and practice, it must have seemed that, apart from the giant exception of Russia, there had been a resounding victory for the cause of parliamentary government. Had not enthusiastic Liberal propagandists on the side of the Allies—including many who deemed themselves Socialists—repeatedly proclaimed that the war was "a war for democracy" as well as "a war to end war"? Had not the two great Empires of Central Europe—two out of the three chief strongholds of autocracy—fallen, and been replaced by "democratic" parliamentary systems modelled on Great Britain and France ? Had not Tsardom too gone the way of all tyrannies ; and would not the obvious and inherent instability of the new Soviet régime speedily lead to its replacement by yet another imitation of English or French Parliamentarism ? For most respectable people in 1920 were prophesying without hesitation the imminent collapse of Bolshevism ; and the Great Powers were still helping, by blockade and assistance to " White " invaders, to give it a few stout pushes in the required direction. The first Russian Revolution had been proclaimed by Mr. Bonar Law in the British House of Commons as heralding the reorganisation of the Russian Empire on impeccably British lines ; and much the same view of it was taken in the United States and other democratic countries, except that in each country the imitation was thought of in terms of its own, rather than anyone else's, democratic institutions.

The hopes centred on Prince Lvov and Kerensky were disappointed ; but it was difficult for opinion in Western Europe or in America to believe that Communism had come to stay. For respectable opinion—including that of most Socialists—all over Western Europe and North America had come to believe that, in broad terms, the central problem of the art of politics—that of the right basis of government for a right-minded State—had been settled for generations to come, if not for all time. States ought to be democratic, which was taken as meaning that they ought to have political institutions based on representative government with the backing of a wide popular franchise. They ought to have Parliaments, preferably of two Chambers, though the right form for the less powerful Chamber was a matter of difficulty and disagreement, and there were some who held to the theory of two co-equal Chambers. These Parliaments were to "represent" the country, so that legislation passed by them could be regarded as expressing the real will of the electorate—even on those occasions when most of the electors appeared to be indifferent, or even hostile. In addition to its Parliament, each State ought to have an executive—a Government—possessing the "confidence of the country." There was a difference of opinion over the question whether the executive ought to be chosen separately by the people, as the President of the United States is chosen, or in effect by the Parliament, or subject to the veto of the Parliament, as it is chosen in the French Republic and in the constitutional monarchy of Great Britain. But in Europe the latter system in general prevailed ; and it became the model for the democratic constitutions of the new post-war States.

There was a wider difference of opinion over the question of the "head of the State." Could a right-minded democratic State consistently have a King or Emperor, or ought it necessarily to be a Republic ? Most of the new States of Europe had little choice in this matter ; for, with the Hapsburgs and the Hohenzollerns ruled out, as well as discredited, there was something of a famine in eligible monarchs. Germany, from among her princelings and their families, had been willing enough to provide when she was planning in advance her distribution of the fruits of victory. But in the actual post-war constitution-making the question of monarchy hardly arose. Only Hungary, after expelling her Bolsheviks, equipped herself with a Regent in lieu of the Hapsburg monarch she was not allowed to have. Elsewhere the problem was settled on republican lines, but as a matter of convenience rather than principle. The new Republics had Presidents ; but in most cases they were meant to be rather ceremonial figure-heads than actual governors, and in some the Prime Minister was allowed to double the parts. There was no imitation of the American system of a President independent of the legislature and at the head of the executive. Where President and Prime Minister are united in the same person, as they are in Estonia and the Irish Free State, the latter position is the source of power, and the holder of the office gets it as the leader of a parliamentary majority or working coalition, and not by direct election at the hands of the people.

The problem of Constitutional Monarchy *versus* Republic

was, however, commonly regarded as of secondary importance, and as not affecting the real character of the State's government. For in theory, though the surviving monarchs in democratic countries still had very wide powers according to the letter of the constitution, they were to exercise these powers only at the will and under the orders of the Government. The Ministers might be, according to the letter of the law, "the King's Ministers"; but in practice the King was to be "the Ministers' King." His functions, apart from his duty of getting himself revered and loved by his people, were to be mainly those of a mannequin combined with a ventriloquist's dummy. This theory of the functions of constitutional monarchy was naturally nowhere fully operative—for, after all, Kings are men—but it is hardly an overstatement to say that it represents accurately the attempt of democratic theorists to reconcile to themselves the inconsistency of remaining monarchists. They defended monarchy on the ground that it did not exist, save only as a harmless and convenient fiction useful for cementing the bonds of Empire, upholding the respect of common democrats for their betters, and above all avoiding the danger of a too powerful President. The State, it was said, must have a head; so, in the name of democracy, let that head be empty.

The accepted pre-war view of the right constitution for a right-minded State thus left aside the secondary question of Monarchy *versus* Republic, and concentrated on what were regarded as the essential political institutions. The core of the problem was the form to be given to the institution of Parliament. The new States were thought of as coming into existence by virtue of the will of their inhabitants; and this will must be provided with the means of making itself effective, first in setting up the formal institutions of the nascent communities, and then in ensuring the continued conformity of these institutions to their will. There must be some sort of Constituent Assembly; and by fiat of this Assembly must arise a Parliament and the means of periodically renewing its life. For both

Assembly and Parliament the franchise ought to be wide ; for all citizens not excluded by some special disqualification ought to have their share in making and working the new State. There remained open the question whether women ought to have votes ; for, in face of a difference of opinion between Great Britain and France on the problem whether women are political beings, the world was unable to dogmatise on so grave a matter. But at any rate all adult men, save for very special reasons shown, ought to vote ; and in fact women at once got votes under all the new constitutions except that of Yugoslavia, where the question was left over to be settled later by ordinary legislation. Finland, the first country to grant woman suffrage (in 1906), Denmark, Holland, and Norway had given women votes before the war ; and Great Britain had followed their example before the war was over. In this matter, the new States took Great Britain rather than France as their model.

Even woman suffrage, however, was commonly regarded as a secondary issue. The democratic theory plainly involved that everybody had the right to vote, unless some very special reason for exclusion could be advanced. The sole question was whether women were persons capable of citizenship. France, under no compulsion to change her constitution, might continue to ignore the obvious answer ; but new States engaged in constitution-making could not, unless they were prepared to depart consciously and manifestly from the democratic principle. Accordingly, almost everywhere women got the vote.

The gospel of the new democracies can therefore be said to begin with Universal Suffrage—since the latter days of the eighteenth century the first article in the international democratic creed. The second part of the gospel is Parliamentarism, based on the idea of popular representation. The people, having votes, are to use them primarily for the choice of a representative Chamber, which is to be the chief source of all legislation. In some cases there were to be two Chambers ; but let us confine ourselves in the first instance to the more directly popular of the two. For on the attitude of this Chamber the complexion of the Government was to depend ; and it was meant to embody the idea of popular sovereignty.

In the pre-war systems of the leading countries, two broadly differing ways of organising parliamentary, or congressional, government were in evidence. In Great Britain and in the United States, the political forces strong enough to count in determining the complexion of the Government were organised mainly in two great rival parties, so that one or other of these two was always in a position of dominance. It was indeed possible under the American system for the executive to be in the hands of one party and the legislature of the other; but this "lame-duck" situation was exceptional, and seldom of long continuance. Such a paralysis of the working of the State machine was not possible where, as in France and Great Britain, there was no application of the principle of the "separation of powers"; for in these countries the executive could remain in office only as long as it could command a parliamentary majority. In Great Britain, despite the dominant position of the two traditional parties—Liberals and Conservatives—it was possible for a Government to hold office without having an independent majority at its back ; for the Irish Nationalists formed a powerful minority party, which could sometimes either keep a Government in office or turn it out, and after 1900 the Labour Party appeared as a second minority group. Actually, between 1910 and 1914 the Liberal Government owed its continuance in office to the support of these two smaller parties. But there was never, before 1914, any question of a Government being formed by any party except the two traditional antagonists ; and Great Britain alternated between Liberals and Conservatives as the United States alternated between Democrats and Republicans—with the difference that there was a sharper, though still narrow, cleavage of policies, along well-known lines, between the British than between the American parties.

In France the situation was very different ; for there parties were far more numerous and loosely organised, so that Governments had always to be formed on the basis of coalitions among a number of distinct political groups. It was easier for groups to dissolve, and for new groups to appear, as situations changed ; and there were always a number of individual deputies whose allegiance was doubtful, and a number of middle parties capable of entering into temporary combinations either to the Right or to the Left. Moreover, the arrangement of parties in the Senate— the Second Chamber—did not necessarily coincide with that in the Chamber of Deputies ; and it was far more possible than in Great Britain or the United States for a particular deputy to ally himself with the Government of the day without necessarily either committing his party or leaving it. The French system was thus far more flexible and easily changeable than the British.

The different practice of the two countries about dissolutions and General Elections was—and is—closely connected with this difference of party systems. Where a Government can hold office only as long as it has the support of Parliament, and most of the Members of Parliament belong to one or other of the two great parties, it follows that, given the composition of Parliament, there is only one possible Government. What, then, is to happen if this Government, owing either to differences in its own ranks or to the manifest unpopularity of its policy in the country, is unable to carry on ? Clearly there must be a dissolution of Parliament, followed by a General Election designed to resolve the difficulty by declaring the will of the electorate. Under the French system, on the other hand, no such necessity exists. For, when the Parliament is split up among a number of groups, and varying combinations are possible among these groups and their members, it is not the case that there is only one possible Government. If one group of Ministers cannot carry on, it may be quite practicable to find another group that can, without any necessity for an appeal to the electors. Consequently, whereas the British Parliament is practically always dissolved in connection with a change of Government, the French Chamber nearly always remains in being for the full term for which it was first elected, and usually outlives in the course of this term a whole succession of different Governments. Of course, the distribution of seats may be such that, in a particular Chamber, any possible Government must have either a "Right" or a "Left" inclination, as the case may be. But within this condition many variations are possible.

It is out of the question, in this matter, to disentangle cause and effect. If pre-war France had been politically dominated by two big parties, like Great Britain, she would have been compelled to provide for the "right of dissolution"—that is to say, to allow a change of Government, actual or prospective, to be accompanied by an "appeal to the country." But was it because France had not two big parties, but many groups, that she did not recognise in her constitution this "right of dissolution"? Or was her group system, at least in part, the result of the "right of dissolution" not being recognised? If Great Britain had possessed, instead of two big parties, numerous small and far less coherent groups, she could not have allowed a General Election every time she needed a change of Government; for General Elections are expensive and unpopular if they come too close together. But is the two-party system cause or consequence of the recognition of the Prime Minister's right to demand a dissolution?

At any rate, the two systems existed ; and there can be no doubt what, in general terms, the consequences were. The British system tended to make Governments strong, and the French tended to make them weak. For under British conditions the Government not only had as a rule a clear majority of its own supporters behind it, but was also able to mitigate the ardours of the critics within its own ranks, or of allied smaller parties, by threatening a dissolution which would cost the individual Member of Parliament money, and might lose him his seat. The French deputy, on the other hand, stood in far less fear of the Government, because it had not the right to appeal to the electorate ; and the French Ministry had always to be conciliating the divergent groups on which it depended for support, and was apt to find in inactivity the line of least resistance. Moreover, the life of a French Cabinet was very often too short to make possible the following of any consecutive or constructive policy.

Accordingly, the case for the British and French systems could almost be re-stated as the case for strong and weak parliamentary institutions. The advocates of strong government and of vigorous party policies upheld the British arrangement, while those who believed that the best guarantee of individual freedom is weak government greatly preferred the French. It is true that the government of France was—and is—a great deal more bureaucratic than that of Great Britain ; but that is a matter of the administrative rather than the legislative system, and it is with legislation alone that we are at present concerned.

If the new States of post-war Europe had been able to choose freely between the British and French parliamentary systems, it is not easy to say which they would have chosen. Actually, their choice went everywhere in favour of methods which resulted in reproducing something far more akin to French than to British parliamentary conditions. For, in deciding in favour of proportional representation, as they did with singular unanimity, they were adopting an electoral arrangement clearly calculated to lead to the multiplication of parties, and therefore to the group basis of French politics rather than the strong party government of Great Britain.

But they had not, in reality, an open choice on the main issue. For the British system implies the prior existence, or immediate potentiality, of two parliamentary parties capable of forming a Government and a major Opposition. But nowhere in Europe did such parties exist, nor could they be called into existence under the prevailing conditions. There were, and there were bound to be at least for some

Tr

time to come, a considerable number of separate groups in the Parliaments of the new States. Governments were bound to depend for their majorities on coalitions among these groups ; and it was impossible to give such coalitions the stability of consolidated parties. A close approximation to the French system therefore arose naturally out of the circumstances ; and the new Chambers, while they tried sometimes to model their behaviour on the " Mother of Parliaments," operated in fact far more like the French *Chambre des Députés*.

This situation was due in part to the development of Socialism. For in most of the new countries the Socialists formed, if not the largest, at least one of the two largest parties in the first post-war Parliaments. They were not, however, strong enough to win a clear majority ; and accordingly they either constituted the main opposition to a broad alliance of *bourgeois* and other non-Socialist groups which together formed the Government, or they themselves entered into coalitions with the more " progressive " of the non-Socialist parties. These other parties were never closely enough agreed to form a solid combination ; for they ranged from representatives of landowning interests, large capitalist interests, clerical interests, petty *bourgeois* interests, peasant interests, and so on, to still more sectionalised groups standing for the rights and claims of the racial and national minorities scattered plentifully over the territories of most of the new States. This situation, in which everything had to be settled *de novo*, and there were no clear precedents to go by, was one which made every sectional interest exceedingly anxious to secure direct representation, as a source of bargaining strength. It therefore made for the vitality of a large number of small parties, each identified with some sectional point of view. Sometimes, as in Czechoslovakia, the series of parties based on conflicting class interests was duplicated for the distinct nationalities ; and in other cases party divisions were based on religious as well as political or class groups. But more often there was one series of class-interest parties drawn mainly from the national elements forming the majority of the population, and a second series of nationalist groups, each representing a confusing medley of class interests. Moreover, this clamjamfry of parties was perpetuated and reinforced by the adoption of P.R., which was adopted by the new States less as a matter of democratic principle according to John Stuart Mill than because each sectional group saw in it the assurance of its own representation and survival.

Stable Governments were, under these circumstances, exceedingly hard to form ; and the democratic Governments of post-war Europe have been for the most part very unstable. The new States have carried on somehow ; and most of them have not substantially altered, though several of them have in fact suspended, the constitutions drawn up on the morrow of the war. But it will hardly be maintained that these constitutions have worked well, or bid fair to serve as permanently satisfactory instruments of government. The most that can be said for them is that, in the circumstances which existed in 1919 and 1920, there was practically no choice. The local Communists lacked the strength to take control, the Socialists were unable to gain a clear majority, and the sectional interests were too sharply divided for a firm anti-Socialist combination to be created ; and accordingly the only possible course was to recognise the group system. At least until the new States had had plenty of time to settle down, and to deal with the vast number of conflicting claims which faced them, the claims of minorities were certain to play a major part in shaping the political system. Proportional representation won the day because it was the most thorough embodiment of the " minority " spirit.

What has been said above applies fully as much to Germany as to new States such as Czechoslovakia or Poland. For post-war Germany seemed to most Germans virtually a new State, or at any rate one in which there had to be a new fundamental settlement of the claims of conflicting classes and sections. Germany, more than any other State, because her combined difficulties in domestic and external politics were greater, felt during the post-war years the repercussions of a political system designed to make difficult the creation of a solid parliamentary majority. The German political situation is discussed in detail elsewhere ; here we are only pointing out that P.R. exaggerated the difficulties inherent in the political situation.

For P.R. amounts, above all else, to the giving of constitutional sanction to the representation of sectional interests. The case put forward on its behalf is that it follows logically from the conception of representative government ; for if the voters are to be represented, each of them ought to be given the largest possible chance of helping to elect someone who really represents his point of view. The system of single-member constituencies and that of the *scrutin de liste* without P.R.—i.e. the method of voting in larger constituencies for party lists of candidates *en bloc*— are alike in ruling out the representation of such minorities as live scattered among the rest of the population, so that their votes are not numerous enough to carry the day in any particular constituency. The second ballot and the alternative vote are further means of wiping out the minority parties. Under these systems, say the advocates of P.R., many votes are wasted ; for the minority groups must either vote for their own men without hope of securing their election, or vote for someone who does not represent them, or not vote at all. P.R., properly worked, ensures that no vote is wasted, and gives each group, large or small, a representation corresponding to the number of votes cast on its behalf. A P.R. Parliament, and no other, therefore really represents the nation. It is, or should be, a perfect mirror of the national consciousness.

So far, so good ; and if the aim of Parliaments were simply to hold the mirror up to national divisions of opinion the case for P.R. would be unanswerable. But one object—not the least important—in electing a Parliament is to provide the community with a workable and effective legislative machine. What if the two aims prove to be inconsistent ?

Which is to be given up ? Is Parliament to become less a legislative instrument in order to be a better mirror, or a worse mirror in order to legislate more efficiently ? The " perfect mirror " theory is tenable only by those who believe that, on the whole, individuals and smaller groups within the State are best left to manage their own affairs, and that the concentration of power in the hands of the central State authority is an evil. Anyone who holds that the State has wide functions of intervention, and that it is necessary for men to be strongly governed, is bound to aim at securing an effective instrument of legislation, even at some cost in its reflecting quality.

In other words, the mirror theory might do well enough in a society so settled in the general character of its social and economic life, and so unvexed by major problems, that it could get on comfortably enough without much controversial legislation, and under the ægis of a weak and unstable Government. Pre-war France was on the whole in this condition ; and perhaps Holland is in it now. But a mirror is essentially passive : it reflects, but it does not originate or decide. A Parliament which mirrors the kaleidoscopic opinions of a diversified community is most unlikely to be good at settling major conflicts of interest among the divergent groups which it represents. But, unhappily, these groups are most likely to be insistent on separate representation at times when their divergencies are most acute, and the problems raised by their conflicts most difficult and fundamental.

These conditions go far towards explaining the almost general dissatisfaction of to-day with the working of the parliamentary system. The strength of Parliamentarism— above all of British and French Parliamentarism—in the latter part of the nineteenth century lay pre-eminently in the fact that it was being used to work a securely established system, on the fundamentals of which nearly all articulate opinion was in agreement. The differences between the recognised parties did not go down to first principles : and therefore a broad continuity of aims and policy was possible between the rival parties. Neither Conservatives nor Liberals in Great Britain, neither Republicans nor Democrats in the United States, wanted or proposed to do anything which seemed to their rivals so dreadful as to threaten the disruption of the body politic, or the dissolution of the social contract. The battle of words might wax fast and furious, and politicians might call one another the most dreadful names ; but all the same the amount of common ground between them was far more extensive than their areas of dispute.

Nor was this all. In the pre-war democratic countries, men were working on the basis of an existing system of settled rights and claims. They might wish to modify these in one or another particular ; but apart from the particular projects of reform over which they wrangled they took the existing conditions for granted. This greatly reduced the pressure from organised sectional interests, and made it possible for each of the great rival parties to put up a plausible claim that it stood for the totality of the national interests. But in post-war Europe nothing could be taken for granted, because there was nothing securely established. Everything had to be affirmed or denied afresh ; and a thousand problems were demanding immediate settlement. Were the old landowners or the peasants to have the land ? Was the State to base its policy on Economic Nationalism, or on Internationalism ? Was it to go Socialist, or at any rate how much of State Socialism was it to embody in its new economic system ? Was it to have an established Church, or to treat all religions alike ; and, if the latter, how was it to treat them ? Was it to compensate those who had lost their savings through the inflation of the currency ? Was it to grant political autonomy to provinces possessing a distinct racial, cultural, economic, or religious character of their own ? Was it to allow racial minorities their own languages, schools, cultural conditions ? These and a host of other questions buzzed like flies round the heads of the statesmen of the new Republics ; and every question furnished a reason for the existence of a fresh political party.

Parliamentarism, then, could not be expected to work in post-war Europe as it had worked in Great Britain when the British social system had the solidity of Victorian mahogany, or in France when the life of peasant and small-scale industrialist went on almost unaffected by the doings of the politicians in Paris. In the post-war period, politics were bound to affect everybody ; and in every community there were political differences too deep for easy reconciliation. This applied even in the States which were not compelled to build up their political institutions afresh from the bottom. British Parliamentarism could no longer be the same with three parties, instead of two, contending for office, and one of these challenging, at least in words, the ark of the capitalist covenant. The oft-expressed desire for the final elimination of the Liberals was based far less on a desire to clear the ground for a straight fight between Capitalism and Socialism—which was not at all desired by most people—than on a hankering to get back to the old simplicity of the two-party system. For, with only two major parties, each capable of securing an independent majority, British people both knew how their political system worked and believed in its efficiency for the limited tasks it had been called upon to perform before the war. They did not like at all the prospect of a succession of Parliaments in which no party would be able to command a majority. But in fact the old conditions could not be recalled ; and the creakings and groanings of the old parliamentary system, now called upon to adapt itself to a new situation, were soon plainly audible.

Great Britain, however, like France, could in the short run carry on with relatively little difficulty, because she did not have to settle everything at once, and also because British Socialism remained Socialism on paper, but was only social reform in practice—a continuation and extension of, rather than a rupture with, the Liberal tradition. Though the cleavage between the parties raised more fundamental questions than before, it did not raise them in forms imperatively demanding immediate solutions. Very slowly, the old British economic and social system was beginning to disintegrate ; but for the time being it was perfectly possible to carry on without any deep disturbance of class relationships or established ways of life. The " Mother of Parliaments " lost much of her glamour ; but she did not lose her ability to survive and "manage" somehow. Even less was French Parliamentarism shaken by the war—that is, shaken visibly and at once. And the American political system remained, to all outward seeming, totally unaffected.

Where, as in Italy, Parliamentarism was a plant of tenderer and more exotic growth, things fell out differently. United Italy, poor and industrially undeveloped, provided herself with a Parliament as the symbol of national unity and respectable Statehood far more than because her citizens had any faith in, or understanding of, the working of parliamentary institutions. Cavour had no successors : Italy developed neither strong and coherent political parties on the British model, nor the power to make a group system in the image of the national character, as it came to be in France. Italian politics remained an affair of superficial dexterities and manipulations, such as Giolitti was adept in, with little relation to the real currents of public opinion or to the real forces shaping the national life. Socialism in Italy became an important political force far less because it was strong than because the rest were weak ; and it never became confident enough of its hold to master the country. After the war, Don Sturzo, with his *Popolari*, challenged it in the field of social reform, and made a real attempt to build up, in face of Papal suspicion, a closely knit Catholic Party transcending class-differences. But Italian Parliamentarism was of too weak and imitative a growth to stand up against the storms and stresses of the post-war years. Confronted for the first time with fundamental cleavages of opinion in the country, it could not make itself the arbiter of these differences. The rival factions did battle outside Parliament, in the streets and in the factories, and not in orderly debates or election meetings ; and the Government, having no idea how to hold the contending forces in check, before long simply gave up trying to govern at all. For some time before the Fascists marched on Rome, Italy had been in effect a country without government.

The demonstrated failure of Italian Parliamentarism, and its fate, served as a salutary warning against the facile optimism of post-war Liberal-Democratic theory. For though the Fascists were ostensibly making war upon Communism and Internationalism, it was the Liberal-Democratic State that they actually overthrew. Their antagonist was, no doubt, this form of State at its weakest and least successful in realising the principles of Liberal Democracy. But the warning was none the less salutary ; for it was a warning against the danger of assuming that parliamentary institutions, set up in the less economically developed countries, would work out as they had worked out in Great Britain or France, or would be in fact either liberal or democratic in practice. It was a warning against the fallacy of generalising about the right forms of government, and against constitutions made by imitative eclecticism instead of the creative impulse of an original and appropriate creed. It was an ironic fortune that equipped the new States of Eastern Europe with the complete paraphernalia of a political system of which its originators in Western Europe were growing more sceptical every year.

§ 2. POLITICS IN GREAT BRITAIN

SOMETHING has been said both of the greater strength of Parliamentary institutions in those countries in which the idea of responsible Parliamentary Government was already well established in the nineteenth century and of the difficulties which Parliamentarism has encountered even in those countries since the war. It was pointed out that countries such as Great Britain and France had been able to carry on without any serious challenge to their

Parliamentary systems despite the growing creakiness of the Parliamentary machine because of two things—first because in these countries economic problems, though pressing, were nothing like so insistent as they were in the new States of Central and Eastern Europe, and secondly, because the Parliamentary system was far more deeply rooted in the habits and ideas of the people. There has been since the war much grumbling at the ineffectiveness of parliamentary government in both Great Britain and France ; but there has been no widespread desire hitherto to tear up Parliamentarism by the roots in order to substitute for it some quite different form of government. In France, indeed, the Parliamentary State has been subjected to a growing fire of criticism from both Right and Left. The Communists have been able to build up a party of some size, and there has been a revival of anti-republican and anti-democratic agitation on the extreme Right. But neither the Communists nor the *Camelots du Roi* and the *Action Française* have been able to shake the solid mass of support behind the Parliamentary parties, ranging from Conservative Republicans to orthodox Socialists. In England there has been even less of a challenge from either side to the established institutions of the Parliamentary State. Communism has so far never risen higher than the return of one solitary member to the House of Commons, and Fascism has made its appearance only in a succession of movements more suggestive of *opéra bouffe* than of serious counter-revolutionary activity.

Nevertheless, even in the countries most used to traditional democratic institutions and to the Parliamentary system, there has been a growing recognition that this system is on the defensive. In the United States, for example, while no third party has succeeded in challenging effectively the far-reaching machinery of the two traditional parties, much less in rallying any large measure of support behind a proposal to change the character of the State, there has been a very great increase of discontent with the working of the party system in both Federal and State affairs, and a marked tendency to dispense with the institutions of nineteenth century democracy in the running of the local government machine. The vastness of the territory and population of the United States, and the existence of a host of separate centres each possessed by a strong spirit of localism, have stood powerfully in the way of the national self-expression of the forces of criticism which have been growing up, and there has been something of a temptation for Americans radically discontented with the existing political institutions of their country to turn their backs on political affairs with a despairing shrug of the shoulders, and give themselves up to the collection of *Americana* in a spirit of purely unconstructive satire. There has been much " muck-raking " and much denunciation of the unfettered authority of big business on the one hand, and on the other, much outcry at the activities of Communists, " criminal Syndicalists " and agitators of foreign origin. But in terms of the constructive rebuilding of political and economic policy all the criticism had amounted to very little up to the moment of President Roosevelt's assumption of office in 1933. Then, indeed, the American political system underwent changes as startling and sudden as any country has ever yet experienced without a revolution ; but it falls outside the scope of this book to attempt even such evaluation of these changes as is possible at the present stage.

Let us begin with an attempt to evaluate the development of the political situation in post-war Britain. As we have seen, right up to 1914 British politics were still being conducted in effect on the basis of a two-party system. There were, indeed, in the House of Commons four parties and not two ; but only the two great traditional parties, Liberals and Conservatives, were in a position to aspire to the right of forming either His Majesty's Government or His Majesty's Opposition. The Labour Party, though it had proclaimed its complete independence, was still in effect little more than a group on the left of the Liberals, and aimed necessarily at using them as the instrument for satisfying its immediate aspirations. The Irish, following a more independent line in some respects, were also tied to the Liberal Party as the only instrument through which they could hope to achieve Home Rule. Neither Labour nor Irish Nationalism offered any challenge to the basis of the Liberal-Democratic State, and even the theoretical Socialism of the Labour Party was still doubtful. Labour was only beginning to emerge from its swaddling clothes as an independent party.

It is obvious that this arrangement presented from the merely administrative point of view very considerable advantages. For it is much easier to manage a Parliamentary machine when all changes of sentiment can be made effective merely by the Government and the Opposition changing places. But, as we have seen, the smooth working of this two-party arrangement depends on the existence between the contending parties of a large amount of common ground. If Government is to succeed Government with a smooth alternation between party and party, both the rival parties must be in agreement on the fundamental nature of the State and the leading institutions which it is to sustain and develop. Where such agreement exists a change of Government, or the election of a new Parliament with a different party complexion, will not involve to any considerable extent the tearing up of the legislation enacted under the authority of the preceding Government. Both sides will be prepared for the most part to accept accomplished facts, and changes will go on by the method of small deviations to the right or to the left rather than by sharp and sudden jerks of policy. If each incoming Government is really determined to undo most of the things that its predecessor has done, and does really regard its rival's policy as threatening the destruction of the country, the Parliamentary system at once ceases to be workable. Parliamentary Democracy is in fact a workable system only on the assumption that the great majority of those who are actually in a position to influence the march of events find themselves in substantial agreement about the matters which lie at the root of political and economic activity.

In Great Britain, as in all other belligerent countries

except the United States, the war seriously upset the old arrangement of parties. There were national coalitions claiming to represent the country as a whole, and these coalitions were the easier to arrange because on the main issues most of the representatives of all the parties did find themselves in agreement. In view of this fundamental agreement, there was little difficulty in arranging for the temporary suspension of party strife, and concentrating upon the measures necessary for the prosecution of the war. A tiny handful of Liberals, including one or two Liberal Ministers, dropped out in 1914 when war was declared, and a small minority of the Labour Party, basing itself on the definitely Socialist Independent Labour Party, took up an anti-war attitude and passed into opposition. But even the I.L.P. did not sever its formal affiliation to the Labour Party despite its disagreement on policy. Apart from these defections, up to the end of 1916 Great Britain was governed on non-party lines—that is to say, on the basis of a suspension of all changes not rendered necessary by the exigencies of war. This solid front of the constitutional parties was broken up at the end of 1916, when Mr. Lloyd George drove Mr. Asquith from office and replaced him at the head of a new coalition from which some of the old Liberal politicians were excluded ; and there was a further rift from 1917 onwards as a larger section of the Labour Party passed into opposition on account of the refusal of the Government to enter into negotiations for a peace based on compromise. Moreover, in the last year of the war, anti-war sentiment was spreading rapidly among the industrial workers in Great Britain, as well as in other countries, as the pressure of the long struggle came to be more acutely felt and the " combing out " of more and more men from the factories provided a stream of increasingly reluctant and unwarlike recruits to the armed forces. Nevertheless Great Britain finished the war under a coalition from which the Labour Party had not even at that stage officially withdrawn ; and although the Labour Party did withdraw and pass into formal opposition as soon as the

Armistice was signed, the " Coupon " election of 1918 was fought on the basis of a continued coalition between the Conservatives and Mr. Lloyd George's Liberal followers.

After the election of 1918 two things were apparent. First, it was clear that the Liberal Party had been damaged, if not irretrievably, at any rate very severely indeed, by the rift between Mr. Lloyd George's followers and the Asquithites. Secondly, the Labour Party, despite its un-preparedness and the big differences which existed within its ranks, found itself called upon to assume the rôle of His Majesty's Opposition in face of the cleavage in the Liberal ranks, and began for the first time to look forward to the day when it would be in a position to take over the govern-ment of the country. Henceforth there were three claimants for the two positions of Government and Opposition. The old simplicity of the two-party system was for the time irretrievably lost.

For Liberalism, divided in counsel and impotent in action as it was during the post-war years, was still an electoral force to be reckoned with. If, indeed, the Liberals associated with the Government had been prepared to merge themselves completely with the Conservatives into a single national party based on the defence of the capitalist system, the two-party arrangement might have been restored ; for the independent Liberals would in that event almost certainly have either disappeared or at least been reduced to an impotent fraction. But this was desired neither by the Liberals nor by a great many of the Conservatives. The Conservatives wanted the spoils of office for themselves, were fully conscious of the superiority of their strategic position, and had no intention of accepting permanently the leadership of Mr. Lloyd George, convenient as they found it in the immediate post-war emergency. The Liberals still cherished the hope that when the immediate turmoils of the post-war period were over they would be able to regain their position as a united party and oust Labour from its status as the official Opposition. Indeed, the leaders of both the old parties for the most part agreed in desiring the return of pre-war political conditions. They much preferred the prospect of a continuation of the gentlemanly battle between rival capitalist parties to the prospect of a struggle between two great parties standing, in theory at least, for radically different forms of economic organisation. Nothing was more likely to turn the Labour Party completely into a Socialist Party than the formation of a united capitalist *bloc* against it.

Moreover, the Labour Party, as it emerged from the war with its new Constitution and programme of 1918, had become a good deal more Socialist, though it was by no means yet Socialist in a thorough-going sense. Labour had first become an independent party in any real sense in 1900, when the tiny group of Socialists organised under Keir Hardie's leadership in the Independent Labour Party induced the Trade Unions to join with them in forming the Labour Representation Committee. This body, which adopted the name " Labour Party " in 1906, was at the outset far more a Trade Union than a Socialist Party ; and right up to 1918 it had made no formal declaration of its Socialist faith, though its driving force came largely from the Socialist—but for the most part non-Marxian— minority within its ranks. But in 1918, under the stimulus of war conditions, the Labour Party radically amended its constitution, so as to base itself on individual members as well as on Trade Union and other collective affiliations ; and at the same time it produced, in *Labour and the New Social Order*, a clearly Socialist programme, though its Socialism remained evolutionary and gradualist, and was far more under the influence of Fabian than of Marxian ideas.

In the excited atmosphere of the period immediately after the war, when men were looking for the new Heaven and the new Earth which Mr. Lloyd George had been foremost in promising them as the fruit of victory, the basic institutions of the capitalist State no longer seemed so firm and so sacred as they had seemed up to 1914. The Bolshevik Revolution in Russia, while it had by no means converted the British workers to Communism, had to a substantial extent influenced their attitude so as to make them doubt the stability of the capitalist State. There were times in 1919 and 1920 when the British Labour Party even began to look like a revolutionary Socialist Party— for example, at the moment when a General Strike was threatened against the danger of British intervention in the war between Poland and Soviet Russia. No doubt the leaders of British Labour remained in their fundamental attitude thoroughly gradualist ; but for the time being the situation made them look a good deal less constitutionalist than of old. They returned speedily enough to a strictly constitutional attitude as the post-war excitement died down and Great Britain succeeded in rebuilding at any rate the façade of her pre-war system. But even so the attitude of the Labour Party was radically changed, in that it thought of itself no longer as a third-party group but definitely as a force aiming within a measurable space of time at taking over the government of the country.

Actually the Labour Party's chance came far sooner than it had expected, and long before it was at all ready for the responsibilities which it was called upon to assume. Mr. Lloyd George's coalition broke down in 1922 and was replaced by a purely Conservative Government. With the Liberals still divided into two contending fractions, the Labour Party was able to maintain its status as the official Opposition. Two years later, Mr. Baldwin, who had succeeded Mr. Bonar Law as the Conservative leader, presented Labour with the opportunity to become a Government by fighting a General Election on the still unpopular issue of Tariff Reform. Labour, in a considerable minority in the House of Commons, could form a Government only if it consented to be kept in office by the votes of the Liberals. But the Liberals were by no means prepared to serve as docile allies to the extent to which the Labour Party had so served them in the years immediately before the war. The Labour Party could therefore govern at all only on condition that it did not attempt to put into effect any of the major proposals included in its official programme. It was in the anomalous position of a nominally Socialist Party taking office on the strict understanding that it would take no step towards the institution of Socialism. Its tenure of office was precarious even from day to day ; and its presence in office under these highly restrictive conditions could have no real effect in interrupting the continuity of British political development. All it could do, if it wished to remain in office, was to carry out a Liberal programme within the assumptions and limitations of the capitalist system.

It is of course a moot point whether under these conditions the Labour Party was right in assuming office at all, or whether, if it had decided to assume office, it should not have courted immediate and certain defeat by putting up at once a challenging Socialist programme which it could have had no prospect of carrying into effect, or even of getting accepted in the House of Commons. In fact neither of these alternatives seems to have been seriously considered. The Party grasped the chance of office both because it wanted office and because it felt that the holding of office as a minority was an indispensable step towards becoming a majority Government—and also, no doubt, because it hoped, even as a minority Government, to carry through certain secondary social reforms which would do something to ameliorate the economic conditions of the workers.

The " gradualism " which the Labour leaders accepted in 1924 and again in 1929 was in effect only another name for the continuity characteristic of British political development for a century past. It implied that, if Socialism was to come, it was to be brought into existence by means of a slow accretion of piecemeal changes in the social and economic structure of society, and not by any sudden reversal of the fundamental assumptions of Capitalism. Even in the long run it did not, in the minds of most of the Socialist leaders, involve any radical change in the form and working of the Liberal-Democratic State.

After the enactment of a few useful but secondary reforms

the Labour Government of 1924 ended in inglorious fiasco. Symbolically, it was brought to disaster by the problem of its handling of Anglo-Russian relations ; for its attempt on the one hand to negotiate a working economic arrangement with the Russians and on the other to present an appearance of firmness in the handling of Communist agitation in Great Britain resulted in practice in placing it in a strategic position difficult for a Socialist Party without a majority behind it. Mr. MacDonald mishandled the incident of the Zinoviev letter not out of sheer muddleheadedness, but because he and his Party were really trying to behave simultaneously in two divergent ways in their handling of the Russian situation. They reaped their reward in the Labour *débâcle* of 1924 ; but even in this *débâcle* it was re-markable to what an extent the Labour vote stood firm. The Labour Government went down not because its own supporters turned against it, but because the fear of " red revolution" brought the vast reserves of non-political voters to the poll.

Thereafter Great Britain experienced five years of Con-servative Government, with Labour ranking still as the major Opposition, and the Liberals, despite the galvanic efforts of Mr. Lloyd George, still hopelessly divided and unable to frame any coherent policy on which more than a fraction of the Party could agree.

The General Election of 1929 reproduced the situation which had arisen in 1924. Once more the Labour Party, though stronger than it had been at its first venture into office, was only in a position to form a minority Govern-ment, and needed the support of the Liberals in order to make its measures effective. It was therefore again pre-cluded from making, even had it desired to make, any attempt at the enactment of really Socialist measures. Once again the Labour Party under Mr. MacDonald's leadership accepted these conditions. Now, in the light of after events, it seems clear that the limitations imposed on Labour policy in 1929 were to its leader and to many of his colleagues positively welcome. For in their view Great

Britain was not ripe for Socialism, but only for some further instalment of social reform. Indeed, in the minds of Mr. MacDonald and quite a number of the other leaders of the Party, Socialism evidently held a place not as something to be fought for, or established speedily by the political action of the workers, but only as a vague utopian pattern for some future society to be realised either at some distant epoch or perhaps not at all. Socialism remained theoretically an aspiration and an inspiration ; but it did not take shape as a practical political policy.

Under these circumstances, even if world conditions had remained favourable to the continuance of the traditional policy of social reform, it is doubtful if the Labour Government could have made much of a showing. For even before the world slump a situation had been reached in Great Britain which made further instalments of social reform very difficult to carry through in face of the increasing embarrassment of British capitalist industry ; and this difficulty had been seriously aggravated by the unfortunate and disastrous decision to return to the gold standard at the pre-war value of the pound sterling, a step which had seriously embarrassed the British export trades and narrowed the scope for the further redistribution of incomes by means of the social services. But in fact the coming of the world slump soon after the Government had assumed office added enormously to the difficulties in its way. Any Government in Great Britain would have found itself seriously embarrassed, and would have been bound to incur a good deal of unpopularity in consequence of the adverse effects of the depression. But these conditions were especially unfavourable to a Government which, in as far as it had a policy at all, based this policy on redistributing some of the surplus incomes of the rich among the poorer sections of the community without disturbing the fundamental institutions which permitted the rich to acquire their wealth. Even so, the Labour Government managed to add to its difficulties by putting at the Exchequer a Minister even more fanatically devoted to the maintenance of the gold standard than the bankers themselves. Thus the one measure of alleviation that might have been applied within the limitations of the Government's changed attitude was excluded from consideration. The second Labour Government ended accordingly in an even more inglorious *débâcle* than that of 1924 ; and on this second occasion the real contradictions and inhibitions inherent in its attitude were openly admitted by the secession of three of its best known leaders and by the reappearance of the Labour Prime Minister at the head of a Coalition Government consisting predominantly of Conservatives and Conservative-minded Liberals.

Abandoned by its best known leaders and thoroughly handicapped by the lack of a constructive policy—for which the rapidly improvised programme of 1931 was but a poor and ineffective substitute—Labour went down in the ensuing General Election to a defeat far more thorough than that of 1924. Even on this occasion the bulk of its working-class supporters still stood firm, despite the bewilderment caused by the defection of Mr. MacDonald and his colleagues. But once more the non-political voters were drawn by panic to the polling booths, and on this occasion a substantial fraction of the better paid workers and a much larger proportion of the black-coated element which had rallied to the Labour Party abandoned its cause and gave their support to the so-called " National " Government. The Labour Party was left after 1931 with but a handful of supporters in the House of Commons, and with the task of policy-building to be done all over again under new leadership. For it was manifest, if not to some of the leaders of the Party at any rate to almost everyone else, that it was necessary at long last to face realities, to recognise the failure of the traditional methods of gradualist social reform, and to devise a totally new policy in the light of the changed economic and political conditions of 1931.

Meanwhile, what of the machinery of Parliamentary Government ? As a machine Parliament remained intact, unchanged since pre-war days save for the great enlargement of the electorate under the Representation of the

People Act of 1918. But the reality behind the form had been radically altered. For this reality consisted far less in the formal structure of Parliament than in the old party system which sustained its practical working. This old system of two parties, agreed upon fundamentals and differing only upon secondary issues, had gone past recall. The eclipse of the Liberals had indeed created a situation in which ever since the war there had been only two possible Governments—on the assumption that Governments were still to be constituted on party lines. But this assumption could not be completely fulfilled when one of the two claimants to office was only in a position to govern with the support of a third party far more closely allied in attitude and policy to its opponents than to itself. Under these conditions the traditional method of working Parliament could be maintained only as long as the Labour Party consented to behave as if it were a direct successor of the pre-war Liberal Party, and to remain within the traditional assumptions of the old party system—that is to say, as long as it refrained from making any attack on the fundamental institutions of British Capitalism.

What has been said is not that Parliament cannot be used as an instrument of radical reorganisation, but only that it cannot be so used without a fundamental change in its character. The present Parliamentary machine is so constructed as to be wholly unsuited in its working to the requirements of a party which sets out to achieve a radical change in the social and economic system. For any such change is bound to involve simultaneous action over a very wide field. It cannot be a question merely of nationalising one or two particular industries, or of passing one or two measures dealing with specific issues, while leaving the rest of the capitalist system to go on working as before. For the passing of a few measures applying Socialist principles to a limited part of the economic life of the country is bound in fact so to dislocate the working of the capitalist machine, with its reliance on automatic adjustments of part to part and its delicately poised equilibrium of economic forces, as to throw the machine out of gear at many points not directly affected by the immediate measures introduced by a Socialist Government. Socialism and Capitalism are not two systems, each dominating its own distinct sphere of economic activity. If Socialism is introduced even at one point on any significant scale it will have to be introduced at many other points in order to keep the system as a whole working at all. Moreover, the transition to Socialism, if it is to be made at all, ought to be made swiftly. For the period which intervenes between the first constructive steps towards the establishment of Socialism and the creation of a Socialist system complete enough to dominate all the major activities of society is bound to be a period of considerable economic dislocation, and to involve a temporary inefficiency which will be able to make the best neither of the old system nor of the new. The case for Socialism speedily if at all is not based merely on being in a hurry. It arises out of the inherent necessities of the transition.

It is obvious that the Parliamentary machine, as it now exists, is an impossible instrument for any such speedy change from one system to another. Even if we leave out of account the obstructive potentialities of the House of Lords and of the Crown, which are both certain to be opposed to the projected change of system, and confine our attention merely to the working of the House of Commons as a legislative instrument, the difficulty remains. Parliament is a body which works on the assumption that the measures placed before it are to be debated line by line with the fullest freedom of criticism on points of detail as well as of principle ; and this involves the further assumption that the body of legislation placed before it will be sufficiently small to enable this democratic condition to be effectively observed. A Government working within the limitations of traditional constitutional practices cannot possibly hope to carry through more than two or three major measures in the course of a Parliamentary session, whereas a Government setting out to establish Socialism may want to carry through in that space of time changes

which, if constitutional forms are to be observed, will need
to be embodied in as many as a hundred separate Parliamentary bills. Of course, if all discussion were ruthlessly
stifled and a Socialist majority made the fullest use of its
sheer voting strength to pass through bill after bill practically without discussion in the forms proposed by the
executive, the required output might be secured from the
House of Commons. But this, as the opposition parties
would at once point out, would mean an entire break with
the constitutional practice of Parliamentary legislation.
It would be to do with the House of Commons what
Mussolini has in fact done with the Italian and Hitler
with the German Parliament—to turn it into a mere
registering machine for decisions made elsewhere, and to
remove from it altogether its function of representing
divergent views and of ventilating grievances as the
guardian of articulate interests.

Yet it is clear that, if Parliamentary forms are to be
retained at all, something widely different from this, maybe,
but still involving a very great departure from past constitutional practice, will have to be done by any party which
sets out to make the difficult voyage from Capitalism to
Socialism without actual revolution. This would involve
the creation of extra-Parliamentary machinery for the
working out and application of Socialist schemes. It would
mean that the executive would be clothed with very much
wider and more authoritative powers than have been conferred on it within the existing Parliamentary system ; but
the executive could in practice delegate these powers to a
large extent to the functional organisations based on the
organised bodies—Trade Unions, Co-operative Societies,
local authorities, and so on—which would be used as its
agents in the actual execution of its schemes. In this way it is
conceivable that the transition to Socialism might be accomplished under the ægis of a reorganised Parliamentary
system ; but this Parliamentary system would have to be
as radically different from the nineteenth century Parliament as chalk from cheese.

Nor must it be forgotten that even this use of the Parliamentary machine for the establishment of Socialism would be practicable only if that machine could be for all practical purposes identified with the House of Commons. For it is utterly out of the question to envisage the House of Lords acquiescing in the adoption of a policy designed to facilitate the institution of a Socialist system by administrative means. This is true of the House of Lords as it stands to-day. And if, as may yet happen, the Conservatives were to use the opportunity of their present tenure of power so to amend the constitution of the House of Lords as to make it irremovable save with its own consent, the last avenue for the attainment of Socialism within the forms of constitutional action would be definitely closed, and any party which set out conscientiously to establish Socialism would have to become definitely unconstitutional in its attitude, however loath it might be to do so.

It is not, however, proposed to follow up further these implications of the advent of Socialism as a practical and immediate policy upon the field of Parliamentary activity. We are here concerned only with the fact that the basic assumptions on which the British Parliamentary system has hitherto rested could certainly not be sustained if the Labour Party set out seriously to establish a Socialist system. British Parliamentarism has continued to work with nothing worse than creakings and groanings of the machine during the past dozen years only because the British Labour Party has not been a Socialist Party in the sense of aiming at the immediate establishment of Socialism. It has not been a Socialist Party in this sense not so much because of the attitude of its leaders, though this has counted for something, as because there has been among its rank and file supporters no insistent pressure upon it to become immediately Socialist.

The British capitalist system has not, indeed, succeeded in re-establishing its old position in the world of Capitalism. Britain's economic supremacy and her prospects of maintaining herself in the future as a great capitalist industrial

State have been seriously undermined. But, although British Capitalism has been on the decline, it has not been overwhelmed by any catastrophe sufficiently far-reaching to make the drastic reorganisation of the economic system an immediately imperative task. British Capitalism, with diminished prestige and prosperity, has been able somehow to carry on ; and it is even true that Great Britain has been affected less than any other great country, with the possible exception of France, by the adversities of the past few years. The British unemployed have felt the pinch of " National Economy," and there has been some wage-cutting and a good deal of piecemeal worsening of conditions. The British rich are not so rich as they were, and the tribute levied by the British investors on the inhabitants of less developed countries has substantially fallen off. But according to the standards of to-day Great Britain remains a relatively prosperous country ; and accordingly the mood of her people is not one of desperation such as would encourage the growth of extreme political views. British Communism is insignificant in the amount of support which it commands for precisely the same reason as has prevented the growth of any substantial Fascist movement. For both these movements are products of an advanced stage in the decay of capitalist civilisation. They do not spring up, or at any rate attain to any considerable influence, where the mass of the people continue to be fairly well fed and to face life with a reasonable degree of equanimity. There are Fascist potentialities not only among the supporters of Sir Oswald Mosley, but to a far more menacing extent on the right wing of the Conservative Party, among those who rally round Mr. Churchill. There are potential Communist elements within the ranks of the Labour Party as well as among the followers of Mr. Pollitt and Mr. Maxton. But neither of these extremes is likely to become really powerful unless and until the disintegration of British Capitalism has gone a great deal further than it seems in the immediate future likely to go, save as the outcome of the plunging of Western Europe into another war.

§ 3. POLITICS IN FRANCE

SINCE the conclusion of the Great War in 1918 seven Governments have held office in Great Britain. Germany, up to and including the Chancellorship of Hitler, has had fifteen ; and France, up to and including the Radical Ministry of Daladier, no less than twenty-three—all within a period of less than fifteen years. Several of these short-lived French Governments have survived for only a few days ; and not one of them has held office for anything like so long as the Baldwin Ministry formed after the General Election of 1924. Clemenceau remained in office from 1917 to the beginning of 1920. Poincaré's second and third Ministries, which were consecutive, lasted from the middle of 1926 to the middle of 1929 ; and Briand was in office from 1921 to 1923 without a break. But otherwise no single Ministry has been of any considerable duration. As far as Governments are concerned, the administration of France has been even more discontinuous than those of most of the new countries which equipped themselves with brand-new constitutions on the morrow of the war.

Nevertheless there has been, despite all the instability of French Cabinets, a considerable degree of continuity in the conduct of French affairs. For many of the changes of Ministry have not carried with them any large shift of policy. This applies most of all in the sphere of foreign affairs ; for after Poincaré's Ruhr adventure of 1923–24 Briand successfully and with only occasional set-backs and interruptions dominated the foreign policy of the French Republic almost up to the time of his death. Nor has there been in home affairs so much instability as the frequent changes of Government would suggest, for many of the changed combinations of the post-war period have been shifts of *personnel* rather than of policy, and have involved no more than a slight edging of the Government to right or left. There have been in France since the war Governments of the Right and Governments of the Left ; and the distinction between the two is at the extremer points sufficiently marked. But no Government has been able to exist unless it could command the support not only of the Left or Right, but also of a substantial part of the Centre, and this necessity has been an important factor in preserving continuity of attitude even between Governments representing predominantly right or left tendencies.

This situation arises from the fact that France carries on her political life not under a two- or three- or four-party system but on the basis of a large number of distinct but to some extent shifting groups. There are, indeed, on the left clear-cut fairly well organised parties, the Socialists and the Radical-Socialists ; and on the support of these two any Government of the Left is bound chiefly to rest. The extreme Right is far less clearly organised and far less important from a numerical point of view. It ranges from the anti-Republican extremists, divided into a number of separate groups, Bonapartists, Constitutional Monarchists, *L'Action Française* and *Les Camelots du Roi*, to so-called Moderate Republicans who are themselves divided into a number of separate groups of varying degrees of Conservatism. Between these parties far to the right and the left-wing parties which have constituted, sometimes formally but more often in effect, a " *Cartel des Gauches*," lie a number of middle groups and parties. In face of the weakness and impracticability of the extreme Right these centre groups are bound to provide the main body of support for any Government of conservative tendencies. For the parties of the extreme Right cannot conceivably in the existing condition of French political opinion become strong enough to provide the necessary support for a Government of their own. Most of these centre groups are in effect Conservative and strongly nationalistic in their outlook ; and mainly from among them were recruited the forces which rallied behind Poincaré immediately after the war and behind Tardieu and Laval between 1929 and 1932. But they also include elements which are prepared on occasion to support, at any rate for a short time, a Government inclining more definitely towards the left ; and in the uncertain poise of French political opinion during most of the post-war period the swing to and fro of these middle elements has been the chief feature in the making and un-making of Governments. Not until the General Elections of 1932 gave the Left parties a clear and decisive majority in the Chamber was it possible for a Government of the Left to exist without the sufferance of some at least of the deputies drawn from the centre groups ; and even to-day this is only possible provided that the Radical-Socialists, as the largest *bourgeois* party of the Left, are able to keep on terms with the Socialist Party. They are in fact always un-easy bedfellows ; for it must be clearly understood that there is nothing Socialist about the Radical-Socialist Party except its name. It is in effect a left-wing *bourgeois* party with the traditional policy of anti-clericalism and individu-alist liberalism, and in no sense a Socialist Party as the term is ordinarily understood.

The Ministry which holds office in France in 1933 is a Radical-Socialist Ministry drawing some of its support from the other groups and parties of the Left, but dependent for its continuance in office on the toleration of the Social-ists. The policy of the Socialist Party has been since the war that of refusing to take part in any Coalition Govern-ment, but of giving its support on terms to any left-wing Government that is prepared to follow a reasonably ad-vanced policy. There is, however, no promise that this sup-port will be maintained, and no pact between the Socialists and the Radicals save at election times. Again and again overtures have been made by the Radicals to the Socialists either for the formation of a Coalition Government which would involve the Socialists in the responsibility for Radical measures, or at least for definite pledges of support from the Socialists to a purely Radical Ministry. But the Socialist terms for any pledge of support have always been higher than the Radicals have been prepared to concede ; and this situation has made the tenure of Radical Governments continually uncertain. When Herriot, the Radical-Socialist leader, assumed office after the fall of Laval and the sweeping left-wing successes in the General Election of 1932, his failure to come to terms with the Socialists was followed by some attempt to lean on the Centre for support, and so to dispense with the aid of the Socialists' voting strength. But there has been ample evidence in the past of the unsatisfactory position of any left *bourgeois* Ministry which relies on the Centre for support ; and the Daladier Government at present in office has swung back further to the Left and is again relying on the voting strength of the Socialists to keep it in office.

The Socialists, for their part, despite their objection to some of the Government's economy measures, have been induced to support it because there is clearly no alternative combination on the Left, and the fall of Daladier would inevitably mean his replacement by a new combination resting upon the Centre, which would be likely to take advantage of the world economic depression for an attack on the social services and the working-class standard of life. Nevertheless, the Daladier Ministry, no less than its predecessors, is essentially unstable, as any Ministry formed in the present condition of French party politics is bound to be. There is no continuity in the Governments of the French Republic because there are no parties powerful enough to keep a Ministry of their own in office, and no alliances sufficiently homogeneous to have any certainty of lasting.

The Governments of France are in consequence of their instability necessarily weak, especially in matters of finance, which most of all require continuous strong administration. Finance wrecked the Radicals in 1924–25 and again in 1926 ; and it was left to Poincaré to carry through, by the strength of his own personality and with the aid of a Ministry supported chiefly by the Right and Centre, the long delayed stabilisation of the franc. While this was doing, and while Poincaré was there with a strong personality to take charge of affairs, the French political situation appeared for a time unwontedly stable ; but after Poincaré's withdrawal the instability returned. Between 1929 and 1932 there were seven distinct Ministries, including two attempts, which both failed at the very outset, to reconstitute Governments based mainly on the Left. The Ministries of Tardieu and Laval during this period did indeed attempt to carry on Poincaré's work in home affairs ; but they were never sure of the support of the Chamber for any length of time, and their somewhat aggressive foreign policy came to be more and more out of tune with the growingly pacific temper of national opinion.

While, however, France changes her Government oftener than any other important country, there is, as has been suggested, an underlying stability in the French Parliamentary system. Weak government does not necessarily imply the weakness of the Parliamentary system itself, and no more than in Great Britain has the system been menaced since the war by any fundamental threat to its continuance. The French Parliament itself is less probably deeply rooted in the life of the nation than the Parliament of Great Britain ; and there are larger elements in France which object fundamentally to the whole constitution of the State. France has her Royalists on the one side and her Communists on the other, whereas Great Britain has but the barest handful of out and out opponents of the constitutional system. But the body of support behind the French Parliamentary system is nevertheless solid and imposing ; and the weakness of the Cabinet system, so far from being regarded by public opinion in France as an argument against a Parliamentary régime, is often counted in its favour. For France is still pre-eminently a nation of small-scale producers, peasants, small employers, independent craftsmen, and traders, with a very influential middle class of *rentiers* living in retirement at a relatively low standard of life. These classes do not want strong government, as long as weak government manages somehow to carry on without taxing them too highly and without chivvying them too much—and, of course, provided that the economic system continues to function without positive breakdown. They take no great account of the doings away at Paris, and they are not even particularly keen on the control of their own local administrations, which are in fact far more dominated from the Centre than the local government of Great Britain. The French are a political people, but their politics still consists very largely in a demand to be let alone ; they have, for example, a quite astonishing power of simply refusing to do things, including, unfortunately for the finances of the French Republic, a remarkable capacity for evading the payment of taxes.

This description of the predominant temper of French political life remains true even in face of the enlargement of the area of France under the Treaty of Versailles and of the rapid development of heavy industry which has taken place in recent years. The *Comité des Forges* has sometimes been regarded as the arbiter of French economic policy ; and its attitude has undoubtedly exerted a strong influence on those Governments which have drawn their support mainly from the Right and Centre. But the *bourgeois* Left and some of the Centre still represent predominantly the point of view of the small-scale producers and traders hostile to large-scale industry and in the last resort to imperialist and militarist policies. The strengthening of the Left at the General Election of 1932 represented the victory of these home-keeping and relatively pacific tendencies over the more aggressive militarism of the Conservative groups. As long as the French are not unduly frightened, their political life tends to incline towards the *bourgeois* Left. If, however, they become nationally frightened, as they did in 1923 and as they have considerable cause to do again just now, the balance is apt to tilt over towards the Right with its greater stress on the military requirements of national defence and its more aggressive policy in external affairs. The danger is that the revival of militarism in Germany under Nazi rule may cause just such a swing back of opinion, and so upset the comparatively internationalist policies followed by the French Governments during the past year.

This strength of the *bourgeois* Radical parties, which get the main bulk of their support from the *petite bourgeoisie,* serves in France as a powerful insurance against the growth of anything in the nature of an influential Fascist movement. For the Radical-Socialists and the parties closely allied to them draw the main body of their support from precisely those elements in the community which Mussolini in Italy and Hitler in Germany succeeded in rallying to Fascism. In both these countries this conversion of the *petite bourgeoisie* to a policy of revolution arose out of the dissolution of *bourgeois* society and the rapid rise of Socialism and Communism among the working classes. Fascism developed first of all as a movement of *petit bourgeois* and peasant self-defence, based on economic and political desperation. But in France the *petite bourgeoisie* has as yet no cause for despair. It has been hit no doubt by the world slump ; but the comparative self-dependence of the French national economy and the pursuance of a policy of protection for French agriculture have combined to maintain relatively well the position of the French peasants and small-scale industrial producers. Large-scale industry has suffered as a result of the slump, and manual workers have begun to suffer seriously in terms both of unemployment and of reduced wages. But there has been no suffering in France at all comparable to the economic distress which has been the regular accompaniment of German political life ever since 1929 ; and accordingly the middle parties between Socialism and revolutionary reaction have been able to maintain their position without any serious difficulty, and to carry on without any immediate threat to the continuance of the Parliamentary system.

Fascism in France will become a dangerous force only if economic depression goes so far as to destroy the basis of life for the French peasantry and the *petite bourgeoisie* of the towns. What has been said of the conditions of French economic life also explains, though to a less extent, the position of the French Socialist and Communist movements. The French worker is feeling the pinch of the depression, for unemployment has risen during the last year at an alarming rate ; but the workers in large-scale industry form a comparatively small section of the French population, and are hardly powerful enough by themselves to upset the stability of French political institutions or to win a majority for constitutional Socialism. French Socialism possesses a considerable degree of strength and has grown substantially in recent years ; but there seems to be no prospect under present conditions of the French Socialist Party being able, either by itself or jointly with the Communists, to win a majority in the Chamber of Deputies. French Socialists are even to-day only one-fifth of the French Chamber, and Socialists and Communists together not much more than one-fourth.

Nor does French Communism show any sign of becoming a really powerful force. In the period of excitement immediately after the war, the majority of the French Socialists actually went Communist. But many of those who declared for Communism at this stage could hardly be regarded as full Communists in the Moscow sense of the term, and the minority which rejected Communism carried with it a majority of the Socialist members in Parliament, and speedily regained its strength as the premier working-class party in the country as well. This is natural enough, for Communism, like Fascism, is only likely to develop as a really powerful force where the capitalist institutions of a country have reached an advanced stage of decay, or under the influence of war as a powerful solvent of established institutions. France, despite her revolutionary history in the nineteenth century, is to-day, with Great Britain, the least revolutionary of countries, and therefore the least favourable ground for the growth of extremist movements on either the right or the left. It is easy enough to criticise the inadequacy of the French Parliamentary system from a constructive point of view. French politics are unconstructive, and French public finance is almost always in a mess. But that is fundamentally because a large section of the French public does not want its politics to be constructive. In home affairs it prefers the relative security it knows to doubtful and dangerous experiments in either a right or a

UR

left direction. And it is not likely to be converted from this point of view until either large-scale industrialism has advanced a good deal further, or the European anarchy so infects the relatively self-contained French economic system as to make the continuance of the existing situation plainly impossible.

§ 4. FASCISM IN ITALY

EVEN WHILE the new States of post-war Europe were beginning to build up their constitutions on the basis of supposedly democratic principles derived from the experience of Western Europe and the United States, the fundamental principles on which they were working were being aggressively challenged in Russia by Lenin and his fellow-Communists, who were working upon a radically different set of underlying assumptions and with a radically different conception of true democracy in their minds. The crumbling of the old feudal autocracies of Central and Eastern Europe was accompanied not only by an extension of the methods and policies of Parliamentary democracy to new areas in Europe, but at the same time by the emergence into the realm of practice of new theories of Government, which challenged the entire basis on which these post-war constitutions were being built. The Russian challenge will be discussed further in a later section of this book. It is mentioned here only because it was in fact prior in time to the other rival which Parliamentary democracy has encountered in its attempt to take charge of European affairs. Fascism, though it emerged later, is treated first because it involves a far less fundamental cleavage with the past than Communism and seeks to alter rather the political structure of society than the underlying economic structure on which, in the view of Marx's Communist followers, political institutions are bound to rest. Fascism is in effect an attempt to change the political organisation of society without radically altering the economic system ; and accordingly the transition from Parliamentarism to Fascism can be made far more easily and with far less disturbance to the working of the social system than the infinitely more drastic purge of economic institutions demanded by the Communists would involve.

Marxism in its Communist form—it is a matter of dispute how far any other form of it can claim to be really Marxism at all—is essentially a cosmopolitan doctrine. It aims at transcending all political and racial frontiers, not merely in the sense of wishing to link up the various nations of the world into a federal unity of free workers' republics, but also in setting out to abolish these frontiers altogether save as purely administrative divisions in a world too large to be managed successfully under a system of unitary government. Against the division of the world into separate political units—nation from nation—Communism sets up the division of men into economic classes based on their differing relations to the powers of production and to the productive system. " Workers of the World, Unite " is its slogan, and it aims at bringing together the whole working-class movement as a cosmopolitan force abjuring all ideas of patriotism and national loyalty and seeking by its united action to establish everywhere a social system based on the abolition of class distinctions. The classless society is its ideal ; and this classless society is to be, not a national society related to other classless societies as the capitalist States of the world are related to one another to-day, but a world society cut up into autonomous groups merely for purposes of administrative convenience.

Parliamentarism, on the other hand, is at most internationalist and not cosmopolitan. The League of Nations is an attempt to group the sovereign States of the world into a loose federation of co-operating nations without any sacrifice of sovereign independence by the member States, save upon a few clearly defined issues. It assumes that the various States which make up the federation can be regarded as possessing Governments whose views can be taken as in some real sense expressing the national will of each country ; and its theory, if not its practice, therefore assumes that each country will possess some form of Government that can be accepted as fulfilling the requirements of democracy. The League itself, with its Council and its Assembly, attempts to reproduce the structure of Parliamentarism on an international scale. Its Council aims at being something like an international Cabinet, and its Assembly something like an international Legislature ; and its affiliated complement, the International Labour Organisation, has been created mainly in accordance with the same set of ideas. If Parliamentarism, basing itself on the recognition of national sovereignty, can become an international force, the League of Nations is its natural instrument. But a federal body formed upon this basis of co-operation between sovereign Governments can clearly never pass over from the international to the cosmopolitan ideal. It is a linking of nations and not in any sense a denial of the ultimate validity of national or racial divisions.

Even so, the League has far too internationalist a tone to please the Nationalists of post-war Europe. They may be able to dominate the League Council or the League Assembly, or at all events to prevent the League from taking any effective action that might menace the absolute self-determination of each individual sovereign State ; but they are well aware that much of the public sentiment in each country which supports the League goes much further than the governing organs of the League are able to go in an internationalist and pacifist direction. For many of the League's unofficial supporters, organised in bodies like the League of Nations Union in Great Britain and the corresponding societies in the Continental countries, do not recognise how thoroughly the structure of the League rests upon an assumption of the absolute sovereignty of each national State. They are trying to edge it towards a more far-reaching internationalism, based not indeed on a denial of the reality or value of national divisions, but at least upon a drastic limitation of sovereign independence in such matters as the making of war and peace. They want to limit armaments, to promote international treaties and arbitration, and to build up on the foundation of the League an international public opinion which shall be effective in checking nationalist or imperialist aggression wherever it makes itself felt. The League, in aspiration if not in fact, embodies the philosophy of liberal Parliamentarism extended from the national to the international scale.

Fascism, however, while it may be consistent with affiliation to the League, as long as the League does nothing to limit ultimate national sovereignty, is by no means prepared to endorse this underlying liberal philosophy of the League's rank and file supporters. For, in as far as Fascism can be regarded as having a philosophy at all, that philosophy is ultimately and aggressively nationalist. It is hostile both to the pacifist internationalism which underlies the attempt to build up the authority of the League of Nations and by that means to put limits to the national self-expression of the member States and, even more thoroughly and fundamentally, to the whole attitude of Communism, which aims at nothing less than the complete sweeping away of the solidarities and loyalties upon which Fascism rests. Fascists have everywhere declared war on internationalism in all its forms ; but their deepest hatred has been reserved for the Communists and for such Socialists as share in the cosmopolitan outlook dictated by the Marxian philosophy. Thus, while, as we saw earlier, Fascism has in practice been the destroyer of the Liberal Parliamentary State, it has really been for the most part marching over the prostrate body of Parliamentarism in order to get at its real enemy, the cosmopolitan philosophy of Communism and Socialism.

The New Nationalism. Nationalism has thus become in the twentieth century the philosophy of new authoritarian groups aiming at the destruction of the Parliamentary system. This is of course a complete reversal of the position which existed in the earlier part of the nineteenth century, when nationalism developed as the ally and inspiration of the very liberal-democratic movements whose destruction it is compassing to-day. Nineteenth century nationalism is associated in our minds with the German Revolution of 1848, with the unification of Italy, and with the building up of Parliamentary institutions based on the idea of responsible government over a large part of Europe. It was the enemy of the old autocracies ; and its constant demand was for the granting by the absolute monarchies upon which it waged war of constitutions embodying the principles of democratic self-government. There were indeed in Mazzini's nationalism large elements of internationalism already present ; and Mazzini can fairly be regarded as the forerunner of the ideas which the more advanced adherents of the League are now attempting to embody in its collective institutions. But Cavour was a very different person from Mazzini ; and the liberal nationalism of the nineteenth century was in practice far more *à la* Cavour than *à la* Mazzini. For, wherever nationalism established itself and succeeded in equipping a country with responsible Parliamentary institutions, it easily became expansionist and imperialist as well as merely nationalist.

Up to the Great War these tendencies were able to develop without requiring any further change in the structure of the State. For it was found that Parliaments were fully as amenable as autocracies to the new philosophy of economic imperialism. But there were in the expansionist and imperialist phase of nationalism which set in in the later part of the nineteenth century already latent the elements which were in due course to prove fatal to the liberalism of the Nation-State. The more successful nationalism was in consolidating the institutions of the States in which it developed, the less liberal it grew and the more it tended to ally itself with the aristocratic and authoritarian elements in society which it had originally set out to fight. Side by side with this gradual conversion of the liberals to authoritarianism and imperialism, there had been going on an opposite conversion of the older aristocracy to nationalism. The Junkers and militarists, the great landed proprietors and aristocrats of the old order, having lost their power to govern society autocratically by their own class authority, set to work to master and turn to their own ends the institutions of the new Parliamentary States. In order to do this they had to find allies ; and these were soon discovered in the great industrialists and bankers and traders, who had appeared as a liberalising influence as long as they continued to be excluded from an effective share in political power. The new nationalism brought together, if not into unified parties, at least into alliances of co-operating political groups, the aristocrats of the old order and the plutocrats of the new. And this process, which had been going on for a long time before 1914, but was still incomplete and largely unrecognised when the war broke out, was speedily completed after the war, when both aristocrats and plutocrats were confronted with the *fait accompli* of the democratic Parliamentary State. Nationalism, which had been in the early nineteenth century a force on the left in European politics, was quite definitely after 1918, and to a considerable extent had become even before 1914, a force standing on the extreme right.

This is not to say that the Junkers and militarists felt any affection for their new allies. At any rate in Germany and Austria-Hungary, where State constitutions had retained large elements of autocracy and aristocracy right up to 1918, the old governing classes retained their traditional ideals and continued to hold that the only appropriate way for men to be governed was by a powerful monarchy upheld by the recognised authority of a privileged aristocratic class. This Junker attitude was at bottom a class and racial attitude even more than a nationalist attitude ; it stood for the national State not so much because it was national as because it embodied a system of class and race privilege, and it withheld any real feeling of loyalty from the new Republics established in the defeated countries on the ruins of the pre-war Empires of Central Europe. It was nationalist only in the sense that it resented external interference with its right to struggle for the regaining of its old exclusive authority, and in the sense that it saw in militant nationalism the best hope of re-establishing autocracy and aristocracy as the pillars of the State. But, while there was no change in the mental attitude of the traditional upholders of class privilege, there was a great change for the time being in their power. They could not hope to regain control by their own unaided efforts, and they had accordingly to ally themselves with any forces which they thought themselves capable of turning to their own ends. This meant at first an alliance with industrial magnates, bankers and merchants, fearful of the rise of Socialism within the post-war Republics. But it came to mean later a willingness to join forces with any movement which seemed to promise the overthrow of democratic institutions without, at the same time, involving any attack on the central position of economic privilege.

Fascism, though in both Italy and Germany it has appeared at a certain stage of its development in alliance with the older nationalism, rests in reality on very different foundations. In Italy Mussolini and his Fascists took over and used for their own purposes in the early stages of building up the new Fascist State the remnants of Conservative nationalism ; but they never allowed their policy to be in any way governed or deflected by the wishes of their conservative allies. In the same way the German Nazis made their Government in coalition with Herr von Papen and Herr Hugenberg ; but even the first few weeks of Herr Hitler's Government showed conclusively that in this alliance the Nazis meant to secure exclusive domination for themselves. Captain Göring, and not his titular chief von Papen, took over the government of Prussia ; and excluded Republican officials and administrators were everywhere replaced by Nazis and not by Nationalists. Moreover in Germany, as in Italy, the nationalists were speedily dissolved as a separate party, and merged in the new movement which they had helped to power. Fascism may be able successfully to absorb into itself in Germany, as it has done to a large extent in Italy, the articulate remnants of the old feudal nationalism ; but it is a great mistake to confuse the two, or to regard them has having anything more than an incidental and temporary community of outlook.

Fascist Philosophy. What, then, is the underlying philosophy of Fascism in post-war Europe ? The question is extraordinarily hard to answer ; for, while there has been no dearth of theorists willing to equip the new movement with an appropriate philosophy, it is clear that the movement came into being first and its philosophy was developed afterwards as an explanation and a justification of its positive doings. There is of course nothing unnatural in this. It is indeed the logical order of development that forces should arise in the world before theoretical explanations of these forces can be put forward. Theory interprets facts as they arise. It is only creative in the secondary sense that the possession of an articulate theory can give added strength and coherence to a force already in independent being. If Fascism had started as a philosophy it might never have become a movement ; starting as a movement, and deriving its power from the actual state of mind which existed widely among men in the years immediately after the war, it was bound before long to grow a philosophy in order to give theoretical sanction to its existence.

We must, then, if we are to understand how Fascism has developed into a powerful force in the life of post-war Europe, begin by looking for its causes in men's state of mind in the years immediately following the war. And we shall have to begin with a paradox. Fascism is essentially an outgrowth of the psychology of disillusionment and defeat. It is perfectly true that it developed first in Italy, and that Italy had been in the war on the victorious side. But, while Italy was the ally of France and Great Britain and the United States, she emerged from the Peace of Versailles with a sense not of victory but of humiliation and defeat. There had been strong opposition in the country itself to participation in the war ; and the *volte face* which brought Italy to change sides and, after dissociating herself from the Triple Alliance, to abandon neutrality in favour of an active part on the side of the Allies, was brought about by lavish promises concerning the spoils of victory. Italy was to be allowed as the reward for her help to emerge from the war as a great imperialist Power with a colonial empire comparable with those of the other great Powers and unlimited prospects of expansion. The disappointment of these hopes, and the scanty rewards which could be anticipated from the exploitation of her largely barren territories in North Africa, caused after 1918 a revulsion of opinion so violent as to threaten the very foundations of a flimsy liberal-democratic State which showed no real capacity for government, or for the handling of the difficult economic problems which confronted the country. The checking of emigration raised up a surplus population seeking an outlet for its energies, and returning soldiers found no means of fitting themselves into an economic structure which appeared to stand in no need of their services. Socialism waxed strong in the industrial centres ; but Italian industry was too little developed for Socialism to become an effective force unless it could either win the peasants over to its side or make up its mind to dominate them in the Communist way, and find means of creating a sufficient mass of agrarian discontent to enable it to seize power. Possibly the Italian Socialists, who developed strong left-wing tendencies after the Russian Revolution, might have succeeded in doing this had it not been for Don Sturzo and his *Popolari*, with their progressive policy of social reform and their wide appeal among the Catholic peasantry. But Don Sturzo and his followers were successful in preventing Socialism from permeating the peasants, and accordingly in interposing barriers, which seemed to most of the Socialist leaders to be absolute, in the way of a successful Socialist revolution. The contest for popular support between the Socialists and Don Sturzo's Catholics thus led to a position of stalemate. The Socialists were too strong to allow the *bourgeois* parties to govern effectively without them ; but they were not strong enough to assume the task of governing themselves. Consequently a hungry and disillusioned population found itself left without any government at all, and a larger and larger number of the younger elements within it were soon in a mood to turn to anyone who promised them a field for immediate activity and a prospect of ending the deadlock in political and economic affairs.

Out of these elements of discontent the ex-Socialist Mussolini proceeded to build up his Fascist following. Benito Mussolini had been before the war an active Socialist leader, belonging to the extreme wing of the party and influenced largely by Syndicalist ideas. When the world crisis arose in 1914 he opposed strongly the intervention of Italy on the side of the Central Powers ; and he soon came over, after a quarrel with the Socialist Party, to the advocacy of intervention on the Allied side. On ceasing to be editor of *Avanti*, the official Socialist paper, he founded the *Popolo d'Italia* for the expression of his own views ; and this paper became one of the influential forces in driving the Italian politicians to intervene in the war. When war had been declared, Mussolini joined the army as a private soldier, and remained on active service until he was wounded in 1917. He then returned to his editorial work, urging in the *Popolo d'Italia* the continued prosecution of the war even after the disaster of Caporetto, and the pressing to the full of Italy's claims to a large share in the spoils of victory.

The Rise of Fascism.

Soon after the Armistice, amid the complete disorganisation which had overtaken Italian economic life, the rapidly rising prices, the widespread unemployment and the general discontent with the policy of the Government at the Peace Conference, Mussolini founded in March 1919 his first *Fascio di Combattimento*, the forerunner of the Fascist Party. At this stage and for some time longer, his policy was still in many respects aggressively Socialist. The Fascist movement began as a force relying on the support of the ex-soldiers, with an aggressive programme of economic demands combined with the

advocacy of an entire reconstruction of the Italian State.
It was republican, democratic, anti-clerical and even to
some extent internationalist. It demanded the convocation
of an " Italian constituent assembly conceived as the
Italian section of an international constituent authority of
the peoples, with a view to proceeding to the radical
transformation of the political and economic foundations of
social life." It proclaimed the doctrine of " popular
sovereignty exercised by the universal equal and direct
suffrage of the citizens of both sexes together with the right
of referendum and popular veto." It demanded the abolition of the Senate and the institution of single chamber
government, severe limitations on the powers of the executive, and a considerable measure of decentralisation in the
affairs of local government. With these demands went
others—for complete liberty of thought, conscience, religion, association, Press and propaganda, the dissolution of
joint-stock companies, the suppression of all speculation, of
banks and of stock exchanges, the nationalisation of credit,
payment of the national debt at the exclusive expense of the
rich, redistribution of the national wealth, including the
division of the land among the peasants, and finally, the
exploitation of industries, transport and public services
under the control of the Unions of technicians and workers.
Internationally, too, this first programme of the Fascists
reads strangely to-day. It demanded the abolition of con-
scription, general disarmament and the prohibition by all
States of the manufacture of arms, the abolition of secret
diplomacy, and similar aspirations of the political left ; and
it laid down that international policy should be " inspired
by the principle of the sovereignty of peoples and their
independence within the confederation of States."

Radical as these demands of the Fascists were, Mussolini
and his friends were throughout at loggerheads with the
orthodox leaders of the Socialist movement. Italian
Socialism immediately after the war had taken a pronounced left-wing turn. In July 1919 there was a political
strike in support of the Soviet Governments of Russia,

Bavaria and Hungary ; and throughout the latter part of 1919 and the early months of 1920 there were constant strikes, including important stoppages on the railways and in the Post Office in June 1920. These movements led up to the great dispute in the metal industry in the summer of 1920. Strikes by the workers in certain establishments were followed by the declaration of a general lock-out by the metal employers ; and the Trade Unions then retaliated, as they had previously on a smaller scale, by a general occupation of the factories. Up to this point, Mussolini and his Fascists, while they were already at variance with the internationalist attitude of the Socialists, were generally on the side of the workers. The Fascists had supported the peasant risings in 1920 in the south of Italy, and they were prepared to support the occupation of the factories by the workers. But the Socialist leaders would have no dealings with Mussolini and his Fascists ; and from this point the quarrel between the two groups became open and bitter. The Socialists and their Trade Union allies, having seized the factories, had to make up their minds what to do next ; for the Government, so far from taking any step to turn them out, merely left them in passive occupation in the hope that the movement would collapse. This indeed it was bound to do unless the Socialists were prepared to go further and embark on positive revolutionary action ; for they had no means of securing supplies of raw materials in order to work the factories themselves, or of disposing of the products if they had been prepared to work them.

The Socialists, however, despite their left-wing policy, shrank from any attempt at open revolution. They had plenty of arms, for Italy was in those days full of arms in private hands, and large quantities of munitions had been seized in the occupied factories. But there was a total lack of military organisation and of military leadership, and finally, in October 1920, the workers, unprepared to take full control of the State, evacuated the factories and returned to work on the basis of a compromise over wages and conditions.

This failure to seize power in the summer of 1920 proved in the long run the undoing of the Italian Socialist movement. It caused violent internal disputes in the party itself. In June 1921, after the Party Congress had refused to commit itself to a revolutionary policy, the Communist wing broke away and formed its own organisation in association with the Third International ; and even so the remainder of the party continued to be split between a right wing, following a strictly constitutional policy, and a left, or "maximalist," wing differing from the Communists only in matters of tactics and revolutionary method. The party split again in October 1922, but long before this its chance had gone.

Meanwhile Fascism had been growing fast. In September 1919 d'Annunzio, at the head of a small unofficial army, had marched on Fiume and occupied the town in defiance of the decisions of the Allied statesmen. There was deep and widespread resentment in Italy at the treatment meted out to the country by President Wilson and the Allied statesmen at Paris ; and a wave of nationalism swept over a large mass of the people, especially among the upper and middle classes. D'Annunzio's dramatic seizure of Fiume helped to fan the flames, and his continued occupation of the city in defiance of the Allied Governments kept the excitement at height throughout 1920. When finally he surrendered Fiume to Italian regulars in 1921, and his forces were disbanded, most of his men speedily went over to the Fascists, thus equipping Mussolini with a powerful reinforcement to the groups of ex-soldiers whom he had already gathered round him. Thereafter Fascismo spread faster still. Already in November 1920 Mussolini had begun the formation of armed Fascist *squadre*, and an intensive guerilla warfare between the Fascists and the Socialists and Communists had set in. After the occupation of the factories had failed Fascist policy became less and less revolutionary in an economic sense, and more and more aggressively nationalist, though it still retained for some time its anti-clerical and anti-monarchical tenets. In November 1921 the Fascist

Congress decided to create a definite political party boy-cotting the existing Italian State and demanding its radical reconstruction. But in forming the party the Fascist Congress laid down no policy for it, merely announcing that its policy was adequately expressed in the utterances of its leader. Mussolini had in fact succeeded in building on the basis of his original organisation of ex-soldiers a powerful, disciplined and armed body of adherents prepared to follow him almost blindly wherever he might choose to lead.

The main strength of Fascism came not from the industrial workers, but from the *petite bourgeoisie* and the peasants. Fascism, like the Nazi movement at a later stage in Germany, recruited itself primarily from those elements in the population which combined hostility to large-scale Capitalism with an intense fear of the coming of a Socialist and still more of a Communist régime. Its adherents, apart from the discontented ex-soldiers, who provided its nucleus of active members, were drawn from the classes whose position was based on the ownership of small property and the carrying on of small-scale industry and agriculture ; and as long as these forces felt Socialism rather than large-scale Capitalism to be the chief enemy threatening their survival, they were willing to ally themselves with large-scale Capitalism in order to overcome the Socialist menace. Mussolini, after the failure of the occupation of the factories, drew large subsidies from the great Italian industrialists as a reward for the intensive warfare which he carried on against the Socialist and Communist groups. It was with the assent and to a large extent the positive co-operation of the Italian industrialists, as well as of the aristocracy, that, despite the declared anti-capitalist attitude of the movement, Fascism actually climbed towards power. Mussolini showed an extraordinary talent for organising the intermediate groups under the inspiration of an *idea nazionale* which often seemed to have no real or positive content. He showed how the middle groups in society could be organised into a force powerful enough to compass at least temporarily the defeat of Socialism ; and similar adventurers in other countries have not been slow to master the lessons of his achievement.

Meanwhile the Italian State remained in the nerveless hands of the old governing groups. Civil war between Fascists, Communists and Socialists raged practically unchecked in the streets of the leading cities, and nothing was done to improve the almost desperate economic situation of the country. More and more the old liberal-democratic order in Italy was dissolving into chaos ; and, since the Socialists had drawn back on the brink of revolution, Fascism remained as the sole effective claimant for political power. The Catholic *Popolari* were too much involved with the old order of Centrists, and too pacific in their methods to deal with a situation so desperate as had arisen in the Italy of 1922 ; for it had become plain that the Italian State lay at the mercy of that party, and of that party only, which was prepared to appeal to force in order to resolve the deadlock. When finally in October 1922 the Fascists marched on Rome, there was not even the shadow of armed opposition, though the army, if it could have been trusted, would have been ample to deal with Mussolini's following. But the army made no move, and the old Ministry yielded up its power without a blow.

This could not indeed have happened had not Fascism, as a prelude to the assumption of power, made certain definite renunciations of its earlier policy. In September 1922 Mussolini, on behalf of the Fascists, definitely expressed his adherence to the monarchy as the symbol of that national unity for which Fascism stood ; and at the same time there was a pronounced relaxation of the anti-clerical propaganda previously associated with the movement. The King was won over to the Fascist side ; and it was largely the King's attitude that made resistance by the old Government impossible. For, while the troops might have obeyed the King if he had given the order to resist, it is quite unlikely that they would have obeyed the

Government against the King's will. With the King's support Fascism was able to assume control of the State without any active opposition. But at the outset Mussolini and his followers did not feel strong enough to attempt to govern alone. Setting a precedent which was followed by Hitler and the Nazis a decade later, they assumed office as the leading element in a coalition Government into which they admitted representatives of the old nationalist and *bourgeois* parties, trusting to their own superior unity and to the force behind them to render these additional elements impotent in effect. In the event the old nationalists were speedily absorbed into the Fascist Party, and the elements which were less capable of absorption were soon liquidated when they had served their original purpose of easing the Fascist assumption of power. Meanwhile, Parliament, with only a tiny handful of Fascists among its members, found itself completely dominated by the new administration. Against the will and opinion of the great majority of the members, it passed in 1923 the new constitutional law demanded by the Government, knowing that a refusal on its part to acquiesce would simply lead to its forcible dissolution. It suited Mussolini to cloak his assumption of dictatorial powers as far as possible in constitutional forms ; and Parliament, rather than provoke a more definitely revolutionary situation, meekly did whatever he and the Fascists ordered.

The new electoral law of 1923 was designed to ensure the Fascists a working majority in the new Parliament, even in face of a state of opinion in the country which would certainly not have secured them that majority under the old system of proportional representation. Under the new system, the party which obtained the largest number of votes, provided that it secured at least twenty-five per cent of all the votes cast, was to be allotted two-thirds of the total number of seats in the new Parliament, the remainder being divided among the other parties in proportion to the votes cast. Under this system the Fascists succeeded in 1924 in securing 65 per cent of all the votes cast, and therewith a Parliament ready to carry out their policy without question.

But at this point the new Fascist State was almost wrecked by the troubles which followed the murder of the Socialist leader Matteotti, who had ventured to denounce the new electoral system as unconstitutional, and had advocated a refusal to recognise the decrees of the new Parliament. The murder of Matteotti caused a great revulsion of feeling throughout the industrial centres of North Italy ; and the Fascists, in order to avoid a revolutionary outbreak, were compelled to make temporary concessions. In 1925 a new electoral law, based on universal suffrage for all citizens over twenty-five and on single-member constituencies, was enacted ; and there were other signs of the impending liberalisation of the Fascist régime. But as soon as the difficulties following on the Matteotti case had been successfully overcome the Fascists once more changed their tactics. In 1926 the opposition was expelled from Parliament, at which it had for some time attended but irregularly and in small numbers ; and in 1928 the electoral law was again changed and a totally new system instituted in accordance with the principles of the " Corporative State " which the Fascists were now setting out seriously to institute. As the electoral law of 1928 still forms the basis of the political structure of Fascist Italy, it will be convenient before we attempt to describe it to say something more generally of the nature of the new corporative society for which Fascism professes to stand.

The Corporative State. Fascism as a theory and as a political policy rests essentially upon its claim to embody the " national idea." As we have seen earlier, the theory of Fascism has grown up gradually, following its practice rather than giving rise to it. Indeed, on the face of the matter Italian Fascism has completely boxed the compass of theory since it originally appeared as a political force. There seems on the face of the matter to be nothing in common between the revolutionary and aggressive economic and political policy advocated by the Fascists in 1919 and the programme which, with the support of the Nationalists and the great employers, as well as the small middle class, they proceeded to put into force in Italy after the march on Rome. These obvious contradictions have led many observers to regard Fascism as essentially an opportunist movement created by Mussolini for his personal ends, and brought to power by his personal genius for focussing contemporary discontents. But this view, while it possesses some substance, is fundamentally mistaken. The Fascists have shown a great capacity for changing their minds and adopting quite contradictory policies at different times ; but behind their opportunism there is a real element of continuity, and it is upon this element, rather than upon their opportunism, that their power is fundamentally built.

For Fascism, even at its first appearance in 1919, was emphatically a nationalist force. Even when it set out to proclaim universal disarmament and the federation of free nations, it was already thoroughly nationalist in its outlook and stood for the independence of each sovereign nation as an ultimate element in the constitution of an international political system. Mussolini succeeded in building up Fascism into a force powerful enough to take over the government of Italy because he realised the possibility of working on emotions in the minds of men sufficiently powerful to create an effective counter-force to the emotional appeal of international Socialism. The mobilisation of discontent with the low position held by Italy among the nations, with her economic backwardness as the cause of her political subjection, and with the supposedly ungenerous treatment meted out to her at the Peace Conference, was the first task which Mussolini and his Fascists took in hand. There were many other elements in their programme at this stage ; and these other elements were important as additional means of enlisting support. But what gave unity to the movement from the first was its aggressive insistence on the unity of the nation as a whole and on the utter failure of the old liberal-democratic State to achieve this unity, or to give Italy a respected and secure status among the nations. There was so far not much philosophical background to this idea of national unity ; but the idea was present and could be filled out in both theory and practice as soon as necessity arose. Actually Fascism took over from Gabriele d'Annunzio a great deal of the romantic nationalism which he embodied in the new constitution which he drew up for the Free State of Fiume during the period of his occupation ; and Hegelian philosophers, such as Gentile, who rallied to the movement at a later stage, soon filled up the gaps on the theoretical side. Fascism may have begun by being mere nationalism ; it soon took unto itself the character of a mystical Hegelian nationalism made up of elements taken from the Constitution of Carnaro and the *Philosophie des Rechts*.

At the basis of this enlarged nationalist theory is the conception of the totalitarian State, that is to say, of the State as taking up into itself and unifying all the institutions of the national life, private as well as public. The Fascists deny, as Hegel denied a century earlier, that there can be any social organism more ultimate and embracing than the national State. They deny the possibility, or at least the validity, of any real international State, or even of any federation of nations embodying a supra-national consciousness. For them the national State is the ultimate being, more real than the individuals and groups which make it up, and with an absolute claim upon the loyalty of every one of its members. But the national State is at the same time not a mere absorption of the many into the one ; for it finds expression naturally and inevitably through the multiplicity of functional organisations, each playing its essential part in the organised life of the entire society, and each responsible to the State for the successful fulfilment of its own particular function. At this point the philosophy of Fascism has obviously certain resemblances both to the Syndicalism which had a substantial influence upon its actual development in Italy and to Guild Socialism. But

Fascism diverges sharply from both Syndicalism and Guild Socialism in that it denies the existence of the class struggle, save under the conditions of *bourgeois* democracy, and claims to remove the necessity for class conflict by assigning to each class and group its significant place and function within the structure of the Corporative State. It is at war with Marxism and internationalism because both doctrines set up claims to loyalty which deny the claims of the national State ; and it is especially hostile to Marxism, because Marxism, far more than *bourgeois* internationalism, not merely denies the ultimate validity of the claims of the national State, but sets up against them a counter-claim to allegiance on a basis of economic class.

According to the Fascist theory, classes exist not independently but only as the corollaries to the distribution of functions within the national State. There is no true community of class extending across national frontiers, because the class as it exists within each State is only a fragmentary expression of the national consciousness of that State, and has no claim to expression at all except in as far as it is fulfilling its assigned function within the national body. The Fascist State recognises Trade Unions, provided that they are built in its own image, and repudiate all connections with Marxism and the class-war ; but it gives equal recognition to associations of employers and to all corporate groups based on professional solidarity. Moreover, its recognition is in all these cases conditional and not absolute. It recognises the Trade Union, or the employers' association, not as a body possessing independent rights against the State, but only as a part of the necessary working machine of the Corporative State itself. The Trade Union and the employers' association thus become parts of the State, each with a definite responsibility and both subject to the controlling power of the State as a whole. The Trade Union may seek to raise wages or improve conditions of work, and the employers' association may seek to reduce wages or to worsen conditions ; but both must bow to the final judgment of the State, and no conflict between group interests must be pushed to the point at which it threatens the security of the State. Compulsory arbitration in industrial matters is therefore an integral part of the Fascist system.

The Fascists contemplate a far more complete disappearance than has actually been secured of the antagonisms between employers and workers. Under the Fascist State employers and workers are to be organised into separate syndicates on a professional basis. But these syndicates are also to come together in corporations representing the industry as a whole, and upon these corporations it was at one time proposed that the responsibility for the conduct of industry should be largely and progressively devolved. With a view to the building up of this new autonomous structure for Italian industry the Fascists established as early as 1923 their Ministry of Corporations ; and in 1926 a National Council of Corporations was brought into being and strengthened subsequently by the legal recognition accorded to it in 1930. But in practice the Council of Corporations has so far worked by bringing together over the whole field of industry the separate associations of employers, manual workers and technicians and professions ; and the unified structure for each industry contemplated in the original scheme has not in fact been brought into effective existence, though some advance towards it has been recently announced. Strikes, since the disturbances which followed the murder of Matteotti, have been few and far between, and the arbitration machinery has worked after a fashion ; but differences between employers and workers have by no means been removed, though their expression has been largely prevented by the complete domination of the Fascist leaders over the new Trade Union movement which they have created.

For in order to advance even as far as they have advanced towards the corporative State the Fascists have been compelled to create a new Trade Union movement of their own. Not content with smashing the machinery of the Socialist and Communist Parties, Fascism also destroyed the existing

Trade Unions of the Italian workers. In their place Mussolini and his colleagues created new Fascist Trade Unions, to which alone were conceded State recognition and the right to enter into collective agreements under the auspices of the Corporative State. Workers were not forbidden to form or belong to other associations standing outside the Fascist system ; but they were compelled to subscribe to the Fascist Unions without acquiring any rights within them unless they became members, and the other associations were reduced to impotence by the refusal of recognition or of the right to make agreements with employers. The old Italian Trade Union movement was thus in process of time almost completely liquidated ; and the new Trade Unions established and maintained under Fascist leadership were fully amenable to the will of the Party which had brought them into existence. Much working-class discontent remained and remains to-day ; but it was left unorganised and without means of expression. The Fascists thus successfully realised, in form at least, their aim of making the Trade Union movement an integral part of the new State.

There is clearly no more than a superficial resemblance between a Trade Union movement thus disciplined and organised under the auspices of the State and the independent self-governing Unions intended by the Syndicalists and Guild Socialists to serve as the effective basis for a new industrial society. Fascism took over from Syndicalism and Guild Socialism something of the idea of self-government in industry ; but it then proceeded to apply this idea in a manner totally inconsistent with either Syndicalist or Guild Socialist aspirations. For although the Guild Socialists, unlike the Syndicalists, did recognise the need for a political State, distinct from the industrial organisation of society, they thought of this State not as a sovereign authority dominating the whole life of society, but as a federal body emanating from the independent economic institutions established for the government of industry. Moreover, both Syndicalism and Guild Socialism contemplated the abolition of class distinctions and the total disappearance of the employing class, and stood for the conduct of industry through self-governing corporations of workers by hand and brain, with the total supersession of private ownership and of the profit motive. Fascism, on the other hand, recognises and seeks to stabilise class distinctions, and sets out to maintain the principles of private property and production for private profit.

On this question of private property and the private exploitation of the means of production the attitude of Fascism is that the State should only interfere with the working of industry to the extent necessary to ensure the stability and success of the social system as a whole. It recognises that there are cases in which interference is necessary and desirable, and that there may be cases in which the State must either directly or through some form of publicly owned corporation take over the actual administration of a particular industry or service, especially where it is in the nature of a monopoly. The ultimate claim of the State to interfere in any field of industry is therefore recognised ; but it is also laid down that interference should in practice occur as seldom as possible, and rest always upon exceptional grounds. Actually, the Fascist State has been led to intervene to a substantial extent, not only in regulating the relations between employers and workers under a system of compulsory arbitration, but also in the actual conduct of industrial enterprise. It has reorganised the banking system with a considerable degree of public participation ; and it has created for the financing of Italian industry the *Instituto Mobiliare Italiano* as a Public Utility Corporation under the supervision of the Ministry of Finance. This new body, set up in November 1931, came into existence largely for the purpose of relieving the *Banca Commerciale* from the burden of its large holdings of industrial shares. These shares were transferred from the bank to a new company, the *Società Finanziaria Industriale*, which was financed mainly by the new *Instituto Mobiliare*. The resources of the *Instituto Mobiliare* itself were drawn in the first instance half from the Post Office Savings Bank of

Italy and half from the private concerns associated in the *Consorzio Mobiliare Finanziario*, which in turn owned a majority of the shares in the *Banca Commerciale*. For additional capital the *Instituto* has power to raise money by means of debentures and interest-bearing bonds ; and it can then grant loans to business enterprises or participate in their share capital. It is thus a sort of semi-public investment trust for the development of Italian industry.

The creation of this body—one of the products of the freezing of the Italian banking system in the course of the world economic crisis—caused considerable misgivings in the minds of some of the Italian capitalists, who feared that it might become the means of realising some of the earlier ambitions of the Fascist leaders towards the nationalisation of industry. Reassuring statements were thereupon issued by the Government ; it was declared emphatically that there was no intention of using the *Instituto* as an indirect instrument of nationalisation, but at the same time the ultimate claim of the Fascist State to intervene in any part of the industrial field in defence of the national interests was emphatically re-affirmed.

The Fascist Party thus combines an insistence on the ultimate right of the State to control every aspect of the economic and social life of the community with a preference for leaving economic matters as far as possible in the hands of the private *entrepreneur*. Drawing its chief support, as it has done in the past, from the *petite bourgeoisie* and the small farmers, Fascism was clearly bound to insist strongly on the rights of private property and on the retention of private enterprise as the basis of the new State. It was able to reconcile this insistence with its totalitarian conception of the State the more easily because of the comparatively undeveloped character of Italian industry and commerce, which still rest largely on a basis of small-scale enterprise. But at the same time, in order to ensure the continued support of the larger capitalist interests, it modified greatly its original bias against large-scale enterprise and accorded the same freedom to the large as to the small employer.

This made it unable to satisfy the aspirations of the industrial workers for improved conditions, and in fact wages have fallen under the Fascist régime, which has consequently but a precarious hold on the support of the industrial workers. It has, however, succeeded in dominating so completely the organisation of the Trade Union movement that working-class discontents, even if they reach a considerable intensity, can find no means of collective expression. Nevertheless, the failure of Fascism to meet the claims of the industrial workers constitutes to-day the chief danger to the stability of the totalitarian State.

The Fascist Party.   Politically, the control exercised by the Fascist Party over the country is complete. As we have seen, the new electoral law of 1928 set up a totally new system of government. Parliament does indeed still exist ; but it has been shorn of almost all its real importance, and so reorganised as to be in fact only a subordinate part of the Fascist machine—a mere registering body for decisions arrived at without consulting it, and occasionally a theatre for the " Duce's " pronouncements. The real power rests with the Fascist Party itself, and the real legislative body in Italy to-day is the Fascist Directory appointed by the head of the State from nominations submitted by a National Council representing the local organisations of the Fascist Party. This Directory works in conjunction with the Fascist Grand Council, a larger body which includes, in addition to a number of Ministers and dignitaries sitting *ex officio*, a body of members also appointed directly by the head of the State, together with four permanent members chosen as a reward for their services in connection with the March on Rome in 1922.

This Grand Council to all intents and purposes chooses the Parliament. The system under which this is done is somewhat complicated. All the syndicates and industrial and professional and cultural organisations recognised by the Fascist State are allowed to submit nominations for membership of Parliament. From the nominations thus gathered

in from the various functional bodies the Fascist Grand
Council then proceeds to select 400, and these 400 then
form the National List of candidates for Parliament put
forward with the approval of the Fascist Party. No other
Party is allowed to nominate candidates, and the entire
electorate is called upon to vote for or against the whole
list of 400 candidates *en bloc*. If the voting goes in their
favour they form the Parliament. If it were to go against
them a new election would have to be held on the basis
of fresh nominations secured in the same way ; but it is
highly improbable that the list would ever be rejected. In
the election following the adoption of this system 90 per
cent of the electorate voted, and nearly 98 per cent of
those who voted voted in favour of the Fascist list.

What else, indeed, were they to do ? For there was no
prospect of securing the return of any alternative candidates. The final stage of the election of candidates for Parliament has thus become practically meaningless, and
Parliament itself has become a body of little or no real
significance in the working of the machine of State. Such
value as the electoral machinery does possess in providing
for the expression of Italian opinion is derived not from the
final voting but from the initial nominations sent forward
by the various associations recognised as integral parts of
the Fascist State. The Fascists claim that this system
secures, in place of the outworn forms of democratic representation under the Parliamentary system, a real representation of those functional groups which have an important
contribution to make to the national life. In place of
the old, and in its view outworn, conception of Parliamentary
democracy it sets up the ideal of functional representation.
Repudiating the democratic theory that each should count
as one and none as more than one, it puts forward instead
a system of functional representation of constituent groups
within the State.

But in practice, as we have seen, the real control rests not
with the Parliament elected in this way, but with the
Fascist Party, which dominates the life of Italy fully as

much as the Communist Party dominates that of Russia. There are, however, important differences between the forms of control exercised by the Communist and Fascist Parties. In the first place, the Fascist Party is far less democratic in its internal methods of organisation than the Communist Party. Built up largely round the personality of Mussolini, it has conferred upon the head of the State enormous powers in choosing his own coadjutors, including not only his colleagues in the Government but all those who are to have an important voice in the councils of the Party. In Russia the Communist Party is a democratic body exercising autocratic authority over non-Communists, whereas Fascism reproduces in the structure of the Party the authoritarian institutions which it has impressed upon the Italian State. In the second place, the authority of the Communist Party in Russia is based on a complete control not only of the political life of the Soviet Republic but also of its economic institutions. Russia has liquidated private capitalism and abolished class distinctions, whereas, in Italy, as we have seen, industry remains under private ownership and State intervention in economic matters continues to be exceptional.

Thus, while there are close resemblances between the position of the Communist Party in Russia and that of the Fascist Party in Italy as far as politics are concerned, in economic matters, which are fundamental, there is little or no resemblance. That is why, whereas the Russian system appears to be established on a secure and permanent basis, it is not possible to affirm with anything like the same certainty that Fascism will endure for long. It has sometimes been suggested that the entire Fascist system depends for its continuance on the personality of Mussolini ; and while this may not be true, it is certainly true that any weakening in the leadership of the Fascist Party could easily cause the entire system to crumble away, for the simple reason that it has not superseded but only been super-imposed upon private Capitalism, and has therefore been compelled to leave in being the underlying antagonisms between economic classes, even while it has successfully checked their expression.

By many critics of the Fascist régime the account here given of it will be deemed far too favourable, on the ground that it accepts to too great an extent the subsequent rationalisation by Fascist advocates of the policy of opportunistic violence actually pursued by the Fascist Party in its march to power. According to these critics, Fascism has no real philosophy or political theory of its own. It is no more than a creed of violence and personal ambition dressed up in the borrowed garments of a belated Hegelianism. It is of course perfectly true that Fascism only found out what its philosophy was when it had already begun to practise it, and that the appeals on which it relied, and continues to rely, in enlisting support have had very little to do with its philosophical basis, save to the extent to which its philosophy has been influential in bringing over a certain percentage of intellectuals to its side. Fascism secured its adherents in its early days by appealing to the resentment, the fears and the violent passions of men who found themselves living in a State devoid of clear purpose, and incapable of sustaining either public order or private welfare. It appealed to the discontented classes with an aggressive economic programme over which it threw a glamour of romantic heroism by its insistence on the national destiny. Though it repudiated the idea of class antagonisms, it nevertheless recruited its adherents largely from classes which rallied to it as a means of defending their class interests against the Socialists ; and it was only able to realise, even to the extent to which it has realised, the totalitarian State by the ruthless suppression of the organisations built up for themselves by the largest class in that State, the manual workers. Though it may claim to express the solidarity of the Italian people, it has to be recognised that this claim still rests on force and not on positive or willing consent. Hence the continued necessity for rigid censorship of Press and opinion, the insistence on strict tests of orthodoxy among the teachers in schools and universities, and the continued elimination of all expressions of opinion hostile to or even critical of the underlying assumptions of the Fascist system.

Nevertheless, Fascism can claim to be a philosophy, even if this philosophy has grown out of events rather than determined their course. For it has successfully set up for the time being a society based on the philosophy of nationalism, and thrown back the attacks launched against nationalism by the cosmopolitan philosophy which underlies the Socialist as well as the Communist doctrine. Socialism and Communism are philosophies based on accepting as ultimate the solidarity of class ; Fascism is a philosophy which attempts to combat these doctrines by appealing to the rival ideal of nationality. And even the Marxists, who believe that in the end economic forces are bound to exert a predominant influence, do not attempt to deny that nationality is a force working in the minds of men and capable, because it is in men's minds, of playing an influential part, at least in the short run, in shaping the course of history.

§ 5. FASCISM IN GERMANY

SINCE the rise of Fascism in Italy there has been a growing tendency to apply the name to a wide variety of political movements in different European countries. Wherever Parliamentary institutions are abandoned or their influence seriously curtailed in favour of some form of dictatorship, this dictatorship is loosely described as Fascist, provided only that it is a dictatorship directed against the influence of Socialist and Communist movements. The name Fascism is thus loosely used to cover a number of political developments differing considerably among themselves. For example, in the Austria of 1933 the dictatorship of the Christian Social Chancellor, Dr. Dollfuss, is commonly described as Fascist, although it is at present in violent conflict with the Austrian section of the Nazis ; and again the dictatorship of Primo de Rivera in Spain was often regarded as a Fascist movement, although it was in reality rather an attempt to preserve the Crown against the combined onslaught of the republican forces than a Fascist movement originating among the nationalist sections of the middle class. We have, then, to make up our minds whether we propose to use the term Fascist in a sense wide enough to cover all the post-war European movements directed from the Right against the institutions of Parliamentarism, or whether we propose to confine its use to such movements as possess a closer community of idea with Italian Fascism.

There is undoubtedly something in common among all the movements of the Right against Parliamentary government, for they are in all cases the product of the failure of the Parliamentary State to face satisfactorily the difficult situations of the post-war world. As we have seen in an earlier section, this failure of the Parliamentary State has been most manifest and complete where Parliamentarism has had the weakest tradition behind it, as in Italy and Germany, and has been made the more unavoidable by the attempt to impress a national democratic character on Parliamentarism by the adoption of proportional represen-tation. For the one chance that Parliamentarism might have stood of successful survival in Central and Southern Europe rested on its ability to create instruments of strong and coherent government, and thus to pursue a steady and continuous line of policy ; and the possibility of this rested in turn on the existence of parties strong enough to com-mand an effective majority. France, with her tradition of democratic self-government, has been able so far to make shift with a succession of weak Governments alternating between the right and left of the middle-class parties ; but French methods of government were bound to prove totally inadequate in dealing with the far more difficult problems which confronted post-war Italy, and, still more, the new German Republic.

While however, some community of character must be recognised among all the non-Socialist reactions away from

Parliamentary government, it is both more convenient and more accurate to confine the use of the term Fascist to a narrower group of post-war movements. Of these by far the most important, after the Italian movement described in the preceding section, is the Nazi movement which has come to full political power in Germany during 1933. For the Nazis, or National Socialists, while their attitude differs in certain respects from that of the Italian Fascists, and they have so far given less indication of having a workable political or economic theory in their minds, have drawn their support largely from the same elements as rallied round Mussolini's Fascist organisations in the years immediately following the war. Nazism is, like Italian Fascism, a movement drawing its main strength from the lower middle classes and the peasants, though it has also rallied round it a considerable amount of support both from military officers of the old régime and sons of the old nobility, and from workmen feeling the pinch of Germany's desperate economic condition, and despairing of any succour from a working-class movement sharply divided between the rival factions of Social Democrats and Communists. Hitler's Brown Army has been, like Mussolini's Blackshirts, from the first a largely military formation, though it has been until lately far shorter of arms than Mussolini's men ever were, largely because of the steps taken to secure the thorough disarmament of Germany under the Peace Treaty. Moreover, attaining to its full strength a decade and a half after the conclusion of the war, it has not drawn its support to anything like the same extent as Mussolini's Fascists drew theirs from the disappointed ex-soldiers demobilised at the conclusion of hostilities. The Nazis, apart from their leaders, are largely young men—too young to have taken any part in the Great War. Their fighting quality is therefore probably substantially lower and their discipline is certainly less than that of Mussolini's armed Fascists at the time of the March on Rome. That they have been able to take control so completely of the situation in Germany and to apply force on so large a scale with so little resistance is attributable far less to their own disciplined prowess than to the weakness or absence of military formations among the forces opposing them. There can be no doubt that if the *Reichswehr* and the *Stahlhelm* organisations had been united with the support of the police in stopping Hitler's Brown Army from unconstitutional excesses, the task would have been well within their powers. That, no doubt, was why the Nazis needed the support of President Hindenburg and of the Nationalists in order to establish their control. For as soon as they had the *Reichswehr* as well as the *Stahlhelm* on their side, or at least definitely precluded from opposing them, there was nothing to stand in their way. The Republican *Reichsbanner* was too weak and practically without arms ; and the Communist organisations had also been successfully deprived of their weapons under the previous régime.

Hitler's Nazis are thus a far less effective military force than Mussolini's Fascists, but the two movements spring largely from a common source. Hitler, like Mussolini, is an ex-Socialist, and, unlike Mussolini, he still retains the word Socialist in the name of his Party. Like Mussolini, he has built up his movement on the appeal to national emotion ; and, again like Mussolini, he has sought his backing chiefly among those elements in the population which can be most easily rallied not only against the international doctrine of the Communists but also against all plans for the socialisation of industry. Hitler's constant denunciations of Jews, bankers and speculators are calculated to appeal not only to the nationalist sentiments of his hearers but also to the peasant and small *bourgeois* groups from which he derived his original strength. Like Mussolini, he began with a programme embodying large elements of Socialism ; but the Socialist features of the Nazi programme have receded more and more into the background, to be replaced, not so far by any clear picture of the Corporative State, but by a vast outpouring of rhetoric attributing Germany's economic troubles to the injustices put upon her by the Treaties of Peace, and to the machinations of the enemies within her gates—the Jewish internationalists, the international Marxians, who are reputed in the last decade to have governed Germany in alliance with the Jews, the great stores, which are accused in one breath of profiteering at the expense of the public and of undercutting the small private trader, and, finally, even the Catholics, who are said to have demonstrated their lack of patriotism by allying themselves in a succession of Governments with the atheistical and internationalist leaders of the Social Democratic Party. Out of the farrago of denunciations that makes up Hitler's speeches it is difficult to make anything like sense. But it is quite unsafe to conclude that an inability to talk sense is any barrier in the way of success in governing a nation, especially under the topsy-turvy economic and political conditions of to-day.

It is true that not all Hitler's lieutenants have been content with a mere whirl of denunciatory words. Gregor Strasser, for example, was long regarded as the real intellectual leader of the Nazis, and the chief exponent of their economic policy ; but Strasser parted company with his fellow leaders, and lost his influence, in 1932, when the Nazis were confronting the choice between entering into a coalition on terms which would have made it impossible for them to carry out the complete " purge " of Germany which they demanded, and holding aloof in the hope that time would allow complete power to fall into their hands. Strasser, advocating coalition at the cost of compromise, was driven from his influential position in the Party ; and the leadership then passed, with Hitler still as figure-head, to extremists of the type of Goebbels and Goering, whose policy, as far as it is at present known, appears to be purely destructive. Conceivably, now that the Nazis have climbed to power, Strasser will come back, or perhaps some able ally such as Schacht will be able to take hold of the dislocated economic machine. But of this there is as yet no sign. The destructive policy of the Nazis is plain enough ; their constructive policy remains an entirely unknown quantity.

The Rise of the Nazis. Nazism began as an organised movement, not in North Germany where it has since attained to its greatest power, but in Bavaria. Hitler, an Austrian by birth, began organising his National Socialists in Bavaria in 1919. As we have seen earlier, the German revolution of 1918 actually began in Bavaria, and it was there that the first revolutionary Government was established under the leadership of Kurt Eisner, the Independent Socialist. But Eisner was assassinated by a royalist fanatic, and after a short-lived Communist insurrection, a Government under Social Democratic leadership assumed office. But Socialism in Bavaria had been fatally weakened by the events of 1919, and soon after the Prussian Kapp Putsch of 1920 the Socialist Ministry resigned and an anti-Socialist Government took its place. At the following elections a large anti-Socialist majority was returned, and, with the support of the new Government, the Communist movement was rigorously suppressed. It was in this atmosphere of revolution and counter-revolution that Hitler created his Nazi organisation, hovering at first between the demand for Bavarian separatism and the creation of a powerful pan-German State.

After 1920 the Nazi movement became more and more pan-German in its attitude ; and in 1923, joined by Ludendorff and the most extreme section of German militarists, it attempted a counter-revolution, designed, setting out from Munich, to overthrow the Weimar Republic. The Bavarian Government, by the use of dictatorial powers, successfully repressed this revolution, and Hitler was condemned in April 1924 to five years' detention in a fortress. He was, however, released within a few months, and set to work immediately to reorganise his National Socialist Party, which thereafter spread gradually from Bavaria to other parts of Germany, although it was some time before it achieved any great importance in German politics, or came to be regarded as in any real sense a menace to the stability of the Weimar Republic. In the general elections of 1924 the Hitlerites, then allied to the *Deutsche Völkische-Freiheits-bewegung*

(German People's Movement for Freedom) gained 32 seats. But in 1928, after it had broken with its late ally, it was only able to return 12 members. Its real chance came only with the world slump ; and by far the most effective recruiting agent for the Hitlerites has undoubtedly been the economic suffering which has overtaken the German people ever since the withdrawal of foreign capital began towards the close of 1928.

Between 1924 and 1928 Germany had maintained an illusory internal prosperity by means of heavy borrowing of capital from overseas. The withdrawal of this capital, chiefly on account of the American boom, left her for the first time since the Dawes Plan faced with the necessity of living upon her own attenuated resources, and at the same time meeting the heavy claims both of her late enemies for reparations and of foreign capitalists for interest on the large sums which she had borrowed. Conditions in 1929 were bad enough, but they became infinitely worse when Germany had to face not only the withdrawal of foreign capital but also the effects of the American crash and the world depression on her export trade. The Nazi movement, a product above all of disillusionment and despair, went ahead by leaps and bounds from the moment when the politicians at the head of the Weimar Republic ceased to be able to maintain tolerable living conditions for the mass of the German people, including the middle classes as well as the manual workers. At the election of July 1932 the Nazis returned 230 members and polled $13\frac{3}{4}$ million votes. Thereafter came a reaction, and at the election of November 1932, on a reduced total poll, the Nazi members fell to 196, and their vote to $11\frac{3}{4}$ millions. It was then widely prophesied that Nazism had already passed its zenith, and was certain rapidly to decline. This prophecy might possibly have been correct, if, as many people then supposed to be likely, there had been a material improvement in the economic situation. But economically things went from bad to worse during the following months, and in February 1933, when Hitler had already become Chancellor and established his Nazi dictatorship, the Nazis polled $17\frac{1}{4}$ million votes and returned 288 members, thus falling not far short of an absolute majority in the Reichstag, and commanding, in the enforced absence of the Communists, an effective majority in conjunction with their 52 Nationalist allies.

It was upon a coalition Government headed by the Social Democrats that the first brunt of the great economic depression fell. Divided internally, the Government had great difficulty in pursuing any coherent policy in face of the depression. In 1929 it found itself seriously at loggerheads with Dr. Schacht, the right-wing President of the Reichsbank. Dr. Schacht's public denunciations of the Hague Conference settlement led to the resignation of Hilferding, the Social Democratic Finance Minister, and to a weakening of the position of the Social Democrats in the country, although continued differences between Dr. Schacht and the Government resulted in the resignation of the former early in 1930. Meanwhile, the financial situation continued to grow worse, and the differences in the Cabinet over the best means of meeting it more pronounced. The parties of the Right, including the People's Party, demanded a drastic curtailment of unemployment benefits and other social services ; and on this issue the coalition Government broke up in March 1930, and was succeeded by a *bourgeois* Government under the leadership of Brüning, a member of the Catholic Centre. This Government, in face of the growing severity of the crisis, was compelled at once to have resort to emergency powers, using the authority of the President to put through its measures by decree even without the co-operation of the Reichstag.

As the depression deepened these measures became more and more severe ; for Germany under Brüning's leadership was making a tremendous effort to build up, even in face of adverse world conditions, a substantial export surplus for the payment of reparations and the meeting of claims arising out of Germany's foreign borrowing since the war. This could be achieved even temporarily only by the most drastic curtailment of imports, and at the cost of a severe and progressive fall in the standard of living of the German people. Nevertheless the Brüning Cabinet carried on, and appeared for a time to be meeting with signal success. But this success was achieved only at the cost of engendering in the minds of a large section of the German people a mood of desperation which boded ill for the future of a Republic connected in the popular imagination with the inflicting of these sacrifices. Brüning's position consequently became more and more difficult to maintain ; and at length in June 1932, in face of the tremendous growth of the Nazi movement and of popular discontent, President Hindenburg dismissed the Chancellor and on his own authority set up a non-party Government of pronounced Nationalist complexion under the leadership of von Papen. Thereafter negotiations began for an accommodation with the Nazis ; but Hitler, after some hesitation, refused to collaborate in a coalition Government in which his Party was not offered a free hand. The new Reichstag, elected in July 1932, was thereupon dissolved, and another election held in November with the result, as we have seen, of a temporary setback to the Nazis. But popular discontent with the aristocratic Nationalist Government of von Papen continued to grow, and in December 1932 President Hindenburg was compelled much against his will to get rid of his unpopular Chancellor, who was replaced by General von Schleicher.

Von Schleicher, who was also associated with the forces of the old Right in Germany, attempted to appease the discontent by following a more moderate policy than von Papen, and did his best to come to terms with the Trade Unions and to obtain at least the tolerance of the Social Democrats. But his Ministry was short-lived. The Nazi movement became more and more menacing, and in January 1933 President Hindenburg at last sent for Hitler and offered him the Chancellorship. The precise conditions on which this offer was made cannot be known ; but it is clear that they included the association with the new

Government under Hitler's leadership of the old Nationalists —President Hindenburg's friends—as well as the Nazis, and that the President relied on von Papen, who was included in the new Government, and the other Nationalist Ministers, to do something to keep the Nazis in order. In practice, however, the entire power passed into the hands of the Nazis ; for although von Papen became Vice-Chancellor and Reichs Commissioner for Prussia (the autonomous Government of Prussia based on a coalition led by the Social Democrats having been superseded by a Commissioner appointed by the Reich under von Papen's Ministry), the real power in Prussia was exercised by the Nazi, Captain Göring, as Deputy Commissioner of the Interior. The new Government immediately instituted a reign of terror. Jews and Social Democrats, as well as Communists, were remorselessly persecuted ; and a thorough weeding out of all officials unsympathetic to the new Nazi régime was begun. The Nazis seized power and installed Commissioners of their own with dictatorial authority not only in the States in which they and their allies commanded a majority in the legislatures, but also in the free cities, such as Hamburg, and even in the German States beyond the Main line, including Catholic Bavaria.

Since then, Nazism has carried the revolution several stages further. It has successfully edged its Nationalist allies out of their positions of influence, merged the Nationalist *Stalhelm* with its own forces, compelled Hugenburg to resign from the Government, and the Nationalist Party itself to dissolve and join the Nazi ranks. It has pursued successfully a vendetta against " political " Catholicism, which it regards as the ally of Dollfuss's Christian Social dictatorship in Austria, and has persecuted and broken up the Catholic Bavarian People's Party and the Catholic Centre. It has set to work to eliminate the Protestant Churches of Prussia, by installing its own nominees in ecclesiastical authority. It has destroyed the largely Socialist Trade Union movement, and begun to set up a new workers' directory under its own authoritative control. In short, it has set itself to dominate, in the name of the Nazi State, every aspect of the life of the German people, and to break up by violence every organisation, secular or clerical, that is capable of offering any sort of opposition to its complete authority.

Wholesale arrests of Communists and Social Democrats, and in some cases of members of the Catholic Centre as well, have been carried out, to the accompaniment of much ruthless brutality ; and the members of the Brown Army, enrolled and clothed with authority as auxiliary police, indulged in an orgy of domiciliary visits to suspected persons, in the course of which a number of Socialists and Communists were brutally shot down. Moreover, in the disorder accompanying the imposition of the new tyranny, numerous murders were committed, and arrests made by bands of Nazis acting without a shadow of public authority. Citizens hostile to the Nazi régime were kidnapped and confined in private houses and subjected to many brutalities. It is indeed impossible at present to estimate accurately the extent of the reign of terror which the Nazis established in Germany during the first weeks of their tenure of power ; but enough news soon filtered across the frontiers, in spite of the rigid censorship, to show that the Nazis were going far beyond the methods practised by the followers of Mussolini on the morrow of their triumph in 1922.

Nazism has thus assumed completely tyrannical power within the frontiers of Germany ; for, although the Nazis are still governing nominally in coalition with ex-Nationalist upholders of the pre-war régime, they have in fact completely eliminated and destroyed their allies, and succeeded in having matters all their own way. Obviously this change in the internal situation of Germany is destined to have far-reaching effects on the European situation as a whole. The Weimar Republic is clearly doomed. For, although it is quite uncertain whether the Nazis intend to restore a monarchical form of government, they have shown that they have no use for the *bourgeois* Republic. And it is hardly less clear that, even if the Nazis are in process of time overthrown, the new organisation of Germany which takes their place will be something very different from the Parliamentary Republic established on the morrow of the Great War. For a time at least the Nazis can be expected to remain in power ; for there is at present certainly no force in Germany capable of standing up against them, even if their alliance with the Nationalists should be broken. The old Social Democratic Party, though its leaders have moved their headquarters to Prague, and are attempting to carry on underground propaganda in Germany from abroad, is clearly dead past recall ; and it is still too soon to say what new force on the Left—whether the Communist Party, or some new body born out of the ashes of Social Democracy, or again some revolutionary force germinated out of Nazism itself, is likely to take its place.

The Nazis have been brought to power on a wave of Nationalist sentiment and profound economic distress. They have made lavish promises of their ability to deal with the situation, which they trace primarily not to the economic disorders of the world as a whole, but rather to the hardships inflicted on Germany by the Versailles Treaty. They are demanding first of all the right for Germany to rearm ; and such hope as there ever was for the successful outcome of the Geneva Disarmament Conference has largely disappeared as a result of their assumption of power. Certainly the Nazis mean to rearm Germany as far as they can afford to do so, and perhaps further, and as fast as they feel strong enough to stand up to the political consequences of defying France and Great Britain. But rearmament is desired not only for its own sake, but also as a symbol of restored German nationhood, and a throwing off once and for all of the enforced repentance exacted from Germany in the Versailles Treaty. Hitler and his followers have again and again denounced the Treaty itself, and the entire territorial settlement embodied in it, as well as the disarmament of Germany. They have never been prepared to recognise the Locarno Treaties or to accept the rearrangement of Germany's frontiers as permanent. They mean, if they are strong enough, to challenge the entire Versailles settlement. They will presumably be wary of picking a quarrel with France over Alsace-Lorraine in the immediate future; for France is bound to remain for some time to come the greatest military Power in Europe. But they have already shown signs of a readiness to pick a quarrel before long with the Poles over the Polish Corridor and the Silesian frontier. To say this is not to suggest that there is an immediate prospect of armed conflict between Poland and Germany; for the Nazis will obviously wish to reorganise their forces before they are ready to begin fighting for their claims. Germany must rearm before she can venture to fight, for the Polish Army is large and well-equipped. What is meant is that the new movement which has come to power in Germany rests on a state of mind of aggressive nationalism which will certainly not in the long run refrain from challenging by armed force the territorial settlement made at Versailles. Nor does it appear possible that the embargo imposed by the Peace Treaty on German rearmament can be maintained, especially in face of the failure of the Allied Powers to implement their own promises that German disarmament would be but the prelude to international measures of disarmament which would once more establish equality.

If, however, a Germany intent on rearmament is to have any hope of satisfying her ambitions she must at all costs find allies. Where, then, is she to seek for help? She must obviously turn to Italy, where another Fascist Government is in power, and where jealousy of France and serious dissatisfaction with the terms of the post-war European settlement also exist. But will the Italians, under Mussolini's skilful leadership, be prepared to respond to the German overtures—at any rate to the extent of threatening Europe seriously with another war? Mussolini, despite many warlike utterances since he assumed power, has never shown in the last resort any wish to take up arms, at all events against any Power that could be regarded as Italy's equal. The question is whether the change in Germany will bring about a change in Italian policy as well, and lead the Italians, now that they are in a position to find allies, towards a more bellicose frame of mind.

Clearly, if there is to be any question of an alliance with military aims between Germany and Italy, the position of Austria, placed between these two Fascist powers, comes to be of vital significance. France, in resisting ever since the war the repeated attempts to bring about an *Anschluss* between Austria and Germany, has had always in mind the danger of an alliance, made stronger by a common frontier, between Germany and Italy. If Austria's present Christian Social Dictatorship were to yield, as many people think it will, to a Nazi dictatorship, based on an alliance between the Austrian Nazis and the Heimwehr, the political union of Austria and Germany would be virtually accomplished even if they remained nominally separate States. The triumph of Fascism in Austria would create a Fascist *bloc* running continuously from the Baltic to the Mediterranean, and shutting off France effectively from the allies she has been at pains to create for herself in Central and Eastern Europe. This Fascist *bloc* would have on one side of it France, Great Britain and the smaller Powers of Western Europe, and on the other Poland and the Little Entente, with Russia watching anxiously from the east the renewal of hostile alliances in capitalist Europe.

At present, the chief obstacle to this development is to be found in Italy ; for the Italians, while they are ready enough to rejoice over the triumph of Fascism in Germany, have at present no desire to precipitate a European conflict, or to have the fresh complication of active German influence and intervention reintroduced into the tangled international politics of Southern Europe. Accordingly Mussolini, while he has shown an attitude of friendship to the new Germany, has evidently declared for the present against a Nazi *coup* in Austria, and has encouraged the Austrian Government to adopt a firm policy in resisting Nazi aggression. How long this attitude will be, or can be, maintained is uncertain ;

but while it lasts it undoubtedly helps to preserve a precarious peace in Europe. For if the Nazis once get Austria, there will be immediate and powerful repercussions on the political situation both in Hungary and in the countries which form the Little Entente—to say nothing of the effect on France of the virtual establishment of the *Anschluss* which she has been resisting ever since 1918.

At a time when speculations such as these are in the minds of every student of European politics, Briand's ideal of a United States of Europe on a capitalist basis seems remote indeed. The Nazi triumph in Germany has made dramatically apparent what was already going on under the surface—a new division of Europe west of Russia into a number of armed camps dominated as in the years before 1914 by the threat of war.

§ 6. THE CHALLENGE OF COMMUNISM

THE FIRST great challenge of which men became aware after the war was that of Russian Communism. From the moment of the Bolshevik victory in the second Russian Revolution of 1917 men were everywhere conscious of the emergence into the field of politics of a great new revolutionary force. For the Russian Revolution was not merely by far the greatest since the French Revolution of 1789, but also as unlike any previous revolution as that of 1789 had been unlike anything which the world had known before. There were indeed certain features in the Bolshevik Revolution of 1917 which recalled the events of the Paris Commune of 1871, to which Socialists had always looked back as the example on a tiny scale of what a Socialist Revolution might be, if it had to come by violent means. But the difference of scale was too vast for the analogy of the Paris Commune to hold good ; and outside a narrow circle of theoretical Socialists people in Western Europe knew little of the detailed history of the Paris Commune or of the political principles which had found expression in it. The Russian Revolution appealed to them, with whatever feelings they regarded it, as something totally new in the history of the world, something fundamentally startling to a degree which compelled them to go back to the first principles of politics in determining their attitude.

The Bolshevik Revolution was fully as startling to most Socialists as to men of other opinions ; for up to 1917 the great majority of Socialists had supposed that Socialism, when it came, would be certain to come first in the most advanced industrial countries, which were held to be the ripest for it because they had advanced furthest along the path of large-scale industrialisation, and had therefore created within themselves the strongest working-class organisations and the most widespread Socialist movements. It seemed altogether contrary to the anticipated course of evolution that Socialism should come first in a country where the vast majority of the people were peasants living on the land at a very low standard of life, where the number of industrial workers was insignificant, and there had been no prior evolution in the direction of Socialism under the capitalist system. On these grounds many Socialists, including the most prominent theorists of German Social Democracy, held that the Russian Revolution could not possibly establish itself permanently as a Socialist Revolution, and indeed that it had no right to have happened at all. It was, according to these Socialists, indispensable that a country on its way towards Socialism should pass through all the stages of evolution belonging to the capitalist phase, and that only when Capitalism had within a country developed its full potentialities and come to be a fetter upon the further advancement of the productive forces would the time be ripe for an attempt to put Socialism into operation. Many Socialists held further that the adoption of a complete form of political democracy was no less indispensable as a forerunner of Social Democracy, and that in a country where the vast mass of the people had never attained to any share in the government it would be wholly impossible to create at a blow the conditions necessary for the operation of a Socialist system. These Socialists —including at this stage many Russian Socialists—would have had the Russian Revolution stop short at the phase which it reached in the first Revolution of 1917, or rather they would have had it halt there on the basis of a *bourgeois* Parliamentary Republic, and then develop gradually through the stages of Capitalism which Russia had still to accomplish to the point at which it would be ripe for Socialists to attempt to take control.

Over this issue there arose on the morrow of the November Revolution of 1917 a bitter controversy between the Russian Bolshevists and the Social Democrats of Western Europe and especially of Germany—a controversy enshrined in the literature of the movement in the vituperative volumes of Lenin on the one side and Karl Kautsky on the other. According to Lenin, the second Russian Revolution was the fulfilment within a particular sphere of the course of action laid down for the proletariat by Marx and Engels : according to Kautsky it was an impudent attempt by a small body of fanatics to seize power long before the conditions for the coming of Socialism had been secured.

Nevertheless the Bolsheviks made their revolution, and made it with immediate success after waiting for a number of months in order to be assured of striking at the moment most favourable to their cause. There had been talk of a Bolshevik Revolution earlier in the year, especially in July. But Lenin had been firm in urging the Party to hold its hand until the conditions of success were present, that is to say, until the Revolution could be made under such circumstances as would place the Bolsheviks at the head of a widespread movement among the mass of the population. Lenin, quite as much as Kautsky, repudiated the idea of a revolutionary *coup d'état*, to be carried through by a small minority of class-conscious persons, irrespective of the ripeness of the general body of working-class opinion for according positive support. He would have nothing to do with the purely insurrectionary theory of revolution ; but he held that the time was ripe in October, as it had not been in July, because by October the Bolsheviks had won over to their side a majority in the Workers' and Soldiers' Councils which had sprung up at the time of the first Revolution, and were therefore in a position to use these mass organisations of the working class as instruments of their policy.

This was indeed the essence of the policy which Lenin and his group were attempting to follow. Their theory was that the mass of the workers must, if revolutionary action was to succeed, be brought under the leadership of a strong and disciplined group which knew what it wanted and was prepared to be ruthless in working for the achievement of its aims. But they held equally that this disciplined group would be powerless, however much determination it might show, unless it could get on its side the mass organisations of the workers, and carry through the Revolution with their positive support. Thus the Bolshevik Revolution was based on the two forces which have been fundamental ever since to the Communist régime in Russia—a strong disciplined party bound together by a common ideology and a common body of revolutionary strategy, and an organised mass movement based upon the workers and capable of being brought under the leadership of the far smaller party.

Given these conditions, Lenin and those who were working with him in the Russian Bolshevik Party saw no reason why the Revolution should not come first in Russia rather than in one of the more advanced industrial countries. They repudiated indeed the view that the Revolution could be thought of at all fundamentally upon national lines. The Revolution which they were making in Russia was only part of a world Revolution destined to come in all capitalist countries, and to carry the world on from the capitalist phase of social evolution to a new Socialist phase. That the Revolution should come first in Russia only meant that the fighting broke out most hotly at that particular point of a firing line that ran round the whole world, and that, at this particular point, the defences of Capitalism were first broken ; because, even if the industrial proletariat was less numerous in Russia than in the more advanced countries, so also was Capitalism far weaker and far more easily exhausted by the experience of three years of war.

The Bolsheviks were not making a *Russian* Revolution. They were making a *world* Revolution, and merely beginning it in their own country because there the opportunity for making it had come first. Lenin indeed recognised that the less advanced character of the Russian economy made it impossible for the Bolsheviks, however thorough their seizure of power might be, to leap straight from an undeveloped Capitalism to a Socialist system. He agreed with Kautsky that Russia would have to pass through all the stages of capitalist evolution before she could arrive at the achievement of Socialism. But, unlike Kautsky, he held that these later stages of Capitalism could be gone through under Socialist instead of capitalist control—and gone through under these conditions much more speedily and far less disastrously for the workers. What Lenin aimed at building immediately for Russia he always described not as Socialism or Communism but as State Capitalism—a State Capitalism to be achieved under the auspices of a proletarian State based upon disciplined Communist control. Russia, according to the Communists, is not to-day a Communist country. It is still completing, with its successive Five-Year Plans and its socialisation of agriculture, the stages of State capitalist development ; and only when this phase has been completed will the creation of a Communist society become possible. Then, in Lenin's phrase, the State—the new proletarian State created by the workers in place of the Capitalist State which they have destroyed —will " wither away." Government of men will give place to administration of things ; and the need for coercion will disappear in proportion as the new classless community is brought effectively into being. The Proletarian State based upon the working class has the object of abolishing itself together with both the class which it is out to destroy and the class by means of which it wields its authority. In

the classless Society of to-morrow there will be no State—
even in a proletarian sense.

Communism and the State.   It is the fundamental
thesis of the Communists, as it was of Marx, that the tasks
which the State has to accomplish in the achievement of
Socialism call for the creation of a totally new kind of
State for their execution. It will never do, Marx and
Lenin alike say, merely to take over, by the capture of a
Parliamentary majority, the political machinery of the
bourgeois State, and to try to use this machinery for the
achievement of Socialism. For the *bourgeois* State has been
designed with quite different objects, and is not capable
of being used for a purpose radically different from that
which brought it into being. The *bourgeois* State was born
with the coming of Capitalism, is suited to the maintenance of Capitalism, rests upon capitalist principles and
ideas, and is therefore not merely useless as an instrument
for bringing the Socialist community into being, but positively destructive of the Socialism of those who attempt to
use it for this purpose.

For deeply embedded in the whole idea of the capitalist
State as it exists to-day is the notion of private property,
and the defence of private property ; and no less deeply
embedded in it is the notion of individualism, expressing
itself through an individual liberty which is also conceived
largely as a property right. Individual liberty and property were chiefly the ideals proclaimed by the French
Revolution ; and the world importance of the French
Revolution lay in creating a new type of State thoroughly
adjusted to the needs of an expanding capitalist system.
The entire code of law which capitalist States administer
is based on the defence of individual property rights. The
police, the Civil Service, the Constitution itself, exist
primarily for the defence of these rights. Even the army
is mainly the instrument for defending the property rights of
one group of nationals against the claims of others, or for
the appropriation of property rights by means of imperialist

exploitation. But the property rights thus embedded in the Capitalist State are not rights in effect belonging to every individual. They are chiefly the monopoly of a single class—the capitalist class—which owns by far the greater part of the social property which the law is called upon to defend, and uses this property as means of exploiting labour. For from the right to exploit labour the value of capitalist property is exclusively derived. If there were no propertyless labourers for the capitalist to employ in his factories or mines these giant instruments of production would be of no value to him, because he could not extract from their use one iota of profit.

Accordingly, in pledging itself to the defence of property, the capitalist State is in effect pledging itself to the defence of the system of capitalist exploitation—to the defence of the property of the " Haves " against the demands of the " Have Nots " for a share in the fruits of social labour. It is impossible, the Communists say, to change the character of a State pledged to the defence of these ultimate capitalist rights. Socialism, which challenges the entire right of property in the means of production, and claims that the entire product of man's social labour upon the means of production ought to be common property in accordance with the essentially social character of the productive process, must create for itself a political instrument based upon these new ideas of socialisation, and therefore actively in opposition to capitalist notions of property and individual rights.

In seeking for a basis for this new instrument of socialisation Communists repudiate not only the capitalist conception of the rights of property but also the capitalist conception of individual liberty. For the effective liberty of the individual depends under Capitalism upon his possession of property. The equal liberty which the law and the State nominally afford him is to a great extent valueless unless he possesses as a basis for its use the economic security which in such a society property alone can give. Moreover, the basis of the new society must be sought not in the individual but in something more closely in accord with the growingly social character of the processes of living. More real than the individual in a political sense is the class—the body of persons who fulfil in the process of production at a given stage of social development a common economic function, and occupy by virtue of that function a common economic status. To the class it is necessary to look for the instrument which is to serve as a basis for the new State needed for the building up of Socialism. In place, therefore, of the insistence on individual rights—the right, for example, of each man and woman to an individual vote—Communism seeks rather to base its new political institutions upon the collective rights of the class through which it attempts to further the coming of Socialism—the working class. It wants a political instrument collectively expressing the will of the working-class; and the question of individual voting seems to it quite secondary to this primary desideratum.

The Communists found the appropriate instrument of which they were in search, not in the pre-existing organisations of the workers—Trade Unions, Co-operative Societies and the like—but in new mass organisations arising in and out of the Revolution. For Trade Unions and Co-operative Societies have alike grown up in order to satisfy the needs of the workers under Capitalism, and have accordingly taken on a character and a point of view largely influenced by the capitalist environment in which they have had to work. Co-operative Societies under Capitalism must compete with the private traders and the Joint Stock Companies, and must, in order to do this, behave largely as capitalists behave. The Trade Unions must bargain with employers or employers' associations and arrive with their adversaries at terms of accommodation which will allow work to proceed and wages to be paid under conditions which capitalists can be induced to accept. Neither of these forms of working-class organisation therefore possesses a revolutionary character, or at least can retain that character when it meets with success and establishes itself as a recognised institution within a capitalist Society. The Trade Unions, and to a less extent, the Co-operative

Societies, have been invaluable training grounds for the workers, and have performed indispensable tasks in bringing them together and giving them a sense of collective strength and authority ; but, though they may still be needed within a revolutionary society, and may indeed find within such a society a greatly expanded sphere of work and influence in giving collective expansion to the social life of the workers, they can hardly be used directly as the foundations for the building up of the new revolutionary instrument of Government.

For this, something far more directly expressive of a revolutionary will among the mass of the workers is clearly needed. In the earlier phases of the Russian Revolution, as in those of the German Revolution a year later, this instrument came almost spontaneously into being, as indeed it had done earlier in that great dress rehearsal for the events of 1917, the Russian Revolution of 1905. The Councils (*Soviets* in Russia, *Räte* in Germany) of Workers, Soldiers and Peasants, were the direct expressions of the general mass of the working class in its revolutionary frame of mind, and were therefore the natural foundation on which the initial structure of the new proletarian State could be built. But these bodies—spontaneous expressions of mass sentiment—had, before they could be used for this task, to be infused with far clearer and more conscious revolutionary conceptions in the sphere of policy as well as of mass feeling. This could be accomplished only if the disciplined revolutionary party which believed itself to be the true expression of the workers' needs and aspirations could take firm hold of them and make them the instruments of its will. Through the middle months of 1917 this was being gradually achieved in Russia as the indispensable preparation for the second and conclusive stage of the Revolution. That it was never achieved in Germany was due partly to the far greater hold of the German Majority Socialists over a large section of the German working class, and partly to the absence in Germany of any strong revolutionary party corresponding to the Bolshevik Party in Russia. For, though the Spartacists possessed the necessary revolutionary will, they had no such basis of common preparation as the Russian Bolsheviks had gained during their years of exile, nor were they nearly strong enough in personnel to make their influence felt to the necessary extent ; while the Independent Socialists, who to a large extent acted with them, had no clear-cut theoretical ideas at all, but hovered between a half-acceptance of the parliamentary and constitutional ideas of the majority on the one hand and a half-allegiance to Communism on the other.

In Russia, on the other hand, the Bolsheviks were strong enough, determined enough and united enough to accomplish their purpose ; but it must not be forgotten that they were greatly helped in this by the comparative weakness of the other Russian Socialist Parties. By far the largest of these was the Social Revolutionary Party, which had its main strength among the peasants. But this party had little coherence and was greatly weakened by the very fact that its supporters were found among the scattered peasantry all over the country rather than among the highly concentrated, though numerically far inferior, groups of the industrial workers. When the time came the Bolsheviks, with the temporary aid of the Left Wing of the Social Revolutionaries led by Spiridonova, were able to sweep aside both the far larger Right Social Revolutionary Party and the Menshevik Social Democrats. These last, sharing the German Social Democratic view that it was necessary to build up the Constitutional Parliamentary State before advancing directly towards Socialism, were prepared to ally themselves with the *bourgeois* parties of the Left, and in doing so largely forfeited their support among the main body of the working class. For the workers, amid the collapse of the old Russian system, were in a definitely revolutionary mood, ready to be led towards the complete seizure of power at which the Bolsheviks were aiming. Above all they wanted peace, because of the sufferings which war had brought with it and from total lack of sympathy with the political aims of Tsardom. The attempt under the right-wing Socialist Kerensky to continue the war was fatal to the hold of the anti-Bolshevik Socialists upon the main body of the industrial workers.

Communism and the Peasantry.   Nor was it less fatal in the case of the peasants ; for above all else the peasants wanted to get home. They were weary of fighting and still more of being half starved in the army, far from home, and often no less far from the scenes of actual warfare ; and, if there was revolution afoot, they wanted to be in their own villages in order to be sure of getting their share of the land in any redistribution or seizure of the large estates that might take place. Accordingly the Bolsheviks were secure of the support of the main mass of both peasants and industrial workers if only they promised peace and the other parties did not. " They have voted with their feet," said Lenin at a later stage, in defending the acceptance of peace on practically any terms ; and there is no doubt that peace was one of the two things the offer of which by the Bolsheviks definitely brought the mass of poor men's opinion over to their side.

The second thing was the offer of the land, for the peasants, even if they had for the most part no political principles and no conscious interest in politics, were at all events strongly interested in getting more land, and in acquiring that good land much of which had been monopolised by the great landowners. Accordingly the Bolsheviks, adapting their policy to the need for securing the support of mass feeling among the peasantry as well as the conscious backing of the main body of the organised workers, were able to carry through the second Revolution and thereafter to use the Soldiers', Workers' and Peasants' Councils as the basis of their power.

What was then widely said in other countries by Socialists and non-Socialists alike was that, although the Bolsheviks had temporarily won power with the aid of the peasants, in the long run authority would rest not with them but with the great mass of peasants who so far outnumbered the industrial workers. The peasant, it was said, might be inarticulate and slow to move, but he was tremendously powerful in defence of his interests ; and in the long run the passive resistance of the peasantry was certain to compel the Bolsheviks either to build up a State in accordance with peasant needs or to yield up power to some alternative Government that would give the peasants what they wanted. What the peasants did want, it was said, was in the first place the land, and then to be let alone—let alone to farm it in their own way, however inefficiently, without being called upon to pay large taxes to a distant central Government in Moscow, or to bother their heads about any problems outside their own village. Russia, it was predicted, would in these circumstances cease to be a political unit at all. It would fall inevitably to pieces, perhaps to be reconstituted as a series of peasant republics, perhaps to fall in part under the sway of despots wielding arbitrary power in particular areas—in fact it would be thoroughly and irretrievably Balkanised. Communism, it was held, could be in a country like Russia only an episode, for however strong and determined the Bolsheviks might be they would be unable for long to stand up against the overwhelming force of peasant numbers.

The Communists for their part fully realised the seriousness of the problem they had to face ; for they were well aware that, though they had secured, on the immediate issues placed before the country, the support of the mass of the peasants, the peasantry were not Communist in any sense, or capable of being made Communist by mere force of oratory or argument. But the Communist philosophy had an answer to this problem. In the view of the Bolshevik leaders the active rôle in the proletarian Revolution belonged to the industrial workers ; and it was upon the Workers' Councils that the primary responsibility for building the new proletarian State must rest. The rôle of the peasants was bound to be largely passive ; but, provided that their craving for land was adequately satisfied, they could be carried along upon the tide, and a central Government strong enough to impose its will on the country as a whole could be brought into being without rousing their collective opposition.

But in order to secure this it would be necessary to divide the peasantry against themselves, by bringing into relief the antagonism between poor peasants who had either no land or far too little to enable them to achieve a tolerable standard of living and the richer peasants who in some cases employed labour, and, even if they did not, had holdings large enough to raise them substantially above the general level of the peasant standard of living. These richer peasants included many who were small traders as well as cultivators of the soil, and often small money-lenders into the bargain. They were thus in a sense capitalistic in their way of living, in that they exacted profit either from hired labour or from buying and selling other men's produce, or from usury, or from all these things. The Communists set themselves from the first to build up their own support in the villages by rallying to their side the poorer peasants, the *bedniaki*, and stirring them up to strong antagonism towards the richer peasants, the *kulaki*. This programme of action was intermitted for a time after the institution by Lenin of the New Economic Policy. But this was done only when the civil war was over, when armed aggression from abroad had ceased, and when the power of the central Soviet Government had been sufficiently consolidated to remove the danger of any serious Counter-Revolution securing peasant support. Moreover, the New Economic Policy was conceived and carried out only for the purpose of according the Communists a breathing space ; as soon as they felt strong enough to resume the offensive the class war in the villages was taken up again, and a little later when the Five-Year Plan seemed sufficiently advanced for a new task to be attempted, the large-scale socialisation of agriculture was instituted and a definite campaign launched both for eradicating the last *kulak* remnants from the villages and for transforming the peasant from a small-scale individual or family cultivator into a unit in a new socialised system of agricultural production.

For according to the Communist theory Socialism can never be established in Russia in any real sense as long as the great mass of the people continue to live on the land under a system of individual cultivation which is bound to breed in them an individualist habit of thought. Socialism involves, in the Communist view, socialising men's minds as well as their ways of working ; and their minds can be socialised only if their ways of working are socialised first of all. Accordingly agriculture as well as industry must be brought within the range of socialisation, not only in order to promote the improvement of agricultural methods but also in order to make the population of Russia thoroughly socialised in thought and attitude. The socialisation of agriculture as well as industry is therefore an essential deduction from the Communist philosophy ; and both these aspects of the Communist policy imply the socialisation of men as well as things—indeed, men even more than things are the objects of socialisation.

The Soviet System.   The Russians, we have seen, set out to build up their new State on the basis of revolutionary organisations created by the workers themselves. This is the Soviet system, which is not fundamentally a method of voting different from that of Parliamentary democracy, but the logical outcome of a different form of social organisation, arising out of the working class as the inevitable expression of its collective consciousness as a class. The Workers' and Soldiers' Councils of the Revolutionary period have indeed now given place to a regular system of local Soviets, extending over the whole country, and it is from these local Soviets, which have now become organs of a new form of constitutional government, that the superior institutions of the Federated Soviet Republics and of the U.S.S.R. as a whole are drawn. To those who have been brought up to think in terms of pre-existing forms of political organisations, the outstanding feature of the Soviet system often seems to be the method of indirect election, that is, of choosing the delegates or representatives who are to sit upon the higher and larger organs of government by indirect election through the smaller local organs. But though this method of indirect election does arise naturally as the means of making the Soviet system effective over the larger areas, it is not the fundamental thing, which is rather that the whole scheme of governmental institutions emerges from class organisations, and is based upon the conception of class unity rather than upon the casting of individual votes. The Soviet system is essentially a system of class government—though that does not prevent it from being based upon a franchise quite as wide as that of nominally democratic countries under the parliamentary system. The difference between the two systems is not that one enfranchises more and the other less people, but that one is conceived in terms of individual voters and their rights, and the other in terms of the collective rights of a dominant social class.

Of course, this class system of voting and the method of indirect election which arises out of it make it far easier than it could be under the parliamentary system for the highly disciplined Communist Party and its local branches throughout the country to establish an effective control over the working of the entire machine. For the Communists, being the one recognised class party, with their own organisation of cells and branches extending to practically every area, are able to exercise a tremendous weight in elections of every sort. They do not, and they do not attempt to, monopolise all the seats upon the local Soviets for Communist Party members ; and when the Central Congress of Soviets meets for the Union as a whole it consists to a considerable extent of delegates who are not members of the party. But the Communist Party is usually in a position to secure the election of any individual whom it particularly wants and to ensure that enough seats are everywhere in its hands to enable its members, with their coherent habit of acting together, to dominate policy. Moreover, the higher up the scale of indirect election one moves, the greater becomes the influence exerted by the

Party, and the greater the proportion of Party members sitting upon the governing bodies. The key positions in the Soviet Union, apart from those technical posts for which it is still necessary to call in outside help, are practically monopolised by Communists ; and the Communist monopoly is likely to extend further and further as, with the growing solidity of the new régime, Party influence and membership become more widespread even than they are to-day. For, despite the recurrent " purges " engaged in by the party, the membership is likely to grow much larger as industrialisation is extended not only by the expansion of industry but also by the progressive socialisation of Russian agriculture.

The socialisation of agriculture is undoubtedly a factor making for a large increase in the direct participation of Party members in the local working of the Soviet system. But, let it be clear, there is no universal Communist monopoly. For example, it is fully recognised as necessary to give effective representation and a large degree of local autonomy to national and cultural minorities within the territory of the Soviet Union. Of course, Communism is fully wide enough to appeal to these minorities, though at present its hold on many of them is less strong than in Russia proper. But the Bolsheviks have felt strong enough, and sure enough of the pervasive influence of their doctrine, to grant autonomy to these groups within the Soviet system.

There has been since the Bolsheviks assumed power a great deal of discussion in Russia concerning the proper relationship between the industrial workers and the peasants within the new system. On the one hand, Lenin and the Communist Party have constantly described the Soviet system as a government of the workers and peasants, and on the other they have spoken of the dictatorship of the proletariat as involving the dictatorship of the industrial workers. How are these two statements to be reconciled ? Are the peasants part of the new ruling class in Russia, or are they not ? The answer given by the Communists is in terms of the distinction between the foundations on which the new State is built up and the character of the leadership under which it is controlled. The workers and peasants together form the foundation of the new Communist State ; industrial workers and peasants alike have created this State and now maintain it under the leadership of the Communist Party. The party represents primarily the industrial workers, and is to be regarded as above all the expression of their point of view. The peasants' rôle is not merely passive ; but it is definitely secondary to the rôle of the industrial workers. Peasants as well as industrial workers are, of course, increasingly found in the ranks of the Communist Party, but the broad character of the Party continues to be industrial ; and its declared object is, by industrialising agriculture as well as industry, to bring the peasants into an attitude of mind in which they can become full partners in the exercise of the dictatorship and in the new Socialist society which is to arise out of it. The separate peasant attitude is to disappear, and in its place is to come a new attitude based on the abolition of the difference between town and country and the comprehensive social-isation of all economic processes, agricultural as well as industrial. But until this has been brought about, the rôle of the peasantry is to serve as allies of the industrial workers in the maintenance of the new State, but in this alliance to be brought under the effective leadership of the industrial workers through the disciplined organisation of the Communist Party.

This clear-cut theory of revolution and of proletarian action in the period following the success of the revolution-ary effort of the proletariat is based throughout on Marxism. The Russian Communists conceive themselves as funda-mentally Marxists, not in the sense of following blindly what Marx and Engels said of the very different circum-stances of eighty or ninety years ago, but rather of applying the fundamental principles of Marxism to the new situation which has arisen with the advance of Capitalism to a new phase. At the time when Marx and Engels were writing, Capitalism was still at a competitive phase of development.

Great Britain was the only really advanced capitalist country ; and there had not developed, as there has since, an acute rivalry in world markets between a number of developed capitalist countries all trying to sell their goods and to assure themselves of the required supplies of raw materials and other products needed for the expansion of the industrial system. In other words, Capitalism had not then become Capitalist Imperialism.

Lenin and Imperialism.   The contribution of the Communists, and above all of Lenin, their outstanding thinker, has been that of carrying Marxism a step further than it was possible for Marx and Engels to carry it, by re-stating it in terms of the new phase of capitalist develop-ment with which the working-class movement has now to deal. Lenin's most important theoretical work is entitled *Imperialism, the Last Stage of Capitalism,* and it is above all in working out afresh the strategy of the Socialist Move-ment in face of the problems created by the rise of Imperial-ist Capitalism that Lenin's new contribution to the Marxist philosophy lies.

According to Lenin's analysis the coming of Imperialism brings to an end the peaceful and even development of Capitalism as a system, and substitutes for the steady technical and economic progress of the earlier period an uneven process of growth marked by the outbreak of serious crises and by a growing clash between the rival Capitalisms of the great industrial countries. This clash, leading inevitably to great imperialist wars, makes possible in Lenin's view the victory of Socialism in particular countries in which Capitalism breaks down under the strain imposed upon it by the imperialist struggle. The strategy of the working-class movement has accordingly to be directed to the building up of an organisation capable of seizing the opportunities created by such imperialist struggles for achieving the revolution. This involves an attitude radically different from that of the orthodox Socialist parties ; for it contemplates the coming of Socialism, not as a result of a gradual evolution of the Parliamentary system, but rather by means of a sharp revolutionary uprising under proletarian leadership.

Lenin does not hold that a Communist or Socialist Party, however strong, can make a revolution merely by organising and preparing for it ; he holds that, in order to achieve a successful revolution, it must await the coming of a situation in which the temporary weakening or breakdown of the capitalist forces gives it the chance of acting in such a way as to command the support of the great mass of the workers in the country concerned. But he holds equally that in the absence of a strong and determined revolutionary party this chance will be bound to pass, or at any rate to be so used that the instinctive revolutionary struggles of the workers will merely become the means whereby the more democratic elements among the middle classes will succeed in re-establishing Capitalism. The proletariat, Lenin insists, through the disciplined working-class party which makes itself its class representative, must seize the leadership of the revolution when the moment for action arrives, and must push ruthlessly out of the way all those *bourgeois* or moderate Socialist groups which cannot be relied upon to press the revolution through to its conclusion in the establishment of a State under full proletarian control. Consequently the strategy of preparing for the revolution must be that of building up this disciplined party ; and ruthless warfare must be waged against all those Labour Parties which seek the support of the working class on the basis of a programme of gradual Parliamentary evolution or of conciliation of the *bourgeoisie*.

From this conception of revolutionary strategy arises the virulence of the Communists when they are speaking of the Social Democratic and Labour Party leaders. For they conceive these leaders and the parties which they control as the chief obstacles in the way of the creation of the revolutionary parties which alone will be competent to seize the moment when it comes, and to put themselves at the head of the entire working class.

It is obvious that this theory was worked out largely in terms of the situation existing in Russia before 1917. Lenin's conception of revolutionary strategy, while it was put forward as universal, was really a plan of action primarily for the Socialist Movement in Russia, or at all events for the Socialist Movement in countries where Socialism was struggling against a semi-autocratic régime to which a substantial section of the middle class found themselves opposed. The insistence that in the absence of clear revolutionary leadership of the proletariat the workers would do the fighting for a revolution, the fruits of which would then be seized by the middle class, is clearly based on envisaging such a situation as that of Russia, or to a less extent pre-war Germany, where the middle class was still largely excluded from political power. In Great Britain or France it is inconceivable that the middle class would want to make a revolution side by side with the workers against the Government, and thereafter to throw over their working-class colleagues and submit them to a new subjection, because already in these countries the middle classes constitute and control the Government. They are already for this reason not a revolutionary force, but a force on the side of the conservation of the *status quo*. In so far as they assume a revolutionary attitude at all, this will be only by way of counter-revolutionary action against the threat of a Socialist victory. They will begin by taking sides, if a revolutionary situation arises, not with, but against the working class. In Russia, on the other hand, and to a less extent in pre-war Germany, the situation which Lenin envisaged did in effect exist ; and, but for the Bolshevik seizure of leadership in November 1917, the revolution of March would have become, in the hands of the *bourgeois* parties and the moderate Socialists such as Kerensky, an instrument for the establishment of a liberal-democratic capitalist régime. This is what actually happened in Germany, where the Spartacists and Independents failed to seize control.

As soon as we begin to think in terms of the liberal parliamentary democracies of Western Europe, the problem

of revolutionary strategy has to be envisaged differently ;
and it is largely the failure to realise this essential difference that has so far made it impossible for Communism to
secure any considerable hold in either Great Britain or
France. Moreover, in post-war Germany, with its far
higher degree of industrialisation, the situation was so
different from that in Russia that, when once the revolutionary moment of 1918 and the early months of 1919
had passed and the *bourgeois* Republic been definitely
brought to birth, the Communist strategy was radically
inappropriate to the conditions of the new Republic and
therefore failed, though in less measure than in either
Great Britain or France, to rally the workers to its side.
The question which Communists seem never to have
thought out is how Marxism ought in the twentieth century to be applied in those countries which are already
equipped with liberal-democratic Constitutions, and have
already large middle classes exercising the predominant
influence in their political affairs.

Communism, thus basing itself upon Marxism, represents a far more fundamental challenge than Fascism to
the institutions of capitalist Europe. For Communism puts
forward only incidentally an alternative form of political
organisation to the parliamentary State. Its fundamental
purpose is not to state a new political theory, or to suggest
new or improved means of working out the implications
of political democracy, but to accomplish a radical change
in the conditions under which political and economic
institutions alike are to operate. It aims at the complete
socialisation of the powers of production, the complete
destruction of social classes, and the establishment of a new
type of society to which the old political conceptions will be
totally irrelevant.

Of course, Communism will be under no less necessity
than any previous system of reconciling the claims of liberty
and authority, and of finding scope for the individual
within a system of institutions making for the greatest
happiness of the greatest number. The old problems which

have been argued about ever since men began to argue at all in political terms will continue to concern it. But these problems will take on radically different forms because the underlying structure of the new society will be altogether different from the old. Take, for example, the question of liberty. So far, men have always been concerned with the safeguarding of human liberty within a society based upon and recognising the economic and class inequality of men. A large part of the claims of libertarians in hitherto existing societies has in fact consisted either of claims which, even if they were granted, would only in practice accord real liberty to the possessors of economic security at a fairly high standard of life or, on the other hand, of claims designed to give those lacking this security some sort of guarantee against the extreme pressure of exploitation by their economic superiors. Within the framework of a society based upon economic equality, or at least upon the complete destruction of class divisions, the problem of liberty will assume a new aspect.

Critics of Russian institutions in capitalist countries are apt to dwell very greatly on the alleged suppression of liberty in Russia to-day, and to base their arguments on the disappearance of the characteristic liberties associated in their minds with the liberal-parliamentary State. But though the Soviet system in its present working does undoubtedly restrict individual liberty very seriously in certain directions—above all in the expression of political views hostile to the system itself—it has resulted in other directions in an enormous extension of the liberties of the great mass of the Russian people. Observers who come back from Russia, unless they are too prejudiced to notice what they see, practically all report that there exists among the Russian people of to-day, in non-political matters, a sense of freedom and of self-expression quite unknown among the mass of the people in any capitalist country. They report, moreover, that the Russian workman's attitude even to the hard discipline of the Five-Year Plans differs radically from the typical attitude of workmen in capitalist societies, and that the Russian workers, or at least the younger generation among them, feel that the industries in which they are working are their common possession. They have therefore towards them an attitude of responsibility which makes hard service in forwarding the success of the plan not a form of servitude but an expression of collective freedom. Liberty, under the restrictions imposed on its political expression by the necessities of the proletarian dictatorship, is finding new forms and new substance within the Russian Workers' State. This is not to say that the restrictions imposed upon it in the interests of the dictatorship are good ; but in setting them down as criticisms of the Soviet system it must not be forgotten that there are very large extensions of liberty to be taken into account on the other side. Above all it does appear that Russian society is permeated by a real hope in the future, and that a large proportion of the Russian workers do feel themselves to be engaged upon a really worth-while task of social construction, in strong contrast to the spirit of disillusionment which pervades all classes in the capitalist world.

We come back now to the question which we left unanswered some time back. If Communism, thought out in and for Russia and taking account primarily of the conditions existing in Eastern Europe, has failed to create a strategy effective in the very different conditions of Western Europe, does this failure imply that Communism is itself inappropriate to Western Europe, or only that its strategy needs to be thought out anew in West European terms ? If by Communism is meant, not the precise system which the Russians have successfully instituted in their own country, but rather a thoroughgoing system of Socialism to be instituted by means of a radical transformation in the class structure of society, the arguments against transplanting Communism in its Russian form to Western Europe are beside the point. If, on the other hand, Communism means that the policy and strategy of the Communist International are to be rigidly applied by working-class parties throughout the world, then Communism is most unlikely to become he instrument of social transformation in the western countries. But this question can be dealt with more easily n a separate section, in which we shall be discussing the position and prospects of Socialism primarily in Western Europe.

§ 7. EUROPEAN SOCIALISM

EUROPEAN Socialism as an organised movement, as distinct from a body of theories, dates effectively from 1848. Before the year in which Marx and Engels issued to the world their famous *Communist Manifesto* Socialism had already a considerable history behind it, and there had been many great Socialist thinkers—Saint Simon and Fourier in France, and above all, Robert Owen in Great Britain. Socialist ideas, too, had played a part in many organised movements in both Great Britain and France, for example in the Owenite Trade Union movement of 1834 and in Chartism. But not until 1848 did there emerge in Europe a continuous agitation based on a clear-cut Socialist philosophy and programme of action. Ever since 1848 the Socialist movement of Continental Europe has been based mainly upon the doctrines contained in the *Communist Manifesto*.

The revolutions of 1848 and the following years contained everywhere Socialist elements ; and in both Germany and France Socialists attempted to wrest the effective leadership from the middle-class revolutionaries. But these attempts were beaten down ; for nowhere except in Great Britain was there yet a proletariat large enough to form the basis of a considerable organised movement, and in Great Britain the power of Chartism had been broken before 1848. With the defeat of the Liberal revolutions in the years after 1848, Socialism underwent persecution and the Socialist movement was to a great extent eclipsed. But it was not long before the work of rebuilding had begun ; and especially in London there continued after 1848 to be a body of revolutionary exiles from Continental countries who kept Socialist thought and agitation alive. Karl Marx was the dominant figure among these Socialist exiles, as was Mazzini among the non-Socialist revolutionaries in London; and in 1864 Marx's chance came to re-create an international movement similar to that which he and Engels had hoped for in the "Year of Revolutions."

In 1864 the International Workingmen's Association, better known as the First International, was born; and Marx at once assumed the leadership. Under the auspices of the First International the work was taken in hand of building up organised Socialist movements in the leading Continental countries, and especially in France and Germany. From this period dates the effective beginning in Germany of the Marxian Social Democratic Party, which had at this stage for its rival the German Workingmen's Association under the leadership of Lassalle. In France the International also established its organisation; but here it found itself opposed on the one hand to the semi-Anarchist followers of Proudhon, who believed in a solution of the social problem by means of Producers' Societies and a reform of the credit system, and the followers of Blanqui, much nearer to the Marxist point of view, but differing from the Marxists in that they advocated the tactics of revolutionary action by a class-conscious minority even in the absence of support from the mass of the workers. In Italy, Marx's movement took less strong root, for there it was opposed not only by the followers of Mazzini but also by powerful Anarchist influences which brought it more under the sway of the great Russian leader, Michael Bakunin. In Russia, Marxism at this stage had relatively little hold; for the main mass of the Russian Socialist movement, attempting to base its agitation on the peasantry in a country as yet quite undeveloped in an industrial sense, found more to meet its needs in the doctrines of Anarchism than in the "Scientific Socialism" of Marx and Engels.

The First International reached the culminating point

of its career with the creation of the Paris Commune in 1871, after the defeat of Napoleon III at the hands of the Prussians. But this short-lived experiment in practical Socialism was wiped out in blood, and its defeat was fatal to the immediate prospects of the Socialist International in Europe. Yet it lived on in the minds of Socialists as the one actual working pattern of the Socialist revolution in action. It profoundly influenced the later thinking both of Marx himself and of his successors who built up the Communist movement in Russia.

After the collapse of the First International the Socialist movement in most parts of Continental Europe underwent a period of repression. Great Britain indeed was unaffected, as she had been amid her growing economic prosperity practically untouched by the wave of unrest which had brought the Marxian International to birth. There was no rise of British Socialism after the fall of the Chartist movement until it was born again in the course of the industrial depression of the late 'seventies and early 'eighties. But on the Continent the movement remained alive, though it was driven underground. In France many of the leaders were in exile or in prison, and in Germany too the movement, after a period of growth, had soon to undergo Government persecution under Bismarck's anti-Socialist laws. In the meantime, however, German Socialism had undergone a highly significant change. At the Gotha Congress of 1875 the Social Democratic Party, created on a Marxian basis by Bebel and Wilhelm Liebknecht, united with the Workingmen's Association, which included the followers of Lassalle. This unity was achieved on the basis of an agreed programme which was a compromise between the views of the rival leaders. The draft of it was sent by the German Marxist leaders to Marx, and Marx replied in the scathing criticism now known as *Comments on the Gotha Programme*. So fatal would the publication of these comments have been to the prospects of German working-class unity that the German Social Democratic leaders suppressed them, and they were not published till long after

Marx's death. For Marx saw in the terms of unity accepted by his German followers a surrender of the revolutionary policy which he had laid down in the *Communist Manifesto* of 1848, and a definite compromise with a form of Socialism which he regarded as essentially reactionary.

The differences between Marx and the Lassallians were many ; but for the purposes of this brief study it is necessary to mention only one. Lassalle had always worked for an extension of State intervention in industry, for the development of social legislation, and for securing the help of the State in the organisation of working men's co-operative societies and similar bodies. Thus, the Lassallian programme embodied a policy of gradualism based on an extension of State control, and demanded for its execution a Parliamentary Socialist Party adopting an evolutionary and compromising attitude. The German Social Democratic leaders, in order to achieve unity, had swallowed a large part of the Lassallian programme, contenting themselves with producing, side by side with these clauses, slogans drawn from the revolutionary philosophy of Karl Marx. Thus from the very moment of its union with the Lassallians, the German Social Democratic Party embarked in principle upon the evolutionary course which was characteristic of its actual achievements when it was called upon after 1918 to assume a part in the Government. The real cleavage between Social Democracy and Communism in Germany goes right back to the controversy over the Gotha programme in 1875 ; for at that time few even of the Marxist leaders saw the real implications of the compromise which they were adopting in the interests of unity.

From the 'eighties onwards Socialism began to grow rapidly in most of the European countries ; and, with the passing of the repressive movements which had followed the Paris Commune, Socialist parties emerged and were able openly to put forward candidates for election to the various national Parliaments. At first these candidates met with little success ; but gradually the electoral strength of the movement increased, and in the early years of the twentieth century the Socialists were already a respectable fraction of the Parliaments in the leading Continental countries. Thus in Germany immediately before the war the Reichstag had 111 Social Democratic members out of a total of 397. In France the Unified Socialist Party had 102 members out of a total of 602, and in many other countries—Italy, Belgium, Holland, Switzerland, Denmark, and Sweden—Socialist parties had risen to positions of considerable influence.

In Great Britain, the course of evolution had been somewhat different. An attempt of the Social Democratic Federation to create a Socialist Party in the 'eighties met with little success, and it was not until 1900 that the Labour Representation Committee, later re-named the Labour Party, came into being. This new party, brought to birth mainly under the influence of Keir Hardie and the more advanced of the Trade Unionists, differed from most of the Continental parties, except that of Belgium, in being based not upon the membership of individual Socialists, but mainly upon the Trade Union movement. Keir Hardie and his group aimed from the first at what they called the " Labour Alliance "—that is to say, at an alliance between the comparatively small body of conscious Socialists and the mass of the workers organised in the Trade Unions. They succeeded in persuading the Trade Unions to join with them in setting up a political party, in which, by virtue of their greater numbers, the Unions possessed the ultimate control, and for which they found the greater part of the funds. This party was not, like the Continental parties, definitely Socialist in principle. It accepted a number of Socialist doctrines, and found its leaders largely among Socialists ; but it was not until after the war a Socialist Party in any clearly defined sense. Even when it became a Socialist Party by the adoption of distinctively Socialist resolutions, the Socialism which it took over from the English Fabians and the followers of Keir Hardie was of a non-doctrinaire and largely non-Marxian sort, stressing

social reform rather than Socialism in its immediate programme and aiming at the achievement of its objects by
means of gradual and constitutional evolution through
Parliament and not by revolution.

On the surface the differences between British Socialism
as it existed in 1914 and Continental Socialism were therefore considerable ; for Continental Socialism was in all
the countries of Western Europe for the most part strongly
Marxist, at least in phraseology. But in practice the differences were far smaller than they appeared ; for, although
the English Socialists and the Continental Socialists were
accustomed to use different phrases and the Continental
phrases sounded by far the more extreme, neither German
nor French Socialism was really more revolutionary in its
methods of action than British Labour. The International
Socialist Bureau, better known as the Second International,
had been constituted in 1901; and in this new international
organisation the British Labour delegates found no difficulty in associating quite harmoniously with their Marxian
Continental colleagues. Indeed, there was in matters of
policy a much sharper cleavage between the Italians and
Spaniards on the one side and the Germans and French
and British on the other than between those who thought
themselves Marxists and those who did not.

In Russia, the situation of Socialism before the war was
radically different, because Russian Socialists continued
to be subjected to the extremes of persecution. Most of the
best-known leaders were either in Siberia or in exile abroad,
and after the defeat of the Russian revolution of 1905
persecution had been intensified. The Russian Socialists
had to conduct their agitation from abroad, and do their
thinking largely on foreign soil. They were divided, apart
from minor fractions, into three considerable parties. The
largest of these was the Social Revolutionary Party, based
mainly upon the peasants and thinking mainly in terms of
a peasant revolution. This party was in reality more Anarchist than Socialist in its fundamental doctrines, and
looked back to Bakunin rather than Marx as the inspirer

of its policy. It was also strongly Slavophil, and therefore followed an individual national line of its own. The two remaining parties both professed to be Marxist ; they were, indeed, two rival groups into which the old Russian Social Democratic Party had split in 1903–4. Of these two, the Bolsheviks, who became the Communist Party and carried through the second revolution of 1917, upheld Marxism in the revolutionary sense of the *Communist Manifesto* of 1848 and of Marx's *Comments on the Gotha Programme* of 1875. On the other hand, the Mensheviks, the smaller of the two groups, had assimilated their doctrines to those of the western Social Democrats and especially of the German Social Democratic Party. They claimed to be Marxists ; but their Marxism had become evolutionary in the sense that they believed that the way to the establishment of Socialism in Russia must lie through the setting up in the first instance of the *bourgeois* democratic State, and the development under its auspices of Russian industrialisation to the point required for the creation of a working class capable of assuming power. The disputes between the rival Russian parties were acute in the years immediately before the war ; but naturally the group most closely in touch with the Social Democrats of Western Europe was the Menshevik group, which had most completely adopted the revisionist version of Marxism current in western Socialist circles.

Post-War Socialism.   The war broke up the Second International. This federation of European Socialist parties had in 1907 pledged the constituent parties to use every possible effort to avert war if it should threaten to break out, and, if it actually broke out in spite of their efforts, to employ the situation created by it for the purposes of advancing the cause of Socialism in their own countries. But when war did come in 1914, although there were Socialist demonstrations against it in each country, the Socialist parties, or the majority of them, rallied in the moment of crisis to the support of their several " national causes." The German, French, and British Socialists alike voted in favour of the war credits demanded by the respective Governments ; and, though there was in each country a Socialist minority opposed to the war, this minority had at the outset no means of common action. Everywhere the main mass of the working-class movement was drawn in to the support of its own nation in arms. Indeed, some of the Socialists on both sides were among the most jingo of all the supporters of the war. Right up to 1918 not one of the leading Socialist parties had withdrawn its support from its own national Government ; and, in both Great Britain and France, Socialists had been members of the respective Cabinets during the greater part of the war. Only lack of opportunity prevented the German Socialists from enjoying a similar doubtful honour. Before long the anti-war minorities in the various Socialist parties attempted to draw together on international lines. At Zimmerwald in September 1915 the first international conference of anti-war Socialists was held ; and this was followed up a little later by a second conference at Kienthal in April 1916. To these two gatherings came Socialists of very different complexions. On the one hand there were Socialists whose opposition to the war was based mainly on pacifist grounds, and whose main object was to bring pressure on the various Governments to make peace at the earliest possible moment. But there were also Socialists who were to be subsequently the leaders of Communism, and among them Nicolai Lenin. This second group did not care a fig for pacifism. What it wanted was to take full advantage of the opportunity created by the crisis in world Capitalism for furthering the cause of revolutionary Socialism. For the moment it suited the second group to work with the first, in order that the agitation for peace might be used to undermine the morale of the various national forces. But there was really nothing in common between the two groups of delegates at Zimmerwald and Kienthal.

A new phase began with the first Russian revolution in the early months of 1917. For even the moderate Russian

Socialists, though some of them were prepared to continue the war in response to the demands of the Allies, passionately desired peace, and were well aware that their country could not stand the strain much longer without absolute collapse. Accordingly, in the course of 1917, Russia became a new force appealing to the workers of every country to agitate for a negotiated peace. Out of this agitation came the project of a great international conference, to be held at Stockholm, at which the united working-class demand for a negotiated peace was to find expression. When the Bolsheviks came to power in Russia they were fully prepared to take the lead in this crusade for peace. For they had even less desire, as well as less ability, to carry on the war of nations than their predecessors in power. Accordingly they took up strongly the demand for international working-class action, and the later agitation for the Stockholm conference became in effect the beginning of the world-wide appeal of the Russian Communists for support among the workers in other countries. The Governments were successful in suppressing it ; but their very success was one of the causes of a great strengthening of Socialist feeling among the working classes in the belligerent countries.

Meanwhile, the Bolsheviks, holding power by a precarious tenure in their own country, were by no means disposed to rest content with a merely pacifist movement, or to remain upon the defensive until world Capitalism was ready to launch a combined attack upon them. They regarded the revolution which they had made as merely the forerunner of a world revolution which was to usher in the new Socialist system for the whole capitalist world ; and they promptly set about drafting a great new appeal to the workers of the world to follow their lead and to join with them in the making of this world revolution. Emphasising the continuity of their movement with the earlier Marxism, they created, in order to further the cause of world revolution, a new International as the successor of the ill-fated Second International, which in their view had shown its incompetence and unsoundness at the outbreak of war. This new Communist International, better known as the Third International, was created at Moscow in 1919, and from it a new *Communist Manifesto* was launched upon the world.

Meanwhile, after the war the inter-allied Socialists took the lead in re-creating the old Second International, this time with the new name of the Labour and Socialist International. There were thus two rival Socialist Internationals, each claiming to represent the working-class movement of all countries ; but these two bodies stood for exceedingly different policies. For, whereas the Third International was definitely calling upon the workers to make a world revolution, the parties associated with the Labour and Socialist International were for the most part attempting to bring about the reconstruction of their own national economies on the basis of further instalments of social reform, and to extend their influence on strictly constitutional and parliamentary lines. But not all the Socialist parties were prepared to associate themselves with either extreme ; and for some time there was great confusion in the camp of international Socialism, with a " Two and a half International," as it was called, attempting to mediate between the " Second " and the " Third."

Especially in Italy was there a sharp division of views. The majority of the Italian Socialist Party had throughout opposed Italian participation in the war, though a minority had broken away and supported intervention. After the war, the Italians, apart from Mussolini and his group, who had broken with the Socialists, were split into three significant factions—the Communists, who had definitely gone over to the Moscow doctrines, the Maximalists, who also proclaimed themselves revolutionaries but were not prepared definitely to throw in their lot with the Third International, and the moderate Socialists, who aligned themselves with the constitutional Socialist parties of Western Europe. We have seen in an earlier section how these differences in Italian Socialism prepared the way for the triumph of Fascism.

Almost everywhere in Europe, as things began to settle down after the war, it was realised that numerically Socialism had become much stronger than it had been in 1914. Everywhere the Socialist parties had been able substantially to increase both their representation and their voting strength. In some cases, as in Great Britain, the real increase of strength did not become manifest till some years after the war ; but as soon as there had been time for the immediate excitement to die down, the gain in Socialist voting strength became everywhere apparent. It was, however, equally clear that, while Socialism had increased its numerical influence, the constitutional Socialist parties were in most countries unlikely in the near future, if at all, to gain clear majorities in their national Parliaments. This prospect was especially remote in those countries, including, as we have seen, practically all the new States, which had adopted in their Constitutions the principle of proportional representation ; for proportional representation is a system admirably calculated to prevent any party from getting a clear majority save under the most exceptional conditions.

The Socialists were thus faced with a new situation. Before the war they had been accustomed to take their exclusion from office as a matter of course ; and, although they had at times to decide whether to support one *bourgeois* Government against another and thus keep it in office when it would otherwise have fallen, no question arose in most countries of their actually sharing in the responsibilities of government. Socialism was before the war almost exclusively a critical force, standing outside the machine of government and aiming at pressing upon it the claims of the working class. After the war, on the other hand, Socialism had become powerful enough in a number of countries for the constitution of any Government of the Left to be virtually impossible without its aid, and for the question of its willingness to take office inevitably to arise. It might be called upon either to enter into coalition with the left *bourgeois* parties, or to give these parties indispensable support for their own tenure of power, or itself to face office as a minority Government, relying on getting its measures adopted with the aid of left *bourgeois* votes. The first of these situations arose above all in Germany, the second in France, and the third in Great Britain, where the break-up of the great pre-war Liberal Party turned the Labour Party into the leading opposition group.

What were the Socialists to do when they were faced with this new situation ? To the extent to which they were social reformers aiming at the improvement of social conditions within the capitalist system it was clearly illogical for them, when the opportunity came, to refuse to take the chance of improving the quality of current legislation, whether this involved actually taking office or only entering into some sort of agreement to support the *bourgeois* parties of the Left. But, as we have seen, the Socialist parties of Western Europe had long been in their essence social reform parties rather than Socialist parties *à l'outrance*. Accordingly even if, as in France, they refused either to enter coalitions or to take office by themselves in a minority, they were only consistent with their earlier attitude when they pursued the path of compromise, and made the accommodations necessary for the furtherance of a policy of social reform, in preference to declaring open war upon the united *bourgeois* parties and making an immediate attempt to establish Socialism—an attempt which most of their leaders regarded as both impracticable at that stage and in itself highly undesirable. For these leaders were, as we have seen, by no means revolutionists ; and they were for the most part even more bitterly hostile to the Communists and to left-wing elements within their own countries than to the more democratic elements in the middle-class parties.

In the period immediately after the war, attention, especially in Great Britain, was for the time concentrated rather on the Trade Unions than on the Socialist parties. Trade Unionism, even more markedly than Socialism, had emerged from the war with greatly added strength in the leading countries. Side by side with the official Trade Union movements, which, like the Socialist parties, supported the war, there had arisen unofficial movements among the Trade Union rank and file in the factories. These movements, led by unofficial shop-stewards and workshop agitators, became the chief voices of industrial unrest during the later years of the war ; and when, after the Armistice, the Trade Unions were released from their self-imposed loyalty to the cause of national unity, there arose among their members a strong demand for aggressive action to raise wages and improve conditions of labour, and movements came into prominence with more definitely Socialist objects centring round the demand for workers' control in industry. At the same time, the industrial situation was complicated by the demobilisation of the returning soldiers ; and in the early months of 1919 the Trade Union movements in the Allied countries took up a strongly aggressive attitude and put forward many projects of socialisation in industry, coupled with the demand for workers' control. The French *Confédération Générale du Travail* came forward with its plan of *nationalisation industrialisée*. In Great Britain the Trade Unions took up the Guild Socialist demand for industrial self-government, and both the miners and the railwaymen pressed for the socialisation of their industries and their transference to representative bodies chosen largely by the workers themselves. But in both countries the Governments were able to gain time by the granting of immediate concessions ; and with the successful completion of the process of demobilisation the revolutionary moment passed, and the Trade Unions found their opportunity gone, especially when the brief post-war boom gave place to the industrial depression of 1920–21.

Thereafter, the Trade Union movements of the various countries had to face serious difficulties. From 1920 onwards, the centre of interest tended to shift back from Trade Unionism to political Socialism. The shop stewards' movement and the unofficial workshop committees which had been influential under war conditions disappeared as these conditions passed away ; and the employers were able by selective dismissals to weed out the more active " agitators." Guild Socialism, with its demand for industrial self-government, ceased to command widespread support as the possibility of aggressive strike action by the workers grew less ; and in the chief western countries Trade Unionism settled down again to the familiar routine of collective bargaining. It was stronger numerically than before the war ; but there was no fundamental change in its policy or in its relation to the employers.

Syndicalism and Guild Socialism. This, however, applies less to the south of Europe than to Great Britain, Germany, and France. For, in the south, Syndicalist and Anarchist influences were far stronger inside the Trade Union movement ; and the Syndicalist tendency, which had been strongest in France in the early years of the twentieth century, had persisted in Spain and Italy after it had lost its original momentum in France and been partly overlaid by the development of large-scale Capitalism. Small-scale industry tends to breed, in contrast to the strong centralised Unions of the more highly industrialised States, a localised and spontaneous type of Trade Unionism, which relies far less on the building up of large-scale permanent organisations than on keeping alive through a relatively small membership a militant spirit among a minority of the workers, in the confidence that, if this minority gives the lead at the right moment, the unorganised majority will be prepared to follow.

This type of Syndicalist unionism was especially strong in Italy and Spain. In Italy it was crushed, together with the Socialist Party and the Socialist Unions, by the Fascist revolution ; but in Spain it remained alive even under the dictatorship of Primo de Rivera, and it played an important part in the Spanish revolution of 1931, surviving thereafter to give a good deal of trouble to the orthodox Socialists who were collaborating with the Radical parties in the consolidation of the new Spanish Republic. In the stimulation of sporadic mass movements among the workers this type of Syndicalist Trade Unionism is highly efficient ; but it lacks sustained power and, above all, the capacity for creating a coherent and disciplined movement over any wide area. It is, therefore, far more effective in carrying on a guerilla warfare against established institutions than in setting up any authority capable of taking over control. It lacks precisely those qualities which enabled the highly disciplined and centralised Communist Party to establish itself in power over the vast territory of Soviet Russia.

Syndicalism, like Industrial Unionism in America, was from the first essentially a movement of agitation, aiming at the stirring up of the general body of the workers and at the creation among them of a continuous revolutionary temper. Guild Socialism, which bears certain superficial resemblances to Syndicalism, was a movement of a widely different character, in that it was not primarily an agitation at all, but rather a theory developed among a relatively small number of Socialist intellectuals and radiating outwards from this small group so as to influence the more active spirits in the Trade Unions. Having this essentially theoretical character, Guild Socialism, although it profoundly influenced the development of Socialist and Trade Union thought and policy in Great Britain—the only country in which it ever developed an organisation of its own—never became a movement of the workers ; and when the conditions which had favoured its development passed away it speedily lost its wider appeal and disappeared as a distinct form of Socialism. Its effects remained in a permanent modification of Trade Union and Socialist policies ; but the Guild Socialist organisation itself—always very minute in comparison with its articulateness and the spread of its influence—dissolved with the coming of unemployment and industrial depression.

Socialism and Social Reform.

We have seen how, when circumstances became adverse to aggressive Trade Union action, the interest in the West European countries shifted back from industrial to political activity, and the hopes of the workers came again to be centred upon the Socialist parties. These parties, as we saw, had by this time resumed their pre-war attitude of pressing for a more developed policy of social reform, and had added to their demands for reform proposals for the socialisation of certain particular industries as a first instalment of an attempt at Socialist construction within the framework of capitalist society. Their policy was thus twofold, and their appeal to the workers had already this dual character. They relied for the getting of votes largely on their promises of immediate social amelioration, while they appealed to the more active elements in the working class, and the middle-class sympathisers with Socialism, with their more constructive Socialist proposals.

But in practice in both these fields the carrying out of their declared policy presented considerable and increasing difficulties. Social reforms cost money ; and it was becoming harder, in face of the growing pressure on public finance in consequence of the enormously increased burden of debts, to extract additional revenues to be spent on a further extension of social reforms. The hopes of the workers had been raised by the lavish promises made to them during the war ; and the Socialist parties after 1918 had embodied in their programmes ambitious schemes of social amelioration. Even before the coming of the world slump it was doubtful how far the Socialists, if they actually took office, would be in a position to implement their promises without so taxing the richer classes as greatly to diminish the incentives on which the capitalist system depends. This difficulty became immensely greater after 1929, when the ability of Capitalism to stand increasing taxation was diminishing just at a time when the maintenance of the growing body of unemployed, even at a very low subsistence standard, was imposing large additional burdens on the national revenues. Most of all did the difficulties of the German financial situation make it out of the question for the German Social Democrats to press for any considerable advances in social legislation in the years immediately before the Hitler *coup*.

Nor were the British Socialists much more happily placed in respect of the constructive part of their programme. It was being borne in upon them to an increasing extent that they could hope further to expand the social services and further to redistribute wealth only if they could, in order to secure the necessary resources, make a real beginning with the socialisation of industry, and thus transfer to the State some at least of the sources of national wealth. But, commanding no independent majority in the national Parliament, and depending for their ability to get measures passed into law on the support of a certain number of middle-class Liberals or Radicals, they were quite unable to bring forward constructive measures of socialisation with any real hope of carrying them into effect.

Accordingly in both aspects the policy of moderate Socialism suffered, especially after 1929, a visible check. In the countries where the Socialists were strong enough to make it difficult for the government to be carried on without them, something like a stalemate ensued ; and where the Parliamentary system was not strongly rooted this led easily to the virtual abrogation of the powers of Parliament and the substitution of more or less complete forms of dictatorial government. In Great Britain, where the hold of Parliamentarism was far stronger, the crisis of 1931— which made clear once and for all the impotence of gradualist Socialism in face of the world depression—drove the Socialists from power and reduced them temporarily to a mere fraction of the representation which they had previously held. In France the Socialists, not having been subjected to the test of office, were still able to maintain their position, and in 1932 to instal and keep in power a new Government of the Left under the successive leadership of Herriot, Paul-Boncour, and Daladier. But this Radical Government, hardly less than the more reactionary Governments in power in other countries, found itself under the necessity of economising at the expense of the social services and of the wages of public employees in order to avoid a hopelessly unbalanced budget.

The Communists regard these difficulties of post-war Social Democracy in the western countries as a decisive exposure of the futility of the entire policy which the non-Communist parties have been endeavouring to pursue. According to them, there is no way of improving the condition of the workers save by the institution of a Socialist system, and no way to establishing Socialism save by a violent revolution. Socialists who think otherwise are merely beating the air, and in effect are serving the interests of Capitalism by standing in the way of the development of the revolutionary consciousness of the working class. But it is exceedingly doubtful whether, in the circumstances of the western countries, this analysis will bear examination. For the proletariats of France and Great Britain and, even to a less extent, of Germany, differ from the pre-revolutionary proletariat of Russia in that they certainly have something to lose besides their chains. There exists in certain especially depressed areas in the advanced industrial countries a poverty-stricken proletariat which has used up all its savings under the pressure of prolonged unemployment and now subsists meagrely and with diminishing physical efficiency upon some form of dole. But this submerged section of the working classes in the western countries is by no means typical of the working class as a whole. For in neither France nor Great Britain has unemployment of this type affected more than a small section of the total industrial population.

It is mainly among these victims of a depressed capitalist system that Communism, at least in Great Britain, has found its rank and file adherents ; but upon such a basis it is quite impossible for any effective nation-wide Communist movement to be built up, unless and until depression over the country as a whole becomes infinitely deeper and more widespread than it has shown any sign of becoming even after four years of slump. Except in these abnormally depressed districts, which form only a small part of the whole industrial area, the majority of the workers are still either regularly employed or subject only to short spells of unemployment, which produce upon them nothing like the same psychological or economic effects. Many of them have savings, own their own houses, are in relatively good jobs which they have no desire to lose, and so far from being prepared to make a revolution because it may better and cannot worsen their situation, hope strongly, even if they hold Socialist convictions, that Socialism can be brought into being painlessly and without an intervening period of chaos and civil war. So far from responding to Communist propaganda based on the idea of the inevitability of revolution, they react strongly against this type of propaganda and give steady support to the moderate Socialist leaders, or, if they despair of moderate Socialism, are more likely to react against Socialism altogether than to go over to Socialism of a more extreme type.

Doubtless the Communist, if he accepts this diagnosis, will answer that his policy is not in any way affected by it, for it is his business to create in Great Britain and France, as in the more distressed countries, a nucleus of revolutionary working-class opinion in preparation for the time when the further worsening of economic conditions will make a far larger proportion of the total working class ready to listen to his appeals. He regards world Capitalism as in definite process of dissolution and decay ; and, while he does not say that there can be no revival from the present world depression, he does hold that even if a revival occurs it can be only temporary and is bound to give place to a still worse depression in the not distant future. If, then, he recognises that he has little chance at present of winning over the mass of workers to his point of view, he holds only that the time is not yet ripe for the realisation of his hopes, without in the least giving up his conviction that his time will come, and that it is his business to prepare the workers for the coming accentuation of class conflict.

Class-Divisions in Modern Society.   This diagnosis, however, leaves out of account the radical difference between the composition of the occupied population in Great Britain and France and in such a country as Russia. In Russia the great mass of the people were deeply impoverished peasants, and even among the industrial workers the proportion of relatively well-paid and skilled workers was very small indeed. Broadly speaking, the whole working class was bitterly oppressed, and suffered in common the social stagnation of a downtrodden class. But in the western countries of Europe, and especially in Great Britain, this is not so. The workers are far more differentiated among themselves, and include a far higher proportion of relatively well-paid craftsmen holding fairly secure jobs. The black-coated proletariat, as it has been called, is infinitely more numerous ; and above the ordinary ruck of black-coated workers stands a very large and rapidly growing body of professionals and technicians enjoying salaries very substantially above the ordinary working-class levels. It is true that many of the lesser black-coats are very badly off, and that unemployment is fairly severe among the clerical grades ; but there remains a formidable body of middle-class workers who live not on interest or dividends but on salaries earned in the professions or in the technical and administrative departments of industry and commerce. These intermediate grades are closely connected by ties of family and marriage with the upper strata of the manual-working class, as well as with the classes above them.

Class differentiation in advanced industrial societies is thus far more complex than the familiar expositions of the doctrine of the class struggle usually allow for. Above all, the *petite bourgeoisie* can no longer be characterised, as Marx and Engels quite correctly characterised it in 1848, as an essentially reactionary class in process of disappearance before the onset of large-scale industry. This *bourgeoisie* which Marx and Engels described still survives, is still numerous, and still lacks, as it lacked in their time, the power of organising any coherent or powerful movement of its own, or of doing more than hover in its allegiance between the classes above and below it. But the whole situation has been transformed by the development, on the basis of modern industrialism, of a new and quite differently situated *petite bourgeoisie*, which grows in number and strength in proportion as the technical development of industry advances. For this new intermediate class possesses precisely the qualities of initiative and leadership which the older *petite bourgeoisie* so markedly lacks ; and it is capable, by placing itself at their head, of transforming them from a merely confusing element in the struggle of classes into a powerful and aggressive force.

This, as we have seen, is precisely what has happened in those countries in which Fascism has risen to power. But it has happened under the guise of Fascism only where these intermediate classes have found themselves threatened with economic ruin by the disintegration of the economic system. Fascism arises where there is no sufficient scope within the industrial system for the new middle class to exercise its talents and to earn an income which it considers appropriate to its economic and social status. As long as an advanced industrial country is able to provide its growing middle classes with these opportunities, they will not go Fascist ; but if in any country Capitalism shows serious signs of dissolution, and Socialism threatens to displace it, they will be likely to take a very active hand in the conflict between the Socialist and the capitalist forces.

On the analogy of what has happened in Germany, and to a less extent in Italy, it may be regarded as inevitable that, when these groups do organise, their action should take a counter-revolutionary form. But this is only because in both Germany and Italy the capitalist system had fallen into such decay, and was suffering under economic difficulties so extreme, as to threaten seriously the position of the industrial middle class. If to-day Capitalism in Great Britain or in France went the way of German and Italian Capitalism, doubtless Fascism would appear as a powerful force in the two former countries as well ; but if, as seems more probable, the power of Great Britain and France to stand up against even a long continuance of the present world depression remains considerable, there is no reason to anticipate this outcome, and the question is rather what the attitude of these middle-class groups is likely to be in a struggle between capitalist and Socialist forces carried on under a capitalist system still comparatively healthy and strong.

Under such conditions it is by no means a foregone conclusion that the rising industrial middle class will throw all its weight on the capitalist side. Doubtless some of it, by virtue of snobbishness and a desire at all costs to preserve a superiority of status and income, will go that way. But there are other things besides these desires that count in the minds of this section of the population. Consisting largely of technicians and professional people, it is more than any other group interested in its job and keen to get the greatest possible scope for carrying on its work under conditions ministering to the fullest efficiency. Some of its members, at any rate, will be inclined to throw their weight on the side of Socialism to the extent to which they are persuaded that Socialism is really working in the interests of technical progress and is, in the Marxian phrase, in accordance with the requirements of the advancing technical powers of production. Many members of this class have been deeply impressed by the conception of Socialist planning in Russia. Doubtless many of them think that the Russian experiment would be very much better if only it were not Socialist, and would greatly prefer a planned capitalist economy to any form of planning under Socialist control. But some of them have been led, by observing the Russian situation, to realise that Russian planning has been made possible only because the Russians have concentrated in the hands of their governing authorities the ownership and control of all the vital means of production in Russia, so that they have been able to direct the material resources available to them in accordance with the requirements of their general economic plan, whereas no such coherent direction of industrial effort is possible where the ownership and control of the means of production remain in the hands of a large number of private capitalist groups which claim the right to do what they like with their own.

Western Socialists, in making their appeals, have therefore strong reason for making them on a basis calculated to attract at any rate a proportion of the technical and professional workers as well as the manual wage-earners. Nor does this involve, as some suppose it does, any watering down of Socialist programmes or policies ; for there is no reason to suppose that the technical or professional worker is less ready to accept an advanced Socialist programme than a large section of the manual workers, who have also something to lose besides their chains. Indeed, the technicians and professionals are likely to be more attracted to a Socialism sufficiently advanced and drastic to hold out real hopes of successful planning than to a continuation of the moderate and unconstructive policies of previous Labour and Socialist Governments. Socialist parties are more likely to succeed in winning over a majority of the electorate to a Socialist policy if they do look as if they mean to embark upon a businesslike attempt to instal a Socialist system than if they bear the appearance of having no more than a half belief in the efficacy of their own doctrines.

PART V: EUROPEAN INTER-NATIONAL RELATIONS

1. Disarmament and Security
2. The League of Nations
3. The International Labour Organisation

§ 1. DISARMAMENT AND SECURITY

BETWEEN 1914 and 1918 the leading countries of the world were engaged in what was commonly described to the peoples on both sides as a " war to end war." It was promised by each Government to its own nationals that, if they would but consent to prosecute the war to the bitter end, so that the causes for which they stood might completely triumph, the world would, when once the victory had been secured, be set free for ever from the threat of future wars. Above all was this promised as a consequence of the victory of the Allied Powers over Germany and her associates. For these Powers professed to stand for a settlement in which self-interest should have no part and everything possible should be done to build up a friendly and co-operating fellowship of nations. The League of Nations, of which President Wilson was the most enthusiastic advocate, was offered to the world on the morrow of the Allied victory as the means whereby these large promises were to be made good ; and in the Treaties of Peace, side by side with punitive clauses which plainly violated the principles for which the Allies had professed to stand, there were other clauses promising disarmament in a world to be freed henceforth from the danger of war. Disarmament, or rather a drastic limitation of armed *personnel* and of war material, was enforced upon the defeated Central Powers by the Treaties of Peace ; but side by side with these

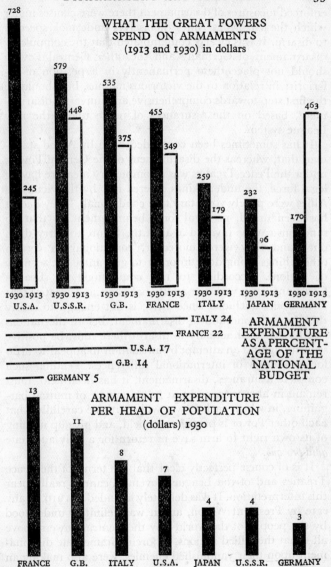

WHAT THE GREAT POWERS
SPEND ON ARMAMENTS
(1913 and 1930) in dollars

728

579

535

463

455

448

375

349

259

245

232

179

170

179

96

1930 1913   1930 1913   1930 1913   1930 1913   1930 1913   1930 1913   1930 1913
U.S.A.   U.S.S.R.   G.B.   FRANCE   ITALY   JAPAN   GERMANY

ITALY 24
FRANCE 22
U.S.A. 17
G.B. 14
GERMANY 5

ARMAMENT
EXPENDITURE
AS A PERCENT-
AGE OF THE
NATIONAL
BUDGET

ARMAMENT EXPENDITURE
PER HEAD OF POPULATION
(dollars) 1930

13

11

8

7

4   4

3

FRANCE   G.B.   ITALY   U.S.A.   JAPAN   U.S.S.R.   GERMANY enforced measures of disarmament there were clauses under which the victorious Allies themselves undertook speedily to disarm. It was clearly contemplated that the compulsory disarmament of Germany and the other Central Powers should not place them permanently in a position of inferiority in relation to the victorious nations, but should be the first step towards comprehensive and universal disarmament, based on the assurances of peace under the new League system.

It has sometimes been contended since by Allied statesmen that, whereas the disarmament of the Central Powers under the Peace Treaties was a compulsory measure having legal force, the undertakings entered into by the victorious Allies were purely voluntary and conditional. They had, it has been urged, no legal force behind them, so that no sanctions can be invoked against the failure to carry them out ; and they were, moreover, conditional on certain other things being done in order to guarantee the security of nations. According to this contention, the League Covenant, even with the additional pacts and treaties that have been concluded since 1919, is not enough to satisfy this implied condition of disarmament. Before the nations can be expected actually to disarm there must be positive security against an attempt by any nation to appeal to arms for a solution of international differences. Pending such complete assurances, disarmament, it has been held, must remain in abeyance, or be at best a matter of mutual bargaining, in which each Power will scrutinise carefully what each other Power is prepared to yield, and give up nothing of its own right to arm save in return for a fully adequate *quid pro quo*.

It is of course perfectly clear that the terms of the Peace Treaties and of the League Covenant cannot really bear this interpretation. It was definitely intended in 1919, at any rate by President Wilson, and it was definitely understood by the peoples of the world—by the Central Powers above all—that the Allied nations, in forcing immediate disarmament upon their vanquished enemies, were also making an unequivocal promise of early disarmament in their own countries. Indeed, any other interpretation would make nonsense of the entire system for the guarantee of peace which it was proposed to set up ; for to make security a prior condition of disarmament amounts to a contradiction in terms. As long as all nations are armed to the teeth, no nation can possibly feel secure. It is an absolute condition of security that disarmament should have already taken place. It can doubtless be contended that the two processes ought to go on side by side, and that while the nations are disarming they should proceed simultaneously to build up the framework of a system of mutual concession and co-operation, in order to realise not merely security in a negative sense, but the removal of the causes of quarrels as well as the prevention of the attempt to settle them by war. But the idea that security can precede disarmament is sheerly fantastic, and as long as it persists it is evident that no real progress in the direction of disarmament is likely to be made.

Fifteen years have now passed since the end of the Great War, and throughout these years the Powers, both through the League of Nations and in other international conferences, have been continually discussing the cognate problems of disarmament and security. As early as 1920, the League of Nations set up a Permanent Advisory Commission to discuss the question of disarmament. The Soviet Union and the Baltic countries met in a special disarmament conference of their own as early as 1922. The Washington Naval Treaty between the United States, the British Empire, France, Italy and Japan was entered into in the same year, and was meant to be the first step towards a drastic programme of naval disarmament over the world as a whole. Since then there has been, up to the Disarmament Conference which is still meeting as we write, an infinite amount of discussing, reporting, presenting of plans and counter-plans, argument about the respective merits of absolute and partial, qualitative and quantitative, unilateral and general disarmament, and an infinite

amount of propaganda in favour of one project after another
for the guaranteeing of peace. But what has it all come to ?
How much nearer are we, after these fifteen years, either to
any sort of security against the occurrence of further wars,
or to any real disarmament, or even to a substantial reduction in the number of men under arms, in the size and
equipment of fleets by sea and air, or in budgetary expenditure, open or concealed, upon the fighting services ?

Armaments and Expenditure.   Let us begin with a few
of the outstanding facts. According to the calculations made
by the staff of the League of Nations for the purposes of the
Disarmament Conference, world expenditure on armaments amounted in 1925 to just under 3,500 million
dollars, and in 1930 to 4,128 million dollars. These figures
are calculated by aggregating in terms of dollars the
annual expenditure of 62 different countries. They cannot
pretend to complete accuracy ; but they are certainly near
enough to the truth to give a realistic picture of the situation as it exists at present. This hardly looks as if, despite all
the conferences, real progress were being made in the direction of world disarmament ; for although the cost of maintaining a given quantity of armaments was undoubtedly to
some extent higher in 1930 than in 1913, it was also undoubtedly lower in 1930 than in 1925 ; so that the real
increase in armaments between 1925 and 1930 was considerably greater than the totals of expenditure show.

No comparison with 1913 is possible for the world as
a whole on the basis of the available figures ; but a comparison can be made for certain of the leading Powers.
Thus if the expenditure on armaments in 1913–14, when
preparedness was at an exceptionally high level in view of
the general expectation that a great war might break out
in the near future, is compared with the expenditure in
1930–31, it will be found that the three leading Allied
countries—Great Britain, France and Italy—together spent
on armaments in 1913–14 just over 900 million dollars,
whereas in 1930–31, despite their complete victory in the

war, and their success in disarming their late enemies, the same three countries spent about 1,250 million dollars, an increase of nearly 40 per cent, which should be compared with a rise of about 18 per cent in dollar prices between the two dates. It is true that this increase is very much less than the increase in the United States, which was comparatively lightly armed before the Great War. The United States spent on armaments 245 million dollars in 1913–14, and 728 million in 1930–31—an increase of practically 200 per cent. Japan increased her expenditure by 142 per cent, from 96 million dollars to 232 millions. The U.S.S.R. showed an increase in armaments expenditure of 29 per cent, from 448 million dollars to 579 millions in 1929–30 ; but in this case the rise in internal prices was very much greater than in the other countries concerned, so that the figures exaggerate the real rate of increase. On the other hand, Germany, compulsorily disarmed by the Peace Treaties, spent in 1930–31 on armaments only 170 million dollars as against 463 millions in 1913–14, a fall of 63 per cent.

Put the position in another way. In 1930–31 Germany was spending only 5 per cent of her total budgetary outgoings on armaments, thanks to the compulsion laid upon her by the Treaty of Peace. Great Britain, on the other hand, was spending 14 per cent, and the United States 17 per cent, while France was spending no less than 22 per cent, and Italy 24 per cent. France had the highest *per capita* expenditure on armaments of any country in the world ; for in 1930 her armaments cost her no less than 13 dollars per head of population. Great Britain came next with 11 dollars, followed by Italy and Holland with 8 dollars ; the United States spent 7 dollars, the U.S.S.R. 4 dollars, and Germany only 3 dollars, while in Austria and Hungary expenditure was only 2 dollars a head, and in Bulgaria only 1 dollar. Certainly, compulsory disarmament, whatever stigma it may be felt to convey, has its compensations from the point of view of its effect on the national budget, though of course these effects were in practice neutralised during the period after the war by the Allied demands for reparations.

It is, however, in some respects misleading to compare national armaments in terms of budgetary expenditure alone ; for a great deal depends upon the nature of the armaments upon which the money is spent, and upon the different forms of military service adopted. Conscript armies are much cheaper per head than long-service standing armies recruited by voluntary enlistment. Naval armaments cost in these days of vastly expensive capital ships more than corresponding land armaments ; and the different standards of life in the various countries affect considerably the cost of maintaining armed forces of any given size. It is therefore necessary to consider not only the amount spent on armaments, but also the number of effectives enrolled in the various armies, and the material equipment of their naval and air forces. It is, however, extraordinarily difficult, as the World Disarmament Conference has already discovered, to obtain from countries any really adequate or comparable account of the numbers and equipment of their armed forces. Many of the European countries have, in addition to their regular armies, numerous auxiliary forces, variously denominated frontier guards, citizen guards, irregulars, and various other ambiguous descriptions. It is hard to know how far trained reserves ought to be counted in estimating the size of the national forces, or what account should be taken of part-time armies such as the Territorial Army in Great Britain in comparison with full-time soldiers. Again there is the question of the colonial forces maintained abroad by the various imperialist Powers. Is a statement of the British forces to include the Indian army, or only the British troops stationed in India, and is the number of the French army to be reckoned by including the large, and from a military point of view undoubtedly valuable, army raised and for the most part stationed in Africa ? These questions admit of no uniform answer likely to command unanimous agreement ; and because of them it is exceedingly difficult to present any comprehensive picture on a comparable basis. All that can be done and all that we have attempted to do is to extract such relevant information as can be extracted from the special tables prepared on the basis of returns from each nation for the use of the Disarmament Conference, and to set side by side with these figures certain figures for earlier years, which unfortunately cannot be made fully comparable with the Disarmament Conference returns.

Let us confine ourselves in the first place to a comparative table for 1913, 1925 and 1928, published in an article by General Sir Frederick Maurice in the issue of the League of Nations periodical *Headway* for December 1929. All these figures are derived from documents published by various bodies connected with the League of Nations. The 1913 figures were originally issued by the Temporary Mixed Commission on Armaments, while the figures for 1925 and 1928 are taken from the League of Nations Armaments Year Book. On the basis of these figures, we see that there had been in Western Europe between 1913 and 1928 at best only an insignificant tendency towards the reduction of armaments. Italy appears, indeed, to have a slightly smaller army, and France a substantially smaller army, than before the war. But for Great Britain there has been an apparent increase, which is, however, largely if not wholly due to the figures being compiled on a different basis. Taking the figures for France and Italy, we get a total force of 1,050,000 comprised in their combined peace establishments before the war, as against 920,000 in 1928, surely a most unsatisfactory percentage reduction for the ten years after the conclusion of the " war to end war " ? Naturally, the Central European countries show a much larger aggregate reduction, as they have for the most part been compulsorily disarmed ; and certain of the Scandinavian countries and also Holland have greatly reduced the size of their armed forces, which were always small. It is to be observed that for the European countries as a whole the total reduction in the peace establishments between 1913 and 1928 amounted to less than one million out of

ARMIES AT PEACE STRENGTH

Approximate only. Including Colonial Armies, but not Irregulars.

Country	Strength
GERMANY	100
G.B.	137
TURKEY	140
U.S.A.	145
CZECHO-SLOVAKIA	150
ROUMANIA	250
INDIA	260
JAPAN	270
POLAND	323
ITALY	491
U.S.S.R.	562
FRANCE	662

EUROPEAN ARMIES IN 1931

Country	Regulars	Gendarmerie	Others
Albania	13,000	—	?
Austria	21,000	17,000* (and police)	—
Belgium	86,000	—	6,000
Bulgaria	19,000	6,000	3,000
Czecho-slovakia	139,000	—	13,000
Denmark	8,000	—	3,000
Estonia	14,000	—	1,000 Civic Guard 29,000
Finland	32,000	—	2,000 Civic Guard 100,000
France	497,000 (662,000 including Colonials)	37,000	18,000
Germany	100,000	—	?
Great Britain	137,000	—	Territorials, etc. 153,000
Greece	65,000	—	?
Holland	55,000	—	4,000
Hungary	35,000	—	12,000
India	260,000	—	74,000
Irish Free State	6,000	5,000 Reserves under training	Civic Guard 7,000
Italy	491,000	90,000	—
Latvia	23,000	—	1,000
Lithuania	18,000	—	?
Luxembourg	—	500	—
Norway	6,000	—	—
Poland	266,000	—	64,000
Portugal	61,000	—	11,000
Roumania	250,000	—	63,000
Spain	195,000	16,000	?
Sweden	25,000	—	—
Switzerland	12,000†	—	—
Turkey	140,000	30,000	—
U.S.A.	145,000	—	?
U.S.S.R.	562,000	—	?
Yugoslavia	184,000	—	28,000

* *Heimwehr* not included.　　† Average daily number in training.

$3\frac{3}{4}$ millions in arms in 1913, and that there were still in 1928 not far short of three million men regularly under arms, apart from those included in the naval and air forces of the countries concerned.

Turn now to the approximate figures for 1931, and consider the absolute numbers under arms in the various countries, again excluding naval and air establishments. Three countries—France, Italy and the U.S.S.R.—possess armies of over half a million men, Poland has over a quarter of a million, and six other European countries have armies exceeding the 100,000 permitted as a maximum to Germany under the Treaty of Peace. Belgium, with her relatively tiny population, is not far behind Germany, with 90,000 men ; and all the neighbours of Austria and Hungary, with their permitted maxima of 12,000, and Bulgaria with 20,000, still have armies many times larger than those allowed to their defeated rivals. How can these vast forces still under arms in every danger spot of Europe possibly be compatible with any sense of security on the European Continent ? It is indeed sometimes contended that the larger the army the greater the security that it will not be used ; but we have yet to find any reasonable person who really believes in this fantastic doctrine after the experience of the years leading up to the outbreak of war in 1914. We were told often enough in those days that a thorough preparedness was the best guarantee of peace ; but it would need some credulity to hold any such opinion to-day.

Turn now from the military forces of Europe to the navies of the leading maritime countries. Navies are expensive things, and only rich and powerful countries can afford the luxury of large and up-to-date naval forces. But every important country that possesses an outlet to the sea still desires to equip itself with a powerful navy, and there is still fully as much rivalry in naval as in military armaments. It is true that the relative strength of the Great Powers in capital ships has been regulated to some extent by international agreement since the Washington Naval Treaty

FLEETS OF THE POWERS, JANUARY 1932

	British Empire	U.S.A.	Japan	France	Italy	U.S.S.R.	Germany
Battleships and Battle Cruisers	15	15	10	9	4	3	4+2
Cruisers	53+7	19+7	31+7	22+5	17+9	4	6
Destroyers and Torpedo Boats	134+20	251+5	110+10	65	99+11	17	26
Minesweepers	32	43	10+2	26	48	6	29
Aircraft Carriers and Flotilla Leaders	24+3	3+1	3+1	14+19	21	—	—
Sloops, Gunboats and Motor Boats	51+10	20	15	65+25	70+3	4	3+1
Submarines	52+10	81+3	67+5	65+45	46+29	16	—

	Denmark	Estonia	Finland	Greece	Latvia	Holland	Norway	Poland	Portugal	Roumania	Spain	Sweden	Turkey	Yugoslavia
Battleships	—	—	—	2	—	—	—	—	—	—	2	—	2	—
Cruisers	3	2	2	2	2	3	—	—	11	—	8	—	2	—
Destroyers	—	—	—	8	—	8	3	2	11	4	17	13	5	1
Submarines	11	—	4	6	2	31	9	3	6	1	16	22	2	4
Coast Defence Ships	—	—	—	3	—	—	4	—	—	—	—	10	—	—

(A *plus* sign (+) indicates vessels under construction)

of 1922 ; and the process of agreeing upon ratios was carried somewhat further, among some only of the leading countries, at the Naval Conference of 1927. But both the Washington Naval Treaty and the subsequent Three-Power Pact were effective, in as far as they were effective at all, rather in preventing a race to increase naval armaments above the existing levels than in actually reducing the armaments already in existence or preventing the replacement of obsolete vessels by new and more powerful engines of destruction. Arrangements for naval parity between Great Britain and the United States, with Japan only a little way behind and ever anxious to catch up and achieve an effective equality in capital ships, are no assurance at all against naval warfare ; for the permitted naval equipment is still large enough to leave each of these countries armed to the teeth, while the maintenance by each of them of a powerful navy not unevenly matched with each of the others serves both as an inducement to the warlike spirit and as a perpetual challenge to those nations which are behind in naval armaments.

France, which comes next after the British Empire, the United States and Japan in capital ships, has a powerful enough navy to play an important part in any war based on rival alliances of Powers ; and Italy, which comes next after France, is only willing to accept measures of limitation provided that she is conceded, in theory at least, the right to build up to whatever tonnage France may be allowed, though her financial power actually to do this, unless the French substantially reduce their existing tonnage, may legitimately be doubted. It was on this issue of Franco-Italian parity that the attempt to make a new Five-Power Naval Pact in 1927 finally broke down. It had been hoped to supplement what had been done at Washington in 1922 in the case of capital ships by a further pact including other classes of vessels. This proved to be impossible in face of Franco-Italian rivalry, except for three countries—Great Britain, the United States and Japan ; and even their agreement was, as we have seen, rather a promise to

AIR FLEETS OF EUROPE, 1932

Great Britain	1,434+127	Spain	462+187
France	2,375	Portugal	159
Italy	1,507	Greece	40+80
Germany	—	Albania	—
U.S.S.R.	750+750(?)	Bulgaria	—
Poland	700	Turkey	50
Czechoslovakia	546+141	Austria	—
Roumania	799	Hungary	—
Yugoslavia	627+263	Switzerland	300
Belgium	195+113	Lithuania	70
Holland	321	Latvia	79
Denmark	78 (reducing to 24)	Estonia	74
Sweden	167	Luxembourg	—
Norway	179	Irish Free State	24
Finland	60		
U.S.A.	1,752+599		
Japan	1,639		

A *plus* sign (+) indicates aeroplanes not fit for active military use
where these are distinguished in the figures.

abstain from fresh competitive building on a gigantic scale than any indication of a willingness actually to reduce their existing tonnage. The size of the armed fleets still maintained by the leading countries in 1932 is indicated in the table on page 709, and while the figures are inevitably to some extent misleading, in that they group together indiscriminately vessels new and old, they are startling enough to indicate plainly the narrow measure of success that has so far accompanied all the output of conversations and agreements on naval disarmament.

As a complement to fleets and armies there has come into existence, for the most part since 1914, a new arm ; and every country now considers it essential to its nationhood to maintain not only a powerful army but also a large fleet of fighting aeroplanes. Owing to the newness of this arm, no comparison with earlier dates is of much use ; for obviously the aeroplane has come into existence not solely as an addition to previous forms of armament, but also to some extent as a substitute for them. When, for example, it is suggested that fighting and bombing aeroplanes should be totally abolished, the reply is at once made, especially by Great Britain, that aeroplanes, provided they do not exceed a certain range and carrying capacity, are to be conceived rather as agencies of police than as offensive military units. Are they not far cheaper and more convenient means than soldiers of keeping recalcitrant tribesmen in order ? Cannot a native village be far more effectively terrorised by dropping bombs than by punitive expeditions by land ? Great Britain is prompt to protest against bomb-dropping upon people whom she regards as civilised ; but mere natives are another matter, and it is even argued that the aeroplane is a merciful weapon because, humanely used, it strikes far more terror than it does material or human damage. In any case, the air fleets of the world have risen to a prodigious size in recent years ; and aeroplanes have from the standpoint of countries struggling with serious budgetary difficulties the supreme merit of being reasonably cheap.

Moreover, apart from fighting planes built directly for the service of the various States, it is always possible in the event of war to press planes built for civil aviation into military use ; and it is a notorious fact that comparatively few of the regular air roads which now run over a great part of the world could be maintained as purely commercial ventures, and most depend for their existence on subsidies which States are prepared to grant in aid of civil aviation on account of its potential military value. Germany, denied all military aeroplanes, has naturally taken up civil flying with enthusiasm. But the Germans are not alone in this. The figures on page 711 showing the approximate strength of the air fleets of Europe in comparison with those of the United States and Japan give unhappily far less than an adequate picture of the potential force that could be put into the air by the various nations in the event of war.

The Traffic in Armaments.

So much for the actual forces under arms by land, sea and air in a Europe supposed to be bound together in a League of Nations based on the guarantee of perpetual peace, and further safeguarded by a host of general and bilateral convenants, pacts and treaties of every sort and kind. No account of the armed camp which Europe still is could be complete unless something were said in addition of the means of making the tools with the aid of which war's mischief is carried on ; for now, as before the war, the armament-makers stand behind the statesmen of Europe, egging them on to arm and counter-arm, and drawing their toll of profit from the mutual fears and suspicions of the nations. On the eve of the war much had already been written by way of exposure of the armament rings which had been a powerful factor in stimulating war feeling in all the leading countries, and in persuading each country to buy more arms in order to get even with its neighbours. For, as has often been pointed out, the sellers of armaments more than any other class of traders have a natural instinct and interest to combine. Almost every other commodity is produced in response to a limited demand, so that the sale of a dose of it by one producer means that less of it remains to be sold by others. But with armaments this is not the case. If an armament firm succeeds in selling to one country some new and deadly engine of destruction, that is a reason why all the other countries which are its rivals in the armaments race should seek immediately to possess themselves of a quota of the same engine of destruction, or if possible of some newer and more devastating engine, the purchase of which will in turn set up a fresh demand from other countries for something newer and deadlier still. Adam Smith said once that all capitalists were in a natural conspiracy against the public ; but of no group of capitalists is this true to anything like the same extent as of the purveyors of armaments. The more they sell the more their products are in demand ; and they would be more than human if, as capitalists, they did not seek in these circumstances to sell as much as they can possibly induce the Governments of the world to buy or if, in their endeavours to sell as much as possible, they did not resort often to methods which even the current standards of business morality condemn.

As many writers have pointed out, the armament firms have shown themselves throughout their history singularly free from merely nationalistic prejudice. They have been perfectly prepared to sell to anybody, and never happier than when they have been in the satisfying position of selling to both sides in some jolly war which has created a gratifying demand for their products. They have been perfectly prepared to sell implements of war which have been used for blowing their own countrymen to bits. For nothing is more profitable than to sell to a potential enemy, since such a sale almost inevitably creates an additional demand for armaments from the home Government. In the Great War many thousands of British and Allied soldiers were killed and wounded by British rifles, British bayonets, British guns ; and in the next war, if it comes in the near future, it is quite certain that the same will be true. For despite all that was known of the armament rings before

1914 and all the experience men had of them during the Great War, they are still left free to pursue their old games, and have even increased their power and degree of combination in the post-war years. One great name indeed has ceased to be prominently associated with the manufacture of armaments since 1914 ; for the disarmament of Germany and the prohibition of the manufacture of war material within her frontiers has caused the disappearance of the great Krupp concern from among the leading armament-makers of the world—though in face of recent changes in the German situation it would be quite unsafe to prophesy that this disappearance is more than temporary. But, if for the moment Krupp has been put out of the game, plenty of other giants remain. The two pre-war British giants, Vickers and Armstrong Whitworth, with their countless subsidiaries, have now joined forces as far as their armaments business is concerned ; and, though they fell on evil days after the war as a consequence of grossly inflationary finance in the course of the immediate post-war boom, financial reconstruction has now set them free, with the continued support of the Bank of England, to go on with their familiar business of supplying the needs of any country that is prepared to order their goods. It is true that arms can only be exported from Great Britain under licence ; but this does not apply to many semi-manufactures which can be worked up into armaments abroad. Nor is any attempt made under normal conditions to prohibit or even to limit the export of arms ; for would not any such policy result in throwing skilled British engineers out of work, and in lowering the profitableness of British business enterprise ? Our rivals sell armaments to all comers, and so do we ; for in these matters a number of blacks are always reckoned as making a white.

It is not suggested for a moment that Vickers-Armstrong is any worse than the corresponding armament firms of other countries. France has its famous Schneider-Creusot combine, with a history extending back to the French Revolutionary Wars in the eighteenth century ; and Schneider-Creusot,

it is well known, is, together with other French armament firms, the great power behind the *Comité des Forges*,
the political representative of French heavy industry
and the close associate of every reactionary Government
that has held office in France since the war. Schneider-
Creusot, moreover, is closely linked up with the armaments
industry in Central and Eastern Europe. M. Eugène
Schneider is a director of the *Banque de l'Union Parisienne*
and president of the *Union Européenne Banque* ; and it is no
accident that the first of these bodies finances an important
credit institution in Hungary, while the second plays an
important part in the control of the Skoda works in Czechoslovakia. France has not been backward in assuring the new
States of Central and Eastern Europe of an adequate supply
of arms. The Skoda firm has its factories in Poland and
Roumania as well as in Czechoslovakia ; and Schneider-
Creusot together with its associated concerns has been most
active in the munitions trade in the Balkan countries as well
as further north. But even here internationalism is not
absent ; for the Schneider-Creusot group does not hesitate
to supply arms to the Hungarians as well as the Czechs,
although these two countries are obviously arming largely
against each other. We say nothing here of the giant Mitsui
armaments concern in Japan, which ranks after Vickers-
Armstrong and Schneider-Creusot as the third greatest
armaments concern in the world ; for there is enough to
occupy our attention in Europe without considering the
position in other Continents. Germany, owing to the Peace
Treaties, can to-day put up no armaments giant to rank
beside these three ; but it must not be forgotten that, since
Germany has been forbidden to manufacture armaments
herself, there has been a remarkable growth of armament
firms in her immediate neighbourhood, in both Sweden
and Poland, or that the Bifors concern in Sweden has close
associations with Krupps, and has been afforded full permission to use the Krupp patents. Dutch armament firms,
too, have German associations ; and the fact that they are
also associated with Vickers-Armstrong is assuredly no

guarantee of any unwillingness on their part to fulfil German orders. But there is no space to pursue in this book the ramifications of the European armaments firms ; those who are in search of further enlightenment must be referred to the exceedingly useful booklet published by the Union of Democratic Control in 1932 under the title of " *The Secret International*." From this booklet have been taken many of the facts and illustrations given in this section.

Armament-makers, if they are to be successful profit-makers as well—and of what use would it be to make armaments if there were no profit in the game ?—must have the ear of statesmen ; and they have always been on the alert to ensure the respectful attention of statesmen to their intelligent anticipations of the danger of war. No sooner does an armament firm secure an order from any one country than its representatives are off in haste to tell the Ministers at the head of the war departments of all the other countries of the sinister intentions of their customer ; and these representatives are sure to be able to return with a refreshing stream of additional requisitions for the means of destruction. In order to ensure the needed attention in high quarters, armament firms are usually very careful in recruiting their directorates. While a mysterious " genius " such as Sir Basil Zaharoff may remain in the background, and prefer the reputation of being the mystery man of Europe to taking a permanent part in the activities of the businesses which he controls, the Boards of Directors of the great armament firms are usually so chosen as to include a sufficiency of persons likely to find favour in high places. Retired army officers with good connections in the War Offices of the various countries usually play a prominent part in the high-class commercial travelling of the armament rings. But the rings have also found it useful to offer a lucrative home to retired civil servants, or even to ex-politicians possessing the necessary official connections. The overhead cost of selling armaments is considerable ; and it is said that in the years immediately before the war certain of the leading firms maintained in the principal Continental capitals private missions of their own, with no other functions than those of hospitably entertaining, and on occasion suitably rewarding, important personalities in a position to influence the placing of orders for their wares. Nor is there any reason to suppose that this practice has ceased to-day, though republican statesmen are perhaps in some cases less open to direct bribery than the predatory hangers-on of the pre-war Russian and Austro-Hungarian imperial courts.

The industry of warfare is, however, by no means confined to the firms which make guns, rifles, armour-plate and the other familiar products of the metal and engineering industries. It is also becoming more and more an affair for the firms manufacturing chemicals and explosives of many different kinds ; and these firms are no less strongly organised and hardly less successful in influencing national policies than the armament makers in the metal trades. Great Britain's solicitude for the maintenance of an effective dyestuffs industry was not mainly due to the importance of an adequate supply of dyestuffs for the textile trades ; and the willingness of the British Government to purchase nearly two million shares in the British Dyestuffs Corporation was an illuminating comment on its belief in the achievements of the " war to end war." Since then the chemical industry of Great Britain has been reorganised on a broader basis, and the British Dyestuffs Corporation has been merged with Brunner Mond, the United Alkali Company, and the great explosives concern of Nobel, into Imperial Chemical Industries Limited, with its issued capital of over £70,000,000, its control over practically the whole chemical industry of Great Britain, and its ramifications in other countries, especially Canada and the United States. I.C.I. has, moreover, a holding in the famous *I. G. Farbenindustrie* of Germany, on whose pre-war experience it was largely modelled. The chemical trade has the advantage over the armament-makers that the plant which it uses to make ordinary commercial products in time of peace can be readily adapted for the manufacture of explosives, poison gases, and other more patriotic products in time of war ; and though the one considerable paper achievement in lessening the horrors of war that has been made by the nations of the world since 1918 is the agreement of 1925 forbidding poison gas, it requires an optimist to believe that, if a great war once breaks out, nations equipped with large chemical factories able to turn out poison gases of unprecedented virulence, will, if they feel their backs against the wall, for long stand out against the temptation of using the forbidden weapons. Each of the Great Powers has set up a special authority for the study and organisation of chemical warfare ; and chemical research is in every country subsidised to some extent by Governments in view of the possibility that it could be turned to profit in case of war.

What can be done in face of the menace to the continuance of civilisation represented by these powerful vested interests, which have the strongest possible motive for inducing the nations to arm one against another ? The danger which threatens the world from this profit-making traffic in the implements of destruction is certainly far greater than the menace of the trade in opium or the White Slave Traffic, which special international institutions have been established to suppress. It is surely clear that, even if armaments ought to be made at all, their manufacture ought to be so controlled and regulated that it is impossible for anyone to have a financial interest in making them. They ought not, at all events, to be made under the inducement of private profit, or under conditions which foster powerful private concerns with a direct interest in stirring the nations up to mutual hatred and to actual war. In other words, the manufacture of armaments, as long as it continues to exist at all, ought to become a public monopoly ; and this system of socialisation ought to be applied not only to the direct manufacture of munitions of war in the narrower sense, but certainly to an industry such as the chemical industry, a large part of whose productive resources is capable of being applied to the ends of war. If this were done, there would no longer be hawkers of armaments and private scaremongers with a direct interest in selling war. Governments would no longer have contracts for war supplies to let out to the citizens of their own or other countries, and the necessity of manufacturing all armaments under public auspices would give at any rate some greater assurance of publicity than exists under the present conditions of an authorised private trade in armaments.

But the socialisation of the industries producing the instruments of war would not solve the entire problem. Indeed, it might even raise new problems of its own. For the smaller countries at present depend for their armaments largely upon factories located in the greater countries, or at all events upon companies organised and financed by groups of capitalists belonging to the great imperialist Powers. If the production of war material were made a public monopoly, the sale of armaments outside their country of manufacture would obviously become to a greater extent than it is to-day a matter of political policy ; for States could hardly follow the example of private firms and sell munitions of war to other States with whom they contemplated the likelihood, or even the possibility, of armed conflict. To a great extent this would be an advantage, in that it would tend to diminish the international trade in arms ; but it would also place many of the smaller countries in the position of depending for their supplies of arms upon the Great Powers. This dependence, while it would strengthen the influence of the Great Powers in preventing minor wars, as long as these Powers were able to act together, might become a source of danger in as far as the Great Powers were working one against another. France for example, instead of supplying the new States of Central and Eastern Europe with the money wherewith to buy arms from the Schneider-Creusot combine, would be in a position to supply these countries with arms directly from her own munitions factories, and to refuse to supply countries of whose policy and aspirations she did not approve. Great Britain might find herself supplying another group of countries and refusing supplies to other countries in the same way, while Germany would have an even more power-ful motive than she has to-day for demanding an equality of treatment which would allow her to resume the manu-facture of war material on the grand scale.

The socialisation of the armament industries might, moreover, induce more of the smaller States to set up arma-ment works of their own, and to give high protection to those industries which are capable of being turned to the production of armaments in the event of war ; and it might thus, over a wide field, especially in the heavy industries, encourage still further the growth of economic nationalism. The socialisation of the armaments industry is certainly not by itself a sufficient means of checking the growth of armaments, or of preventing States from arming one against another or ranging themselves in imperialistic groups and rival European alliances ; but the dangers involved in a policy of socialisation, while they are real, are very much less than the dangers of leaving things as they are. For it is better, if dangers exist, that they should be brought out into the open and that the responsibility for guarding against them should be put definitely on the Governments of the world, than that they should be covered up from public view because they are under the control of private profit-making concerns for which the Governments which encourage their operations are in a position to disclaim responsibility.

There is, indeed, one very difficult problem of the present time which is intimately connected with this question of the socialisation of the armament industries. At present the largest importer of arms from the rest of the world is China, which draws supplies from practically all the countries in which important armament works are situated. China has practically no armaments industry of her own ; she depends almost entirely on supplies brought in from abroad. On the other hand, Japan, as we have seen, has a very powerful armament industry under the leadership of the Mitsui combine. Japan also imports arms, and imports to a much larger extent semi-manufactured materials out of which arms can be made. But she is in a far better position to dispense with external assistance in the equipment of her forces than her chief rival in the Far East. If the European countries were to socialise their armaments industries and then refuse to supply arms to China, they would in effect be putting that country at the complete mercy of Japan. On the other hand, if they continued to supply China from their socialised armament factories, this would at once involve political complications in their relations with Japan, though, since Japan has announced her withdrawal from the League of Nations, she would no longer be in a position to raise the issue before the League even if she desired to do so. In face of the League's recent judgment on Japanese intervention in Manchuria, it would be obviously and grossly unfair to refuse to supply the Chinese with arms if Japan were to launch a further attack upon them—and it would be in practice no less unfair to impose an embargo on the export of arms to both combatants, as Great Britain did for a brief period early in 1933—for Japan can get along without the imports, whereas China obviously cannot. But in this case too it would be worth while to face the political complications involved in the socialisation of the armament industries in order to do away with the sinister influence upon world affairs at present emanating from the vested interests of the great armament firms.

Projects of Disarmament.

We have seen that, ever since the Peace Treaties were concluded and the Covenant of the League of Nations drawn up, the countries of the world have been continuously engaged in the discussion of proposals for disarmament. Ever since the Permanent Advisory Commission on Armaments and the Temporary Mixed Commission on Disarmament were set up in 1920 discussions have been going on either among technical experts or among statesmen themselves. As long ago as 1925 the League Council created a special Preparatory Commission of twenty-six members with instructions to prepare the ground for a World Disarmament Conference, and this committee reported in 1927, shortly after Germany had become a member of the League. In this year, the U.S.S.R., invited together with the United States to take part in the discussions on disarmament, brought forward, for the first time in a general assembly of the nations, a proposal for a draft convention based on universal and complete disarmament. The practically unanimous rejection of this scheme by the larger countries induced the U.S.S.R. to try again ; and in 1928 M. Litvinov came forward with a proposal for partial disarmament, which met with no better success. Not until February 1932 did the World Disarmament Conference finally begin, under the presidency of Mr. Arthur Henderson ; and as we write the World Conference is still in session, and seems likely to remain in session a long while yet.

In the meantime, as we have seen, there have been separate discussions on the question of naval disarmament, beginning with the Washington Five-Power Treaty of 1922 and leading on to the Three-Power Pact of 1927 between Great Britain, the United States and Japan, to which France and Italy were also signatories in respect of certain of the clauses. But the failure of the negotiations of 1927 compelled the advocates of naval disarmament to recognise that little progress could be made in this field unless military disarmament were also taken into account. For the two problems cannot in effect be separated ; and the obstacles to success are in both cases to a great extent the same. Accordingly the World Disarmament Conference of 1932 was called to deal with the naval as well as the military aspects of the question ; and in the long succession of rival plans which have been laid before it during the past year, questions of naval and military armaments have been constantly considered in relation to each other. The problem of naval disarmament is indeed technically the simpler, in that it is for the most part of vital concern only to a small number of Great Powers ; for the navies of the smaller countries are, in relation to the fleets of the Great

Powers, of very little importance or fighting value, whereas the armed forces even of the smaller States constitute potential contingents in the military forces of great rival European alliances, and the complications of military disarmament are far greater because of the difficulty of defining the permissible number of effectives on a uniform basis for different countries with widely varying military systems and conditions of service.

In all this succession of discussions on the question of disarmament it has been impossible to isolate this one issue from other problems arising out of the relations between nation and nation. Thus, discussion on disarmament has been constantly mixed up with, and affected by, the simultaneous negotiations over such matters as security, arbitration, mutual assistance, and the renunciation of war as a means of settling international disputes. The draft Treaty of Mutual Assistance, which came under discussion in 1922, arose out of the work of the Temporary Mixed Commission to which reference has already been made. In the revised draft of this projected treaty, presented to the League after an accommodation between the French and British points of view, it was proposed to limit the assistance promised by all the signatory States to any country which found itself in the position of resisting aggression by another State, to those nations which had actually reduced their armaments in reliance upon the promise of assistance given by the Treaty. The two questions of disarmament and security were thus linked together at an early stage in the discussion of the problem ; and they have throughout been very closely connected, especially in the minds of the French, who have continually insisted that they cannot be expected to disarm save on the basis of some firm assurance that other countries will come to their help in face of any threat of invasion of their territory.

The Third Assembly of the League in 1923 recommended acceptance of the revised draft of the Treaty of Mutual Assistance ; but there was no readiness to accept it among the leading countries included in the League, and its rejection by most of the countries concerned, and especially by Great Britain, which was not prepared to involve herself in any obligation binding her in certain circumstances to go to war on behalf of another State, called for the making of a new start.

The next attempt came from certain of the smaller States of Europe, which at the fifth League Assembly in 1924 brought forward the Geneva Protocol. This project, most closely associated with the name of Dr. Benes of Czechoslovakia and with the short-lived British Labour Government of 1924, was based on an explicit renunciation of war by the signatory States, and on the recognition of the compulsory jurisdiction of the Permanent Court of International Justice, set up at the Hague in 1920 as a part of the new post-war machinery of international collaboration. The Geneva Protocol did not involve the submission of all disputes to the Hague Court, for it was recognised that disputes would arise which it would not be possible to settle by judicial methods ; but it did involve both a definite renunciation of war and an agreement to submit to the compulsory authority of the Court all matters admitting of judicial decision. Eighteen States, including France, Belgium, Czechoslovakia, and Yugoslavia, signed the Geneva Protocol ; but the fall of the British Labour Government at the end of 1924 was followed by its rejection by Great Britain, largely on the ground that its acceptance involved obligations over and above those contained in the Covenant of the League, especially in the provisions for applying economic sanctions to States which the League Council held to be in the wrong. Great Britain, as a naval Power, held that the burden of these economic sanctions would in practice be placed largely upon her, and was not prepared to commit herself to an absolute undertaking to blockade any State designated by the League as the aggressor in an international dispute. This British attitude was fatal to the prospects of the Geneva Protocol, since without British participation it could be of but little value, especially in view of the absence of the United States from the League and their refusal to recognise the jurisdiction of the International Court.

The rejection of the Geneva Protocol involved yet another fresh start ; and this time the initiative was taken by the Great Powers, and especially by Great Britain, which, having refused to accept the system proposed in the Protocol, was compelled, in view of the continued demand of France for guarantees of security after the end of the Ruhr struggle, to put forward some alternative proposal. This alternative was worked out in the Locarno Pacts, which became effective in 1926 after the admission of Germany to the League of Nations. Under the Locarno agreements Great Britain, France, Belgium, Germany and Italy all bound themselves by guarantees against any attempt to alter by force the territorial settlement set up in Western Europe by the Peace Treaties. Under the Locarno settlement all war between Germany, France and Belgium was to be abolished, and no changes could be made in their respective frontiers in Western Europe by an appeal to force. This mutual settlement was further guaranteed by Great Britain and Italy, which bound themselves to go to the assistance of any State suffering as a result of the violation of the pledge given by the three countries directly involved. In addition to this the Pacts concluded at Locarno included a series of arbitration treaties between Germany and her neighbours in both east and west. Such treaties were signed not only with France and Belgium, but also with Czechoslovakia and Poland ; and at the same time France signed treaties of mutual assistance with Poland and Czechoslovakia. But in these further treaties Great Britain was not involved, as she was not prepared to give any guarantee of the integrity of the eastern frontiers established under the Treaties of Peace.

The Locarno Pacts were acclaimed at the time by Sir Austen Chamberlain as the " real dividing line between the years of war and years of peace " ; they were to remove for the future all danger of any attempt by Germany to regain her lost territories in the West by an appeal to arms, and they were intended to be the foundation of a new friendship between the French and German peoples. In order to secure a settlement on these lines Great Britain gave up her objection to entering into any commitment that might conceivably involve her in going to war on the Continent of Europe ; but the chance of the obligation which she undertook having actually to be fulfilled seemed in 1925 to be relatively small. Thus France secured under the Locarno settlements some part of the international guarantees of security which she had been demanding ever since the conclusion of the war. But in fact the Locarno settlements, though they remain in force, have by no means succeeded in establishing the cordial relations hoped for between Germany and France, or in diverting permanently the current of either German or French foreign policy. France has not felt the security given to her under the Pacts to be complete enough to remove the need for asking for further guarantees ; and while the German Republican Government renounced on behalf of Germany any attempt to alter the western frontiers of the Peace settlement by force, propaganda for frontier revision continued unabated inside Germany, and it by no means follows that German Governments of a very different complexion will be prepared permanently to honour the signature of the German Government of 1925. While, therefore, Locarno undoubtedly did something for a time to settle the acute unrest which had accompanied the Ruhr struggle of 1923–24, it by no means removed the danger of war in Europe or established any effective system for the guarantee of future peace. For one thing, the problem of the Eastern frontier remained open ; and for another, no one was at all certain how much the signatures appended at Locarno would really be worth if the European situation underwent any considerable change. Accordingly, there was no real change in the policy of France ; and before long the return of more nationalistically-minded Governments in France caused the French demand for further guarantees as the indispensable condition of any approach to disarmament to be quite as loudly expressed as it had been by M. Poincaré in the days of the Ruhr occupation.

For the time being, however, the chief centre of European unrest shifted from Western to Eastern and Central Europe. Ever since the end of the war, France had been building up there a system of alliances and pacts for mutual defence and political collaboration. Hard upon the heels of the Franco-Belgian military pact of September 1920 came the Franco-Polish Treaty of Mutual Defence concluded in February 1921. Meanwhile, the succession States bordering upon Hungary had been drawing together in the series of pacts which developed into the Little Entente. In August 1920 Czechoslovakia and Yugoslavia formed a defensive alliance directed against the possibilities of Hungarian aggression or a Hapsburg restoration in Hungary ; and later in the year a looser agreement was made between Czechoslovakia and Roumania on the same lines. In March 1921 the ex-Emperor Karl made his first attempt to establish himself on the Hungarian throne ; and this at once led to action by the Little Entente countries, and was followed by the conclusion in April of a definite alliance between Czechoslovakia and Roumania, and in June by a similar alliance between Roumania and Yugoslavia. Karl's second attempt in October 1921 further cemented the alliance of the three Little Entente Powers ; and France, in pursuit of her policy of alliances in the east, began to build up a system of mutual engagements with the Little Entente States, as well as with Poland. Thus in June 1924 France, which had already made an arrangement with Roumania, entered into treaties of alliance and mutual help with both Czechoslovakia and Yugoslavia, the treaty with Yugoslavia following upon the agreement reached between Italy and Yugoslavia in the same month. Poland and Roumania had also made a defensive alliance in March 1921, so that, in the absence of an Eastern Locarno, the countries which felt themselves threatened either by potential German aggression in the East, or still more by any attempt to restore the Hapsburgs and lay the foundations of a new Austro-Hungarian Empire, were bound together in close connection with France into an East European system closely corresponding to the Western system which underlay the main Locarno Pact. But these agreements in Eastern Europe were far more in the nature of military alliances than of attempts to bring together into a system of security countries with opposing interests and attitudes ; and accordingly, while they might be temporarily effective in keeping the peace, they were clearly aimed at achieving this result by the threat of force rather than by the establishment of any sort of international co-operation.

Accordingly the League of Nations was before long back at its work of trying to promote some more intensive agreement for ensuring peace and promoting disarmament all over Europe. In 1925, as we have seen, the League Council created a commission to prepare the way for a Disarmament Conference ; and in 1927 it set up a Special Committee on Arbitration and Security. Numerous agreements for arbitration by the Permanent Court of International Justice at the Hague had been reached between particular countries from 1921 onwards ; but these referred only to disputes turning upon juridical issues, and they were often hedged round with a great many reservations which considerably limited their value. The question primarily before the League after Locarno was that of so amending the League Covenant, or so reinforcing it by pacts or treaties, as to build up real and effective guarantees for the preservation of peace, and thus to make possible some substantial achievement in the field of international disarmament. It is not proposed in this book to follow through their successive stages the countless negotiations and projects of the next few years—from the proposal of the U.S.S.R. for universal disarmament in 1927 and its more limited disarmament proposals of 1928, to the General Convention for Improving the Means of Preventing War which was passed by the League in 1931, but has not yet reached the stage of extensive ratification. It suffices to make a general review of the main problems, achievements and failures of the years between the Locarno Pacts and the Disarmament Conference of 1932.

Means of Preventing War.

This discussion is bound to turn mainly upon three instruments designed to improve the chances of world peace. These are the Optional Clause, the General Act, and the Kellogg Pact—the first two emanating from the League of Nations, and the third from the independent initiative of the Government of the United States. It is simplest to begin with the Kellogg Pact of August 1928. This American proposal, which has been, on paper at least, universally accepted, involves the nations of the world in a complete renunciation of all wars save wars of defence. It is meant as a symbolic and declaratory agreement indicating the determination of the countries which sign it to keep the peace. But it is unaccompanied either by any sanctions in the event of its violation, or by any definition of what constitutes a defensive as against an aggressive war. Indeed, the United States, standing outside the League of Nations and also refusing until 1930 to adhere to the Court of International Justice, could hardly propose any international agreement involving either sanctions or the setting up of machinery for the determining of the aggressor in face of a threat or actual outbreak of war. It could only propose that the nations should consult together when the occasion arose, and be guided in their action not by any pledges given in advance—for the United States Government would have had no power to give any such pledges, and Congress would certainly have refused to place any such authority in its hands—but by the actual circumstances of the moment. This, of course, constitutes a fatal weakness in the Kellogg Pact, in the opinion of all those who believe in the League system of endeavouring to preserve the peace by means of an organised association of States, and with the aid of machinery and rules created in advance of the actual situations with which they are intended to deal. All the Governments, including that of the U.S.S.R., signed the Kellogg Pact ; but the appending of their signatures to it made little or no difference to their attitudes or to their beliefs in the effectiveness of the means available for the prevention of war.

At the time when the American Government came forward with the proposals which resulted in the Kellogg Pact, the League of Nations was already engaged in the discussions which led up to the formulation of the General Act ; and this new instrument filling out the terms of the League Covenant was actually adopted by the League in September 1928, the month after the signing of the Pact. Before the drafting of the General Act, the chief instrument existing under the League Covenant for the preservation of peace was embodied in the Optional Clause. This Clause, which had been accepted in full at the beginning of 1928 by fifteen States, involved the recognition of the power of the Permanent Court of International Justice to make binding decisions on all disputes of a legal character concerning the interpretation of treaties and on any question of international law arising between States accepting the Clause. But the Optional Clause dealt only with disputes in relation to which a decision could be arrived at by the legal interpretation of existing treaties or in accordance with the established principles of international law. The General Act was designed to fill in the very large gaps thus left in the framework of the system of international arbitration and judicial settlement of disputes. Under it signatory States were given the alternative of sending disputes of a justiciable character (i.e. arising out of the interpretation of existing treaties or turning on questions of international law) either to the International Court or by agreement to a special arbitration tribunal. But provision was also made for dealing with non-justiciable disputes. These were to be sent in the first instance to a conciliation commission, which might be either a standing body or constituted *ad hoc* ; and a failure by this commission to settle the dispute was to involve its reference to an arbitral tribunal of five members, of whom two were to represent the States directly concerned, and three were to be appointed from the nationals of other countries. This arbitral tribunal was to have power to give a binding decision, and any State adhering to the General Act entered into an obligation to accept the decision so made.

The General Act, unlike the Optional Clause, thus aimed at establishing a complete framework of arbitration in disputes of all kinds arising between nations. But it was open to States to adhere to it not only generally but also subject to such reservations as they might choose to make in respect of their national sovereignty or of any particular class of disputes ; and although France and Italy, as well as Great Britain under the second Labour Government, accepted the General Act, the acceptance was made subject, especially by France and Great Britain, to so many reservations as largely to destroy its effect. For example, France felt that the reservation excluding from the obligations imposed under the General Act disputes already in existence before it was signed removed the entire range of differences arising out of the Treaties of Peace outside the new machinery of pacific settlement which it laid down ; and France would certainly have refused to sign the General Act if she had thought that there was any chance of the question of territorial revision of the Peace Treaties of 1919 and 1920 being successfully raised under it. Great Britain also made a reservation in respect of disputes arising prior to her accession to the General Act " or relating to situations or facts prior to the said accession "—an exception so wide that almost anything might be held to come under it ; and the British adhesion, like the French, was subject to a whole string of further reservations, of which the most important were those which excluded questions which by international law lie within the domestic jurisdiction of States, disputes between Great Britain and other countries within the Empire, and disputes " in regard to which the parties to the dispute have agreed or shall agree to have recourse to some other method of peaceful settlement."

Thus the General Act, almost equally with the Kellogg

Pact, amounted in face of the reservations which the leading States attached to their signatures to little more than a gesture. No more than the Kellogg Pact could it be regarded as any real guarantee of the maintenance of peace among the nations of Europe. Yet even in this truncated form it is doubtful whether it would have been signed had not the second British Labour Government remained in office long enough to carry it through. Moreover, it is significant that, even before the ratifications of the General Act had begun to come in, the League was already engaged in discussing the draft of yet another attempt to promote European security—the General Convention for Improving the Means of Preventing War.

While these discussions on the question of security were proceeding, the League was already engaged in a somewhat desultory series of preparatory conversations and negotiations in preparation for the projected Disarmament Conference. As we have seen, attention in this field had from the Washington Treaty of 1922 been concentrated largely upon the question of naval disarmament. The Three-Power Naval Pact of 1927, with its failure to secure agreement between France and Italy, had left the situation in this field extraordinarily unsatisfactory ; and the Five-Power Naval Conference of 1930 was a renewed attempt to secure agreement between the principal naval Powers. At this Conference the French at once brought up the question of the interdependence of naval and military armaments, and demanded the right to increase their navy on a very large scale in the absence of effective guarantees of security by both land and sea. Great Britain proposed an extension of the naval holiday which had been agreed upon at Washington in 1922 for a period of ten years, up to 1935. The proposal to abolish submarines was strongly opposed by the French, while Italy demanded parity with any other Continental Power. Thus the failure of 1927 was repeated in 1930 ; for no method was found of accommodating the French and Italian claims. A Three-Power Treaty between Great Britain, the United States and Japan was indeed arrived at, and this definitely fixed the relative quotas of cruisers and submarine strength as well as of capital ships, subject to a saving clause allowing the signatory Powers to increase their fleets if other countries actually increased theirs. The provisions for a further naval holiday in respect of capital ships were signed by France and Italy as well as by the three Powers which signed the main part of the Treaty ; and an attempt was made to regulate and human-ise submarine warfare. But the naval armaments allowed to the three principal Powers still remained at an exceedingly high level, so that the Treaty, like its predecessors, was rather a conditional guarantee against a new race in naval armaments than any assurance of effective reduction ; and in any case the failure to reach a Franco-Italian agreement far overshadowed any success which was reached in the negotiations between Great Britain, the United States, and Japan. The whole question of naval armaments was left in an exceedingly unsatisfactory position, to be handed over to the General Disarmament Conference of 1932 along with the still almost untouched problem of armaments by land and air.

The Disarmament Conference.   After the years of preparation to which reference has been made already, the World Disarmament Conference at last met on February 2nd, 1932, with Mr. Arthur Henderson in the chair—for Mr. Henderson retained the presidency of the Conference, which had been offered to him personally, despite the fall of the British Labour Government in the previous Sept-ember. After the opening formalities it did not take long for the assembled delegates to make plain the profound divergences of view which still existed among them, despite all the preparatory work that had been done on most of the major issues. No review will be attempted here of the long series of proposals and counter-proposals put forward in the course of 1932 and 1933 on behalf of the various delegations, or of the successive attempts which were made to produce compromise drafts on which some limited agreement could be based. It seems more useful to try to set out in the broadest possible way the attitudes adopted at the Conference by the chief Powers and to attempt to draw from these differences of attitude certain conclusions about the prospects of world disarmament as a result of international negotiation.

Although the lesser Powers, whose most frequent spokesman was the Conference Reporter, Dr. Benes, took at times an important part in the deliberations, most of the attention at the Conference was inevitably concentrated upon the divergent views of the Great Powers. Great Britain, France, Italy, Germany, the United States and Russia had their distinctive points of view as well as their mutual jealousies ; and each of them was prone to insist on the abolition or drastic limitation of those forms of armament which favoured its rivals, while maintaining its own right to keep the almost unrestricted use of those armaments which told most in its favour. This difference of view arose most obviously over the discussion of what is called qualitative disarmament—that is, over the attempt to ban certain weapons and forms of warfare as contrary to the international code of civilised warfare. But the differences were by no means confined to these points. They went so far as to involve in the minds of the different delegations totally different conceptions of the way in which the question of armaments ought to be approached, and of the appropriate relationship between disarmament and security.

At the one extreme stood the Soviet Union with its proposal for complete disarmament by all nations. It has often been suggested that the Soviet Union put forward this proposal only because it knew that it would not be taken seriously, and hoped to gain the support of pacifist opinion throughout the world by a gesture which it would not be called upon to implement. Soviet Russia is, indeed, inevitably in the existing state of her foreign relations, a heavily armed country ; and it is not likely that she would agree to disarm unless she were sure that other countries were disarming too. But there is no doubt that Russia has a very

strong interest in being allowed to pursue her internal
policy of building up a Socialist system without the danger
of foreign military interference, and that accordingly she is
as deeply interested as any Power can possibly be in
forwarding the cause of international disarmament. Even
if the Russians had no anticipation that their proposal of
complete disarmament would be accepted, and even if they
meant to put this proposal largely to propagandist use,
there is no reason to question their profound desire for the
largest possible measure of international disarmament that
there is any hope of securing. The Russians are certainly
prepared to go as far as other nations can possibly be
induced to go in the direction of general disarmament,
and in the complete prohibition of special types of warfare
or forms of military equipment. Moreover, the U.S.S.R.
took the lead at the Disarmament Conference in pressing for
a plain agreed definition of what constitutes " aggression " ;
and in the summer of 1933 the Russians signed pacts embodying a far-reaching definition and thus implementing
the earlier " pacts of non-aggression," with a succession of
countries including the Baltic States, Poland, the Little
Entente, Turkey and other " border " States.

It is most convenient to take next the attitude of the
United States ; for in this case again there is no ground for
questioning the desire for a large measure of actual reduction of armaments, and not merely of agreed limitation on a
basis which might enable countries to retain their present
armaments and even to increase them. President Hoover's
proposal of a cut of nearly a third in all armaments, subject
to certain minimum provisions for the preservation of order,
was undoubtedly made sincerely ; and its unfavourable
reception by some of the other delegations, and notably by
the British Government, was one of the worst setbacks
which the Conference encountered. The Americans, moreover, were prepared to go a long way in order to meet the
point of view of other countries. For example, whereas
they were in the first instance opposed to any system of
budgetary limitation, on the ground that this would react

unfairly upon them in face of their higher level of costs, they expressed at a later stage their willingness to accept the principle of budgetary limitation side by side with that of quantitative limitation of effectives and equipment, and the qualitative restriction of permitted types of warfare. The Americans did undoubtedly try hard to make the Conference a success ; and, while they were not prepared for unilateral methods of disarmament, they did try their hardest to push Europe in the direction of an actual cutting down of its armed forces.

Italy put forward, next to the U.S.S.R., the most drastic proposals for disarmament. Italy was prepared, according to her spokesmen, to go as far in the direction of disarmament as other nations could be induced to go with her in practically any direction, quantitative and qualitative. But there was one condition which accompanied all the Italian proposals, whether it was stated openly or only implied. This was that the disarmament of France must proceed as fast as the disarmament of Italy, or even faster, through the abolition of certain types of armament in which France has at present the advantage. For instance, Italy wished to abolish all capital ships ; for to do this would have given her a far better chance of making actually effective the parity with France which she claimed at the Naval Conference of 1927—when, it will be remembered, the claim was the principal cause of the failure to arrive at a Five-Power Naval Pact. Yet it is not necessary to question the sincerity of the Italians' desire for an actual restriction of armaments, provided that France restricts hers to at least an equal extent. For undoubtedly the burden of armaments expenditure presses very heavily on a country which is endeavouring to carry an international weight beyond her internal economic strength.

Great Britain appeared on the face of the matter, and was largely in reality as well, the country least willing among the Great Powers to accept a drastic scaling down. The British spokesmen claimed that Great Britain had to a large extent disarmed herself already, and that in the

ZR

military sphere and in the air her forces were no longer more than barely sufficient, and perhaps not even barely sufficient, to enable her to maintain her imperial commitments and connections. She was prepared to go some distance further towards disarmament provided that she could be sure that other countries would disarm as well, and that she would not be asked to reduce her arms below what she regarded as the necessary minimum in those fields in which her imperial commitments were greatest. She was prepared in naval disarmament for considerable further reductions in capital ships, but inclined to maintain, again on imperial grounds, a stiff attitude in face of attempts to secure a drastic limitation in the smaller types of craft. Again and again the British stressed the point that Great Britain could not be regarded as a nation at all heavily armed, and that accordingly special consideration ought to be given to her claims in relation to any proposal such as President Hoover's for scaling down all armaments by one-third or some other fixed proportion.

But these were not the only points on which Great Britain took a line certain to breed dissension in the Conference. For example, her spokesmen, together with those of the United States, Italy and Germany, advocated the complete abolition of submarines ; but they were unwilling to accept the complete abolition of bombing from the air, although they wanted a limitation on the number and size of military aircraft, because they demanded as an exception the right to use bombing aircraft for police purposes in outlying districts. Again, while Italy, Russia, Germany and the United States all wished to abolish the tank as an undoubtedly offensive weapon, Great Britain refused to accept this proposal unless she were allowed to keep tanks up to a maximum size which in fact included practically all the effective tanks which she at present possesses. The British spokesmen insisted throughout on the importance of qualitative disarmament, not only in the sense of protecting the civil population against aerial bombardment and chemical warfare, but also in the sense of limiting armaments as far as possible to means of defence, and excluding those implements of war and those methods of warfare which are most susceptible of being used for purposes of offence. But when it came to definitions, and the question which were mainly offensive and which mainly defensive weapons was referred to expert commissions for report, it soon appeared that each country was inclined to regard as defensive those weapons in which it enjoyed a superiority, and as offensive those whose unrestricted use was more likely to favour its rivals. This applies particularly to the French unwillingness to abolish the submarine and to the British unwillingness to abolish the tank ; and it also applies to the British insistence on the need for restricting the size of land forces as against their less oncoming attitude in the matter of naval armaments.

The German case, as it was stated at the Disarmament Conference, turned mainly upon the question of equality. Under the Peace Treaty German armaments had been subjected to severe quantitative limitation ; and the use of certain particular forms of armament, including tanks, heavy guns and military aeroplanes, had been totally forbidden. Germany's civil aviation and her manufacture of substances which might be turned to military use had been placed under control, her navy had been taken away, and her right to build fresh vessels had been restricted as to both size and number. The Germans wanted to escape from the stigma of inequality which all these special restrictions had placed upon them. They were prepared to accept the continuance of certain restrictions on condition that the Allies would implement the promises contained in the Treaty by applying the same restrictions themselves. That is to say, the Germans would not insist on rearming with the forbidden weapons if their abolition could be made an agreed international measure ; but if other countries intended to go on making and using the forbidden forms of armament, the Germans claimed their right to do the same, and the refusal of this right caused at one stage the withdrawal of the German Government from further

participation in the Conference. The crisis thus created in
the affairs of the Conference was finally ended by the agreement reached by Great Britain, France, Italy and the United
States with the von Schleicher Government in December
1932. Under this agreement, the claim of equality was
conceded in principle, on the understanding that it could
not be fully applied at once, but only by stages, but that the
special restrictions imposed on Germany by the Peace
Treaty were at once to be replaced by limitations to be
included, for Germany as well as for other countries, in the
convention to be drawn up by the Disarmament Conference. Germany would thus no longer be subjected to any
form of restriction different in kind from those applying to
other countries. Having gained this point, the Germans
returned to the Conference ; but the von Schleicher
Government did not last long, and its replacement by the
Nazi régime soon raised fresh difficulties. The concession
to Germany had come too late ; for it is quite possible that
if the claim granted in December had been granted earlier
in the year, the Brüning Government would never have
fallen, and the advance of the Nazis might have been
checked or reversed. The late Allies had therefore largely
themselves to thank for the growing difficulties in the way
of disarmament presented by the German attitude of 1933.
For, though the Nazi Government subsequently withdrew
its wrecking proposals, and agreed to accept the terms
endorsed by its predecessor, the fears aroused by the
militaristic temper of its leaders remain.

Among the Great Powers we come last to France,
because the French attitude to disarmament differs
radically from any of those so far described. France has
throughout insisted upon the close connection between
disarmament and security. She is willing to disarm only
to the extent to which she feels that the need for armaments
is reduced by the provision of some effective alternative
means of national defence. Moreover, unlike the other
countries described, she conceives of national disarmament
as consisting not solely in a reduction in the quality or

quantity of the military personnel or implements of war at the disposal of each individual nation, but also in the possible provision of an armed force, at the disposal not of any one nation but rather of the League of Nations itself, as an instrument for the forcible preservation of world peace. Both the Tardieu Government's plan, put forward at the beginning of the Disarmament Conference, and the later plans favoured by the Radical Socialist Governments which succeeded it, have embodied this project of an international security force to be used exclusively for the preservation of world peace.

Briefly, the French plan of November 1932 proposed in the first place that the guarantees against war embodied in the Kellogg Pact and the Covenant of the League should be strengthened by actual guarantees of action against the aggressor. The French held that any violation of the Kellogg Pact, or of any of the other undertakings entered into under the League Covenant or under separate treaties, ought to involve the breaking off of economic and financial relations with the aggressor by all the other signatories. They advocated, in addition to the general engagements to ensure peace entered into through the League and under the Kellogg Pact, that there should be within the League a distinct pact of European Powers defining the conditions under which each State would have the right to the assistance, military as well as moral, of the other signatories. They held that all countries entering the European pact must adhere to the General Act, and that the guarantees of mutual help should come into action as soon as any one Power was attacked or invaded by another.

As a basis for this proposed European pact, the French proposed a uniform type of army in Continental Europe—a short-service army with a limited personnel—and the limitation of the equipment to be provided for this army so as to make it more effective in defensive than in offensive warfare. All heavy war material capable of serving as a basis for offensive warfare should, the French held, be kept under the control of the League in separate dumps set up in each country, and should be earmarked exclusively for the use of the States which found themselves the victims of aggression. At the same time there was to be international control of the manufacture of war material, and each country was to set aside a special armed force, to which alone the heavier types of armaments would be reserved, to be placed at the League's disposal for use against an aggressor. Aerial bombardment was to be wholly forbidden, and bombing aeroplanes totally suppressed ; but these measures were to be conditional on the effective international control of civil aviation through a European Air Transport Union. For naval disarmament a further special pact between the chief Powers interested in Mediterranean affairs was proposed, on the basis of leaving intact the relative strength now existing between these Powers—that is to say, the Italian claim for naval parity was again rejected. In addition, each State possessing a navy was to agree to place a part of its navy at the disposal of the League for use against an aggressor by the same method as was suggested in the case of military forces.

This ambitious French plan, linking together the two questions of disarmament and security, was conceived on totally different lines from the plans put forward by the other Powers ; for none of the others was prepared to contemplate either the creation of a special international armed force, or the earmarking of certain armaments and contingents for the service of the League under the direct orders of an international authority. It was obviously impracticable to secure any sort of agreement on the basis of the French plan in face of the hostile attitude of the other Powers ; but the French were equally unwilling to give way and to agree to any considerable limitation of armaments—though they did in fact under the Radical Governments of 1932–33 take some steps towards a reduction of military expenditure—unless countries not only bound themselves to the preservation of the peace by stronger covenants than they had been prepared to enter into as yet, but also provided for the definite use of armed forces against any country held guilty of breaking the peace.

There was thus, among the major Powers, a complete deadlock, which, by successive compromises and agreed resolutions evading the main issues, it was vainly attempted to conceal. By the end of 1932 it had become obvious that, despite the temporary removal of the immediate obstacle to a convention caused by the German demand for equality, there was no real prospect of a convention which would bring with it any considerable advance in the direction of general disarmament. All that could be hoped for at that stage was some practical progress in the field of qualitative disarmament, especially in respect of the abolition of gas and chemical warfare, and of severe restrictions on aerial bombing, including the prohibition of the use of aircraft deliberately against the civil population. But it remained very doubtful how far, in face of the continued mainten-ance of general armaments at a very high level, covenants prohibiting or restricting the use of particular weapons would in fact be adhered to if war actually broke out, and a country found itself facing the prospect of defeat through the denial to itself of some particular prohibited form of war. In 1933 the Conference, recognising the futility of trying to agree upon any inclusive general convention in the immediate future, settled down to consider a less ambitious draft, dealing largely with qualitative disarmament, and decided to leave the major points of difference for discus-sion at a later stage, creating for this purpose some sort of permanent Disarmament Commission, and agreeing to resume the discussions later on in the hope that some way of overcoming the obstacles might before long be found.

Throughout the Conference there was considerable dis-content among the delegates of the smaller Powers, which found themselves continually pushed into the background, while the Conference adjourned in order to enable the major Powers to hold private conversations of their own in the hope of bridging their differences. Some at any rate of the smaller countries, particularly those of Western

Europe, are keenly anxious to press disarmament to the furthest possible lengths ; and these countries resented strongly the domination which the Great Powers were attempting to exercise. Nor was this the only serious diplomatic cause of offence which occurred at the Conference ; for again and again, especially when the German claim to equality was under discussion, Great Britain, France and the United States adjourned to negotiate and discuss, to the exclusion not only of the smaller Powers, but also of Italy. Italy had been prepared from the first to grant the German claim to equality, whereas France had not ; and Great Britain had been unwilling to take any clear line except in agreement with France. It was natural enough under these circumstances for the British and French to meet together and discuss their attitude, and for them to desire to have the co-operation and countenance of the United States ; but the result of excluding Italy was unfortunate, for it tended to align the Italians more definitely with the Germans, and also to give the Italian Government a strong desire to take the first opportunity of asserting its claim to be fully consulted in the deliberations of the Great Powers.

In fact the exclusion of Italy from the conversations of 1932 over German equality and the general question of disarmament was, it is to be feared, the immediate cause of the use made by Mussolini of MacDonald's visit to Rome early in 1933 in quest of a Four-Power Pact ; for at Rome Mussolini turned the tables on the British and French by raising openly, for the first time since the war, the issue of Treaty revision, and thus stirred up all the smaller States of Europe, which had acquired their present territories under the Treaties of Peace, to a strong antagonism to the attempt to create a Four-Power Pact among the great western countries, and so keep in check the dangers to European peace created by the revival of militarism in Germany. MacDonald's attempt may have been perfectly well intentioned ; but in allowing Mussolini to use the occasion in order to proclaim the doctrine of Treaty revision, so far from helping to further the cause of European peace, he stirred up fresh sources of discord and created additional antagonisms between the smaller and greater Powers, besides making the entry of France into any pact of the kind contemplated far more difficult than it need have been. Even though the difficulties were smoothed over, and an emasculated Four-Power Pact initialled by the four States, this did not undo the damage.

Treaty Revision. For France cannot, without forfeiting her position of ally and protector to a number of the smaller States of Central and Eastern Europe, enter into any pact in which the revision of the Treaties is proclaimed as one of the principal objects. Throughout Central Europe Treaty revision means, in the minds of most people, the loss by the new States of the position which they gained at the end of the world war, the renewed aggrandisement of Hungary, and the possible reconstruction of the Austro-Hungarian Empire. In Poland it means the threatened loss of the Corridor, and of her rights in Danzig ; while in the Balkans it means the threat of a renewal of the military power of Bulgaria. Moreover, the Great Powers which were thus speaking of Treaty revision showed no sign of a willingness to give up any of their own war conquests. They might be prepared to concede territorial readjustment in favour of Germany or Hungary at the expense of the smaller Continental States ; but they did not indicate that they were prepared to hand back to the Germans any of the colonial territories which they acquired under mandates in 1919. In these circumstances Treaty revision, as it was put forward in the early months of 1933, seemed to the smaller States of Central and Eastern Europe a barefaced attempt by the Great Powers to compel them to make sacrifices in the interests of Germany and Hungary, without giving up anything themselves.

Nevertheless, it is undoubtedly true that the Peace Treaties ought to be revised, and that many of the territorial settlements made in a spirit of vindictiveness and of " spoils to the victors " after the conclusion of the world war were palpably unjust as well as inexpedient. Hungary was restricted within frontiers far too narrow on either national or economic grounds ; Austria was left in an impossible economic situation. There is no logical or rational defence of the continuance of the Polish Corridor under the existing conditions ; Poland has no right on national grounds to retain territories inhabited largely by Ukrainians ; nor can the present frontiers of Bulgaria be upheld on any principle of national justice. There are all over Europe countless wrongs crying for redress—wrongs created by the Treaties of Peace in the attempt to make a compromise between the irreconcilable spirits of national self-determination and " spoils to the victors." Nor is there any valid ground, if other countries are to be allowed to possess colonial empires, why a Germany readmitted to equality of status should be denied that right. In Europe it is arguable that the frontiers created in 1919 and 1920 did far less violence to the principle of national self-determination than the frontiers which existed in 1914 ; but the degree of violence which they do to this principle to-day is a sign not only that the principle of national self-determination was not carried out so completely as it might have been, but also that in face of the intermingling of European populations and the interpenetration of national groups, it is impossible to make any satisfactory settlement of European frontiers that will not hopelessly violate at many points the nationalist principle, even if no account is taken of the highly important factor of preserving the unity of coherent economic areas.

In effect, nationalism as a basis for the territorial organisation of Europe is bound to break down if and as long as the attempt is made to carry it into effect on the principle of the absolute independence and sovereignty of each national State. Each national minority is acutely conscious of its grievance, not only because it is often persecuted by the representatives of the national majority which dominates the State in which it is included, but also because it resents being shut up absolutely and finally within the frontiers of a national State regarded as finally self-governing and sovereign in all respects. The grievances of national minorities are greatly aggravated in many areas by deliberate persecution ; but they will exist even in the absence of persecution as long as States are regarded not merely as convenient territorial divisions of the European Continent, but as absolute national entities with full rights of disposal over the lives and means of existence of all their citizens, with regard only to their own interests and with no regard at all to the claims of a wider pan-European or world unity. The multiplication of independent sovereign States, which the attempt to establish the principle of national self-determination in Europe involved, has in effect brought with it problems insoluble within the limited conditions of State sovereignty—problems which can be solved only by the universal admission that States have only limited rights in relation to their subjects, and must admit the claims of some authority transcending merely national boundaries.

This great issue of nationalism and internationalism, which will have to be discussed more fully in a subsequent section, is inevitably raised here because it is closely involved with the whole question of disarmament. The French demand for security is by no means unreasonable or to be rejected out of hand, however much the methods by which the French propose to realise security may be rejected as impracticable. Nations will not disarm, though they may agree within narrow limits to restrict their armaments or their armaments expenditure on an agreed basis, as long as they continue to be nations in the sense of claiming complete national sovereignty. For the whole idea of absolute sovereignty involves in the last resort the right to do anything which may be held to serve the interests of the nation regarded as an ultimate unit, irrespective of the consequences which the doing of it may have for the rest of the world. This right includes necessarily and inevitably the right to make war in the national interest. For, as long as nations continue to exist as nations in the sense just given to the term, there will continue to be causes of war between them, if only because there will be territories to which more than one nation considers that it possesses an indefeasible national right. Under these conditions no territorial settlement can ever be permanent, and no security of peace can ever exist. But where there is no security there cannot be any real measure of disarmament ; for the sense of insecurity will lead inevitably to the endeavour of each nation, save those few small countries which see their best protection in being completely defenceless, to make itself strong enough to ensure its own safety. In fact, no nation ever is or can be strong enough to achieve this object ; for, even if it is stronger than its immediate neighbours or than any other single Power, it can never be strong enough to be sure of resisting successfully any combination of Powers that may be formed against it.

There is accordingly no limit to the quantity of armaments that a country may hold itself to require as the necessary minimum for its own defence. For no nation can tell against how many other Powers or with what allies it may be called upon to defend itself. Under these conditions, even if limitations of armaments are agreed upon internationally, nations will inevitably tend not only to create armaments right up to the permitted limits, but also to evade the spirit of the limitations by devising new and more powerful means of warfare within the letter of their engagements. There will be a qualitative if not a quantitative race in armaments ; and in these days of invention the qualitative factor is coming to count for more and more. It may be worth while to hold disarmament conferences in the hope of achieving at least some limitation, and of checking from time to time the armaments race, much as the World Economic Conference of 1927 did check for a time the upward movement of European tariffs. But it is out of the question to expect much more than this, save as a result of a far-reaching change in the entire structure of the European State system. For this there is no sign that either statesmen or peoples are as yet prepared.

For it is difficult indeed for those who have grown up in the tradition of national sovereignty to think in any different terms, and the whole idea of sovereignty is so deeply embedded in the political ideas of the modern world, and in its economic as well as its political relationships, that it will hardly be driven out save as the result of some sharp and desperate shock to the existing structure of European society. Nor should it be forgotten that this idea of State sovereignty, inconsistent as it is with the conception of any real League of Nations as an organ of effective international co-operation, is deeply embedded in the Covenant of the present League, which has been based throughout on the attempt to bring together sovereign States, and not at all designed to break down national sovereignty in the interests of a wider conception of world, or even of European, unity. The League of Nations is in fact a League of Governments, each of which regards itself as representing an altogether independent and self-determined sovereign State ; and no Government feels itself entitled, or is prepared, to give away anything that might result in an abrogation of any part of its sovereignty. Hence the unanimity rule, by which many of the most important functions of the League are conditioned. For, as Lord Cecil said in the course of the original discussions at which the form of the League Covenant was decided, " all international decisions must of their nature be unanimous," a sharp and unequivocal proclamation of the doctrine of national sovereignty, and at the same time a plain declaration that the new House of Nations at Geneva was being built upon the sand.

§ 2. THE LEAGUE OF NATIONS

THE LEAGUE OF NATIONS formed at the conclusion of the Great War and as a part of the Peace settlement consisted at the end of 1932 of fifty-seven member States. Of these, twenty-seven, or rather less than half, were in Europe, and eighteen in America. The total included, besides Great

Britain, the great self-governing Dominions—Canada, Australia, New Zealand, South Africa, and Ireland, and also British India ; so that the British Empire collectively, if it chooses to act together, is able to exert a considerable voting influence within the League. The most notable absentees from the League are the United States and the U.S.S.R., and next after these Egypt and Brazil. Brazil, which was at one time in the League, resigned some years ago without at the same time relinquishing her membership of the International Labour Organisation. Otherwise the membership of the two bodies is the same ; but, in both cases, States not members, and especially the United States, are often asked to send delegates or observers to particular conferences. The European countries included in the League range from the Great Powers to Albania and Luxembourg ; but certain tiny independent States, such as Monaco, San Marino, and Liechtenstein, are outside the League. Most of the South American States, with the exception of Brazil, belong ; but Costa Rica and Ecuador are two further exceptions. Japan, which had been in the League from the outset, gave notice of withdrawal in 1933 as a result of the League's action over the Manchurian dispute ; but, of the other Asiatic Powers, China, Persia, and Siam, as well as India, are inside the League, while Afghanistan, Arabia, Nepal, and Manchukuo are non-members. Thus, with the important exceptions of the United States, Japan and the U.S.S.R., the League can be regarded as fully representing the countries which play a leading part in the world's international affairs.

It was of course intended, when the League was first created, that the United States should be a member of it. Indeed, the whole idea of the League largely came from President Wilson, who took a larger part than any other man in pressing the idea on the Great Powers at the conclusion of the war, and in formulating the principles underlying the Covenant. But President Wilson found it beyond his strength to induce the politicians of his own country or American public opinion to accept the commitments which they conceived to be involved in membership of a League inevitably centred upon Europe and involved in the tangled mutual relationships of the European States. Nor did a clause specially inserted in the Covenant to affirm the continued validity of the Monroe Doctrine reconcile American opinion to the possibility of League interference between the United States and its smaller neighbours in Central and South America. The United States stood aloof ; and this by itself sufficed to make the League much less than a representative international organisation for the world as a whole, and greatly to increase its concentration upon European affairs. For, with the United States outside, the remaining Great Powers associated with it, with the exception of Japan, were all European Powers ; and inevitably the League was from the outset largely concerned with complications arising out of the peace settlement of 1919 and with relationships along the new frontiers constituted in Europe under the Treaties of Peace.

The exclusion of the U.S.S.R. is no less important than that of the United States. At the time when the League was formed the Soviet Union was still widely regarded as certain to disappear in the near future, and civil war was still in progress on all the Russian frontiers. Statesmen in capitalist countries were entirely unwilling to recognise that the victory of Communism in Russia could be permanent, or that a country basing both its internal and its external relations on principles so widely different from their own might have to be accepted into the comity of nations. They hoped for, and were actively engaged in fostering, the victory of the counter-revolutionary forces upon Russian soil ; and the admission of Russia to the League was regarded as no more than deferred pending the establishment of a settled and acceptable form of government over her vast territories. Nor were the Russians in 1919 in a mood that would have made easy their acceptance of the obligations involved in League membership. For, while capitalist opinion was still looking forward confidently to the overthrow of Communism in Russia, the Russian Communists were still hoping for a rapid victory of the revolutionary forces all over Europe, and regarded their own revolution as only the first instalment of a world revolution which was due speedily to arrive. In these circumstances their desire and aspiration were, not to ensure the maintenance of the *status quo*, but to forward as rapidly as possible the triumph of the world revolution ; and for this reason the League and Russia were not merely incompatibles, but from the first antagonistic, in that the Allied Powers inside the League were in their several ways actively forwarding the cause of the various counter-revolutionary generals who were overrunning one part or another of Russian territory.

The situation has changed since then, and the Soviet Government in Russia is now recognised *de jure* or *de facto* by a considerable number of Powers, though this recognition remains precarious, and the deeply rooted hostility of the capitalist States towards Russia retains undiminished force. But the recognition of the Soviet Government by one after another of the capitalist Powers has not made the way plain for the entry of Russia into the League, though Soviet representatives have participated in a number of the special conferences held under its auspices, including both the World Economic Conferences of 1927 and 1933 and the Disarmament Conference. Russian statesmen no longer hope for the speedy triumph of the revolution all over Europe ; and they have largely modified, as the indispensable condition of being let alone to pursue their own economic development, their attempts to stimulate revolutionary movements in other countries. But they have not in the smallest degree abandoned their hopes, or reconciled themselves to the maintenance of the *status quo*. World revolution remains in their view, now as much as in 1919, the only solution of the world's economic and political problems. The Russians have, however, shown themselves willing to recognise that this end cannot be gained by the maintenance of unfriendly relations with their capitalist neighbours, or by any attempt to impose their revolutionary ideas by force. They have accordingly been fully prepared to work for the maintenance of world peace, and to conclude, with any country that is willing, non-aggression pacts based on the renunciation of all attempts to overturn Governments or make territorial changes by armed force. By July 1933 Pacts of Non-Aggression, usually amplified by further pacts so defining the aggressor as to exclude all forms of military action, had been signed by the U.S.S.R. with nearly all the border States, including the Little Entente, Poland, most of the Baltic States and Turkey. They have perforce reconciled themselves to a far slower pace than they once hoped for in the development of the world revolution ; but to defer hope is not to abandon it, and the gulf between Russia and the capitalist States of the world remains as impassable as before in terms of ultimate ideals, if not of immediate policy.

The absence of Russia from the League has had serious consequences on its claim to speak with a voice representative of world opinion ; for there has been a constant danger that the European Powers included in the League might attempt to use it as an instrument not merely for the preservation of the *status quo* in their own countries, that is to say, as a guarantee against revolution at home, but also positively against Russia. At one time the French especially were full of the idea of a sanitary cordon, to be drawn across Eastern Europe, shutting off the territory of the Soviet Union from those of the Powers west of the dividing line. Of late this idea has fallen into the background ; but even to-day, when plans are put forward for a European Union such as Briand advocated, there is a constant danger that the union may be less a means for the preservation of world peace than a league of capitalist States directed against Socialist Russia.

The participation of the States of Central and South America in the League was largely an assertion on their part of their independence in foreign politics of the United States. But in practice the League has not dealt either very much or very effectively with American affairs. The United States, as we have seen, secured in the League

Covenant a recognition of the continued validity of the Monroe Doctrine ; and in pursuance of this policy the Americans have remained suspicious of League intervention in American affairs, and the European Powers which have dominated League policy have seen the need for walking warily where America is concerned. Thus League intervention has been largely ineffective in checking the outbreak of little wars on the South American Continent, even when the attempt has been made to join forces with the United States for their prevention.

Nor has the League been happier in its dealings with the affairs of the Far East. In this case, indeed, the great European Powers are all far more closely concerned than they are with what happens over the greater part of South America. But the League countries cannot move in the Far East without the full participation of the United States, which is quite as deeply concerned as any of them—indeed far more deeply concerned than any other country save Great Britain. Moreover, Japan, though she has been up to 1933 a member of the League, has been determined throughout in the last resort to have her own way in Far Eastern affairs, and by no means to accept European dictation in her dealings with China. The attempt of the League, tardy and hesitant as it was, to interfere in the Manchurian dispute of 1932-33 only served to drive Japan into open revolt against the public opinion of Europe as expressed in the League declarations, to the extent of actually severing her membership. It is, indeed, more than probable that if the European Powers had acted more promptly and decisively than they did in the case of Manchuria, so as to make their joint influence and determination felt before Japan had taken the step of recognising the so-called independent State of Manchukuo, their action might have been far more effective ; for Japan was at that time far more open to influence than she is to-day, now that the weakness of League action has been plainly shown.

The real truth is that the Western Powers were not

prepared to act unitedly on behalf of China against Japanese aggression, however clearly the Japanese action violated the principles laid down in the Covenant of the League. Some of the European statesmen more than half sympathised with Japan ; while others, who took what is called the " League view," were unprepared to involve their countries in the risk of open conflict with the Japanese, especially as they felt no assurance that their League partners would act solidly with them. Consequently, Japan was allowed to flout the League in the Far East ; and the demonstration of weakness thus given to the whole world not only undermined its influence in Japan and in Asia generally, but also went far to undo such authority as it had managed to build up for itself even in Europe.

Despite the fact that nearly half the member States of the League are situated outside Europe, the League is predominantly a European affair, and concerns itself predominantly with European relationships. It is in fact to a great extent a loose association of the Great Powers of Western Europe to which the smaller Powers of Central, Southern, and Eastern Europe are admitted upon a footing in which inferiority and equality are curiously blended. In one sense all the League Powers are formally equal, since they have all an equal voice in the League Assembly, which is the body wielding in theory the ultimate control. But real power in the League resides far more in the Council than in the Assembly, and upon the Council there is a sharp differentiation between the greater and the smaller Powers. In the original Constitution of the League, provision was made for the five Great Powers which were then expected to be included in it to have direct representation upon the Council. These were the United States, the British Empire, France, Italy, and Japan. All the other States together were to have only four representatives upon the Council, selected by the Assembly from time to time at its discretion. In the first instance the four representatives from the smaller Powers were selected from Belgium, Brazil, Greece, and Spain ; and in view of the withdrawal of the United

States, this meant that the League Council had from the first an overwhelmingly European composition.

Since its original constitution the personnel of the League Council has been substantially modified. First, in 1922, the number of members to be selected by the Assembly from the Powers to which direct representation was not given was raised from four to six, and later, in 1926, this representation was raised again from six to nine, and at the same time Germany was nominated a permanent member of the Council. In theory the election of Council members by the Assembly to the seats not reserved for the principal Powers is an entirely open matter ; but in practice an unwritten rule seems to have grown up. Since Canada secured a seat on the Council in 1927 one seat has been in practice reserved for the British Dominions, the Irish Free State having taken Canada's place in the election of 1930. Three seats have been given to Latin America. Spain and Poland, despite the original understanding that there should be rotation among the States not granted permanent membership, have been continuously represented, while the remaining three seats have been scrambled for by the other European countries and the Asiatic States other than Japan. This has meant in practice that the representatives of the small countries have stood little chance of securing election unless they have been able to build up a kind of electoral *bloc* by some form of agreement to support one another's candidates at successive elections. With the exception of Germany the States defeated in the late war have stood virtually no chance of securing representation.

Some sort of inequality was of course inevitable if the League was to be made to work at all ; for the Great Powers would certainly never have accepted a League in which their rights were to be no greater than those of, say, Albania or Siam or Luxembourg. They were bound to insist on some form of inequality, despite the theoretical principle of the absolute independence of sovereign States on which the League has been built up. But in reality the element of inequality in the League has been far greater than the representation on the Council shows. The Great Powers are in a minority on the Council, and in theory the small Powers might combine so as to out-vote them on the Council as well as in the Assembly. But what happens in fact is that the decisions of the League are very often taken as a result, not mainly of discussions in the Council, but of private consultations held among the Great Powers, and apart from the recognised machinery of the League. Again and again, when some important issue has come up, the Great Powers have first met and endeavoured to decide what their attitude was to be, and have then gone to the League and secured the acceptance of the policy upon which they had already reached agreement.

This, too, is impossible to avoid in the present state of the world's international relations. For, as long as force potentially counts in international affairs, the last word is bound to be with the Great Powers, which alone are in a position to employ force in matters of primary importance. It would be of no use for the smaller League countries to out-vote the Great Powers on any issue on which the Great Powers were able to agree ; for they would have no means of making their vote effective, and if they persisted in their attitude the only possible result would be to destroy the League altogether, and therewith remove such protection as it does give to their frontiers and such guarantees as it provides against their being the victims of aggressive war. Accordingly, though the smaller countries often grumble at the attitude assumed by the Great Powers, in the last resort they have to take what the Great Powers please to give them, and the League inevitably becomes more a piece of machinery for registering the decisions of the Great Powers associated with it than a real organ of world-wide international collaboration. This is not the fault of the individuals who dominate the Council, though it doubtless expresses pretty accurately the point of view of those of them who sit there as representatives of the larger countries. It is not primarily anyone's fault ; it is simply the outcome of the existing condition of international politics and of the continued acceptance of State sovereignty as a basis for the government of the world's affairs.

It is even misleading to think of the League as predominantly a federation formed to bring together the nations of the world with a view to co-operative action in the interests of the world as a whole. It was not created primarily as an organ of world government even in the most rudimentary sense, but, as the terms of the Covenant and the discussions which accompanied its formation alike make sufficiently clear, as an instrument for the prevention of war, and the peaceful settlement of disputes between nation and nation. These functions are primarily arbitral and judicial, and only to a quite minor extent those of positive collaboration in constructive tasks. The League has indeed developed through its economic and financial organisation some activities making in the direction of a more constructive form of collaboration. But these are still in a very rudimentary stage ; and even the influence which the League exerted in persuading the countries of Europe to return to the gold standard after the war could only take the form of a gentle suasion made effective far more by the action and attitude of the great Central Banks than through the instrumentality of the League itself. The League's economic activities are still largely statistical and informative ; and the World Economic Conferences of 1927 and 1933 have demonstrated the difficulty of translating into positive action even those recommendations upon which the representatives of all the assembled countries are able to agree. The I.L.O. has gone somewhat further in a constructive direction ; but its achievements and shortcomings can be more conveniently discussed in a later section.

Positive collaboration in dealing with world problems through the League has gone furthest in the fields most remote from the major issues of politics and economics. It is in the sphere of public health, of the suppression of the traffic in drugs, and of the White Slave Traffic, in the improvement through suasion of the standards of hygiene and public morals in the more backward countries, that the League has so far done its least spectacular but most efficient work. But the success achieved in these fields is the result of the ability to handle such matters without raising large political complications, or stirring up vested economic interests too strong to be interfered with without provoking political reactions. In these fields the League is undoubtedly useful and doing excellent work ; but however important what it has done in these respects may be in itself, clearly it is but secondary in relation to the main objects which all believers in any real form of inter-nationalism have at heart.

The League Covenant. The fundamental weakness of the League of Nations, as it exists at present, is that it is based upon a full recognition of the absolute independence and sovereignty of the States composing it, or at any rate of the Great Powers which in practice dominate its activities. Or perhaps it would be truer to say that this is not so much the weakness of the League as a fatal defect in the existing system of international relationships—a defect from which no international body constructed within the prevailing system of ideas about the rights of nations can possibly escape. It would be unfair to blame the League for embody-ing the principles of national sovereignty and independence as long as these principles continue to be firmly insisted upon by the States which make it up. But it would also be mere self-delusion to imagine that the League can become an effective instrument of positive international collabora-tion as long as these principles of autarchy remain intact.

That the League is based firmly on the idea of State sovereignty appears again and again through the successive clauses of the Covenant in the stress laid on the unanimity rule. There is, indeed, some departure from this rule, but only at the expense of the smaller States. As far as the Great Powers are concerned it is insisted upon throughout as the very basis of the Covenant save in mere matters of procedure, in relation to which any organisation that is to work at all must have some power of determining its action by a majority vote. Thus Article 5 lays down that, except where it is otherwise expressly provided, " decisions at any meeting of the Assembly or of the Council shall require the agreement of all the members of the League represented at the meeting." This clause plainly proclaims at the outset the doctrine of State sovereignty, subject only to such modifications as are introduced by the terms of the Covenant itself.

What, then, are these modifications ? We need not concern ourselves with those which deal purely with matters of procedure, but only with those which may involve important issues of international policy. The most important of these are embodied in Article 15, which deals with the action to be taken by the League in handling any disputes which are not actually submitted for arbitration or judicial settlement to the Permanent Court of Justice or to some specially constituted tribunal. Under Article 15 the members of the League undertake to submit any disputes not so referred to consideration by the League Council, and it is open to any member of the League to bring a dispute to the notice of the Council and to insist on investigation by the Council. When a dispute is thus submitted, the first duty of the Council is to endeavour to effect an amicable settlement ; but if this cannot be done the Council must take action in the form of making a report, not only reviewing the facts of the dispute, but also making recommendations for its adjustment. This report can be made by the Council either unanimously or by a majority vote ; but unless the report is made unanimously by all the members of the Council, except those who represent actual parties to the dispute, no obligation rests upon the members of the League to carry out the recommendations embodied in the report. They are left free under the Covenant to do precisely what they like, with only the academic recommendation that their actions must be taken in such a way as to further " in their own opinion the maintenance of right and justice." If, however, the Council is able to make a unanimous report, or one in which all the members other than those who represent States directly parties to the dispute are prepared to concur, a definite obligation is imposed upon all member States ; for all the members agree under the Covenant that in these circumstances of unanimity " they will not go to war with any party to the dispute which complies with the recommendations of the report." Observe that even in these circumstances they are not committed, under Article 15, to take any action against the State which fails to comply with the recommendations of the League, but only to refrain from hostile action against the State which does carry out the League's proposals.

The Council may, however, instead of taking the responsibility itself, refer any dispute with which it is called upon to deal to the Assembly of the League, upon which all States are represented and all have alike one vote, irrespective of their size and importance. If such a reference to the Assembly is made, the power to issue a report and to make recommendations for the settlement of the dispute is thereby transferred from the Council to the Assembly. In this case the unanimity rule is not insisted on ; for it would clearly be out of the question to rely on unanimity among the large number of separate nations included in the League, especially as one or another of them, without being directly a party to the dispute in question, would almost certainly be in such close relations with the offending State as to back it up almost automatically, or at least to abstain from voting so as to destroy the unanimity required for League action against it. A curious procedure has therefore been worked out for the application of Article 15 where a dispute is referred by the Council to the Assembly. The Assembly can take a decision in such a case by a majority vote ; and the decision so taken can become binding upon all members of the League, but only on one very important condition. This condition is that the representatives at the Assembly of all those States which have members on the League Council, except the States which are directly parties to the dispute, must vote unanimously in favour of the Assembly's report and recommendations, and there must be also a clear majority of the other members of the League. Thus each great State, unless it is itself a party to the particular dispute which is under consideration, maintains its absolute right of veto upon any action which it is proposed to take under Article 15.

There is doubtless some invasion of the principle of State sovereignty in the fact that under Article 15 a State which is itself a party to a dispute can be overriden by the verdict of other States, even if it is one of the Great Powers represented on the Council. But this is as far as the Great Powers have been prepared to go in limiting their absolute sovereign rights ; and, as we have seen recently in the case of the Manchurian dispute, the attempt to put the machinery of Article 15 in motion against a Great Power has merely caused that Power to give notice of withdrawal from the League, and has not induced the remaining Powers to take any action which would compel the recalcitrant Great Power to observe the recommendations embodied in the League's report. The exception in these circumstances in effect confirms the rule. Even the small invasion of the claims of absolute State sovereignty embodied in Article 15 is hedged round with so many restrictions as to make its operation very difficult under the League's rules of procedure ; and if, finally, these difficulties are overcome, it remains open for a Great Power which finds its sovereignty invaded to regain all its rights by withdrawal from the League.

It is true that Article 1 lays down that a State may only withdraw from the League after giving two years' notice of its intention, and subject to the proviso that all its international obligations and all its obligations under the Covenant shall have been fulfilled at the time of its withdrawal. But what are the obligations of a State under Article 15 ? Article 15 does not say that any State is compelled to carry out the terms of the recommendations issued by the Council or the Assembly. It only lays down that the members of the League will not go to war with any State which does comply with the recommendations. It says nothing about their going to war with, or employing any lesser sanctions against a State which does not. Therefore, as far as Article 15 is concerned, it is perfectly open for Japan, or any other Power which may find itself in a similar situation, to argue that in refusing to accept the recommendations of the Council or the Assembly it is not in any way violating the League Covenant or impairing even technically its right to resign from the League under the terms of Article 1.

This question of sanctions is dealt with in Article 16. The governing words of the Article are those with which it opens. They run as follows : " Should any member of the League resort to war in disregard of its covenants under Articles 12, 13, or 15, it shall *ipso facto* be deemed to have committed an act of war against all other members of the League, which hereby undertake immediately to subject it to the severance of all trade and financial relations, and the prohibition of all intercourse between their nationals and the nationals of the Covenant-breaking State, and the nationals of any other State, whether a member of the League or not." This sounds drastic enough in all conscience, since it envisages the complete boycott of the offending State not only to the extent of the severance of relations with it by all the other League States and their nationals, but even to the point of blockading it completely against all intercourse with the rest of the world. But under what conditions can these drastic obligations upon the League's members arise ? We have seen already that the only circumstances in which they can arise under Article 15 is the action of a member of the League in going to war with a party to the dispute which complies with the recommendations of the League's report. Doubtless as a matter of plain common sense most people would hold that Japan is at present at war with China. But the Japanese firmly maintain that this is not the case. There has not been, and is not likely to be in the circumstances, any

formal declaration of war : there are merely certain operations of a military character, designed primarily for the
suppression of brigandage, and any act involving a formal
state of warfare can doubtless be carried out under the
convenient auspices of the new State of Manchukuo, which
is not a member of the League. The art of wholesale murder
without making formal war thus acquires a new political
significance ; and as there is no authority entrusted with
the duty of deciding what does constitute making war and
what does not, the Japanese, or any other State similarly
situated, can easily put up at least a technical case for
urging that the obligations envisaged under Article 16
cannot be invoked in consequence of anything they have
done to violate the terms of Article 15. Doubtless if the
League chose to declare through the Council or the
Assembly, with the required degree of unanimity, that the
Japanese were engaged in making war on China, and that
China had complied with the recommendations of the
League, the obligations envisaged in Article 16 would then
arise. But the Council is not under any compulsion to do
this, and is in practice most unlikely to do it at the expense
of any Great Power.

There remains to be considered the reference in the words
quoted from Article 16 to disregard of covenants under
Articles 12 and 13. Article 12 binds the members of the
League, if any dispute likely to lead to a rupture arises
between them, to " submit the matter either to arbitration
or judicial settlement or to enquiry by the Council " ; and
the members of the League agree " in no case to resort to
war until three months after the award by the arbitrators
or the judicial decision or the report by the Council."
Here again the sole obligation is not to resort to war, and
there is still no definition of what constitutes a resort to
war, so that the same difficulty arises as in the case of
Article 15. Article 13 relates only to disputes which the
members of the League concerned " recognise to be suitable for submission to arbitration or judicial settlement " ;
and it is left to the parties themselves to determine whether

or not a particular dispute does come within this definition, subject only to the proviso that " disputes as to the interpretation of the Treaty, as to any question of international law, as to the existence of any fact which, if established would constitute a breach of any international obligation, or as to the extent and nature of the reparation to be made for any such breach, are declared to be among those which are generally suitable for submission to arbitration or judicial settlement." But the value of this proviso is largely destroyed by the word " generally," which clearly leaves it open to any State to declare that in the particular dispute in which it is concerned an exception should be made to this general proviso, even if the circumstances are such as to bring the dispute within the broad terms of the article.

Under Article 13 the members of the League agree " that they will carry out in full good faith any award or decision that may be rendered, and that they will not resort to war against a member of the League which complies therewith." But this obligation refers only to disputes which they have themselves agreed in advance to submit to arbitration or judicial decision in accordance with the terms of Article 13, and therefore does not constitute any invasion of their independent sovereignty, or impose upon them any obligation to carry out the decisions of the League upon any question which they do not regard as suitable for arbitration or judicial settlement.

The conclusion to be drawn from this somewhat complicated review of the most vital clauses of the League Covenant is that in setting up the League of Nations the Powers which agreed upon the draft of the Covenant most carefully refrained from subjecting themselves to any obligation to carry out the decisions of the League, even when these decisions have been unanimously made by all the League Powers which are not directly parties to the dispute. The most they bound themselves to accept was that they would not go to war with any party to the dispute which did comply with the recommendations made unanimously by the League Council. Even this would of course be a very valuable concession if there were any means of securely implementing it ; but, as the Japanese dispute has plainly shown, it is possible for a Great Power to violate quite openly the decisions made by the Council or the Assembly in full accordance with the terms of the Covenant without incurring any of the drastic penalties laid down against offenders in Article 16. The most that can be said is that, if all the Great Powers except one were really determined to take action against the remaining Great Power, and this one Great Power did, in spite of their determination, go to war with a League member contrary to the terms of the Covenant, the remaining Powers could, by declaring that the offending Power had taken this course and thereby implicitly defining the act of going to war, bring into force against it the sanctions of Article 16.

It is, however, clear that the extremely drastic character of the sanctions contemplated in Article 16, and the failure to provide for any less drastic sanctions as an alternative form of pressure upon the offending State, make it impossible for the League to invoke the Article unless all the Great Powers not directly involved are prepared actually to go to war with the offender and to place their forces at the disposal of the League, not only for the carrying out of a universal blockade but also, if necessary, for the actual levying of war at the League's orders. Indeed, this levying of war is clearly contemplated under the second clause of Article 16, which lays down that where the obligation to enforce a boycott under the first clause of Article 16 arises " it shall be the duty of the Council to recommend to the several Governments concerned what effective military, naval or air force the members of the League shall severally contribute to the armed forces to be used to protect the Covenants of the League " ; and it is further laid down in Section iii. of the same Article that the members of the League " will afford passage through their territory to the forces of any of the members which are co-operating to protect the covenants of the League "—a provision which incidentally raised considerable difficulties in the way of the entry of Switzerland into the League on account of the determination of the Swiss Government to maintain inviolable the historic neutrality of Swiss territory.

Short of the readiness actually to make war upon the offender, or at all events to threaten war and be prepared actually to make war if the threat is not effective, the League is unable under the Covenant to apply lesser sanctions. It seems clear that this insistence that sanctions, if they are applied, must take so extreme a form, must have been deliberately designed, by excluding the employment of less extreme sanctions, to make the use of Article 16 as difficult as possible, and thereby to prevent the League from taking measures of a less forcible character by way of pressure against an offending country. For it is evident that sanctions which can only be applied by the threat of actually making war and involve the handing over by the individual Powers of their armed forces to the control of the League for this purpose are exceedingly unlikely to be used in practice, in face of the insistence of national sovereignty which marks the Covenant as a whole, and is deeply rooted in the attitudes of the States which make up the League's membership.

Sanctions and Armaments. This question of sanctions is of course very closely connected with the attitude which successive French Governments have consistently taken up in relation to all proposals for disarmament. The French have recognised the inadequacy of the provisions of Article 16 and of the Covenant as a whole for the purposes which they have in view, and desire, in pursuance of their policy of insisting on adequate guarantees of national security as a condition precedent to any substantial measure of disarmament, to add to the Covenant fresh international obligations within the general framework of the League binding the League States together for the common enforcement of a peace based upon the territorial *status quo*.

The French, as we have seen, want not only additional promises that the other League States will come to their assistance against any aggressor who attempts to upset the existing territorial arrangements in Europe, but also the definite establishment of an armed force composed of national contingents under the control of the League, and the setting up of a number of internationally controlled " dumps " of those heavier munitions of war whose use it is proposed to restrict in the disarmament convention—these " dumps " to be guarded for the exclusive use of the League itself or of national contingents operating under the League's orders and in defence of the conditions embodied in the Covenant. But no other Power has shown any willingness to accept this broadening of the obligation to use the collective force of the member States in support of the *status quo*, although in the absence of some such scheme as the French Government put forward to the Disarmament Conference of 1932 the sanctions provided for in Article 16 of the Covenant are likely to remain ineffective.

How far, then, is any scheme of the sort proposed by the French at the Disarmament Conference really practicable ? If certain types of armaments are either prohibited or drastically limited under a Disarmament Convention, is it practicable or desirable to maintain a supply of these forbidden armaments to be used exclusively under the League's control ? These armaments would have to be kept somewhere, that is to say, upon the territory of some State belonging to the League. The French suggest that there should be a number of separate " dumps " for the keeping of these armaments ; but in practice would any State in the event of a resort to war refrain from using all the arms at its disposal, even if some of them were nominally reserved for use at the orders of the League exclusively, and were forbidden to it unless it were actually making war on the League's behalf ? It seems most unlikely that if war had actually broken out any great State would in fact accept such a limitation upon its effective fighting force. But if one State seized and used the armaments contained in the

" dump," other States would obviously follow its example ; for it would be out of the question for them to deny themselves the use of a type of armament which was being used by their adversaries. In practice, therefore, the reserved arms, if they were allowed to remain in existence at all, would certainly be used ; and the proposal to reserve them exclusively for use at the orders of the League would inevitably break down.

Nor does there seem to be any greater hope in the proposal that each country should establish a special contingent of heavily armed troops to be used only in the service of the League ; for the conditions which apply to the establishment of special " dumps " of armaments subject to this condition apply with even greater force to national contingents of soldiers, sailors and airmen. It would be impossible in the event of war to restrict the use of any such contingents by the nations to which their members belonged, and therefore to prevent them from being added in effect to the armed forces of the belligerents. The French answer to these objections would doubtless be that, even if they are valid, the establishment of the proposed " dumps " and contingents of men would nevertheless equip the League with an armed force upon which it could call for service against a State guilty of serious offence against the comity of nations. In the French view the League is nothing as an authority with power to apply sanctions as long as it has no armed force of its own. The logical deduction from this view would be that an international army should be established for the enforcement of peace under the direct auspices of the League, and not responsible in any way to any national State. But even the French recognise that the establishment of such a force would involve the abrogation of the principle of national State sovereignty, for which they stand equally with other nations, and that it is quite impracticable in the present condition of national opinion. They therefore advocate a half measure which is plainly unworkable. Their proposal, so far from furthering the cause of disarmament, would in practice add to the armed forces at the disposal of each State concerned, and, instead of excluding the use of certain weapons which it is desired to abolish by agreement upon qualitative disarmament, would perpetuate the existence of these weapons and make their use inevitable in the event of war actually breaking out. The French proposal will not work ; but despite its unworkability, it has to be recognised as the nearest approach that any Great Power has been prepared to make towards a real attempt to render the League an effective instrument for the enforcement of peace, and to transcend the limitations imposed upon its action by the insistence on national sovereignty.

There is in the last resort no halfway house between absolute national sovereignty and the recognition of a supra-national authority with the right to issue decisions upon which individual nations are under an obligation to act. Nor, as long as the use of armed forces continues to be regarded as a final resort when persuasion and non-military sanctions have failed, is there any halfway house between the recognition of the right of national States to make in the last resort war without limit and the setting up of a supra-national armed force under supra-national control, powerful enough to apply coercion to any national State or combination of States which attempts to resist its authority. As long as war is still to be contemplated as a possible contingency by the Governments of the separate nations, no international authority can be assured of the power to prevent it or to override the limits of national sovereignty, unless that authority is so equipped as to be able to make war itself with a convincing superiority of force. But there is absolutely no possibility of a supra-national force, armed with power of this order, being brought into existence. For if the States of the world were prepared to allow such a force to come into being this could be only because they had already given up the claim to resort to national war, and were already prepared to recognise the right of a supra-national authority to override their national views.

As long as States continue to insist upon State sovereignty

they cannot agree to the creation of a super-State. As long as they continue to believe in the necessity for national armies capable of making war they cannot agree to the creation of a supra-national army strong enough to defeat their own forces. If the conditions existed for bringing into being a supra-national military power strong enough to enforce peace, those conditions would of themselves have made the existence of any such supra-national power unnecessary. The French policy, which attempts to approach the idea of a supra-national armed force without going outside the limitations of State sovereignty, is self-contradictory ; but any attempt to remove the contradiction by proposing the establishment of a real supra-national authority would be doomed to defeat because within the nations the conditions required for the acceptance of such a proposal do not yet exist.

If, then, there is no real question of arming the League itself either with a supra-national force powerful enough to coerce the national States or with a force based on national contingents restricted to use under the auspices of the League, what advance is possible beyond the highly unsatisfactory situation which exists under the terms of the present Covenant ? The most obvious answer is that the League can become a real organ of international government, even in the sense of preventing war, only to the extent to which in each country and above all in each of the Great Powers the spirit of nationalism can be conquered, and so strong a spirit of internationalism substituted for it in the minds of the peoples as to compel the Governments to abandon the idea of national sovereignty, to accept the principle that national rights and claims should be subject to the overriding rights of the world as a whole, and accordingly to give up armies and navies as the logical consequence of the abandonment of the idea of national sovereignty and of the thought of a resort to war in support of national claims. In other words, the obvious answer is that the League can be made effective as an organ of international government, even in the limited sphere of preventing war, only in as far as public opinion in the great States turns pacifist and internationalist, and is prepared to subordinate national to world considerations and to accept the overriding authority of some body representing not one nation alone but the comity of civilised peoples. When we speak of pacifism in this connection we are thinking not of that extreme form of pacifism which repudiates altogether the resort to force, but only of a pacifism which definitely rejects the idea of international war under any circumstances. Accordingly we are not suggesting that public opinion must reach a point at which it would refuse to tolerate the maintenance by the Governments of any armed forces at all, but only one at which it would definitely insist on disarmament down to the point—already reached in Denmark—of preserving only the minimum forces required for the preservation of internal order and only those forms of armament required for this purpose, to the exclusion of all forms of armament designed for other than police purposes.

Is it possible to contemplate in the near future so great an advance of pacifist sentiment in the leading countries of the world as this large approach to complete disarmament would connote ? The answer clearly is that it is not ; for the conditions required for the development of such a pacifist attitude on the part of the peoples of the great States are not fulfilled within the existing framework of European society. In the first place, the peoples of Europe are not, in the existing State system, prepared to accept the present frontiers of the various States as permanent. It is true that, under the Locarno Pacts, Germany joined with the other Western Powers in guaranteeing not to resort to war for the alteration of her existing western frontiers—in other words, not to make war for the reconquest of Alsace-Lorraine and the smaller areas taken from her under the Peace Treaty. But she has given no similar guarantee concerning her frontiers in the east—that is to say, in relation either to Upper Silesia or to the Polish Corridor. Nor have the other Powers defeated in the Great War given any guarantees corresponding to those given by Germany at Locarno. Hungary, for example, is certainly not prepared to accept as final the manifestly unjust territorial settlement forced upon her after the war. Turkey may be ; for Turkey has successfully reconstructed her State on a new basis within her amended frontiers, and the exchange of populations has done much to remove the menace of Turkish irredentism. But Bulgaria is no more prepared than Hungary to bind herself permanently to the acceptance of the territorial *status quo*.

Moreover, it is highly uncertain whether the undertakings entered into by Germany at Locarno can be regarded as preserving their value in face of the dramatic change in the German political situation, and of the wave of nationalist sentiment which has swept over the German people during the past year. Everyone knows that the existing territorial settlement in Europe is inherently unstable, and that no peace based upon its absolute and unqualified maintenance stands any chance of being so accepted by the peoples of Europe as to be compatible with the development in their minds of a pacifist spirit that can serve as a basis for a real internationalist attitude. Nationalism will continue to menace the peace of Europe and to sustain the idea of State sovereignty as long as the existing States of Europe remain in being with their existing frontiers and their existing political relationships.

It must not of course be forgotten that in an exceedingly cautious fashion the League Covenant does recognise that the necessity for territorial readjustments may arise. It is not based on the absolute assertion of the permanence of the existing European frontiers. Thus, Article 19 of the Covenant lays down that " the Assembly (not, it should be observed, the Council) may from time to time advise the reconsideration by members of the League of treaties which have become inapplicable, and the consideration of international conditions whose continuance might endanger the peace of the world." But these cautious words clearly contemplate the reconsideration of treaties and the readjustment of frontiers only by mutual agreement, and subject to the unanimity rule which is the basis of the League Covenant as a whole. The Covenant provides no means whereby frontiers can be readjusted or the Peace Treaties reconsidered save on this basis of unanimity. Article 10 binds all members of the League " to respect and preserve as against external aggression the territorial integrity and existing political independence of all members of the League " ; and, in the absence of any special provision permitting the reconsideration of existing treaties or frontiers by a procedure not involving unanimity, the clause of Article 5 which lays down the rule demanding agreement of all members of the League represented when a question is under discussion, clearly precludes any such reconsideration in the absence of unanimity among the States concerned.

The League is thus tied not absolutely, but in default of agreed revision, to the existing territorial settlement of Europe ; and the fact that it is so tied means that States which are determined to bring about a readjustment of their frontiers will be unwilling to bind themselves to a greater extent than they are bound already under the Covenant to observe the decisions of the League. The difficulty which arises over this issue has come out very plainly in consequence of Mussolini's action in raising the question of Treaty revision in connection with the pact proposed between the four Western Powers in the early months of 1933. For, as we have seen, Mussolini's dictum at once led to an insistence by certain of the League States, and notably by France, Poland and the Little Entente, that any pact which they could agree to recognise must be arrived at " within the framework of the League "—in other words, that it must be of such a sort as to preclude territorial revisions of the Treaty except on the basis of unanimity provided for in the Covenant. This, however, by no means suits Germany or the other States which are desirous of territorial readjustment ; for these States are well aware that their claims are not in the least likely to be accepted voluntarily by the Little Entente or Poland or any of the countries at whose expense the territorial readjustments are being sought. The fact that the League is in its conception an instrument not merely for the prevention of war in general, but specifically for the prevention of any attempt by war to alter the territorial settlement embodied in the Treaties of Peace, has been brought out very plainly indeed by the discussions which have centred round the Four-Power Pact of 1933.

Thus, while some members of the League see its chief value in the guarantees which it gives them for the preservation of the existing frontiers of Europe, other members regard it as valuable only if it can be used for the purpose of altering these frontiers, and regard it as a positive nuisance to the extent to which it stands in the way of their desire for territorial readjustments. But, it may fairly be asked, if the existing frontiers of Europe carry no authority which the nations of Europe are prepared to accept, would any alteration of frontiers be likely to improve the situation? Are such problems as that of the Polish Corridor or the drawing of frontiers through the territories occupied by inextricably mingled national elements in Central and Eastern Europe capable of solution at all on a basis of mutual consent, or on any basis at all that will prevent fresh attempts to alter them by war when occasion offers?

The answer is that within the existing system of sovereign States there is no possibility of a territorial settlement which will remove the danger of wars aiming at territorial readjustment. For there are numerous areas to which more than one State can put forward a claim which is bound to seem valid from the nationalist point of view; and as long as States continue to be regarded as ultimate sovereign entities claiming the final allegiance of their subjects, there is no arbitrament save that of war to which in the last resort these rival claims can be submitted.

It does not, however, follow that the desire to abolish war is merely utopian, or that no political system that would remove the danger of war from this cause is possible on the European Continent. What does follow is that the danger of war can be removed only by changing the character and the mutual relationships of the States of which Europe must continue to be made up. It is of course out of the question to propose that all Europe should be merged into a single State governed from one common centre. The needs and situations and the national traditions of the various peoples are far too wide apart to admit of any such simple solution. The problem must be solved, if it is to be solved at all, along federal lines, under some system which will allow each country to retain its internal autonomy in the management of those affairs which are vital to its national culture and traditions, while providing a common government for the whole of Europe, or at least for a large part of it, in respect of those matters which require co-ordinated action over a wider field. There is no real impossibility in looking forward to a European federation powerful enough to take over from the separate States the administration of many vital services, while leaving to each individual country a degree of autonomy amply sufficient to safeguard its special national needs. But the creation of any such European federation involves that it must be built round the fulfilment of common services for the peoples of Europe, and not concentrated upon purely political issues or upon the attempt to prevent war.

The Foundations of Internationalism.   Take for example the position of the European system of transport. Europe has already the nucleus of a system of internationalised waterways ; and common action in respect of those rivers, such as the Danube, which serve the needs of a number of separate countries has been forced upon these countries by the impracticability of treating each stretch of the river that flows through the territory of a particular State as its own special property, and still more by the necessity of providing some form of common administration where the river is itself the boundary between two States. The Danube and a number of other rivers have accordingly their international commissions, which have now been brought under the auspices of the League of Nations. But in no sphere save that of river transport has the process of internationalisation even begun, unless account is to be taken of the safeguarding of the rights of a number of different nations in certain particular ports. It is, however, clearly desirable in the common interest of all the European peoples that the co-ordinated control of transport should be pushed much further. Air services in particular are clearly unsuitable for independent national control. Even apart from the obvious danger that aeroplanes built for civil transport may be turned to military uses in time of war, there is a very strong case for the complete internationalisation of civil aviation, at any rate as far as the main European airways are concerned. This has been actually proposed at the Disarmament Conference, with the object of preventing the use of commercial aeroplanes in time of war ; but this is the wrong way of tackling the problem. It ought to be envisaged from the standpoint of equipping Europe with a common system of air services linking every quarter of the Continent together.

Or take again the question of the railways. There are necessarily arrangements between the railway systems of the various countries for the regulation of through traffic, both for goods and passengers ; but at present each country maintains its entirely independent railway system, usually under public ownership, though in some countries the actual administration is entrusted to one or more private companies. Many of the newer States are exceedingly ill-equipped with railway facilities ; for the railway systems built before the war were designed in relation to the pre-war frontiers and are often both unsuitable and inadequate in relation to post-war economic and political needs. Clearly it would be very much to the advantage of Europe as a whole if a unified railway system could be developed, and if capital for the building of new lines and the improvement of those already in existence could be provided on an international basis against the security of the railway receipts. For under present conditions the countries which stand most in need of improved railway facilities are precisely those which have the greatest difficulty in raising the capital necessary for financing the construction of new lines. Apart from this, if the whole railway system of Europe could be co-ordinated under international control it would be possible greatly to improve the efficiency of services for both passengers and goods ; and the certain consequence of this improvement would be to make it harder for the separate States to maintain many of the restrictions which they now impose upon the free movement of goods and persons. Nothing would have so great an influence towards the unification of Europe as the internationalisation of the main transport services by rail and air. At the same time the existing international postal convention which links together the national postal systems of the various countries could be made the basis for a corresponding internationalisation of the means of communication.

Any real advance towards European collaboration, and incidentally towards removing the possibility of war between nations, involves above all the development of common economic services over the whole area of Europe, or over as large a part of it as can be brought within a comprehensive federation on these lines. Briand's famous project of European union was faultily conceived and certain to prove abortive in that it attempted to bring about a political union of the European States without giving it any firm basis of common economic service. The French plan was to begin with political unification, in the hope that some form of economic unification would follow—at least to the extent of the mutual lowering of tariff barriers and the encouragement of trade between European countries. But to begin in this way is to take hold of the wrong end of the stick. Collaboration, if it is to be fruitful, must begin in the economic field ; and if it can be made successful in economic matters, political collaboration will follow. Even the Committee for European Union, set up by the League as a consequence of Briand's project, soon ceased to talk in the barren terms of political unification and set itself to the consideration of certain of the major economic problems facing the European States. It began to discuss the possibilities of lowering tariff barriers, of creating an international Agricultural Mortgage Corporation in order to relieve the indebtedness of the farming communities, of taking steps for the revalorisation of cereals, through the preferential admission of European wheat into the importing countries and the creation of an international guarantee fund. These plans have so far proved no less unrealisable than the original project of political union ; but is not that largely because they have attempted to take hold of the economic problem precisely at those points at which the apparent interests of the separate European States are most divergent, instead of trying to find common services which could be developed under unified European, or at least Continental, control ?

It is not suggested that it would be at all easy to persuade the European States to agree to hand over any of their vital services to the control of an international authority. How difficult this is has indeed been illustrated by the discussions at the Disarmament Conference of the proposal to establish an international control of civil aviation ; and any plan for the internationalisation of the railways would certainly encounter even stronger resistance. Yet railway internationalisation does offer to all the Continental States the possibility of very great positive economic benefits and offers these most of all to those smaller States in Eastern and Central Europe whose economic difficulties are most acute, and whose political antagonisms constitute a no less constant threat of war than the mutual hostilities of the greater Powers. Yet, despite all the advantages that projects of economic unification may offer, they are not at the present time in the least likely to be accepted. National hostilities are just now too strong for any of the States of Europe to agree to allow any vital service to pass, if it can help it, out of its exclusive national control.

If, however, a solution of the European problem is at present impossible, even on these lines, are we not compelled to go deeper and to question the entire validity of the European State system as it at present exists ? If States, organised as they are to-day, cannot overcome their national antagonisms, or agree, in spite of obvious economic and political advantages, on any constructive measures of political unification, must there not be something radically wrong with the entire European State system ? There is something radically wrong ; and the wrong is that each State, with the possible exception of Soviet Russia, is governed to-day not in the common interest of the entire community for which it professes to stand, but rather in the interest of certain limited classes which rest their claims upon vested interests and traditional rights. In effect, as long as States are governed either by autocracies based on hereditary privilege, or by plutocracies arising out of the development of modern Capitalism, the vested interests created or sustained by their existing constitutions are certain to prove too strong for them to be induced to agree to any real measure of internationalisation. Only if States are administered in accordance with the interests of the whole body of their inhabitants, and under the control of Governments representing this communal point of view, will real internationalism become possible. For only so will forces be created in each State sufficiently powerful to overcome the sectional interests which look askance at all efforts to promote real international collaboration, because the success of these efforts would prejudice their power to administer the national affairs in accordance with their sectional point of view. This means that the essential prelude to any real collaborative commonwealth of Europe is the establishment of some form of Socialism in each European country, or at least in all those which are important enough to influence the general movement of European affairs. For Socialism, putting first the interest of the common people, would necessarily bring with it a willingness to carry out those measures of economic unification which are plainly calculated to make Europe as a whole wealthier and better governed.

But at this point comes the objection that the very forces which have of late destroyed the Socialist movements of Italy and Germany claim, equally with Socialism, to put the class point of view behind them, and to bring into being Governments which do stand essentially for the point of view of the nation as a whole. The claims of Fascism as a doctrine of national solidarity have been discussed in an earlier section. Here we are concerned with it solely in connection with its effects on international relations. The most profound difference between Fascism and Socialism is precisely the difference between nationalism and internationalism which we have just been discussing. For, whereas Fascism bases itself absolutely and without qualification upon the idea of the Nation State as something ultimate, with a right to command the entire and undivided loyalty of its subjects, Socialism is at its very basis an international doctrine, affirming the solidarity immediately of the working classes throughout the world, but also, from the moment of its successful establishment, of all peoples. For Socialism recognises class differences only for the purpose of abolishing them. There could, of course, arise a bastard "National Socialism" which denied this fundamental doctrine of world solidarity, and sought merely to socialise the conduct of the essential economic services of a particular State in order to strengthen that State as an absolute authority. Nazism in Germany, for example, claims to be National Socialism ; and though the Socialist part of its doctrine was little stressed during the later stages of its rise to power, undoubtedly the Nazis are capable, as the Fascists have been capable in Italy, of increasing the amount of State intervention in industry, and of affirming the right of the State to take over essential economic services for the purpose of strengthening the nation in relation to the outside world. But this type of National Socialism is not really Socialism at all. It is based not on the attempt to abolish social classes and to establish a classless society, but rather on the principle of admitting class differences and recognising class privileges, provided they are made subordinate to the claims of the nation, which is regarded not as a means of promoting human welfare, but essentially as a metaphysical being, with power as its most valuable attribute and its highest achievement in the attainment of supreme military strength.

This bastard " National Socialism " has nothing in common with Socialism, which is fundamentally internationalist and pacific, seeks to link together the workers of all countries for the establishment of a classless international community broken up only for convenience into territorial divisions, and is totally uninterested in the conception of national power. " National Socialism " is merely the so-called Bismarckian " State Socialism " of the nineteenth century re-written in terms appropriate to the class divisions and political perplexities of the twentieth century.

If these contentions are correct, the one hope of making the League of Nations into an effective instrument of internationalism lies in the victory of Socialism in enough of the countries which make it up totally to change its character, and to convert it from an instrument designed to prevent war between sovereign States into an organ of international government actually in charge of those vital economic functions which need for their efficient conduct administration upon an international scale. Just as the Nation-States of Europe have gradually taken over from the smaller communities out of which they have been built up one vital function of economic organisation after another, and have been compelled to do this because the evolution of the economic powers of mankind has irresistibly demanded the creation of larger administrative units, so now in the twentieth century the time is ripe for the creation of still larger organs of economic administration. Nationalism, with its cherished doctrine of State sovereignty, may once have been an instrument of economic progress, in that it did help to bring about the unification of territories too small to stand by themselves under the economic conditions of the modern world. But Nationalism in its turn has now become a fetter upon the developing productive powers of mankind ;

and it too is destined in due course—not to pass away any more than localism has passed away with the coming of the Nation-State—but to be superseded in a large number of the functions which are at present organised on a national basis by larger forms of administration more suitable to the conditions of our time.

How this will come about it is of course impossible to predict. If Socialism is able peaceably to conquer power in each of the great States of Europe, it will be possible for Socialist Governments to turn the League of Nations from what it now is into an effective organ of positive economic collaboration, or to create within it a real European union having this object. If, on the other hand, Socialism comes not by a process of peaceful conquest of power in each country, but as the result of a further world convulsion brought about by the inability of one nationalism to live at peace with another, the course of evolution will probably be quite different ; for the coming of such a convulsion will certainly sweep away the League of Nations and all the elaborate structure of pacts and treaties built up since the conclusion of the Great War. Europe will then have to make a new start ; and this new start will have to be made far more in the sphere of economic realities and far less in terms of obsolete and obstructive nationalist ideas than the attempt to which President Wilson pinned his faith but not his country in 1919.

We have spoken so far of Europe in an inclusive sense, as if we were envisaging the advent of a single federation wide enough to embrace the entire European Continent. This may indeed be the form in which European internationalism will be realised ; but not even an approach towards an inclusive federation of this type is possible under existing political conditions. For, apart from the difficulties which have been considered already, two countries stand in so different a relation to the rest of the world from the remaining States of Europe that their position raises special difficulties and calls for special comment. These countries are Great Britain and the U.S.S.R.

Great Britain and the League.   The position of Great Britain is obviously complicated, because, while on the one hand she is linked up with Europe by close ties both of economic intercourse and of cultural relations, she has also, by virtue of her possession of an Empire scattered over every Continent, extra-European connections which she cannot afford to sacrifice as long as this Empire remains in being. Whenever the question of European collaboration comes up she is divided between her deep interest in European affairs and her desire to strengthen as far as possible her existing imperial connections. When, for example, the European countries meet in order to discuss common action for the lowering of tariffs and other barriers in the way of trade, Great Britain has a deep interest in getting these tariffs lowered and the strongest possible reason for wishing not to be excluded from any preferential arrangements which the European countries may make among themselves for the admission of one another's goods. But Great Britain is not prepared to admit the goods of other European countries on more favourable terms than goods coming from Empire countries ; nor, since the Ottawa Conference, has she been prepared or able, in view of her imperial commitments, to admit European goods even on the same terms. The Ottawa decisions in fact commit Great Britain for a period of years to imperial tariff preference, and thereby shut her out from even the possibility of becoming a member of a European tariff union. This may seem to be the less important because there appears to be no early prospect of the European countries agreeing to create such a union, ready as they may be to discuss it from time to time. But if the European States did show some real disposition to lower their tariffs against one another's goods, so as to grant preferential treatment to European products, Great Brtain would inevitably be torn between her fears of exclusion from the European market and her desire to maintain the preferences accorded to her by the Empire countries. She was so divided in mind at the time of the World Economic Conference of 1927, and again when

Briand's plans for European union were under discussion ; and the fact that she has, under the National Government, committed herself temporarily to a thorough-going policy of Empire preference by no means proves that the question is settled once and for all.

For Great Britain, despite the decline in recent years of her trade with the European Continent, still sells a highly important proportion of her exports in the European market, and, what is more important, looks to this market, even more than to the Empire market, for an expansion of her exports in the event of any substantial recovery in world trade. It is arguable that in the long run the sparsely populated Empire countries may so increase their demand as to afford a sufficient outlet for British manufactures ; but no one in his senses supposes that this can be true in the short run, and it is with the short run that British commercial interests are inevitably most concerned. They are quite prepared to make concessions to the Empire, to the extent to which these concessions can be made without involving exclusion from the markets of Europe ; but if such exclusion did really threaten, there would be a considerable cooling in British commercial circles of such enthusiasm as at present exists for the Ottawa agreements.

Somewhat similar considerations arise when the countries of Continental Europe begin discussing any system of mutual guarantees of peace on the lines of the French proposal for mutual pacts of security. For in this case again Great Britain is torn between her desire not to lose her political and economic influence in Europe, and not to be faced with a *bloc* of European countries from which she is excluded, and her equally strong desire to keep free of Continental entanglements and to maintain close political connections with the countries of the Empire. The French, recognising the impossibility of inducing Great Britain to join in any comprehensive European pact involving military guarantees, proposed in their second scheme laid before the Disarmament Conference in 1932 that there should be a Continental Pact, which Great Britain would not be asked to join, as a complement to a wider and looser pact based upon the League as a whole. But this project was only less unwelcome to Great Britain than the request to join a Continental Pact ; for, if she does not wish to become involved in such a pact, neither does she desire a pact to be made without her, on terms which might possibly result in an alliance of European States detrimental to her special interests.

Thus both politically and economically Great Britain stands poised between a policy of full collaboration in the affairs of Europe and one of imperial unity in an exclusive sense. She has been enabled so far to walk this tight-rope successfully, in the first place because she is an island, and in the second because the Continental States have not so far succeeded in reconciling their own differences sufficiently to present a united front. If they did this, she would have to determine her attitude one way or the other ; and at present she would almost certainly decide, however reluctantly, to remain outside a *bloc* formed in Continental Europe, while endeavouring to make the best terms she could for her commerce with the countries forming the *bloc*.

Thus for the present at least the idea of a confederal Europe has to be conceived in terms which leave out Great Britain on the west ; but this is solely due to the continued existence of the British Empire as a political and economic unit. If Great Britain lost India, if a number of her colonies fell away or were taken from her, if the self-governing Dominions pressed somewhat further their established right to take their own line in international affairs as well as in matters of internal government, Great Britain, reft of her imperial sovereignty, would be inevitably drawn into the circle of the Continental system. There is no likelihood of these things happening at the moment ; but if another world war did break out, no one can prophesy that Great Britain would be able to come through such a war with her Empire intact or even surviving at all.

Moreover, Socialism is inconsistent with Empires as they are now conceived. It is not in the least inconsistent with the existence of federations of self-governing countries bound together solely upon a basis of mutual consent ; and to the extent to which the British Empire can survive this test there is no reason why Socialism should modify in any way the relations at present existing between Great Britain and the self-governing Dominions. But in such a reformed Empire India would have to be a member, if at all, on terms of political and economic equality ; and the other colonial possessions of the British Crown could be retained only to the extent to which their retention could be justified in the interests of their own inhabitants. In Africa, for example, the victory of Socialism in Europe would almost certainly bring with it the sweeping away of the separate colonial administrations at present maintained by the various European countries in favour of some sort of international administration within which the existing colonies and mandated areas would be re-grouped, irrespective of their present imperial affiliations. The British Empire might survive ; but an Empire so reconstituted as this survival would imply would no longer possess the character of an exclusive political or economic unity, or bar out a country belonging to it from entering into the closest political and economic associations with countries standing outside. Great Britain might be a member of the British Empire, and yet at the same time belong to a European group of States ; and Canada might retain political affiliations with Great Britain, and yet build up close economic and political relationships with the United States.

The U.S.S.R. and the League. At the opposite end of Europe from Great Britain is the Soviet Union, stretching across the Continental frontier without a break to the Far East. The mass of the population of Soviet Russia still lives in Europe ; but the larger part of Russian territory lies beyond the Urals, and the development both of Russian industry and of Russian agriculture is being so carried on under the Soviet Government as to remove the centres of economic activity further from the western frontiers and nearer to the huge undeveloped tracts of the east. Russian industries are being developed in and beyond the Urals, and a steadily increasing population is being settled in Asiatic Russia. It will inevitably take a long time for this great shifting of the centre of Russian economic and political life to produce its full effects. But there is no doubt at all that it is going on, or that it is being done deliberately by the Soviet Government as a means both of opening up the vast new territories remote from western Europe, and of lessening the danger to the Russian system from war upon the western frontiers. Russia, confronted by a hostile Europe determined to maintain the capitalist system and protect itself from the infection of Communism, is reciprocating by such withdrawal from European complications as lies within her power.

The Russians, of course, cannot, and would not if they could, disinterest themselves in the affairs of Europe ; they are inevitably interested very closely in the settlement of European affairs and in the maintenance of the peace of Europe, as well as in finding outlets for their exports, and the means of purchasing manufactured goods in the markets of Western Europe. Nor can the western countries afford to ignore Russia, both because they too are interested in the Russian market and because, even apart from their unwillingness to disarm as long as they feel the menace of Communism in the east, Russian ideas can percolate across their frontiers even without the aid of Russian soldiers. But, though Russia must interest herself in the affairs of Europe, and other European countries must interest themselves in the affairs of Russia, though Russian delegates must be invited to attend, and must actually attend, international conferences on questions of disarmament and economic relations, there is no real possibility, as long as the rest of Europe remains capitalist, of the entry of Russia into any closer union with the European States. The difference between the Communist form of Socialism which is now dominant in Russia and the Capitalism which still holds the field over the rest of Europe is far too profound to be bridged by any merely mechanical union. The Russians, as we have seen, do still stand for the idea of world revolution, though they have abandoned the notion of fostering it by active intervention in the affairs of the European States ; and the capitalist Powers still hope for the disappearance of Russian Communism, though they have abandoned for the time at least, in face of their own troubles and antagonisms, the idea of trying to overthrow it by force. Between these two divergent points of view there can be no accommodation ; and it would be impracticable for a Socialist Russia to be administered under the same international control with a capitalist Europe. Socialist Russia could not hand over any vital service to an international control, to be operated mainly under the auspices of a federation of capitalist States ; nor politically could Russia join in guaranteeing the integrity of a State system and of State frontiers whose validity she denies. Of course the triumph of Socialism in Europe would alter this situation so as to make collaboration possible. But for the present Russia is bound to go her own way in the East to an even greater extent than Great Britain in the West. Such immediate approaches as can be made towards closer European union have therefore to be thought of in terms of the Continental States which lie between the Russian frontier and the Atlantic Ocean.

It has, however, to be remembered that the U.S.S.R., under its existing Constitution, is not a closed but an open federation. The draughtsmen of the Russian Constitution deliberately left the way open for fresh units to join the U.S.S.R. if they were prepared to accept the principles of Communism and the overriding control of the Soviet Union as a whole in matters of general policy. It is therefore quite within the bounds of possibility that the result of any upsetting of the present European State system would be among other things the voluntary linking up of new territories in Eastern Europe with the U.S.S.R. ; so that Russia might on a federal basis regain part at least of the territory which was lost to her through the creation of

new States at the conclusion of the war. Just as the small
Republics of Georgia, Azerbaijan and Armenia have disappeared and been merged into the Soviet Union as one
of its constituent Republics, so some of the border States
might, if they underwent Communist revolutions of their
own, prefer to forgo their present independent status, and
link up with Soviet Russia. For there is no essential element
of permanence in the existing frontiers between the
U.S.S.R. and the rest of Europe. Peasants on the Russian
side of the frontier, especially in the southern part of
Poland, are, as we have seen, much the same as the peasants
of the Ukraine ; and if the smaller States of Eastern Europe
went Communist, without a similar change to some form
of Socialism in Europe as a whole, they would be compelled to seek the support of their great eastern neighbour,
probably to the extent of accepting some form of political
unification, subject to autonomy in the management of
their own local affairs. In that event, Communism, even
if it did not fulfil the hopes of the Third International by
conquering Europe as a whole, would be brought far more
closely into contact with the West by the disappearance as
separate entities of the smaller States which at present bar
off Soviet Russia from the Great European Powers.

§ 3. THE INTERNATIONAL LABOUR
ORGANISATION

THE INTERNATIONAL LABOUR ORGANISATION
was set up in 1919 as a part of the Peace settlement ; and
the statutes by which it is governed form Part XIII of the
Versailles Treaty. This part of the Treaty opens with a
preamble declaring the motives which have led the " high
contracting parties, moved by sentiments of justice and
humanity as well as by the desire to secure the permanent
peace of the world," to establish the Organisation. The
preamble declares that " conditions of labour exist involving

such injustice, hardship, and privation to large numbers of people as to produce unrest so great that the peace and harmony of the world are imperilled and the improvement of those conditions is urgently required." The International Labour Organisation was established as a means of remedying these evils. In amplification of these objects certain principles which are to govern the action of the I.L.O. are set out in Article 437 of the Versailles Treaty. First among these comes " the guiding principle . . . that labour should not be regarded merely as a commodity or article of commerce " ; and further principles are designed to safeguard the right of association by both employers and workers. These include the payment of adequate wages and the limitation of the working day, the abolition of child labour, equal pay to men and women for work of equal value, the protection of the rights of foreign labour, and the setting up of an adequate system of inspection for the enforcement of industrial laws.

It is nowhere clearly laid down in the statutes of the International Labour Organisation how wide the scope of its activities is meant to be. Thus there arose at an early stage the question whether the regulation of conditions in agriculture as well as industry came within its province. The French Government among others desired to exclude agriculture ; but in the end this objection was overridden, and the conventions and recommendations adopted at subsequent International Labour Conferences have dealt with the condition of agricultural workers, seamen and other special classes of labour as well as with industry in a narrower sense. A further question arose at an early stage about possible overlapping between the International Labour Organisation and the Economic Section of the League of Nations. The I.L.O. was established in order to deal with questions of labour and employment. It was clearly impossible to isolate these questions from other matters relating to industry ; and one of the earliest activities of the International Labour Office, the permanent machinery set up within the Organisation, was to institute an ambitious " Enquiry into Production." To this strong objection was taken on the ground that, in the questions asked, the Office was travelling far outside its limited terms of reference. But the matter was never settled by any formal decision, the I.L.O. agreeing to restrict its enquiry in order to avoid a ruling which might have seriously limited its future work. Since then on a number of occasions the International Labour Organisation has collaborated with the Economic Section of the League in particular pieces of work, notably in the attempt to deal with the coal-mining situation in Europe. Where necessary, conferences are convened jointly by the two bodies ; and the I.L.O. is called into consultation when the Economic Section of the League is dealing with matters of direct concern to Labour.

In general, the International Labour Organisation consists of the same States as are members of the League of Nations, and membership of the League automatically carries with it membership of the International Labour Organisation. But there is nothing to prevent the I.L.O. from admitting countries which are not members of the League. Thus Germany and the other Central Powers belonged to the International Labour Organisation for some time before their admission to the League ; and when Brazil withdrew from the League she retained her membership of the I.L.O., to which she still belongs. With the single exception of Brazil the membership of the two bodies is at present the same.

There is, however, a very notable difference between these two related international organisations. The League is in form purely an association of Governments, whereas the International Labour Organisation, though its members are States, includes provision for the representation not only of Governments but also of the organisations of employers and workers in each country. Each State which belongs to the I.L.O. has four representatives at the International Labour Conferences. Two of these are appointed by the Government as its own representatives ;

but the other two have to be appointed by the Government
" in agreement with the industrial organisations, if such
organisations exist, which are most representative of employers or workpeople as the case may be, in their respective countries." The Conference as a whole is thus made
up as to one half of Government representatives and as to
the other half of representatives of employers and workers
in equal numbers.

Usually no difficulty arises in carrying out the provisions
for the appointment of employers' and workers' representatives ; but a peculiar problem exists in those countries
in which there is no Trade Union movement in the ordinary
sense. Thus there have been difficulties over the appointment of Labour representatives in Japan ; and, when
Fascist Italy destroyed the largely Socialist Trade Union
movement and substituted for it a system of Fascist Unions
as an integral part of the " Corporative State," the workers'
representatives at the International Labour Conference
challenged the right of the delegate appointed from the
Fascist Union to serve as a working-class representative
and refused him admission to the discussions of the workers'
group. This protest was overridden at the Conference itself ;
for under the Statutes of the International Labour Organisation it requires a two-thirds majority of the votes cast to
exclude any delegate who has been duly appointed by his
Government, and this majority could not be secured. But
the workers' group has maintained its position of refusing
to select an Italian representative upon any committee, or
to act with the Italian " workers' representative " in any
way. A similar situation has now arisen in the case of Germany, and obviously it is bound to be reproduced in the
event of any other country passing under Fascist domination.

The Governing Body of the International Labour
Organisation reproduces the structure of the Assembly, in
that it too consists as to one half of Government representatives, while the other half is appointed by and from the
employers' and workers' delegates at the Conference.
In making these appointments the representatives of the

employers and workers vote as separate groups ; so that their representatives sit upon the governing body not as national representatives but as representing the employers' and workers' groups as a whole. A significant departure is thus made from the principle adopted in the League of Nations that the whole structure should be built up on the representation of separate sovereign States ; for the constitution of international groups of employers and workers inside the I.L.O. involves the recognition of claims of class solidarity cutting across national boundaries. In practice, both on the Governing Body and at the Conferences of the International Labour Organisation, the workers' and employers' groups do as a rule take collective decisions and vote solidly for or against particular resolutions or conventions, though occasionally a particular delegate dissents from the views of the majority of his class colleagues and casts an opposing vote. In the composition of the Governing Body, apart from this question of the special representation of workers and employers' interests, much the same problems have arisen as in the case of the League of Nations. In the International Labour Organisation as in the League, a differentiation is made between the principal and the less important countries ; but in the I.L.O. the countries to be accorded special representation on the governing body are selected in accordance with their industrial importance rather than with their position as Great Powers in a political sense.

The Governing Body consists in all of twenty-four members. Twelve of these, as we have seen, are selected in equal numbers by the employers' and workers' groups acting internationally. The remaining twelve seats have to be allotted to the Governments. Eight of these seats are at present reserved for the leading countries. In the list originally drawn up at the Washington Conference of 1919 the countries selected for special representation were Belgium, France, Germany, Great Britain, Italy, Japan, Switzerland and the United States. The United States, however, was no more prepared to join the International Labour

Organisation than the League ; and in order to secure American representation on the Governing Body Canada was accorded a seat in its place. India also put forward strong claims for representation, and succeeded in displacing Switzerland from the group of countries enjoying special treatment. With these two changes the original suggestions were accepted, and these eight countries accordingly are always represented upon the Governing Body. Only four seats are therefore left to be allotted among all the remaining Governments. These are at present occupied by Brazil, Denmark, Poland and Spain. At an early stage strong complaints arose from the smaller countries, and especially from the countries of South America, that they were accorded no adequate representation ; and at the Conference of 1922 it was proposed to amend the Constitution so as to increase the membership of the Governing Body from twenty-four to thirty-two, thus allowing four extra seats for Governments and two each for the employers' and workers' groups. Moreover, it was proposed to do this without increasing the number of countries granted special representation, so as to give half the Government seats on the Governing Body to the smaller countries. This amendment, however, required, in accordance with the Constitution of the I.L.O., the ratification of no less than forty-two separate States. Forty-one of these ratifications have now been received, but up to the end of 1932 Italy was still blocking the amendment, which has therefore not so far come into force.

The International Labour Organisation is often loosely described as a body for the purpose of passing international labour laws. But in the true sense it has no legislative powers ; for in labour matters as in political affairs each State insists on reserving its separate sovereignty, and is not prepared to surrender power to any international body. The International Labour Conference can only propose and cannot enact. It can pass recommendations and urge their adoption by the various States ; and it can draw up Draft Conventions which the Governments of the member

States are under an obligation to submit to the competent legislative authorities in their countries within a definite period of time. But the obligations of the Governments are limited to this act of submission ; and if the legislative authority in a particular country does not choose to ratify the Conventions proposed by the International Labour Organisation it is perfectly free to reject them, or to take no action. Indeed any Government is itself perfectly free to advise the rejection of a convention, even if its own representatives at the International Labour Conference have previously voted in its favour. On a number of occasions Conventions formally adopted by the International Labour Conference have been subsequently rejected outright by certain of the member States. But more often what happens is that either the Government merely submits the Draft Convention to its Parliament or similar body without any recommendation, and no action is taken either to accept or reject it, or else ratification is postponed or adjourned or made conditional on prior ratification by those countries which are most directly in competition with the State concerned.

The Work of the I.L.O.   Between 1919 and the end of 1931 the International Labour Conference adopted 31 separate Conventions, apart from recommendations and resolutions ; and all these have been submitted for ratification to the member States. Of these 31 Conventions there had been, in June 1933, 505 ratifications by member States, less than 9 ratifications per Convention as against a total of 58 member States. It thus appears that a large number of States have failed to ratify any considerable number of Conventions. Actually 20 States are not recorded as having finally ratified even a single Convention. But all these States are non-European, unless Turkey be counted as a European State, no less than 14 of them being situated in Central or Southern America. Thus, Great Britain and France have each ratified 18, Italy, Poland and Roumania 17, Germany and Sweden 16, and Holland 15. Spain has the highest record, with 30 ratifications, but is apparently soon to share this record with Uruguay, which has just agreed, as we write, to ratify 30 conventions all in a lump, having previously ratified none at all. Luxembourg and Bulgaria come next, with 27 each, followed by Belgium, Yugoslavia and the Irish Free State, with 21. Czechoslovakia, with 12 ratifications, comes low in the European list, level with Japan. Denmark surprisingly has ratified only 10 Conventions in all, Switzerland only six, and Albania only four. The Swiss difficulty arises largely from the federal structure of the Swiss State. Portugal and Lithuania are also low, with only five ratifications; but most of the remaining European States have ratified much the same number as the greater European Powers. Naturally the number of ratifications is as a rule greatest in the case of the Conventions adopted during the earlier years of the International Labour Organisation's existence ; for it often takes a long time to get a Convention embodied in the national law even of a State which is prepared to ratify it. But some of the earlier Conventions, even of those adopted in 1919, still fall very far short of complete ratification—notably the Convention on hours of work in industry, under which the establishment of a universal maximum working week of 48 hours was proposed. This is by far the most important Convention yet adopted by the International Labour Conference ; and the difficulties over its ratification have been the most serious setback encountered by the International Labour Organisation during its fourteen years of activity.

The Washington Hours Convention was the first measure adopted by the International Labour Organisation at its inaugural conference at Washington in 1919. After many years of effort only nine European countries and two outside Europe have definitely ratified it. The only important industrial countries included in this list are Belgium and Czechoslovakia, the others being Luxembourg, Spain, Portugal, Greece, Roumania, Bulgaria and Lithuania. The non-European countries are Chile, the Dominican Republic, and India. In this last case ratification does not imply the adoption of the 48 hours working week, as special provision was made in the Convention for the recognition of an appreciably longer working week in Asiatic countries. Four other States—France, Italy, Austria and Latvia—have agreed to ratify the Convention only on condition of its acceptance by the other leading countries. A number of other countries have approved the Convention, but have not yet brought it into effect ; while five—Great Britain, Germany, Poland, Denmark and Estonia—have reserved action, and five others have either rejected the Convention outright or in some other way successfully shelved it, the absolute rejections being those of Sweden and Switzerland.

Since the Convention was adopted, there have been numerous attempts by the I.L.O. and also by certain Governments, under strong pressure from the workers' group, to secure general ratification ; and on several occasions special conferences of the Labour Ministers of the leading countries have been held in order to see whether agreement for simultaneous ratification could be secured. The employers, on the other hand, have been for the most part strongly opposed to ratification, even in those countries in which the existing working week does not in most trades exceed 48 hours. Just before the coming of the world slump a further attempt at ratification was being made, largely on the initiative of the British Labour Government ; and the employers, backed by certain of the Governments, were pressing for modifications relaxing the severity of the clauses relating to overtime. These modifications were strongly resisted from the workers' side ; but the world slump swept away the hope of securing early ratification in any form. For although it meant that in practice a large proportion of the workers in the various countries were working much less than 48 hours a week, the employers, with the support of most of the Governments, became increasingly reluctant to see the Convention passed into law because it would have meant difficulties with the Trade Unions over the readjustment of wage-rates in accordance with the shortening of the working hours, and in some cases payment for overtime where this was not already being made. Thus, at a time when the countries' situation made possible, and even imperatively called for, a reduction in working hours, it became paradoxically far more difficult than when industry was busier to secure an agreed limitation.

An attempt was, however, made in 1932 to approach the question of the limitation of hours in a somewhat different way. Among the workers especially it was being urged that in view of the world depression steps ought to be taken for a fairer sharing out of the available amount of employment among the employed populations of the various countries. For this purpose it was proposed that, at any rate for the duration of the slump, a maximum working week of 40 hours should be accepted by all States in accordance with the terms of a new Convention to be drafted by the International Labour Organisation. The Italian Government, with a few others, gave its support to this proposal, which came up for consideration at a special International Labour Conference. At this gathering the employers strongly resisted the proposal, on the ground that it would have the effect of raising costs of production and thus further hampering industry at a time when it was already labouring under considerable difficulties. For it was strongly insisted by the workers' group that the reduction in hours must not involve any reduction in earnings, and that accordingly wage-rates must be left intact where they were fixed on a weekly basis, and scaled up where hourly payment or piecework is at present in force. The majority of the Governments, while they were not prepared to accept the workers' proposal that no reduction in wages should be permitted in any case, gave a general endorsement to the workers' point of view, to the extent of urging that if an agreed reduction of hours was brought about steps must be taken to safeguard wage rates. Finally, by the joint action of the Governments' and workers' representatives and against the opposition of the employers' group, it was decided that further consideration should be given to the whole proposal, and a resolution was passed referring the matter for inquiry by the International Labour Office, with a proviso that the inquiry should include the problem of safeguarding wages as well as that of bringing about a reduction in working hours. In the middle of 1933 the project came up for further consideration at the International Labour Conference ; but with the British Government, backed by Nazist Germany, taking the lead against it with the full support of the employers' group, the requisite majority for carrying it further could not be secured, and it was shelved for another year.

There the matter now stands. It will presumably come up for consideration at subsequent meetings of the International Labour Conference ; but in view of the divergence of attitudes and especially of the strong hostility expressed by the British Government to any Convention at all, it seems most unlikely that an agreed solution will be reached. Indeed, even if a Convention is in the end drafted the situation which arose over the Washington Hours Convention of 1919 seems likely to be reproduced, and the British Government may perhaps be again the principal obstacle to its adoption by the leading industrial nations.

The Conventions adopted by the International Labour Organisation are of very unequal importance. Some of them relate only to particular classes of workers, or to industrial problems of secondary importance. In especial, the practice has grown up of devoting special sessions of the Conference to questions affecting seamen ; and two conferences have been largely specialised to dealing with agricultural questions. After the Washington Hours Convention the most important general Conventions are those dealing with unemployment and the minimum wage. The Unemployment Convention, which provides for the setting up by each State which ratifies it of some form of provision by way of insurance or otherwise for the maintenance of the unemployed, has been ratified by 25 States, including most of the leading industrial countries. But the Minimum Wage Convention, which was adopted in 1919 and provides for the establishment of some sort of minimum wage-fixing machinery in each country, has so far received in all only 10 ratifications, though its obligations are by no means onerous. In general, while the output of Conventions has been considerable, very great difficulty has been experienced in securing their acceptance by the member States ; and even where they have been adopted this has often been because they went no further than the States concerned had gone already on a basis of purely national legislation.

The actual influence of the International Labour Organisation in improving standards of labour legislation in the more advanced industrial countries has been exceedingly small. Such valuable results as it has so far achieved in this field have been mainly in pulling up certain of the less advanced countries to a standard somewhat nearer to that of the more advanced nations than they would probably have reached if the I.L.O. had not existed. But even in this field the achievements up to the present have been disappointingly meagre, especially outside Europe ; and there is no doubt that the principal cause of this slow rate of progress is to be found in the unresponsive attitude of the leading industrial countries to those Conventions which would involve any improvement in their own national laws. In particular the failure of the advanced countries to accept the Washington Hours Convention has immensely weakened the prestige of the I.L.O. among the lesser States, and has made the task of securing ratifications far more difficult than it need have been. Moreover, the refusal of the United States to enter the I.L.O. was almost as serious a blow to its prospects of effective work as the corresponding refusal to enter the League of Nations was to the wider cause of international collaboration.

Nevertheless, it is beyond dispute that the I.L.O. has done much useful work, though this has been rather in the field of promoting international discussion and spreading information about the various countries than in the direct improvement of industrial legislation by means of its Conventions. Undoubtedly in such fields as inspection, factory legislation and administration, the regulation of child labour, the prevention of night work, and the promotion of industrial hygiene, the existence of the I.L.O. has been an important factor in inducing countries to make at least some elementary provision in their own national codes of law. In addition the existence of the I.L.O., with the distinct recognition accorded to the international solidarity of interests among workers' as well as employers' representatives, has to some extent helped to promote common action by the Trade Unions in the various countries, and thus to supplement the activities of the International Federation of Trade Unions. It would be foolish to expect that action in the sphere of labour legislation by international agreement could advance much faster than international consciousness among the nations, or that the I.L.O. could successfully transcend that spirit of insistence on national State sovereignty which, as we have seen, has been so fatal an obstacle in the way of the development of the League of Nations as a real organ of international government. More clearly than the League of Nations, the I.L.O. is worth while. Even if its achievements are small, they make definitely in the right direction and have some effect in improving the condition of the workers in those countries which are most backward in safeguarding the interests of labour.

Like the League Covenant, the constitution of the I.L.O. makes provision for the application in certain cases of sanctions against a State which fails to comply with the obligations of membership. The case for sanctions can arise, however, only if a State fails to comply with obligations into which it has voluntarily entered. In joining the I.L.O. a State undertakes, as we saw, the definite obligation to submit for consideration by its own legislative authority any Convention adopted by the International Labour Conference, whether its own representatives at the Conference have voted in favour of the proposed Convention or not. Failure to submit a Convention is accordingly an offence against the constitution of the Organisation. But in effect this obligation can be easily complied with in such a way as to procure the rejection or shelving of any Convention which the Government in question does not like ; and there-fore no Government is likely to be particularly anxious to evade it. A State cannot become guilty of any sort of default by refusing to accept a Convention, for there is no obliga-tion upon any State to accept any Convention unless it wishes to do so. In practice therefore default is only likely to arise where a State, having voluntarily ratified a par-ticular Convention, thereafter fails to secure its enforcement.

If this happens, a complaint can be lodged by any other State concerned against the offending State. The matter has then to be referred to a special commission of Inquiry constituted on the suggestion of the Governing Body of the I.L.O. by the Secretary-General of the League of Nations from a panel of representatives of Governments, employers and workers. This Commission may report to the Inter-national Labour Organisation what its recommendations, if any, are in respect of the complaint, and may include in its report a proposal for the application of sanctions of an economic character against a defaulting State. When such a report has been made, it is open for the Government accused of default to refer the question to the Permanent Court of International Justice, which can then issue a binding award. The Permanent Court, moreover, may itself recommend the application of economic sanctions against a State guilty of breach of its international obliga-tions. But the enforcement of these economic sanctions is left purely to the voluntary initiative of the other member States, any of which is free if it so chooses, but is in no way compelled, to put into force the economic measures sug-gested by the Commission or by the Permanent Court. Clearly these hesitant provisions are not very likely to be invoked in practice, and there would be extreme difficulty, even if sanctions were recommended in a particular case, in getting them applied by agreement between the countries which are members of the I.L.O.

We have seen in the case of the Washington Convention that special provisions were included for the modification of the 48 hours week in its application to Asiatic countries.

This was in accordance with the general scheme laid down in the Constitution of the I.L.O. Article 405 provides that " in framing any recommendation or draft convention of general application the Conference shall have due regard to those countries in which climatic conditions, the imperfect development of industrial organisations, or other special circumstances, make industrial conditions substantially different, and shall suggest the modifications, if any, which it considers may be required to meet the cases of such countries." It is further provided in Article 421 that the member States must apply those Conventions which they themselves ratify to their own colonial possessions which are not fully self-governing, subject to similar modifications to those laid down in Article 405. This last provision is one of the most valuable embodied in the International Labour Organisation's Constitution ; for it does at least make a beginning of applying some sort of industrial legislation to the colonial empires of the Great Powers. Unhappily, this has not so far meant much in practice, owing to the very slow progress which has been made in getting Draft Conventions accepted by the leading countries.

It may seem remarkable that a large part of the opposition to Conventions proposed at the successive International Labour Conferences and to the ratification of Conventions actually approved has come from the more advanced industrial nations, in which economic conditions are on the whole more satisfactory than in the less developed countries. This arises partly from the fact that these countries have for the most part their own codes of industrial legislation and that sometimes a Convention, even if it does not in general lay down standards as high as those already in force in the country concerned, differs in certain material particulars in the methods which it prescribes from the provisions of the existing national legislation, so that it seems to involve inconvenient changes in national law without any corresponding advantage. But the objections raised by the advanced countries are also influenced in many cases by their fears that, even if a particular Convention is generally ratified, there will be great differences between one country and another in the extent to which it is actually observed and enforced. The more advanced countries, and especially Great Britain and Germany, have had higher standards than most other countries in the actual enforcement of the laws which they place upon their Statute Books, though even in the most developed countries labour inspection still leaves much to be desired. A country like Great Britain may therefore express a fear that other countries which agree to ratify a particular Convention will not in fact enforce its observance to anything like the same extent as it will be enforced if Great Britain embodies it in her national code of law. Again, the advanced industrial countries are often unwilling to accept a particular Convention unless there is an assurance that it will be simultaneously ratified by their chief industrial competitors ; and these fears are apt to result in each country waiting for others to act first, with the consequence that in the end no one acts at all, and the Convention remains a dead letter.

But these excuses are by no means sufficient to explain the extraordinary attitude adopted by Great Britain in relation to the Washington Hours Convention of 1919 ; for Great Britain had of all countries by far the most to gain from the acceptance of a limitation of hours which had been secured in the great majority of her own industries. There is little doubt that, if she had promptly ratified the Washington Convention, most other countries, including her leading competitors, would speedily have followed suit, and that the 48 hours week would have become a general standard at least over Western Europe, with the safeguard of national legislation behind it in each of the leading countries. It was indeed suggested in support of the refusal or ratification that the drafting of the Washington Hours Convention was such as to make difficult its reconciliation with the industrial agreements reached by certain British Trade Unions with their employers, and particularly that acceptance of its terms would upset the railwaymen's agreements. But this difficulty could in fact easily have been overcome within the framework of the Convention ; and it seems clear that the real opposition to ratification came from the British employers, who, though they had conceded the 48 hours week in the period of industrial unrest immediately following the war, were not prepared to regard this victory of the Trade Unions as permanent to the extent of allowing it to be embodied without opposition in the national code of law. This attitude on the part of the British employers was extraordinarily short-sighted ; for by their failure to secure the ratification of the Convention by Great Britain, and thus to make easier its acceptance by other countries, they have imposed on themselves competitive handicaps which have become more severe in the course of the present world depression.

Throughout its career the International Labour Organisation has owed a great deal to the forcible person who was placed in 1919 at the head of the International Labour Office. M. Albert Thomas, a former French Socialist leader who had been Minister of Munitions in France during the war, showed extraordinary energy and resource both in developing the authority of the I.L.O. and in beating back assaults upon it by Governments and employers' associations desirous of diminishing its influence. To him is due to a great extent the authority which, in face of much opposition, the International Labour Organisation has actually succeeded in building up ; and his death in 1932 was a serious blow to the cause of international action for the safeguarding of the rights and conditions of labour in accordance with the principles laid down in the Treaty of Peace. For it is clear that under less energetic and skilful management in its early years the I.L.O. might speedily have been reduced to insignificance in the slump of 1921 and the following years, and that, although M. Thomas often provoked criticism by his outspoken and autocratic methods, his presence at the head of the Organisation was one of the chief factors compelling Governments to respect its activities.

Part VI : THE EUROPEAN OUTLOOK

ONLY FOOLS venture, in the present situation, upon confident prophecy about the economic outlook. So far, among those who have ventured upon prophecy since the world depression began, the pessimists have always been right, and it is tempting to assume that they will go on being right, and to say that there is no prospect of an early recovery from the slump, or even of any sustained upward turn. But we are not prepared to make so confident a prophecy even about the immediate future ; all we will venture to say is that there is as we write no clear sign of an improvement calculated to lead directly to a real world recovery. It is true that there has been a big improvement in prices and production in the United States since the suspension of the gold standard, that some small reduction has occurred in the surplus stocks of raw commodities, and that agricultural output has begun in some measure to decline in response to the sharp fall in prices. There is probably a greater reduction in the volume of stocks of finished and semi-finished goods held by traders ; and to this extent the situation is more favourable, in that the stimulus given to production by any favourable conjuncture would be more rapidly passed on to the producing industries and would lead to a more rapid expansion of employment than at any time since the slump set in.

This, however, is only to say that the conditions would be more favourable if forces making for durable recovery were present and able to assert themselves. We look in vain for the clear emergence of such forces. Indeed the last few months have brought in Europe, largely as a result of economic adversity, political complications and new threats of war which make strongly against that revival of confidence on which the upholders of Capitalism rely for an improvement in world trade and production. Moreover, although the United States, where the world depression began, has emerged without positive collapse from the banking crisis of the opening months of 1933, and has been able to engineer, under President Roosevelt's astute leadership, a considerable upward movement of a speculative sort, the effect of this crisis and of the measures taken to deal with it is still too uncertain for any confident prediction to be made either about the future course of American economic policy, or about the long-run repercussions on the American economic system. Great Britain indeed has escaped far more lightly than most other countries during the later phases of the world slump ; for her departure from the gold standard in 1931 did give her a substantial measure of relief. But such advantages as she enjoys are purely relative ; and there is no sign of the coming from Great Britain of any force leading in the direction of world recovery.

Nor are the hopes once based upon the World Economic Conference now anywhere confidently held ; and although, the Conference is actually in session as we write, and a whole series of discussions about the economic future is taking place between the representatives of the leading countries, it does not appear, at any rate on the surface, that the participants in the conference are equipped with any agreed or workable plan for promoting a general revival. In these circumstances there is assuredly no sufficient reason for prophesying a speedy end of the slump ; but we hesitate to say with any assurance that it is bound to continue. What we are prepared to assert is that, even if recovery does come in the near future, that will be by no means the end of Europe's economic problems ; for any such recovery as is foreshadowed by the measures at present proposed is likely, so far from being permanent, to lead on in the not distant future to a new depression fully as disastrous as that through which the world is passing to-day.

Capitalist Combination and State Control. To this point we shall recur ; but before we attempt to discuss the future of European Capitalism, it seems best to deal with those tendencies which have emerged during the post-war years both before and after 1929. If the present organisation of the capitalist system is compared with its organisation in 1914, certain very large differences at once come into view. There has been in the first place a very great increase in industrial combination. Employers were drawn or driven together into large combines or associations during the years of war because such combination was absolutely necessary in order to secure a co-ordinated effort for the supplying of war needs. The organisations thus brought into being to a great extent survived the emergency, and were reconstituted after the war as private combinations and associations of business firms. But the large element of control which had been exercised over them by the various States between 1914 and 1918 was for the most precipitately removed under suspicion that it was tainted with Socialism. Since 1918, combination in industry has been the rule rather than the exception, though the forms of combination differ widely from case to case, and are of very varying intensity, from the great trusts under completely unified financial control, through the cartels which are the characteristic feature of the German economic system, to much looser trading associations among firms which preserve their independence.

But this growth of combination, while it has sometimes created organisations of international scope, has for the most part proceeded along national lines and even on a basis of nationalist and imperialist policy. It has resulted in the creation in most of the leading industries of powerful national or imperialist groups of producers, often in sharp rivalry one with another throughout the markets of the world ; and these combined groups of producers have been able to a far greater extent than before the war to rely on their respective States for support in their commercial adventures and antagonisms. Thus business combination, so far from unifying the world and making more remote the danger of national wars, has become for the most part an ally of nationalism and imperialism, and has helped to increase national antagonisms by binding them up more closely with private capitalist interests. This tendency has both strengthened and been strengthened by the movement towards higher tariffs and increasing restrictions upon international trade ; and the two forces combined have helped to create a series of State systems administered by Governments more directly responsive than before the war to the economic claims of large vested interests organised upon a national scale. Such tendencies towards internationalism as do exist in the capitalist world have been far too weak to stand up against these nationalist forces. They have been for the most part either inclusions of smaller countries within the spheres of influence of the industries of the great imperialist Powers, or arrangements almost in the nature of commercial treaties between great national capitalist groups. The Continental Steel Cartel, for example, is an arrangement between a number of groups of steel producers each organised upon a purely national basis. The Royal Dutch Shell, with its ramifications in many parts of the world, represents rather a penetration of British imperialist influence in the petroleum industry than any movement towards international capitalist action.

Side by side with this growth of capitalist combination upon a national basis there has gone a great increase in the amount of State control over industry and of State intervention in the economic field. The countries which precipitately abolished in 1919 the forms of control over industry which they had established during the war have been compelled by force of circumstances to reintroduce them to a substantial extent, or to impose new controls in the interests of more efficient industrial organisation. In Great Britain a large part of the electrical industry has been socialised in the hands of the Central Electricity Board ; and the industry as a whole has been brought under public control. Railway rates have been regulated on a more comprehensive basis than before the war ; and a substantial beginning has been made with the State control of road transport. The mines have remained in private hands ; but the mine-owners are now organised into State-controlled associations for the fixing of output and prices. The British agricultural industry is also passing under a form of State regulation through a whole series of marketing schemes for particular products. Sugar-beet growing and wheat growing are subsidised by the State. The import of dyestuffs is regulated by a licensing system designed in the interests of maintaining an industry supposed to be vital for military purposes ; and, finally, the new British tariff is being used, at any rate to a certain degree, as an instrument for bringing about the compulsory reorganisation of industry. There is a Commission with compulsory power to amalgamate coal mines ; and it looks as if there would be another soon for the compulsory regulation of iron and steel. Yet Great Britain is one of the countries less affected than most by the post-war movement towards State control in industry.

This movement has gone further in Italy, where the Government, through the *Instituto Mobiliare Italiano* and the *Società Finanziaria Industriale*, has taken a large share in the task of financing Italian industry ; and large schemes of land reclamation and improvement have been undertaken by the Fascist State. But it is in Germany that the process has advanced to the furthest point. There the threatened collapse of the entire banking system compelled the Government to come to the assistance of the banks and to put up new capital for them under conditions which involved bringing them under a drastic form of State control. The Prussian State was before the war a large colliery owner ; and, since the war, State ownership and operation of coal mines has been supplemented by many other ventures of the State into the field of industrial ownership, either as sole owner or as part owner of " mixed " enterprises in partnership with other agencies. The great German steel industry has passed to a substantial extent under State control ; and almost the entire German economic system has come, during the past few years, to be regulated by a most drastic system of emergency decrees to which the Nazis, with their doctrine of " National Socialism," have now fallen heirs. In the smaller countries, too, there has been a substantial amount of taking over by the State, especially in the sphere of banking and industrial financing and of the disposal of agricultural produce. If State control of industry were Socialism, Europe would be to-day a far more socialistic Continent than before the war.

Nor has State intervention spread only or even mainly in this field of the control of industry. There has been also a very large development of social services and of the use of the tax system as a means of redistributing incomes. State after State has been compelled, usually much against the will of its Government, to make provision on a large scale for the maintenance of the unemployed ; and there has been a considerable extension also in the sphere of public health services and of insurance against sickness and incapacity. Far larger sums than before the war are paid out now in the budgets of most European countries for the social services. But this form of redistribution of the national income by taxation is by no means the only form of which account has to be taken ; for over against it as a factor tending in the opposite direction there is the enormous increase in the volume of national debts, which compels States to levy greatly increased taxes and to hand back a large part of the product of these taxes in the form of interest to the debt-holders. Thus, whereas social service expenditure tends to redistribute incomes through taxes to the poorer sections of the community, national debt interest, despite the diffusion of holdings, has on the whole the opposite effect ; and the pressure of the debt burden upon the national finances has been one of the factors aggravating the tendency towards high protective duties in order to raise larger sums from the poorer sections of the community by means of taxes on commodities.

The burden of national debts is of course very unevenly

spread over Europe, in accordance with the terms on which the post-war stabilisation of currencies took place. Thus, whereas Great Britain by the terms of her return to the gold standard involved herself in an enormous burden of interest to the holders of the debt, Germany, by practically wiping out her old currency, largely released herself from this burden ; while France, by reducing the franc to one-fifth of its pre-war value, also largely relieved the budget at the expense of the debt-holders. In 1930 the National Debt of Great Britain was more than ten times, and that of the United States nearly fifteen times, as great as before the war ; whereas the French National Debt, allowing for the depreciation of the currency, was less than three times as great, and the German debt only twice as great, and in Italy the increase was only 6 per cent. This German figure, however, makes no allowance for reparations, which had, up to 1931, taken the place in the German economy of the debt burden displaced by inflation and the change in the currency system. In absolute terms Great Britain had in 1930 by far the heaviest debt per head, not far short of twice that of France, more than six times that of the United States, and more than seven times that of Italy, while Germany's burden in pounds per head was less than one-twentieth of the British burden.

All these changes, whatever their social consequences, involved increased State intervention in the affairs of the individual citizens. The individual taxpayer became more conscious of the existence of the State as his burdens increased ; and the individual recipient either of debt interest or of social services also took an increased interest in the problems of public finance. Moreover the State, through its intervention in industry both internally and through the regulation of foreign trade by tariffs and by other methods, far more directly and constantly affected the position of both employers and workers than under pre-war conditions. Many people have regarded these manifestations of increasing State interference as forms of Socialism ; and it is perfectly correct to say that they foreshadow a transition from a system of private enterprise to one of national planning under the auspices of the State, and thus anticipate the entry of the capitalist world upon a new phase of development. But they certainly are not Socialism in any sense in which it is advocated by Socialists, but only in the sense in which men spoke in the nineteenth century of the State Socialism of Germany under Bismarck. For although they extend the power of the State they give no guarantee that this power will be used in the interests of the working class ; and, so far from being based on the internationalist principles on which Socialism rests, they have been for the most part aggressively nationalist in their conception and administration. State intervention is not Socialism : indeed, up to a certain point it is the very negation of Socialism, for the State needs to intervene in the affairs of industry and commerce at many points precisely because these affairs are in private and not in public hands.

Where industry and trade are socialised, as they are in Russia, there is no need for tariffs. Indeed, the entire tariff system becomes meaningless ; for the State, if it did impose tariffs, would only be taxing itself. Similarly, if industry were carried on under a Socialist system a large part of the existing codes of industrial legislation would come to be, if not unnecessary, at any rate rather internal acts of State administration than legislative measures to be enforced upon employers.

Moreover, even where industries are actually taken over by the State either wholly or in part, their operation under present conditions is usually so organised as to make them minister as much as possible to the service of other industries which still remain in private hands. The British Central Electricity Board has been so designed as to involve the minimum of actual public operation, and to leave both the generation of electricity and its retail distribution in the hands of private concerns where they were not already publicly owned by municipal bodies.

To a great extent, the State intervention of recent years

has been not a step taken because those who took it actually desired or thought it desirable to increase the element of State control in the economic life of society, but because, much against their will, they were driven to its adoption by the threatened breakdown of the institutions of private enterprise. Governments have advanced towards State control unwillingly, and often regarding it purely as an emergency measure on which they would like to go back at the earliest possible moment. Consequently, driven to administer a system in which they do not believe, they have often administered it very badly, and this has tended to give State control a bad name. Nor is this the only cause tending to make it unpopular ; for, as it is usually introduced in order to deal with a serious breakdown in some part of the economic system, it is commonly regarded as responsible for the bad condition of the enterprises which it has taken over, even if this condition would in fact have been much worse, or the enterprises have ceased to exist at all, in the absence of State action. Above all in the field of the regulation of international commerce, the increase in State intervention has obviously had the effect over the world as a whole of strangling and not of stimulating industrial activity and the exchange of goods. For here, too, its object has been essentially the combating of an emergency ; and each country has found itself driven into expedients for which there was no defence save that they were necessary measures of self-protection against similar steps taken in other countries, or against the complete collapse of the national currency.

It is in these circumstances not surprising that there has gone up from a considerable section of the middle-class public, with the backing of many of the theoretical econmists, a loud demand for a return to *laissez-faire*, not only in the sphere of external trade, but over the whole industrial field. Economists in many countries have argued that if only the nations of the world would remove their restrictions on international trade, repeal their minimum wage laws and much of their recently enacted social legislation, and leave economic forces freedom to assert themselves, the disequilibria which exist in the economic world to-day would speedily disappear, and industry and trade be everywhere re-established before long upon a sound footing. This would involve, in the view of those who advocate this policy, a drastic scaling down of wages, which would speedily come about if the protective social laws at present in force were swept away. For the pressure of unemployment, in the absence of any public system of maintenance, would cause such a scramble for jobs as to compel the workers to accept lower wages. In an earlier chapter we have examined the fallacies involved in this doctrine, and we need not repeat the argument now. What concerns us here is that, even if this policy were sound in itself and not, as we believe it to be, radically unsound, there would be very formidable obstacles in the way of its adoption.

Rentiers and Workers. The two outstanding obstacles to the return to pure *laissez-faire* are the creditor classes and the working classes. The creditor classes would put up a most formidable resistance to any attempt drastically to scale down their claims. But in the absence of such a scaling down the *laissez-faire* system could not possibly work out to a new equilibrium. For it involves an even further fall in prices, and would thus make the burden of debt even more intolerable than it is to-day. The creditor classes are, however, an exceedingly influential element in practically every State, and above all in France and in Great Britain ; and it would need a Government very different from any which has yet held power in either of these countries effectively to challenge their determined opposition. The second obstacle lies in the working classes, who would strongly resist both any drastic reduction in wage-rates and any attempt to go back on a large scale upon the social services developed since 1914. The resistance of the working classes to lower wages might perhaps be overcome ; for this would have to express itself through industrial action, and the effect of depression and rationalisation alike has been to weaken the Trade Union movement. But really drastic economies in the social services would call out the determined opposition of the working classes not merely in their Trade Unions but also as voters. It would therefore be exceedingly difficult to carry through in any country working under a system of Parliamentary democracy.

Both Great Britain and France as well as many of the lesser countries have, it is true, had their " economy campaigns " during the world depression, and have scaled down the social services to some extent ; but the amount which they have dared to do in this field is infinitely smaller than would be required if the policy of a whole-hogging return to *laissez-faire* were seriously in contemplation. Even the National Government in Great Britain, though it came to power with large ambitions of " national economy," has of late shown a growing tendency to go slow in this field of retrenchment.

Largely, the relative decline in the power of the workers' industrial organisations is in the democratic countries balanced by the growth of their political power. In as far as European countries remain under a system of Parliamentary democracy, the pressure from the working-class electors for improved social services will be maintained ; and it is even bound to increase to a substantial extent, especially as rationalisation in industry advances, and there is growing need for new protective measures in the interests of the older workers who are thrown upon the industrial scrap-heap.

Capitalism and the Standard of Life.
Can Capitalism, in the countries where Parliamentary democracy exists, meet these increasing political claims of the poorer sections of society ? There is clearly no reason in terms of the power to produce wealth why it should not. For the power to produce in all countries has increased, is increasing, and in the opinion of many capitalists ought to be diminished. But this is of course no answer to the question ; for events

have already abundantly illustrated the truth that an increasing power to produce does not necessarily mean an actual increase in production. In fact, the ability of Capitalism to grant an improving standard of life to the workers depends, however much productive capacity may increase, upon international co-operation. For no one capitalist country can, under the existing conditions, easily advance its working-class standards far beyond the others, either by raising wages and so directly adding to the costs of production, or by improving the social services, which will have to be financed partly at least by the imposition of additional taxes upon the capitalist producers. International competition between capitalist countries at present bars the way to an improvement in the standard of living, and indeed impels each country to set about reducing wages where it can in order to improve its competitive position.

What, then, are the prospects of international capitalist co-operation for the common improvement of living standards among the working classes ? The road to this obviously sensible course of procedure seems to be increasingly blocked by those countries in which the institutions of Parliamentary democracy have been destroyed. One fruit of Mussolini's power in Italy has been the maintenance of an exceedingly low wage standard among the Italian workers. Italy, it is true, matters comparatively little because her products do not enter largely into competition with those of the great industrial nations. But Germany matters a great deal ; and the new German Revolution may easily lead to an intensification of the efforts which Germany has made in recent years to improve her competitive position in the markets of the world by lowering the standard of life of the German people. The Nazis have no doubt made large promises of economic concessions in the course of their climb to power ; but now that they have got the German working classes by the short hairs, nationalist feeling will probably be used to justify low standards of living in the interests of the extension of German overseas trade. Political rivalry with the other great industrial nations will moreover probably accentuate this tendency towards lowering the German cost of production at any expense to the working-class standard of life.

The Outlook for European Socialism.

One capitalist country, we have said, cannot afford to advance far beyond its rivals in improving the standard of living, and can therefore find no way of escape from the present economic impasse. Nor does there seem to be much prospect of capitalist countries combining to find a way out. What, then, would be the position of one advanced industrial country if it went Socialist ? Could it, by applying Socialism on a national scale, escape from the limiting conditions of capitalist competition and raise the standard of living of its people in accordance with the growing magnitude of its productive power ? To a certain extent it could, provided that its Socialist system was introduced under conditions admitting of its efficient operation and not as the result of a devastating civil war involving large destruction of economic values. For there is no reason why Socialism in some countries and Capitalism in others should not exist temporarily side by side. The experience of Russia in recent years has shown, despite the extreme challenge which Communism presents to the capitalist world, that this can be done ; and both Russia and many of her neighbours have recognised the fact during the past few years by the mutual signing of pacts of non-aggression. Of course any Socialist system applied within a single nation could only achieve this raising of the standard of life, up to the level made possible by its productive power, on condition that it worked with the aid of a complete monopoly of foreign trade in all essential commodities, and developed in place of the existing methods of restricting trade new methods of bulk purchase, international barter, and regulated exchange of commodities. But these controls would not need to be merely restrictive, as tariffs inevitably are, but could be made the foundations of a system of regulated international economic co-operation. Clearly, then, the success of any one country in escaping from the impasse of international competition by applying Socialist measures will depend on its adopting not merely a few socialistic measures but a thoroughgoing Socialist system ; and nothing short of thoroughgoing Socialism will enable it to go far ahead of other countries in improving the standard of life.

Thoroughgoing Socialism, however, does not imply Communism in the Russian sense. We have given reasons in earlier chapters for holding that Communism in its Russian form is unlikely to prevail in Western Europe, though it might extend much further than it has yet done in the countries of Eastern Europe—for example in Poland, Roumania, and the predominantly agricultural States of the south. Perhaps the destruction of German Social Democracy may now have made it, over at any rate a large part of Germany, the sole alternative to the Nazi dictatorship. There is only one condition on which Communism would be likely to prevail in other western countries without a radical change in its form and methods of action. That condition is the coming of a new world war sufficiently devastating to break up the capitalist economy of the West, and leave no other alternative. What is implied, then, in the insistence that only a thoroughgoing Socialism could achieve the desired result is not Communism in the Russian sense, but a thoroughgoing Socialism appropriate to the conditions of Western Europe.

The Danger of War. Something must be said at this point about the possible exception just indicated. Is a new world war likely ? It is clearly impossible to base much hope of an assured European peace upon the League of Nations, or upon those separate pacts and treaties, such as the agreements made at Locarno, which have been designed to prevent war. For the Peace Treaties and the European settlement which emerged from them in the first place were, and remain, unjust in themselves in many of their most vital features, and in the second place have created exceedingly powerful vested claims, both political and economic, whose consequences it is bound to be exceedingly difficult to undo. It is certainly out of the question in the present state of European feeling to seek to remedy the territorial abuses created by the Peace Treaties by any method of agreed readjustment of national frontiers ; for countries are far too jealous and fearful one of another to admit of any increase in one another's national strength if they can possibly help it. Accordingly, both the injustices created by the Peace Treaties and the vested interests and nationalistic sentiments which they have entrenched have permeated Europe to-day with a spirit of militarism far too strong to yield to the treatment prescribed for it in draft disarmament conventions and draft treaties of international security.

Moreover, the Nazi revolution in Germany does almost certainly mean German rearmament ; for, though the Germans profess their willingness to remain disarmed if other countries will disarm to an equal extent, there is obviously little chance of this condition being satisfied, and the inevitable concession of equality to the Germans therefore means that Germany will be allowed to rearm. Nor, if rearmament in Germany does begin, is there likely to be any effective way of keeping it under control. In these circumstances, German rearmament is practically certain to lead to a renewed demand for the increase of armaments elsewhere. A straw sometimes shows which way the wind is blowing ; and it is significant that in the French Socialist Party, which has been strongly pressing for disarmament for some time, a crisis should have arisen on this issue in April 1933. A majority of the French Socialist Deputies on this occasion voted, against the wishes of the leaders of the Party, in favour of a modification in the proposals for disarmament put forward a month or two before.

But after the experience of the years before 1914 no one

is likely to doubt that the greater the armaments the greater the danger of war. The danger of a new European war on the grand scale is not perhaps immediate, for the combatants are not yet ready for it ; but it is very real. Moreover, the next war looks like being even more terribly destructive than the last, especially to the civilian populations and to the industries of the belligerent countries— unless, of course, the use of the more destructive weapons can be limited in advance by some effective form of international agreement. But how much prospect is there of qualitative disarmament being agreed to, or of any such agreement being actually preserved if war does break out ? As we have said, when countries believe themselves to be fighting for their national existence, conventions limiting the use of arms are likely to be speedily overridden.

The course at present adopted by the statesmen of Europe is to play for time in the hope of something turning up, and of European countries somehow settling down again. But what signs are there that this is likely to happen ? It is perfectly true that a substantial economic recovery would for the time being greatly reduce the danger of war, in that most countries would be too busy trying to take full advantage of it to think quite so much about national glory or national grievances. But in the present state of Europe this would be only a respite ; for economic recovery would have the effect of making it easier for the nations to rearm, and in the present state of European relationships only poverty prevents them from being far more heavily armed than they are to-day. If we are successfully to prevent war we must remove the causes of war, which lie fundamentally in capitalist nationalism and capitalist imperialism. By removing these causes we may succeed in separating the question of territorial rearrangements from questions of national prestige and power and national economic advantage. This involves the establishment of Socialism, not merely as a national, but above all as an international force. But how can we set to work to bring this force into effective operation ?

Nationalism and Internationalism. Evidently, although the Socialism which is needed must be international Socialism, it will have to be worked for largely along national lines. The international spirit is vital to it; but the Socialists of the world are under the necessity of acting, until they achieve power, largely within the framework of the existing national States, with the object of conquering power in each country as a means to breaking down the isolated sovereign independence of each national group. An immense mass of cosmopolitan feeling exists in the world to-day, especially among the younger members of the European community. It is true that a vast mass of nationalist feeling exists as well, and that internationalism, or rather cosmopolitanism, as a world force cannot expect an easy victory over militarist nationalism and the capitalist imperialism with which it is intimately connected. But this mass of cosmopolitan feeling can become a most important ally as well as a driving force for the international working-class movement, for it is potentially Socialist, and will become actually Socialist as soon as it can be convinced that Socialists mean by Socialism a force making definitely for world peace and international collaboration.

The working-class movements of the world, which alone can provide the necessary instruments for the achievement of Socialism, are not at present giving an effective lead to these cosmopolitan forces. The Communists are trying to give such a lead ; but their methods are self-destructive because, by working for a revolution of violence in each country, they positively increase the strength of nationalist feeling and create an ever-increasing danger of nationalist counter-revolution in the shape of Fascism. What is needed is the permeation of the working-class movement with the cosmopolitan spirit of Socialism—in other words, a new cosmopolitan driving force, Socialist in its aims and basing itself upon the working-class movement in the widest sense of the term as the necessary instrument for the achievement of its purpose.

Mr. H. G. Wells has done good service by stressing the

vital importance of cosmopolitanism as a basis for thinking in terms of the new world order. But he has so far shown an inadequate sense of the need for something more than thinking and personal devotion to the cosmopolitan cause. Thought and idealism, if they are to be effective, must find a body, must embody themselves in an institution strong enough to enable them to count in the world of practical affairs. Mr. Wells's cosmopolitanism wanders round the world to-day as a disembodied spirit. But clearly the one body in which it can hope to find an instrument to its purpose is the international working-class movement, broadened and deepened so as to bring within its range not only the manual workers but also all those among the technical and professional groups who put constructive activity before profit, and are prepared to ally themselves with the manual workers on the basis of a cosmopolitan appeal.

Production and Consuming Power. The building up of such a movement requires firm economic and philosophical foundations. In an earlier section we have attempted an analysis of the fundamental doctrines of Marxism without there essaying any criticism of these doctrines. Broadly speaking, we believe the Marxian philosophy to be essentially true, though its expression needs at many points to be modified in the light of later thinking and of practical experience. Above all, it is true that in the world of to-day the " powers of production " upon which the whole Marxian conception depends are fast advancing beyond the possibilities of the economic system within which their operation is still confined. The plain evidence of this is in the failure of the system of distribution characteristic of the present economic order, and based on monopoly and class privilege. For the present economic order, pursuing above all things the profit of the owners of capital, is compelled to seek scarcity and not abundance, because out of scarcity alone comes the value of which the capitalist is in search. Manifestly the overmastering need of our time is to release the powers of production from their present thraldom by means of a new and more adequate system of distributing wealth. The world must have a system of distribution which will enable it to make full use of all the opportunities for production which lie ready to its hand.

This must involve changes not only in the distributive system but also in the control of production. For to alter the system of distribution without altering the control of the productive forces would be to establish a new and irreconcilable contradiction in the working of the economic order. If distribution is to be arranged on such a basis as to make plenty and not scarcity the object of men's economic activities, the powers of production and distribution must be brought under a co-ordinated control in the hands of the entire community. Incomes must be distributed and production arranged for so as to establish a balance between consuming power and the volume of goods that can be made available for consumption. This, however, clearly cannot be accomplished in a satisfactory way upon a merely national scale, for to shut up each country within a rigidly drawn economic frontier of its own is to deny the basic principle that the object of social organisation must be plenty and not scarcity. Economic nationalism is essentially based upon the maintenance of scarcity, because it involves denying men the greatly increased total productivity which arises out of international exchange. Not merely Socialist control within a single country, therefore, but international or rather cosmopolitan Socialism is the logical next step in the evolution of the economic order—the step corresponding to the point which the powers of production have already reached.

Parliamentarism and Revolution.   Evidently the next question is that of means. If cosmopolitanism is to be made the basis of the new economic system, the capitalist State must be broken, for the capitalist State is essentially nationalist in its foundations. If Socialism is to be achieved the capitalist State must be broken no less, for it rests upon the assumption of monopolistic property rights. The coming of the age of plenty demands a new way of organising the communities of the world. The Soviet system, as it has developed in Russia, may be, and we think is, largely inappropriate to the conditions of Western Europe. It was not, even in Russia, something thought out in advance by the theorists of Communism, and then applied to the practical circumstances of 1917 in accordance with a preconceived theory, but something which arose spontaneously, and even to a large extent unexpected by the Communists themselves, in the Russian situation of 1917. Not for some time after the first Russian Revolution did the Communists raise the cry "All Power to the Soviets." They were thinking in the earlier stages far more in terms of factory committees, and were even in the midst of the Revolution largely unconscious of the new forms which the State was destined to assume in their hands. If Socialism comes in Western Europe, the appropriate forms for the organisation of the West European sections of the new cosmopolitan society will have to be developed in the course of the change itself : they cannot be worked out in advance with any certainty.

If, for example, Socialism comes, as we hope it will in Western Europe, not through violent revolution but by a transition devoid of bloodshed, the first stages towards it will in all probability be parliamentary, in the sense that the Socialists will begin by using the parliamentary machine built up by capitalist democracy, and applying this machine, unsuitable as it will doubtless prove to be in the long run, to the achievement of their immediate purposes. This may not now be the case in Germany, where the parliamentary machine has perhaps been too utterly shattered by the events of the past two decades to serve or to be needed as the instrument of constructive change. But unless the dissolution of parliamentary institutions in Great Britain and France and in some of the smaller western countries goes much further than it has gone as yet, the coming of Socialism in these countries is likely to take in the first instance the form of a parliamentary change. The appropriate organisation of the new States of the transition period and of the new Society which is to arise out of this period will have to depend on the circumstances under which the transition actually occurs, and not on any preconceived theory of the detailed strategy of the advance towards Socialism.

The Devolution of Functions. Nevertheless, certain elements in this new Society can be foreseen. It is clear that under the new conditions there will have to be much devolution of powers ; for otherwise the new functions collectively assumed by the community will involve an impossible degree of congestion in the working of the central administrative machine, which is over-burdened already with the tasks which fall upon it under the existing system. This devolution of responsibility will have, however, to proceed even more upon functional than upon local lines. It will have to consist largely in entrusting the conduct of particular services to responsible bodies, appointed in accordance with the requirements of the whole Society and then left free in the detailed working out of their administrative methods. Within this system of functional devolution there will have to be a very large element of workers' control, not merely in the sense of entrusting wide powers to chosen leaders of the working class, but in the fuller sense of permeating the entire body of workers with a sense of responsibility for the successful operation of the new régime. This will be indispensable ; for the bad incentives upon which the world has relied for getting work done under the capitalist order cannot be simply swept away : they must be replaced by new incentives more powerful in getting men to give of their best. These new incentives will have to rest upon the principles of communal service and responsibility ; and there can be no sense of responsibility without a large element of self-government. At the same time there will have to be strong central co-ordination ; for all the different industries and services, and indeed every branch of the new system of socialised industrialism, will have to be closely related to every other, and there will be required a very close relationship between the working of industry and the financial mechanism as a whole, if the indispensable adjustment of production and consumption is to be secured. Thus the banking system and public finance will have to be closely linked up with the industries and services supplying consumers' needs in order to achieve the correct balance. Moreover, while each country will doubtless retain administrative autonomy both in general and in the operation of each industry and service, there will have to be a very high measure of international co-operation—nay more, an actual breaking down of national barriers and an administration of an increasing number of services under international control. Finally, in the new order, means will have to be found of removing from democracy the reproach that it involves the government of the old ; for the new Society will have to base itself upon the control of those whose powers are developing and whose minds are receptive to new ideas and methods of work.

If, however, this is the Society which is clearly needed for the building up of a world Organisation corresponding to the stage already reached by men's productive power, there is still an arduous road to be travelled towards its establishment. We have said earlier that we do not predict as a necessary outcome of the present situation the immediate breakdown of the capitalist order, or even an indefinite prolongation of the present world slump. We have then to ask again whether Capitalism cannot in fact so reconstruct itself as to meet the demand for plenty in place of scarcity, and so bring itself into adjustment with the growing productive powers of mankind. This involves attempting to answer two questions : first, what stands in the way of immediate capitalist recovery, and secondly, how far is Capitalism, even if it can recover from the present slump, capable of so altering its character as to meet the needs of the coming generation.

The Obstacles to Capitalist Recovery. The immediate obstacles to the recovery of Capitalism have been stressed in earlier sections of this book. The first and most obvious of them is the burden of debt : indeed debts occupy so large a place in creating the present difficulties of the capitalist world that one is tempted to say that nothing else really matters. Secondly there is the problem of prices, of price-levels too low to enable production to be carried on upon a sufficient scale under capitalist conditions. But the fall of prices during the past few years is essentially a symptom rather than the disease from which the capitalist world is suffering. It is true enough that by concerted action the capitalist countries could take steps which would be effective in raising the levels of world prices, and that the galvanic effect of these measures would, at any rate if the debt problem were also successfully dealt with, bring about a substantial recovery of capitalist industry. But it is no less clear that such a recovery would be highly precarious, and that the measures taken in order to raise prices would be of such a nature as to lead on to a new world crisis, to be followed by a new and prolonged depression, unless steps were taken to bring the distributive system and the consuming power of the world's peoples into harmony with the magnitude of the world's productive forces. The only way suggested for the effective raising of world prices is some form of monetary inflation ; but monetary inflation under Capitalism, while it may achieve its immediate objects, results inevitably in rebuilding industry upon unsound foundations and will bring into operation again the very forces which led in 1929 to the outbreak of the world depression.

Thirdly, the capitalist world, as a step towards even temporary recovery, will have to get rid of, or greatly to reduce, the present obstructions in the way of international trade. The tariffs, restrictions, quotas, embargoes, exchange controls, and all the other manifestations of economic nationalism which have been discussed earlier in this book are also symptoms of the disease of Capitalism rather than the disease itself. They would disappear or be greatly modified if any revival of capitalist prosperity were to take place ; but it is no less certain that they would be speedily reimposed if a new crisis developed. Fourthly, there is the problem of the relations between Europe and the United States. But this is only the problem of debts and the problem of tariffs over again ; for it is manifestly impossible for European countries to go on making large payments to a creditor who is unwilling to receive his due in the form of goods. Fifthly, there is the question of peace ; for manifestly even a temporary capitalist recovery could not be engineered under the permanent threat to confidence involved by the constant fear of the outbreak of a new war. Capitalism, then, in order to achieve even a temporary revival, would have to succeed somehow in damping down at least for a time the threat of war. If this could be done even for a brief period the existence of more favourable economic conditions would, as we have seen, at least for a short time tend to diminish the war danger by diverting men's thoughts from national grievances to immediate economic opportunities. Yet in the long run, in the present condition of Europe, greater economic prosperity would probably lead to still heavier armaments, and thus recreate the danger of war.

It will be admitted that the obstacles in the way of a successful tackling even of these immediate problems, which must be successfully tackled if Capitalism is to achieve even a temporary world revival, are very formidable. But formidable as they are, they are not finally insuperable. Let us assume that they have been overcome, and that by a variety of methods co-operatively pursued by the leading nations, Capitalism has got back to where it stood, say, ten years ago. What is to happen then ? If economic forces are allowed to develop as they developed between 1923 and 1929 the world will merely be heading towards a new crisis based on the mal-distribution of consuming power and the inability of the present system to find means of distributing the volume of commodities which it is equipped to produce. Can Capitalism find any remedy for this situation ? There are numerous voices now upraised in favour of a planned national economy still retaining the salient features of Capitalism. Each industry, it is urged, or at least each vital industry, should be organised into a closely knit national corporation, while remaining under capitalist ownership. All industries should be closely knit together in terms of a general plan drawn up under the auspices of the national State, and through the instrumentality of capitalist representatives from each industry. Both national States and the organised industries within them should make with other States and with similar groups in other countries collective arrangements for the sharing out of markets and for the carrying on of international exchange. There should be international combinations governing the operations of world Capitalism and dealing in particular with the steps necessary for opening up fresh markets in the less developed countries by means of international lending. In other words, there should be a sort of Bismarckian " State Socialism " in each country, linked together by means of international arrangements between capitalist States and capitalist industrial groups.

Is world Capitalism likely to adopt such a system, or at all events to adopt it in time ? There have been abundant illustrations during the past dozen years of the slow progress made by capitalist rationalisation in face of the obstruction of individual property owners and of the pronounced individualism which is characteristic—which has indeed been in the past the strength—of the business world. To achieve the collective organisation even of a single industry is a painful process involving intense opposition among those whose position is to be disturbed by the change. It is sometimes possible to achieve this in a single industry, where the interests of capitalists in other industries lie in getting it done ; but to achieve it for the whole world of capitalist industry is surely a task far beyond the powers of any State under capitalist domination, let alone of all the leading States of the world acting in unison.

Moreover, even if capitalist planning of this sort could be

achieved both nationally and internationally, to what purposes would it be applied ? Where industries have been closely combined under Capitalism up to the present the chief use to which they have put their new power has been that of restricting supply in order to maintain prices. In other words, they have continued to act in the spirit of the gospel of scarcity and to seek the value which comes of scarcity rather than the plenty which the world requires. Planned Capitalism under the auspices of capitalist States would be likely to press this policy still further. Moreover, Capitalism and nationalism are, as we have seen, close allies ; and it is far more likely that Capitalist States adopting a planned economy would then proceed to compete and dispute bitterly one with another than that they would join together in any widespread system of economic collaboration.

Capitalism and Imperialism.   For Capitalism in its latest manifestations is imperialism as well ; and the last thing an imperialist is willing to believe is that an empire can prosper save at the expense of its rivals. Above all, we find it inconceivable that even the most intensely planned Capitalism would take the indispensable step of setting to work deliberately to raise the purchasing power of the mass of the peoples of the world in order to secure an outlet for the highest possible production. For this course simply could not be made consistent with the active interests of the capitalists in whose hands *ex hypothesi* industries would still be left. Planned capitalism on a world-wide scale seeking plenty rather than scarcity and abandoning imperialist rivalries in favour of cosmopolitan co-operation is a contradiction in terms. Yet only on a basis of cosmopolitan planning can the world hope for a permanent escape from the contradictions in its present situation.

The world, then, *can* recover temporarily even under Capitalism ; but any such capitalist recovery as is at present projected will sow the seeds of new depressions and new imperialist and nationalist rivalries in the future. Capitalist reconstruction gives no assurance of any recovery that can be lasting, and no sign of any ability to achieve world peace. But, some people will say, is Socialism in these respects any better ? Is it not fully possible for Socialism to establish itself on a national basis, and to pursue on such a basis the policy of economic nationalism, thus denying the world the plenty which is within its grasp, and perhaps sowing the seeds of war and imperialist rivalry as surely as Capitalism has sown them during the past fifty years ? We agree that, if Socialism could be conceived as a purely national movement, arising simply as a change in the mechanism of particular national societies and not as a change in the mind and spirit animating the peoples of the world in which it arises, Socialism *in this sense* would be no cure for the world's ills. But Socialism, in the minds of all those who believe in it and are prepared to work for it in all countries, is essentially and absolutely an international doctrine, repudiating the limitations of the national sovereign State and aiming at the creation not of a limited system of collectivism within one country, but of a world-wide system of economic and political collaboration. There is and can be no real and sufficient cause of quarrel between the workers, or between the main masses of the people, in different countries. The conflicts of nationalism and imperialism arise not from real causes of quarrel between the peoples of one country and another, but from a playing upon the passions and ignorances of the mass of the people by powerful economic interests cloaking their search for wealth and power under national and imperial forms, or from that sheer despair—the product of economic adversity —which arises in men's minds when everything seems to be going wrong and they must ease their spirits by finding someone or somebody whom they can blame for their misfortunes. The passions of nationalism are fed on the one hand by imperialist Capitalism and on the other by economic adversity. Displace imperialism, and set the world's feet firmly on the path towards a fuller use of the productive resources at its command ; and the main sources of national hatred and suspicion will at once disappear, setting the world free to embark upon a course of constructive collaboration. This, to our mind, is the moral of the present situation in Europe ; but whether the forces making for cosmopolitan Socialism will be strong enough to build up the new Society before sheer disaster overtakes the peoples of Europe—that remains to be seen. We can only hope and strive to bring this about : we cannot confidently predict success.

Square, where 20,000 people tried to chair him.

TO BREAK A RECORD

Object in visiting England: To break Land's End to John o' Groats record, 866 miles, now held by J. W. Rossiter in 2 days 13 hours 22 minutes, and accounts it hardest ride he has yet essayed. Will ride 120 miles daily in training until early July, when attempt is due.

B. Small will manage; R. Sweeting will arrange relay of description for hourly broadcast throughout Australia.

Says "Oppy": "Your towns are too large and your streets too narrow, but your countryside is the cyclist's 'never-never-land' come true."

MOTHER SAVED FROM RIVER WITH CHILDREN

DRAGGED DOWN BANK BY PRAM

A mother and her three children fell into the river Don at Tinsley, near Sheffield, yesterday and were rescued by boathooks.

Mrs. Stacey, of Newmarch-street, Tinsley, was pushing a perambulator containing two children, aged five and 18 months, with a third riding on the step.

★ *Achievements of Fascism*

WE are led to believe that Hitler is the saviour of Germany, and that Mussolini has rendered a similar service to Italy.

But here are facts:

Germany: Unemployment is estimated at 6,000,000. Decline in trade is £35,000,000. Taxation has greatly increased Retail prices are abnormally high. Wages are down 20 per cent.

Herr Hitler

Italy: Official statistics give unemployment as 1,000,000, but the real figure is much higher. Decline in trade last year was £50,000,000. Budget deficit last year was £70,000,000. and this year is estimated at £30,000,000 down.

Wages being paid in Italy are probably the lowest in the industrial world.

Why, then, do we need a Hitler or a Mussolini in this country?

G. MULVEY OUSELEY.
28, Greenford-road,
Middlesex.

BIBLIOGRAPHY

Needless to say, this book-list is highly selective. Those who want further references may be referred to the bibliographies contained in :

(a) for the *History*   The Encyclopædia Britannica, the Cambridge Modern History
(b) for the *Separate Countries*   The Statesman's Year Book, the Encyclopædia Britannica
(c) for the *Economic Section*   G. D. H. Cole   The Intelligent Man's Guide through World Chaos
(d) for the *Political Section*   Works there listed, by Headlam-Morley, Laidler, and as under (b)
(e) for the *International Section*   Works there listed, by Bailey, Woolf

The most useful atlas is *The Times Atlas*. See also the valuable maps in I. Bowman, *The New World*, Philips' *Historical Atlas*, Bartholomew and Lyde's *Atlas of Economic Geography*, and the *Plebs Atlas*.

Part I. HISTORICAL OUTLINE

H. G. WELLS   The Outline of History   *revised edition 1923*

M. M. KNIGHT   Economic History of Europe   *n.d.*

W. CUNNINGHAM   Western Civilisation in its Economic Aspects (Vol. II. : Medieval and Modern Times)   *1904*

P. BOISSONNADE   Life and Work in Medieval Europe   *1927*

J. W. THOMPSON   History of the Middle Ages   *1931*

D. OGG   Europe in the Seventeenth Century   *1925*

G. N. CLARK   The Seventeenth Century   *1929*

G. SLATER   The Growth of Modern England   *1932*

H. SÉE   Esquisse d'une Histoire du Régime Agraire en Europe aux 18 and 19 Siècles   *1921*

C. DAY   Economic Development in Modern Europe   *1933*

L. KNOWLES   Economic Development in the Nineteenth Century   *1932*

F. A. KIRKPATRICK, ed.   Lectures on the History of the Nineteenth Century   *1904*

S. HERBERT   Modern Europe, 1789–1914   *1916*

J. A. HOBSON   Evolution of Modern Capitalism   *revised edition 1926*

A. VIALLATE   Economic Imperialism   *1923*

P. Ashley Modern Tariff History *1910*
H. Feis Europe the World's Banker *1930*

[Reference can be made throughout to the *Cambridge Modern History*, the *Histoire Générale* of Lavisse and Rambaud, the old and new editions of the *Encyclopædia Britannica*, and to old editions of the *Statesman's Year Book*]

POST-WAR HISTORY

C. Delisle Burns A Short History of the World, 1918–1928 *1928*
R. L. Buell Europe, A History of Ten Years *1929*
A. J. Toynbee The World after the Peace Conference *1926*
I. Bowman The New World *revised edition 1930*
S. D. Schmalhausen, ed. Recovery through Revolution *1933*

Part II. THE COUNTRIES OF EUROPE

GENERAL

The Statesman's Year Book
The Statistical Year Book of the League of Nations (and the Monthly Bulletin)
The Europe Service (loose-leaf)
The Annual Register
The Survey of International Affairs, annual (ed. A. J. Toynbee)
Documents on International Affairs, annual (ed. J. W. Wheeler-Bennett)
The Encyclopædia Britannica (old and new editions)
Department of Overseas Trade, Reports on Economic Conditions in the various countries, published at irregular intervals, annual for the leading countries

[See also the Statistical Year Books published by the various Governments, also the Guide Books such as the *Guide Book of the Soviet Union* and numerous others ; numerous publications of the League of Nations, the International Labour Organisation, the International Institute of Agriculture, the United States Department of Commerce, the Royal Institute of International Affairs, and the (American) Council on Foreign Relations; the volumes of the *Carnegie Social and Economic History of the World War*, H. W. V. Temperley's *History of the Peace Conference*. Of special value for current information are the *Economist* (London), *Monde* (edited by H. Barbusse, Paris), *Current History* (New York), the *Monthly Summary* of the League of Nations (Geneva), the *Board of Trade Journal* (London), the *International Labour Review* (Geneva), the *Federal Reserve Bulletin* (Washington), *Notre Temps* (Paris), and the *Manchester Guardian*]

BALTIC STATES

O. RUTTER   The New Baltic States and Their Future   *1925*
F. WESTERINEN   Agricultural Conditions in Estonia   *1923*
P. MEYER   Latvia's Economic Life   *1925*
E. J. HARRISON   Lithuania   *1928*
H. SPAULL   The Baltic States   *1931*

POLAND

COUNT SKRYNSKY   Poland and Peace   *1923*
F. BUJAK   Poland's Economic Development   *1926*
W. K. KOROSTEWITZ   The Re-birth of Poland   *1928*
R. MACHRAY   Poland, 1914–1931   *1931*

ROUMANIA

V. CLARK   Greater Roumania   *1922*
T. W. RIKER   The Making of Roumania,   *1931*
J. L. EVANS   The Agrarian Revolution in Roumania   *1924*
D. MITRANY   The Land and Peasant Reform in Roumania   *1930*

BULGARIA

J. BUCHAN, ed.   Bulgaria and Roumania   *1924*
L. PASVOLSKY   Bulgaria's Economic Position   *1930*

YUGOSLAVIA

J. BUCHAN, ed.   Yugoslavia   *1923*
BEARD and RADEN   The Balkan Pivot—Yugoslavia   *1929*

GREECE

W. MILLER   Greece   *1928*
A. ANDREADES   Les Effets Economiques de la Guerre en Grèce   *1929*
JOHN MAVROGORDATO   Modern Greece   *1931*

AUSTRIA

W. T. LAYTON and C. RIST   The Economic Situation of Austria   *1926*
C. A. MCCARTNEY   The Social Revolution in Austria   *1926*
J. D. NEWTH   Austria   *1931*

HUNGARY

O. Jaszi   Revolution and Counter-Revolution in Hungary
   1924
B. Kalman   The International Position of Hungary   *1931*

SWITZERLAND

R. C. Brookes   Government and Politics of Switzerland   *1920*

CZECHOSLOVAKIA

J. César and F. Parkeny   The Czechoslovak Republic   *1922*
T. G. Mazaryk   The Making of a State   *1926*
J. O. Crane   The Little Entente   *1931*

GERMANY

H. Stroebel   The German Revolution and After   *n.d.*
W. H. Dawson   Germany under the Treaty   *1933*
M. Sering   Germany under the Dawes Plan   *1929*
J. W. Angell   The Recovery of Germany   *1929*
H. R. Knickerbocker   Germany, Fascist or Soviet ?   *1932*
H. G. Moulton and C. E. McGuire   Germany's Capacity to
   Pay   *1923*
H. G. Daniels   The Rise of the German Republic   *1927*
J. King   The German Revolution, its Meaning and Menace
   1933

SCANDINAVIA

P. Drachmann and H. Westergaard   The Industrial Develop-
   ment and Commercial Policy of the Three Scandinavian
   Countries
G. G. Hardy   Norway   *1925*
D. Heathcote   Sweden   *1927*
H. Jones   Modern Denmark   *1927*
K. Gilmour   Finland   *1931*

BELGIUM

T. H. Reed   The Government and Politics of Belgium   *1924*
E. Mahaim   La Belgique Restorée   *1926*

HOLLAND

A. J. Barnouw   Holland under Queen Wilhelmina   *1923*
L. Nemry   Les Pays Bas après la Guerre   *1925*

FRANCE

A. Siegfried France, a Study in Nationality *1930*
R. H. Soltan French Parties and Politics *1930*
W. F. Ogburn and W. Jaffé The Economic Development of Post-war France *1930*
D. S. Saposs The Labour Movement in Post-war France *1931*
A. Fontaine French Industry during the War *1926*

SPAIN

S. de Madariaga Spain *1930*
F. B. Deakin Spain To-day *1924*
H. R. G. Greaves The Spanish Constitution *1933*

ITALY

F. L. Ferrari Le Régime Fasciste Italien *1928*
C. Haider Capital and Labour under Fascism *1930*
C. E. McGuire Italy's International Economic Position *1926*
G. Salvemini The Fascist Dictatorship in Italy *1927*
T. Sillani, ed. What Fascism Is, and Why *1931*
L. Villari The Expansion of Italy *1930*
L. Villari The Fascist Experiment *1926*

GREAT BRITAIN

A. Siegfried England's Crisis *1931*
A. Siegfried Post-war Britain *1923*
G. D. H. Cole British Trade and Industry, Past and Future *1932*
G. D. H. Cole A Short History of the British Working-Class Movement *re-issued 1932*
W. Dibelius England *revised edition 1930*
F. A. Ogg English Government and Politics *1929*

RUSSIA

J. Mavor Economic History of Russia *revised edition 1925*
C. B. Hoover The Economic Life of Soviet Russia *1931*
G. T. Grinko The Five-Year Plan of the Soviet Union *n.d.*
M. H. Dobb Russian Economic Development since the Revolution *revised edition ?1931*
M. S. Miller Economic Development of Russia, 1905–1914 *1926*
L. Trotsky History of the Russian Revolution, 3 vols. *1932–3*
M. Hindus Humanity Uprooted *1929*
M. Hindus Red Bread *?*

M. Hindus The Great Offensive *1933*
M. I. Cole, ed. Twelve Studies in Soviet Russia *1932*
A. W. Field Protection of Women and Children in Soviet Russia *1932*

Part III. ECONOMIC CONDITIONS

G. D. H. Cole The Intelligent Man's Guide through World Chaos *1932*
G. D. H. Cole, ed. What Everyone Wants to Know About Money *1933*
G. D. H. Cole British Trade and Industry, Past and Future *1932*
A. L. Bowley The Economic Consequences of the War *1930*
J. M. Keynes The Economic Consequences of the Peace *1919*
A. Loveday Britain and World Trade *1931*
J. H. Richardson Economic Disarmament *1931*
League of Nations The Course and Phases of the World Economic Depression *revised edition 1932*
League of Nations World Economic Survey *1932*
Sir A. Salter Recovery *1932*
Sir A. Salter and others The World Economic Crisis *1932*
Sir A. Salter The United States of Europe *1933*
Royal Institute of International Affairs Agriculture, a World Survey *1933*
League of Nations The Agricultural Crisis, 2 vols. *1931–2*
H. G. Moulton and L. Pasvolsky War Debts and World Prosperity *1932*
J. W. Wheeler-Bennett The Wreck of Reparations *1933*
L. Pasvolsky Economic Nationalism of the Danubian States *1928*
R. G. Hawtrey The Art of Central Banking *1932*
D. T. Jack The Restoration of European Currencies *1927*
T. E. Gregory The Gold Standard and its Future *1932*
F. W. Hirst Wall Street and Lombard Street *1931*
C. H. Kisch and W. A. Elkin Central Banks *revised edition 1932*
H. H. Tiltman Slump, a Study of Stricken Europe *1932*
H. R. Knickerbocker Can Europe Recover? *1932*
F. Henderson The Economic Consequences of Power-Production *1931*
H. V. Hodson Economics of a Changing World *1933*
R. F. Harrod International Economics *1933*
B. Whale International Trade *1932*
R. A. Hodgson An Introduction to International Trade and Tariffs *1932*
International Labour Organisation Year Books

INTERNATIONAL LABOUR ORGANISATION Unemployment Problems in 1931 *1931*

[There are many important reports published by the League of Nations and the International Labour Organisation in addition to those mentioned above. Among the periodical publications of these bodies may be mentioned the annual *Review of World Trade and Production* (League of Nations). See also the Year Book of the International Institute of Agriculture, and its yearly Reports on the Agricultural Situation. There are also many useful supplements published by the *Economist*, especially those dealing with German Debts and with the World Economic Conference]

Part IV. POLITICAL SYSTEMS

A. HEADLAM-MORLEY The New Democratic Constitutions of Europe *1929*

M. W. GRAHAM The New Governments of Central Europe *1924*

H. J. LASKI Democracy in Crisis *1933*

H. J. LASKI Liberty in the Modern State *1930*

H. J. LASKI Communism *1927*

J. S. BARNES The Universal Aspects of Fascism *1927*

F. L. FERRARI Le Régime Fasciste Italien *1927*

J. STRACHEY The Coming Struggle for Power *1932*

A. ROTHSTEIN, ed. The Soviet Constitution

N. LENIN The State and Revolution (various editions)

J. STALIN Leninism, 2 vols. *1932 and 1933*

H. W. LAIDLER A History of Socialist Thought *1927*

KARL MARX Capital (ed. G. D. H. Cole) *Everyman's Library 1933*

SOCIALIST LEAGUE Problems of a Socialist Government *1933*

H. DE MAN The Psychology of Socialism *1928*

G. D. H. COLE The Next Ten Years in British Social and Economic Policy *1929*

F. DELAISI Political Myths and Economic Realities *1925*

L. S. WOOLF After the Deluge *1931*

[See also under the various countries]

Part V. INTERNATIONAL RELATIONS

The Peace Year Book

LEAGUE OF NATIONS Armaments Year Book

L. BLUM Peace and Disarmament *1932*

P. J. NOEL BAKER Disarmament *1928*

INTER-PARLIAMENTARY UNION What Would Be the Character of a New War ? *1932*

D. P. MYERS World Disarmament *1932*

N. ANGELL The Unseen Assassins *1932*

N. ANGELL The Great Illusion *new edition 1933*

J. W. WHEELER-BENNETT Disarmament and Security since Locarno *1932*

UNION OF DEMOCRATIC CONTROL The Secret International *1932*

H. N. BRAILSFORD The War of Steel and Gold *1914*

H. N. BRAILSFORD If We Want Peace *1932*

LEONARD WOOLF, ed. The Intelligent Man's Way to Prevent War *1933*

S. H. BAILEY The Framework of International Society *1932*

R. L. BUELL International Relations *1931*

P. B. POLTER Introduction to International Organisation *1928*

LEAGUE OF NATIONS Ten Years of World Co-operation *1931*

F. V. MORLEY The Society of Nations *1932*

J. L. BRIERLY The Law of Nations *1928*

INTERNATIONAL LABOUR ORGANISATION The I.L.O. : The First Decade *1931*

INDEX

GREAT
BRITAIN
&
NORTHERN
IRELAND

IRISH
FREE
STATE

NORTH

DENMARK

SEA

ATLANTIC

OCEAN

NOR

H.
BEL.
GER
LUX.
S.B.

FRANCE
SWITZ

PORTUGAL

SPAIN

MEDITERR

EURO